CONSUMER GUIDE™
AUTOMOBILE BOOK

ALL NEW 1998 EDITION

CONTENTS

INTRODUCTION

The first step to becoming an informed, confident shopper... A-6

USING THE BUYING GUIDE

Getting the most out of our comprehensive 1998 new-car reports... A-7

SHOPPING TIPS

The smart-buyer's guide to negotiating the best purchase or lease... A-8

WARRANTIES AND SERVICE CONTRACTS

How the manufacturers back their products, advice on extra coverage... A-17

SAFETY

The latest on automotive crashworthiness and life-saving features... A-19

CONSUMER COMPLAINTS

What to do when things go wrong... A-25

INSURANCE

Determine how much insurance you need and get the best rates... A-28

1998 BEST BUYS

The top values in cars, minivans, and sport-utility vehicles... A-31

CONTENTS

INTRODUCTION

Buying a new car, minivan, sport-utility vehicle, or truck means making decisions. Selecting a make and model is just the start. You also have to pick a dealer, investigate options, think about warranties and financing—and consider how you might be protected if something goes wrong later.

Some shoppers base their choice almost on price alone. Others focus on a vehicle's styling, its performance, even its interior room. Most buyers toss comfort, safety, fuel economy, insurance costs, warranties, and reputation for reliability into the mix.

No matter which factors are important to you, the *Automobile Book* helps you make a better-informed decision. It furnishes a range of important information—from the pros and cons of leasing versus buying in the Shopping Tips section, to a discussion of air bags in the Safety section, to federal Environmental Protection Agency (EPA) fuel economy estimates in the Buying Guide. Also explored are such innovations as "one-price" selling and the trend toward less-aggressive sales tactics.

Smart shoppers know the more information they have, the easier it is to make the right decisions—decisions they'll be locked into once they sign a contract to buy that new car. If you want to find the right vehicle at the right price while avoiding some car-buying pitfalls, you've come to the right place.

Using the Buying Guide

Most of the *Automobile Book* is devoted to the Buying Guide section, which this year covers more than 165 passenger cars, minivans, sport-utility vehicles, and light trucks.

One caution: The opening "overview" section of each report is based on information supplied by the automakers. Each year, some promises made by the car companies never materialize. Engines, certain options, even new models are delayed or scrapped as the market changes. If something described in this issue conflicts with what you're seeing on vehicles at a dealership, contact us and we will do our best to provide up-to-the-minute information.

Our judgments in the Performance, Accommodations, Build Quality, and Value for the Money segments of each report are based on full road tests, driving impressions of new models, and feedback from owners of earlier models.

Where possible, we note actual fuel-economy figures recorded by our auto staff during road testing. EPA fuel-economy estimates give a good idea of what to expect, but they are derived from laboratory simulations. Though increasingly accurate, we find that the EPA numbers often are higher than what a vehicle achieves in real-world driving.

Best Buys

In addition to the judgments in the reports, the Auto Editors of Consumer Guide™ select Best Buys and Recommended vehicles in 16 size and market categories. An important criterion in making these choices is price, or more precisely, which vehicles offer the most value per dollar spent. Most vehicle classes contain 15 or more different models. Besides the "best" and "recommended" cars in such large groups, there are generally several "good" ones that also deserve consideration, particularly those that are especially keenly priced. In order to point out these value-per-dollar cars, we add a third ratings category: Budget Buys. After all, there's nothing wrong with buying a good car that meets your needs and, at the same time, fits neatly into your budget.

Price Advice

One of the ways our readers get the most for their money is by taking advantage of the price lists in the Buying Guide. These lists include manufacturer's suggested retail prices and dealer invoice prices.

We make every effort to ensure that the prices are accurate and are the latest available at the time of publication.

Prices are not listed for some new models because the manufacturer had not announced 1998 prices when this issue went to press. For some models, we list only the suggested retail prices because the dealer invoice price was not available.

Some prices may be for 1997 models because the manufacturers hadn't announced 1998 prices in time for this issue.

• The retail prices in this issue are manufacturer's suggested retail prices as set by the factory. They are just that—suggestions. Though these are the numbers that appear on the federally mandated window sticker, nothing binds you to paying them. Most shoppers expect—or hope—to pay somewhat less.

• The invoice prices shown are what the dealer pays to buy the car from the factory. Invoice prices generally include advertising fees charged to dealers (discussed in the Shopping Tips section).

• The destination charge is the cost of shipping the car to the dealership from the factory or port of entry. Only in rare instances do the suggested retail and dealer-invoice prices in this book include the destination charge, though a growing number of manufacturers incorporate it in advertised prices. Where the destination charge is listed separately, it must be added to the price of the car. Dealers pay the exact amount shown on the manufacturer's price sticker (explained in Shopping Tips).

Supply, demand, and competition determine the selling price. Market conditions can vary greatly for different cars in different parts of the country. You will have to determine the best price in your area by shopping for the same car at two or more dealers.

We do all we can to make certain that the prices in this issue are accurate. Car companies, however, are free to change their prices at any time. If a dealer claims that our prices are incorrect, contact us and we'll do our best to help you out.

Good luck in buying your next new car. The editors invite your questions and comments:

Consumer Guide™
7373 N. Cicero Ave.
Lincolnwood, IL 60646-1682

USING THE BUYING GUIDE

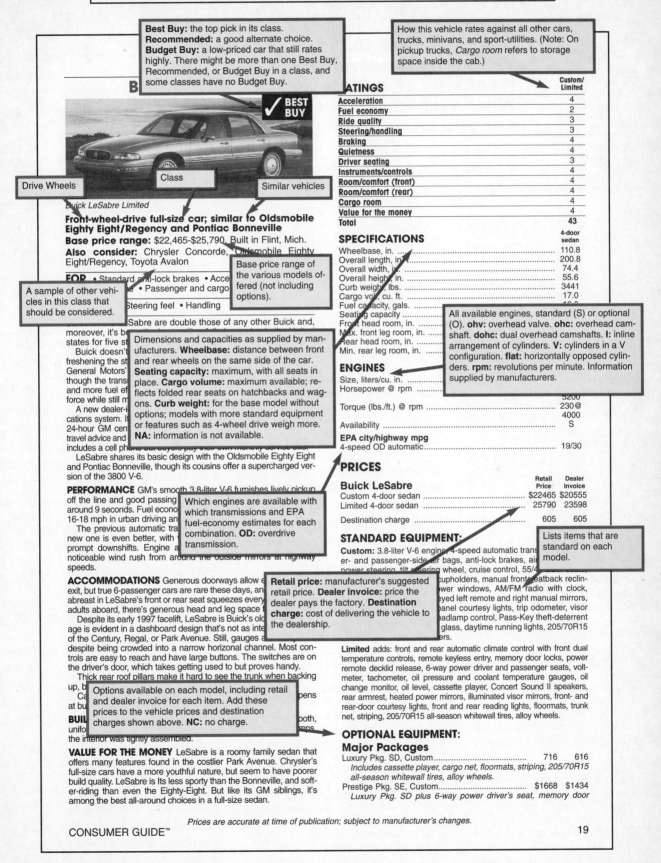

Best Buy: the top pick in its class.
Recommended: a good alternate choice.
Budget Buy: a low-priced car that still rates highly. There might be more than one Best Buy, Recommended, or Budget Buy in a class, and some classes have no Budget Buy.

How this vehicle rates against all other cars, trucks, minivans, and sport-utilities. (Note: On pickup trucks, *Cargo room* refers to storage space inside the cab.)

Drive Wheels

Class

Similar vehicles

Buick LeSabre Limited

Front-wheel-drive full-size car; similar to Oldsmobile Eighty Eight/Regency and Pontiac Bonneville
Base price range: $22,465-$25,790. Built in Flint, Mich.
Also consider: Chrysler Concorde, Oldsmobile Eighty Eight/Regency, Toyota Avalon

Base price range of the various models offered (not including options).

A sample of other vehicles in this class that should be considered.

FOR • Standard anti-lock brakes • Acceleration • Passenger and cargo ... • Steering feel • Handling

...Sabre are double those of any other Buick and, moreover, it's be... ...states for five st...

Buick doesn't... ...freshening the st... General Motors'... ...though the trans... and more fuel ef... force while still m...

A new dealer-i... cations system. I... 24-hour GM cen... travel advice and... includes a cell ph...

LeSabre shares its basic design with the Oldsmobile Eighty Eight and Pontiac Bonneville, though its cousins offer a supercharged version of the 3800 V-6.

PERFORMANCE GM's smooth 3.8-liter V-6 furnishes lively pickup off the line and good passing... ...around 9 seconds. Fuel econo... 16-18 mph in urban driving an...

The previous automatic tra... new one is even better, with... prompt downshifts. Engine a... noticeable wind rush from around the outside mirrors at highway speeds.

Which engines are available with which transmissions and EPA fuel-economy estimates for each combination. **OD:** overdrive transmission.

ACCOMMODATIONS Generous doorways allow e... exit, but true 6-passenger cars are rare these days, an... abreast in LeSabre's front or rear seat squeezes every... adults aboard, there's generous head and leg space f...

Despite its early 1997 facelift, LeSabre is Buick's old... age is evident in a dashboard design that's not as int... of the Century, Regal, or Park Avenue. Still, gauges a... despite being crowded into a narrow horizontal channel. Most controls are easy to reach and have large buttons. The switches are on the driver's door, which takes getting used to but proves handy.

Thick rear roof pillars make it hard to see the trunk when backing up, b...

Ca... at bu...

Options available on each model, including retail and dealer invoice for each item. Add these prices to the vehicle prices and destination charges shown above. **NC:** no charge.

BUIL... uniro... the interior was tightly assembled.

VALUE FOR THE MONEY LeSabre is a roomy family sedan that offers many features found in the costlier Park Avenue. Chrysler's full-size cars have a more youthful nature, but seem to have poorer build quality. LeSabre is lts less sporty than the Bonneville, and softer-riding than even the Eighty-Eight. But like its GM siblings, it's among the best all-around choices in a full-size sedan.

RATINGS

	Custom/Limited
Acceleration	4
Fuel economy	2
Ride quality	3
Steering/handling	3
Braking	4
Quietness	4
Driver seating	3
Instruments/controls	4
Room/comfort (front)	4
Room/comfort (rear)	4
Cargo room	4
Value for the money	4
Total	**43**

SPECIFICATIONS

	4-door sedan
Wheelbase, in.	110.8
Overall length, in.	200.8
Overall width, in.	74.4
Overall height, in.	55.6
Curb weight, lbs.	3441
Cargo vol., cu. ft.	17.0
Fuel capacity, gals.	
Seating capacity	
Front head room, in.	
Max. front leg room, in.	
Rear head room, in.	
Min. rear leg room, in.	

Dimensions and capacities as supplied by manufacturers. **Wheelbase:** distance between front and rear wheels on the same side of the car. **Seating capacity:** maximum, with all seats in place. **Cargo volume:** maximum available; reflects folded rear seats on hatchbacks and wagons. **Curb weight:** for the base model without options; models with more standard equipment or features such as 4-wheel drive weigh more. **NA:** information is not available.

ENGINES

Size, liters/cu. in.	
Horsepower @ rpm	
	5200
Torque (lbs./ft.) @ rpm	230@
	4000
Availability	S

All available engines, standard (S) or optional (O). **ohv:** overhead valve. **ohc:** overhead camshaft. **dohc:** dual overhead camshafts. **I:** inline arrangement of cylinders. **V:** cylinders in a V configuration. **flat:** horizontally opposed cylinders. **rpm:** revolutions per minute. Information supplied by manufacturers.

EPA city/highway mpg
4-speed OD automatic 19/30

PRICES

Buick LeSabre	Retail Price	Dealer Invoice
Custom 4-door sedan	$22465	$20555
Limited 4-door sedan	25790	23598
Destination charge	605	605

Retail price: manufacturer's suggested retail price. **Dealer invoice:** price the dealer pays the factory. **Destination charge:** cost of delivering the vehicle to the dealership.

STANDARD EQUIPMENT:

Lists items that are standard on each model.

Custom: 3.8-liter V-6 engine, 4-speed automatic trans... er- and passenger-side air bags, anti-lock brakes, air... power steering, tilt steering wheel, cruise control, 55/4... ...cupholders, manual front seatback reclin-... ...wer windows, AM/FM radio with clock,... ...eyed left remote and right manual mirrors,... ...panel courtesy lights, trip odometer, visor... ...eadlamp control, Pass-Key theft-deterrent... ...glass, daytime running lights, 205/70R15... ...rs.

Limited adds: front and rear automatic climate control with front dual temperature controls, remote keyless entry, memory door locks, power remote decklid release, 6-way power driver and passenger seats, voltmeter, tachometer, oil pressure and coolant temperature gauges, oil change monitor, oil level, cassette player, Concert Sound II speakers, rear armrest, heated power mirrors, illuminated visor mirrors, front- and rear-door courtesy lights, front and rear reading lights, floormats, trunk net, striping, 205/70R15 all-season whitewall tires, alloy wheels.

OPTIONAL EQUIPMENT:

Major Packages

Luxury Pkg. SD, Custom	716	616

Includes cassette player, cargo net, floormats, striping, 205/70R15 all-season whitewall tires, alloy wheels.

Prestige Pkg. SE, Custom	$1668	$1434

Luxury Pkg. SD plus 6-way power driver's seat, memory door

Prices are accurate at time of publication; subject to manufacturer's changes.

SHOPPING TIPS

Before making the rounds of dealerships, answer some basic questions: What kind of vehicle do you want? What kind do you need? How much can you afford to pay?

Several car companies are holding the line on prices for 1998, and some have even cut prices on selected models.

Affordability remains a serious concern, however. The average transaction price for a new vehicle reached a record $22,200 in 1997, according to the National Automobile Dealers Association.

Car prices are simply too high for many Americans to afford a new model. Many respond by turning to leasing, hoping to avoid a hefty down payment (See "Lease or Buy—Which is Better?"). Rebates are still around, too, as car companies find they have to lay cash on the hood to get more buyers interested.

With so many models available, the choices can be baffling. More buyers than ever are jumping into trucks, and sales of traditional passenger cars are shrinking. Minivans—the favorite family hauler of the 1980s—are losing ground to the phenomenally popular sport-utility vehicles.

To get the best car at the best price, it's more important than ever to do some homework before starting to shop. Start with the basics. Should the vehicle have front-wheel drive, rear-drive, or 4-wheel drive? How big and how flashy should it be? Small cars are generally cheaper to buy and operate, yet big ones tend to protect occupants better in collisions—though some recent subcompacts can actually be safer than older full-size models.

You may also need to consider the price of insuring a particular vehicle. Rates for high-performance cars and sport-utility vehicles are substantially higher than for family sedans. Young drivers crave sporty models, but high insurance premiums can put these cars out of reach.

Fuel costs are important and include not only miles per gallon but whether the car requires expensive premium-grade gas. Many current engines do—and not just in sporty or luxury cars.

Maybe the right "car" for you isn't a car. Perhaps you should buy a minivan or a sport-utility vehicle. Whatever the case, it pays to do preliminary research and then visit as many dealerships as possible.

Take the process in steps:

• Choose a model and options that suit your needs—not just your desires. The Buying Guide contains information and advice on each model and the latest prices.

• Decide how much you can afford and how much you are willing to pay before you shop for a vehicle. Since most people don't pay cash for a car, this involves shopping for a loan.

• Once you've settled on a vehicle, shop at least three dealers to compare prices. Price is important, but look for dealers that appear to provide the best service after the sale.

Be a Smart Shopper

Informed shoppers have an edge. To get the best deal, plan your moves and take your time.

• Arm yourself with as much information as possible about the car you want, and how much it should cost.

• Know what you want, but be flexible. That's not conflicting advice. Narrow your list to two or three models that best suit your needs and pocketbook, but don't be rigid. You won't get the best price if you insist on a particular color or specific equipment, such as a blue coupe with a sunroof.

• Shop competing dealers to compare prices on the same car with the same equipment. Given the ever-widening range of options available, this can be a challenge. Get written price quotes that are good next week, not just today.

Warning: Never be pressured into putting a deposit on a car just to get a quote. When a deposit is required to order or hold the car you intend to buy, keep it small: $50 to $100 is plenty. Get a written statement that you will get your deposit back if the deal turns sour.

• Manufacturers frequently group options in packages. This often reduces the cost of all the included items, but to get the feature you want, you may have to purchase some options you don't. Are they worth the extra cost?

• Size up supply and demand for the car you want. A good deal on a slow-selling model might be below dealer invoice, while a popular car may command full suggested retail price.

Unfortunately, no simple formula spells this out. Selling prices depend on supply and demand for that model in your area and how much competition exists among dealers. The only way to wind up with a "good deal" is to get prices from several dealers.

• Consider resale value. How much will your car be worth when it's time to sell? To get an idea of which models hold their value best, consult used-car price guides, such as the Consumer Guide™ *Used Car Book*, or residual-value guidebooks, which are available at the library.

• Test drive the exact car you decide on—before you buy. Think you want manual shift and a sport suspension? A 15-minute test drive might convince you to go with automatic and softer springs and shocks. Don't settle on engines, transmissions, or other major features until you've tried them on the road.

• Keep your trade-in separate from the new-car price. Some dealers lure customers with a high trade-in allowance, only to inflate the price of the new vehicle. If you're trading in your old car, it's best to talk about that after you receive a price on the new one. That will help you compare price quotes among dealers and decide if you would rather sell your old car yourself.

Dealing with Dealers

Some dealers cling to traditional hard-sell methods. Others take a gentler, more modern approach. If a dealer makes you uncomfortable, look elsewhere. Buying a car should be a pleasant experience, so find a dealer who makes it one.

Even at dealerships where the atmosphere is congenial, the salespeople aren't on your side. Their job is to make as much money as possible on each sale. Your quest as a consumer is to get the lowest possible price on the car you want. What you want to find is a happy medium between getting a good deal and allowing the dealer to make a reasonable profit.

When you're at the dealership, keep these tips in mind:

• Dealers make money not only from the sale itself but by selling financing, insurance, and add-ons. As profits from actual new-car sales decline, dealers try harder to push these "back-end" items.

Popular moneymakers include such options as rustproofing, "protection packages," burglar alarms, powerful audio systems, and extended-service contracts. Dealers pay little for these and mark them up sharply. You can usually buy them elsewhere for less money—and you might not need them at all. (See "Warranties and Service Contracts" section on page A-17.)

• Because today's market is so competitive, try to get dealers to "bid" for your business through lower prices. Let them know you're interested in one of their cars, but that you'll go elsewhere—or buy a different car—to get a better price or fairer treatment.

As a rule, don't tell Dealer A how much Dealer B quoted you on the car you want. Just let each know that you will buy from the one who gives the lowest price and best all-around service.

• For a good deal, find a good dealer. Price is important, but it shouldn't be your only consideration. A dealership with a reputation for good service and giving customers the benefit of the doubt may deserve a few hundred dollars more on the purchase price.

Ask friends and neighbors about their experiences with various dealers. If you spot a car wearing a certain dealer's promotional license-plate frame, ask the owner how he or she was treated. Your local Better Business Bureau can provide a Reliability Report, stating whether complaints have been lodged against a specific dealership. Watch for a pattern of complaints or for signs that problems remain unresolved.

• Look for signs of nefarious sales techniques. Notice how you're approached when you arrive at a dealership, and whether the same salesperson stays with a customer through the entire transaction. Avoid showrooms where a "closer" or "turnover" expert takes over from the original salesperson at some point during the transaction—clear evidence of high-pressure tactics. Beware of dealers who tack a supplementary price sticker onto every car, listing high-profit extras you may not want.

• Look for salespeople who exhibit real product knowledge, not just rattle off a set speech, and are neither pushy nor overly friendly. If you feel bulldozed or intimidated, shop elsewhere. You should expect—and get—professional treatment.

• Check out the service department of the dealership. Ask some people who are having their cars serviced if they are happy with their buying experience and treatment after the sale.

• Many dealers continue to treat women differently from men. Studies have found that females and minorities are less likely to be offered the lowest price on a car. Look for dealers and salespeople who treat every customer with an equally professional approach.

• Don't let yourself be "qualified." That means the salesperson asks pointed questions to see if you're ready to buy right now and are financially able to do so. If you are merely shopping, you might get a quick brush-off. Watch out for questions like, "What will it take for you to buy this car today?"

• Special-ordering the exact car and equipment you desire is usually possible only on domestic models. Import dealers can search other dealers for the model you want and can sometimes install options once the car arrives but can seldom order from the factory.

Even domestic dealers might be reluctant to order a car. Delivery can take six weeks—usually longer—though some manufacturers, led by Cadillac, are speeding up the process. Though the dealer may demand a deposit to order a car, he has no guarantee you won't back out of the deal, leaving him stuck with a car he might have trouble unloading.

The dealer has a financial interest in selling a car that is in stock. Storing the car on his lot is costing him money. In addition, rebates and incentives generally apply only to vehicles "in dealer stock."

If you're not happy with the selection, a dealer can usually search the inventories of counterparts in nearby areas by computer to see if they have what you're looking for.

Rebates and Incentives

Find out exactly what incentives are available and to which cars they apply. Beware of "catches."

Incentives are placed on specific models for a specified period. They come three ways: cash rebates direct to the customer; low interest rates on loans; and cash incentives to the dealer to sell a particular car. In each case, the manufacturer—not the dealer—is the source of the incentive. Remember, too, that rebates are designed to spur sales of specific, slow-selling models.

Customer-direct cash rebates are usually well advertised and consist of a check made out from the automaker to the buyer. As an alternative, you might get a manufacturer-arranged cut-rate loan—low annual percentage rate (APR) financing—that's often available instead of a cash rebate. Rates typically range from 2.9 percent to 7.9 percent APR and traditionally are lowest for shorter-term loans. You will have to do the math to determine which option is best—low-APR financing or a cash-back rebate.

Dealer incentives are trickier. It can be difficult to find out whether a manufacturer is offering dealers cash to sell certain cars, though the business section or automotive pages of some newspapers run lists periodically.

If you learn that a dealer incentive is in effect, try to negotiate the price of the car down by more than that sum. Remember, incentives come out of the manufacturer's pocket, not the dealer's.

If you decide to accept a cash rebate, should you take the money up front and use it as part of your down payment or have the manufacturer mail you a check? There is no real advantage either way, but you might rather have the money now and use it as part of the deal.

When a dealer suggests that you sign the rebate check over to him, that doesn't mean he's trying to steal your money. As long as the rebate is reduc-

Lease or Buy—Which is Better?

Leases account for about one-third of new-car sales overall and more than half of luxury-model transactions, and the number grows annually. Sadly, many consumers resort to leasing for the wrong reason—because they can't afford to buy the new vehicle of their dreams.

Lease contracts have been notorious for cryptic and incomplete language. Federal regulations that took effect October 1, 1997, require clearer language in lease contracts and advertising. The rules also require disclosure of costs such as the total amount due at lease signing, the total amount due over the term of the lease, and the "capitalized cost." Capitalized cost is the equivalent to the selling price of a car and the starting point for lease calculations.

Even if you master all the terms and facts of a particular lease, there's an even bigger issue: Is leasing better than buying? It depends on your particular financial situation, so you may have to consult a tax adviser.

For most consumers, leasing a car every two or three years is more expensive than buying one and keeping it for a time after the final payment. Leasing lets you drive a newer car and one that's always under warranty—and those benefits are likely to cost you money, not save it for you.

On the other hand, many people still purchase simply because they're more comfortable with "owning" a car than leasing. Some financial advisers argue that most advantages to owning a car have disappeared, making leasing more attractive. For example, the interest on car loans is no longer tax deductible.

Here are some guidelines:

• Leasing is most beneficial if you claim your car as a business expense. Generally, all leasing expenses attributed to business purposes can be deducted. Leasing also ties up less capital than buying.

• If you buy a car for business, you can still write it off, but there are more limitations. If you can't claim car expenses for business use, then leasing is probably more expensive than buying. Consult a tax adviser to find out which route is best for you.

• A large down payment (or "capital cost reduction") isn't required for most leases. Monthly lease payments also are generally lower than a loan payment for an equivalent car.

When you buy, banks typically want a down payment of 20 percent. With the average transaction price of a new car around $22,000, that means $4400 in cash or trade-in value on your old car. If you don't have that much, a lease that requires only $1000 down might be a better bet.

• One major disadvantage to leasing is that unless you eventually buy a car, you'll always be making a monthly payment. At the end of a lease you have the option of giving it back to the leasing company or buying it. Unless you decide to make do without a car, you will be stuck with another car payment.

• While monthly payments may be lower on a lease, in the long run it is usually cheaper to buy and keep cars five years or longer. If you pay off a car loan in four years and keep the car another three years, your only expenses after the final payment will be for maintenance, repairs, and insurance.

• On the other hand, would you rather drive a 6-year-old car or a much newer one? A 2- or 3-year lease gives you the option of having a new car more often. The car you drive will be under warranty, and you don't have the hassle of selling or trading in an old car. The majority of leases are for three years, and several companies promote 2-year agreements.

• For the lowest monthly payments, look at cars with high "residual value" or resale value. Most of the cost of a lease is depreciation, so a car that depreciates less will have a lower monthly payment.

Read the Fine Print

If you're enticed by ads that shout "No money down, $299 a month" for a lease on a $25,000 car, take a closer look. It should explain that you could be liable for the following:

• Most leases allow 12,000 miles a year. Over 12,000 miles, you'll pay a penalty of 10 to 15 cents a mile. A lower penalty may be negotiable when you sign the lease, or you might be able to raise the mileage limit by increasing your monthly payment. Some companies promote "low-mileage" leases at tempting rates, but be sure you won't exceed the limit.

• On most leases, you have to pay up front the first month's payment and a refundable security deposit. You may also get hit with an "acquisition fee," in effect, paying the leasing company to process your credit application.

• Most states charge sales tax on the total of the monthly lease payments, not the capitalized cost. A handful of states require that the lessee—that's you—pay sales tax on the "cap cost" or even the full suggested retail price of the car. If the tax is eight percent and you're leasing a $30,000 car, that is $2400.

You usually can roll the sales tax into your monthly payment, but you will have to pay it each time you sign a new lease. If you buy the car at the end, you might have to pay tax again on the purchase price. Check local tax laws.

• Early termination fees: Before signing, learn whether you can terminate the lease early and how much of a penalty you must pay. It might cost thousands of dollars to get out of a lease.

• End-of-lease costs: You could be liable for "excessive wear" or for having the car prepped for resale. Dents, ripped upholstery, and accessories that don't work are examples of damage you will have to pay for. Since "excessive wear" is open to interpretation, it pays to take good care of a leased car so it passes inspection when you turn it in.

If you don't buy the vehicle at the end of the lease, you might have to pay a "disposition fee."

Shop for a Lease

Nearly all major car companies offer national lease programs through their dealers. The "No money down, $299 a month" lease advertised in San Diego also should be available in Toledo. The deal should be the same everywhere, but one dealer might waive the down payment or reduce your monthly payment to convince you to lease from them.

Just as it pays to shop when you're buying, shop for a lease and have dealers compete for your business. Make sure you're comparing costs for identical vehicles. A lease with low monthly payments that requires a hefty down payment might cost more in the end than one with higher monthly payments but little or no money down.

ing his selling price, there is nothing wrong with letting him get the money. In some states, if you sign a rebate over to the dealer, you may not have to pay sales tax on that sum. Check local tax laws.

New Ways to Shop for Cars

Some people love to haggle, but others dread the prospect. Now, there are ways for you to minimize—or even skip— that part of the process.

Only 24 percent of buyers paid the

The Shorter the Loan, the Less You Pay

The sooner you pay off a car loan, the less you will pay in interest. Lenders usually charge lower interest rates on shorter loans. Here are some examples of monthly payments and the amount you will pay in interest and in total for a $16,000 loan. Some figures are rounded off.

Interest Rate	No. of Months	Monthly Payment	Total Interest	Total Payment
2.9	24	$687.00	$488.00	$16,488.00
6.9	24	715.64	1175.00	17,175.00
2.9	36	464.59	725.00	16,725.00
6.9	36	493.30	1759.00	17,759.00
8.0	36	500.80	2029.00	18,029.00
8.0	48	390.40	2739.00	18,739.00
9.0	48	398.16	3112.00	19,112.00
10.0	48	406.40	3507.00	19,507.00
9.0	60	332.80	3968.00	19,968.00
10.0	60	339.20	4352.00	20,352.00
11.0	60	347.20	4832.00	20,832.00

Similar Models

It is common for manufacturers to use the same automotive platform—a car's basic architecture—for more than one vehicle. It is also typical for these "similar models" to share major mechanical components, including engines. However, they usually have individualized styling and are sold under different model names or even different brand names. Choosing the least-expensive member of the group might save you hundreds, even thousands, of dollars.

Chrysler Corporation

Plymouth	Dodge	Chrysler	Eagle	Other Brand
—	—	—	Talon	Mitsubishi Eclipse
—	Avenger	Sebring coupe	—	—
Breeze	Stratus	Cirrus, Sebring convertible	—	—
Neon	Neon	—	—	—
—	Intrepid	Concorde	—	—
Voyager	Caravan	Town & Country	—	—

Ford Motor Company

Ford	Mercury	Lincoln	Other Brand
Escort, ZX2	Tracer	—	—
Taurus	Sable	—	—
Crown Victoria	Grand Marquis	—	—
Contour	Mystique	—	—
—	Villager	—	Nissan Quest
Explorer	Mountaineer	—	—
Ranger	—	—	Mazda B-Series
Expedition	—	Navigator	—

American Isuzu Motors Inc.

Isuzu	Other Brand
Rodeo	Honda Passport
Trooper	Acura SLX
Oasis	Honda Odyssey

Nissan Motor Corporation USA

Nissan	Infiniti
Sentra, 200SX	—
Maxima	I30
Pathfinder	QX4

posted asking price for their last vehicle, according to a survey by The Dohring Company, a market research firm, while 75 percent negotiated the purchase price of their vehicle. Indeed, the average manufacturer's suggested retail price of a new vehicle in 1995 was $22,965, according to the National Automobile Dealers Association. That contrasts with an average transaction price of $20,450. Some analysts believe true transaction prices are even lower.

More interesting yet, the Dohring survey showed, close to two-thirds of buyers liked their most recent haggling encounter, and 48 percent said they prefer to negotiate. Only one-third said they would rather face a "one-price"

situation.

If you're uneasy about negotiating with a dealer, shop for a "one-price" model, such as a Saturn. Or, pick dealers that advertise "no-dicker" sales practices. Then, the price you see posted is the price you will pay. Period. That will reduce the stress and let you concentrate on finding the model that best meets your needs. You might pay more than you hoped, but at least you can be satisfied no one else paid less.

"One-price" selling, a highly-publicized trend a few years ago, has not taken off, partly because some of those "no-haggle" prices were too high. And to make that method work effectively, salespeople have to be paid a salary rather than a commis-

sion—a change most dealers resist.

Another trend that's lost steam is the "value-priced" vehicle, which typically has more standard features at a lower price than a regular model. The practice was most common in California and other western states, where domestic car companies are trying to attract buyers who favor imported vehicles.

The latest trend in pricing and packaging is something many consumers have requested for years—equip vehicles with the features buyers are most likely to want as standard equipment. That reduces the number of optional features consumers have to consider and makes price haggling less of an issue.

GM is using that approach on recently introduced models such as the Chevrolet Malibu and Oldsmobile Cutlass. Ford Motor Company is taking it a step further by offering most of its 1998 Ford and Mercury passenger cars in a 2-model lineup. For example, the Escort sedan comes in base LX and more-expensive SE models and the ZX2 coupe comes in "Cool" and "Hot" models. The drawbacks are potentially higher base prices and a situation in which you might have to buy the more-expensive version to get certain options, such as a sunroof or alloy wheels.

Major new players in the new-car business are changing the way vehicles are sold. So far, the highly-touted "big-box superstores" such as CarMax and AutoNation have concentrated on used-car sales. They have obtained dozens of franchises to sell new vehicles, however, and hope to become a one-stop source for everything automotive, providing a hassle-free, uniform buying experience for several brands of vehicles. This has motivated car companies and individual dealers to improve their sales techniques to compete in this new environment.

More than 11 percent of car shoppers use a buying or pricing service, according to a survey by J.D. Power. In California, it is more than 25 percent. Some are considered brokers, others agents, and others don't quite fit either category as the definitions get hazy.

Brokers typically receive payment from dealers for steering business their way. Some are dealers themselves, or they purchase cars from dealers for resale later. Brokers are banned in seven states, and 10 states require they be licensed.

Toyota Motors Sales, USA

Toyota	Lexus
Camry	ES 300
Land Cruiser	LX 450

General Motors

Chevrolet	Pontiac	Oldsmobile	Buick	Cadillac	Other Brand
—	—	Aurora	Riviera, Park Avenue	Seville	—
Malibu	—	Cutlass	—	—	
	Gr. Prix	Intrigue	Century, Regal		—
Lumina, Monte Carlo	—	—	—	—	
—	Bonneville	Eighty Eight, Regency	LeSabre	—	—
Camaro	Firebird	—	—	—	
Cavalier	Sunfire	—	—	—	
Metro	—	—	—	—	Suzuki Swift
—	Grand Am	Achieva	Skylark	—	—
Prizm	—	—	—	—	Toyota Corolla
Venture	Trans Sport	Silhouette	—	—	—
Astro	—	—	—	—	GMC Safari
Blazer	—	Bravada	—	—	GMC Jimmy
Tahoe	—	—	—	—	GMC Yukon
C/K Pickup	—	—	—	—	GMC Sierra
S-10 Pickup	—	—	—	—	GMC Sonoma, Isuzu Hombre
Suburban	—	—	—	—	GMC Suburban
Tracker	—	—	—	—	Suzuki Sidekick

Saturn Corporation

SC (Coupes)	SL (Sedans)	SW (Station Wagons)

Volkswagen United States Inc.

Golf, Jetta

Every car sold in the U.S. must display in its window a "Monroney sticker" showing the manufacturer's suggested retail price for the vehicle and all of its options. Many dealers also affix a second price sticker containing items added at the dealership. And since October 1, 1994, federal law has required that all cars also display a parts-content label, which may appear as part of the Monroney document or as a separate sticker. See the "Window Stickers" section of the text for details.

Ford
Quality is Job 1.

ESCORT

1998 LX 4 door
5-passenger
2.0L engine
5-speed manual transmission

VIN **3FALP1136WR105289**

EXTERIOR: LASER RED METALLIC
INTERIOR: MEDIUM GRAPHITE CLOTH

STANDARD EQUIPMENT
THE FEATURES LISTED BELOW ARE INCLUDED AT NO EXTRA CHARGE IN THE STANDARD VEHICLE PRICE SHOWN AT RIGHT

EXTERIOR
• FULL BOLT-ON WHEEL COVERS
• SOLAR TINTED GLASS
• INTERVAL WINDSHIELD WIPERS
• DUAL MANUAL MIRRORS
INTERIOR
• CLOTH AND VINYL RECLINING BUCKET SEATS
• CENTER CONSOLE WITH CUPHOLDERS
• SPLIT FOLDING REAR SEAT
• PASSENGER-SIDE VISOR MIRROR
• COOLANT TEMPERATURE GAUGE
• TRIP ODOMETER
• AM/FM RADIO
• DIGITAL CLOCK
• DOOR MAP POCKETS

FUNCTIONAL
• 2.0L SPLIT PORT IND 4 CYL ENGINE
• 100,000 MILE TUNE UP INT.
• POWER RACK-AND-PINION STEERING
• 5-SPD MANUAL O/D TRANSAXLE
• FRONT WHEEL DRIVE
• GAS CHARGED MACPHER. STRUTS
• QUADRALINK REAR SUSPENSION
• FRONT DISC BRAKES
• 185/65R14 TIRES
SAFETY/SECURITY
• DRIVER & PASS AIR BAGS
• HEIGHT-ADJUSTABLE SAFETY BELTS (FRONT)
• LOW-FUEL WARNING LIGHT
• CHILD SAFETY REAR DOOR LOCKS
• 24-HOUR ROADSIDE ASSISTANCE

FOR ADDED PROTECTION, THIS VEHICLE IS EQUIPPED WITH A DRIVER & RIGHT FRONT PASSENGER AIR BAG SUPPLEMENTAL RESTRAINT SYSTEM (SRS)

Compare this vehicle to others in the Free GAS MILEAGE GUIDE available at the dealer.

PRICE INFORMATION — Manufacturer's Suggested Retail Price

STANDARD VEHICLE PRICE	$11,280
OPTIONAL EQUIPMENT	
ANTI-LOCK BRAKES	400.00
AIR CONDITIONING	795.00
REAR DEFOGGER	190.00
REMOTE KEYLESS ENTRY	135.00
FLOORMATS	55.00
TOTAL VEHICLE & OPTIONS	12,855.00
DESTINATION & DELIVERY	415.00
TOTAL	$13,310.00

Gas Mileage Information

CITY MPG **28**

HIGHWAY MPG **37**

Actual Mileage will vary with options, driving conditions, driving habits and vehicle's condition. Results reported to EOA indicate that the majority of vehicles with these estimates will achieve between

18 and **24** mpg in the city and between **22** and **30** mpg on the highway.

1998 ESCORT LX
4 CYL. 2.0L (121 CID)
MULTIPORT FUEL INJECTION
5-SPEED MANUAL
TRANSMISSION

Estimated Annual Fuel Cost: $621

For Comparison Shopping, all vehicles classified as

SUBCOMPACT

have been issued mileage ratings ranging from

18 to **30** mpg city and
16 to **38** mpg highway

TOTAL **$13,310.00**

FOR ADDED PROTECTION, ALL FORD MODELS EXCEED FEDERAL BUMPER STANDARDS AND ARE EQUIPPED WITH A 5-MPH FRONT AND REAR BUMPER SYSTEM AT NO CHARGE.

PARTS CONTENT INFORMATION

FOR VEHICLES IN THIS CARLINE:
U.S./CANADIAN PARTS CONTENT: 70%
MAJOR SOURCES OF FOREIGN
PARTS CONTENT: ....MEXICO: 15%
FOR THIS VEHICLE:
FINAL ASSEMBLY POINT: ....WAYNE, MICHIGAN, U.S.
COUNTRY OF ORIGIN:
ENGINE PARTS: ........................U.S.
TRANSMISSION PARTS: ....JAPAN

NOTE: PARTS CONTENT DOES NOT INCLUDE FINAL ASSEMBLY, DISTRIBUTION, OR OTHER NON-PARTS COSTS.

Above: The federally mandated price sticker shows the manufacturer's suggested retail price for the vehicle and all of its options.

Left: Federal law requires the contents label to show the percentage of U.S. and Canadian parts in the vehicle; the final point of assembly; the foreign country or countries responsible for producing more than 15 percent of the parts; and the country in which the engine and transmission were built.

Right: This is an example of what a second price sticker originated by the dealer might look like.

XYZ MOTORS

PROTECTION PKG	$389
A.D.P.	225
RUSTPROOFING	226
ADVERTISING	200
DEALER PREP	121
SUBTOTAL	1161
XYZ MOTORS TOTAL PRICE	$14,471

Study the Fine Print

Not all of the statements and numbers in retail car ads mean quite what they appear to.

This is a composite advertisement for fictional models, but it contains examples of advertising techniques you should watch for in real ads.

Who declared this dealer #1? Even if true, compared to how many other dealers?

All sales of new cars are "factory authorized." And is this really a liquidation?

An attractive price, but you must surrender all rebates, put a minimum amount down, and pay additional fees. Plus, the deal is based on a 60-month loan to "qualified buyers." Are you one of them? Could you get better terms elsewhere? The dealer sets the value of your trade-in. Who determines whether you qualify for the rebates and the 7.95 percent loan rate? Note, too, that only cars in dealer stock are included.

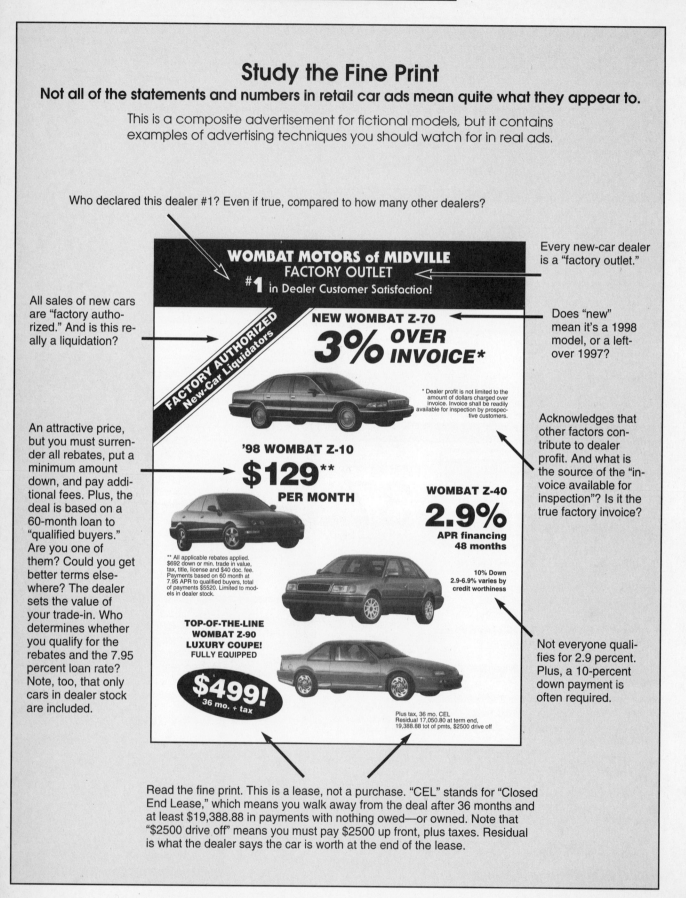

WOMBAT MOTORS of MIDVILLE
FACTORY OUTLET
#1 in Dealer Customer Satisfaction!

FACTORY AUTHORIZED
New-Car Liquidators

NEW WOMBAT Z-70
3% OVER INVOICE*

* Dealer profit is not limited to the amount of dollars charged over invoice. Invoice shall be readily available for inspection by prospective customers.

'98 WOMBAT Z-10
$129 PER MONTH

** All applicable rebates applied. $692 down or min. trade in value, tax, title, license and $40 doc. fee. Payments based on 60 month at 7.95 APR to qualified buyers, total of payments $5520. Limited to models in dealer stock.

WOMBAT Z-40
2.9% APR financing 48 months

10% Down
2.9-6.9% varies by credit worthiness

TOP-OF-THE-LINE WOMBAT Z-90 LUXURY COUPE!
FULLY EQUIPPED

$499!
36 mo. + tax

Plus tax, 36 mo. CEL
Residual 17,050.80 at term end, 19,388.88 tot of pmts, $2500 drive off

Every new-car dealer is a "factory outlet."

Does "new" mean it's a 1998 model, or a leftover 1997?

Acknowledges that other factors contribute to dealer profit. And what is the source of the "invoice available for inspection"? Is it the true factory invoice?

Not everyone qualifies for 2.9 percent. Plus, a 10-percent down payment is often required.

Read the fine print. This is a lease, not a purchase. "CEL" stands for "Closed End Lease," which means you walk away from the deal after 36 months and at least $19,388.88 in payments with nothing owed—or owned. Note that "$2500 drive off" means you must pay $2500 up front, plus taxes. Residual is what the dealer says the car is worth at the end of the lease.

Members of the National Association of Buyers Agents charge a specific fee to the shopper but are prohibited from receiving any payment from dealers. If a buying service charges no fee, they might receive a fee or commission from the dealer to which they direct you. After all, they have to earn a profit somewhere, so it pays to ask about their source of revenue. You might also ask yourself, am I really getting a great deal through this service or should I shop more?

Technology is beginning to change the buying process, and many consumers now buy or shop for a car by computer to bypass all or some traditional routes. The day of ordering a car by computer and having it delivered to your door has not arrived but could be coming soon.

For now, several on-line services transmit purchase requests to a participating dealer, who then responds with the "best" price for the vehicle sought. More dealers are getting involved in such programs, but the price you receive through the World Wide Web may not be the lowest available, so it still pays to shop more than one store.

The trend toward a "virtual showroom" is growing. Nearly every automaker has established a site on the Internet to provide product information. Some are entertaining and informative, allowing you to "build" your vehicle of choice, obtain a complete retail price list, even apply for a loan and make an appointment with a dealership. Others are no more helpful than the usual sales brochures. Hundreds of new-car dealerships now have Web sites to dispense information about their operation and vehicles in stock.

Interactive kiosks also are springing up, serving as a no-pressure information source before you encounter a salesperson. Situated in dealerships, shopping malls, banks, and credit unions, the kiosks use touch-screen computers to display details of available vehicles. In some installations, you can pick up a phone next to the kiosk to make an appointment for a test drive at a nearby dealership.

The bottom line is that the retail end of the automobile business is changing rapidly—and mainly for the better if you consider how much information is at your fingertips now compared to just 10 years ago. You don't have to traipse from dealer to dealer just to see what features and colors are offered. Help is available by phone direct from the car companies, dealers, and the Internet.

Even with all these choices, eventually, you'll probably have to go to a dealership to complete the deal. That being the case, why not shop the old-fashioned way at the same time you are surfing the Web for a new set of wheels? Seeing, touching, and driving a vehicle is much more informative than a "virtual reality" display on a computer screen. A face-to-face meeting with a salesperson may also get more answers than an on-line service can provide.

Our advice is to explore the new ways of shopping for a car, but don't abandon the traditional approaches. Use both and you'll be better informed and more likely to find what you want at the lowest price.

Window Stickers

"Window shopping" can tell you a lot about a particular vehicle—from the suggested retail price to how much "domestic content" it has.

All cars sold in the U.S. must have posted on a side window what is called a "Monroney sticker" (named for the congressman responsible for that requirement). This law does not apply to light trucks, including passenger vans, and most sport-utility vehicles. Most dealers voluntarily put the manufacturer's price sticker on trucks. You decide if you want to do business with one that doesn't.

The Monroney sticker must show:
• The manufacturer's suggested retail price (MSRP) for the vehicle and all its factory-installed options.
• A destination charge for shipping to the dealer from final assembly point or port of importation.
• EPA fuel economy estimates.

Many dealers add a second window sticker listing accessories installed at the dealership, and/or other charges. Balk at paying for anything on this "addendum" sticker. It's very likely the add-ons are of dubious value or grossly overpriced.

Such add-on stickers typically include:
• Rustproofing: Most manufacturers advise against extra-cost rustproofing (see "Warranties and Service Contracts").

• Protection packages: These usually consist of dealer-applied paint sealers and fabric protectors, often in addition to rustproofing. They are of little or no value or duplicate the substances applied at the factory or those you can apply yourself for far less cost.
• Documentary (or "doc") fees: These are supposed to cover the cost of getting the title transferred into your name. Except for normal state title and license fees, these expenses are part of the dealer's cost of doing business—not the consumer's. Some states now limit the documentary fees dealers can charge. Check with local consumer protection agencies.
• M.V.A., A.D.P. (or another abbreviation or code): These are smoke screens for dealer-invented profit-generators. M.V.A. stands for "Market Value Adjustment," and A.D.P. is "Additional Dealer Profit." Both sound official but are created by dealers to squeeze more money out of you. "Currency Valuation Fee" and "Import Tariff" are similar. Some dealers are imaginative in coming up with new names for old add-on charges, such as a "Procurement Fee."
• Advertising fee: See separate subhead on page A-16.
• Dealer prep charge: Dealers claim this covers their cost of cleaning the vehicle and readying it for delivery. Domestic manufacturers reimburse the dealer for these expenses by including them in the retail price of the car. Some imports also include prep in the price. Don't pay it twice. Ask for a summary of what was done, and inspect the car to be sure it was "prepped" and not just washed.

There also are legitimate if unexpected charges associated with the purchase of some vehicles. Two federal taxes affect car prices. First, a gas-guzzler tax is levied on cars that average less than 22.5 mpg in combined city/highway mileage base on EPA estimates. Some manufacturers include the gas-guzzler tax in the base price; other list it separately. Guzzler taxes range from $1000 to more than $3000, so they can have a substantial impact on the purchase price.

Second, an eight-percent federal "luxury tax" is levied on cars selling for more than $36,000. The tax applies only to the amount over $36,000, so a car that sells for $40,000 will be taxed $320 and one that sells for $50,000 will be taxed $1120. The tax applies to the final transaction, or sale, price of the vehicle, not the suggested retail price. In addition, the tax is figured on the full purchase price before any trade-in value is deducted.

Rather than arguing over individual charges like dealer prep consider the "bottom line" approach. Simply ask for a final price—the total amount you'll have to pay—and compare it to the price offered by competing dealers.

Advertising Fees

Dealers might add a separate charge for advertising. Challenge this extra fee.

Many manufacturers do levy an advertising fee on some or all cars. Dealers also join associations to promote their vehicles with regional advertising—though not every dealer participates.

Dealers often post ad fees that are round numbers, like $200. However, the fees are usually assessed as a percentage of each car's invoice price: typically 1 to 1.5 percent for domestic models, as high as 3 percent for other manufacturers. How can 1.5 percent of the invoice price work out to $200 on every vehicle?

In most cases, the ad fee has been incorporated into the invoice price—the amount the dealer paid for the car. So it's already taken into account when he determines the lowest selling price he will accept. Some car companies reimburse part of the ad fee to the dealer later on.

All businesses factor in advertising costs when setting a retail price, but how many others openly try to charge you separately for it? If a salesperson adds such a fee, argue that it is the dealer's cost of doing business, not yours.

Buying "Below Invoice"

Yes, it is possible to buy a car at or below invoice price, but that doesn't mean the dealer goes without a profit.

In some instances, a dealer can obtain a vehicle for less than its actual invoice price. This is possible because many manufacturers refund a small percentage of the invoice price to their dealers. Ford, Chrysler, and General Motors refund three percent of the invoice price. Imports such as BMW, Isuzu, Jaguar, Mitsubishi, Nissan, Saab, Subaru, and Volkswagen also are in the two-to-three-percent range. Known as "holdbacks," these refunds are distributed to dealers as a lump sum several times a year.

Manufacturers also offer dealers various cash incentives to sell specific cars. With these twin "safety nets," dealers can make a profit even if they sell the car at or below invoice price.

Additionally, the invoice that a dealer shows a customer may not be the actual factory document but a padded version compiled on his own computer. A dealer might even attempt to include on his invoice such non-factory items as rustproofing or pinstriping.

Whether the final price is near invoice or not, careful shopping assures that it will be at least well below the sticker price (MSRP)—unless you're seeking a highly popular model, which could indeed sell for full list price.

Before You Sign That Contract

Rushing to complete a deal invites a dealer to take advantage of you.

• Before you sign anything, read the entire contract and be certain you understand exactly what you're buying. The dealership isn't the best place to do this. The salesperson will likely pressure you to sign to get a legally binding contract that sets the terms of your purchase. Worse, you may be in a hurry because you're eager to drive off in your new car. But once you sign that document, it's difficult, if not impossible, to get it changed.

• Take the contract home. Go over it at your own pace, and be sure to contact the dealer if you have questions. If a dealer doesn't want you to take the contract home, get a written purchase agreement that spells out all the details. Once you're satisfied with that agreement, it can be written into a contract.

Here's what a contract should spell out:

Sale price: The amount you've agreed to pay for the car and optional equipment, plus any dealer-installed accessories.

Dealer prep: Explained in "Window Stickers" section.

Down payment: How much you have to pay immediately, either in cash or combined with your trade-in.

Trade-in value: The amount you're getting for your old car.

Destination charge: Sometimes called freight, this is the cost of shipping the car to the dealer. Many automakers now advertise prices that include the destination fee, but it's listed as a separate item on the official window sticker. Dealers get no discount; they pay the amount listed, and so will you. Just don't pay this charge twice.

Sales tax: Check with your state or local government to determine how tax is assessed in your area. Most states levy sales tax on the full purchase price of the new vehicle. In some states, sales tax is calculated on the net price after trade-in value has been deducted.

Total cost: Be sure the all-important "bottom line" is filled in, so you know your total price including options, accessories, destination charge, dealer prep, and taxes. If a dealer leaves this portion blank, you can end up paying more than you bargained for.

Loans: Federal regulations require lenders to disclose all charges. Be sure you know how much you're actually borrowing, the interest rate, your monthly payment, the length of the loan (in months), and the total amount you will pay over the course of the loan.

Domestic Content Labels

Federal law requires all cars and light trucks to display their U.S. and Canadian parts content.

The data may appear as part of the Monroney sticker or on a separate label.

The label must show the following:

• The quantity of U.S. and Canadian parts—considered the "domestic" content—as a percentage of the total parts in the vehicle.

• The foreign country or countries that furnish the most parts, but only if that foreign country supplies 15 percent or more of the total parts on the vehicle. A maximum of two foreign countries may be listed.

• The final assembly point of the vehicle (city, state, and country).

• The countries of origin for the engine and transmission.

WARRANTIES AND SERVICE CONTRACTS

You shouldn't choose a car based only on its factory warranty. Before you buy extended coverage, weigh the costs against the likely benefits.

A factory warranty is the manufacturer's pledge to absorb certain repair or replacement costs until the car has accumulated a stated number of miles or a specified period of time elapses. Here's an overview of how manufacturers' warranties work and what they generally cover.

Basic warranty: "Bumper-to-bumper" coverage for the entire car. Generally excludes tires and the battery (which are warranted by their manufacturers), but certain automakers include tires in their warranties.

Some manufacturers, such as Audi, BMW, and Volkswagen, include routine maintenance and will change oil and filters, wiper blades, and other items during the coverage period. Most automakers do not cover such items. Here's a list of typical exclusions of most basic warranties:

• Normal wear and maintenance items (oil, filters, brake linings).
• Damage from the environment: hail, floods, "acts of God."
• Damage from improper maintenance, such as incorrect fuel or lubricants.
• Damage caused by the owner or vehicle occupants.

Extended warranty: Factory coverage for a specified period beyond the basic warranty. It usually applies to the powertrain, which consists of such major components as the engine, transmission, drive shafts, and related parts.

Corrosion warranty: Factory warranty against "perforation" rust, in which metal is eaten through. Typical exclusions include surface corrosion caused by hail, stone chips, and industrial pollution.

Roadside assistance: Most new vehicles now come with some form of on-the-road help. Some manufacturers enroll the owner in an auto club during the basic warranty period; other programs are independent. Details vary widely, but some plans cover everything from towing and help with flat tires or mechanical breakdowns, to filling an empty tank. A few provide assistance if you're locked out or even reimbursement for an interrupted trip. Some offer a loaner car while yours is being serviced.

Transfers: All factory warranties may be transferred to subsequent owners at no charge for as long as the warranty is in effect. Specific second-owner exclusions may apply to leased and fleet vehicles, and there may be other restrictions that apply to warranty transfers.

Other warranty provisions: Separate coverage required by the federal government applies to emissions and restraint systems.

Service Contracts and Rustproofing

Beware of these extra-cost items. Service contracts are loaded with loopholes, and aftermarket rustproofing is not necessary.

Service contracts are insurance policies, not real warranties. The manufacturers and independent agents that underwrite them gamble that they'll pay out less in repairs than you paid for the contract. They usually win.

Extra-cost contracts, which run from a few hundred dollars to more than $1000, extend coverage for the car's powertrain beyond the duration of the manufacturer's warranty. Sure, powertrain components cost plenty to fix, but they're also among the least likely to need repair or replacement during the manufacturer's warranty.

Some plans do cover items not protected under factory warranties, such as electrical parts. And if you expect to put a lot of miles on the car, a plan that extends the mileage limit of the basic warranty could be worth the price.

Be careful, however. With most policies, it's the underwriter who determines if an item is covered by the extended warranty. Most plans have a deductible of $25 to $100 per service visit. In some, all work must be performed by an authorized dealership and approved beforehand.

A decade ago, new-car dealers sold service contracts to 35 percent of their customers. But one estimate says it has dropped to around 20 percent. Many independent service-contract firms have gone out of business in recent years, leaving both dealers and their customers stranded. A contract issued by the vehicle manufacturer may cost more, but at least the automaker will be around for the next few years.

Scrutinize any service contract at home. Get a copy of the actual contract, not a brochure summarizing coverage. Bear in mind that any service contract duplicates coverage provided by the manufacturer's basic warranty. If the manufacturer includes an extended warranty, you may never need the service contract. It's not always necessary to buy a service contract immediately; the offer should be good for several weeks after you take delivery.

Modern anti-corrosion techniques allow most automakers to provide rust warranties of at least five years and as many as 11. Extensive use of 2-sided galvanized steel, sealed body seams, high-tech factory rustproofing, and anti-chip paint help combat rust.

Despite these advances, many dealers still push aftermarket rustproofing. Why? Because it can cost the dealer less than $50, but they charge you $200 to $400—maybe more. Also, rustproofing warranties are notorious for loopholes that make it difficult to obtain promised repairs.

Toyota's statement is typical: "Application of additional rust-inhibiting materials is not necessary." General Motors goes further, warning that "after-manufacture rustproofing products may create an environment which reduces the corrosion resistance built into your vehicle." Holes drilled into doors and fenders to apply rustproofing may actually promote rusting and void your factory anti-corrosion warranty.

1998 Manufacturers' Warranties

MAKE/MODEL	BASIC WARRANTY (YRS/MILES)	EXTENDED WARRANTY (YRS/MILES)	CORROSION WARRANTY (YRS/MILES)	ROADSIDE ASSISTANCE
Acura	4/50,000	None	5/unltd.	Yes
Audi	3/50,000	None	10/unltd.	Yes
BMW	4/50,000	None	6/unltd.	Yes
Buick	3/36,000	None	6/100,000	Yes
Cadillac	4/50,000	None	6/100,000	Yes
Chevrolet	3/36,000	None	6/100,000	Yes
Chrysler	3/36,000	None	5/100,000	Yes
Dodge	3/36,000	None	5/100,000	Yes
Eagle	3/36,000	None	5/100,000	Yes
Ford	3/36,000	None	5/unltd.	Yes
General Motors EV1	3/36,000[1]	None	6/100,000	Yes
GMC	3/36,000	None	6/100,000	Yes
Honda	3/36,000	None	5/unltd.	No
Hyundai	3/36,000	5/60,000 powertrain	5/100,000	Yes
Infiniti	4/60,000	6/70,000 powertrain	7/unltd.	Yes
Isuzu	3/50,000	5/60,000 powertrain	6/100,000	Yes
Jaguar	4/50,000	None	6/unltd.	Yes
Jeep	3/36,000	None	5/100,000	Yes
Kia	3/36,000	5/60,000 powertrain	5/100,000	Yes
Land Rover	4/50,000	None	6/unltd.	Yes
Lexus	4/50,000	6/70,000 powertrain	6/unltd.	Yes
Lincoln	4/50,000	None	5/unltd.	Yes
Mazda	3/50,000	None	5/unltd.	Yes[2]
Mercedes-Benz	4/50,000	None	4/50,000	Yes
Mercury	3/36,000	None	5/unltd.	Yes
Mitsubishi	3/36,000	5/60,000 powertrain	7/100,000	Yes
Nissan	3/36,000	5/60,000 powertrain	5/60,000	No
Oldsmobile	3/36,000	None	6/100,000	Yes
Oldsmobile Aurora	4/50,000	None	6/100,000	Yes
Plymouth	3/36,000	None	5/100,000	Yes
Pontiac	3/36,000	None	6/100,000	Yes
Porsche	2/unltd.	None	10/unltd.	Yes
Saab	4/50,000	None	6/unltd.	Yes
Saturn[3]	3/36,000	None	6/unltd.	Yes
Subaru	3/36,000	5/60,000 powertrain	5/unltd.	No
Suzuki	3/36,000	None	3/unltd.	No
Toyota	3/36,000	5/60,000 powertrain	5/unltd.	No
Volkswagen	2/24,000	10/100,000 powertrain	6/unltd.[4]	Yes
Volvo	4/50,000	None	5/unltd.	Yes

1. Includes battery pack and 220-volt charging system. 2. Roadside assistance on Millenia and MPV models only. 3. Saturn has a 30-day/1500-mile money back guarantee. 4. 11 years/unlimited miles on Passat.

SAFETY

When air bags, which are supposed to save lives, started taking lives, there was rapid and widespread demand to make these devices safer. Changes are being made on 1998 vehicles, and more are on the way.

At least 80 people have died from air-bag deployments since 1990, including 29 in 1996 alone. The National Highway Traffic Safety Administration, the federal agency that creates and enforces our motor vehicle safety regulations, says most of these deaths occurred because occupants were improperly wearing their safety belts or were not wearing safety belts.

Reports of the deaths stunned safety officials and shocked consumers, some of whom already doubted the value of air bags.

Of the 80 victims, 44 were children riding in the front passenger seat. Twelve were infants in rear-facing child seats, which are not supposed to be placed in a vehicle's front seat, and 30 were unbelted or improperly belted, leaving them too close to the air bag when it deployed at maximum force.

For example, a 7-year-old child riding in the front passenger seat of a minivan suffered a skull fracture because he was wearing only the lap portion of his lap/shoulder belt, allowing his upper body to pitch forward just inches from a deploying air bag.

Eighteen of the 33 drivers killed were unbelted, and three others were improperly belted. Only nine wore seatbelts. It is unknown if the other three were belted.

Of three adult passengers killed, only one was wearing a seatbelt.

Despite evidence that most victims were not properly restrained, there was a disturbing fact: Thirteen of the drivers and one passenger were adult women who were 5-foot 2-inches or shorter.

Federal safety officials, the insurance industry, and the automakers concurred that air bags were deploying with too much force, and children and small adults were most at risk. As a result, here are the major changes made for 1998 by NHTSA:

• The force with which frontal air bags deploy can be reduced 20 to 35 percent. Federal requirements for occupant protection have not changed, but a new testing procedure allows auto manufacturers to certify the lower-powered air bags in time for their 1998 models. The test procedure is discussed later in this section, under "Crash Tests."

Most automakers are depowering their air bags for 1998. Others are planning to phase in reduced-force bags, but some are staying with their present systems.

This is being done as an immediate but interim solution until more advanced air bags are developed (see "Smart Air Bags" in this section).

• More prominent warning labels about the dangers of air bags are required on the sun visors of all vehicles, and a larger, removable label on the dashboard at the time of delivery.

• Safety officials and car companies are stepping up warnings that children under 13 should ride in back, small adults should move as far back as possible from air bags, and everyone should buckle up.

How Air Bags Work

Lost in the recent furor over air bags is that they have saved 2430 lives, according to NHTSA, and reduced fatalities in head-on crashes by 30 percent.

All passenger cars and nearly all light trucks sold this year are required by federal regulations to have dual front air bags.

An air bag is an inflatable device that remains concealed in the steering-wheel hub or, with a passenger-side air bag, in the dashboard, until it is activated by a crash.

In a frontal impact of about 12 mph or more, sensors send an electrical signal to trigger the explosive release of a gas that inflates the fabric bag. All this happens in less than one-tenth of a second, and the bags inflate at speeds of up to 200 mph.

The inflated bag creates a protective cushion between the person and the steering wheel, dashboard, and windshield. After a fraction of a second, the bag deflates, restoring visibility and allowing the driver to continue steering the car to a safe stop.

It is vital to recognize that steering wheel and dashboard air bags are designed to open only in frontal collisions,

which account for about 40 percent of the total crashes and more than half the deaths. Frontal air bags have no effect in side or rear impacts.

Many people incorrectly believe an air bag is the only type of restraint needed. As NHTSA discovered in studying the deaths caused by air bags, people who aren't properly restrained by seatbelts can end up perilously close to an air bag.

Use of the lap/shoulder belt is imperative, even with an air bag. Seatbelts provide the initial and primary protection in frontal crashes, in rear and side impacts, and in rollovers.

NHTSA studies of fatal collisions show a combination of 3-point lap/shoulder belts and air bags offers the greatest chance of survival. Lap/shoulder belts are considered 45-percent effective in cars, and 60-percent effective in light trucks in preventing occupant deaths. Air bags increase the survival rate an additional 11 percent in cars and 27 percent in trucks.

Jim Hackney, director of NHTSA's Office of Crashworthiness Standards, warns that the depowered air bags in 1998 models will still claim lives if consumers do not place infants and children in back and fail to make sure all occupants are properly buckled in.

"Depowered air bags are not going to solve the total problem," Hackney said. "There is still the possibility for people who aren't properly restrained to be out of position, and small occupants or children can be on top of the bag in a deployment. With rear-facing child seats in front, there is tremendous danger."

Hackney acknowledged that air-bag technology needs improvement to prevent the deaths of more motorists.

"Air bags are saving thousands of lives and preventing thousands of injuries," he said. "We still cannot stand by and see people killed and injured by a safety device."

Air Bags and Cutoff Switches

NHTSA is considering rules that will allow wider use of

cutoff switches that disable air bags and make it easier for consumers with special needs, such as medical conditions that make air bags dangerous, to have them turned off by dealers.

Currently, only pickup trucks and certain passenger cars can have cutoff switches. On other vehicles, NHTSA reviews requests from consumers to disable air bags on a case-by-case basis.

NHTSA expects to announce soon a decision on whether to allow manufacturers to install cutoff switches on more vehicles or give consumers more choice in disabling air bags.

During 1995, NHTSA approved installing an on-off switch for the passenger-side air bag on pickups, 2-seat passenger cars, and cars with back seats too small to hold a child safety seat. The reasoning was that in these vehicles, children and infants must ride in front, where they are exposed to the full force of the passenger-side air bag.

Currently, only a small number of pickups have key-operated switches on the dashboard that allow turning the passenger-side air bag on and off as desired. No manufacturer has installed a cutoff switch on any of its passenger cars, but that could change during this model year.

Mercedes-Benz and Porsche have child-seat recognition systems that can automatically disable the passenger-side air bag (see "Smart Air Bags" later in this section).

Crash Tests

Federal crash-test rules have changed for 1998 to allow depowered air bags, but critics believe the federal rules need more drastic change.

All vehicles sold in the U.S. are required to pass a 30-mph crash test into a fixed barrier, but this test is not conducted by the federal government. It is carried out by the car companies themselves, and this is the test that has changed for 1998 models.

Most people are more familiar with the New Car Assessment Program, a 35-mph crash test conducted by the government on 40 to 50 vehicles per year as a consumer-information service.

Here's how the two programs operate:

30-mph crash: Every car, light truck, and sport-utility vehicle sold in the United States must pass this test, which until this year required a head-on crash into a fixed barrier.

The tests are done with both belted and unbelted dummies placed in the front seats. Sensors transmit signals to electronic monitoring devices that detect the extent of the injuries people would have suffered to their head, chest, and upper legs.

The unbelted test is the one that prompted automakers to design so much deployment force into air bags so they opened fast enough to cushion unbelted occupants before the occupants moved out of position.

For 1998, all vehicles still must pass this 30-mph test using belted dummies.

However, car companies can now conduct the test for unbelted dummies with a simulated crash called a "sled test." The dummies are placed in a vehicle mounted on a sled. Instead of crashing into a barrier, the sled travels a short distance on rails and comes to a sudden stop.

This rapid deceleration simulates the forces generated in a 30-mph crash. But the sled test is not as severe, insists Jim Hackney, director of NHTSA's Office of Crashworthiness Standards.

"They're not crushing the front of the vehicle, but using the sled is a much faster testing procedure than the crash test," Hackney said. "It is less severe, but it can be done in a much shorter time and allows them more flexibility in depowering the air bags."

The federal limits for head, chest, and leg injuries have not changed, but Hackney said vehicle manufacturers should still be able to meet these regulations even with air bags depowered by 20 to 35 percent.

For example, the head injury criterion, one of the measurements, still allows a maximum score of 1000 to pass. Hackney said that vehicles previously were averaging 400 to 500 in this test and for 1998, the scores will likely increase because of the depowered air bags.

"We can't say yet what the difference is," he said. "We have not tested production vehicles with the depowered air bags."

The vehicle manufacturers do their own tests and "self-certify" that they meet the 30-mph safety requirements, Hackney said. NHTSA will conduct its own tests on about 30 production vehicles later this year as an audit to learn how much "injuries" to the test dummies have increased.

35-mph crash: This test is head-on into a concrete barrier, and it's conducted by NHTSA using production vehicles. Results of the 35-mph tests are released to the public periodically during the year.

Vehicles are not required to pass this test, which NHTSA conducts on 40 to 50 vehicles each year as a "consumer information program." Results for other vehicles, tested in previous model years and not significantly changed in design, are presumed to remain valid.

Belted dummies are monitored for forces to the head, chest, and upper legs. Vehicles are crashed at 35 mph—a speed that generates 36-percent more energy (and potential for injury) than the required 30-mph test.

This test is intended to illustrate the differences between vehicles and is used by the government as a basis for evaluating the relative safety of the cars tested. Each tested vehicle gets a rating of one to five "stars," with the highest number of stars indicating the best protection against head and chest injury in a head-on collision.

NHTSA does not advise consumers to use its 35-mph crash results to choose one car over another or to judge that a vehicle is safe or unsafe. The tests are intended only as a narrow comparison of vehicles of similar size and weight (within about 500 pounds).

The 35-mph test results have been criticized for not reflecting real-world collisions because:

• Actual crashes are rarely head-on into flat barriers that involve the full width of the car. More often, frontal collisions occur at an angle. Many safety advocates argue that testing at an offset angle is more valid.

• Dummies represent an average-size male. A larger or smaller person might produce different results. Some automakers use dummies of various size for their own tests.

• Test results often differ from death and injury rates compiled by the insurance industry and even NHTSA itself.

"No matter what kind of test you do, you're only going to simulate one situation," responds NHTSA's Hackney. "The goal is to use a simulation that brings about improvements to the safety of the vehicles.

"The full frontal barrier test puts more stress on the restraint system than any other test. An offset test focuses more on intrusion into the passenger compartment. When we started this program in 1979, there was a lot more intrusion than there is now. The manufacturers have done a lot of things to reduce intrusion considerably."

Seatbelts: Still the Most Effective Restraint

The car companies, the government, and the insurance industry don't see eye-to-eye on all safety matters. One thing they agree on is that all vehicle occupants should be securely buckled.

Though more attention has focused recently on the benefits and risks of air bags, seatbelts remain the most effective safety feature required by the government. Seatbelts are the primary restraints in motor vehicles. Air bags are supplementary restraints.

The federal government estimates seatbelts have saved more than 90,000 lives since 1975—10,414 in 1996 alone. Air bags, which are newer and less common, are credited with saving 2430.

Any discussion of auto safety should include the caveat that all vehicle occupants need to be buckled. Last year, according to NHTSA, 64 percent of passenger-vehicle occupants killed in crashes were unrestrained.

Rear-seat passengers who aren't buckled are tossed about inside a vehicle in a collision or rollover, exposing themselves and the driver to injury. Unbelted passengers also can be thrown from a vehicle

and risk being hit by other cars or trucks. Seventy-three percent of those ejected from vehicles die.

NHTSA estimates that 68 percent of Americans buckle up, a dramatic improvement from about 40 percent in the last 10 years. Seatbelt usage is still far lower in the U.S. than in countries such as Canada, Germany, and Australia, where more than 90 percent of vehicle occupants buckle up. The goal in the U.S. is to achieve 90 percent by the year 2005.

Part of the reason for this disparity is, unlike in those other countries, there is no national law in the U.S. that mandates seatbelt use or sets uniform penalties for violations. Instead, each state sets its own laws and punishment, and most have chosen to adopt weak laws with small fines.

New Hampshire—whose motto is "Live Free or Die"—is the only state that does not require adults to use seatbelts. Of the other 49 states that do, 36 have "secondary enforcement" laws, which means a motorist cannot be stopped because they are not wearing a seatbelt. A ticket for not wearing a seatbelt can be written in those states only if an officer stops a vehicle for another violation.

Thirteen states and the District of Columbia have "primary enforcement" laws that allow stopping motorists for not wearing belts. The states are California, Connecticut, Georgia, Hawaii, Iowa, Louisiana, Maryland, New Mexico, New York, North Carolina, Oklahoma, Oregon, and Texas.

However, even in some states with primary enforcement, fines are as low as $10—hardly a deterrent—and most are $25 or less. Oregon has the stiffest fine at $75, and New York and the District of Columbia are next at $50.

Twelve states and Washington, D.C., require all occupants be buckled, yet here, too, each state is free to define which vehicles are covered by the law. In some, it applies to all motor vehicles; in others, it's just passenger cars. Pickups, vans, and sport-utility vehicles—which account for more than 40 percent of new-vehicle sales—are not covered by the seatbelt laws in some states.

Even if more states adopt stronger laws, Brian O'Neill, president of the Insurance Institute for Highway Safety, fears that lack of enforcement would make them ineffective.

"We tend to pass a law and then sit back and claim victory," he said. "Passing the law is the easy part. Enforcing the law is the hard part. You have to enforce laws to make them effective."

The penalty in North Carolina for not wearing a seatbelt is only $25, but O'Neill

Auto Safety Hotline

The federal National Highway Traffic Safety Administration (NHTSA) operates a toll-free Auto Safety Hotline for information on government crash tests, safety recalls, and other safety-related questions. Consumers can also call this number to report safety problems with their cars. Hours are 8 a.m. to 10 p.m. Eastern time, on regular business days. An answering system is available after hours.

NHTSA Auto Safety Hotline
1-800-424-9393

Hearing-impaired persons may call:
1-800-424-9153

Consumers can also write to:
National Highway Traffic Safety
Administration
400 7th Street, SW
Washington, DC 20590

Types of Fatal Crashes

Principal Impact type	Percent of all Fatal Crashes
Frontal	51
Left Side	15
Right Side	15
Rear	4
Top/undercarriage	3
Other and unknown	12

(Crashes in which a vehicle rolled over accounted for 30 percent of all passenger-vehicle accident deaths in 1996.)

Passenger-Car Deaths by Size of Vehicle

Category	Wheelbase (in.)	Deaths per 1 million Registered Autos
Small	under 95	296
	96–99	233
Mid-size	100–104	201
	105–109	120
Large	110–114	112
	over 114	110

(Figures are for cars 1–3 years old.)

SOURCE: NHSTA, Insurance Institute for Highway Safety. Figures include both single- and multiple-vehicle crashes of passenger vehicles during 1996.

said strict enforcement of the law has increased usage to 80 percent, among the highest in the country.

"Encouragement doesn't work," he said. "People who don't use belts don't think they'll be in a crash. You can't convince some people to use their belts. You can convince them they'll get a ticket."

All vehicles come with manual 3-point lap/shoulder belts for the outboard seating positions. Most also have 2-point lap belts for the inboard seats, though an increasing number of passenger vehicles furnish a 3-point belt for the center rear seat.

Seatbelts should fit snugly. Shoulder belts should pass over the shoulder and across the chest, with no more than an inch or so slack.

Belts can bother shorter people and children because they rest on the side of the neck or even across the face, and this often is the excuse for not wearing a belt.

To help solve this problem, the NHTSA requires height adjustable shoulder belt anchors for the front seats on 1998 models. This allows adjusting the upper anchor points vertically to suit occupants of various heights. Some manufacturers also provide height adjustments for the rear seatbelts, and others provide "comfort guides," a small clip that routes the belt to a more comfortable position.

If belts lie across the neck of your child, use a booster seat, which usually are designed for youngsters between 40 and 70 pounds. Booster seats elevate a child enough so seatbelts lie comfortably across the shoulder.

Keeping Children Safe

Youngsters may squawk about not riding in front, but safety experts strongly recommend they stay in the back seat until age 13.

Passenger-side air bags are hazardous to children 12 and younger in the front seat—even when they're belted. They are too small and fragile to be so close to a violently deploying air bag.

The risks are greatest for infants. Safety officials warn that a rear-facing child seat should never be used in the front seat of a vehicle with a passenger-side air bag.

Putting children under the age of 13 in the back seat not only eliminates the risks from air bags, it also reduces the risks of injury in frontal crashes—the most common type of collision—because they will be further from the impact.

Several European countries mandate that children ride in the back, but there is no such law in the U.S.

All 50 states and the District of Columbia require infants and toddlers to be placed in a child safety seat when riding in a car. Many laws apply to children up to three or four years of age, but the age cutoffs vary widely. Some cover people as old as 16. A few state laws apply specifically to children weighing 40 pounds or less.

Despite these laws, more than 2100 children age 15 and younger died in motor vehicle accidents last year. NHTSA estimates 40 percent were unrestrained. Child seats can reduce the death risk by 70 percent, yet NHTSA says only one-third are used properly.

Children who weigh less than about 40 pounds and are four feet tall or shorter should ride in a child safety seat. Bigger children can ride in back without a special seat if the shoulder belts fit. If the belts rub their neck or face, then a booster seat is recommended.

More than 100 models of infant carriers and child seats are available, and they vary in design and attachment. That's one reason so many are improperly installed. As a rule, the child is held to the carrier or seat by straps for each shoulder and another between the legs. All child seats are secured by the lap portion of a car's seatbelts, but there is no uniform method of securing them. How and where to properly install them varies by seat and vehicle manufacturer.

Safety experts recommend consulting the instructions for both the child seat and the vehicle manufacturer to be sure you're installing the seat correctly. The owner's manual for new vehicles usually has ample information on installing child seats. The first step is to secure the seat so that it will not move excessively in a collision. The next is to properly secure the child with the belts attached to the seat.

NHTSA is developing new rules for anchoring child seats in passenger vehicles that will cover how seats will be secured, where they can be placed, and the design of the seats themselves.

The new rules will require a tether anchor point built into the rear bulkhead of cars and perhaps separate belts specifically designed for child seats. Some child seats have a tether strap that bolts to the rear of the car and prevents the seat from tipping forward or sideways in a crash. The tether anchor is currently required in Canada but not in the U.S. Consumers with small children should investigate whether an anchor can be installed on a vehicle they are considering.

Built-in child safety seats are a factory option on a number of vehicles, including many minivans and some sport-utility vehicles, though some manufacturers have dropped them because of low demand. This handy feature is integrated with the rear-seat seatback and folds out when needed. Some automakers also offer approved child seats as accessories.

Side Air Bags

A growing number of manufacturers now offer door- or seat-mounted side air bags that protect occupants in side collisions.

Side impacts account for about 30 percent of passenger-vehicle deaths. More than 15,000 fatal or serious head injuries occur yearly because occupants strike a side window, roof pillar, or external object.

Most car companies are introducing side air bags on luxury and "near-luxury" models that cost $30,000 and more. But side air bags for the front seats are standard for 1998 on General Motors' front-drive minivans, the Toyota Avalon, and Volkswagen Passat, all of which are under $30,000, and optional on less-expensive cars such as the mid-size Toyota Camry and subcompact Toyota Corolla and Chevrolet Prizm.

Side air bags may be smaller that front air bags but have to deploy quicker than frontal bags because the crush zone is much narrower. Sensors must detect impact in 4 to 5 milliseconds, versus 15-20 milliseconds in a frontal crash. They must inflate within 20 milliseconds, versus the usual 60-75 milliseconds.

Volvo was the first to introduce side air bags, in 1995, as a standard feature on its 850 sedan and wagon. The following year Volvo made side air bags standard on all its models. Triggered by a mechanical sensor, the side air bags are mounted in the outboard side of the front seatbacks.

Last year, Audi became the first manufacturer to equip a car with six air bags. The A8, a luxury sedan available in limited numbers in the U.S., comes with dual front air bags and side air bags for the four outboard seating positions. Side air bags for the front seats are standard on less-expensive Audis for 1998, including the A6 sedan and all A4 models. Rear side air bags are a new option on the A6 sedan.

BMW has added side air bags for the rear seats on its 1998 7-Series sedan as a $385 option. BMW says it made the side air bags optional because children are more likely to ride in back than adults, and children are more vulnerable to injury from deploying air bags.

BMW also has added side head protection on the 1998 7-Series and 5-Series sedans as a standard feature. Called the Head Protection System (HPS), this is a cloth tube that inflates to reduce head injuries to front-seat occupants in side impacts. Side air bags in the front doors also are standard on the 5- and 7-Series.

Other manufacturers are planning features similar to HPS. Mercedes has developed what it calls a "window bag," an air cushion that inflates along the length of the passenger compartment to protect occupants from hitting a side window or roof pillar. Mercedes says the window bag could appear on U.S. models in early 1999.

Volvo is developing what it calls an "inflatable curtain" that deploys at head level along the sides of the interior. The company says it expects to offer the inflatable curtain by the year 2000.

Smart Air Bags

NHTSA is developing rules that will require manufacturers to use "smart air bags" that would deploy based on the severity of the collision and the person being protected.

NHTSA envisions air bags that will rely on sensors to detect not only whether a seat is occupied but also the size, weight, and position of the occupant to determine when an air bag should be deployed and with how much force. The hope is that this will reduce or eliminate risks to small adults and children from air bags that deploy with too much force.

Both the government and the insurance industry are optimistic the technology for smart—or "advanced"—air bags can be developed to appear on some 1999 models.

The car companies generally aren't as optimistic that this advanced technology can be developed so quickly, but there are already some "semi-smart" systems on the market.

BMW and Mercedes-Benz, for example, have dual-threshold air bag systems. Though the systems differ in details, they generally work like this: If the front-seat occupants are not belted, the air bags will deploy in a collision of about 12 mph. The air bags will not deploy until 15 mph (18 mph in Mercedes' case) if they are belted. The passenger-side air bag will not deploy if a sensor detects the seat is not carrying at least 25 pounds.

Audi is changing its front air bags to a dual-threshold type during the 1998 model year.

Mercedes also offers the BabySmart child-seat recognition system on all its models except the ML320 sport-utility vehicle. It employs a special child seat sold by Mercedes and a company called Britax. A sensor in the front passenger seat detects when the special child seat is in use and automatically disables the air bag. Without the special child seat, a second sensor disables the air bag if there's less than 26 pounds in the passenger seat.

Porsche offers a similar system, but it requires a dealer to reprogram the air bag control unit and install an adapter to recognize a special child seat that comes in three sizes: infant, toddler, and booster.

Real-World Statistics

NHTSA's crash tests do not always portray accurately how a vehicle will fare in the real world. Fatality rates suggest that, all else being equal, a large, heavy vehicle offers the most occupant protection.

Size, weight, handling qualities, and standard or optional safety features all play a role in occupant protection.

The Insurance Institute for Highway Safety studied driver deaths in popular 1991- to 1995-model vehicles. Vehicles with the highest (worst) driver death rates were small cars, small pickups, mini sport-utility vehicles, and sports cars. Those with the lowest death rates were big station wagons, minivans, large and mid-size luxury cars, and large and mid-size sport-utility vehicles.

The worst vehicle, the Chevrolet Camaro, scored nearly three times the average, while the best, the Ford Windstar, had one-fourth the average death rate.

This study's value is limited when choosing a 1998 model. Some of the 1991-95 vehicles with the worst scores did not have air bags, including all the mini SUVs and most compact pickups.

Several of the vehicles have been redesigned since 1995 and have new features such as anti-lock brakes and traction control, and they may also have improved structurally to make them safer.

The Highway Loss Data Institute (HLDI), an insurance trade and lobbying group affiliated with the Insurance Institute for Highway Safety, ranks cars by the number of injury claims filed.

Insurance-based data reflects only claims experience, and cannot prove design flaws. The HLDI ratings show that size alone doesn't guarantee how a car will fare in real-world driving: Some small cars have fewer injury claims than some mid-size cars.

Death rates and injury claims are influenced not only by the size and type of vehicle but by who drives them and how they are driven.

Large, expensive cars most often are driven by older, more experienced drivers, and minivans are usually driven by adults who have children—people who tend to have fewer accidents than the population as a whole.

Small cars and mini SUVs, on the other hand, are used primarily by younger, less experienced drivers—who tend to have more accidents that involve death or injury.

While the information gathered by the insurance industry can be helpful, it may not directly relate to current models or how a vehicle will be driven by your family.

Copies of the brochures, "Driver Death Rates" and "Injury and Collision Loss Experience," are available from:

Highway Loss Data Institute
1005 N. Glebe Road
Arlington, VA 22201

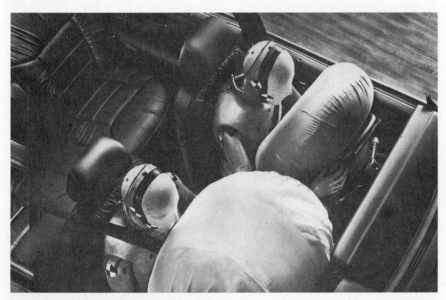

Nearly all new vehicles are equipped with dual air bags.

Light Trucks and Safety

Trucks historically have had fewer safety requirements than cars, but those differences are disappearing. For the 1999 model year, federal regulations will require light trucks to meet the same major safety requirements as cars, including dual front air bags and identical side impact standards.

For 1998, all trucks must have some sort of passive restraint for the front seats, so rather than meet this rule with a stop-gap measure such as automatic seatbelts, most manufacturers installed dual air bags ahead of schedule. That means nearly all 1998-model light trucks have dual air bags. The main exceptions are heavy-duty pickups and vans that are exempt from this requirement.

Many drivers feel safer in a truck than a car. They argue that trucks and vans weigh more than most cars, and weight provides more protection in a collision. You also sit higher in a truck or a van, so you can see trouble coming. This adds to a sense of security, and is one of the key reasons women cite for buying sport-utility vehicles.

According to NHTSA, however, death rates are higher in small pickups and mini SUVs than all classes of vehicles except small passenger cars. The insurance industry reports that personal injury claims are traditionally higher for small pickups and mini SUVs than other types of vehicles.

One key reason: While small pickups are engineered as cargo-hauling vehicles, the majority are driven unloaded, used in place of cars for daily transportation. Empty, a small pickup's cargo bed is extremely light, increasing chances that the rear brakes will lock prematurely in a panic stop. Also, stability is compromised on some trucks because of a higher center of gravity.

By far the deadliest risk facing truck occupants is an accident in which the vehicle rolls over. In 1996, the death rate from rollovers was more than twice as high in SUVs than in passenger cars, and nearly twice as high in pickups.

Rollovers are directly related to a vehicle's stability in turns. That stability is influenced by the relationship between the center of gravity and the track width (distance between left and right wheels). A high center of gravity and narrow track can make a vehicle unstable in fast turns or sharp changes of direction—increasing the odds it will tip over once it begins to skid sideways. The problem is most pronounced in 4-wheel-drive pickup trucks and sport-utility vehicles, which have higher ground clearance for off-road driving.

Despite charges that some SUVs—particularly the smallest ones—tip too easily, NHTSA has found that rollovers are a problem common to all 4WD vehicles, due largely to the way they're driven. Most fatal 4WD rollovers are single-vehicle accidents occurring on weekend nights. The drivers are most frequently males under 25 years of age, and alcohol is usually involved.

In two out of three fatal rollovers, the victims were ejected from the vehicle, indicating they weren't wearing a seatbelt.

Neither cars nor trucks are subject to a federal rollover standard. In June 1996, NHTSA dropped its plan for developing such a standard, claiming that the cost would exceed the agency's cost-benefit limit. However, sport-utility vehicles must carry warnings that they handle and maneuver differently than passenger cars, both on and off the road.

Active Safety Features

While air bags and seatbelts are designed to protect you in the event of a collision, active safety features such as anti-lock brakes and traction control can help you avoid accidents.

More than 40 million vehicles on the road have anti-lock braking systems—or ABS. It's standard on many new vehicles and well worth the extra expense when offered as optional equipment.

ABS is designed to help maintain steering control and prevent skids during braking in rain, snow, and even on dry pavement. A computer controls braking force to prevent the wheels from locking, which results in skidding and robs the driver of steering control.

When ABS brakes are applied, the computer senses when a wheel is about to lock up and then "pumps" the brakes many times per second—much faster than a human foot could. The wheels continue to rotate while slowing the car and the driver maintains steering control.

Stopping distances with ABS may not be any shorter—and on some surfaces may be longer—but the degree of control is dramatically higher. To let drivers know when ABS is activated, the brake pedal pulsates noticeably, sometimes accompanied by a clicking noise.

Many drivers do not understand how ABS works and in an emergency become alarmed by the pedal pulsations. Then, they mistakenly let up on the pedal or begin to "pump" it manually. The correct method, as recommended by NHTSA, is to "stomp and steer." Keep your foot down hard on the pedal, and continue to steer

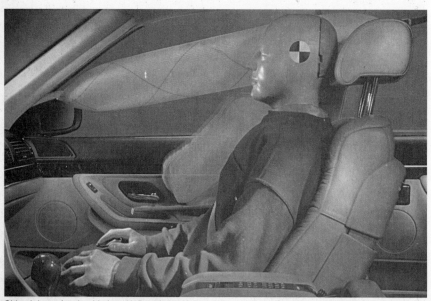

Side air bags (at shoulder) and inflatable head restraints are being offered in an increasing number of vehicles. (BMW photo)

the car around hazards.

Some recent studies have questioned the value of ABS in preventing accidents, and some insurance companies have reduced or eliminated discounts for this feature based on their claims experience. Other studies, however, have concluded that vehicles equipped with ABS are involved in fewer accidents and have fewer injuries.

Consumer Guide™ supports anti-lock brakes enthusiastically and encourages shoppers to buy vehicles equipped with this feature.

Essentially working in the reverse of ABS is traction control, which uses the ABS sensors to detect wheel slip on acceleration. The system then applies the brake to the driving wheel, cuts engine power, or does both, to retard wheel slip until traction is restored. Traction control is optional on many cars and standard on others. It is particularly worthwhile on rear-wheel-drive cars, which tend to lose traction more easily on slippery surfaces.

The Consumer's Role

Motor vehicle deaths declined from 50,894 in 1966 to 41,907 in 1996. This reduction occurred even though Americans drive more now than 30 years ago and millions more cars and trucks are on the road.

The death rate has declined from 5.5 deaths per 100 million miles driven in 1966 to 1.7 in 1996. The death rate was 7.6 per 100 million miles in 1950.

Pushed by federal safety rules, prodded by the insurance industry, and pressed by consumers, the auto industry is forced to build much safer vehicles today. Many car companies exceed the federal safety requirements on their own and, through their own research and innovation, find new ways to make vehicles even safer.

Would safety be the priority it is today without government rules forcing the issue? Probably not, and certainly not on the accelerated schedule required by the government.

However, no matter what safety features the government requires or the car companies offer, motor vehicle safety to a large extent depends on who is driving and how they are driving.

Alcohol was involved in 41 percent of traffic deaths in 1996, which means more than 17,000 people died because somebody drove after they had too much to drink. Speeding was a factor in 30 percent of fatal crashes last year. The total blame—or even any blame—for those deaths cannot be placed on unsafe vehicles or lack of regulation.

Despite the best efforts of the government and auto industry, we continue to kill ourselves by driving recklessly, ignoring traffic laws, refusing to wear seatbelts, and driving while impaired by drugs or alcohol.

CONSUMER COMPLAINTS

Auto complaints top the list of consumer grievances. The best time to attack new-car problems is before you take delivery. But if trouble does develop, a good relationship with the dealer can eliminate the need for more serious action.

Before You Drive Away . . .

Take steps now, to prevent problems early on.

Nothing beats buying a car with a track record of reliability, from a dealer with a reputation for good service. Cars and dealers are improving all the time, but problems still occur. Good treatment during the sale doesn't guarantee the same reception when you return for service, but it's often a good predictor. Here are some tips on addressing problems before they become

major hassles:

• Always test drive the car before taking final delivery.

• Take delivery of the car in the daytime. Artificial light can hide scratches or blemishes.

• Make sure it is the car you paid for. Match the title and all other documents to the Vehicle Identification Number (VIN) atop the dashboard and to the information on the window sticker.

• Is every option you purchased listed on the window sticker? Are they all on the car and in working order?

• Inspect paint, trim, and body panels. Look for evidence of body repair, such as a color mismatch; glass frag-

ments on the floor; loose or missing pieces. Cars can be damaged in transit, and dealer prep work isn't always perfect.

• See that doors, hood, and trunk open and close easily. Examine upholstery and interior trim.

• Insist that all problems get fixed before you drive away. Why should you have to come back for something that is not your fault?

• Check for vital items such as the spare tire, jack, and owner's manual.

• Do you have copies of all documents, including the bill of sale, warranty papers, licensing materials, etc.?

• Do you know where to go and

Government Agencies and Consumer Groups

The auto arbitration programs, government agencies, and consumer groups listed below may be able to help with car problems. Many states and some local governments have their own consumer protection agencies that may be able to act faster than a federal agency.

Better Business Bureau

Provides reports on dealers and other businesses and operates the Auto Line arbitration service for defects covered by a manufacturer's warranty. Check your local phone book for the nearest office or call 1-800-955-5100 for information on the Auto Line program.

Center for Auto Safety
2001 S Street, NW
Washington, DC 20009

Non-profit consumer group lobbies on behalf of consumer interests regarding vehicle safety and quality, and highway safety. Also provides information on lemon laws and has a lawyer referral service. Send a letter explaining your request with a self-addressed stamped envelope.

Chrysler Customer Center
P.O. Box 21-8004
Auburn Hills, MI 48321-8004
1-800-992-1997

Handles complaints not resolved at the dealer or zone-office level and provides information about Chrysler's regional customer arbitration boards.

Federal Trade Commission
601 Pennsylvania Avenue, NW
Washington, DC 20580
(202) 326-2222
Web Site: www.ftc.gov

Provides information on arbitration and consumer complaints and publishes brochures with advice on loans, leasing, and other auto-related topics. Regional offices are in major cities.

Ford Motor Company
Customer Assistance Center
P.O. Box 43360
Detroit, MI 48243
1-800-392-3673 (Ford and Mercury)

1-800-521-4140 (Lincoln)

Handles complaints not resolved at the dealer or regional-office level and provides information on Ford's arbitration program.

Highway Loss Data Institute (HLDI) and
Insurance Institute for Highway Safety (IIHS)
1005 N. Glebe Road
Arlington, VA 22201
(703) 247-1500

Insurance industry lobbying group compiles information on vehicle and highway safety.

National Automobile Dealers Association
AUTOCAP
8400 Westpark Drive
McLean, VA 22102
(703) 821-7000

NADA headquarters will refer you to a local office to answer questions on the AUTOCAP arbitration system and inform you if your dealer is a member.

National Highway Traffic Safety Administration
400 7th Street, SW
Washington, DC 20590
Web Site: www.nhtsa.dot.gov

NHTSA investigates safety defects and enforces federal safety regulations. Call the toll-free consumer hotline for information on crash tests and safety recalls and to report safety problems: 1-800-424-9393.

U.S. Department of Energy
1-800-363-3732
Web Site: www.doe.gov

Distributes free single copies of the EPA Gas Mileage Guide. Copies of the guide also are supposed to be available at car dealers.

U.S. Department of Justice
Office of Consumer Litigation
P.O. Box 386
Washington, DC 20044
(202) 307-0092

This office enforces federal laws covering price labeling of new cars.

whom to contact if service is needed?

• Do you have a copy of the recommended maintenance schedule?

• If a dealer-installed option isn't available at the time of delivery, get installation details in writing.

• Don't sign the contract until you're satisfied that everything you're paying for is accounted for and operating to your satisfaction.

• Be sure you know how to start the engine properly, and how to operate all controls and accessories. If the dealership doesn't volunteer to take you on a "tour" of your new vehicle, ask them to do it.

Service Visits

A few simple steps can

increase the chances your car will be fixed right the first time.

When you drive in for maintenance or repair work, be prepared to discuss the problem in detail. Make certain the service advisor writes a complete and correct description of each problem you've noticed—technicians rely on that service order.

No need to apologize if you can't make the problem appear during a test drive with the service advisor. It happens all the time. Just describe the symptoms and explain the circumstances under which they occur. Insist that service people examine the car under conditions in which the problem is likely to surface. That usually means leaving the car overnight.

If parts must be ordered, the process might take a day or even a week, so don't expect miracles. Parts for low-volume models often take longer.

Letting the dealer conduct routine servicing, such as oil changes, may be wise. Regular customers tend to get prompt attention when a problem appears. Your car also will be up to date in the dealer's records—a point in your favor if a serious flaw develops.

Don't leave the dealership until you're satisfied that all service work has been done correctly.

Keep a detailed record of service visits, including all receipts. Always be prepared to:

• Provide full vehicle data: mileage, date of purchase, and Vehicle Identification Number.

• Describe the problem and what's been done to correct it.

• If you are displeased with the service, provide an explanation of why and the solution you're seeking.

Mediation and Beyond

Third-party dispute programs should be a last resort. They seldom produce miracles.

In a dispute over service or the performance of your new vehicle, we advise that you exhaust each rung up the ladder of solutions before considering bringing in a third-party. This will strengthen your case, should you proceed to mediation or beyond.

If the dealer can't solve your problem, take it to the manufacturer's district or regional representative (your owner's manual should contain this address and phone number). The final avenue should be a mediation or arbitration program.

A few automakers mediate customer disputes internally, but most participate in a program that allows dissatisfied

owners to seek resolution through an independent third party.

These programs usually pit the consumer against the manufacturer, not against the dealer. The consumer presents a complaint, supported by documentation (repair receipts, correspondence, etc.), to a mediation or arbitration panel. The manufacturer's representative presents its side of the story. Then, the panel renders a decision or a recommendation.

Some findings are binding on the manufacturer. Remedies could range from providing the customer's car with a new paint job to, in rare cases, providing the customer with a new vehicle. But when a panel sides with the manufacturer's position, pursuing the complaint grows difficult for the consumer.

Two mediation/arbitration services handle the bulk of cases, but certain manufacturers use other programs.

• The Council of Better Business Bureaus operates the Auto Line program, which combines mediation and arbitration on vehicles that are still covered by the manufacturer's warranty. Most claims are successfully resolved to the satisfaction of both parties in the mediation stage. Many dealers also use this service to resolve disputes that don't involve a manufacturer.

Consumers should first contact the Better Business Bureau (BBB) headquarters at 1-800-955-5100. You will be referred to the appropriate automaker. After a certain number of days, if no agreement has been reached, it goes to a local bureau for a hearing.

• Mediation alone is provided by the Automotive Consumer Action Program (AUTOCAP), a service directed by the National Automobile Dealers Association (NADA) but performed by state or local dealer associations. Panels are made up of consumer representatives and dealers and seek to get both parties to agree to a resolution. BMW, Acura/Honda, Jaguar, Nissan/Infiniti, Mitsubishi, Isuzu, Rolls-Royce, and Volvo use the AUTOCAP resolution program.

Each organization's staff will first try to settle the dispute informally. Recommendations are not binding on either party, but the vast majority of cases are resolved in this informal stage. Unsettled complaints progress to panels made up of consumer volunteers and representatives of manufacturers or dealer organizations. Their findings, too, are not binding.

If you're dissatisfied with a mediator's recommendation, the next option is arbitration. Some manufacturers run their own arbitration programs. Others work through an outside group. Your owner's manual should tell you which program will be used.

In any program, you'll present your case orally and/or in writing. You'll need complete records, including work orders, letters, receipts, and notices. You must prove the car doesn't work properly, that both dealer and manufacturer have failed in several attempts to fix it, and that you've exhausted all other avenues. The manufacturer and/or dealer will then present its case through a representative familiar with repair problems.

Arbitration is similar to a court hearing, but less formal. The panel's decision is binding only on the company. You can accept the verdict, or go on to the next step: formal legal action.

Less than one-third of consumers have a dispute settled wholly their way. In most mediation/arbitration cases, however, the decision at least partially satisfies both sides.

Lemon Laws

Every state now has some form of "lemon law," but the promise usually outweighs the results.

Manufacturers can be ordered to refund the purchase price of a new vehicle or replace a car that's proven critically flawed. Such dramatic results are rare, however. In most states, you must exhaust all other possible remedies first. That means making a specified number of tries—typically three—at the dealership, then passing through arbitration without successful resolution.

You will have to retain a lawyer. To qualify for consideration, a car generally has to be inoperable for at least 30 days during its first 12 months or 12,000 miles. Details vary, so inquire at your state attorney general's office, a consumer protection agency, or the Center for Auto Safety.

Lemon laws typically stipulate that a manufacturer be given one last chance to remedy the complaint. Even if you "win," the automaker nearly always can deduct from your award compensation for the mileage you've put on the vehicle.

INSURANCE

The cost of insurance can influence your car-buying decision. Shop for the best rates, and learn which cars carry higher premiums.

Law and common sense dictate that responsible drivers carry proper automotive insurance coverage. But the amount you'll pay depends on a variety of factors—not all of them related to driving.

Where you live plays a big role in the cost of your coverage. Insurance premiums in mainly urban New Jersey—traditionally the most-expensive state—might run three times higher than those in North Dakota, a rural state with the lowest average premiums. New Jersey's average annual premium of $1169 is about 50 percent higher than the national average.

Though all but seven states require motorists to carry personal liability coverage, no company has to sell it to you. In fact, only motorists with poor driving records are "guaranteed" insurance. They are placed in a high-risk pool, where all insurers share the risk, and premiums range from high to gigantic.

Nearly half the states have no-fault insurance provisions. Under these, an insurance company pays for its client's personal injury claims regardless of who was at fault in an accident. No-fault states allow motorists to file lawsuits for damages in drastic cases or if claims exceed a specified sum. A handful of no-fault states also include property damage.

Insurers Set the Rates

Each state has its own insurance regulations and some limit how much insurers can charge, but premiums are ultimately determined on a state-by-state basis by the insurance companies, which consider an array of information about the drivers and the vehicle to be insured.

Insurers insist there's no consistency in data from state to state to help set rates. Nor can they be certain a motorist is truthful about how many miles they drive annually or other important details that affect risk. So the insurance companies depend on three basic factors to set rates. These may not be the best predictors of risk, but they are relatively easy to determine:

• Who you are: Your age, gender, driving record, and other factors.

• Where you live: Areas with greater population density and more traffic get higher rates.

• What you drive: This is used mainly to set rates for collision and comprehensive coverage and includes the cost of replacement parts and the vehicle's theft history.

Single males under the age of 25 pay the highest rates. Statistics show they are involved in the most accidents. Married men, who have fewer accidents, usually pay less. A handful of states do not allow insurance companies to set rates based on sex or age, but that prohibition has tended to bring on higher rates for women.

Because accident rates are higher in urban areas, insurers charge stiffer premiums to drivers who live in or near a major city. Rates in and around New York City or Los Angeles can be five to 10 times higher than those in rural Nebraska.

Some companies will increase premiums if you receive a single traffic violation or are involved in a minor accident. Others tend to shy away from anyone with a blemished driving record.

Some Cars Cost More

The cost of collision and comprehensive coverage is based largely on the price of the car when new. Insurers add surcharges or offer discounts for others, depending on their claims experience (see chart on Costly-to-Insure Models).

Types of Coverage

Six types of coverage are included in most insurance policies:

Bodily injury liability: Covers injury and/or death claims against you, and legal costs if your car injures or kills someone.

Property damage liability: Covers claims for property that your car damages in an accident.

Liability coverage is expressed by three figures: "100/300/50," for example, means $100,000 bodily injury coverage per person, $300,000 total coverage per accident, and $50,000 for property damage. Because liability coverage protects the other party, it is required in most states.

Medical payments: Pays for injuries to yourself and to occupants of your car. It is optional in some states. In no-fault states, personal injury protection replaces medical payments as part of the basic coverage.

Uninsured motorist protection: Covers injuries caused to you or the occupants of your car by an uninsured or hit-and-run driver; in some states, damage to your property is included. "Underinsured" coverage also is available to cover claims you may make against a driver who has inadequate insurance.

Collision coverage: Covers damage to your car up to its "book" value. Collision coverage carries a deductible, which is the amount per claim you have to pay before the insurance takes effect. The lower the deductible, the higher the premium. While legally it is optional, a lending institution or leasing company will usually require it.

Comprehensive (physical damage): Covers damage to your car from theft, vandalism, fire, wind, flood, and other non-accident causes. Comprehensive also carries a deductible.

Insurers typically begin by assigning each car model a numbered code based on its initial selling price. They then use claims experience with that model to place it in a higher or lower "rating group."

Such rate adjustments are based in part on how expensive the car is to repair, including parts and labor. In addition, surcharges are applied to certain cars that are frequently involved in accidents or suffer a higher-than-average theft rate.

The Highway Loss Data Institute, which is funded by the insurance industry, classifies cars by injury and collision-loss experience. Insurers use that data and other factors as a guide to set rates. In general, according to the Highway Loss Data Institute, "the lowest (best) injury loss results come from large station wagons and passenger vans, standard-size pickup trucks, and large utility vehicles." Small 2- and 4-door cars suffer the worst injury and collision losses.

Since surcharges apply only to collision and comprehensive coverage, they don't always amount to a large sum. State Farm Insurance Company, for instance, adds 10 to 45 percent to the basic rate for cars with a "bad" claims record, and lops off like amounts for those with claim rates lower than average. Domestic models—particularly full-size sedans and wagons—are most likely to warrant a discount. At the other end, some exotic models are almost uninsurable and at the very least demand a massive premium.

High insurance costs have been blamed for sagging sales and even the ultimate demise of some sporty models, such as the Nissan 300ZX and Toyota MR2. Young males in urban areas who want to drive a sporty vehicle must pay dearly. Insuring a high-performance car could cost two or three times the amount charged for an ordinary model—provided the insurer elects to cover it at all.

Sport-utility vehicles also tend to have higher insurance rates than mid- and full-size cars. One reason for this is higher theft rates. Another is that SUVs tend to cost more to buy than mid- or full-size cars, and are more expensive to repair after an accident. Four-wheel-drive systems can be among the most expensive repairs in a collision.

However, insurance companies set rates based on their own experience. If Company A has more collision and theft claims for a particular vehicle than Company B, Company A will charge more for the same coverage. It boils down to a company's actual experience with a particular vehicle or category of drivers.

How Much Coverage Do You Need?

Minimum-level insurance is seldom enough. Without insurance, all your property is put at risk for even a modest accident.

State laws may require liability coverage as low as $15,000 per person, $30,000 per accident, and $5000 property damage—called 15/30/5 in insurance lingo. Some states require as much as 50/100/15. If you can afford it, buy more than the minimum. After all, $10,000 for property damage may not be enough if you rear-end a $100,000 Mercedes-Benz.

The more assets and income you have, the more insurance you need. State Farm recommends at least 100/300/50 for a "middle class family with assets to protect." Better to save money on other parts of the policy than to cut corners on liability. A lawsuit could bring financial ruin.

Some insurers also recommend a $1 million "personal liability umbrella" policy that is issued in conjunction with homeowner coverage. The cost is $200 to $300 per year, and it can protect a family from major lawsuits.

It's also important to shop for insurance. Depending on the underwriter, you could pay anywhere from $500 or $2000 annually for the same coverage.

You can shop for insurance any time, but a good time is when you are shopping for a new vehicle. Instead of just calling your current agent to have your new wheels insured, why not see what other companies charge?

Another good time is when your annual premium renewal arrives in the mail spelling out your coverage and how much it costs. With your current bill handy, you can make direct comparisons with other companies to see who has the best rates for the same amount of coverage.

Shop for insurance by consulting two or three of the largest insurers, such as

Eight Ways To Cut Insurance Costs

1. Buy a vehicle that qualifies for a discount, or at least doesn't carry a surcharge. Before you buy, ask your insurance agent about the cost of insuring vehicles in which you're interested.

2. Take public transportation instead of driving to work. Your insurance premium will go down. Out of the question? Try car pooling. The less you drive, the lower your insurance. Most companies give a break to those who drive fewer than 7500 miles annually.

3. Make certain you're getting every discount to which you are entitled. You might qualify if you car has an anti-theft alarm, air bags, or anti-lock brakes (though some insurers no longer offer discounts on anti-lock brakes). Discounts might also be available if you insure your cars and home with the same firm. People who have taken a defensive-driving class or don't smoke or drink often get discounts.

Review the status of all the drivers in your family with your agent. Most discounts apply to only one portion of the policy, so don't expect dramatic savings.

4. Increase your deductible for collision and comprehensive. Switching from a $100 deductible to $500 could slash your collision and comprehensive premiums by 25 percent. Going to a $1000 deductible might cut it in half. You're still covered for catastrophes, but you foot the bill for fender-benders. Also, think twice about filing small claims with your insurance.

5. Shop around. Before renewing, study the fine print to see if its conditions—or your situation—have changed. Another company might have a better deal, but you won't know unless you shop. Many insurers market policies by mail or phone, or via computer, making it easy to compare rates.

6. Discontinue collision coverage on older cars. Claims are limited to "book" value, so you're not likely to get much anyway. A good rule of thumb is to drop collision when the annual premium reaches 10 percent of your car's value.

7. Be a good driver. Avoid accidents and traffic violations and you'll be rewarded with good-driver discounts ranging from 10 percent to 20 percent of the total premium.

8. Drop coverage for such extras as towing costs or the expense of renting a car while yours is in the shop. Savings here might be small, but these benefits could be duplicated by your new-car warranty's roadside assistance provision.

State Farm and Allstate, and then contact one or two independent agents who can give you premium quotes from more than one company. There are also direct-marketing companies, such as GEICO and Amica, which do business over the phone rather than through agents, and offer some of the lowest rates. Ask for an itemized list of coverage and costs.

In addition to low price, you'll want a company that can provide quick, efficient claims service. Contact your state insurance department or local consumer protection agency to see which companies have been the subjects of complaints.

Most state insurance departments also publish guidelines on the types of coverage required in your state, recommended amounts of coverage, and shopping advice. More than half the states provide rate comparisons using typical drivers as examples to compare premiums from several companies. None of the examples may apply directly to you, but they can give you an idea which companies have the lowest premiums.

Costly-to-Insure Models

Your age, where you live, and your driving record are among the key factors that determine how much you pay for auto insurance. You can't do anything about your age, and you can't always live where you would like to. How you drive and what you drive are under your control, and both affect your insurance premiums.

While all makes and models of vehicles are involved in crashes, some are involved more often and cost more to repair. Insurance companies look at the history of collision and comprehensive claims for each model when determining rates. Those that have a history of more frequent and expensive claims will cost more to insure.

The collision and comprehensive portions of your coverage are a major chunk of your premium, often 50 percent or more of the total cost.

A claims history by car model is compiled by the Highway Loss Data Institute, an arm of the insurance industry's national lobbying group, the Insurance Institute for Highway Safety. Individual insurance companies consult the HLDI data when setting their rates, but they also use their own data from claims made by their policyholders in deciding how much to charge.

Each insurer has its own list of vehicles that qualify for a discount from the standard rate and another for vehicles that warrant a surcharge based on their own claims.

Listed below are some of the models in each category, as determined by State Farm Insurance Company, the nation's largest. It applies to 1997 models and may be different for 1998 models.

1997 MODELS WITH LOWER-THAN-AVERAGE COLLISION/COMPREHENSIVE PREMIUMS

BMW 7-Series
Buick Century, LeSabre, Park Avenue, Regal, Riviera
Cadillac DeVille, Eldorado, Seville
Chevrolet Astro, Corvette coupe, Lumina, Suburban, Tahoe
Chrysler Concorde, LHS, Sebring convertible, Town & Country
Dodge Caravan
Eagle Vision
Ford Crown Victoria, Explorer, F-150, Taurus, Windstar
GMC Safari, Suburban, Yukon

Hyundai Elantra wagon
Infiniti Q45
Isuzu Hombre, Trooper
Jaguar XJ Sedan, XK8
Jeep Grand Cherokee
Lexus ES 300, GS 300, LS 400
Lincoln
Mercedes-Benz
Mercury Grand Marquis, Mystique, Sable, Villager
Nissan Quest
Oldsmobile Aurora, Eighty Eight
Plymouth Breeze, Voyager
Pontiac Bonneville, Grand Prix, Sunfire convertible
Saab 900
Saturn wagon
Toyota Avalon, Land Cruiser, RAV4
Volvo

1997 MODELS WITH HIGHER-THAN-AVERAGE COLLISION/COMPREHENSIVE PREMIUMS

Acura Integra
Audi Cabriolet
BMW 3-Series, 8-Series
Chevrolet Blazer, Camaro, Cavalier, S-10
Dodge Avenger, Neon, Ram 1500
Eagle Talon
Ford Escort, Mustang, Probe, Ranger
Geo Metro, Prizm, Tracker
GMC Jimmy, Sonoma
Honda Civic, del Sol, Prelude
Hyundai Accent, Elantra sedan, Sonata
Jeep Wrangler
Kia Sephia, Sportage
Lexus SC 300
Mazda MX-6, Protege, 626
Mercury Tracer
Mitsubishi Eclipse, Galant, Mirage, Montero, 3000GT
Nissan Altima, Pathfinder, Sentra, 200SX, 240SX
Plymouth Neon
Pontiac Firebird, Sunfire coupe and sedan
Porsche 911
Saturn coupe
Suzuki Swift, Sidekick
Toyota Celica, Corolla, Paseo, Supra, Tercel, Tacoma, 4Runner
Volkswagen Golf

1998 BEST BUYS

The auto editors of Consumer Guide™ have selected "Best Buys" and "Recommended" vehicles in 15 categories of passenger cars, minivans, pickup trucks, and sport-utility vehicles. In some categories there also are models designated "Budget Buys."

At least one Best Buy has been chosen in each category as the vehicles the editors rank as the best overall choices. Models labeled Recommended also are highly worthy of consideration. Budget Buys are competent vehicles that sell for significantly less than the average for their category.

Vehicles are assigned to one of the 15 categories based on their size, price, and market position. Thus, a $13,000 subcompact competes against other low-priced small cars, not against $45,000 luxury cars.

Results of road tests conducted by the Consumer Guide™ auto editors play a major role in the selection of Best Buys. Other factors include price, cost of ownership, manufacturer's warranties, the vehicle's reputation for reliability, and safety features.

Only models that have been road tested by the editors are considered. Some new or redesigned models, such as the new Lexus RX 300 sport-utility vehicle, weren't available for testing in time to be considered for this issue.

BEST BUY	RECOMMENDED	BUDGET BUY
SUBCOMPACT CARS Chevrolet Prizm Ford Escort Honda Civic Mercury Tracer Toyota Corolla	Chevrolet Cavalier Pontiac Sunfire Saturn Sedan and Wagon Mazda Protege	Dodge/Plymouth Neon
COMPACT CARS Mazda 626 Nissan Altima	Ford Contour Mercury Mystique	
MIDSIZE CARS Ford Taurus Honda Accord Mercury Sable Toyota Camry	Chevrolet Malibu Nissan Maxima	Chevrolet Lumina Dodge Stratus Plymouth Breeze
FULL-SIZE CARS Buick LeSabre Oldsmobile 88/Regency Pontiac Bonneville	Toyota Avalon	
NEAR-LUXURY CARS Infiniti I30 Lexus ES 300	Buick Park Avenue	Audi A4
LUXURY CARS Lexus LS 400 Mercedes-Benz E-Class	Acura RL BMW 5-Series Cadillac De Ville/Concours Cadillac Seville	Lincoln Town Car

BEST BUY	RECOMMENDED	BUDGET BUY
LUXURY COUPES Lexus SC 300/400	Cadillac Eldorado	Buick Riviera
SPORTS COUPES Honda Prelude	Chrysler Sebring Dodge Avenger	Ford Escort ZX2 Saturn Coupe
SPORTS & GT CARS Chevrolet Corvette Mazda Miata	BMW Z3 Mercedes-Benz SLK230	Chevrolet Camaro Ford Mustang Pontiac Firebird
MINIVANS Dodge Caravan Plymouth Voyager	Chevrolet Venture Ford Windstar Oldsmobile Silhouette Pontiac Trans Sport Toyota Sienna	
COMPACT SPORT-UTILITY VEHICLES Honda CR-V	Toyota RAV4	Jeep Wrangler
MIDSIZE SPORT-UTILITY VEHICLES Ford Explorer Mercedes-Benz ML320 Mercury Mountaineer	Chevrolet Blazer Toyota 4Runner GMC Jimmy Jeep Grand Cherokee	Jeep Cherokee
FULL-SIZE SPORT-UTILITY VEHICLES Ford Expedition	Chevrolet Tahoe GMC Yukon	
COMPACT PICKUP TRUCKS Dodge Dakota	Chevrolet S10 Ford Ranger GMC Sonoma Mazda B-Series	
FULL-SIZE PICKUP TRUCKS Ford F-150	Chevrolet C/K 1500 Dodge Ram 1500	

ACURA CL

Acura 2.3CL

Front-wheel-drive luxury coupe
Base price range: $22,110-$26,460. Built in Marysville, Ohio.
Also consider: BMW 3-Series, Mercedes-Benz CLK, Volvo C70

FOR • Ride • Steering/handling • Acceleration (3.0 CL)

AGAINST • Automatic transmission performance • Acceleration (2.3CL with automatic)

Acura believes there's a market for a sporty $30,000 coupe with a roomy interior, usable trunk, and a healthy dose of standard amenities. Hence the CL, which slots between Acura's Integra and TL lines in size and price. Honda's upscale division introduced this "contemporary luxury" coupe in spring 1996 as the 1997-model 2.2CL; a V-6 3.0CL arrived last fall.

This year, the 2.2 becomes a 2.3CL by switching from a 145-horsepower 2.2-liter 4-cylinder engine to the 150-horsepower 2.3-liter four that powers Honda's 1998 EX and LX Accord models. The 4-cylinder comes with manual or automatic transmission, the V-6 with automatic only.

On hand for both CLs are new wheels, a revised grille, steering-wheel audio controls, and an engine immobilizer that prevents "hot wiring." The Premium Package now includes a Homelink transmitter for operating garage-door openers and other devices.

PERFORMANCE That the CL acts and feels much like an Accord is no surprise, since it uses many of the same components. That means it's a smooth, generally quiet midsize coupe with a firm but comfortable ride and poised, sporty handling.

The new 2.3-liter engine is about as quick and efficient as the 2.2. With manual transmission, that one ran our 0-60 mph test in a so-so 9.5 seconds while logging a creditable 22.2 mpg overall. Unhappily, the 2.3 has little additional power and torque, so acceleration with automatic transmission should remain adequate rather than brisk. The V-6, by contrast, delivers ample punch. With either engine, the automatic tends to shift with a jolt under hard throttle and in stop-and-go driving can get confused about which gear to be in.

ACCOMMODATIONS The CL has space enough to seat four adults in reasonable comfort, but no more usable passenger room than an Accord coupe. The interior design is pure Acura/Honda, with a comfortable driving position, unobstructed visibility, and simple, convenient instruments and controls.

The driver's seat in the 3.0 model automatically powers fore and aft to assist rear entry/exit. It does so quite quickly via a special electric motor, and it can sense obstructions and reverse direction automatically. However, this capability would be of greater benefit on the front passenger seat, which is used to access the back more frequently.

Cargo space is more than adequate, but there's only a pass-through opening to the trunk instead of a folding rear seatback. Interior stowage for small items is okay, but not exceptional.

BUILD QUALITY We expect top-notch workmanship from Honda's premium brand, and the CL delivers. It feels solidly robust even on rough roads, exhibits good detail finish, and features generally high-quality materials, though some interior plastics look low-budget.

VALUE FOR THE MONEY Though both CLs are competent, pleasant, and well built, neither impresses us as an outstanding value. The 3.0 at least offers 6-cylinder smoothness for less money than rivals such as the BMW 3-Series or Mercedes' new CLK.

RATINGS

	Acura 2.3CL	Acura 3.0CL
Acceleration	3	4
Fuel economy	4	3
Ride quality	4	4
Steering/handling	4	4
Braking	4	4
Quietness	4	4
Driver seating	4	4
Instruments/controls	4	4
Room/comfort (front)	4	4
Room/comfort (rear)	2	2
Cargo room	3	3
Value for the money	3	3
Total	**43**	**43**

SPECIFICATIONS

	2-door coupe
Wheelbase, in.	106.5
Overall length, in.	190.0
Overall width, in.	70.1
Overall height, in.	54.7
Curb weight, lbs.	3009
Cargo vol., cu. ft.	12.0
Fuel capacity, gals.	17.1
Seating capacity	4
Front head room, in.	37.4
Max. front leg room, in.	42.9
Rear head room, in.	35.9
Min. rear leg room, in.	31.0

ENGINES

	ohc I-4	ohc V-6
Size, liters/cu. in.	2.3/137	3.0/183
Horsepower @ rpm	150@ 5700	200@ 5500
Torque (lbs./ft.) @ rpm	152@ 4900	195@ 4700
Availability	S[1]	S[2]

EPA city/highway mpg

4-speed OD automatic	NA	20/28

1. 2.3CL. 2. 3.0CL.

PRICES

1997 Acura CL

	Retail Price	Dealer Invoice
2.2CL 2-door coupe 5-speed	$22110	$19647
2.2CL 2-door coupe automatic	22910	20358
2.2CL 2-door coupe w/Premium Pkg., 5-speed	23160	20580
2.2CL 2-door coupe w/Premium Pkg., automatic	23960	21291
3.0CL 2-door coupe automatic	25110	22313
3.0CL 2-door coupe w/Premium Pkg., automatic	26460	23512
Destination charge	435	435

STANDARD EQUIPMENT:

2.2CL: 2.2-liter 4-cylinder engine, 4-speed automatic transmission or 5-speed manual transmission, anti-lock 4-wheel disc brakes, driver- and passenger-side air bags, cruise control, variable-assist power steering, automatic climate control, moquette front bucket seats, rear trunk pass-through, 6-way power driver seat w/manual lumbar adjustment, center storage armrest, rear center armrest, cupholders, digital clock, tilt steering wheel, rear defogger, leather-wrapped steering wheel, passenger seatback pocket, 6-speaker AM/FM/CD player, remote keyless entry, security system, power windows and door locks, power mirrors, power moonroof, integrated antenna, illuminated visor mirrors, variable intermittent wipers, remote decklid and fuel-door release, door pockets, courtesy and map lights, front and rear stabilizer bars, front mud guards, 205/55VR16 tires, alloy wheels.

3.0CL adds: 3.0-liter V-6 engine, 4-speed automatic transmission, 8-way power driver seat, Bose sound system, heated outside mirrors.

2.2CL w/Premium Pkg. adds to 2.2CL: leather upholstery, seatback

---

Prices are accurate at time of publication; subject to manufacturer's changes.

pocket. **3.0CL w/Premium Pkg.** adds to 3.0CL: leather upholstery, heated front seats, seatback pocket.

Options are available as dealer-installed accessories.

ACURA INTEGRA

Acura Integra LS hatchback

Front-wheel-drive subcompact
Base price range: $16,200-$22,400. Built in Japan.
Also consider: Ford Escort/Escort ZX2, Honda Civic, Volkswagen Golf/Jetta

FOR • Fuel economy • Steering/handling • Acceleration (with manual transmission)

AGAINST • Rear seat room • Road noise • Acceleration (with automatic transmission)

Derived from the Civic, this smallest and most-affordable offering from Honda's upscale division was last redesigned for 1994 and has been little changed since. Given usual Honda practice, a new Integra should appear for 1999, but some sources say it won't arrive before 2000 or 2001.

For '98, Integra drops its base-trim RS sedan, and other models return with minor front and rear styling tweaks. Besides the RS 2-door hatchback coupe, the lineup again offers LS, GS and GS-R coupes and sedans, plus the Type R coupe, a high-performance limited edition model introduced last year, mainly for amateur racers. A tilt- and height-adjustable driver's seat is now standard for all but the RS and Type R. GS models add a leather-covered steering wheel and shift knob, and LS and GS-R get new-design wheels.

As before, all Integras have 1.8-liter twin-cam 4-cylinder engines, but the GS-R and Type R carry more powerful versions with Honda's VTEC variable-valve-timing system. A manual transmission is standard and automatic is optional except on GS-R and Type R.

PERFORMANCE Integra engines rev like crazy, but don't have enough low-speed torque to pull with much gusto when linked to automatic transmission—itself a rough shifter in hard acceleration. With manual, they're quick. We timed an LS at 8.3 seconds 0-60 mph and a GS-R at 7.6. Fuel economy is also commendable with the 5-speed. Our LS returned nearly 25 mpg over 250 city/freeway miles; the GS-R gave us 28.3 mpg overall. Expect less with the automatic.

All Integras suffer a fair amount of engine noise at higher speeds, but are fairly quiet cruisers bar the Type R, which omits some sound deadening to reduce weight. Tire noise is also prominent on most surfaces in any model.

Like its Civic parent, Integra is fun to drive, thanks to sharp steering and nimble cornering. Ride, however, can be rather bouncy on coupes because of their shorter wheelbase.

ACCOMMODATIONS The Integra coupe isn't as roomy as Honda's latest Civic hatchback. It's fine in front for medium-size folk, but only pre-teens fit in the rear. A longer wheelbase makes the sedan a more practical people-mover, but you still don't get a really spacious back seat. Cargo room is okay in sedans and pretty good in coupes, though the latter have a high liftover due to their rear-end styling.

As expected of Honda designs, Integra features a low-but-comfortable driving stance and a handy, simple dashboard layout. All-round visibility is good, though it's slightly restricted to the rear in coupes. A high "wing" spoiler clutters things further in the Type R.

BUILD QUALITY Integras lack the heavyweight feel of larger Acuras, but are solid and robust even on rough roads. Detail finish is exemplary, though some interior plastics look a bit low-buck.

VALUE FOR THE MONEY Integra is a premium small car that offsets relatively high prices with fine reliability, strong resale value, and plenty of driving fun. Acura also offers a longer warranty and more comprehensive customer service than many makes, Honda included. Forget the Type R unless you're a track racer. It's pricey, too high-strung for normal driving, and scarce (only 500 or so available).

RATINGS

	RS 2-dr	LS/GS 4-dr	GS-R 2-dr	Type-R
Acceleration	4	4	5	5
Fuel economy	4	4	4	3
Ride quality	3	3	3	3
Steering/handling	4	4	4	5
Braking	4	4	4	4
Quietness	3	3	3	2
Driver seating	4	4	4	4
Instruments/controls	4	4	4	4
Room/comfort (front)	3	3	3	3
Room/comfort (rear)	2	3	2	2
Cargo room	3	2	3	3
Value for the money	4	4	4	3
Total	**42**	**42**	**43**	**41**

SPECIFICATIONS

	2-door hatchback	4-door sedan
Wheelbase, in.	101.2	103.1
Overall length, in.	172.4	178.1
Overall width, in.	67.3	67.3
Overall height, in.	52.6	53.9
Curb weight, lbs.	2529	2628
Cargo vol., cu. ft.	13.3	11.0
Fuel capacity, gals.	13.2	13.2
Seating capacity	4	5
Front head room, in.	38.6	38.9
Max. front leg room, in.	42.7	42.2
Rear head room, in.	35.0	36.0
Min. rear leg room, in.	28.1	32.7

ENGINES

	dohc I-4	dohc I-4	dohc I-4
Size, liters/cu. in.	1.8/112	1.8/110	1.8/110
Horsepower @ rpm	142@ 6300	170@ 7600	195@ 8000
Torque (lbs./ft.) @ rpm	127@ 5200	128@ 6200	130@ 7500
Availability	S[1]	S[2]	S[3]
EPA city/highway mpg			
4-speed OD automatic	24/31		
5-speed OD manual	25/31	25/31	23/28

1. RS, LS, GS. 2. GS-R. 3. Type R.

PRICES

Acura Integra	Retail Price	Dealer Invoice
RS 2-door hatchback, 5-speed	$16200	$14475
RS 2-door hatchback, automatic	17000	15190
LS 2-door hatchback, 5-speed	19200	17155
LS 2-door hatchback, automatic	20000	17870
LS 4-door sedan, 5-speed	20000	17870
LS 4-door sedan, automatic	20800	18585
GS 2-door hatchback, 5-speed	20850	18630
GS 2-door hatchback, automatic	21650	19345
GS 4-door sedan, 5-speed	21400	19121
GS 4-door sedan, automatic	22000	19836
GS-R 2-door hatchback, 5-speed	21300	19032
GS-R 2-door hatchback w/leather, 5-speed	22100	19747
GS-R 4-door sedan, 5-speed	21600	19300
GS-R 4-door sedan w/leather, 5-speed	22400	20014
Destination charge	435	435

STANDARD EQUIPMENT:

Rating Scale: 5-Excellent; 4-Above average; 3-Average; 2-Below average; 1-Poor

RS: 1.8-liter dohc 140-horsepower 4-cylinder engine, 5-speed manual or 4-speed automatic transmission, driver- and passenger-side air bags, 4-wheel disc brakes, variable-assist power steering, tilt steering column, cloth reclining front bucket seats w/driver-side lumbar adjustment, 50/50 split folding rear seat, center console w/armrest, power windows, power mirrors, tachometer, coolant temperature gauge, AM/FM/CD player w/six speakers, power antenna, remote fuel-door and decklid/hatch releases, rear defogger, rear wiper/washer, intermittent wipers, cargo cover, tinted glass, fog lights, 195/60HR14 tires, wheel covers.

LS adds: anti-lock brakes, air conditioning, cruise control, tilt/height-adjustable driver seat, one-piece folding rear seat (4-door), power moonroof, power door locks, map lights, color-keyed bodyside moldings, Michelin 195/60HR14 tires, alloy wheels, deletes cargo cover and rear wiper/washer (4-door).

GS adds: leather upholstery, rear spoiler (hatchback), 195/55VR15 tires.

GS-R adds to LS: 1.8-liter dohc VTEC 170-horsepower engine, wood-grain console (4-door), rear spoiler (hatchback), 195/55VR15 tires.

GS-R w/leather adds: leather upholstery, leather-wrapped steering wheel and shift knob.

Options are available as dealer-installed accessories.

ACURA RL

RECOMMENDED

Acura 3.5RL

Front-wheel-drive luxury car
Base price: $41,000. Built in Japan.
Also consider: Cadillac Seville, Lexus GS 300/400, Mercedes-Benz E-Class

FOR • Acceleration • Steering/handling • Ride

AGAINST • Rear head room • Steering feel

The flagship sedan from Honda's upscale division goes its own way in the luxury class, using a V-6 engine and front-wheel drive while most rivals have rear-wheel drive and some offer V-8s. Acura believes its design provides comparable luxury in an more-efficient package.

For '98, the RL loses its optional Premium Package, but adds two features from it as standard equipment: heated door mirrors and a 255-watt 8-speaker Bose sound system. The standard alloy wheels are of a new design, and a 3-point rear-center safety belt replaces a lap belt.

The powertrain consists of a 3.5-liter V-6 and automatic transmission. A leather-trimmed interior is standard. Options include traction control, heated mirrors and front seats, and an in-dash satellite-linked navigation system with a touch-screen color display. Currently, the navigation system delivers audio and visual route instructions for urban areas in California and Nevada. Acura says it is being expanded to included selected sites in the Midwest and Southwest.

PERFORMANCE Though it doesn't feel that snappy, the RL has good grunt for a premium sedan. We timed our test car at 8.05 seconds 0-60 mph. The single overhead-cam V-6 is hushed at cruising speed and emits a subdued, rich-sounding snarl in hard acceleration. It's also pretty efficient. We averaged 19.8 mpg with last year's model, including some 900 miles on a highway trip, where we averaged 21 mpg. Our around-town average was 18 mpg. As expected in cars like this, the RL requires pre-mium fuel.

Ride quality is firm yet supple, and the RL sails over most irregularities with nary a shudder or rattle. This is also a pretty agile big sedan, with only modest body lean in tight corners and quick, precise steering that could nevertheless use more road feel. The brakes provide short, straight stops from high speeds; ours halted from 60 mph in 120 feet. Wind noise is modest, but tire noise is louder than it should be for a $40,000-plus car.

ACCOMMODATIONS Typical of Honda, the RL offers a comfortable, easily tailored driving position; clear sightlines all around; and driving controls that are large, well placed, and intuitive. Rear leg and knee room are more than adequate. The same goes for front head room, though 6-footers in back will find their heads just brushing the roof.

The interior has plenty of spaces for bric-a-brac, while the flat-floor trunk is usefully shaped, if not unusually roomy. The optional onboard navigator is accurate and easy to use, but fingerprints and certain light conditions can render its display almost unreadable.

BUILD QUALITY The RLs we've seen have been consistently solid and well built, with little to criticize in the way of fit-and-finish.

VALUE FOR THE MONEY The 3.5RL is a pleasant luxury sedan that does everything well, but it lacks a few features found on some rivals, such as a 5-speed automatic transmission. It's also no great value in this class (similar money buys a Mercedes-Benz E320, for example). Still, the RL deserves a look as an intelligently designed car that's well executed and rewarding to drive.

RATINGS

	3.5RL
Acceleration	4
Fuel economy	3
Ride quality	4
Steering/handling	4
Braking	4
Quietness	4
Driver seating	4
Instruments/controls	4
Room/comfort (front)	4
Room/comfort (rear)	3
Cargo room	4
Value for the money	3
Total	**45**

SPECIFICATIONS

	4-door sedan
Wheelbase, in.	114.6
Overall length, in.	195.1
Overall width, in.	71.3
Overall height, in.	56.6
Curb weight, lbs.	3660
Cargo vol., cu. ft.	14.0
Fuel capacity, gals.	18.0
Seating capacity	5
Front head room, in.	38.6
Max. front leg room, in.	42.2
Rear head room, in.	36.7
Min. rear leg room, in.	35.5

ENGINES

	ohc V-6
Size, liters/cu. in.	3.5/212
Horsepower @ rpm	210@ 5200
Torque (lbs./ft.) @ rpm	224@ 2800
Availability	S

EPA city/highway mpg

4-speed OD automatic	19/25

PRICES

Acura RL	Retail Price	Dealer Invoice
3.5RL 4-door sedan	$41000	$35190

Prices are accurate at time of publication; subject to manufacturer's changes.

	Retail Price	Dealer Invoice
Destination charge	$435	$435

STANDARD EQUIPMENT:

3.5-liter V-6 engine, 4-speed automatic transmission, driver- and passenger-side air bags, anti-lock 4-wheel disc brakes, front and rear automatic air conditioning, interior air filter, variable-assist power steering, tilt/telescopic steering wheel w/memory, leather-wrapped steering wheel and shifter, cruise control, leather upholstery, power front seats w/memory, driver-seat lumbar support, center console, cupholders, rear-seat trunk pass-through, rear armrest, power moonroof, power windows, power door locks, remote keyless entry, heated power mirrors w/memory, Acura/Bose 8-speaker AM/FM/cassette player w/anti-theft, digital clock, integrated antenna, maintenance interval reminder, rear defogger, remote fuel-door and decklid releases, speed-sensitive intermittent wipers, illuminated visor mirrors, map lights, rear reading lights, alloy wheels, tinted glass, theft-deterrent system, fog lamps, mud guards, 215/60R16 tires.

OPTIONAL EQUIPMENT:

Major Packages

Premium Pkg.	3000	2575

Traction Control System, heated front seats, Acura/Bose sound system w/6-disc CD changer, burled walnut interior trim.

Comfort and Convenience

Navigation System	2000	1717

Requires Premium Pkg.

ACURA SLX

Acura SLX w/Premium Pkg.

4-wheel-drive full-size sport-utility vehicle; similar to Isuzu Trooper

Base price range: (1997 model) $35,300-$38,300. Built in Japan.

Also consider: GMC Yukon, Lincoln Navigator, Lexus LX450

FOR • Passenger and cargo room

AGAINST • Fuel economy • Ride • Entry/exit

SLX is an Acura-badged version of the Isuzu Trooper. It's built by Isuzu and stands apart from the Trooper with a different grille, wheels, and trim, plus more standard luxury features. Last summer, the National Highway Traffic Safety Administration (NHTSA) found no merit in allegations that the SLX/Trooper was more prone to tipping over than other sport-utility vehicles. The charges had hurt sales of the vehicles.

This year's SLX features most of the changes made for the '98 Trooper. These include revised front-end styling, a standard "Torque on Demand" 4-wheel-drive system, and a new 3.5-liter twin-cam V-6 with 25 more horsepower and 42 more pound-feet of torque than the previous single-cam 3.2-liter engine. Automatic remains the sole transmission. "Torque on Demand" allows switching between 2-wheel and 4-wheel High mode "on the fly" via a dashboard button instead of a lever. A 2-speed transfer case again provides Low-range 4WD gearing.

Last year's Premium Package is gone but some of its features are now standard, including leather upholstery, woodgrain interior accents, heated power front seats, and an overhead console. The SLX's

performance will mirror that of a similarly equipped Isuzu Trooper. **See the Isuzu Trooper report for an evaluation of the SLX.**

RATINGS

	Acura SLX
Acceleration	3
Fuel economy	2
Ride quality	3
Steering/handling	3
Braking	3
Quietness	3
Driver seating	4
Instruments/controls	3
Room/comfort (front)	4
Room/comfort (rear)	4
Cargo room	5
Value for the money	2
Total	**39**

SPECIFICATIONS

	4-door wagon
Wheelbase, in.	108.7
Overall length, in.	183.5
Overall width, in.	72.4
Overall height, in.	72.2
Curb weight, lbs.	4315
Cargo vol., cu. ft.	90.2
Fuel capacity, gals.	22.5
Seating capacity	5
Front head room, in.	39.8
Max. front leg room, in.	40.8
Rear head room, in.	39.8
Min. rear leg room, in.	39.1

ENGINES

	dohc V-6
Size, liters/cu. in.	3.5/214
Horsepower @ rpm	215@ 5400
Torque (lbs./ft.) @ rpm	230@ 3000
Availability	S

EPA city/highway mpg

4-speed OD automatic	14/18

PRICES

1997 Acura SLX

	Retail Price	Dealer Invoice
4-door wagon, 4WD	$35300	$30833
4-door wagon w/Premium Pkg., 4WD	38300	33453
Destination charge	435	435

STANDARD EQUIPMENT:

3.2-liter V-6 engine, 4-speed automatic transmission, anti-lock brakes, driver- and passenger-side air bags, variable-assist power steering, air conditioning, cruise control, cloth reclining front bucket seats with folding armrests, 60/40 split folding rear seats, AM/FM/cassette with six speakers, CD player, tilt steering column, power door locks and windows, power heated mirrors, remote keyless entry system, power moonroof, rear defogger, tachometer, coolant temperature and oil pressure gauges, voltmeter, trip odometer, digital clock, tinted windows, leather-wrapped steering wheel, tilt steering column, theft deterrent system, center storage console with cupholders, cornering lights, rear storage compartment, cargo lights, map lights, front and rear stabilizer bars, skid plates, rear step bumper, rear air deflector, mud guards, 245/70R16 all season tires, 5-spoke alloy wheels, full-size spare tire.

Premium Pkg. adds: heated power front seats, leather upholstery, power fold-in outside mirrors, simulated woodgrain interior trim, electronic multi-meter, limited-slip differential, integrated fog lamps, 6-spoke alloy wheels.

Options are available as dealer-installed accessories.

Rating Scale: 5-Excellent; 4-Above average; 3-Average; 2-Below average; 1-Poor

ACURA TL

Acura 3.2TL

Front-wheel-drive near-luxury car

Base price range: (1997 model) $28,450-$35,500. Built in Japan.

Also consider: Infiniti I30, Lexus ES 300, Mazda Millenia

FOR • Acceleration (3.2TL) • Steering/handling • Visibility

AGAINST • Engine noise (2.5TL) • Automatic transmission performance • Road noise (3.2 TL)

Like their big brother, the 3.5RL, Acura's mid-range TL sedans ("Touring Luxury") now come in a single trim level that includes most features from last year's optional Premium Packages.

As before, this 4-door sedan is offered in two versions. With an inline 5-cylinder engine, it's the 2.5TL. With a V-6, it's the 3.2TL. Both models again come only with an automatic transmission and include anti-lock brakes, automatic climate control, and a CD sound system in the base price.

This year, the 2.5TL adds leather interior, power moonroof, keyless entry/security system, and heated mirrors and front seats to its standard equipment list. The 3.2TL adds heated front seats; it already had the other features now included on the 2.5. Traction control and 4-way power passenger seat are 3.2TL options.

PERFORMANCE TLs have precise steering, competent handling, good grip and a firm but comfortable ride. It all makes for a sporty driving feel, though performance and refinement depend on model.

The 5-cylinder engine emits a throaty, coarse growl at odds with the TL's near-luxury mission, and though the 2.5 is no slouch in acceleration, the 3.2 is discernibly livelier, its V-6 smoother and quieter. However, the 3.2 rides on more-aggressive tires that generate more road noise than the 2.5's, though both TLs are pretty quiet overall. At least the V-6 doesn't exact a big mileage penalty. In a mix of city, suburban, and highway driving, we averaged 19.2 mpg with a 2.5TL against 18.3 mpg with a 3.2TL. Both models require premium fuel.

One of our main complaints about any TL concerns the automatic transmission. It's slow to downshift for passing and often upshifts harshly in hard acceleration.

ACCOMMODATIONS The TL's passenger space is unexceptional for a car this size, a result of Acura's typical low-profile styling that also complicates entry/exit for taller persons. Head room all around and rear leg room are just adequate for 6-footers, and there's little toe space beneath the front seats. At least visibility is good to all directions.

Controls are simple and intuitive, though not all are easy to find, and there's no lighting for power window and lock buttons. The trunk has a usefully low, wide opening, but utility suffers from sidewalls that narrow sharply about halfway forward.

BUILD QUALITY Our most recent test TL was solid and rattle-free. Its paint was deep and glossy, and trim was applied with care inside and out.

VALUE FOR THE MONEY The TLs have their good points, but don't do any single thing well enough to stand out in the competitive near-luxury segment. Acura has bolstered its customer service programs in an effort to retain buyers defecting to other luxury brands. That makes the TL attractive, but play the field; there are good alternatives in the same price range.

RATINGS

	Acura 2.5TL	Acura 3.2TL
Acceleration	3	4
Fuel economy	3	3
Ride quality	3	3
Steering/handling	4	4
Braking	5	5
Quietness	3	4
Driver seating	4	4
Instruments/controls	4	4
Room/comfort (front)	3	3
Room/comfort (rear)	3	3
Cargo room	4	4
Value for the money	4	4
Total	**43**	**45**

SPECIFICATIONS

	4-door sedan
Wheelbase, in.	111.8
Overall length, in.	191.5
Overall width, in.	70.3
Overall height, in.	55.3
Curb weight, lbs.	3252
Cargo vol., cu. ft.	14.1
Fuel capacity, gals.	17.2
Seating capacity	5
Front head room, in.	39.1
Max. front leg room, in.	43.7
Rear head room, in.	36.9
Min. rear leg room, in.	35.2

ENGINES

	ohc I-5	ohc V-6
Size, liters/cu. in.	2.5/152	3.2/196
Horsepower @ rpm	176@ 6300	200@ 5300
Torque (lbs./ft.) @ rpm	170@ 3900	210@ 4500
Availability	S[1]	S[2]
EPA city/highway mpg		
4-speed OD automatic	20/25	19/24

1. 2.5TL. 3.2TL.

PRICES

1997 Acura TL	Retail Price	Dealer Invoice
2.5TL 4-door notchback	$28450	$24993
2.5TL 4-door notchback w/Premium Pkg.	30500	26794
3.2TL 4-door notchback	32950	28947
3.2TL 4-door notchback w/Premium Pkg.	35500	31187
Destination charge	435	435

STANDARD EQUIPMENT:

2.5: 2.5-liter 5-cylinder engine, 4-speed automatic transmission, driver- and passenger-side air bags, anti-lock 4-wheel disc brakes, variable-assist power steering, automatic climate control, cruise control, cloth reclining front bucket seats, 8-way power driver seat w/lumbar adjuster, front console with armrest, rear armrest, tilt steering column, leather-wrapped steering wheel, tinted glass, power windows and door locks, power mirrors, AM/FM/cassette/CD player, rear defogger, variable intermittent wipers, theft-deterrent system, map lights, visor mirrors, fog lights, 205/60HR15 tires, alloy wheels.

Premium Pkg. adds: leather upholstery, power moonroof. **3.2** adds: 3.2-liter V-6 engine, power passenger seat, remote keyless entry, 205/65VR15 tires.

Premium Pkg. adds: traction control, heated front seats, heated mirrors.

Options are available as dealer-installed accessories.

AUDI A4

BUDGET BUY

Front- or all-wheel-drive near-luxury car

Base price range: $23,790-$30,465. Built in Germany.

Also consider: BMW 3-Series, Lexus ES 300, Mercedes-Benz C-Class, Nissan Maxima

---

Prices are accurate at time of publication; subject to manufacturer's changes.

Audi A4 1.8T

FOR • Ride • Handling • Side air bags • Optional all-wheel drive • Standard traction control (front-drive 2.8)

AGAINST • Rear seat room • Steering feel

Long owned by Volkswagen, Audi has spent the last few years rebuilding its U.S. sales base. That effort has been boosted by the A4, Audi's entry-level sedan that arrived for 1996 with a 172-horsepower V-6. A lower-cost 1.8T model with a turbocharged 1.8-liter 4-cylinder engine was added last year, followed by an improved V-6 with five valves per cylinder (versus two) and 190 horsepower.

This year, Audi adds a V-6 4-door wagon, the A4 2.8 Avant, and adopts the Porsche-designed 5-speed Tiptronic as the A4's automatic transmission. Replacing a conventional 5-speed automatic, Tiptronic allows sequential manual gear selection via a special shift gate. It's mandatory on the front-drive Avant and optional for other A4s in lieu of manual transmission.

All A4s offer front-wheel drive with standard traction control ("FrontTrak" to Audi) or extra-cost Quattro all-wheel drive.

Other changes for '98 include a revised gauge cluster and a choice of three interior color/trim combinations called Ambition, Ambiente, and Advance. A4s have "dual-threshold" dashboard air bags that deploy with lesser force if an occupant is not belted up, plus standard front side air bags.

PERFORMANCE Audi's 2-valve V-6 was smooth, just not very potent. We haven't tested the new 5-valve V-6, but expect it to be far stronger at low speeds yet no less refined. The turbo four is best appreciated with manual shift, but provides adequate go with automatic. We logged nearly 24 mpg on a long highway trip with a manual 1.8T Quattro, so you'll be lucky to average 20-21 mpg overall.

Engines aside, the A4's manual transmission is easy to operate, while adding Tiptronic makes an already-smooth automatic even better. Quattro works with no driver input to provide great traction in any situation. However, the lighter front-drive models get better mileage and, with now-standard traction control, have all the grip most people need.

There's little wind noise, but the V-6 models' high-performance tires thrum on rough pavement and the turbo-four growls at higher speeds. Plus, a 1.8T Quattro we tested emitted an annoying drivetrain drone in 65-mph cruising.

A4's suspension soaks up dips and bumps, and body lean is modest in cornering. The power steering is a bit too light and numb. The brakes seem touchy at first, but they stop the car short and straight. The optional Sport Package adds a firmer suspension and higher-performance wheels and tires that sacrifice some ride comfort for a small extra measure of cornering grip and handling agility.

ACCOMMODATIONS Like BMW's 3-Series and the Mercedes C-Class, the A4 provides good passenger room in front but not in back. Rear leg space all but vanishes without the front seats moved forward, and all-around head room is only adequate with the optional sunroof, which steals about two inches of clearance. Cargo space in sedans is good but not great; at least the trunk lid opens wide at bumper level. The new Avant looks more casual hauler than big-load mover.

The A4 caters nicely to drivers of all sizes. Gauges and most switchgear are clear and well placed, but the climate control panel is needlessly busy and mounted too low.

BUILD QUALITY There's no more solid small sedan than the A4, which smothers bad bumps and potholes with quiet disdain. Detail finish is exemplary inside and out, as are interior materials, though a few molded plastic parts look chintzy.

VALUE FOR THE MONEY The A4 is good enough to stand comparison with its German rivals, as well as near-luxury Japanese sedans such as the Lexus ES 300. It's also the only car in this class offering all-wheel drive. And with free scheduled maintenance for 3 years/50,000 miles, the A4 earns our nod.

RATINGS	1.8T	2.8	2.8 Avant
Acceleration	3	4	4
Fuel economy	3	3	3
Ride quality	4	4	3
Steering/handling	4	4	4
Braking	4	4	4
Quietness	3	3	3
Driver seating	4	4	4
Instruments/controls	3	3	3
Room/comfort (front)	4	4	4
Room/comfort (rear)	3	3	3
Cargo room	3	3	5
Value for the money	4	4	3
Total	**42**	**43**	**43**

SPECIFICATIONS	4-door sedan	4-door wagon
Wheelbase, in.	103.0	103.0
Overall length, in.	178.0	176.7
Overall width, in.	68.2	68.2
Overall height, in.	55.8	56.7
Curb weight, lbs.	3087	3289
Cargo vol., cu. ft.	13.7	NA
Fuel capacity, gals.	16.4	16.4
Seating capacity	5	5
Front head room, in.	38.1	38.1
Max. front leg room, in.	41.3	NA
Rear head room, in.	36.8	37.8
Min. rear leg room, in.	33.4	NA

ENGINES	Turbo dohc I-4	dohc V-6
Size, liters/cu. in.	1.8/107	2.8/169
Horsepower @ rpm	150@ 5700	190@ 6000
Torque (lbs./ft.) @ rpm	155@ 1750	207@ 3200
Availability	S[1]	S[2]
EPA city/highway mpg		
5-speed OD manual	23/25	20/27
5-speed OD automatic	21/30	18/28

1. A4 1.8T. 2. A4 2.8.

PRICES

Audi A4	Retail Price	Dealer Invoice
1997 1.8T 4-door sedan	$23790	$20942
1998 2.8 4-door sedan	28390	24944
Avant 4-door wagon	30465	26839
Avant Quattro 4-door wagon	31040	27464
Destination charge	500	500

STANDARD EQUIPMENT:

1.8T: 1.8-liter turbocharged 4-cylinder engine, 5-speed manual transmission, Electronic Differential Lock, driver- and passenger-side air bags, front side-impact air bag, anti-lock 4-wheel disc brakes, automatic air conditioning, interior air filter, power steering, tilt/telescoping steering wheel, leather-wrapped shifter and boot, cruise control, reclining front seats with height adjustment, 60/40 split folding rear seat, velour or leatherette upholstery, front storage console w/cupholders, folding rear storage armrest, tachometer, trip odometer, coolant-temperature and oil-temperature gauges, voltmeter, outside temperature display, service interval indicator, analog clock, 8-speaker AM/FM/cassette, integrated antenna, power windows, power door locks, heated power outside mirrors, rear defogger, remote decklid and fuel-door releases, intermittent wipers, illu-

Rating Scale: 5-Excellent; 4-Above average; 3-Average; 2-Below average; 1-Poor

CONSUMER GUIDE™

minated visor mirrors, front and rear reading lights, floormats, tinted glass, theft-deterrent system, headlight washers, front and rear fog lights, 205/65R15 tires, alloy wheels.

2.8 adds: 2.8-liter V-6 engine, 8-way power driver seat w/lumbar adjustment, leather-wrapped steering wheel, jacquard satin or leatherette upholstery, adjustable front armrest, cellular phone prewiring, interior wood trim, 205/55HR16 tires.

Avant adds: permanent 4WD (Avant Quattro), roof rails, ski sack.

OPTIONAL EQUIPMENT:

	Retail Price	Dealer Invoice
Major Packages		
All-Weather Package, 1.8T, 2.8	$630	$548
Avant, Avant Quattro	470	409
Includes heated driver-side door lock, heated front seats, heated windshield washer nozzles, ski sack (1.8T, 2.8).		
Sport Pkg., 1.8T	750	653
2.8, Avant, Avant Quattro	400	348
Leather-wrapped sport steering wheel, sport suspension, 205/55ZR16 tires (2.8, Avant, Avant Quattro), 205/55ZR16 tires (2.8), 7-spoke alloy wheels.		
Powertrains		
5-speed Tiptronic automatic transmission	1075	1025
Quattro IV all-wheel-drive system	1650	1650
Comfort and Convenience		
Audi/Bose 8-speaker sound system, 2.8	660	574
6-disc CD changer	1200	1044
Includes Audi/Bose sound system.		
Leather upholstery	1320	1148
NA 1.8T.		
Leather-wrapped sport steering wheel	160	139
Trip computer	250	218
Power sunroof and remote keyless entry	1190	1035
Appearance and Miscellaneous		
Pearlescent metallic paint	570	496
Cool Shades paint	460	400
Metallic/mica paint, 1.8T	460	400
2.8	NC	NC

AUDI A6

Audi A6 sedan

Front- or all-wheel-drive near-luxury car
Base price range: $33,750-$34,400. Built in Germany.
Also consider: Acura TL, Infiniti I30, Lexus ES 300

FOR • Standard anti-lock brakes • Steering/handling • Passenger and cargo room • Side air bags

AGAINST • Rear visibility • Climate controls

This is Audi's best effort yet at matching mid-line BMW and Mercedes-Benz models in prestige and performance. Replacing a car that debuted for 1992, the '98 A6 displays the new VW/Audi corporate look of arched rooflines and prominent semi-circular wheel openings. It debuts as a sedan with a choice of front drive or optional Quattro all-wheel drive. Wagon versions should appear in late '98 as 1999 models.

Though the A6 is the midsize Audi, it's built as a scaled-up version of the German automaker's compact A4 and thus relates to this year's similarly derived new Volkswagen Passat.

Against its predecessor, this A6 is about three inches longer

in wheelbase but a half-inch shorter overall. It's also slightly wider and taller.

As in some other cars, the A6's dashboard air bags have "dual deployment" operation and pop out with lesser force if an occupant is not wearing a seatbelt. Front side air bags are standard and rear side air bags are optional.

The only engine is a V-6 with five valves per cylinder and the only transmission is Audi's 5-speed Tiptronic automatic, which offers manual shift capability via a secondary selector gate.

PERFORMANCE Unlike the previous A6, which felt lethargic off the line and lazy around town, the new one fairly leaps away from stops and is eager to slice through traffic. Part of the transformation is the way in which the throttle is set to deliver lots of go in the first inch or two of pedal travel. It's a technique used by some American automakers, but here it seems slightly out of place, turning a classy European sedan into a stoplight charger. Still, there's no arguing with results, and overall, acceleration is satisfying.

So is handling. The firm steering communicates well in turns and helps the car arrow effortlessly down the Interstate. There are few front-wheel-drive sedans that corner with more poise or grip. The payback is a suspension that glides over pavement craters, but notices most every small bump and tar strip, making for a busy ride on many surfaces.

The brakes are strong, with progressive pedal feel. Wind noise is very low, but the tires thump and whine, and the engine, while not ragged sounding, doesn't purr like a BMW or Mercedes-Benz six.

ACCOMMODATIONS The cabin is a breezy, sophisticated mix of color-matched surfaces, walnut trim, and touches of brightwork on the dashboard, doors, and console. It's also roomier than that of the rival BMW 5-Series or Mercedes E-Class. Front seaters have an abundance of head, shoulder, and leg room. In back is a supportive bench seat and plenty of knee clearance, toe space, and head room.

Saucer-sized main gauges are complemented by intuitive controls that move with satisfying precision, though the down-low climate system panel forces the driver's eyes from the road when adjustments are required.

Too-small outside mirrors hamper lane changes, but visibility is otherwise good. The trunk is cavernous and there's plenty of interior storage, including map pockets on every door.

BUILD QUALITY Our test car's dark green paint was lustrous, panel gaps were precise inside and out, and materials were top-notch.

VALUE FOR THE MONEY An A6 sedan with leather and moon-roof options still costs thousands less than a BMW 528i or Mercedes E320 while delivering a similar sense of Teutonic solidity and driving feel. Don't spend over $35,000 on a sedan without driving this one first.

RATINGS	A6 sedan	Quattro sedan
Acceleration	4	3
Fuel economy	3	2
Ride quality	4	4
Steering/handling	4	4
Braking	4	4
Quietness	4	4
Driver seating	5	5
Instruments/controls	4	4
Room/comfort (front)	4	4
Room/comfort (rear)	4	4
Cargo room	4	4
Value for the money	4	3
Total	**47**	**45**

SPECIFICATIONS

	4-door sedan
Wheelbase, in.	108.7
Overall length, in.	192.0
Overall width, in.	71.3
Overall height, in.	57.2
Curb weight, lbs.	3473
Cargo vol., cu. ft.	17.2
Fuel capacity, gals.	18.5

Prices are accurate at time of publication; subject to manufacturer's changes.

	4-door sedan
Seating capacity	5
Front head room, in.	39.3
Max. front leg room, in.	41.3
Rear head room, in.	37.9
Min. rear leg room, in.	37.3

ENGINES

	dohc V-6
Size, liters/cu. in.	2.8/169
Horsepower @ rpm..	200@ 6000
Torque (lbs./ft.) @ rpm.................................	207@ 3200
Availability	S
EPA city/highway mpg	
5-speed OD automatic..................................	17/28

PRICES

Audi A6

	Retail Price	Dealer Invoice
A6 4-door sedan	$33750	$29697
A6 4-door wagon	34400	30250
Destination charge	500	500

Wagon requires Quattro Value Pkg.

STANDARD EQUIPMENT:

Sedan 2.8-liter V-6 engine, 5-speed automatic transmission, Electronic Differential Lock, driver- and passenger-side air bags, front side-impact air bags, anti-lock 4-wheel disc brakes, automatic air conditioning w/dual zone controls, speed-sensitive power steering, tilt/telescoping steering column, leather-wrapped steering wheel, cruise control, Jacquard satin cloth upholstery, reclining front bucket seats with height and lumbar adjustments, 8-way power driver seat, center storage console with cupholders, adjustable front storage armrest, split folding rear seat, rear folding armrest, walnut interior trim, outside-temperature indicator, tachometer, oil-temperature and coolant-temperature gauge, trip odometer, analog clock, service-interval indicator, Active Auto Check System, power windows, power door locks, heated power mirrors, remote fuel-door and decklid release, AM/FM/cassette, integrated antenna, reading lights, illuminated visor mirrors, rear defogger, rear heat ducts, intermittent wipers, ski sack, floormats, tinted glass, theft-deterrent system, front and rear fog lights, 195/65R15 tires, alloy wheels.

Wagon adds: quattro all-wheel drive, power moonroof, 2-place rear seat, roof-mounted antenna, rear wiper/washer, remote tailgate release, retractable rear window sunshade, cargo-area cover and net, roof rack, 205/55R16 tires.

OPTIONAL EQUIPMENT:

Major Packages

Quattro Value Pkg.	2490	2360
Quattro all-wheel-drive system, power sunroof, 205/55R16 tires.		
Comfort and Convenience Pkg., wagon	860	748
Power front passenger seat, memory driver seat and outside mirrors, remote keyless entry.		
Convenience Pkg., sedan	1500	1305
Memory mirrors, automatic day/night rearview and driver-side mirror, power sunroof.		
Enhanced Security Pkg., sedan	950	827
Rear side-impact air bags, Xenon headlights.		
Warm Weather Pkg., sedan	1800	1566
Insulated glass, power rear sun shade, manual rear side shade, solar panel sunroof.		
Cold Weather Pkg., sedan	750	653
Heated front seats, heated steering wheel, ski sack.		
All-Weather Pkg., wagon........................	520	452
Heated front seats, heated windshield washer nozzles, heated front door locks, headlight washers.		

Powertrains

Quattro IV all-wheel-drive system, sedan................................	1650	1650

Comfort and Convenience	Retail Price	Dealer Invoice
Power moonroof, sedan	$1000	$870
Leather upholstery..........................	1550	1349
Audi/Bose audio system, wagon......	660	574
6-disc CD changer, sedan...............	1300	1131
Includes Audi/Bose sound system.		

Appearance and Miscellaneous		
Pearlescent metallic paint	600	522
16-inch alloy wheels........................	225	196
Includes 205/55R16 tires.		

AUDI A8

1997 Audi A8 3.7

Front- or all-wheel-drive luxury car
Base price range: $57,400-$65,000. Built in Germany.
Also consider: BMW 5-Series, Lexus LS 400, Mercedes-Benz E-Class

FOR • Ride • Quietness • Acceleration • Side air bags

AGAINST • Price • Fuel economy • Control layout

Audi's latest flagship slots in size between the BMW 7-Series and smaller Mercedes-Benz E-Class, but the A8's use of aluminum for most frame and body panels means it weighs 300- to 500-pounds less than comparable luxury sedans.

The A8 3.7 has a 3.7-liter V-8 and front-wheel drive with standard traction control. The A8 4.2 Quattro has a 4.2-liter V-8 and permanently engaged all-wheel drive. Both A8s have six air bags: dual cushions in front and a smaller air bag in each of the four doors.

Dual-pane "acoustic" glass is newly standard for '98, a glass moonroof replaces last year's aluminum sunroof, and the mandatory 5-speed automatic transmission is now a Porsche-designed Tiptronic unit with manual-shift feature. Also on hand is a new option package with high-intensity Xenon-gas headlamps.

PERFORMANCE Aluminum structure or not, A8s aren't lightweights, yet we ran 0-60 mph in just under 8 seconds with a '97 3.7 model. We haven't timed a 4.2 Quattro, but Audi's 6.9-second 0-60 claim seems a half-second optimistic, as the bigger V-8's extra power is partly offset by 220 extra pounds of all-wheel-drive componentry. Fuel economy is a wash. The 3.7 returned 18 mpg in hard city/freeway driving; the Quattro 18.2 in more gentle running.

Both have polished road moves. Handling falls just short of BMW-sporty, but cornering is grippy and predictable—about like that of the biggest Mercedes—and the A8 feels far better planted at high speed than a Lexus LS 400. Wind and engine noise are Lexus-low, but there's mild tire drone over coarse pavement. Ride quality is excellent. The A8 irons out rough spots as well its German rivals and with better body control than the Lexus. "Panic" braking is short and undramatic, though pedal action is somewhat doughy.

ACCOMMODATIONS The A8 packs all the amenities expected in top-drawer cars, and you can almost make it a limousine by opting for the Cold Weather, Warm Weather, and/or Convenience Packages. It doesn't quite match the biggest Mercedes and BMWs for rear passenger room, but head clearance is adequate for 6-footers, leg space borders on generous, and there's enough width for three medium-size adults. All seats

Rating Scale: 5-Excellent; 4-Above average; 3-Average; 2-Below average; 1-Poor

CONSUMER GUIDE™

are firm and supportive, but the front buckets let you slide around some in hard turns.

The dashboard has more buttons and switches than most high-zoot cars and low-set climate controls are particularly tricky to operate while driving. Visibility is constricted over the shoulder because of the roof styling, but is good elsewhere.

Cargo space is ample and lift-over low, but the trunk is rather narrow due to bulky side panels. The interior provides plenty of small-items stowage, though the dashboard glovebox isn't as big as it looks.

BUILD QUALITY Audi says aluminum adds strength while saving weight, and the A8 does feel rock-solid on most any surface. Paint, interior materials, and detail fit and finish were all great on our test cars, as well they should be given A8 prices.

VALUE FOR THE MONEY We like the A8, but can't recommend it because it's overpriced for what it offers. Aluminum construction demands more hand labor than steel, so the A8 costs more than other cars of similar size and power. The Quattro model boasts a class exclusive with its all-wheel drive, but we doubt most buyers need that any more than the aluminum structure that makes these cars so costly. Unless you're willing to pay dearly for the latest in automotive high tech, shop other brands for better value in a big premium sedan.

SPECIFICATIONS

	4-door sedan
Wheelbase, in.	113.0
Overall length, in.	198.2
Overall width, in.	74.0
Overall height, in.	56.7
Curb weight, lbs.	3682
Cargo vol., cu. ft.	17.6
Fuel capacity, gals.	23.7
Seating capacity	5
Front head room, in.	38.9
Max. front leg room, in.	41.3
Rear head room, in.	38.2
Min. rear leg room, in.	38.4

ENGINES

	dohc V-8	dohc V-8
Size, liters/cu. in.	3.7/226	4.2/255
Horsepower @ rpm	230@ 5500	300@ 6000
Torque (lbs./ft.) @ rpm	235@ 2700	295@ 3300
Availability	S[1]	S[2]
EPA city/highway mpg		
5-speed OD automatic	17/26	17/25

1. A8 3.7. 2. A8 4.2.

RATINGS

	3.7	4.2 Quattro
Acceleration	4	4
Fuel economy	2	2
Ride quality	4	4
Steering/handling	4	4
Braking	5	5
Quietness	4	4
Driver seating	4	4
Instruments/controls	3	3
Room/comfort (front)	4	4
Room/comfort (rear)	4	4
Cargo room	4	4
Value for the money	2	2
Total	44	44

PRICES

Audi A8	Retail Price	Dealer Invoice
3.7 4-door sedan	$57400	$50183
4.2 4-door sedan	65000	56795
Destination charge	500	500

STANDARD EQUIPMENT:

3.7: 3.7-liter DOHC V-8 engine, 5-speed Tiptronic automatic transmission, Electronic Differential Lock, Anti-Slip Regulation system, driver- and passenger-side air bags, front and rear side-impact air bags, anti-lock 4-wheel disc brakes, dual-zone automatic air conditioning w/air filter, speed-sensitive power steering, power tilt/telescoping steering wheel, leather-wrapped steering wheel and shifter, cruise control, steering wheel), leather upholstery, 14-way power front bucket seats w/lumbar adjustment and power headrests, memory functions (driver seat, outside mirrors, center storage console with cupholders, two adjustable front armrests, rear folding armrest, walnut interior trim, power sunroof, trip computer, outside-temperature indicator, tachometer, coolant-temperature gauge, trip odometer, digital clock, service-interval indicator, Active Auto Check System, power windows, power door locks, heated power mirrors w/automatic day/night, automatic day/night rearview mirror, remote keyless entry, remote fuel-door and decklid release, AM/FM/cassette, power antenna, reading lights, dual pane acoustic glass, illuminated visor mirrors, rear defogger, rear heat ducts, intermittent wipers, floormats, tinted glass, theft-deterrent system, heated washer nozzles, headlight washers, front and rear fog lights, 225/60HR16 tires, alloy wheels.

4.2 adds: 4.2-liter DOHC V-8 engine, Quattro all-wheel-drive system, Audi/Bose sound system.

OPTIONAL EQUIPMENT:

	Retail Price	Dealer Invoice
Major Packages		
Warm Weather Pkg.	$2000	$1740

Power solar sunroof, insulated glass, power rear-window sunshade, manual rear-side-window sunshades.

Cold Weather Pkg.	1000	870

Heated front and rear seats, heated steering wheels, ski sack.

Electronics Group	700	609

Automatic day/night mirrors, power rear seat lumbar support and headrests.

Comfort and Convenience		
Audi/Bose 6-disc CD changer, 3.7	1400	1218
6-disc CD changer, 4.2	540	470

Appearance and Miscellaneous		
Pearlescent metallic paint	600	522
Polished alloy wheels and 225/55R17 tires	1000	870

AUDI CABRIOLET

1998 Audi Cabriolet

Front-wheel-drive luxury coupe

Base price: $34,600. Built in Germany.

Also consider: BMW 3-Series, Mercedes-Benz SLK230, Saab 900

FOR • Steering/handling

AGAINST • Acceleration • Rear seat room • Cargo room

Cabriolet is what Germans call a convertible. This one is a 2-door soft-top version of the compact Audi 90 sedan that was replaced three years ago by the A4. Though a replacement A4-based Cabriolet would seem likely, its status is unknown.

Meantime, the old model soldiers on, but will no longer be sold in California, Connecticut, Massachusetts, or New York, owing to those states' stiffer emissions standards. The only other changes involve a new-design ignition key, sport steering wheel, and wiper switch.

The Cabriolet has been a slow seller since its 1993 debut. Last year, Audi tried to perk up interest with a $2200 price cut,

Prices are accurate at time of publication; subject to manufacturer's changes.

achieved by making options of the once-standard leather uphol-stery and power top. It didn't help.

As a holdover from the 90 line, the Cabriolet uses Audi's old 2-valve, single-overhead-cam 2.8-liter V-6, not the more potent 5-valve twin-cam version used in A4s. Drive is to the front wheels through an automatic transmission.

PERFORMANCE As ever, the Audi Cabriolet is somewhat underpowered. Though its V-6 is smooth and fairly quiet except near maximum rpm, there's not enough low-speed torque for strong off-the-line launches (0-60 mph takes a little over 10 sec-onds) and quick passing bursts. In addition, shift quality is lethar-gic. Still, this powertrain is acceptable in day-to-day driving, and highway cruising is pretty relaxed.

Ride quality is firm but not harsh, although the shortish wheel-base and low-profile tires can make things jittery over bad pave-ment. There's good grip and little body lean in turns, steering is responsive, and brakes are strong.

ACCOMMODATIONS There's adequate front leg and torso space for average-size adults, plus better top-up head room than most convertibles. But the 90 sedan never had much rear room or cargo space, and the Cabriolet has even less because is has to provide for top stowage. The back seat is thus better left to toddlers, while the small trunk means traveling light. Controls are handy and simple for the most part, but the climate system is more complicated than it needs to be and its panel is too low for easy operation.

Power or manual top, the plastic rear window is prone to early wrinkling and clouding in time-honored convertible fashion. Some less-expensive competitors have a glass window with electric defogger, versus the Audi's less-efficient blower-type air defogger.

BUILD QUALITY Though well crafted in the German way, the Cabriolet has more body flex than most modern convertibles. It's not severe, but it does betray its "converted sedan" construction and does nothing to convey a feel in line with its price.

VALUE FOR THE MONEY Even at its lower base price, the Audi Cabriolet shakes too much and stirs the soul too little to compete with rivals like the BMW 3-Series convertible or a turbocharged Saab 900 ragtop. A replacement model can't come too soon.

RATINGS

	Cabriolet
Acceleration	3
Fuel economy	3
Ride quality	4
Steering/handling	4
Braking	4
Quietness	4
Driver seating	4
Instruments/controls	3
Room/comfort (front)	4
Room/comfort (rear)	2
Cargo room	2
Value for the money	2
Total	**39**

SPECIFICATIONS

	2-door convertible
Wheelbase, in.	100.6
Overall length, in.	176.0
Overall width, in.	67.6
Overall height, in.	54.3
Curb weight, lbs.	3364
Cargo vol., cu. ft.	6.6
Fuel capacity, gals.	17.4
Seating capacity	4
Front head room, in.	38.3
Max. front leg room, in.	40.7
Rear head room, in.	36.4
Min. rear leg room, in.	26.5

ENGINES

	ohc V-6
Size, liters/cu. in.	2.8/169
Horsepower @ rpm	172@ 5500
Torque (lbs./ft.) @ rpm	184@ 3000

	ohc V-6
Availability	S
EPA city/highway mpg	
4-speed OD automatic	19/24

PRICES

Audi Cabriolet	Retail Price	Dealer Invoice
Cabriolet 2-door convertible	$34600	$30424
Destination charge	500	500

STANDARD EQUIPMENT:

Cabriolet: 2.8-liter V-6 engine, 4-speed automatic transmission, driv-er- and passenger-side air bags, anti-lock 4-wheel disc brakes, air conditioning, variable-assist power steering, leather-wrapped steering wheel and shifter, cruise control, cloth/leather upholstery, reclining front seats with height adjustment, center storage console w/cuphold-ers, power windows, power door locks, heated power mirrors, tachometer, coolant-temperature gauge, trip odometer, digital clock, AM/FM/cassette, power antenna, rear defogger, power remote deck-lid and fuel-door releases, illuminated entry, rear heat ducts, intermit-tent wipers, illuminated visor mirrors, ski sack, floormats, tinted glass, theft-deterrent system, headlight washers, front and rear fog lights, manual folding top, 195/65R15 tires, alloy wheels.

OPTIONAL EQUIPMENT:

Major Packages

Premium Equipment Pkg.	3700	3219

Leather upholstery, power folding top, remote keyless entry, wal-nut interior trim.

All-Weather Package	470	409

Includes heated front door locks, heated front seats, heated wind-shield washer nozzles.

Comfort and Convenience

High-back sport bucket seats	1190	1035

Includes power seat-height adjusters. Requires Preferred Equipment Pkg.

Interior windscreen	400	348

Appearance and Miscellaneous

Pearlescent metallic paint	570	496
Cool Shades paint	460	400
Competition-style alloy wheels	400	348

Includes 205/65R15 tires. Requires Preferred Equipment Pkg.

BMW Z3

RECOMMENDED

BMW Z3 1.9

Rear-wheel-drive Sports and GT

Base price range: $29,425-$35,900. Built in Spartanburg, S.C.

Also consider: Mazda Miata, Mercedes-Benz SLK230, Porsche Boxster

FOR • Standard traction control •Steering/handling •Acceler-ation (6-cyl.) • Braking

AGAINST • Acceleration (4-cyl. w/automatic) • Noise • Car-go space

BMW's first sports car in 40 years bowed in spring 1996 in

Rating Scale: 5-Excellent; 4-Above average; 3-Average; 2-Below average; 1-Poor

CONSUMER GUIDE™

response to the "retro roadster" craze ignited by Mazda's Miata. The 4-cylinder Z3 1.9 was soon joined by a 6-cylinder 2.8 model. Both are built at BMW's plant in South Carolina and borrow drivetrains, chassis design, and other components from the German maker's 3-Series line.

Next spring, BMW will add the M roadster, a Z3 packing the 3.2-liter 6-cylinder engine from the high-performance M3 sedan and coupe. A hatchback derivative, the M coupe, should go on sale in fall '98.

Meantime, existing Z3s gain standard rollover bars and offer more heavily bolstered sports seats as a new option. A new Premium Package option delivers wood interior trim and a power soft top, plus, on the 1.9, leather upholstery. Wood trim and the power top (previous Z3s had only a manual top) are also available separately.

PERFORMANCE The Z3 1.9 amounts to a slightly bigger, heavier Miata with a larger, more-potent 4-cylinder engine. But it isn't as quick, running our 0-60 mph sprints in a slightly disappointing 9.3 seconds with manual shift versus Mazda's 8.5. With automatic, the 1.9 takes more than 10 seconds 0-60, unimpressive for the price. The 2.8 accelerates with more authority, but is still no neck-snapper. Its advantage is greater torque for less shifting around town with either transmission.

Premium fuel is required and in hard city/freeway driving with 5-speed test cars we got 22.3 mpg from the 1.9 and 21.1 from the 2.8.

The 4-cylinder offsets its tepid performance by being smooth and not too noisy except when working hard (which is most of the time). The six is even quieter and creamier. But these are sports cars, so wind, road, and engine noise all rise markedly with speed.

Both Z3s have firm suspensions that permit little lean in turns and provide stable cornering. Ride is supple considering the high cornering limits, but it's jiggly except on glass-smooth surfaces and the Z3 isn't as good as Mercedes' SLK in smothering bumps. Braking is straight and short—about 105 feet in 60-mph "panic" stops.

ACCOMMODATIONS Larger folks may feel cramped in the Z3 cockpit, which exceeds Miata's for usable room but is tighter than the SLK's. Getting in and out of the low-slung car is no picnic. A standard power seat allows most drivers to get comfortable, but the steering wheel is mounted rather high and—surprising for these prices—isn't adjustable. Trunk space is meager except by sports-car standards, but interior storage is relatively good and includes a pair of locking bins behind the seats.

The folding top is easy to raise and lower, and many buyers will like the new power option. However, the plastic back window is prone to easy wrinkling, and the roof's wide rear quarters inhibit over-the-shoulder visibility.

BUILD QUALITY The Z3's no-frills interior is appropriate for a sports car, but the 1.9's standard leatherette upholstery looks none too classy. Some plastic interior moldings seem equally cut-rate. In structural stiffness the Z3 is good but some bumps that don't look bad can induce a surprising amount of body shake.

VALUE FOR THE MONEY In performance or equipment it's hard to justify the extra cost of the Z3 1.9 over a Miata, mostly because the Mazda is such a great sports car. The 6-cylinder Z3 is more convincing, but also more expensive. For sports-car fans who can afford to indulge an appreciation of BMW design, the Z3 is rewarding. For the rest of us, Miata's the better value.

RATINGS

	1.9	2.8
Acceleration	3	4
Fuel economy	3	3
Ride quality	3	3
Steering/handling	4	4
Braking	5	5
Quietness	2	2
Driver seating	3	3
Instruments/controls	3	3
Room/comfort (front)	3	3
Room/comfort (rear)	1	1
Cargo room	2	2
Value for the money	3	3
Total	**35**	**36**

SPECIFICATIONS

	2-door convertible
Wheelbase, in.	96.3
Overall length, in.	158.5
Overall width, in.	66.6
Overall height, in.	50.7
Curb weight, lbs.	2701
Cargo vol., cu. ft.	5.0
Fuel capacity, gals.	13.5
Seating capacity	2
Front head room, in.	37.6
Max. front leg room, in.	41.8
Rear head room, in.	—
Min. rear leg room, in.	—

ENGINES

	dohc I-4	dohc I-6
Size, liters/cu. in.	1.9/116	2.8/170
Horsepower @ rpm	138@ 6000	189@ 5300
Torque (lbs./ft.) @ rpm	133@ 4300	203@ 3950
Availability	S[1]	S[2]

EPA city/highway mpg

4-speed OD automatic	23/31	18/25
5-speed manual	23/31	19/27

1. Z3 1.9. 2. Z3 2.8.

PRICES

BMW Z3	Retail Price	Dealer Invoice
1.9 2-door convertible	$29425	$25915
2.8 2-door convertible	35900	31455
Destination charge	570	570

STANDARD EQUIPMENT:

1.9: 1.9-liter 4-cylinder engine, 5-speed manual transmission, All Season Traction, driver- and passenger-side air bags, anti-lock 4-wheel disc brakes, roll bar, air conditioning, variable-assist power steering, leather-wrapped steering wheel/shifter/handbrake, cruise control, leatherette upholstery, 4-way power driver seat, 2-way power passenger seat, center storage console, cupholders, 6-speaker AM/FM/cassette with weather band and amplifier, digital clock, power windows, power mirrors, tachometer, trip odometer, coolant-temperature gauge, intermittent wipers, tinted glass, fog lights, tool kit, 225/50ZR16 tires, alloy wheels.

2.8 adds: 2.8-liter DOHC 6-cylinder engine, limited slip differential, leather upholstery, wood interior trim, Harman Kardon sound system, flared rear fenders, front spoiler.

OPTIONAL EQUIPMENT:
Major Packages

Premium Pkg., 1.9	2000	1680
2.8	950	790

Power convertible top, leather upholstery (1.9), wood interior trim.

Powertrains

4-speed automatic transmission	975	925

Comfort and Convenience

Leather upholstery, 1.9	1150	945

Includes 4-way power passenger seat.

Extended leather upholstery, 2.8	1200	990

Includes color keyed leather steering wheel, instrument cluster hood, console sides, door upper ledges & pulls.

Wood interior trim	400	330
Heated seats	500	410

Includes dual heated mirrors.

Sport seats	400	330

Requires heated seats.

Harman Kardon sound system, 1.9	675	555
Onboard computer	300	250
Power convertible top	750	615

Appearance and Miscellaneous

Chrome trim	150	125
Special/metallic paint	475	390
Sport alloy wheels, 2.8	1125	935

Includes 225/45R17 front tires, 245/40R17 rear tires.

Prices are accurate at time of publication; subject to manufacturer's changes.

BMW 3-SERIES

BMW 323is

Rear-wheel-drive near-luxury car
Base price range: $21,390-$41,500. Built in Germany.
Also consider: Audi A4, Lexus ES 300, Mercedes-Benz C-Class

FOR • Acceleration (exc. 318i/ti) • Steering/handling • Standard traction control • Side air bags

AGAINST • Rear seat room • Cargo room

Once a yuppie status symbol and still widely regarded as the best small sports sedan, the 3-Series is BMW's entry-level car and its best-seller in the U.S.

This year, a new 6-cylinder 323i coupe and convertible replace the previous 4-cylinder 318i versions. Despite their name, the 323s use a 2.5-liter version of the 2.8-liter 6-cylinder that powers the 328i sedan, coupe, and convertible. Rounding out the line are the price-leader 4-cylinder 318ti 2-door hatchback and 318i sedan, as well as the high-performance M3 coupe and sedan.

Front side air bags are now standard except on the 318ti, where they're optional. A fully automatic power top is a new option for convertibles, as is a Premium Package for 323s and 328s. The latter comprises leather upholstery, keyless entry/alarm, power sunroof or convertible top, and either front center armrest (323s) or wood trim (328s). A similar package is available for the 318i sedan.

A new-generation 3-Series sedan will bow about a year from now. Redesigned coupe and convertible models should begin appearing during calendar 1999.

PERFORMANCE Sporty handling remains one of the 3-Series' biggest assets. All models tame twisty roads with ease, aided by fluid, precise steering and the reassuring presence of standard traction control. Suspensions are firm, and while the M3s can be moderately jarring, ride quality is better than on many cars with sporty pretensions. Braking is terrific, but noise levels are nothing special. Tire roar intrudes on M3s, while other models suffer more engine whine in hard acceleration than some buyers might like.

Performance and economy depend greatly on powertrain. The 328s excel in both; we clocked a manual-shift sedan at just 7.2 seconds 0-60 mph and averaged a decent 22.7 mpg. We've yet to try one of the new 2.5-liter 323s, but suspect they will be only a little slower and perhaps a bit thriftier. The 4-cylinder 318s remain marginally underpowered with automatic transmission and are thus best left to enthusiasts who don't mind lots of manual shifting; even then, these Bimmers will be outsprinted by some cheaper cars, though they compensate with easy 25-mpg fuel economy. M3s are real hot rods—close to 6 seconds 0-60—but a heavy right foot can send mileage below 20 mpg. All 3-Series models require premium fuel.

ACCOMMODATIONS With a price of around $40,000 as equipped, it's tough to justify the 328i's cramped rear seating. Head room is generous front and back, and adults get plenty of front leg room in firm bucket seats that secure occupants during hard cornering. But if tall front-seaters move back even a little, the seatbacks quickly eat up rear knee space. Adding to the rear-seat problem are back doors that don't open wide enough for easy ingress and egress.

Thin roof pillars, lots of glass, and large mirrors make for fine outward visibility in traffic, though it's difficult to see the trunk when parking.

Large analog gauges are well placed and legible. No control is far out of the driver's reach, but BMW's logical approach seems to fall apart with an almost overwhelming array of small buttons for the audio and climate systems and the on-board trip computer. Likewise, power window and seat-heater controls are inconveniently arrayed around the shift lever.

A low bumper liftover provides access to a flat-floored and fairly large trunk. However, a narrow trunk opening requires that wide objects be lifted high before they can be stored. The split fold-down rear seats are handy for carrying longer cargo.

BUILD QUALITY Like most German cars, the 3-Series comes across as solid and robust. However, we've noticed the odd squeak and rattle even in brand-new test examples, and the interior is Teutonically austere, with lots of hard plastic that's at odds with prices BMW charges.

VALUE FOR THE MONEY The 3-Series is hard to beat for driving enjoyment, so it's too bad BMW hasn't matched the quality and customer-satisfaction ratings of rivals like Lexus and Infiniti. However, with standard traction control, free scheduled maintenance for the basic warranty period, and little-changed prices, you'd be wise to give these cars a look.

RATINGS

	318i/ti	323i	328i	M3
Acceleration	3	4	4	5
Fuel economy	4	3	3	2
Ride quality	4	4	4	3
Steering/handling	4	4	4	5
Braking	5	5	5	5
Quietness	3	4	4	3
Driver seating	3	3	3	3
Instruments/controls	4	4	4	4
Room/comfort (front)	4	4	4	4
Room/comfort (rear)	2	2	2	2
Cargo room	2	2	2	2
Value for the money	3	3	3	3
Total	**41**	**42**	**42**	**41**

SPECIFICATIONS

	2-door hatchback	2-door sedan	4-door sedan	2-door convertible
Wheelbase, in.	106.3	106.3	106.3	106.3
Overall length, in.	165.7	174.5	174.5	174.5
Overall width, in.	66.9	67.3	66.9	67.3
Overall height, in.	54.8	53.8	54.8	53.1
Curb weight, lbs.	2745	2976	2976	3131
Cargo vol., cu. ft.	15.0	9.2	10.3	8.9
Fuel capacity, gals.	13.7	16.4	16.4	16.4
Seating capacity	5	5	5	4
Front head room, in.	38.7	37.8	38.1	38.1
Max. front leg room, in.	41.1	41.2	41.1	41.2
Rear head room, in.	37.0	36.6	37.3	36.3
Min. rear leg room, in.	32.6	32.7	34.0	28.1

ENGINES

	dohc I-4	dohc I-6	dohc I-6	dohc I-6
Size, liters/cu. in.	1.9/116	2.5/152	2.8/170	3.2/192
Horsepower @ rpm	138@ 6000	168@ 5550	190@ 5300	240@ 6000
Torque (lbs./ft.) @ rpm	133@ 4300	181@ 3950	206@ 3950	225@ 3800
Availability	S[1]	S[2]	S[3]	S[4]
EPA city/highway mpg				
4-speed OD automatic	22/31	NA	20/29	20/28
5-speed manual	23/31	NA	19/26	
5-speed OD automatic				19/28

1. 318i models. 2. 323i models. 3. 328i models. 4. M3 models.

PRICES

BMW 3-Series

	Retail Price	Dealer Invoice
318ti 2-door hatchback	$21390	$19225
318i 4-door sedan	26150	22930
323is 2-door notchback	28700	25160
323i 2-door convertible	34700	30410

Rating Scale: 5-Excellent; 4-Above average; 3-Average; 2-Below average; 1-Poor

CONSUMER GUIDE™

	Retail Price	Dealer Invoice
328i 4-door sedan	$33100	$29010
328is 2-door notchback	33200	29095
328i 2-door convertible	41500	36355
M3 4-door sedan	39700	34780
M3 2-door notchback	39700	34780
Destination charge	570	570

STANDARD EQUIPMENT:

318 models: 1.9-liter DOHC 4-cylinder engine, 5-speed manual transmission, All Season Traction, driver- and passenger-side air bags, front side-impact air bags (318i), anti-lock 4-wheel disc brakes, variable-assist power steering, air conditioning, automatic dual climate control (318i), cruise control (318i), cloth upholstery (318ti), leatherette upholstery (318i), 6-way manual reclining bucket seats with height/tilt adjustments, split folding rear seat (2-door), cupholders, front seatback storage nets, power windows, power door locks, heated power mirrors, 10-speaker AM/FM/cassette, heated windshield washer jets, diversity antenna (318i), tachometer, trip odometer, digital clock, fuel-economy indicator (318i), outside temperature indicator (318i), speed-sensitive intermittent wipers, rear defogger, Service Interval Indicator, map lights (318i), rear reading lights, cargo-area storage box, tool kit, full-size spare tire (318i), 185/65TR15 tires, wheel covers.

323 models add: 2.5-liter DOHC 6-cylinder engine, leather-wrapped steering wheel and shifter, rear storage armrest w/rear cupholders (323i convertible), manual folding top (323i convertible), fog lights, 205/60HR15 tires, alloy wheels.

328 models add: 2.8-liter DOHC 6-cylinder engine, Active Check Control system, front reading lights, rear reading lights (4-door), 8-way power front seats, front center armrest, fully automatic power folding top (328i convertible).

M3 adds: 3.2-liter DOHC 6-cylinder engine, limited-slip differential, leather upholstery, 8-way manual sport seats (4-door), 12-way manual sport seats (2-door), upgraded brakes, sport suspension, 225/45ZR17 front tires, 245/40ZR17 rear tires, M double-spoke alloy wheels, deletes 8-way power front seats, front center armrest, cruise control.

OPTIONAL EQUIPMENT:

Major Packages

	Retail	Dealer
Active Pkg., 318ti	1350	1150

Cruise control, leather-wrapped steering wheel and shifter, remote keyless entry, theft-deterrent system, onboard computer, 205/60HR15 tires, alloy wheels, metallic paint. NA with Sports Pkg.

318ti Sports Pkg., 318ti	2940	2500

Sport suspension, cloth/leather upholstery, sport seats, leather-wrapped steering wheel and shifter, fog lights, M-Aerodynamic bumpers and rocker panels, 225/50ZR16 tires, alloy wheels. NA with Active Pkg.

323 Sports Pkg., 323is	990	820
323i conv.	750	625

Fog lights, sport suspension (323i), 225/50ZR16 tires, cross-spoke alloy wheels.

328 Sports Pkg., 328i 4-door, 328is	2125	1750
328i conv.	1775	1465

Leather sport seats, sport suspension (328i 4-door, 328is), 225/50ZR16 tires, double-spoke alloy wheels.

318i Premium Pkg., 318i	1900	1575

Leather-wrapped steering wheel and shifter, front armrest, remote keyless entry, theft-deterrent system, power sunroof, alloy wheels.

323 Premium Pkg., 323is	2125	1765
323i conv.	2750	2285

Leather upholstery, front armrest, power sunroof (323is), power convertible top (323i conv.), remote keyless entry, theft-deterrent system.

328 Premium Pkg., 328i, 328is	2125	1765
328i conv.	1600	1330

Leather upholstery, wood trim, power sunroof (328i, 328is), remote keyless entry, theft-deterrent system.

Powertrains

4-speed automatic transmission	975	925
NA on M3.		
5-speed automatic transmission, M3 4-door....	1200	1140

Safety Features

	Retail Price	Dealer Invoice
Rollover Protection System, convertible	$1450	$1190

Comfort and Convenience

Cruise control, 318ti, M3	475	390
Leather upholstery, 318, 323, 328............	1450	1190

318ti and 318i 4-door include leather-wrapped steering wheel and shifter. 4-doors include rear storage armrest with cupholders when not ordered with split folding rear seat. 328 includes wood interior trim (NA with 328 Sports Pkg.) and onboard computer. NA 318ti Sports Pkg.

Power front seats, M3	945	775
Heated front seats	500	410
M3 includes heated mirrors.		
Split folding rear seat,		
318i 4-door, 328i 4-door, M3 4-door	300	245
NA w/ski sack.		
Ski sack, 318i 4-door, 328i 4-door	300	245
NA w/folding rear seat.		
Harmon Kardon audio system..................	975	800
Includes CD changer. NA 318ti.		
Fog lights, 318i, 323is,		
323i conv.,	260	215
Onboard computer, 318ti..........................	300	250
328, 323, M3	500	415
Power sunroof	950	780

Appearance and Miscellaneous

Hardtop, convertible	2295	1885
California top, 318ti	1600	1380
Metallic paint, 318, 323, 328...................	475	390
M3	NC	NC
Rear spoiler, M3	650	535
Sport suspension, 318i	350	290
318i 4-door requires 205/60R15 tires and alloy wheels.		
Alloy wheels, 318i	850	700
Forged alloy wheels, M3	1450	1190
M-Contour alloy wheels, M3.....................	NC	NC

BMW 5-SERIES

RECOMMENDED

BMW 528i

Rear-wheel-drive luxury car
Base price range: $38,900-$53,300. Built in Germany.
Also consider: Acura RL, Lexus GS 300, Mercedes-Benz E-Class

FOR • Side air bags • Acceleration (540i) • Steering/handling • Ride • Quietness • Head Protection System

AGAINST • Low-speed acceleration (528i) • Rear seat comfort

The 5-Series is BMW's "in-between" 4-door: larger than a 3-Series sedan but almost as agile, and only a bit less luxurious than the big 7-Series.

This year, both the 6-cylinder 528i and V-8 540i offer optional rear side air bags to complement their standard dashboard and front side "torso" air bags. Both also gain BMW's exclusive new Head Protection System as standard. This consists of two tubular "bags" that inflate in a side impact, popping out just above each front door to cushion the heads and shoulders of front-seat occupants.

Prices are accurate at time of publication; subject to manufacturer's changes.

Other changes include a new Sport Package option for the 528i and the automatic-transmission 540i. This delivers black exterior trim, sport-tuned suspension, and 17-inch wheels, all of which are standard on the 540i with 6-speed manual shift. On the price front, the 528i is unchanged from its closing '97 sticker; the 540i automatic goes up $1000, the 6-speed model $950.

PERFORMANCE Not as quiet as a Lexus or BMW's own 7-Series, the 5s are nonetheless nearly free of wind noise at 65 mph and suffer intrusion from road noise over only the coarsest surfaces. The 528i accelerates and cruises quietly; the 540i has a huskier exhaust note but is still quite serene.

The 6-cylinder needs to wind above 3000 rpm before it provides any zip, so the 528i with the optional 4-speed automatic transmission feels slightly winded climbing hills or in quick passing sprints. We prefer the slick-shifting 5-speed manual version. By contrast, the 540i's smooth V-8 has plenty of muscle for quick launches and spirited passing with its 5-speed automatic.

Mileage can vary a lot depending on drivetrain and your driving. In hard city/highway work, we averaged 20.9 mpg with a manual 528i, but only 18.8 with an automatic. An automatic 540i returned just under 16 mpg despite a fair dose of moderate-speed freeway running. All models demand premium fuel.

Any 5-Series is surefooted in corners despite a fair amount of body lean. Steering is quick and precise, but some of our testers label it too sensitive at highway speeds. Helped by a stout structure, the standard suspension smothers bumps and provides a comfortable, stable ride. The tighter sport suspension gives more jiggle and thump on less-than-perfect pavement, so try it before deciding.

ACCOMMODATIONS The 5-Series is tighter inside than most rivals and four adults is the practical limit. The rear seat has ample head and leg room, but only because the seat cushion is low and short, which makes long rides uncomfortable. The trunk isn't wide, but it has a long, flat floor, and there's an optional folding rear seat for additional cargo space.

We continue to like this BMW's take-charge driving stance. Some minor controls aren't so likable, especially the complex audio/climate/trip computer display that takes a while to sort out.

BUILD QUALITY The old "bank-vault solid" cliche aptly describes the 5-Series' driving feel. Workmanship and interior materials are first-class, as they ought to be at these prices.

VALUE FOR THE MONEY The 5-Series is luxurious, but tilts toward enthusiasts who demand premium engineering and superior road manners. They are great drives, especially the potent 540i, but they're not great value. The 528i is short on power for what it costs, while the 540i is over $50,000. Still, if you've got the money and appreciate traditional BMW virtues, the 5-Series is a Recommended sports sedan choice.

RATINGS

	528i	540i
Acceleration	3	5
Fuel economy	3	2
Ride quality	4	4
Steering/handling	4	4
Braking	5	5
Quietness	4	4
Driver seating	5	5
Instruments/controls	3	3
Room/comfort (front)	4	4
Room/comfort (rear)	3	3
Cargo room	3	3
Value for the money	4	4
Total	**45**	**46**

SPECIFICATIONS

	4-door sedan
Wheelbase, in.	111.4
Overall length, in.	188.0
Overall width, in.	70.9
Overall height, in.	56.5
Curb weight, lbs.	3450
Cargo vol., cu. ft.	11.0
Fuel capacity, gals.	18.5
Seating capacity	5
Front head room, in.	37.4
Max. front leg room, in.	41.7

	4-door sedan
Rear head room, in.	37.5
Min. rear leg room, in.	34.2

ENGINES

	dohc I-6	dohc V-8
Size, liters/cu. in.	2.8/170	4.4/268
Horsepower @ rpm	190@ 5300	282@ 5700
Torque (lbs./ft.) @ rpm	207@ 3950	310@ 3900
Availability	S[1]	S[2]

EPA city/highway mpg

4-speed OD automatic	18/26	
5-speed manual	19/28	
5-speed OD automatic		18/24
6-speed OD manual		15/24

1. 528i. 2. 540i.

PRICES

BMW 5-Series	Retail Price	Dealer Invoice
528i 4-door sedan	$38900	$34490
540i 4-door sedan, 6-speed manual transmission	53300	46675
540i 4-door sedan, 5-speed automatic transmission	50500	44225
Destination charge	570	570

540i w/6-speed manual transmission add Gas Guzzler Tax: $1300

STANDARD EQUIPMENT:

528i: 2.8-liter DOHC 6-cylinder engine, 5-speed manual transmission, All Season Traction, driver- and passenger-side air bags, front side-impact air bags, side head protection system, anti-lock 4-wheel disc brakes, variable-assist power steering, power tilt/telescopic steering wheel, leather-wrapped steering wheel, shift knob and hand brake, steering wheel mounted radio and telephone controls, cruise control, air conditioning with dual automatic climate controls, filtered ventilation, 10-way power front seats (with power head restraints and memory driver's seat, steering wheel and outside mirrors), leatherette upholstery, rear center storage armrest, cupholders, 10-speaker anti-theft AM/FM stereo cassette, diversity antenna, power windows, power door locks, heated power mirrors, power sunroof, tachometer, trip odometer, outside temperature display, onboard computer, theft-deterrent system, map lights, intermittent wipers, remote decklid release, rear defogger, seatback and door storage, front and rear reading lights, Service Interval Indicator, Active Check Control system, fuel economy indicator, illuminated visor mirrors, tool kit, 225/60HR15 tires, alloy wheels.

540i adds: 4.4-liter DOHC V-8 engine, 5-speed automatic transmission, Dynamic Stability Control, 14-way power front seats, leather upholstery, burl walnut interior trim, power moonroof, automatic day/night rearview mirror, remote keyless entry, upgraded onboard computer, metallic paint, 225/55HR16 tires, deletes Active Check Control System.

540i 6-speed adds: 6-speed manual transmission, front sport seats, Shadowline exterior trim, sport suspension, 235/45WR17 tires, 7-spoke composite alloy wheels, deletes Dynamic Stability Control.

OPTIONAL EQUIPMENT:
Major Packages

Premium Pkg., 528i	3450	2520

Leather upholstery, wood interior trim, metallic paint, cross-spoke alloy wheels. NA with Sport Pkg.

528i Sport Pkg., 528i	3450	2865

Leather upholstery, Technical Surfaca interior trim, metallic paint, Shadowline exterior trim, sport suspension, cross-spoke alloy wheels, 235/45WR17 tires.

540 Sport Pkg., 540i automatic	3115	2585

Sport seats, Shadowline exterior trim, sport suspension, cross-spoke alloy wheels, 235/45WR17 tires.

Powertrains

4-speed automatic transmission, 528i	975	925

Safety Features

Rear side-impact air bags	385	320

Rating Scale: 5-Excellent; 4-Above average; 3-Average; 2-Below average; 1-Poor

Comfort and Convenience

	Retail Price	Dealer Invoice
Power moonroof, 528i	$1050	$865
Navigation system, 528i	2690	2420
540i	2500	2250
528i includes wood interior trim.		
Comfort 16-way power front seats	1200	965
Includes power lumbar support. 528i requires Premium Pkg.		
Power lumbar support, 528i,		
540i automatic	400	325
NA with sport seats.		
Sport seats, 540i automatic	NC	NC
Requires Sport Pkg.		
Split folding rear seat	575	470
Includes ski sack. 528i requires Premium Pkg.		
14-speaker audio system	1500	1240
Includes upgraded amplifier and digital signal processor.		
Heated front seats	500	410
Heated front seats and steering wheel	650	535
Power rear and manual rear side sunshades	575	470

Appearance and Miscellaneous

Metallic paint, 528i	475	390
540i	NC	NC
Sport alloy wheels, 540i manual	300	245

BMW 7-SERIES

BMW 740i

Rear-wheel-drive luxury car
Base price range: $61,500-$91,530. Built in Germany.
Also consider: Infiniti Q45, Lexus LS 400, Mercedes-Benz S-Class

FOR • Acceleration • Ride • Steering/handling • Passenger room/comfort • Side air bags

AGAINST • Fuel economy • Control layout

The 7-Series is to BMW what the S-Class is to Mercedes: big, luxurious German flagship sedans that are part "executive express," part technical showcase. BMW offers three models: the V-8-powered 740i and its long-wheelbase companion, the 740iL; and V-12 750iL.

The 1998 versions went on sale last June with only two changes from '97: optional rear side air bags (dashboard and front side air bags remain standard) and a new Head Protection System that BMW claimed as a safety first. Also standard on '98 5-Series BMWs, the Head Protection System employs a tubular air bag that inflates in a side impact, popping out from just above each front door to protect occupant heads and shoulders. Three more changes occurred last fall: a power-adjustable steering wheel that now automatically tilts up on opening a door to facilitate entry/exit; an improved version of BMW's Dynamic Stability Control anti-skid system (also standard); and break-resistant security glass as a new option for the two iL models.

PERFORMANCE All 7-Series sedans are quiet, comfortable, and enjoyable to drive—really "enthusiast limousines." The V-8 models have a tad more engine and road noise than a Lexus LS 400, but they're at least as quiet as other rivals. They're also surprisingly agile in corners, with slightly more responsive steering

and a bit less body lean than corresponding S-Class Mercedes.

Ride quality is excellent, a benefit of sophisticated suspension design and bump-flattening weight. Happily, the brakes are well up to the heft, capable of short, stable emergency stops in most any situation.

Performance-wise, the 740s have enough low-end muscle to accelerate briskly from standstill and for swift passing at highway speeds. In fact, the V-8 is strong enough and so silky that we see little need to pay so much more for the V-12 750.

Fuel economy doesn't usually concern buyers in this price league, but it's still discouraging to average just 13.2 mpg in a 750iL, with about one-third of our driving on highways. A 740iL returned 18.8 overall, but more than half of our travel was on highways.

ACCOMMODATIONS The 740i doesn't lack for interior or cargo space, but the long-wheelbase iL models have more passenger room than most luxury sedans, plus unusually easy all-around entry/exit. Seats on all 7s are supportive and comfortable for long drives. Other pluses include clear gauges, controls strategically placed for easy access, and a multitude of standard amenities. Unfortunately, a lot of gizmos means a lot of buttons and switches, not all of which are clearly marked. The worst offender is the combined climate/audio/cell phone display, which can be as confusing to new users as Windows 95.

BUILD QUALITY Flawless workmanship is expected of top-echelon cars, and the 7-Series has it. All models feel stout and substantial from behind the wheel, and detail finish is exemplary everywhere you look.

VALUE FOR THE MONEY Luxury car sales in general have been soft the past few years, so the 7-Series models should be available at discounts. Before you buy, though, look at alternatives, especially the LS 400 and the S-Class. BMW builds great cars, but so do the other guys.

RATINGS

	740i	740iL	750iL
Acceleration	4	4	5
Fuel economy	3	3	2
Ride quality	5	5	5
Steering/handling	4	4	4
Braking	5	5	5
Quietness	5	5	5
Driver seating	5	5	5
Instruments/controls	3	3	3
Room/comfort (front)	5	5	5
Room/comfort (rear)	4	5	5
Cargo room	4	4	4
Value for the money	3	3	3
Total	**50**	**51**	**51**

SPECIFICATIONS

	4-door notchback	4-door notchback
Wheelbase, in.	115.4	120.9
Overall length, in.	196.2	201.7
Overall width, in.	73.3	73.3
Overall height, in.	56.5	56.1
Curb weight, lbs.	4255	4288
Cargo vol., cu. ft.	13.0	13.0
Fuel capacity, gals.	22.5	22.5
Seating capacity	5	5
Front head room, in.	37.7	37.7
Max. front leg room, in.	41.9	41.9
Rear head room, in.	38.1	38.1
Min. rear leg room, in.	36.7	41.9

ENGINES

	dohc V-8	ohc V-12
Size, liters/cu. in.	4.4/268	5.4/328
Horsepower @ rpm	282@ 5700	322@ 5000
Torque (lbs./ft.) @ rpm	310@ 3900	361@ 3900
Availability	S[1]	S[2]
EPA city/highway mpg		
5-speed OD automatic	17/24	15/20

1. 740i, 740iL. 2. 750iL.

PRICES

BMW 7-Series

	Retail Price	Dealer Invoice
740i 4-door sedan	$61500	$54495
740iL 4-door sedan	65500	57345
750iL 4-door sedan	91530	80610
Destination charge	570	570

750iL add Gas Guzzler Tax: $1700

STANDARD EQUIPMENT:

740i: 4.4-liter DOHC V-8 engine, 5-speed automatic transmission w/Adaptive Transmission Control, All Season Traction, driver- and passenger-side air bags, front side-impact air bags, side head protection system, anti-lock 4-wheel disc brakes, variable-assist power steering, power tilt/telescopic steering wheel with memory, cruise control, air conditioning, automatic climate control system with dual controls, interior air filtration system, 14-way power front seats with driver-side memory system, 4-way lumbar support adjustment, leather upholstery, walnut interior trim, door and seatback pockets, folding rear seatback, power windows, power door locks, heated power mirrors with 3-position memory, remote keyless entry, remote decklid release, variable intermittent wipers, heated windshield-washer jets, heated driver-side door lock, rear head rests, front and rear storage armrests, automatic day/night rearview mirror, front and rear reading lamps, illuminated visor mirrors, tachometer, trip odometer, Service Interval Indicator, Active Check Control system, onboard computer, rear defogger, power moonroof, 10-speaker AM/FM/cassette with diversity antenna and steering wheel controls, cargo net, Electronic Damping Control, theft-deterrent system, tinted glass, fog lamps, tool kit, 235/60HR16 tires, cast alloy wheels.
740iL adds: 16-way power Comfort Seats, 6-inch longer wheelbase.
750iL adds: 5.4-liter V-12 engine, ASC+T traction control with Dynamic Stability Control, heated seats, heated steering wheel, power rear seats with power lumbar adjustment, power rear headrests, cellular telephone, 14-speaker premium sound system w/CD and digital sound processor, 6-disc CD changer, power rear sunshade, parking distance control, ski sack, self-leveling rear suspension, ventilated rear disc brakes, Xenon headlamps, headlight washers, forged alloy wheels.

OPTIONAL EQUIPMENT:

Powertrains

Cold Weather Pkg., 740i, 740iL	825	685

Heated steering wheel, headlight washers, ski sack.

Safety Features

Rear side-impact air bags	385	320
Break-resistant security glass, 740iL, 750iL	2600	2160

Comfort and Convenience

Heated front seats, 740i, 740iL	500	410
16-way power Comfort Seats, 740i	1200	965

Includes 2-way power upper backrest adjustment, power lumbar support.

Navigation system	2500	2250
14-speaker premium sound system, 740i, 740iL	2100	1745

Includes CD player and digital sound processor.

Parking distance control, 740iL	900	750
Power rear sunshade, 740iL	740	615

Appearance and Miscellaneous

Self-leveling rear suspension, 740iL	1100	915
Electronic Damping Control, 740i, 740iL	2000	1660

BUICK CENTURY

Front-wheel-drive midsize car; similar to Buick Regal, Oldsmobile Intrigue, and Pontiac Grand Prix
Base price range: $18,215-$19,575. Built in Canada.
Also consider: Honda Accord, Mercury Sable, Toyota Camry

FOR • Standard anti-lock brakes • Passenger and cargo room

Buick Century Limited

AGAINST • Handling • Ride

Century shares its basic design with the Buick Regal, Pontiac Grand Prix, and Oldsmobile Intrigue, but where those cars are cast as sporty sedans, Buick aims this version at a conservative, comfort-oriented audience.

Century last year got its first full redesign since the front-wheel-drive model was introduced in 1982. Wheelbase grew more than four inches and overall length increased more than five. Flowing lines replaced boxy contours and the station wagon body style was dropped.

Changes are few for '98. As in all Buicks, the dual air bags have reduced inflation power. These bags deploy with less force but still meet federal safety standards. A new dealer-installed option is General Motors' OnStar communications system. It links the car by satellite and cellular telephone to a 24-hour GM center from which advisors can provide directions and travel advice and can notify local authorities in an emergency. The $895 price includes a cell phone but not installation or monthly service fees.

Both the base Custom and plusher Limited models have a V-6 engine and automatic transmission. Front and rear bench seats provide 6-passenger capacity; buckets aren't offered.

PERFORMANCE Packaged to provide a taste of Buick luxury at an affordable price, Century performs admirably. It won't excite the enthusiast driver, but it is quiet, comfortable, and economical for a 6-passenger car.

A soft suspension that easily absorbs most bumps is common to both models. Unfortunately, the body keeps bouncing well after the bumps have passed and over really rough pavement, the Century can feel queasy. Body lean in turns is pronounced, and the relatively narrow tires furnish modest cornering grip. The steering isn't sloppy, but some Century drivers are likely to wish for less power assist and more road feel.

It growls when asked to furnish passing power, but the V-6 is otherwise a peaceful runner and nicely suited to this duty. Acceleration is adequate off the line and in highway merging and overtaking. Smooth gear changes and rapid downshifts help. Our test car averaged a laudable 28.1 mpg, but 800 of our 1000 test miles were on the highway. Expect to average in the low-to-mid-20s in an even mix of city-freeway travel. Wind and road noise are low at highway speeds.

ACCOMMODATIONS The interior provides adult-size space and its rounded forms are far more pleasing than the squared-off design of the previous Century.

Entry and exit are eased by tall, wide doors, but the softly padded standard cloth seats offer little support for the thighs or lower back. The optional leather seats might prove firmer.

Monotone interior hues are set off by easy-to-use instruments and controls in black plastic housings. Instrumentation is limited to a speedometer and fuel and coolant gauges. Climate controls are mounted low in the center of the dashboard, where they interfere with a center passenger's knees.

The roomy trunk has a wide, flat floor, but loading and unloading requires you to stretch over a wide bumper-level shelf.

BUILD QUALITY Models we've tested have been tight, solid, and well finished.

VALUE FOR THE MONEY Century is a modern, well-thought-out sedan that manages to retain the no-surprises formula that made its predecessor a darling of older buyers. We don't consider it so much a toned-down version of the Regal as much as a cut-rate copy of Buick's own LeSabre. On those terms, it's worth a look.

Rating Scale: 5-Excellent; 4-Above average; 3-Average; 2-Below average; 1-Poor

CONSUMER GUIDE™

RATINGS

	Custom/Limited
Acceleration	3
Fuel economy	3
Ride quality	4
Steering/handling	3
Braking	3
Quietness	4
Driver seating	3
Instruments/controls	3
Room/comfort (front)	4
Room/comfort (rear)	4
Cargo room	4
Value for the money	3
Total	**41**

SPECIFICATIONS

	4-door sedan
Wheelbase, in.	109.0
Overall length, in.	194.6
Overall width, in.	72.7
Overall height, in.	56.6
Curb weight, lbs.	3335
Cargo vol., cu. ft.	16.7
Fuel capacity, gals.	17.0
Seating capacity	6
Front head room, in.	39.3
Max. front leg room, in.	42.4
Rear head room, in.	37.4
Min. rear leg room, in.	37.5

ENGINES

	ohv V-6
Size, liters/cu. in.	3.1/191
Horsepower @ rpm	160@5200
Torque (lbs./ft.) @ rpm	185@4000
Availability	S

EPA city/highway mpg
4-speed OD automatic	20/29

PRICES

Buick Century	Retail Price	Dealer Invoice
Custom 4-door sedan	$18215	$17031
Limited 4-door sedan	19575	18303
Destination charge	550	550

STANDARD EQUIPMENT:

Custom: 3.1-liter V-6 engine, 4-speed automatic transmission, driver- and passenger-side air bags, anti-lock brakes, daytime running lamps, power steering, tilt steering wheel, air conditioning, cloth reclining 55/45 front bench seat, front storage armrest w/cupholders, rear armrest w/cupholders, automatic power door locks, power windows, power mirrors, coolant-temperature gauge, trip odometer, AM/FM radio, digital clock, rear defogger, interior air filter, remote keyless entry, variable intermittent wipers, visor mirrors, rear heat ducts, tinted glass, solar-control windshield and rear window, Pass-Key theft-deterrent system, 205/70R15 tires, wheel covers.

Limited adds: variable-assist power steering, dual automatic climate control, body-colored heated power mirrors, illuminated visor mirrors, retained accessory power, rear courtesy/reading lights, floormats, striping.

OPTIONAL EQUIPMENT:

Major Packages

	Retail	Dealer
Popular Pkg. SB, Custom	330	283

Cruise control, cargo net, map lights on inside rearview mirror, floormats.

Premium Pkg. SC, Custom	830	714

Popular Pkg SB plus 6-way power driver seat, cassette player.

Luxury Pkg. SE, Limited	525	452

Cruise control, rear storage armrest with cupholders, cassette player, map lights on inside rearview mirror, cargo net.

	Retail Price	Dealer Invoice
Prestige Pkg. SF, Limited	$1620	$1393

Luxury Pkg. SE plus dual automatic climate control, 6-way power driver and passenger seats, upgraded cassette player with automatic tone control and anti-theft feature, Concert Sound II speakers, steering-wheel radio controls, integrated antenna, automatic day/night inside mirror.

Safety Features

Integrated child seat, Custom	100	86

Comfort and Convenience

OnStar System	895	761

Includes Global Positioning System, voice-activated cellular telephone, roadside assistance, emergency services. Requires dealer installation charge and monthly service charges.

Dual automatic climate control, Custom w/Pkg. SC	45	39
Leather upholstery, Limited	550	473

Includes leather-wrapped steering wheel.

6-way power driver seat	305	262
Cruise control	225	194
Power glass sunroof	695	598

Custom requires Premium Pkg. SC, automatic day/night inside mirror, and illuminated visor mirrors. Limited requires Prestige Pkg. SF.

Automatic day/night inside mirror, Custom	217	187
Limited	80	69

Custom includes illuminated visor mirrors. Custom requires Premium Pkg. SC. Limited requires Luxury Pkg. SE.

Heated power mirrors, Custom	58	50

Requires option pkg.

Illuminated visor mirrors, Custom w/Pkg. SC	137	118
Rear storage armrest with cupholders, Limited	45	39
Cassette player	195	168

Upgraded cassette player,
Custom w/Pkg. SB, Limited	220	189
Custom w/Pkg. SC, Limited w/Pkg. SE	25	22

Includes automatic tone control and anti-theft feature. Requires Concert Sound II speakers.

CD player, Custom w/Pkg. SB, Limited	320	275
Custom w/Pkg. SC, Limited w/Pkg. SE	125	108
Limited w/Pkg. SF	100	86

Includes automatic tone control and anti-theft feature. Requires Concert Sound II speakers.

CD/cassette player, Custom w/Pkg. SB, Limited	420	361
Custom w/Pkg. SC, Limited w/Pkg. SE	225	194
Limited w/Pkg. SF	200	172

Includes automatic tone control and anti-theft feature. Requires Concert Sound II speakers.

Concert Sound II speakers	70	60

Custom requires option pkg.

Integrated antenna	40	34

Requires option pkg.

Steering-wheel radio controls	125	108

Requires upgraded cassette player, CD player, or cassette/CD player. Requires cruise control. Custom requires option pkg.

Trunk-mounted CD changer prep pkg.	50	43

Requires upgraded cassette player, CD player, or cassette/CD player. Custom requires option pkg.

Cargo net	30	26
Floormats, Custom	45	39

Appearance and Miscellaneous

Striping, Custom	75	65
Engine-block heater	18	15
Alloy wheels	375	323
205/70R15 whitewall tires	150	129

BUICK LeSABRE ✓ BEST BUY

Front-wheel-drive full-size car; similar to Oldsmobile Eighty Eight/Regency and Pontiac Bonneville

Base price range: $22,465-$25,790. Built in Flint, Mich.

Also consider: Chrysler Concorde, Oldsmobile Eighty Eight/Regency, Toyota Avalon

Prices are accurate at time of publication; subject to manufacturer's changes.

Buick LeSabre Limited

FOR • Standard anti-lock brakes • Acceleration • Transmission performance • Passenger and cargo room

AGAINST • Steering feel • Handling

Sales of the LeSabre are double those of any other Buick and, moreover, it's been the best-selling full-size sedan in the United States for five straight years.

Buick doesn't mess with success for '98, changing little after freshening the styling slightly for 1997. The sole powertrain remains General Motors' 3800 V-6 hooked to an automatic transmission, though the transmission itself is new and designed to be smoother and more fuel efficient. The standard dual air bags inflate with less force while still meeting federal safety standards.

A new dealer-installed option is General Motors' OnStar communications system. It links the car by satellite and cellular telephone to a 24-hour GM center from which advisors can provide directions and travel advice and can notify local authorities in an emergency. The price includes a cell phone but buyers pay their own monthly service bills.

LeSabre shares its basic design with the Oldsmobile Eighty Eight and Pontiac Bonneville, though its cousins offer a supercharged version of the 3800 V-6.

PERFORMANCE GM's smooth 3.8-liter V-6 furnishes lively pickup off the line and good passing power. Our test car did 0-60 mph in around 9 seconds. Fuel economy is reasonable for a full-size sedan: 16-18 mph in urban driving and in the mid-20s on the highway.

The previous automatic transmission was hard to fault, but the new one is even better, with virtually seamless gear changes and prompt downshifts. Engine and road noise are low, but there's noticeable wind rush from around the outside mirrors at highway speeds.

Buick aims LeSabre at a mature audience seeking room, comfort, and quietness. Its road manners are not sloppy, but in soaking up bumps, the soft base suspension allows the body to bound and float on wavy roads. The light, vague steering provides little feedback in spirited driving and in tight turns, body lean and tire squealing are noticeable. The optional Gran Touring Package adds a tauter suspension, wider tires, and more-precise steering for a more disciplined feel, but at some sacrifice in ride comfort.

The standard anti-lock brakes provide short, straight stops. Our test car averaged 127 feet in 10 stops from 60 mph.

ACCOMMODATIONS Generous doorways allow easy entry and exit, but true 6-passenger cars are rare these days, and putting three abreast in LeSabre's front or rear seat squeezes everyone. With four adults aboard, there's generous head and leg space for all.

Despite its early 1997 facelift, LeSabre is Buick's oldest car and its age is evident in a dashboard design that's not as integrated as that of the Century, Regal, or Park Avenue. Still, gauges are easily read despite being crowded into a narrow horizonal channel. Most controls are easy to reach and have large buttons. The headlight switches are on the driver's door, which takes getting used to but proves handy.

Thick rear roof pillars make it hard to see when backing up, but visibility is otherwise good.

Cargo volume is ample at 17.0 cubic feet, and the trunk lid opens at bumper level to a flat floor that's wide and long.

BUILD QUALITY Our most-recent LeSabre test car had smooth, uniformly glossy paint. Other than a few minor rattles over bumps, the interior was tightly assembled.

VALUE FOR THE MONEY LeSabre is a roomy family sedan that offers many features found in the costlier Park Avenue. Chrysler's full-size cars have a more youthful nature, but seem to have poorer build quality. LeSabre is less sporty than the Bonneville, and softer-

riding than even the Eighty-Eight. But like its GM siblings, it's among the best all-around choices in a full-size sedan.

RATINGS

	Custom/Limited
Acceleration	4
Fuel economy	2
Ride quality	3
Steering/handling	3
Braking	4
Quietness	4
Driver seating	3
Instruments/controls	4
Room/comfort (front)	4
Room/comfort (rear)	4
Cargo room	4
Value for the money	4
Total	**43**

SPECIFICATIONS

	4-door sedan
Wheelbase, in.	110.8
Overall length, in.	200.8
Overall width, in.	74.4
Overall height, in.	55.6
Curb weight, lbs.	3441
Cargo vol., cu. ft.	17.0
Fuel capacity, gals.	18.0
Seating capacity	6
Front head room, in.	38.8
Max. front leg room, in.	42.6
Rear head room, in.	37.8
Min. rear leg room, in.	40.4

ENGINES

	ohv V-6
Size, liters/cu. in.	3.8/231
Horsepower @ rpm	205@ 5200
Torque (lbs./ft.) @ rpm	230@ 4000
Availability	S

EPA city/highway mpg

4-speed OD automatic	19/30

PRICES

Buick LeSabre	Retail Price	Dealer Invoice
Custom 4-door sedan	$22465	$20555
Limited 4-door sedan	25790	23598
Destination charge	605	605

STANDARD EQUIPMENT:

Custom: 3.8-liter V-6 engine, 4-speed automatic transmission, driver- and passenger-side air bags, anti-lock brakes, air conditioning, power steering, tilt steering wheel, cruise control, 55/45 cloth seats, front storage armrest with cupholders, manual front seatback recliners, power door locks, power windows, AM/FM radio with clock, intermittent wipers, color-keyed left remote and right manual mirrors, rear defogger, instrument panel courtesy lights, trip odometer, visor mirrors, Twilight Sentinel headlamp control, Pass-Key theft-deterrent system, solar-control tinted glass, daytime running lights, 205/70R15 all-season tires, wheel covers.

Limited adds: front and rear automatic climate control with front dual temperature controls, remote keyless entry, memory door locks, power remote decklid release, 6-way power driver and passenger seats, voltmeter, tachometer, oil pressure and coolant temperature gauges, oil change monitor, oil level, cassette player, Concert Sound II speakers, rear armrest, heated power mirrors, illuminated visor mirrors, front- and rear-door courtesy lights, front and rear reading lights, floormats, trunk net, striping, 205/70R15 all-season whitewall tires, alloy wheels.

OPTIONAL EQUIPMENT:
Major Packages

Luxury Pkg. SD, Custom	716	616

Includes cassette player, cargo net, floormats, striping, 205/70R15 all-season whitewall tires, alloy wheels.

Rating Scale: 5-Excellent; 4-Above average; 3-Average; 2-Below average; 1-Poor

CONSUMER GUIDE™

	Retail Price	Dealer Invoice
Prestige Pkg. SE, Custom......................................	$1668	$1434

Luxury Pkg. SD plus 6-way power driver's seat, memory door locks, remote keyless entry, voltmeter, tachometer, oil-pressure and coolant-temperature gauges, oil-life and oil-level monitor, power mirrors, Lighting Pkg. (illuminated visor mirrors, map lights), power remote decklid release, Concert Sound II speakers, door-edge guards.

Limited	659	567

Includes automatic level control, starter interrupt, automatic day/night left outside rearview mirror, cassette player with automatic tone control, steering-wheel radio controls, cornering lamps.

Gran Touring Pkg., Custom w/Pkg. SE, Limited	512	440
Limited w/Pkg. SE	337	290

Includes variable-assist power steering, Gran Touring Suspension, 3:06 axle ratio, automatic level control, leather-wrapped steering wheel, 215/60R16 touring tires, alloy wheels. Requires traction control.

Powertrains

Traction control system, Custom w/Pkg. SE, Limited	175	151

Comfort and Convenience

OnStar System	895	761

Includes Global Positioning System, voice-activated cellular telephone, roadside assistance, emergency services. Requires dealer installation charge and monthly service charges.

Leather upholstery, Custom	995	856
Limited	550	473

Custom requires option pkg. Custom with Luxury Pkg. SD requires power mirrors, 6-way power driver's seat, remote keyless entry, memory door locks, remote decklid release.

6-way power driver's seat, Custom.........................	305	262

Requires power mirrors and cruise control. With luxury Pkg. SD, requires power mirrors, remote keyless entry, memory door locks, remote decklid release.

6-way power passenger seat, Custom w/Pkg. SE..	305	262
Power mirrors, Custom	78	67

Requires 6-way power driver's seat and cruise control. With Luxury Pkg. SD, requires 6-way power driver's seat, remote keyless entry, memory door locks, and remote decklid release.

Automatic day/night mirror, Limited.........................	70	60

Includes compass.

Lighting Pkg., Custom w/Pkg. SD	116	100

Map lights, illuminated visor mirrors.

Power remote decklid release, Custom w/Pkg. SD	60	52

Requires remote keyless entry, 6-way power driver's seat, power mirrors, and memory door locks.

Remote keyless entry, Custom w/Pkg. SD	135	116

Requires remote decklid release, 6-way power driver's seat, power mirrors, and memory door locks.

Memory door locks, Custom w/Pkg. SD	25	22

Requires remote decklid release, remote keyless entry, 6-way power driver's seat, and power mirrors.

UN6 audio system, Custom	195	168

Includes cassette player with clock.

UL0 audio system, Custom w/Pkg. SE, Limited	150	129

Includes cassette player with clock, automatic tone control, and steering-wheel radio controls.

UN0 audio system, Custom w/Pkg. SE, Limited.....	250	215
Limited w/Pkg. SE	100	86

Includes CD player with clock, automatic tone control, and steering-wheel radio controls.

UP0 audio system, Custom w/Pkg. SE, Limited	350	301
Limited w/Pkg. SE	200	172

UN0 audio system plus cassette player.

Appearance and Miscellaneous

Starter interrupt, Limited...	159	137
Cornering lamps, Limited	60	52
Engine block heater	18	15
Automatic level control, Custom w/Pkg. SE, Limited	175	151
Alloy wheels, Custom	325	280

	Retail Price	Dealer Invoice
205/70R15 whitewall tires, Custom.........................	$76	$65

NA with Gran Touring Pkg.

205/70R15 self-sealing whitewall tires, Custom	226	194
Custom w/option pkg., Limited	150	129

BUICK PARK AVENUE

RECOMMENDED

Buick Park Avenue Ultra

Front-wheel-drive luxury car
Base price range: $30,675-$35,550. Built in Lake Orion, Mich.
Also consider: Infiniti I30, Lexus ES 300, Oldsmobile Aurora

FOR • Standard anti-lock brakes • Acceleration • Passenger and cargo room • Steering/handling (Ultra)

AGAINST • Fuel economy (supercharged V-6) • Steering/handling (base suspension) • Rear visibility

Buick's flagship sedan gets enhanced safety and convenience features for '98. Park Avenue was redesigned for 1997, gaining three inches in wheelbase, an inch in overall length, and about 250 pounds. But its styling was an evolution of earlier themes.

This full-size sedan comes in base trim or as the plusher Ultra. Both have a 3.8-liter V-6, but the Ultra's is supercharged to produce 240 horsepower, 35 more than the base model's.

As in all Buicks, the dual air bags have reduced inflation power to deploy with less force but still meet federal safety standards. Newly standard on Ultra and optional on the base model is a right-side rear view mirror that aids visibility backing up by tilting down when reverse gear is engaged.

A new dealer-installed option is General Motors' OnStar communications system. It links the car by satellite and cellular telephone to a 24-hour GM center from which advisors can provide directions and travel advice and can notify local authorities in an emergency. The $895 price includes a cell phone but buyers foot the cost of cell service, installation, and monthly service fees.

PERFORMANCE This is a quiet, substantial-feeling car whose performance is especially impressive in supercharged form. Helped by the automatic transmission's subtle, alert shifting, both models distribute ample power over a wide range of engine speeds. Acceleration with the supercharged Ultra is more than a match for 6-cylinder competitors and feels much like a small V-8. Buick recommends premium gas for the Ultra, and we averaged 15.3 mpg with one in predominantly city driving. Our base Park Avenue averaged 19.8 mpg on regular-grade fuel.

The standard steering and suspension settings favor low-effort comfort, but that makes for steering that's too light at freeway speeds and floaty body motions over undulating surfaces. Optional on both models is a Gran Touring setup that does a fine job of soaking up bumps with little jarring while maintaining a flat, stable ride. It also quells undue body lean and front-end plowing in corners, and its magnetic variable effort steering feels natural and responsive, with good straight-line stability. Stopping power feels strong, and though simulated emergency stops brought on pronounced nose dive, there was no loss of stability or control. The Ultra does a great job of muffling wind, road, and engine noise.

ACCOMMODATIONS Head and leg room are abundant, though with six on board, everyone is shoulder-to-shoulder. The

Prices are accurate at time of publication; subject to manufacturer's changes.

seats are comfortable but are not sufficiently contoured to give occupants good lateral support when the road turns twisty. Front lap and shoulder belts are anchored to the seat itself and move with the seats. They're handy to grab and always fit just right.

Gauges and switches are generously sized and we like the use of a simple dashboard pull-knob for the headlights. On the debit side, the horn buttons are beneath the thick air-bag cover and require substantial force to activate. Wipers triggered by moisture on the windshield are standard on the Ultra and optional on the base Park Avenue; they don't work as efficiently as traditional delay systems. OnStar and the available tire pressure monitor are worthwhile features, but we don't feel the same about the head-up display, which projects speedometer and other readings onto the windshield. Outward vision is good, and the roomy trunk has a low liftover.

BUILD QUALITY Park Avenues we've tested have had good fit and finish inside and out. However, an Ultra we drove in sub-freezing weather emitted creaks from the suspension when traversing speed bumps or entering driveways.

VALUE FOR THE MONEY In a near-luxury category dominated by imports, Park Avenue delivers traditional American virtues of roominess, power, and amenities at a competitive price. Buick's customer satisfaction ratings aren't as strong as those of such rivals as Infiniti and Lexus, but there's enough goodness here to warrant serious consideration.

RATINGS

	Base	Ultra
Acceleration	4	4
Fuel economy	2	2
Ride quality	3	4
Steering/handling	3	4
Braking	4	4
Quietness	4	4
Driver seating	3	3
Instruments/controls	4	4
Room/comfort (front)	4	4
Room/comfort (rear)	4	4
Cargo room	4	4
Value for the money	4	3
Total	**43**	**44**

SPECIFICATIONS

	4-door sedan
Wheelbase, in.	113.8
Overall length, in.	206.8
Overall width, in.	74.7
Overall height, in.	57.4
Curb weight, lbs.	3740
Cargo vol., cu. ft.	19.1
Fuel capacity, gals.	18.5
Seating capacity	6
Front head room, in.	39.8
Max. front leg room, in.	42.4
Rear head room, in.	38.0
Min. rear leg room, in.	41.1

ENGINES

	ohv V-6	Supercharged ohv V-6
Size, liters/cu. in.	3.8/231	3.8/231
Horsepower @ rpm	205@ 5200	240@ 5200
Torque (lbs./ft.) @ rpm	230@ 4000	280@ 3600
Availability	S[1]	S[2]

EPA city/highway mpg
4-speed OD automatic	19/29	18/27

1. Base model. 2. Ultra.

PRICES

Buick Park Avenue

	Retail Price	Dealer Invoice
Base 4-door sedan	$30675	$27761
Ultra 4-door sedan	35550	32173
Destination charge	665	665

STANDARD EQUIPMENT:

Base: 3.8-liter V-6 engine, 4-speed automatic transmission, driver-

and passenger-side air bags, anti-lock 4-wheel disc brakes, daytime running lights, air conditioning w/automatic climate control with dual temperature controls, rear-seat climate controls, interior air filtration, power steering, tilt steering wheel, cruise control, 10-way power 55/45 cloth front seat, front storage armrest with cupholders, rear armrest with cupholders, rear head restraints, rear seat pass-through, power windows with passenger lockout, power door locks, power mirrors, remote keyless entry with perimeter lighting, overhead console, rear defogger, tachometer, trip odometer, coolant-temperature gauge, AM/FM/cassette player, Concert Sound II speakers, rear-window antenna, remote decklid and fuel-door releases, front and rear reading and courtesy lights, illuminated visor mirrors, intermittent wipers, Twilight Sentinel headlamp control, cargo net, floormats, automatic level-control suspension, Pass-Key theft-deterrent system with starter interrupt, solar-control tinted glass, cornering lamps, 225/60R16 tires, alloy wheels.

Ultra adds: supercharged 3.8-liter V-6 engine, traction-control system, leather upholstery, memory driver seat and memory mirrors w/parallel park assist passenger-side mirror, memory climate control and radio presets, heated mirrors w/driver-side automatic day/night mirror, Seating Pkg. (power lumbar adjustment, heated front seats, power front and manual rear articulating headrests), rear-seat storage armrest with cupholders, leather-wrapped steering wheel, cellular phone readiness pkg., moisture-sensing windshield wipers, driver information center (tire- and oil-pressure warning, oil life and oil-level monitors, low-washer-fluid, low-coolant, and door-ajar indicators, and trip computer), CD player with automatic tone control and steering-wheel controls, rear illuminated vanity mirrors, wood door trim, Concert Sound III speakers, 4-note horn.

OPTIONAL EQUIPMENT:

	Retail Price	Dealer Invoice
Major Packages		
SE Prestige Pkg., Base	$890	$765

Memory driver-seat and mirrors w/parallel park assist passenger-side mirror, heated mirrors, automatic day/night driver-side mirror, automatic day/night rearview mirror, universal garage door opener, UL0 audio system (AM/FM/cassette player with clock, seek and scan, automatic tone control, and steering-wheel radio controls), moisture-sensing windshield wipers, driver information center (tire- and oil-pressure warning; volt, oil-life, and oil-level monitors; low-washer-fluid, low-coolant, and door-ajar indicators; and trip computer).

	Retail Price	Dealer Invoice
Gran Touring Pkg., Base w/SE Pkg.	240	206
Ultra	105	90

Includes Gran Touring suspension, aluminum wheels, and 225/60R16 touring tires. Base w/option pkg. also includes 3.05 axle ratio and leather-wrapped steering wheel. Base also includes variable-assist power steering. Requires automatic day/night mirror. Base also requires traction control.

Powertrains

	Retail Price	Dealer Invoice
Traction-control system, Base w/SE Pkg.	175	151

Comfort and Convenience

	Retail Price	Dealer Invoice
OnStar System	895	761

Includes Global Positioning System, voice activated cellular telephone, roadside assistance, emergency services. Requires dealer installation charge and monthly service charges.

	Retail Price	Dealer Invoice
UL0 audio system, Base	150	129

Includes AM/FM/cassette player with clock, seek and scan, automatic tone control, and steering-wheel radio controls.

	Retail Price	Dealer Invoice
UN0 audio system, Base	250	215
Base w/Pkg. SE	100	86

Includes AM/FM/CD player with clock, seek and scan, automatic tone control, and steering-wheel radio controls.

	Retail Price	Dealer Invoice
UP0 audio system, Base	350	301
Base w/SE Pkg.	200	172
Ultra	100	86

UN0 audio system plus cassette player.

	Retail Price	Dealer Invoice
Trunk-mounted CD changer, Ultra	595	512
Concert Sound III speakers, Base w/SE Pkg.	250	215
Automatic day/night rearview mirror w/compass	70	60

Base requires SE Pkg.

	Retail Price	Dealer Invoice
Electric sliding sunroof	995	856

Base requires SE Prestige Pkg.

	Retail Price	Dealer Invoice
Seating Pkg., Base	380	327

Power lumbar adjustment, heated front seats, and power front articulating headrests.

Rating Scale: 5-Excellent; 4-Above average; 3-Average; 2-Below average; 1-Poor

	Retail Price	Dealer Invoice
Convenience Console/Five Person Seating Pkg. ...	$185	$159

Bucket seats, console with writing surface and accommodations for phone and fax, cupholders, and auxiliary power outlets. Base requires leather upholstery, rear storage armrest, Cellular Phone Readiness Pkg.

Leather upholstery, Base.........	600	516
Cellular Phone Readiness Pkg., Base	75	65

Requires optional radio.

Eye Cue head-up display	275	237

Base requires cellular phone readiness pkg., SE Prestige Pkg.

Appearance and Miscellaneous

Four-note horn, Base w/SE Pkg.	28	24
Engine-block heater	18	15
Chrome-plated alloy wheels...........	695	598
225/60R16 whitewall tires, Base	85	73

NA with Gran Touring Pkg.

BUICK REGAL

Buick Regal GS

Front-wheel-drive midsize car; similar to Buick Century, Oldsmobile Intrigue, and Pontiac Grand Prix

Base price range: $20,945-$23,690. Built in Canada.

Also consider: Honda Accord, Mercury Sable, Nissan Maxima, Toyota Camry

FOR • Acceleration • Ride • Passenger and cargo room • Instruments/controls • Standard anti-lock brakes and traction control

AGAINST • Fuel economy (supercharged engine)

Regal shares its underskin design and basic interior with the Century but is marketed as a sportier and more-powerful sedan. Buick introduced this Regal as a 1997½ model to replace slightly smaller 2- and 4-door models that dated from 1988.

The only powertrain is a 3.8-liter V-6 and automatic transmission. The base Regal LS has 195 horsepower, the supercharged GS has 240. The GS also gets a firmer suspension, a body-colored grille, and leather upholstery.

Both Regals have front bucket seats and a console-mounted floor shifter (versus Century's bench seat and column-mounted lever). Separate right- and left-side climate controls, magnetic variable assist power steering, and anti-lock 4-wheel disc brakes are standard.

For '98, the GS gets a standard power driver's seat and an antenna embedded in the rear window. As in all '98 Buicks, the air bags deploy with reduced force but still meet federal safety standards. GM's OnStar communications system, a new dealer-installed option, links the car by satellite and cellular telephone to a 24-hour GM center from which advisors can provide travel advice and summon emergency help. The price includes a cell phone but not service fees.

PERFORMANCE GM is justifiably proud of its smooth 3.8-liter V-6 and the engine feels great in the Regal, furnishing good acceleration at low speeds and plenty of passing power. Performance is even better with the supercharged edition, but we're not convinced it's worth paying $2700 more for the GS model to get it. We averaged 17.6 mpg with our GS test car. Transmission behavior with either engine is sparkling.

Buick pitches the Regal as a sports sedan, but the car favors comfort over ultimate handling prowess. Steering response is a bit slow in quick changes of direction, and the body floats slightly over high-

speed dips that wouldn't fluster European sport sedans. However, body lean is moderate and large bumps are soaked up with little intrusion on passengers. Regal's biggest shortfall in highway driving is the presence of some wind noise.

ACCOMMODATIONS Regal's cabin is a nice place to be. There's good room front and rear and the comfortable front seats support nicely even in spirited driving. One negative is the fold-down center rear armrest: It's too low to be of much use, yet its width intrudes on outboard passenger space.

Gauges are large and unobstructed, but some of our testers complained that the climate controls were needlessly complicated. And, to pick a nit, the remote keyless entry fob contains a trunk-lid release, but there's none in the cabin.

Interior storage includes small map pockets at all seating positions, and a large locking console bin whose cover unfortunately has a lip design that can pinch fingers.

The lid to the large trunk opens 90 degrees on hinges that don't intrude on luggage space, though you have to stretch over a wide bumper shelf to load and unload. The standard seatback passthrough is nice, but a split-folding rear seat would be more useful.

BUILD QUALITY We're impressed by the quality of the interior materials and the solidity of a body free of squeaks and rattles.

VALUE FOR THE MONEY Regal doesn't match the overall refinement or proven record of reliability of midsize Best Buys such as the Honda Accord and Toyota Camry, nor does it benefit from the deep price discounts available on the Ford Taurus and Mercury Sable. But its high levels of standard equipment, solidity, and performance earn it a look.

RATINGS

	LS	GS
Acceleration	4	5
Fuel economy	3	2
Ride quality	4	4
Steering/handling	3	4
Braking	4	4
Quietness	3	3
Driver seating	4	4
Instruments/controls	4	4
Room/comfort (front)	4	4
Room/comfort (rear)	4	4
Cargo room	4	4
Value for the money	4	4
Total	45	46

SPECIFICATIONS

	4-door sedan
Wheelbase, in.	109.0
Overall length, in.	196.2
Overall width, in.	72.7
Overall height, in.	56.6
Curb weight, lbs.	3447
Cargo vol., cu. ft.	16.7
Fuel capacity, gals.	17.0
Seating capacity	5
Front head room, in.	39.3
Max. front leg room, in.	42.4
Rear head room, in.	37.4
Min. rear leg room, in.	36.9

ENGINES	ohv V-6	Supercharged ohv V-6
Size, liters/cu. in.	3.8/231	3.8/231
Horsepower @ rpm	195@ 5200	240@ 5200
Torque (lbs./ft.) @ rpm	220@ 4000	280@ 3600
Availability	S[1]	S[2]
EPA city/highway mpg		
4-speed OD automatic..........	19/30	17/27

1. LS. 2. GS.

PRICES

Buick Regal	Retail Price	Dealer Invoice
LS 4-door sedan	$20945	$19165
GS 4-door sedan	23690	21676
Destination charge	550	550

Prices are accurate at time of publication; subject to manufacturer's changes.

BUICK

STANDARD EQUIPMENT:

LS: 3.8-liter V-6 engine, 4-speed automatic transmission, traction control, driver- and passenger-side air bags, anti-lock 4-wheel disc brakes, daytime running lamps with Twighlight Sentinel, magnetic variable assist power steering, leather-wrapped tilt steering wheel, cruise control, air conditioning, dual zone manual climate control, air filtration system, cloth reclining front bucket seats, front console w/dual cupholders and auxiliary power outlet, rear armrest w/dual cupholders, remote keyless entry, programmable automatic power door locks, lockout protection, power windows w/driver's express down feature, trip odometer, tachometer, temperature gauge, warning lights for door ajar and trunk ajar, intermittent wipers, Pass-Key theft-deterrent system, color-keyed heated power mirrors, rear defogger, rear seat pass-through, courtesy/map lights on inside rearview mirror, visor vanity mirrors, AM/FM/cassette player with clock, retained accessory power, low fuel reminder tone, solar-control tinted glass, integral fog lamps, 215/70R15 tires, wheel covers.

GS adds: supercharged 3.8-liter V-6 engine, heavy-duty 4-speed automatic transmission with driver selectable shift control, traction control, leather seats, power driver seat, front and rear floormats, rear courtesy and reading lamps, automatic radio tone control, Concert Sound II speakers, dual illuminated visor vanity mirrors, driver information center (oil change monitor, oil level, fuel/engine information), Gran Touring suspension, bright exhaust outlets, 225/60R16 touring tires, alloy wheels.

OPTIONAL EQUIPMENT:

	Retail Price	Dealer Invoice
Major Packages		
Luxury Pkg. SB, LS	$587	$505

Includes front and rear floormats, reading/map lights, dual illuminated visor vanity mirrors, 6-way power driver's seat, integrated rear window antenna, trunk convenience net.

| Prestige Pkg. SC, LS | 887 | 763 |

Luxury Pkg. plus automatic day/night rearview mirror, cassette player, steering-wheel mounted radio controls, automatic radio tone control, Concert Sound II speakers.

| Luxury Pkg. SE, GS | 330 | 284 |

Includes dual zone automatic climate control, steering wheel mounted radio controls, integrated radio antenna, reading/map lights, illuminated visor mirrors, trunk convenience net.

| Prestige Pkg. SF, GS | 915 | 787 |

Luxury Pkg. SE plus cassette/CD player with automatic tone control, automatic day/night rear view mirror, 6-way power passenger's seat.

| Gran Touring Pkg., LS | 552 | 475 |

Consists of Gran Touring suspension and 225/60R16 blackwall tires, alloy wheels. Requires option pkg.

Safety Features		
Integrated rear child safety seat	100	86
Comfort and Convenience		
OnStar System	895	761

Includes Global Positioning System, voice-activated cellular telephone, roadside assistance, emergency services. Requires dealer installation charge and monthly service charges.

| Dual zone automatic climate control, GS | 145 | 125 |

Requires Luxury Pkg. SE.

| Cellular phone prewire package | 75 | 64 |
| Driver information center, LS w/Pkg. SC | 75 | 65 |

Includes oil change monitor, oil level, fuel/engine information center.

Rear window antenna, LS w/Pkg. SB	40	34
Steering-wheel mounted radio controls	125	108
CD player prep package	50	43
ULO audio system, LS	95	82

Includes automatic tone control and Concert Sound II speakers.

| UPO audio system, LS | 295 | 254 |
| LS w/Pkg. SC, GS | 200 | 172 |

Includes CD/cassette player and Concert Sound II speakers.

| Power moonroof | 695 | 597 |

Includes automatic day/night rearview mirror, map lights. Requires option pkg.

	Retail Price	Dealer Invoice
Leather bucket seats, LS	$550	$473

Requires option pkg.

| Heated front seats | 225 | 193 |

LS requires leather seats.

| 6-way power driver's seat, LS | 305 | 262 |
| 6-way power passenger's seat | 305 | 262 |

LS requires Prestige Pkg. SC.

| Trunk convenience net | 30 | 26 |
| Electrochromatic rearview mirror | 80 | 69 |

LS requires Luxury Pkg. SB.

Appearance and Miscellaneous

| Alloy wheels, LS | 375 | 323 |
| 16-inch chrome alloy wheels | 650 | 559 |

LS requires Gran Touring Pkg.

BUICK RIVIERA

BUDGET BUY

Buick Riviera

Front-wheel-drive luxury coupe
Base price: $32,500. Built in Orion, Mich.
Also consider: Acura CL, Cadillac Eldorado, Lexus SC 300/400

FOR • Standard anti-lock brakes • Acceleration • Ride • Steering/handling

AGAINST • Instruments/controls • Rear visibility • Entry/exit • Fuel economy

Buick is finally admitting that a large car with two, long heavy doors and a cramped rear seat is not for everyone. In fact, it's pitching Riviera as an impractical, indulgent reward for upscale achievers.

In keeping with this new theme, Buick has shelved the base 205-horsepower 3.8-liter V-6 and made standard the previously optional 240-horsepower supercharged version. Likewise, the standard front bench seat is dumped and all Rivs now come with the previously optional front buckets, so "practical" 6-passenger seating is out.

As in all Buicks, the air bags deploy with less force but still meet federal safety standards. A new dealer-installed option is GM's OnStar communications system. It links the car by satellite and cellular telephone to a 24-hour GM center from which advisors can provide directions, travel advice, and notify authorities in an emergency. The $895 price includes a cell phone but not service fees.

PERFORMANCE Eight of 10 Riviera buyers already were paying the extra $1195 for the supercharged engine option, obviously realizing that, given this big coupe's substantial weight, it was needed for performance that matched the sporty, sophisticated styling. Indeed, the supercharged 3.8 provides fine power across a wide range of speeds and teams with the smooth-shifting transmission for a highly refined powertrain. Premium fuel is required, and we averaged 17.7 mpg.

Riviera feels balanced in turns, with moderate body lean and good grip. Steering response isn't as sporty-sharp as in such rivals as the Lexus SC 300, though it is reasonably precise.

The comparatively soft suspension and long wheelbase provide a comfortable ride but not the athletic poise of the SC 300 or Acura 3.0CL. Despite suspension revisions for '98, wavy roads still set the nose to bouncing more than is necessary. The brakes feel strong and there is no undue nosedive in hard stops.

ACCOMMODATIONS Riv buyers also had a strong preference for the previously optional front buckets, but these seats look sportier than

Rating Scale: 5-Excellent; 4-Above average; 3-Average; 2-Below average; 1-Poor

22   CONSUMER GUIDE™

they are; our drivers find them soft and lacking in lateral support.

In front, head room is generous and even 6-footers have space to stretch. There's more rear-seat room than in most coupes, but head and leg clearance are not abundant for a car that's longer than a Park Avenue. The doors are cumbersome in tight parking spaces and climbing in or out of the back seat requires stooping to clear the roof and front shoulder belts.

The dashboard design spaces the speedometer and tachometer wide of the steering column, so the driver's eyes don't fall naturally to either. It's a stretch to the climate and audio panels, a problem addressed by the optional steering-wheel-mounted auxiliary controls.

A tall rear parcel shelf and thick rear roof pillars interfere with the driver's view aft and over the shoulders.

Riviera has more cargo space than most rivals. Its trunk is wide and goes well forward, but is not deep enough to accommodate objects taller than grocery bags, and the liftover is high.

BUILD QUALITY Our most-recent test car had lustrous black paint with only a small amount of bumpy orange-peel texture. Interior materials were generally of high quality, but the turn signal stalk and some other controls felt flimsy.

VALUE FOR THE MONEY As luxury coupes go, Riviera's cargo and passenger room make it quite functional. As an indulgence, it's more reasonably priced than most rivals while still delivering style, comfort, and performance. Plus, dealers should be discounting.

RATINGS

	Riviera
Acceleration	4
Fuel economy	2
Ride quality	3
Steering/handling	4
Braking	4
Quietness	4
Driver seating	3
Instruments/controls	2
Room/comfort (front)	4
Room/comfort (rear)	2
Cargo room	4
Value for the money	4
Total	**40**

SPECIFICATIONS

	2-door coupe
Wheelbase, in.	113.8
Overall length, in.	207.2
Overall width, in.	75.0
Overall height, in.	54.6
Curb weight, lbs.	3699
Cargo vol., cu. ft.	17.4
Fuel capacity, gals.	20.0
Seating capacity	5
Front head room, in.	38.2
Max. front leg room, in.	42.6
Rear head room, in.	36.2
Min. rear leg room, in.	37.1

ENGINES

	Supercharged ohv V-6
Size, liters/cu. in.	3.8/231
Horsepower @ rpm	240@ 5200
Torque (lbs./ft.) @ rpm	280@ 3600
Availability	S
EPA city/highway mpg	
4-speed OD automatic	18/27

PRICES

Buick Riviera	Retail Price	Dealer Invoice
2-door coupe	$32500	$29413
Destination charge	665	665

STANDARD EQUIPMENT:

Base: 3.8-liter supercharged V-6 engine, 4-speed automatic transmission, driver- and passenger-side air bags, anti-lock 4-wheel disc brakes, variable-assist power steering, leather-wrapped tilt steering wheel, cruise control, automatic air conditioning with dual climate controls, rear-seat heating vents, leather upholstery, cloth 6-way power front bucket seats with power recliners, front storage armrest with cupholders, rear-seat armrest, power windows, power heated mirrors, automatic power door locks, remote keyless entry system (w/perimeter lighting, security feedback and instant alarm), tachometer, coolant-temperature gauge, illuminated passenger-side visor mirror, remote fuel door and decklid releases, AM/FM/cassette/CD player with clock, Concert Sound II speakers, power antenna, intermittent wipers, rear defogger, front and rear reading and courtesy lights, Twilight Sentinel headlamp control, cargo net, automatic level control suspension, Pass-Key theft-deterrent system, trip odometer, solar-control tinted glass, daytime running lights, 225/60R16 all-season tires, alloy wheels.

OPTIONAL EQUIPMENT:

	Retail Price	Dealer Invoice
Major Packages		
SE Prestige Pkg.	$1145	$985

Traction-control system, driver-seat and passenger-seat power lumbar adjustment, automatic day/night rearview and driver-side mirrors, steering-wheel-mounted radio controls, driver-side illuminated visor mirror, theft-deterrent system, universal garage door opener, cornering lamps, striping.

Comfort and Convenience		
Power sunroof with sunshade	995	856
OnStar System	895	761

Includes Global Positioning System, voice-activated cellular telephone, roadside assistance, emergency services. Requires dealer installation charge and monthly service charges.

Memory/heated front seats	415	357

Includes memory outside mirrors.

Automatic day/night rearview mirror	70	60

Includes compass. Requires SE Prestige Pkg.

Appearance and Miscellaneous		
Bright white diamond paint	395	340
Engine block heater	18	15
Chrome alloy wheels	695	598

Requires supercharged engine.

CADILLAC CATERA

Cadillac Catera

Rear-wheel-drive near-luxury car

Base price range: $29,995-$32,995. Built in Germany.
Also consider: Infiniti I30, Lexus ES 300, Mercedes-Benz C-Class

FOR • Standard anti-lock brakes and traction control • Passenger and cargo room • Steering/handling • Acceleration

AGAINST • Rear visibility

Compact and midsize sedans in the $29,000-$40,000 range are the fastest-growing segment of the luxury-car market. Cadillac has turned to Germany and General Motors' Opel subsidiary for a European flavored sedan that fits into this "near-luxury" niche.

Catera, based on the Opel Omega, is the only rear-wheel-drive Cadillac and the only one without a V-8 engine, using instead Opel's 3.0-liter V-6 linked to an automatic transmission. Anti-lock brakes and traction control are standard, but unlike an increasing number of rivals, Catera doesn't offer side air bags. Leather upholstery and a power sunroof are options and for '98, are joined by a power rear-window sunshade. The extra-cost Bose audio system gains radio data system (RDS) capability. RDS enables the radio to display such broadcast information as station call letters and song titles, as well as to break into programming with emergency broadcast system alerts.

A new dealer-installed option is GM's OnStar system. This links the car by satellite and cellular telephone to a 24-hour GM center from which advisors provide directions and travel advice and can notify local authorities in an emergency. The $895 price includes a cell phone but buyers pay their own service bills.

PERFORMANCE Catera gets away from a stop briskly and, with liberal use of the throttle, provides spirited acceleration. The V-6 can't match a V-8's burst of power in the 40-60-mph range, but the transmission downshifts crisply to furnish adequate passing response. We averaged 20 mpg in a mix of city, suburban, and highway driving.

Credit Cadillac with preserving Catera's sporty European genes. The steering is precise and the car feels alert in changes of direction, cornering with modest body lean and good balance. The taut suspension resists wallowing and floating and absorbs bumps with minimal disturbance.

Braking power is strong, with good pedal modulation and little nosedive in sudden stops.

Catera's twin-cam V-6 emits a sporty snarl under hard throttle but otherwise goes about its work quietly. At freeway speeds, wind rush around the side windows is louder than it ought to be and the tires thump loudly over bumps and tar strips.

ACCOMMODATIONS The driveline hump intrudes on the rear seat's center position, so Catera offers comfortable room for four adults on softer seats than in the typical European car.

The steering wheel is mounted further away from the driver than in other Cadillacs, imparting a sportier feel. But the steering column is angled slightly toward the center of the car, forcing some drivers to sit in a position that's tiring on long drives.

Main instruments and controls are logically placed, though the cruise control buttons on the end of the turn signal stalk are tiny and hard to use.

Convenient touches include a modestly sized glovebox that's refrigerated by the air conditioner and a one-touch moonroof control. Demerits to the cupholding contraption that pops out of the center console; it's awkward to use yet renders the console useless when stored.

Large rear headrests and a narrow rear window limit the driver's view aft. Split folding rear seats increase the versatility of the roomy trunk.

BUILD QUALITY Fit and finish on Cateras we've tested have been about par for the class, with generally good-quality materials and a touch of fake wood on doors and console. One test car had an occasional rattle in the dashboard and the suspension squeaked over speed bumps and in steep driveway entrances.

VALUE FOR THE MONEY Cadillac comes to a hotly contested market with a quiet, solid feeling car with a relatively spacious interior and athletic moves. Catera's list of standard equipment is impressive for its base price, and a loaded example runs about $36,000. It's a fresh approach for Cadillac and worth looking at.

RATINGS

	Catera
Acceleration	4
Fuel economy	2
Ride quality	3
Steering/handling	4
Braking	4
Quietness	3
Driver seating	4
Instruments/controls	3
Room/comfort (front)	4
Room/comfort (rear)	3
Cargo room	4
Value for the money	3
Total	**41**

SPECIFICATIONS

	4-door sedan
Wheelbase, in.	107.4
Overall length, in.	194.0
Overall width, in.	70.3
Overall height, in.	56.3
Curb weight, lbs.	3770
Cargo vol., cu. ft.	14.5
Fuel capacity, gals.	18.0
Seating capacity	5
Front head room, in.	38.7
Max. front leg room, in.	42.2
Rear head room, in.	38.4
Min. rear leg room, in.	37.5

ENGINES

	dohc V-6
Size, liters/cu. in.	3.0/181
Horsepower @ rpm	200@ 6000
Torque (lbs./ft.) @ rpm	192@ 3600
Availability	S

EPA city/highway mpg	
4-speed OD automatic	18/25

PRICES

1997 Cadillac Catera	Retail Price	Dealer Invoice
4-door notchback	$29995	$28645
Destination charge	640	640

STANDARD EQUIPMENT:

3.0-liter DOHC V-6 engine, 4-speed automatic transmission, anti-lock 4-wheel disc brakes, dual-zone automatic climate control w/outside temperature indicator, driver- and passenger-side air bags, variable-assist steering, traction control, cloth front bucket seats, 8-way power driver seat with power recliner, passenger-seat power height adjuster, split folding rear bench seat, front articulating and rear headrests, front console w/storage armrest and cupholders, rear armrests, power windows, automatic power door locks, remote-keyless entry system, heated power mirrors, cruise control, AM/FM/cassette with eight speakers, integrated rear window antenna, steering-wheel radio controls, tinted glass, wood interior trim, intermittent wipers, leather-wrapped tilt steering wheel, Driver Information Center, analog instrument cluster, tachometer, coolant-temperature and oil-pressure gauge, voltmeter, trip odometer, remote fuel-door and decklid release, rear defogger, anti-theft system, automatic day/night inside mirror, illuminated visor mirrors, front and rear reading lights, illuminated entry, automatic parking-brake release, dual exhaust, Twilight Sentinel headlamp control, wiper-activated headlights, cornering lamps, daytime running lamps, fog lights, trunk mat and cargo net, floormats, 225/55HR16 tires, alloy wheels, full-size spare.

OPTIONAL EQUIPMENT:

Comfort and Convenience

Comfort Convenience Pkg.	3000	1875

Leather upholstery, 8-way power front passenger seat, memory seats and mirrors, theft-deterrent system.

Heated front and rear seats	400	340
Power sunroof	995	846
Universal garage-door opener	107	91
8-speaker Bose sound system	723	615

Appearance and Miscellaneous

5-spoke alloy wheels	355	156
5-spoke chrome wheels	1195	523

CADILLAC DEVILLE   ▮RECOMMENDED▮

Front-wheel-drive luxury car

Base price range: $37,695-$42,295. Built in Hamtramck, Mich.

Also consider: Buick Park Avenue, Lincoln Continental, Lincoln Town Car

FOR • Side air bags • Standard anti-lock brakes and traction control • Acceleration • Passenger and cargo room

Rating Scale: 5-Excellent; 4-Above average; 3-Average; 2-Below average; 1-Poor

Cadillac De Ville

AGAINST • Fuel economy • Climate controls (base De Ville and d'Elegance)

With last year's demise of the Fleetwood, the DeVille series took over as Cadillac's only full-size luxury sedan. For '98, these front-wheel-drive 4-doors tout safety enhancements as they face a redesigned Lincoln Town Car, which retains traditional rear-wheel drive.

All three DeVilles use Cadillac's Northstar V-8. The base model and gold-ornamented d'Elegance have 275 horsepower, the performance-oriented Concours has 300. All come with automatic transmission, traction control, and front side air bags.

Returning as standard on Concours, and newly optional on the others, is Cadillac's Stabilitrak system, which activates the front brakes individually to enhance control in emergency maneuvers. New optional radios include radio data system (RDS) capability, which allows broadcasters to transmit text and emergency messages along with the audio signal.

A dealer-installed option is GM's OnStar, which links the car by satellite and cellular telephone to a 24-hour GM center from which advisors provide directions and travel advice and can notify local authorities in an emergency. The $895 price includes a cell phone but buyers pay their own installation and monthly service bills.

Concourse and d'Elegance add heated front seats and a CD player as standard for '98. Concours also gains fresh alloy wheels.

PERFORMANCE The Northstar V-8s are models of smooth power, providing snap off the line and working with the excellent transmission to furnish satisfying passing response. Most rivals aren't as fast. Our base-model test car did 0-60 mph in 6.8 seconds, but averaged just 16.8 mpg in a mix of driving conditions. Premium gas is required.

The standard Road Sensing Suspension automatically adjusts firmness to driving conditions. It allows more than a trace of float over dips at highway speeds, but overall, DeVille and d'Elegance are secure, stable, and absorbent. The stiffer-riding Concours feels more buttoned down at speed and has firmer steering, but the others suit a wider range of drivers and roads. The long wheelbase saddles these big sedans with a 41-foot turning radius, so parking is sometimes a chore. The brakes feel strong: Our test Concours stopped in an average of 134 feet in 10 stops from 60 mph with minimal nosedive.

ACCOMMODATIONS There's space for six adults if middle passengers brush shoulders with their companions. Head room is generous, and there's leg stretching room in the rear seat. Ingress and egress are good, despite rear doors that open only about 70 degrees.

Concours has a fresh, European-inspired dashboard design with analog gauges and easy-to-reach controls. The others get a digital speedometer and hard-to-reach climate-system buttons, though steering-wheel controls are provided for some climate and audio functions. RDS works as advertised, though currently, just 700 of America's 7000 radio stations broadcast a compatible signal. Our experience with OnStar suggests it's a worthwhile option, and the price does includes a voice-activated cell phone.

Thick rear roof pillars and small outside mirrors make it hard to park and safely change lanes.

The trunk opens at bumper level and has a wide, flat floor that holds lots of luggage. Interior storage space is adequate.

BUILD QUALITY Our latest test cars were free of flaws. Interior materials and workmanship are the highest quality of any domestic car.

VALUE FOR THE MONEY The base model accounts for 70 percent of DeVille sales, with good reason: It's the best value in this range of Cadillacs and among the better buys among large luxury cars in general. It has a satisfying blend of performance, room, comfort, and features at a reasonable base price of around $37,000. It also seems clearer about its mission than the similarly priced Lincoln Continental.

RATINGS

	Base/d'Elegance	Concours
Acceleration	4	4
Fuel economy	2	2
Ride quality	4	4
Steering/handling	3	3
Braking	4	4
Quietness	4	4
Driver seating	4	4
Instruments/controls	3	4
Room/comfort (front)	5	5
Room/comfort (rear)	5	5
Cargo room	4	4
Value for the money	4	4
Total	**46**	**47**

SPECIFICATIONS

	4-door sedan
Wheelbase, in.	113.8
Overall length, in.	209.7
Overall width, in.	76.5
Overall height, in.	56.0
Curb weight, lbs.	4012
Cargo vol., cu. ft.	20.0
Fuel capacity, gals.	20.0
Seating capacity	6
Front head room, in.	38.5
Max. front leg room, in.	42.6
Rear head room, in.	38.4
Min. rear leg room, in.	43.3

ENGINES

	dohc V-8	dohc V-8
Size, liters/cu. in.	4.6/279	4.6/279
Horsepower @ rpm	275@ 5600	300@ 6000
Torque (lbs./ft.) @ rpm	300@ 4000	295@ 4400
Availability	S[1]	S[2]
EPA city/highway mpg		
4-speed OD automatic	17/26	17/26

1. DeVille. 2. Concours.

PRICES

Cadillac DeVille	Retail Price	Dealer Invoice
Base 4-door sedan	$37695	$34646
d'Elegance 4-door sedan	41295	37940
Concours 4-door sedan	42295	38855
Destination charge	665	665

STANDARD EQUIPMENT:

Base: 4.6-liter DOHC V-8 275-horsepower engine, 4-speed automatic transmission, traction control, driver- and passenger-side air bags, front side-impact air bags, anti-lock 4-wheel disc brakes, daytime running lamps, dual-zone automatic climate control w/outside temperature indicator, Magnasteer variable-assist steering, tilt steering wheel, leather-wrapped steering wheel, cruise control, cloth 8-way power front seats with power recliners, front storage armrest w/cupholders, front and rear articulating headrests, overhead storage compartment, power windows, programmable power locks w/valet lockout, remote-keyless entry system, illuminated entry, heated power mirrors w/driver-side automatic day/night, AM/FM/cassette with six speakers and Theftlock, power antenna, steering-

Prices are accurate at time of publication; subject to manufacturer's changes.

wheel radio and climate controls, driver-side visor storage, illuminated front visor mirrors, intermittent wipers, Driver Information Center, trip odometer, power decklid release and pulldown, remote fuel-door release, rear defogger, Pass-Key II theft-deterrent system, automatic day/night inside rear-view mirror, front and rear reading lights, Integrated Chassis Control System, automatic parking-brake release, Twilight Sentinel headlamp control, wiper-activated headlights, trunk mat and cargo net, floormats, automatic level-control suspension, tinted glass, cornering lamps, striping, 225/60R16 all-season whitewall tires, alloy wheels.

d'Elegance adds: Comfort/Convenience Pkg. (heated seats, Memory Pkg. [memory seats, mirrors, climate control and radio presets], dual power lumbar adjustment), leather upholstery, Zebrano wood trim, Active Audio System with cassette/CD player and 11 speakers, automatic windshield wipers, rear illuminated visor mirrors, gold trim/badging, chrome alloy wheels.

Concours adds: 4.6-liter DOHC V-8 300-horsepower engine, dual exhaust, front bucket seats, front floor console, rear storage armrest w/cupholders, analog instrument cluster, tachometer, coolant-temperature gauge, fog lights, continuously variable Road-Sensing Suspension, Stabilitrak, 225/60HR16 blackwall tires, and deletes: front storage armrest, gold trim/badging, striping, chrome alloy wheels.

OPTIONAL EQUIPMENT:

	Retail Price	Dealer Invoice
Major Packages		
Comfort/Convenience Pkg., Base	$867	$737
Heated seats, Memory Pkg. (memory seats, mirrors, climate control, radio presets), dual power lumbar adjustment.		
Safety/Security Pkg., Base, d'Elegance	752	639
Concours	502	427
Electronic compass, StabiliTrak (Base, d'Elegance), universal garage-door opener, theft-deterrent system.		
3000-lb. Trailer Towing Pkg.	110	94
Includes trailer wiring harness, engine oil cooler.		
Comfort and Convenience		
OnStar System	895	761
Includes Global Positioning System, voice-activated cellular telephone, roadside assistance, emergency services. Requires dealer installation charge and monthly service charges.		
Leather upholstery, Base	785	667
Power sunroof	1550	1318
Concours, d'Elegance delete rear visor mirrors.		
U1R Active Audio Sound System, Base	670	570
AM/FM/cassette/CD with 11 speakers.		
UM5 Active Audio Sound System, Base	770	655
d'Elegance, Concours	100	85
Includes AM/FM/cassette/CD, digital signal processing, and 11 speakers.		
12-disc CD changer	595	506
Trunk storage system	265	225
Appearance and Miscellaneous		
White diamond or pearl red paint	500	425
Chrome alloy wheels, Base, Concours	795	507

CADILLAC ELDORADO

RECOMMENDED

Cadillac Eldorado Touring Coupe

Front-wheel-drive luxury coupe
Base price range: $38,495-$42,695. Built in Hamtramck, Mich.

Also consider: Buick Riviera, Lexus SC 300/400, Lincoln Mark VIII

FOR • Standard anti-lock brakes and traction control • Acceleration • Steering/handling

AGAINST • Fuel economy • Rear visibility • Climate controls (base model)

Eldorado spent most of the last 20 years as essentially a 2-door version of the 4-door Seville, but Seville graduates to a new platform for 1998, leaving the Eldo as we know it with a cloudy future. Reports have this front-wheel-drive coupe switching to rear-wheel drive sometime after 1999.

Both the base car and the sportier Eldorado Touring Coupe (ETC) come with a V-8 that's rated at 275 horsepower in the base model, 300 in the ETC. Automatic transmission, anti-lock brakes, and traction control also are standard.

New audio systems have radio data system (RDS) capability, which allows broadcasters to transmit program and emergency messages. A carried-over option is the OnStar, which links the car via satellite and cell phone to a 24-hour GM center from which operators can furnish travel advice and other services.

StabiliTrak enhances stability during emergency-avoidance maneuvers by activating the front brakes selectively; it's standard on the ETC and newly optional on the base Eldo. The ETC includes heated front seats for '98 and its steering increases effort not only as vehicle speed rises but now as cornering forces build.

PERFORMANCE Both models have outstanding acceleration, but differ in the way power is delivered. The ETC musters its best punch at high engine speeds, so it shines on stretches of open road. The base Eldo's V-8 is tuned to produce more torque at low speeds, so it's more eager to provide quick bursts of acceleration in congested city and suburban driving. Both use premium gas. In a mix of driving, our test ETC averaged 15.2 mpg, our base version 18.

The base Eldo changes direction with little drama, if not much athleticism. The Touring Coupe floats less over undulations and takes corners with minimal body lean and good grip, but its firmer ride is uncomfortable over big bumps. The ETC's steering is more precise, though it feels slightly artificial off center. StabiliTrak adds a welcome margin of safety. Our test cars stopped short and with good control. Noise levels are low, though the engines do emit a refined growl under hard throttle.

ACCOMMODATIONS Room is ample in front and adequate for two adults in the rear, though as in most coupes, it's a chore to climb in and out of the back. Wide, heavy doors require lots of room to open fully.

A stylish, functional dashboard puts the ETC's interior at the head of the luxury-coupe class. The base model's less-efficient dashboard design hides the climate controls behind the steering-wheel rim. Doors lack map pockets, but cupholders and storage space are in the center armrest. However, the armrest is awkward to open while driving. The trunk holds at least two golf bags, and a low liftover makes loading easy. Extra caution is required when changing lanes because of the massive rear roof pillars.

BUILD QUALITY Eldorados we've recently tested were trouble-free and handsomely finished inside and out.

VALUE FOR THE MONEY The ETC is jazzy, but its price is up by $1500 over last year. You'll save a few dollars without any meaningful loss of performance with a base model, which rises $500. Sales are slow on both, so discounts should be available.

SPECIFICATIONS

	2-door coupe
Wheelbase, in.	108.0
Overall length, in.	200.6
Overall width, in.	75.5
Overall height, in.	53.6
Curb weight, lbs.	3843
Cargo vol., cu. ft.	15.3
Fuel capacity, gals.	20.0
Seating capacity	5
Front head room, in.	37.8
Max. front leg room, in.	42.6

Rating Scale: 5-Excellent; 4-Above average; 3-Average; 2-Below average; 1-Poor

	2-door coupe
Rear head room, in.	38.3
Min. rear leg room, in.	35.5

RATINGS

	Base	Touring Coupe
Acceleration	4	4
Fuel economy	2	2
Ride quality	4	3
Steering/handling	3	4
Braking	4	4
Quietness	4	4
Driver seating	3	3
Instruments/controls	3	4
Room/comfort (front)	4	4
Room/comfort (rear)	2	2
Cargo room	3	3
Value for the money	4	4
Total	**40**	**41**

ENGINES

	dohc V-8	dohc V-8
Size, liters/cu. in.	4.6/279	4.6/279
Horsepower @ rpm	275@ 5600	300@ 6000
Torque (lbs./ft.) @ rpm	300@ 4000	295@ 4400
Availability	S[1]	S[2]
EPA city/highway mpg		
4-speed OD automatic	17/26	17/26

1. Base. 2. Touring Coupe.

PRICES

Cadillac Eldorado	Retail Price	Dealer Invoice
Base 2-door notchback	$38495	$35378
Touring Coupe 2-door notchback	42695	39221
Destination charge	665	665

STANDARD EQUIPMENT:

Base: 4.6-liter DOHC V-8 275-horsepower engine, 4-speed automatic transmission, traction control, dual exhaust, anti-lock 4-wheel disc brakes, driver- and passenger-side air bags, daytime running lamps, wiper-activated headlights, Magnasteer variable-assist steering, leather-wrapped steering wheel with controls for radio and climate, tilt steering wheel, automatic climate control air conditioning, cruise control, cloth 8-way power front bucket seats, center console with armrest and storage bins, overhead storage compartment, power windows, automatic power locks, remote keyless entry system, heated power mirrors w/driver-side automatic day/night, rear defogger, automatic day/night rearview mirror, AM/FM/cassette player with six speakers, power antenna, remote fuel-door and decklid release, power decklid pull-down, trip odometer, tachometer, Driver Information Center, Zebrano wood trim, driver-side visor storage flap, intermittent wipers, automatic parking-brake release, Twilight Sentinel headlamp control, illuminated entry, reading lights, illuminated visor mirrors, floormats, trunk mat and cargo net, Integrated Chassis Control System, automatic level control, solar-control tinted glass, valet lockout, Pass-Key II theft-deterrent system, fog lamps, cornering lamps, 225/60R16 tires, alloy wheels.

Touring Coupe adds: Comfort/Convenience Pkg. (Memory Pkg. [memory seats, mirrors, climate control, and radio presets], power lumbar adjustment, heated front seats.), high-output 4.6-liter DOHC V-8 300-horsepower engine, CD player w/Bose sound system, leather upholstery, rear-seat storage armrest with cup holders, analog instrument cluster, coolant-temperature gauge, automatic windshield wiper system, theft-deterrent system w/alarm, continuously-variable Road-Sensing Suspension, Stabilitrak, 225/60HR16 tires.

OPTIONAL EQUIPMENT:

Major Packages

	Retail Price	Dealer Invoice
Comfort/Convenience Pkg., Base	$867	$737

Memory Pkg. (memory seats, mirrors, climate control, and radio presets), power lumbar support, heated front seats.

	Retail Price	Dealer Invoice
Safety/Security Pkg., Base	$502	$427
Touring Coupe	207	176

Electronic compass, universal garage-door opener, theft-deterrent system w/alarm (Base).

Comfort and Convenience

OnStar System	895	761

Includes Global Positioning System, voice-activated cellular telephone, roadside assistance, emergency services. Requires dealer installation charge and monthly service charges.

Power sunroof	1550	1318
U1R Bose Sound System, Base	1119	951

Includes AM/FM/cassette/CD player, four Bose amplified speakers, Theftlock.

UM5 Bose Sound System, Base	1219	1036
Touring Coupe	100	85

Includes AM/FM/weatherband/cassette/CD player, digital signal processing, and four Bose amplified speakers, Theftlock.

12-disc CD player	595	506
Leather upholstery, Base	785	667
Trunk storage system, Touring Coupe	225	205

Appearance and Miscellaneous

White diamond or red pearl paint	500	425
Striping, Base	75	64
StabiliTrak, Base	250	213
225/60R16 whitewall tires, Base	76	65
225/60ZR16 tires, Touring Coupe	250	213
Chrome alloy wheels	795	507

CADILLAC SEVILLE

RECOMMENDED

Cadillac Seville STS

Front-wheel-drive luxury car

Base price range: (est.) $42,000-$47,000. Built in Hamtramck, Mich.

Also consider: BMW 5-Series, Infiniti Q45, Lexus LS 400, Mercedes-Benz E-Class

FOR • Acceleration • Side air bags • Automatic transmission performance • Handling/roadholding • Interior storage space • Standard anti-lock brakes and traction control

AGAINST • Fuel economy • Rear visibility

Moving to recapture the "Standard of the World" title it admits it lost, Cadillac unveils a redesigned Seville intended to better the quality and value of such brands as Mercedes-Benz and Lexus.

Like its predecessor, the 1998 model has front-wheel drive and Cadillac's Northstar V-8, which is rated at 275 horsepower in the base SLS model, 300 in the sportier STS. The new Seville shares some underbody structure with the Buick Riviera and Park Avenue and Oldsmobile Aurora. Styling is evolutionary, but body length shrinks 3.1 inches while wheelbase stretches 1.2 inches. All Sevilles are again built in Michigan, but about 20 percent will go to overseas markets. The car was designed with both left- and right-hand drive.

Carried-over standard features include StabiliTrak, which aids

Prices are accurate at time of publication; subject to manufacturer's changes.

control in evasive maneuvers by selectively applying the front brakes. Also back is an electronic suspension that reads the road surface and continuously adjusts to soften the ride and control body motion.

A redesigned interior introduces to Seville front-seat mounted side air bags. New safety belts attach to the seat frame and include the first belt pretension system in a U.S.-made car. An STS option is Cadillac's new Adaptive Seat System in which 10 air cells in the front seats adjust automatically to suit body styles.

Standard on the STS and optional on the SLS is radio data system (RDS) capability, which displays song title and other broadcast information and can interrupt programming with emergency messages. The OnStar satellite communication system is optional.

Estimated base prices at time of publication were $42,000 for the SLS and $47,000 for the STS. That's about $3000 over the '97s.

PERFORMANCE With unaltered Northstar V-8s and little change in curb weights, acceleration again is among the class leaders. Behavior of the smooth automatic transmission is beyond reproach, and the STS has the advantage of new technology Cadillac calls Performance Shift Algorithm, which adjusts to an array of driving conditions; it can even downshift as the car negotiates a corner and hold the lower gear to enhance acceleration out of the turn.

A stiffer body structure, steering effort keyed both to vehicle speed and cornering force, and a new rear suspension give Seville fine ride and handling qualities, though neither model quite matches the European-bred composure of a BMW 5-Series. The SLS feels appropriately soft without being sloppy, while the STS, with its tauter suspension, aggressive tire tread, and lower ride height, responds more quickly to steering inputs and corners flatter.

Cadillac claims Seville is as quiet as a Lexus LS 400. We detected little wind noise or objectional tire roar on our preview test drives, but the STS's engine sounds noticeably gruffer than the SLS's in hard acceleration, and both cars suffer more exhaust noise than a Mercedes-Benz E-420

ACCOMMODATIONS Four adults is the practical limit, and rear-seaters must tuck their legs and swivel their ankles to negotiate narrow door bottoms. Front-seat space is generous. Rear-seat leg room is only adequate and Cadillac's decision to raise the height of the back seat cushion for better visibility has tall riders brushing the headliner. Exceptionally comfortable are the STS's optional adaptive seats, which subtly but effectively adjust support even as the occupant changes position.

A new instrument panel illuminated by florescent backlighting and LED needles gives the gauges terrific definition, and the driver can extinguish the lighting, leaving only a digital speed readout. Switchgear is logically arrayed (cruise control gets its own stalk, just like at Mercedes), though the climate controls are too low. Both models have a console shifter that now moves through a serpentine slot—again like Mercedes.

Wide rear roof pillars and a tall trunk limit the driver's view aft and over the shoulders. The trunk is spacious. Inside, Seville goes from what Cadillac acknowledges was almost no storage room to a class-leading array of 19 separate pockets, boxes, and pouch. Included is space for an umbrella beneath the front passenger seat, a two-tier front armrest with room for an optional 6-disc CD changer, and an optional sectioned trunk bin.

BUILD QUALITY Cadillac has lofty goals for Seville, promising that it'll be among the top 10 cars in the influential J.D. Power Initial Quality Survey of owners. Pilot production cars we drove seemed well assembled, but there was a cheap feel to the plastic covers of the accessory power source and the rear armrest console.

VALUE FOR THE MONEY We're already impressed enough with Seville's performance, features, solidity, and target price to recommend its consideration. If Cadillac delivers on its quality pledges, the '98 could be a Best Buy in a very competitive segment.

RATINGS

	SLS	STS
Acceleration	4	4
Fuel economy	2	2
Ride quality	4	4
Steering/handling	4	4
Braking	4	4
Quietness	5	4
Driver seating	4	5
Instruments/controls	4	4
Room/comfort (front)	4	4
Room/comfort (rear)	4	4
Cargo room	4	4
Value for the money	4	4
Total	**47**	**47**

SPECIFICATIONS

	4-door sedan
Wheelbase, in.	112.2
Overall length, in.	201.0
Overall width, in.	75.0
Overall height, in.	55.7
Curb weight, lbs.	3972
Cargo vol., cu. ft.	15.7
Fuel capacity, gals.	18.5
Seating capacity	5
Front head room, in.	38.1
Max. front leg room, in.	42.5
Rear head room, in.	38.0
Min. rear leg room, in.	38.2

ENGINES

	dohc V-8	dohc V-8
Size, liters/cu. in.	4.6/279	4.6/279
Horsepower @ rpm	275@ 5600	300@ 6000
Torque (lbs./ft.) @ rpm	300@ 4000	295@ 4400
Availability	S[1]	S[2]
EPA city/highway mpg 4-speed OD automatic	17/26	17/26

1. SLS. 2. STS.

PRICES

Cadillac Seville	Retail Price	Dealer Invoice
SLS 4-door sedan	$—	$—
STS 4-door sedan	—	—
Destination charge	665	665

Retail, dealer invoice, and some options prices not available at time of publication.

STANDARD EQUIPMENT:

SLS: 4.6-liter DOHC V-8 (275-horsepower) engine, 4-speed automatic transmission, traction control, driver- and passenger-side air bags, front side-impact air bags, anti-lock 4-wheel disc brakes, daytime running lights, air conditioning w/dual zone climate control, outside temperature display, interior air filter, rear heat/air conditioning outlet with fan, MAGNASTEER variable-assist steering, leather-wrapped steering wheel with controls for radio and climate system, cruise control, leather upholstery, 8-way power front seats with power recliners, front and rear articulating headrests w/power height adjustment for front headrests, center storage console with armrest, rear armrest w/storage, overhead console, Zebrano wood interior trim, power windows, programmable power door locks, valet lockout, remote keyless entry, illuminated entry, heated power mirrors w/driver-side automatic day/night, automatic day/night rearview mirror, Bose AM/FM/cassette/CD with eight speakers and Theftlock, diversity antenna, map lights, illuminated visor mirrors, visor storage flaps, Driver Information Center, tachometer, coolant-temperature gauge, trip odometer, automatic parking brake release, remote fuel door and decklid releases, trunk pass through, intermittent wipers, wiper-activated headlights, Twilight Sentinel headlights, rear defogger, floormats, trunk mat and cargo net, cornering lights, Pass Key III theft-deterrent system, solar-control tinted glass, continuously variable Road-Sensing Suspension, Stabilitrak, automatic level control, 235/60R16 tires, alloy wheels.

Rating Scale: 5-Excellent; 4-Above average; 3-Average; 2-Below average; 1-Poor

STS adds: 4.6-liter DOHC V-8 (300-horsepower) engine, Performance Shift Algorithm, Memory Pkg. (two-driver memory seats, mirrors, climate control, and radio presets), power lumbar adjusters, power tilt and telescoping steering wheel, Curb-View passenger-side mirror, Rainsense automatic wipers, compass, universal garage door opener, sound system with digital signal processing/weatherband/automatic volume control, fog lights, STS suspension tuning, 235/60HR16 tires.

OPTIONAL EQUIPMENT:

	Retail Price	Dealer Invoice
Major Packages		
Convenience Pkg., SLS	$—	$—
Includes power lumbar support for front seats, Rainsense automatic wipers, compass, universal garage door opener.		
Personalization Pkg., SLS	—	—
Convenience Pkg. plus Memory Pkg. (two-driver memory for seats, mirrors, climate control, and radio presets), heated front and rear seats, power tilt and telescoping steering wheel.		
Heated Seat Pkg., STS	—	—
Heated front and rear seats, compass, universal garage door opener. NA with Adaptive Seat Pkg.		
Adaptive Seat Pkg., STS	—	—
Adaptive front seats, compass, universal garage door opener.		
Comfort and Convenience		
OnStar System	895	761
Includes Global Positioning System, voice-activated cellular telephone, roadside assistance, emergency services. Requires dealer installation charge and monthly service charges.		
Power sunroof	1550	1318
UM5 Bose sound system, SLS	—	—
Includes AM/FM/Weatherband/cassette/CD with digital signal processing, automatic volume control.		
UM9 Bose sound system	—	—
Includes AM/FM/weatherband/cassette/mini CD player with digital signal processing, automatic volume control.		
6-disc CD player	—	—
Wood trim pkg.	—	—
Wood trimmed steering wheel and shift knob.		
Trunk storage system	—	—
Appearance and Miscellaneous		
Striping, SLS	75	64
Engine block heater	—	—
Chrome alloy wheels	—	—
235/60ZR16 tires, STS	—	—

CHEVROLET ASTRO

Chevorlet Astro LT AWD

Rear- or all-wheel-drive minivan; similar to GMC Safari

Base price range: $19,638-$21,838. Built in Baltimore, Md.
Also consider: Chevrolet Venture, Dodge Caravan, Ford Windstar

FOR • Standard anti-lock brakes • Passenger and cargo room • Trailer towing capability

AGAINST • Fuel economy • Entry/exit • Ride

After two years of fairly extensive changes, Astro alterations are limited to new colors, the addition of Chevy's Passlock theft-deterrent system, and revisions to the automatic transmission.

Astro was Chevrolet's first attempt at a minivan and adheres to the truck-based school of small van building rather than the newer, car-based front-wheel-drive designs. GMC sells a nearly identical truck as the Safari

Astro comes with rear-wheel drive or permanently engaged all-wheel drive in a single body length with a passenger-side sliding door. Buyers have a choice of two side-hinged rear doors or rear "Dutch" doors with a separate-opening tailgate. Seats for up to eight are optional. A cargo version also is available.

The sole powertrain is a 190-horsepower V-6 with automatic transmission. Dual air bags and anti-lock brakes are standard.

For 1998, Chevy adds two new exterior colors and says the clearcoat finish is changed to better withstand environmental etching. The new Passlock theft-deterrent system has been in use for several years in other GM products. It disables the starter for 10 minutes if anyone tries to start the car with anything but the ignition key. Changes to the automatic transmission include a new case designed to reduce noise and an electronically controlled clutch intended to improve efficiency.

PERFORMANCE Astro and Safari are better suited to heavy-duty work than are front-drive minivans. For example, Astro's 5500-pound trailer towing capacity is 2000 pounds more than that of the front-drive Chevrolet Venture minivan. The penalty for this brawn is a rough, bouncy ride that's less car-like than the front-drive minivans. Steering and handling aren't as nimble, either, though Asto doesn't feel as ponderous as a full-size van. It's noisier than sleeker car-based minivans, however, with high levels of road and wind noise at freeway speeds.

The V-6 and automatic transmission work together to provide fine acceleration and smooth shifts. Downshifts are prompt and passing power is very good. On the downside, the V-6 consumes lots of gas. Expect no better than 15 mpg in urban driving—less with the AWD models.

The all-wheel-drive system requires no input from the driver. It automatically sends power to the wheels with the most traction and is well worth considering if you live in the snowbelt.

ACCOMMODATIONS Entry/exit to the front seats is hampered by a tall step up and doorways that are narrow at the bottom. Once aboard, front-seat riders contend with uncomfortably narrow footwells. Head room is abundant throughout, and there's good passenger space in the middle and rear rows, though getting to the rear-most bench is difficult. Astro's seats aren't as easy to remove as the lighter modular seating in GM's front-drive minivans, but once out, there's plenty of cargo space. Unlike the swing-out rear doors, the optional dutch doors allow an unobstructed rear view, and include the convenience of lift-open glass and an available defogger.

The dashboard has a convenient layout with lots of built-in storage. All controls are within reach of both the driver and front passenger and are easy to operate. Chevrolet offers a dual sound system that allows front- and rear-seat passengers to listent to separate audio programming.

BUILD QUALITY Astro's interior is solidly assembled and has generally high-grade materials. Squeaks and rattles are minimal. The fit of the exterior panels is unexceptional, but Astro's new clearcoat process should improve the paint finish.

VALUE FOR THE MONEY Consider the Astro/Safari twins if you're looking for a minivan to haul cargo and handle light-duty towing. If you want one primarily for passenger use, go with alternatives such as the Venture, Dodge Caravan, Ford Windstar, or Plymouth Voyager.

SPECIFICATIONS

	3-door van
Wheelbase, in.	111.2
Overall length, in.	189.8
Overall width, in.	77.5
Overall height, in.	76.0
Curb weight, lbs.	4197
Cargo vol., cu. ft.	170.4
Fuel capacity, gals.	25.0
Seating capacity	8

Prices are accurate at time of publication; subject to manufacturer's changes.

	3-door van
Front head room, in.	39.2
Max. front leg room, in.	41.6
Rear head room, in.	37.9
Min. rear leg room, in.	36.5

RATINGS

	LT 2WD
Acceleration	4
Fuel economy	1
Ride quality	3
Steering/handling	3
Braking	3
Quietness	3
Driver seating	3
Instruments/controls	4
Room/comfort (front)	3
Room/comfort (rear)	4
Cargo room	5
Value for the money	3
Total	39

ENGINES

	ohv V-6
Size, liters/cu. in.	4.3/262
Horsepower @ rpm	190@ 4400
Torque (lbs./ft.) @ rpm	250@ 2800
Availability	S
EPA city/highway mpg	
4-speed OD automatic	16/21

PRICES

Chevrolet Astro	Retail Price	Dealer Invoice
2WD 3-door van	$19638	$17772
AWD 3-door van	21838	19763
Destination charge	585	585

STANDARD EQUIPMENT:

4.3-liter V-6 engine, 4-speed automatic transmission, anti-lock brakes, driver- and passenger-side air bags, front air conditioning, variable-assist power steering, 5-passenger seating (reclining high-back vinyl front bucket seats, 3-passenger bench seat), coolant-temperature and oil-pressure gauges, voltmeter, trip odometer, solar-control tinted glass, intermittent wipers, AM/FM radio, digital clock, dual manual outside mirrors, visor mirrors, remote fuel-door release, front and rear auxiliary power outlets, rear storage compartments, daytime running lamps, 215/75R15 tires.
AWD model has permanent 4-wheel drive.

OPTIONAL EQUIPMENT:

Major Packages

Preferred Equipment Group 2 (1SB)	263	226

Cruise control, tilt steering wheel, cargo net.

Preferred Equipment Group 3 (1SC)	1455	1251

Group 1SB plus power windows and door locks, dome and reading lamps, deep-tinted glass, 8-passenger seating (front bucket seats, second- and third-row bench seats), Seat Pkg. (cloth upholstery, front seat armrests, map pocket, manual driver-seat lumbar adjuster), floormats, bodyside moldings, styled steel wheels.

LS Preferred Equipment Group 4 (1SF)	1988	1710

LS Decor Group (cruise control, tilt steering wheel, 8-passenger seating, Seat Pkg., power door locks, power windows, deep-tinted glass, reading lamps, lower bodyside cladding, chrome-accent grille, cargo net, styled steel wheels, floormats).

LS Preferred Equipment Group 5 (1SG)	2628	2260

Group 1SF plus power mirrors, passenger-side underseat storage compartment, overhead console, illuminated visor mirrors, remote keyless entry, roof rack.

LS Preferred Equipment Group 6 (1SH)	3016	2594

Group 1SG plus 6-way power driver seat, alloy wheels.

	Retail Price	Dealer Invoice
LT Preferred Equipment Group 7 (1SK)	$4631	$3983

LT Decor Group (LS Decor Group plus deep-tinted side windows, power mirrors and windows, remote keyless entry, adjustable split second bench seat with fold-down center console, upgraded cloth upholstery, overhead console with compass and outside temperature indicator, leather-wrapped steering wheel, illuminated visor mirrors, striping, alloy wheels), 6-way power driver seat, roof rack.

Comfort and Convenience

Rear air conditioning	523	450
Rear heater	205	176
Dutch doors	364	313
ordered with LS or LT Decor Group	305	262

Includes rear wiper/washer and electric release.

7-passenger seating	969	833
ordered with Group 1SC	406	349
ordered with Group 1SF, 1SG, or 1SH	318	273
ordered with Group 1SK	NC	NC

Front and second-row bucket seats, third-row bench seat, Seat Pkg.

8-passenger seating	395	340

Front bucket seats, second- and third-row bench seats.

Manual lumbar adjusters for second-row bucket seats	100	86
6-way power driver seat	240	206

Requires Preferred Equipment Group and cloth upholstery.

6-way power passenger seat	240	206

Requires 6-way power driver seat. Requires Preferred Equipment Group.

Seat Pkg.	168	144

Front seat armrests, map pocket, manual driver-seat lumbar support. Requires cloth upholstery.

Leather seat trim	950	817

Requires LT Preferred Equipment Group 1SK.

Dual integrated child seats	240	206

Requires cloth upholstery. NA with Group 1 SK or 7-passenger seating.

Rear defogger	154	132

Requires dutch doors.

Power door locks	223	192
Leather-wrapped steering wheel, ordered w/Group 1SF, 1SG, or 1SH	54	46
Deep-tinted glass	290	249
Remote keyless entry	135	116

Base and base with Group 1SB require power door locks.

Power mirrors, ordered with Group 1SC or 1SF	98	84
Homelink garage-door opener, ordered with 1SG, 1SH, or 1SK	107	92
Cassette player	147	126
Cassette player w/automatic tone control	307	264

Requires Group 1SC, 1SF, 1SG, 1SH, or 1SK.

CD player w/automatic tone control	407	350

Requires Group 1SC, 1SF, 1SG, 1SH, or 1SK.

Cassette and CD players w/automatic tone control	507	436

Requires Group 1SC, 1SF, 1SG, 1SH, or 1SK.

Rear radio controls, ordered w/LS or LT Decor Group	158	136

Requires Group 1SF, 1SG, 1SH, or 1SK. Requires cassette player with automatic tone control or cassette and CD player w/automatic tone control.

Floormats	47	40
ordered with 7- or 8-passenger seating	69	59

Appearance and Miscellaneous

Chrome accent grille	150	129
Roof rack	126	108
Cold Climate Pkg.	46	40

Includes engine-block heater and coolant protection.

Bodyside moldings, base, base with Group 1SB	121	104
2-tone paint	NC	NC

Requires Group 1SF, 1SG, 1SH, or 1SK.

Rating Scale: 5-Excellent; 4-Above average; 3-Average; 2-Below average; 1-Poor

Special Purpose, Wheel and Tires

	Retail Price	Dealer Invoice
Locking differential	$252	$217
Touring Suspension Pkg., 2WD	306	263
Gas shock absorbers, rear stabilizer bar, 235/65R15 white outline letter tires.		
Trailering Special Equipment, heavy duty..............	309	266
Platform trailer hitch, 8-lead wiring harness.		
215/75R15 whitewall tires	60	52
NA with Group 1SH, 1SK, or alloy wheels.		
215/75R15 white outline letter tires........................	88	76
Alloy wheels	340	292
ordered with Group 1SC, 1SF, or 1SG	248	213
Chrome wheels	340	292
ordered with Group 1SC, 1SF, or 1SG	248	213
ordered with Group 1SH or 1SK	NC	NC
Styled steel wheels	92	79

CHEVROLET BLAZER

RECOMMENDED

Chevrolet Blazer LT 4WD 4-door

Rear- or 4-wheel-drive midsize sport-utility vehicle; similar to GMC Jimmy and Oldsmobile Bravada

Base price range: $21,663-$25,176. Built in Moraine, Ohio, and Linden, N.J.

Also consider: Ford Explorer, Jeep Cherokee, Nissan Pathfinder, Toyota 4Runner

FOR • Standard anti-lock brakes • Acceleration • Passenger and cargo room • Ride

AGAINST • Rear seat comfort • Fuel economy

A revised interior with Blazer's first passenger-side air bag and the addition of standard anti-lock 4-wheel disc brakes keynote functional changes to this popular SUV. Outside, styling is freshened with a new grille and front and rear bumpers, composite headlamps, step bumpers, and bodyside moldings. On the debit side, permanently engaged 4-wheel drive is no longer available.

Blazer is built from the same design as the GMC Jimmy and Oldsmobile Bravada, but differs in styling and some features. It's available as a 2- and 4-door wagon with 2- or 4-wheel drive. A drop-down tailgate with a separate swing-up rear window is standard. A one-piece, top-hinged liftgate with independently opening glass is available on 4-door models at no extra cost.

All Blazers use a 190-horsepower 4.3-liter V-6. Automatic transmission is standard and a 5-speed manual is optional on 2-doors. Last year's permanently engaged 4WD system was an option on 4-door models. The surviving system can be shifted between 2- and 4-wheel drive on the fly via a dashboard button but is not designed for use on dry pavement. Among trim levels available on 2-door Blazers is the ZR2 off-road package that adds a raised suspension.

Blazer's revamped dashboard inclues new controls for the heating and air conditioning system, new gauges, and a glove box below the passenger-side air bag. The new split rear bench seat has self-stowing outboard headrests that do not require removal when the seatback is folded down.

PERFORMANCE Blazer feels energetic because its V-6 makes the lion's share of its power where most drivers need it—at low speeds. Acceleration is lively from a standstill and mid-range passing power is strong. The engine is generally quiet and smooth except on cold mornings, when it's loud and rough until it warms up. The automatic transmission changes gears smoothly during acceleration and downshifts promptly for passing.

Fuel economy is no bargain. In a 21,000-mile long-term test of a 4-door 4WD Blazer we netted an average of 15.2 mpg, with a high of 22.4 mpg on the highway and a low of 12 mpg in city driving. This is typical of sport-utility vehicles, though we've averaged below 12 mpg with rival V-8 models.

Abandoning permanently engaged 4WD puts Blazer at a competitive disadvantage against the Ford Explorer and Jeep Grand Cherokee, both of which offer 4WD systems that can be used on dry pavement. Though it's less convenient than permanent 4WD, Blazer's part-time system can be engaged or disengaged while underway and does a fine job in snow.

The optional "premium ride" suspension allows Blazer to absorb bumps with less harshness than the Explorer, and Blazer handles better—more like a car than a truck. Steering feel is firm, body lean is moderate in turns, and overall balance is good. The brakes on our long-term tester were a continuous source of aggravation because the pedal had a spongy feel and suffered excessive travel. Overall stopping ability was only adequate. Road and wind noise are moderate at highway speeds, making Blazer one of the quieter-cruising SUVs.

ACCOMMODATIONS Blazer and Jimmy have less interior room than the Explorer, but there's ample space for four adults and just enough width to squeeze a fifth person into the middle of the rear seat. With the new self-stowing headrests, Blazer matches Explorer for split rear seats that easily fold to increase cargo space. On both vehicles, however, stiff rear seatbacks are too short to provide much shoulder support.

Thanks to spare-tire stowage below the rear underbody, cargo room is good with the rear seatback up and generous with it folded. We're pleased to be given a choice of two tailgate styles. We prefer the liftgate because you don't have to stretch over the drop-down tailgate to reach into the cargo hold, and it retains the convenient independently opening glass.

Blazer drivers enjoy the high seating position that attracts so many people to SUVs, but it's still hard to judge where the corners of the vehicle are when parking. In addition, the center and rear roof pillars are thick, and the dark tint of the rear windows cuts outward visibility at night.

A low step-in height makes getting in and out of the Blazer's front seats easy. As expected, it's difficult to access the rear seat in the 2-door model, but narrow rear doors make it harder than it should be on 4-door versions.

BUILD QUALITY During its year-long test period, our Blazer required a new fuel pump and starter and repairs to a leaky cooling system—all covered by warranty. The interior and exterior held up well, and the body felt solid at the end of the test, though the black paint did not retain a uniform luster.

VALUE FOR THE MONEY Blazer's biggest assets are ride comfort and low noise levels. It clearly beats the Explorer in those areas, and it has a much stronger base engine. Explorer counters with more convenient 4WD and an optional V-8 engine, giving it the edge overall. Blazer is still a good choice and, when similarly equipped, can be less expensive than its Ford rival.

RATINGS

	2-dr. 4WD	4-dr. 4WD
Acceleration	4	4
Fuel economy	2	2
Ride quality	3	4
Steering/handling	3	3
Braking	3	3
Quietness	3	3
Driver seating	4	4
Instruments/controls	4	4
Room/comfort (front)	4	4
Room/comfort (rear)	2	3
Cargo room	4	5
Value for the money	4	4
Total	**40**	**43**

SPECIFICATIONS

	2-door wagon	4-door wagon
Wheelbase, in.	100.5	107.0
Overall length, in.	176.8	183.3

Prices are accurate at time of publication; subject to manufacturer's changes.

	2-door wagon	4-door wagon
Overall width, in.	67.8	67.8
Overall height, in.	64.9	64.3
Curb weight, lbs.	3515	3685
Cargo vol., cu. ft.	66.9	74.1
Fuel capacity, gals.	19.0	18.0
Seating capacity	4	6
Front head room, in.	39.6	39.6
Max. front leg room, in.	42.5	42.4
Rear head room, in.	38.2	38.2
Min. rear leg room, in.	36.3	36.3

ENGINES

	ohv V-6
Size, liters/cu. in.	4.3/262
Horsepower @ rpm	190@4400
Torque (lbs./ft.) @ rpm	250@2800
Availability	S

EPA city/highway mpg

4-speed OD automatic	17/23
5-speed OD manual	18/25

PRICES

Chevrolet Blazer	Retail Price	Dealer Invoice
2-door wagon, 2WD	$21663	$19605
2-door wagon, 4WD	23651	21404
4-door wagon, 2WD	23188	20985
4-door wagon, 4WD	25176	22784
Destination charge	515	515

STANDARD EQUIPMENT:

2-door: 4.3-liter V-6 engine, 4-speed automatic transmission, driver- and passenger-side air bags, anti-lock 4-wheel disc brakes, daytime running lights, power steering, air conditioning, cloth front bucket seats with manual lumbar adjustment and console, split folding rear bench seat, trip odometer, coolant-temperature and oil-pressure gauges, voltmeter, automatic day/night rearview mirror, AM/FM radio, digital clock, automatic headlights, cupholders, intermittent wipers, floormats, cargo-area tiedown hooks, Passlock theft-deterrent system, solar-control tinted glass, dual outside mirrors, bright grille, 5-lead trailer wiring harness, Smooth Ride suspension, 205/75R15 all-season tires, 4WD adds Insta-Trac part-time 4WD, electronic-shift transfer case, tow hooks.

4-door adds: cloth 60/40 split front bench seat with storage armrest, **4WD** adds: Insta-Trac part-time 4WD, electronic-shift transfer case, tow hooks.

OPTIONAL EQUIPMENT:
Major Packages

	Retail Price	Dealer Invoice
Preferred Equipment Group 1SB	643	553
Manufacturer's discount price, (credit)	(57)	(49)

Cassette player, tilt steering wheel, cruise control.

LS Preferred Equipment Group 1SC, 2-door	2855	2455
Manufacturer's discount price	1455	1251

Group 1SB plus cassette player with automatic tone control, map lights, illuminated visor mirrors, leather-wrapped steering wheel, overhead console, tachometer, 2 power outlets, power windows and door locks, heated power mirrors, deep-tinted tailgate glass, rear defogger, rear wiper/washer, power tailgate release, color-keyed grille and front bumper, touring suspension, 235/70R15 tires, alloy wheels.

LS preferred Equipment Group 1SC, 4-door	3556	3058
Manufacturer's discount price	2156	1854

Group 1SB plus cassette player with bucket seats, automatic tone control, map lights, illuminated visor mirrors, leather-wrapped steering wheel, overhead console, tachometer, 2 power outlets, power windows and door locks, heated power mirrors, liftgate, deep-tinted tailgate glass, rear defogger, rear wiper/washer, power tailgate release, color-keyed grille and front bumper, body side moldings, rear cargo shade, Premium Ride Suspension Pkg., 235/70R15 tires, alloy wheels.

LS Preferred Equipment Group 1SD, 2-door	3490	3001

	Retail Price	Dealer Invoice
Manufacturer's discount price	$2090	$1797

2-door Group 1SC plus 6-way driver seat, remote keyless entry, Homelink universal garage door opener.

LT Preferred Equipment Group 1SD, 4-door	5529	4859
Manufacturer's discount price, 4-door	4129	3551

4-door Group 1SC plus 6-way power driver seat, front power lumbar adjustors, leather upholstery, remote keyless entry, Homelink universal garage door opener, front air dam, fog lights.

Convenience Pkg.	395	340

Cruise control, tilt steering wheel.

Convenience Group, 2-door	535	460
4-door	710	611

Power windows, door locks, and mirrors.

Rear-Window Convenience Pkg.	322	277

Rear defogger, remote tailgate release, rear wiper/washer.

ZR2 Wide Stance Performance Pkg., 2-door 4WD	1850	1591

Heavy-duty wide stance chassis, heavy-duty suspension, Bilstein shock absorbers, Shield Pkg. heavy-duty differential gears and axles, fender flares, 31X10.5R15 tires, full-size spare. Requires LS Group, limited slip differential. NA w/Trailering Special Equipment.

Off-road suspension, 2-door 4WD	634	545
2-door 4WD with Group 1SC or 1SD	245	211

Includes gas shock absorbers, uprated torsion bar, jounce stabilizer bar, full-size spare tire, 235/75R15 on/off-road white outline letter tires (w/o Group 1SC or 1SD).

Trailering Special Equipment	210	181

Includes platform hitch, heavy-duty flasher. 2WD models require automatic transmission.

Powertrains

5-speed manual transmission, 2-door (credit)	(890)	(765)

Requires tachometer.

Locking differential	252	217

Comfort and Convenience

6-way power driver seat, w/Group 1SC	240	206

Requires remote keyless entry.

Heated front seats, 4-door	225	194

Requires leather upholstery.

Cloth upholstery, 4-door w/LT Group (credit)	(600)	(516)
Power sunroof	695	598

Requires overhead console.

Homelink universal garage-door opener	130	112

Includes trip computer, compass, outside-temperature indicator. Requires overhead console.

Remote keyless entry system	150	129

Requires Group 1SC and 6-way power driver seat.

Overhead console	147	126

NA with bench seat. Requires power sunroof when ordered without a Preferred Equipment Group or with Group 1SB.

Tachometer	59	51
Cassette player	122	105
CD player	100	86

Requires Group 1SC or 1SD.

Cassette/CD player	200	172

Requires Group 1SC or 1SD.

Rear cargo shade, 2-door 4WD with LS Decor Group	69	59

Requires exterior spare-tire carrier.

Appearance and Miscellaneous

Roof rack	126	108
Fog lights, 2WD, 4WD 4-door	115	99
Rear liftgate, 4-door	NC	NC

Requires ZQ6 convenience group and rear-window convenience pkg. when ordered without a Preferred Equipment Group or with Group 1SB.

Custom 2-tone paint, 4-door	197	169

Requires LS Decor Group or LT Decor Group.

Cold Climate Pkg.	89	77

Includes heavy-duty battery, engine block heater.

Rating Scale: 5-Excellent; 4-Above average; 3-Average; 2-Below average; 1-Poor

Special Purpose, Wheels and Tires

	Retail Price	Dealer Invoice
Shield Pkg., 4WD	$126	$108
Includes transfer case and front differential skid plates, fuel tank and steering linkage shields. NA with all-wheel drive.		
Heavy-duty battery	56	48
Smooth Riding suspension (credit)	(275)	(237)
Requires Group 1SC or 1SD.		
Touring suspension	197	169
w/Group 1SC or1SD	NC	NC
Includes gas shock absorbers.		
Premium suspension, 4-door	197	169
Includes gas shock absorbers.		
Exterior spare-tire carrier, 2-door 4WD	159	137
Includes full-size spare tire and cover.		
Alloy wheels	280	241
205/75R15 all-season white letter tires.................	121	104
235/70R15 all-season tires	192	165
235/70R15 all-season white letter tires.................	325	280
w/Group 1SC or1SD	133	114
235/75R15 on/off-road white letter tires, 4WD......	335	288
4WD w/Preferred Equipment Group....................	143	123
Requires off-road or touring suspension. Includes exterior spare-tire carrier.		

CHEVROLET CAMARO

BUDGET BUY

Chevrolet Camaro Z28 hatchback

Rear-wheel-drive sports and GT; similar to Pontiac Firebird

Base price range: $16,625-$27,450. Built in Canada.

Also consider: Chevrolet Corvette, Ford Mustang, Mitsubishi Eclipse

FOR • Standard anti-lock brakes • Acceleration (Z28) • Handling

AGAINST • Fuel economy (Z28) • Ride (Z28) • Rear seat room • Wet weather traction (without traction control) • Rear visibility

Chevrolet's pony car out paces the Ford Mustang in performance-per-dollar, but can't catch its arch rival in the sales race. Chevy fights back for '98 with a restyled nose and—you guessed it—even more power.

The rear-drive Camaro comes as a 2-door hatchback or 2-door convertible, both in base or Z28 trim. Dual air bags, 4-wheel anti-lock disc brakes, and air conditioning are standard. Convertibles have a power-operated top that features a full headliner and glass rear window with electric defogger. Pontiac's Firebird shares Camaro's mechanical components but has different styling.

Camaro's new nose comes courtesy of a fresh fascia, composite reflector headlamps, and a restyled hood and fenders. Underhood, the Z28 gets a version of the Corvette's aluminum V-8 with 305 horsepower, 20 more than last year's cast-iron V-8. The base model has a 200-horsepower V-6. A 5-speed manual transmission is standard with the V-6 engine and a 6-speed manual is standard with the V-8. Automatic is optional with both. Traction control is optional on the Z28.

The Corvette-based V-8 also is new for the Z28-based SS package; it makes 320 horsepower through special tuning. Other SS features include a functional hood scoop, larger tires, a special rear spoiler, and an upgraded suspension.

PERFORMANCE With its V-8, the Z28 has outstanding acceleration with either transmission and easily out-powers the rival Mustang GT. Yet, driven gently, it's relatively docile and easy to live with. Our last test of an automatic-transmission Z28 coupe included drives in several snow storms, where the optional traction control proved invaluable. Fuel economy was less satisfying; just 15.1 mpg in mostly city driving.

With 200 horsepower, the base-model's V-6 outmuscles Mustang's base V-6 and nearly matches the acceleration of the Mustang GT. It's also cheaper to insure than V-8 models and gets better mileage, averaging 18.6 mpg with a 5-speed in our last test.

With either Camaro, body lean is minimal, steering sharp, and grip ample. On the downside, the Z28's high-performance tires generate lots of noise at highway speeds and add to the harsh ride. The suspension has been softened this year, yet there's still a tendency for the stiffly sprung back end to skip sideways on patched pavement. The brakes have strong stopping power and good pedal modulation.

We expect lots of mechanical ruckus in a car like this, but the Z28's exhaust rumble is so prominent as to be tiresome.

ACCOMMODATIONS You'll never mistake Camaro for a family car. Entry/exit into the low cockpit is difficult, and the wide, heavy doors require lots of room to open. Wide rear roof pillars block the driver's view when backing up or changing lanes, and the low seating position further hurts visibility. Rear leg room, limited to begin with, is nearly nonexistent if the front seats are more than halfway back.

The rear of the cargo area is deep enough for two sets of golf clubs and the rear seat folds to create a floor, but a high liftover makes loading and unloading difficult.

No gauges are obstructed, the radio and climate controls are easy to reach, and the power window and door lock switches are conveniently mounted on the driver's armrest. But the turn-signal stalk also governs the cruise control system, wipers and washers, and high-beam headlights. That's too many functions for one control.

BUILD QUALITY Our test cars had minimal squeaks and rattles, despite jarring suspensions. The gaps between body panels were even, and paint was smooth. In exchange for open-air fun, the convertible's body flexes over bumps more than most modern ragtops.

VALUE FOR THE MONEY Think of the Z28 as a Corvette with a back seat. SS models are expensive, but deliver on their promise of exceptional performance. At around $16,625, the base Camaro is an excellent sporty-car value that should have substantially lower operating costs than the Z28.

RATINGS

	Base	Z28
Acceleration	4	5
Fuel economy	2	1
Ride quality	3	2
Steering/handling	4	5
Braking	4	4
Quietness	2	2
Driver seating	3	3
Instruments/controls	4	4
Room/comfort (front)	4	4
Room/comfort (rear)	2	2
Cargo room	3	3
Value for the money	3	3
Total	**38**	**38**

SPECIFICATIONS

	2-door hatchback	2-door convertible
Wheelbase, in.	101.1	101.1
Overall length, in.	193.5	193.5
Overall width, in.	74.1	74.1
Overall height, in.	51.3	52.0
Curb weight, lbs.	3331	3468
Cargo vol., cu. ft.	12.9	7.6
Fuel capacity, gals.	15.5	15.5
Seating capacity...........................	4	4

Prices are accurate at time of publication; subject to manufacturer's changes.

	2-door hatchback	2-door convertible
Front head room, in.	37.2	38.0
Max. front leg room, in.	42.9	42.9
Rear head room, in.	35.3	39.0
Min. rear leg room, in.	26.8	26.8

ENGINES

	ohv V-6	ohv V-8	ohv V-8
Size, liters/cu. in.	3.8/231	5.7/346	5.7/346
Horsepower @ rpm	200@ 5200	305@ 5200	320@ 5200
Torque (lbs./ft.) @ rpm	225@ 4000	335@ 4000	345@ 4400
Availability	S[1]	S[2]	S[3]

EPA city/highway mpg

4-speed OD automatic	19/29	17/25	17/25
5-speed OD manual	19/30		
6-speed OD manual		18/27	18/27

1. Base. 2. Z28. 3. SS.

PRICES

Chevrolet Camaro

	Retail Price	Dealer Invoice
Base 2-door hatchback	$16625	$15212
Base 2-door convertible	22125	20244
Z28 2-door hatchback	20470	18730
Z28 2-door convertible	27450	25117
Destination charge	525	525

SS standard equipment, options, and prices unavailable at time of publication.

STANDARD EQUIPMENT:

Base: 3.8-liter V-6 engine, 5-speed manual transmission, driver- and passenger-side air bags, anti-lock 4-wheel disc brakes, daytime running lamps, air conditioning, power steering, tilt steering wheel, cloth reclining front bucket seats with 4-way adjustable driver seat, center storage console with cupholders and auxiliary power outlet, folding rear seatback, automatic headlights, intermittent wipers, AM/FM/cassette, digital clock, day/night rearview mirror with dual reading lights, tachometer, voltmeter, oil-pressure and coolant-temperature gauges, trip odometer, low-oil-level indicator, visor mirrors, front floormats, solar-control tinted glass, left remote and right manual sport mirrors, Pass-Key theft-deterrent system, rear spoiler, 215/60R16 all-season tires, wheel covers.

Base convertible adds: rear defogger, premium speakers, power folding top, 3-piece hard boot with storage bag.

Z28 adds to Base hatchback: 5.7-liter V-8 engine, 6-speed manual transmission or 4-speed automatic transmission, limited-slip differential, 2-way adjustable driver seat, low-coolant indicator system, performance ride and handling suspension, black roof and mirrors, 235/55R16 tires, alloy wheels.

Z28 convertible adds: rear defogger, premium speakers, 4-way adjustable driver seat, rear floormats, power folding top, 3-piece hard boot with storage bag, color-keyed power mirrors.

OPTIONAL EQUIPMENT:

Major Packages

Preferred Equipment Group 1SB, Base hatchback	565	486

Includes cruise control, remote hatch release, power door lock, fog lights.

Preferred Equipment Group 1SC, Base hatchback	1231	1059

Pkg. 1SB plus power windows, power mirrors, leather-wrapped steering wheel, remote keyles entry, illuminated entry, theft-deterrent system.

Preferred Equipment Group 1SE,		
Base convertible	1306	1123

Includes cruise control, remote decklid release, power door locks and windows, power mirrors, leather-wrapped steering wheel, remote keyless entry, illuminated entry, theft-deterrent system, bodyside moldings, rear floormats, fog lights.

Preferred Equipment Group 1SG/H,		
Z28 hatchback	1576	1355
Z28 convertible	NC	NC

Includes cruise control, power door locks and windows, power mirrors, 6-way power driver seat, remote hatch/decklid release, leather-wrapped steering wheel, rear floormats, remote keyless entry, illuminated entry, theft-deterrent system, bodyside moldings, fog lights.

	Retail Price	Dealer Invoice
Appearance Pkg., Base	$1755	$1509
Z28	1480	1272

Front and rear body moldings, 235/55R16 tires (Base), alloy wheels (Base).

Performance Handling Pkg., Base	225	194

Limited slip differential, performance axle ratio (w/automatic transmission), dual exhaust, sport steering ratio. Requires option pkg., 235/55R16 tires, and alloy wheels.

Performance Pkg., Z28 hatchback	1175	1011

Larger stabilizer bars, stiffer springs and bushings, dual adjustable shock absorbers, power steering fluid cooler. Requires 245/50ZR16 performance tires, performance axle ratio w/automatic transmission. NA w/removable roof panels.

Powertrains

4-speed automatic transmission, Base	815	701
Traction control, Z28	450	387

Requires Preferred Equipment Group.

Performance axle ratio, Z28	300	258

Requires automatic transmission and 245/50ZR16 tires.

Comfort and Convenience

AM/FM/cassette with automatic tone control,		
hatchback	350	301
convertible	215	185
AM/FM/CD with automatic tone control, hatchback	450	387
convertible	315	271
12-disc CD changer	595	512

Requires AM/FM/cassette with automatic tone control.

Remote keyless entry, Base hatchback	225	194

Includes theft-deterrent system. Requires Preferred Equipment Group 1SB.

6-way power driver seat, Base	270	232
Leather bucket seats	499	429

Z28 hatchback requires preferred equipment group.

Rear defogger, hatchback	170	146
Removable roof panels, hatchback	995	856

Includes locks, storage provisions, and sun shade. NA Performance Pkg.

Rear floormats, Base hatchback	15	13

Appearance and Miscellaneous

Engine-block heater	20	17
Color-keyed bodyside moldings, Base hatchback	60	52
235/55R16 tires, Base	132	114

Requires alloy wheels.

245/50ZR16 performance tires, Z28	225	194
245/50ZR16 all-season performance tires, Z28	225	194
Alloy wheels, Base	275	237

Requires 235/55R16 tires.

Chrome alloy wheels, Base	775	667
Z28	500	430

CHEVROLET CAVALIER

Chevrolet Cavalier LS 4-door

Front-wheel-drive subcompact; similar to Pontiac Sunfire

Base price range: $11,610-$19,410. Built in Lordstown, Ohio; Lansing, Mich; and Mexico.

Also consider: Chevrolet Prizm, Dodge Neon, Ford Escort, Hyundai Elantra

---

Rating Scale: 5-Excellent; 4-Above average; 3-Average; 2-Below average; 1-Poor

FOR • Standard anti-lock brakes • Fuel economy • Acceleration (2.4-liter) • Visibility

AGAINST • Rear head room • Seat comfort

Cavalier's convertible goes full-sport for 1998, switching from a luxury-oriented LS model to the performance-minded Z24 model. This is Chevrolet's best-selling car and comes as a 2-door coupe, a 4-door sedan, and a 2-door convertible with a standard power top. The sporty Z24 version had previously been available only as a coupe, with the convertible confined to the LS trim level.

All Cavaliers have a 4-cylinder engine. Base, RS, and LS versions use a 115-horsepower overhead-valve 2.2-liter. Internal revisions designed to make it run smoother result in a loss of 5 horsepower for '98. Standard on the Z24 and optional on LS models is a 150-horsepower dual-overhead camshaft 2.4-liter. Manual transmission is standard on base, RS, and Z24 Cavaliers. A 3-speed automatic is optional on the base version, while a 4-speed automatic is standard on the LS and optional on other Cavaliers. Traction control is included with the 4-speed automatic. Dual air bags and anti-lock brakes are standard on all.

Among other changes for 1998, Chevy says a redesigned manual transmission shifter provides a sturdier feel, and the LS sedan is available with a rear spoiler. Cavalier shares its mechanical design with the Pontiac Sunfire, but differs in styling.

PERFORMANCE This year's base engine is indeed quieter, and the loss of 5 horsepower doesn't seem to affect performance. Acceleration is still adequate, and while the automatic tranmission provides smooth, prompt shifts, it leaves the engine with no power to spare.

The 2.4-liter provides noticeably faster acceleration and workes better with automatic than many twin-cam fours. But it becomes noisy when pushed hard before settling down to a peaceful level at cruising speeds. In any Cavalier, wind and road noise are evident on the highway, but no more than in most subcompact cars.

We averaged 23.8 mph in a base Cavalier sedan with automatic transmission. That's not great given this car's economy mission, but nearly all our driving was in rush-hour commuting. Expect more than 30 mpg in highway cruising.

Base, RS, and LS Cavaliers corner with adequate grip and moderate body lean, but ride quality is above the subcompact-class average. Most bumps and ruts are soaked up with little trouble, though they're often accompanied by a loud thump. Z24 models ride more harshly in exchange for an improvement in handling.

Braking performance is good. The pedal is firm and the brakes engage smoothly, with the anti-lock feature kicking in quickly in hard stops on wet pavement.

ACCOMMODATIONS Cavalier's interior is as roomy and accommodating as that of most any competitor. Head room is generous in front, though that's partly because the front bucket seats are mounted so low that you almost fall into them. Still, shorter drivers on our staff reported they could easily see over the dashboard. Visibility also is good to the sides and rear.

Rear leg room is adequate for adults. The back seat isn't wide enough to hold more than two grownups, but three children fit comfortably.

The dashboard holds clear gauges and audio and climate controls that are easily reached while driving. Interior storage is ample. The center console has open and covered bins and two cupholders, the front doors have small map pockets, and the dashboard has a large glovebox.

The trunk opening is too small to easily load large objects, but otherwise cargo space is more than adequate and the rear seatback folds for extra room, though it can't be locked to separate trunk and interior.

BUILD QUALITY Smooth paint and neatly applied trim on our most-recent test car gave the exterior a pleasing appearance. The dashboard has a padded top—unusual for this price class—but also some flimsy plastic trim. Molded plastic door panels are an obvious cost-cutting measure.

VALUE FOR THE MONEY Cavalier doesn't match the refine-

ment of the Toyota Corolla or the fun-to-drive character of the Dodge/Plymouth Neon. However, it's without glaring faults and offers dual air bags and anti-lock brakes at a price just over $12,000 including destination charges.

RATINGS

	Base 4-dr.	RS 2-dr.	LS 4-dr.	Z24 conv.
Acceleration	2	2	2	4
Fuel economy	4	4	4	4
Ride quality	3	3	3	3
Steering/handling	3	3	3	4
Braking	4	4	4	4
Quietness	3	3	3	3
Driver seating	3	3	3	3
Instruments/controls	4	4	4	4
Room/comfort (front)	3	3	3	3
Room/comfort (rear)	3	2	3	2
Cargo room	3	3	3	2
Value for the money	5	4	4	4
Total	**40**	**38**	**39**	**40**

SPECIFICATIONS

	2-door coupe	2-door convertible	4-door sedan
Wheelbase, in.	104.1	104.1	104.1
Overall length, in.	180.7	180.3	180.7
Overall width, in.	68.7	67.4	67.9
Overall height, in.	53.0	53.9	54.7
Curb weight, lbs.	2584	2899	2630
Cargo vol., cu. ft.	13.2	10.5	13.2
Fuel capacity, gals.	15.2	15.2	15.2
Seating capacity	5	4	5
Front head room, in.	37.6	38.1	38.9
Max. front leg room, in.	42.3	42.4	42.3
Rear head room, in.	36.6	37.6	37.2
Min. rear leg room, in.	32.7	32.6	34.4

ENGINES

	ohv I-4	dohc I-4
Size, liters/cu. in.	2.2/134	2.4/146
Horsepower @ rpm	115@ 5000	150@ 5600
Torque (lbs./ft.) @ rpm	135@ 3600	155@ 4400
Availability	S¹	S²
EPA city/highway mpg		
3-speed automatic	24/31	
4-speed OD automatic	25/34	22/32
5-speed OD manual	25/37	22/33

1. Base, RS, LS. 2. Z24; optional, LS.

PRICES

Chevrolet Cavalier	Retail Price	Dealer Invoice
Base 2-door notchback	$11610	$10855
Base 4-door sedan	11810	11042
RS 2-door notchback	12870	12033
LS 4-door sedan	14250	13324
Z24 2-door notchback	15710	14689
Z24 2-door convertible	19410	18148
Destination charge	500	500

STANDARD EQUIPMENT:

Base: 2.2-liter 4-cylinder engine, 5-speed manual transmission, driver- and passenger-side air bags, anti-lock brakes, daytime running lights, power steering, cloth and vinyl reclining front bucket seats, folding rear seat, storage console with armrest, AM/FM radio, digital clock, intermittent wipers, tinted glass, left remote and right manual mirrors, theft-deterrent system, 195/70R14 tires, wheel covers.

RS adds: cruise control, tilt steering wheel, easy-entry front passenger seat, tachometer, trip odometer, visor mirrors, variable intermittent wipers, remote decklid release, floormats, trunk net, color-keyed fascias and bodyside moldings, front mudguards, rear decklid spoiler, 195/65R15 tires.

LS adds to Base: 4-speed automatic transmission, traction control, tilt steering wheel, cruise control, air conditioning, cloth upholstery, tachometer, trip odometer, cassette player, digital clock, visor mirrors, front reading lamps, variable intermittent wipers, remote decklid release, floormats, trunk net, color-keyed fascias and bodyside

Prices are accurate at time of publication; subject to manufacturer's changes.

moldings, front mud guards, 195/65R15 tires.

Z24 adds: 2.4-liter DOHC 4-cylinder engine, 5-speed manual transmission, easy-entry front passenger seat, power windows, power door locks, power mirrors, power top (convertible), rear defogger (convertible), daul map lights, sport suspension, rear decklid spoiler, fog lights, 205/55R16 tires, alloy wheels, deletes 4-speed automatic transmission, traction control, and mudguards.

OPTIONAL EQUIPMENT:

	Retail Price	Dealer Invoice
Major Packages		
Preferred Equipment Group 1, Base 2-door	$515	$464
Base 4-door	498	448
Remote decklid release, variable intermittent wipers, visor mirrors, color-keyed fascias and body moldings, front mudguards, cargo net, floormats, 195/65R15 tires, special wheel covers. 2-door adds easy-entry front passenger seat.		
Preferred Equipment Group 2, Base 2-door	990	881
Group 1 plus cruise control, tilt steering wheel, power mirrors.		
Preferred Equipment Group 1, RS	714	643
LS	819	737
Power windows and door locks, remote keyless entry, power mirrors, power decklid release.		
Powertrains		
2.4-liter DOHC 4-cylinder engine, LS......................	450	405
3-speed automatic transmission, Base	600	540
NA with Preferred Equipment Group 2.		
4-speed automatic transmission, Base, RS, Z24....	780	702
Includes traction control. Base 2-door requires Preferred Equipment Group 1.		
Comfort and Convenience		
Air conditioning, Base, RS	795	716
Adjustable lumbar support, convertible	50	45
Requires vinyl bucket seats.		
Rear defogger	180	162
Std. convertible.		
Power sunroof, 2-door notchback	595	535
Includes mirror-mounted front map light. Base requires Preferred Equipment Group.		
Power door locks, Base 2-door, RS	220	198
Base 4-door, LS..	260	234
AM/FM/cassette, Base, RS	165	149
AM/FM/cassette with automatic tone control,		
Base, RS..	220	198
LS, Z24	55	50
Includes premium speakers.		
AM/FM CD player with automatic tone control,		
Base, RS..	320	288
LS, Z24	155	140
Includes premium speakers.		
Appearance and Miscellaneous		
Rear spoiler, LS..	125	113
Alloy wheels, RS, LS...	295	263

CHEVROLET C/K1500

RECOMMENDED

Chevrolet K1500 Silverado w/optional third door

Rear- or 4-wheel-drive full-size pickup; similar to GMC Sierra 1500

Base price range: $14,930-$26,099. Built in Arlington, Tex.; Ft. Wayne, Ind.; Pontiac, Mich.; and Canada.

Also consider: Dodge Ram 1500, Ford F-150, Toyota T100

FOR • Standard anti-lock brakes • Acceleration (V-8 engines) • Cargo and towing ability

AGAINST • Fuel economy (V-8 engines) • Ride quality

Chevrolet makes few changes to the 1998 edition of its full-size pickup as it prepares an all-new replacement for the 1999 model year. GMC's version, badged the Sierra, also is slated for a '99 redesign.

Called the C/K, Chevy's truck comes in three series, with designations based on payload capacity: 1500 for a half-ton rating; 2500 for three-quarter ton; 3500 for one ton. This report discusses only the 1500 series.

Regular- and extended-cab models are offered and both are available with a "Fleetside" slab-sided cargo bed or a "Sportside" flared-fender bed. Beds come in 6.5- and 8-foot lengths. Rear-drive models have a "C" prefix and 4-wheel-drive models a "K" prefix.

A swing-open passenger-side rear door is optional on C/K1500 extended-cab short-bed models. The door is available only with the top-line Silverado equipment.

A 3-place front bench seat is standard. Front buckets are optional. Extended-cab models get a 3-place rear bench. Dual air bags are standard on models below 8600 pounds gross vehicle weight, which includes all 1500s. A dashboard switch can deactivate the passenger-side air bag when a rear-facing infant seat is used. Anti-lock brakes and daytime running lights are standard.

The base engine is a 200-horsepower V-6. Two gas V-8s are available on the 1500-series: a 5.0-liter with 230 horsepower and a 5.7-liter with 255 horsepower. Two 6.5-liter turbocharged diesel V-8s are optional, one making 180 horsepower and the other 195. Manual transmission is standard, and a 4-speed automatic is optional. K models have GM's Insta-Trac on-demand 4WD, a part-time, shift on-the-fly system not for use on dry pavement. Maximum towing weight is 7500 pounds for 1500-series models.

Changes for 1998 include the addition of GM's PassLock theft-deterrent system. The system disables the vehicle for ten minutes if anything other then the key is used to start the truck. Other changes include new exterior colors and changes to the automatic transmission designed to increase its durability.

PERFORMANCE We're leery of doing much heavy work with the base V-6, though it feels adequate with the manual transmission. The 5.0-liter V-8 is powerful enough for routine use but not the best choice if you do much towing or heavy hauling. The 5.7-liter is among the best V-8s in the industry. It furnishes strong acceleration and has the muscle for heavy-duty work. It's our engine of choice in the C/K line. Both V-8s, however, will guzzle lots of gas; expect less than 15 mpg in urban driving.

Steering is firm and natural feeling and ride quality is tolerable, but the more you raise the payload capacity, the more bouncing you'll experience with an empty cargo bed. The brake pedal on several of our test C/Ks has had a mushy feel, reducing our confidence in overall braking performace.

ACCOMMODATIONS These pickups have wide, spacious cabs with ample room in front for even the largest occupants. Regular-cab models don't have as much room for storing items behind the seats as the regular-cab F-150 or Dodge Ram. As with all big pickups, the rear seat on extended-cab C/Ks is wide, but the seatback is uncomfortably vertical and there's little knee room, so it's not the place to ride on a cross-country journey. The extended-cab's rear door is a convenience, but it's available only with a V-8 engine and automatic transmission so you have to spend a lot to get one.

The dashboard has unobstructed gauges, large controls for the headlamps and climate systems, and audio controls mounted within easy reach of the driver. The optional center armrest has a roomy and versatile storage compartment, but the lid is cumbersome to open while driving.

BUILD QUALITY The last Chevy K1500 we tested was well assembled, free of squeaks and rattles, and had excellent exterior fit and finish.

Rating Scale: 5-Excellent; 4-Above average; 3-Average; 2-Below average; 1-Poor

VALUE FOR THE MONEY Chevy's C/K pickup perennially finishes second to Ford's F-Series as the top-selling vehicle—car or truck—in the United States. Both the F-Series and the Dodge Ram are newer designs with more modern interior features, but the Chevy pickups are still highly competitive in ride quality, price, and equipment.

RATINGS

	Reg. cab V-6	Ext. cab 5.7 V-8
Acceleration	3	4
Fuel economy	2	1
Ride quality	2	2
Steering/handling	2	2
Braking	3	3
Quietness	3	3
Driver seating	4	4
Instruments/controls	4	4
Room/comfort (front)	5	5
Room/comfort (rear)	—	2
Cargo room	1	3
Value for the money	4	4
Total	**33**	**37**

SPECIFICATIONS

	Reg. cab short bed	Reg. cab long bed	Ext. cab short bed	Ext. cab long bed
Wheelbase, in.	117.5	131.5	141.5	155.5
Overall length, in.	194.5	213.4	218.5	237.4
Overall width, in.	76.8	76.8	76.8	76.8
Overall height, in.	70.8	70.0	70.6	70.1
Curb weight, lbs.	3869	4293	4140	4387
Maximum payload, lbs.	2030	2755	2040	1656
Fuel capacity, gals.	25.0	34.0	25.0	34.0
Seating capacity	3	3	6	6
Front head room, in.	49.9	39.9	39.9	39.9
Max. front leg room, in.	41.5	41.7	41.7	41.7
Rear head room, in.	—	—	37.5	37.5
Min. rear leg room, in.	—	—	34.8	34.8

ENGINES

	ohv V-6	ohv V-8	ohv V-8	Turbodiesel ohv V-8
Size, liters/cu. in.	4.3/262	5.0/305	5.7/350	6.5/395
Horsepower @ rpm	200@ 4400	230@ 4600	255@ 4600	180@ 3400[1]
Torque (lbs./ft.) @ rpm	255@ 2800	285@ 2800	330@ 2800	360@ 1800[1]
Availability	S	S[2]	S[3]	O[3]

EPA city/highway mpg

4-speed OD automatic	16/21	15/21	NA	NA
5-speed OD manual	17/22	15/20	NA	

1. HD diesel, 195 @ 3400 and 430 @ 1800. 2. K1500 Ext. cab long bed; optional C/K 1500. 3. C/K 1500.

PRICES

Chevrolet C/K 1500

	Retail Price	Dealer Invoice
C Sportside, short bed, 4.3	$16930	$14814
C Fleetside, short bed, 4.3	16355	14311
C Fleetside, long bed, 4.3	16655	14573
C Fleetside, W/T short bed, 4.3	14930	13512
C Fleetside, W/T long bed, 4.3	15250	13801
K Sportside, short bed, 4.3	19930	17439
K Fleetside, short bed, 4.3	19355	16936
K Fleetside, long bed, 4.3	19655	17198
K Fleetside, W/T short bed, 4.3	18630	16860
K Fleetside, W/T long bed, 4.3	18950	17150
C Sportside extended cab short bed, 5.0	23099	20212
C Fleetside extended cab short bed, 4.3	18355	16060
C Fleetside extended cab long bed, 5.0	19150	16756
K Sportside extended cab short bed, 5.0	26099	22837
K Fleetside extended cab short bed, 4.3	21355	18686
K Fleetside extended cab long bed, 5.0	22150	19381
Destination charge	625	625

C denotes 2WD; K denotes 4WD. Sportside ext. cab requires third door.

STANDARD EQUIPMENT:

C: 4.3-liter V-6 engine, (5.0-liter V-8 engine C/K Fleetside extended cab long bed), 5-speed manual transmission, driver- and passenger-side air bags, anti-lock brakes, daytime running lights, variable-assist power steering, 3-passenger vinyl bench seat (regular cab), 60/40 split 3-passenger vinyl bench seat (extended cab), fold-down rear seat (extended cab), cupholders, intermittent wipers, cloth headliner (extended cab), passenger-side visor mirror, AM/FM radio, coolant-temperature and oil-pressure gauges, tachometer, voltmeter, dual auxiliary power outlets, cargo box light, swing-out rear quarter windows (extended cab), solar-control glass, dual outside mirrors, Passlock theft-deterrent system, underhood storage box, 7-lead trailer wiring harness, full-size spare tire, 235/75R15 tires.

Sportside extended cab, short bed models add: 5.0-liter V-8 engine, 4-speed automatic transmissiom, Silverado Decor Pkg. (power windows, power door locks, leather-wrapped tilt steering wheel, custom cloth upholstery, carpeting, cruise control, door map pockets, cassette player, floormats, air conditioning, chrome grille, chrome rear bumper, power mirrors, bright bodyside and wheel opening trim, rally wheels), third door.

K adds: part-time 4-wheel drive, tow hooks, 245/75R16 tires.

OPTIONAL EQUIPMENT:

Major Packages

	Retail Price	Dealer Invoice
Preferred Equipment Group 1SW, W/T	NC	NC
Manufacturer's discount price,		
w/manual transmission (credit)	($500)	($430)
Includes standard equipment.		
Cheyenne Group 1SA	NC	NC
Manufacturer's discount price,		
ordered w/manual transmission, Convenience Pkg., and Bright Appearance Pkg. (credit)	(1200)	(1032)
ordered w/manual transmission and Convenience Pkg. (credit)	(1000)	(860)
ordered w/manual transmission and Bright Appearance Pkg. (credit)	(700)	(602)
ordered w/manual transmission (credit)	(500)	(430)
ordered w/automatic, transmission, Convenience Pkg., and Bright Appearance Pkg. (credit)	(700)	(602)
w/automatic transmission and Bright Appearance Pkg. (credit)	(200)	(172)
ordered w/4-speed automatic transmission and Convenience Pkg. (credit)	(500)	(430)
Includes standard equipment. NA W/T.		
Silverado Group 1SB	3036	2611
Manufacturer's discount price,		
ordered w/5-speed manual transmission	1786	1536
ordered w/automatic transmission	2286	1966
Silverado Decor Pkg. (adds to std. Cheyenne Decor: power windows and door locks, leather-wrapped tilt steering wheel, custom cloth upholstery, carpeting, floormats, cruise control, door map pockets, cassette player, air conditioning, chrome grille and rear bumper, power mirrors, bright bodyside and wheel opening trim, rally wheels).		
Silverado Group 1SC, regular cab	4505	3874
Manufacturer's discount price,		
w/manual transmission	3255	2799
w/automatic transmission	3755	3229
1SB plus remote keyless entry, power driver seat, leather upholstery, split/reclining bench seat, compass, automatic day/night mirror.		
Silverado Group 1SC, extended cab	4571	3931
Manufacturer's discount price,		
w/manual transmission	3321	2856
w/automatic transmission	3821	3286
1SB plus remote keyless entry, power driver seat, leather upholstery, compass, automatic day/night rearview mirror.		
Convenience Group, Cheyenne	385	331
Tilt steering wheel, cruise control.		
Comfort and Convenience Pkg., Cheyenne	1337	1150
Air conditioning, tilt steering wheel, cruise control, cassette player.		
Bright Appearance Pkg., Cheyenne		
Fleetside	483	415
Sportside	452	389
Bodyside molding, chrome grille and bumpers, rally wheels.		
Appearance Pkg., Cheyenne	191	164
Chrome grille, composite halogen headlights, dual horns.		
Snow Plow Prep Pkg., 4WD regular cab	158	136
with Off-Road Pkg.	55	47
Heavy-duty shock absorbers and front springs. NA W/T short bed or with 6.5-liter turbodiesel engine.		

Prices are accurate at time of publication; subject to manufacturer's changes.

	Retail Price	Dealer Invoice
Off-road Pkg., Silverado 4WD	$270	$232

Includes front differential and transfer case skid plate. Requires LT245/75R16C tires or 265/75R16C tires. NA with heavy-duty shock absorbers.

Heavy-duty trailering equipment	339	292
ordered with Snow Plow Prep Pkg.		
or Off-Road Pkg.	299	257
ordered with diesel engine or 3.73 rear axle ratio	204	175
ordered with diesel engine or 3.73 rear axle ratio, and Off-road or Snow Plow Prep Pkg.	164	141

Trailer hitch, heavy-duty shock absorbers, engine-oil cooler. Long bed models require rear step bumper. 6-cylinder-equipped models require 4-speed automatic transmission. NA extended cab with Bilstein shock absorbers.

Powertrains

5.0-liter V-8	495	426

Std. extended cab long bed, Sportside extended cab, short bed. NA W/T.

5.7-liter V-8	1195	1028
with extended cab long bed	700	602

NA W/T.

6.5-liter V-8 turbodiesel, 4WD extended cab	4055	3487
4WD extended cab long bed	3560	3062

Includes heavy-duty chassis, engine-oil cooler, 235/75R15 tires (regular cab). Requires bumper guards. NA W/T.

4-speed automatic transmission	970	834

Std. Sportside extended cab, short bed.

Heavy-duty 4-speed automatic transmission	970	834

NA W/T.

Cheyenne/Silverado w/optional engine	135	116

Includes engine-oil cooler.

Locking differential	252	216
Electronic transfer case, 4WD	150	129

Requires automatic transmission, and ZQ3 convenience group or Silverado Group.

Comfort and Convenience

OnStar System	895	761

Includes Global Positioning System, voice-activated cellular telephone, roadside assistance, emergency services. Requires dealer installation charge and monthly service charges.

Air conditioning, Cheyenne	805	692
Remote keyless entry, Silverado Group 1SB	150	129
Power door locks, Cheyenne	156	134
Cassette player, W/T, Cheyenne	147	126
Cassette player with automatic tone control, Silverado	90	77

Includes enhanced speaker system.

CD player with automatic tone control, Silverado	190	163

Includes enhanced speaker system.

CD/cassette players w/automatic tone control, Silverado w/automatic transmission	290	249

Includes enhanced speaker system.

Power driver seat, Silverado extended cab	240	206

Requires split bench or bucket seats, and custom cloth or leather upholstery.

Leather bench seat, Silverado regular cab	1000	860
Custom cloth 60/40 split bench seat, Silverado regular cab with Group 1SB	174	150

Includes storage armrest and power lumbar adjustment.

Leather 60/40 split bench seat,		
Silverado regular cab with Group 1SB	1174	1010
Silverado extended cab with Group 1SB	1000	860

Includes storage armrest and power lumbar adjustment.

Custom cloth bucket seats,		
Silverado regular cab with Group 1SB	386	332
Silverado extended cab with Group 1SB	270	232
Leather bucket seats,		
Silverado extended cab with Group 1SC	270	232
Silverado extended cab with Group 1SB	1270	1092
Automatic day-night mirror, Silverado Group 1SB	145	125

Includes 8-point compass.

Rear defogger, Silverado extended cab	154	132

NA with sliding rear window.

Appearance and Miscellaneous

	Retail Price	Dealer Invoice
Third door, Silverado extended cab short bed	$420	$361

Requires 5.0- or 5.7-liter engine, 4-speed automatic transmission. NA with heavy-duty 4-speed automatic transmission, deluxe two-tone paint, vinyl upholstery, carpeting delete.

Bedliner, Fleetside models	225	194
Camper-type exterior mirrors, Cheyenne	53	46
Silverado (credit)	(45)	(39)
Deep-tinted glass,		
regular cab with sliding rear window	35	30
extended cab	107	92
extended cab with rear defogger	72	62
NA W/T.		
Sliding rear window	115	99
NA with rear defogger.		
Two-tone paint, Silverado	190	163
Deluxe two-tone paint, Silverado Fleetside	275	237

Special Purpose, Wheels and Tires

Heavy-duty chassis equipment, 4WD extended cab	230	198

Requires 6600-lbs. GVWR.

Bilstein gas shock absorbers, 2WD	225	194

NA extended cab with heavy-duty trailering equipment.

Heavy-duty shock absorbers	40	34

NA with Off-road Chassis Pkg., 6.5-liter turbodiesel engine, or W/T short bed.

Heavy-duty front springs, 4WD	63	54

NA with Off-Road Pkg.

Front differential and transfer case skid plates, 4WD	95	82
Engine-oil cooler, gasoline-engine models	135	116

Cheyenne and Silverado 4WD short bed and regular cab long bed require V-8 engine.

Heavy-duty transmission cooler	96	83

Requires 5.7-liter V-8 or 6.5-liter turbodiesel V-8 engine, automatic transmission.

Auxiliary battery	134	115

Requires 5.0-liter or 5.7-liter V-8 engine. NA with W/T.

235/75R15 white letter tires, each axle, 2WD	50	43
spare	25	22
NA W/T.		
265/75R16C on/off road white letter tires,		
each axle, 4WD	104	89
spare	52	45
NA W/T.		
LT245/75R16C on/off road white letter tires,		
each axle, 4WD	72	62
spare	36	31
245/75R16 white letter tires, each axle, 4WD	50	43
spare	25	22
Chrome wheels, 2WD W/T, Cheyenne	310	267
Cheyenne w/Bright Appearance Pkg., Silverado.	250	215
Alloy wheels, Cheyenne	400	344
Cheyenne w/Bright Appearance Pkg., Silverado.	340	292

CHEVROLET CORVETTE

Chevrolet Corvette convertible

Rear-wheel-drive sports and GT
Base price range: $37,495-$44,425. Built in Bowling Green, Ky.
Also consider: Chevrolet Camaro, Dodge Viper, Porsche

Rating Scale: 5-Excellent; 4-Above average; 3-Average; 2-Below average; 1-Poor

Boxster, Toyota Supra

FOR • Acceleration • Steering/handling • Instruments/controls • Standard anti-lock brakes and traction control

AGAINST • Fuel economy • Ride (Continuous Variable Real Time Damping Suspension) • Rear visibility

When Chevrolet designers set about creating the fifth-generation Corvette that debuted for 1997, they engineered it to accommodate a convertible body with no added structural bracing. That planning comes to fruition for 1998 as a convertible joins the coupe in the lineup of this 2-seat sports car.

Both use a 345-horsepower aluminum V-8 linked to a standard automatic transmission or optional 6-speed manual. Traction control is standard. The convertible, expected to account for about 45 percent of sales, has a manual folding top with a glass rear window and defroster. It's the first 'Vette convertible with a traditional trunk since the 1962 model.

Corvette's body remains fiberglass and is 1.2 inches longer overall than the version it replaces on a wheelbase longer by 8.3 inches. The transmission is located at the rear axle and there's no spare tire: The standard tires can run for up to 200 miles with no air pressure.

Changes for '98 include optional magnesium wheels, revisions to quiet the fuel pump, and a provision that allows the automatic transmission to start in second gear for cleaner slippery-surface getaways.

PERFORMANCE Zero-60 mph acceleration of about 4.7 seconds and a top speed around 172 mph put Corvette among the world's fastest cars. The better news is that all this muscle is relatively easy to control thanks to suspension revisions made in the '97 redesign.

Steering and smooth-road handling are racer-like, and the tail is now less likely to skitter sideways when encountering bumps in a turn. A chassis that's stiffer than the one it replaces allows Chevy to fit softer springs, so ride quality is good enough to qualify the 'Vette as everyday transportation. Of three suspension choices, the base setup is by far the best all-around choice.

Part of this car's personality is a booming exhaust note, lots of engine roar in hard acceleration, and copious tire noise. With it's inner-lined soft top, at least the convertible is hardly noisier overall than the coupe.

We averaged 16.5 mpg in a test of an automatic-transmission coupe. A 6-speed averaged 19.5 mpg with substantially more freeway driving, including a best of 26.3 mpg in one 350-mile highway jaunt.

A puncture in a test car's left-front tire helped demonstrate the run-flat technology. An instrument-panel warning message alerted us that the tire had deflated, and the car tracked true at 55 mph to a service center.

ACCOMMODATIONS The current chassis eliminates the earlier Corvette's tall door-frame sills, making the new car about as easy to get into and out of as less-racy sports coupes. There's generous room for two adults, even good leg space since the rear-mounted transmission frees up footwell width. Instruments and controls are sensibly designed and conveniently located.

The convertible's roof folds neatly beneath a hard tonneau (which flows into an intriguing body-colored panel between the seats), but the system's weight and the location of some release points mean you have to stand outside the car to raise and lower the top. Wind buffeting with the top down is less than in most open sports cars.

Thick roof pillars hurt visibility to all corners, but a low cowl creates a clear field of vision forward. Both bodies have sufficient rear cargo room to hold two sets of golf clubs, but cockpit storage space is limited to a tiny glovebox and a minuscule center console compartment.

BUILD QUALITY Our test Corvettes have had solid structures, but suffered a myriad of detail flaws, including a loose driver's seat, occasional squeaks from interior trim (some of which isn't richly finished enough for the car's price), and mismatched paint and body-panel fit.

VALUE FOR THE MONEY If you like your high-performance sports cars big, bold, and brawny, there's no better all-around

performance value than a Corvette. Neither model is inexpensive, but the convertible's base price is actually some $600 under that of the last 'Vette ragtop.

RATINGS

	Coupe	Conv.
Acceleration	5	5
Fuel economy	2	2
Ride quality	3	3
Steering/handling	5	5
Braking	5	5
Quietness	2	2
Driver seating	3	3
Instruments/controls	4	4
Room/comfort (front)	3	3
Room/comfort (rear)	—	—
Cargo room	4	3
Value for the money	4	4
Total	**40**	**39**

SPECIFICATIONS

	2-door hatchback	2-door conv.
Wheelbase, in.	104.5	104.5
Overall length, in.	179.7	179.7
Overall width, in.	73.6	73.6
Overall height, in.	47.7	47.7
Curb weight, lbs.	3245	3246
Cargo vol., cu. ft.	24.8	13.9
Fuel capacity, gals.	19.1	19.1
Seating capacity	2	2
Front head room, in.	37.8	37.6
Max. front leg room, in.	42.7	42.8
Rear head room, in.	—	—
Min. rear leg room, in.	—	—

ENGINES

	ohv V-8
Size, liters/cu. in.	5.7/350
Horsepower @ rpm	345@ 5600
Torque (lbs./ft.) @ rpm	350@ 4400
Availability	S

EPA city/highway mpg
4-speed OD automatic: 17/25
6-speed OD manual: 18/28

PRICES

Chevrolet Corvette	Retail Price	Dealer Invoice
2-door hatchback	$37495	$32808
2-door convertible	44425	38872
Destination charge	565	565

STANDARD EQUIPMENT:
Base: 5.7-liter V-8 engine, 4-speed automatic transmission, Acceleration Slip Regulation traction control, limited slip differential, driver- and passenger-side air bags, heavy-duty anti-lock 4-wheel disc brakes, daytime running lights, low tire-pressure warning system, air conditioning, Magnasteer variable-assist power steering, leather-wrapped tilt steering wheel, cruise control, oil-level indicator, cupholder, remote keyless entry, remote hatch/decklid release, analog gauges, digital driver information center in 4 languages, AM/FM/cassette, integrated antenna (hatchback), power antenna (convertible), rear defogger, reclining leather bucket seats, power driver's seat, center console, auxiliary power outlet, heated power mirrors, power windows with driver and passenger express down, power door locks, intermittent wipers, rearview mirror with reading lights, Pass-Key theft-deterrent system, solar-control tinted glass, body-color removable roof panel (hatchback), manually folding top (convertible), Goodyear Eagle GS-C extended mobility tires (245/45ZR17 front, 275/40ZR18 rear), alloy wheels.

OPTIONAL EQUIPMENT:
Major Packages
| Memory package | 150 | 129 |

Includes settings for driver's seat, exterior mirrors, radio presets, and climate control.

Prices are accurate at time of publication; subject to manufacturer's changes.

	Retail Price	Dealer Invoice
Performance Handling Package	$350	$301

Sport suspension (Bilstein shock absorbers, stiffer springs, stabilizer bars and bushings), special wheels. Automatic transmission requires performance axle ratio. NA with Continuously Variable Real Time Damping Suspension.

Powertrains

6-speed manual transmission	815	701
Performance axle ratio	100	86

Comfort and Convenience

Dual zone air conditioning controls	365	314
Perforated leather sport seats.................................	625	538
6-way power passenger seat	305	262
AM/FM/CD player..	100	86
12-disc CD changer	600	516
Luggage shade and parcel net, hatchback.............	50	43
Floormats	25	22

Appearance and Miscellaneous

Transparent roof panel, hatchback.........................	350	559
Dual roof option, hatchback	950	817

Standard solid removable roof panels and transparent roof panels.

Color-keyed bodyside mouldings	75	65
Fog lamps...	69	59
Continuous Variable Real Time Damping Suspension	1695	1458
Magnesium wheels...	3000	2580

CHEVROLET LUMINA

BUDGET BUY

Chevrolet Lumina LTZ

Front-wheel-drive midsize car; similar to Chevrolet Monte Carlo

Base price range: $17,245-$19,745. Built in Canada.

Also consider: Dodge Stratus, Ford Taurus, Toyota Camry

FOR • Quietness • Passenger and cargo room • Ride • Acceleration (3.8-liter) • Instruments/controls

AGAINST • Steering feel • Fuel economy (3.8-liter)

A new V-6 option and availability of General Motors' OnStar navigation system head the list of changes to Lumina. This is basically a 4-door sedan version of the Chevy Monte Carlo. All Luminas have dual air bags. Anti-lock brakes are standard on all but the base model, where they're optional.

Base, LS, and sporty LTZ models are offered, all with a 160-horsepower 3.1-liter V-6 standard. Replacing last year's 215-horsepower 3.4-liter V-6 as an LTZ option is GM's 200-horse-power 3.8-liter V-6. LTZs ordered with the 3.8 get 4-wheel disc brakes instead of rear drums. The only transmission is an automatic that Chevy says has been redesigned to provide smoother, prompter shifts.

Six-passenger seating is standard, with front buckets optional on the LTZ. A child safety seat that folds out of the rear seatback is optional.

Other changes for 1998 include revised daytime running lights that automatically switch to regular headlights when it gets dark. And the optional Ride and Handling suspension and Soft-Ride suspension get revisions intended to enhance control.

OnStar links the car by cellular telephone and satellite to a 24-hour GM center from which operators can provide directions and other assistance and can summon emergency help. The $895 cost of the dealer-installed option includes a cell phone, but buy-ers must pay installation and service fees.

PERFORMANCE Lumina's 3.1-liter V-6 feels a little slow getting away from a stop, but otherwise delivers adequate acceleration and smooth passing power. We averaged 20.1 mpg with the LS in driving evenly split between surface roads and expressways. The 3.8 is a noticeable improvment over the 3.1 and the underachieving twin-cam 3.4 it replaces. Low- and mid-range power is robust, though the penalty is a few miles per gallon in fuel economy.

Both engines are smooth, quiet, and linked to a transmission that changes gears smoothly and downshifts promptly when passing power is needed.

Lumina is substantially quieter on the highway than most of its competition. Suspension tuning is spot-on for the car's role as a family sedan. It allows the LS to soak up bumpy pavement without harshness or excessive bouncing. Any model handles competently, but we recommend the LTZ suspension if you prefer a firmer ride and slightly sharper responses in changes of direction. Unfortunately, Lumina's steering is light, loose around center, and has little road feel.

Our most-recent test car was an LS and its standard anti-lock brakes stopped it in adequately short distances and with good control.

ACCOMMODATIONS There's ample room for four adults and, with the standard front bench seat, six can squeeze in if nobody minds crowding. Head room is adequate and there's generous rear leg room in the outboard positions. Entry to the rear seat is easy through the tall doors.

Lumina's dashboard has a clean, contemporary design with simple controls that are easy to see and reach. A rotary knob left of the steering column governs the lights and three rotary knobs in the center of the dash regulate the climate system.

Deep side windows and relatively narrow roof pillars give the driver a good view to all directions.

Interior storage includes small map pockets on the doors, an adequate-size glovebox, and, with the front bench seat, a folding center armrest. Lumina has a roomy 15.5-cubic-foot trunk with a flat floor that goes well forward.

BUILD QUALITY Our Lumina test cars have been well assembled. Most controls feel solid and operate smoothly.

VALUE FOR THE MONEY This is a pleasant, competent family sedan that deserves a close look from midsize-car shoppers. It takes a more-conservative approach to design and performance than the Ford Taurus. We find that appealing. And it's also less expensive.

RATINGS	Base/ LS	LTZ w/3.8 V-6
Acceleration	3	4
Fuel economy	3	2
Ride quality	4	4
Steering/handling	3	3
Braking	4	4
Quietness	4	4
Driver seating	4	4
Instruments/controls	4	4
Room/comfort (front)	4	4
Room/comfort (rear)	4	4
Cargo room	4	4
Value for the money	4	4
Total	**45**	**45**

SPECIFICATIONS

	4-door sedan
Wheelbase, in.	107.5
Overall length, in.	200.9
Overall width, in.	72.5
Overall height, in.	55.2
Curb weight, lbs.	3330
Cargo vol., cu. ft.	15.5
Fuel capacity, gals.	16.6
Seating capacity	6
Front head room, in.	38.4
Max. front leg room, in.	42.4
Rear head room, in.	37.4
Min. rear leg room, in.	36.6

Rating Scale: 5-Excellent; 4-Above average; 3-Average; 2-Below average; 1-Poor

CONSUMER GUIDE™

ENGINES

	ohv V-6	ohv V-6
Size, liters/cu. in.	3.1/191	3.8/231
Horsepower @ rpm	160@ 5200	200@ 5200
Torque (lbs./ft.) @ rpm	185@ 4000	225@ 4000
Availability	S	O[1]
EPA city/highway mpg		
4-speed OD automatic	20/29	19/30

1. Optional, LTZ.

PRICES

Chevrolet Lumina

	Retail Price	Dealer Invoice
Base 4-door sedan	$17245	$15779
LS 4-door sedan	19245	17609
LTZ 4-door sedan	19745	18067
Destination charge	550	550

STANDARD EQUIPMENT:

Base: 3.1-liter V-6 engine, 4-speed automatic transmission, driver- and passenger-side air bags, daytime running lamps, air conditioning, power steering, tilt steering wheel, 60/40 cloth reclining front seat with center armrest and 4-way manual driver seat, seatback storage pocket, cupholder, AM/FM radio with digital clock, power door locks, visor mirrors, reading lights, trip odometer, intermittent wipers, Pass-Key theft-deterrent system, tinted glass, left remote and right manual mirrors, color-keyed grille, bodyside moldings, 205/70R15 touring tires, wheel covers.

LS adds: anti-lock brakes, power windows, power mirrors, custom cloth upholstery, tachometer, cassette player with automatic tone control, illuminated passenger-side visor mirror, cargo net, QNX 225/60R16 touring tires, alloy wheels.

LTZ adds: rear spoiler, color-keyed outside mirrors, sport alloy wheels.

OPTIONAL EQUIPMENT:

Major Packages

Preferred Equipment Group 1, Base	758	675
Power windows and mirrors, cruise control, power decklid release, cargo net, floormats.		
LS	645	574
Remote keyless entry, dual zone heater/air conditioner controls, cruise control, power decklid release, floormats.		
LTZ	816	726
Remote keyless entry, cruise control, dual heater/air conditioner controls, steering-wheel radio controls, power decklid release, floormats.		
Sport Performance Pkg., LTZ	450	401
3.8-liter V-6 engine, ride and handling suspension, 4-wheel disc brakes, sport alloy wheels, 225/60R16 tires.		

Safety Features

Anti-lock brakes, Base Lumina	575	512
Integrated child safety seat, Lumina	125	111
Base requires custom cloth 60/40 seat.		

Comfort and Convenience

OnStar System	895	761
Includes Global Positioning System, voice-activated cellular telephone, roadside assistance, emergency services. Requires dealer installation charge and monthly service charges.		
Power windows, Base	328	292
Rear defogger	170	151
Cruise control	225	200
Remote keyless entry, Base, LS	220	196
Requires Preferred Equipment Group 1.		
Cassette player, Base	232	206
Includes automatic tone control.		
CD player, Base	325	289
LS, LTZ	93	83
Includes automatic tone control.		
Steering-wheel-mounted radio controls, LS, LTZ	171	152
Includes leather-wrapped steering wheel.		

	Retail Price	Dealer Invoice
Power driver seat	$305	$271
Custom cloth 60/40 seat, Base	150	134
Front bucket seats w/center console, LTZ	200	178
Leather 60/40 seat, LS, LTZ	645	574
Leather front bucket seats, LTZ	695	619
Power sunroof	700	623
LTZ requires a Preferred Equipment Group. NA Base.		
Front floormats	20	18
Rear floormats	20	18

Appearance and Miscellaneous

Engine block heater	20	18
QNX 225/60R16 touring tires, Base	175	156
Requires alloy wheels.		
Chrome wheel covers, Base	100	89
White alloy wheels, LTZ	NC	NC
Requires white paint.		
Alloy wheels, Base	300	267
Requires QNX 225/60R16 touring tires.		

CHEVROLET MALIBU

RECOMMENDED

Chevrolet Malibu

Front-wheel-drive midsize; similar to Oldsmobile Cutlass

Base price range: $15,670-$18,470. Built in Oklahoma City, Okla., and Wilmington, Del.

Also consider: Honda Accord, Nissan Altima, Toyota Camry

FOR • Standard anti-lock brakes • Passenger and cargo room • Ride • Fuel economy (4-cylinder)

AGAINST • Engine noise (4-cylinder) • Steering feel

This new midsize sedan with the breezy '60s name debuted last year, slotting between the Cavalier and Lumina in size and price. Malubu comes in base and LS trim levels and the addition of optional leather upholstery for the LS is among the few changes for '98.

Malibu's wheelbase is almost three inches longer than the subcompact Cavalier sedan's and just a half-inch shorter than the midsize Lumina's. Overall length is 10 inches longer than the Cavalier but 10.5 shorter than the Lumina.

Inside, Malibu has slightly more front head room than its Chevrolet companions, but the biggest difference is rear leg room, where Malibu has 3.5 inches more than the Cavalier and nearly 1.5 inches more than the Lumina. Malibu and Cavalier seat five, while Lumina offers a front bench seat for 6-passenger capacity.

Standard on the base Malibu is a 150-horsepower dual-camshaft 2.4-liter 4-cylinder. Optional on the base model and standard on the LS is a 155-horsepower 3.1-liter V-6. The only transmission is an automatic with a floor-mounted shift lever.

New aluminum wheels and an optional 6-way power seat for the base model round out this year's changes. Dual air bags, anti-lock brakes, air conditioning, power steering, a tilt steering wheel, tachometer, and daytime running lights are standard on both Malibu models.

PERFORMANCE Malibu's 4-cylinder engine provides good acceleration and should be more than adequate for the majority of owners. However, it's quite loud in hard acceleration. The V-6 is stronger off the line and around town, but doesn't feel significantly more energetic than the 4-cylinder at highway speeds—

though it is substantially smoother. The automatic transmission shifts without jarring but doesn't always downshift promptly to furnish passing power. Our 4-cylinder test car averaged 22.5 mpg in a mix of city and expressway driving. Our test of a V-6 Olds Cutlass netted 22.8 mpg in similar use.

Charging down a freeway off-ramp brings on tire scrubbing and substantial body lean, and the steering is a little slow and vague in spirited cornering. But in daily driving situations, Malibu feels agile, maneuverable, and secure.

The suspension absorbs rough pavement well, though there's a lot of suspension and tire thumping over ruts and potholes. The highway ride is stable and comfortable. Wind noise is low, but the level of engine and tire noise makes for less-than-serene cruising.

Our test car had adequate stopping power, good pedal modulation, and moderate nose dive in hard baking.

ACCOMMODATIONS Front head room is generous, and leg room is more than adequate all around. Rear head room is sufficient for those under 6-feet tall. The front bucket seats are firm and nicely contoured, but the rear bench is harder and flatter than it ought to be.

Malibu's dashboard is a gently curved model of efficiency, with unobstructed analog gauges, convenient stalks for wipers and headlamps, and large, accessible audio and climate controls. We like the radio's simple knobs for volume and tuning and the armrest grouping of switches for power windows, locks, and mirrors.

Interior storage is above average, with a large glovebox, generously sized center console/armrest, and front-door map pockets. A cupholder is molded into the console and another slides out from the dashboard to the the driver's left. Trunk space also is generous and augmented by a flat floor, huge opening, and a near-bumper-level sill.

Thin roof pillars and large outside mirrors provide good visibility, though the parcel shelf is high enough to block the driver's view of the trunk when backing up.

BUILD QUALITY Our test cars had glossy paint and carefully applied exterior trim. They were rattle-free, and the interiors had a tasteful blend of fabrics, plastics, and padded surfaces that gave the Malibu the feel of a more-expensive car.

VALUE FOR THE MONEY Malibu isn't exactly a cut-rate Camry, but it delivers an admirable mix of utility, driving fun, and features at an attractive price. This is an intermediate-sized sedan that deserves serious consideration.

RATINGS

	Base w/4-cyl.	LS
Acceleration	3	4
Fuel economy	4	3
Ride quality	4	4
Steering/handling	3	3
Braking	5	5
Quietness	3	3
Driver seating	4	4
Instruments/controls	4	4
Room/comfort (front)	4	4
Room/comfort (rear)	3	3
Cargo room	4	4
Value for the money	4	4
Total	45	45

SPECIFICATIONS

	4-door sedan
Wheelbase, in.	107.0
Overall length, in.	190.4
Overall width, in.	69.4
Overall height, in.	56.4
Curb weight, lbs.	3100
Cargo vol., cu. ft.	17.0
Fuel capacity, gals.	15.0
Seating capacity	5
Front head room, in.	39.4
Max. front leg room, in.	41.9
Rear head room, in.	37.6
Min. rear leg room, in.	38.0

ENGINES

	dohc I-4	ohv V-6
Size, liters/cu. in.	2.4/146	3.1/191
Horsepower @ rpm	150@ 5600	155@ 4800
Torque (lbs./ft.) @ rpm	155@ 4400	180@ 3200
Availability	S[1]	S[2]
EPA city/highway mpg		
4-speed OD automatic	23/32	20/29

1. Base. 2. LS; optional, base.

PRICES

Chevrolet Malibu	Retail Price	Dealer Invoice
Base 4-door sedan	$15670	$14338
LS 4-door sedan	18470	16900
Destination charge	525	525

STANDARD EQUIPMENT:

Base: 2.4-liter 4-cylinder engine, 4-speed automatic transmission, driver- and passenger-side air bags, anti-lock brakes, daytime running lights, air conditioning, power steering, tilt steering wheel, cloth upholstery, reclining front bucket seats, storage console w/armrest, cupholder, tachometer, coolant-temperature gauge, trip odometer, AM/FM radio, digital clock, intermittent wipers, visor mirrors, remote decklid release, auxiliary power outlet, rear heat ducts, dual outside mirrors w/driver-side remote, tinted glass, Passlock II theft-deterrent system, 215/60R15 tires, bolt-on wheel covers.

LS adds: 3.1-liter V-6 engine, cruise control, custom cloth upholstery, power driver seat, split folding rear seat, power windows, power door locks, remote keyless entry, power outside mirrors, cassette player, rear defogger, illuminated passenger-side visor mirror, dual reading lamps, passenger assist handles, cargo net, floormats, fog lamps, alloy wheels.

OPTIONAL EQUIPMENT:

Major Packages

Preferred Equipment Group 1, Base	700	630
Power windows and door locks, power outside mirrors.		
Preferred Equipment Group 2, Base	1100	990
Group 1 plus cruise control, remote keyless entry, dual reading lamps.		

Powertrains

3.1-liter V-6 engine, Base	495	446

Comfort and Convenience

Cruise control, Base	225	203
Requires Preferred Equipment Group 1.		
Power sunroof	635	572
Includes reading lights. Base requires Preferred Equipment Group 2.		
Custom cloth upholstery, Base	225	203
Includes split folding rear seat, cargo net. Requires Preferred Equipment Group.		
Leather upholstery, LS	475	428
Includes leather-wrapped steering wheel.		
Power driver seat, Base	310	279
Cassette player, Base	220	198
CD player, Base	320	288
LS	100	90
CD/cassette player, Base	420	378
LS	200	180
Remote keyless entry, Base	150	135
Requires Preferred Equipment Group.		
Rear defogger, Base	180	162
Floormats, Base	40	36

Appearance and Miscellaneous

Mud guards	60	54
Base requires Preferred Equipment Group.		
Engine block heater	30	27
Alloy wheels, Base	310	572
Requires Preferred Equipment Group.		

Rating Scale: 5-Excellent; 4-Above average; 3-Average; 2-Below average; 1-Poor

CHEVROLET METRO

Chevrolet Metro LSi 4-door

Front-wheel-drive subcompact; similar to Suzuki Swift

Base price range: $8655-$10,055. Built in Canada.

Also consider: Hyundai Accent, Nissan Sentra, Toyota Tercel

FOR • Optional anti-lock brakes • Fuel economy • Maneuverability • Visibility

AGAINST • Rear seat room • Ride • Noise • Acceleration (3-cylinder)

Moving over from the now-defunct Geo line, Metro continues into 1998 with Chevy bow tie badges, a revised engine, and minor appearance changes. Metro is built from the same design used for the Suzuki Swift. Both cars are assembled at a General Motors/Suzuki assembly plant in Canada.

Metro comes as a 2-door hatchback and a 4-door sedan. With a curb weight of 1895 pounds, the hatchback is among the lightest cars sold in the U.S. It comes in base and LSi trim. The sedan is an LSi. Dual air bags are standard and anti-lock brakes are optional on all Metros.

A 55-horsepower 1.0-liter 3-cylinder powers the base hatchback. LSi models have a 1.3-liter 4-cylinder that's revised to produce 79 horsepower, 9 more than last year. Manual transmission is standard. A 3-speed automatic is optional in the LSi.

Composite headlamps, redesigned radios, and new seat fabrics, complete the changes for '98.

PERFORMANCE Metro's light weight and modest dimensions are evident in the way bumps jar the suspension and create kickback through the steering wheel. Road noise is high, and there's also lots of wind roar and mechanical ruckus.

Ride quality can get harsh over badly broken pavement. The short wheelbase makes Metro very agile around town, but the skinny tires run out of grip quickly in high-speed turns.

The 4-cylinder engine is much livelier than the 3-cylinder, but it certainly doesn't turn Metro into a hot rod. Step on the gas and there's considerable noise—and only modest progress. We averaged 25.8 mpg with an automatic-transmission LSi 4-door. Nearly all our driving was city and suburban commuting, but that's still not great for a car sold as a fuel miser. If you're looking for high mileage, stick with the 3-cylinder hatchback, but be warned that acceleration is excruciatingly slow and passing power is nil at highway speeds.

Braking performance was only adequate on our test car, which lacked the anti-lock option. In simulated panic stops, the rear brakes locked well before the fronts did.

ACCOMMODATIONS Metro's sedan body has a surprising amount of interior room for its petite dimensions. The rear seat provides adequate head room and leg room for two medium-size passengers. Things are tighter inside the hatchback, and it's hard to get in or out of the rear seat, regardless of body style.

Tall windows and slim roof pillars give the driver great visibility. A simple dashboard layout puts controls where they're easy to see and reach. This year's new radios have much better controls and feature large dials and oversized buttons.

Cargo space is a little better then average for cars in this class, but the sedan's trunk opening is small.

BUILD QUALITY Metro's low cost dictates modest interior trim

and lots of hard plastic. However, they're solidly put together and have better paint finishes than some costlier subcompacts.

VALUE FOR THE MONEY Metro is worth considering if low cost is your overriding priority. But a larger, more substantial car—even a used one—is a smarter choice in the long run.

RATINGS

	Base	LSi 2-door	LSi 4-door
Acceleration	1	2	2
Fuel economy	5	4	4
Ride quality	2	2	3
Steering/handling	3	3	3
Braking	2	2	3
Quietness	2	2	2
Driver seating	3	3	3
Instruments/controls	3	3	3
Room/comfort (front)	3	3	3
Room/comfort (rear)	2	2	3
Cargo room	3	3	3
Value for the money	3	3	3
Total	**32**	**32**	**35**

SPECIFICATIONS

	2-door hatchback	4-door sedan
Wheelbase, in.	93.1	93.1
Overall length, in.	149.4	164.0
Overall width, in.	62.6	62.6
Overall height, in.	54.7	55.4
Curb weight, lbs.	1895	1984
Cargo vol., cu. ft.	22.5	10.3
Fuel capacity, gals.	10.6	10.3
Seating capacity	4	4
Front head room, in.	39.1	39.3
Max. front leg room, in.	42.5	42.5
Rear head room, in.	36.0	37.3
Min. rear leg room, in.	32.2	32.2

ENGINES

	ohc I-3	ohc I-4
Size, liters/cu. in.	1.0/61	1.3/79
Horsepower @ rpm	55 @ 5700	79 @ 6000
Torque (lbs./ft.) @ rpm	58 @ 3300	75 @ 3000
Availability	S[1]	S[2]

EPA city/highway mpg

3-speed automatic		30/34
5-speed OD manual	44/49	39/43

1. Base 2-door. 2. 4-door and 2-door LSi.

PRICES

Chevrolet Metro	Retail Price	Dealer Invoice
Base 2-door hatchback	$8655	$8153
LSi 2-door hatchback	9455	8812
LSi 4-door sedan	10055	9371
Destination charge	340	340

STANDARD EQUIPMENT:

Base: 1.0-liter 3-cylinder engine, 5-speed manual transmission, driver- and passenger-side air bags, daytime running lights, cloth/vinyl reclining front bucket seats, folding rear seat, console with cupholders and storage tray, coolant-temperature gauge, dual outside mirrors, 155/80R13 tires.

LSi adds: 1.3-liter 4-cylinder engine, upgraded cloth/vinyl upholstery, intermittent wipers, trip odometer, passenger-side visor mirror, color-keyed bumpers, bodyside moldings, wheel covers.

OPTIONAL EQUIPMENT:
Major Packages

Preferred Equipment Group 2, Base	179	159

Easy-entry passenger seat, remote outside mirrors, bodyside moldings, floormats, wheel covers.

Preferred Equipment Group 3, Base	1294	1152

Group 2 plus air conditioning, AM/FM radio with digital clock.

Preferred Equipment Group 2, LSi 2-door	1375	1224

Air conditioning, AM/FM/cassette with digital clock, floormats.

Prices are accurate at time of publication; subject to manufacturer's changes.

	Retail Price	Dealer Invoice
LSi 4-door	$1665	$1482

Air conditioning, power steering, AM/FM/cassette with digital clock, floormats.

| Convenience Pkg., LSi .... | 125 | 111 |

Easy-entry passenger seat (2-door), split folding rear seat (4-door), remote outside mirrors, remote decklid release (4-door), cargo cover (2-door), trunk light (4-door).

Powertrains

| 3-speed automatic transmission, LSi .... | 595 | 530 |

Safety Features

| Anti-lock brakes .... | 565 | 503 |

Comfort and Convenience

Air conditioning	785	699
Power steering, 4-door	290	258
AM/FM radio	330	294

Includes seek and scan, digital clock, four speakers.

AM/FM/cassette	550	490
Base w/Group 3	220	196
AM/FM/CD player	650	579
Base w/Preferred Group 3	320	285
LSi w/Preferred Group 2	100	89
Radio provisions	100	89

Includes speakers, antenna.

Power door locks, 4-door	220	196
Rear defogger	160	142
Rear wiper/washer, LSi 2-door	125	111

Requires rear defogger.

| Tachometer .... | 70 | 62 |

Includes trip odometer on base.

| Floormats .... | 40 | 36 |

Appearance and Miscellaneous

| Bodyside moldings, Base .... | 50 | 45 |

CHEVROLET MONTE CARLO

Chevrolet Monte Carlo Z34

Front-wheel-drive sports coupe; similar to Chevrolet Lumina

Base price range: $17,795-$20,295. Built in Canada.

Also consider: Acura CL, Chrysler Sebring, Dodge Avenger

FOR • Standard anti-lock brakes • Acceleration (3.8-liter) • Instruments/controls • Ride

AGAINST • Entry/exit • Rear visibility

This is basically a Lumina sedan in 2-door-coupe clothing and gets the same changes as its more-popular sibling, including a new top-of-the-line V-6 and GM's OnStar navigation system.

Dual air bags and anti-lock brakes are standard Monte Carlo, comes in LS and Z34 trim. The LS has a 160-horsepower 3.1-liter V-6. Replacing a 215-horsepower dual-overhead-cam 3.4-liter V-6 on the Z34 is GM's overhead-valve 3.8-liter V-6 with 200 horsepower. Both engines use automatic transmission. Four-wheel disc brakes are standard on the Z34.

Six-passenger seating is standard on the LS. Front buckets are optional on the LS, standard on the Z34. Both have split folding rear seatbacks. Among other '98 changes are daytime running lights that automatically switch to regular headlights when it gets dark. Additionally, the Z34's standard Ride and Handling suspension is

revised to provide more ride control, and the LS's Soft-Ride suspension gets a larger stabilizer bar intended to quell body lean in turns.

OnStar is a new dealer-installed option that links the car by cellular phone and satellite to a 24-hour GM center from which operators can provide directions and other services and summon emergency help. The system's $895 cost includes a cell phone, but not installation and monthly service fees.

PERFORMANCE The LS's 3.1 V-6 is slow to get this big coupe away from a stop, but otherwise delivers adequate acceleration and smooth passing power. We averaged 20.1 mpg in driving split between surface roads and expressways.

The Z34's 3.8 liter is smoother and stronger than the old 3.4 and outshines the 3.1 in low- and mid-range power, but at the penalty of a few miles per gallon in fuel economy. Both engines team with a transmission that changes gears without fuss and alertly downshifts for good passing power.

Benefitting from genuine midsized-car heft, Monte Carlo is quieter on the highway than most of its smaller rivals. It's also better at smothering bad pavement. The base suspension is reasonably absorbent with no excessive bouncing. The Z34 rides more firmly but seldom uncomfortably. Handling is modest on the LS, sharper on the Z34, though the steering feels disconnected from the road at times. The standard anti-lock brakes stopped our test cars in adequately short distances and with good control.

A high parcel shelf and fat rear-roof pillars combine with undersized outside mirrors for poor rear visibility.

ACCOMMODATIONS There's ample room for two in front and two in back. Any more and everyone's pressing shoulders. Head room is adequate and there's generous rear leg room. Entry to the rear seat is difficult and it's hard to open the wide doors in tight parking spaces.

Monte Carlo's dashboard has a clean, contemporary design with simple controls that are easy to see and reach. Three rotary knobs in the center of the dashboard regulate the climate system. Interior storage includes small map pockets on the doors, an adequate-size glovebox, and, with the front bench seat, a folding center armrest.

BUILD QUALITY Our test cars were well assembled and free from squeaks and rattles. The interior materials are appropriately smart for this price range.

VALUE FOR THE MONEY Monte Carlo's size makes it more of a personal-luxury 2-door than a coltish sporty coupe. Chevy has a redesigned model in the wings and we feel it's overdue. Meantime, there should be some good deals to be made on the Monte of your choice.

RATINGS

	LS	Z34
Acceleration	3	4
Fuel economy	3	2
Ride quality	4	4
Steering/handling	3	4
Braking	5	5
Quietness	4	4
Driver seating	4	4
Instruments/controls	4	4
Room/comfort (front)	4	4
Room/comfort (rear)	3	3
Cargo room	4	4
Value for the money	4	3
Total	44	45

SPECIFICATIONS

	2-door coupe
Wheelbase, in.	107.5
Overall length, in.	200.7
Overall width, in.	72.5
Overall height, in.	53.8
Curb weight, lbs.	3239
Cargo vol., cu. ft.	15.5
Fuel capacity, gals.	16.6
Seating capacity	6
Front head room, in.	37.9
Max. front leg room, in.	42.4
Rear head room, in.	37.4
Min. rear leg room, in.	34.9

Rating Scale: 5-Excellent; 4-Above average; 3-Average; 2-Below average; 1-Poor

ENGINES

	ohv V-6	ohv V-6
Size, liters/cu. in.	3.1/191	3.8/231
Horsepower @ rpm	160@	200@
	5200	5200
Torque (lbs./ft.) @ rpm	185@	225@
	4000	4000
Availability	S[1]	S[2]
EPA city/highway mpg		
4-speed OD automatic	20/29	19/30

1. LS. 2. Z34.

PRICES

Chevrolet Monte Carlo	Retail Price	Dealer Invoice
LS 2-door notchback	$17795	$16282
Z34 2-door notchback	20295	18570
Destination charge	550	550

STANDARD EQUIPMENT:

LS: 3.1-liter V-6 engine, 4-speed automatic transmission, driver- and passenger-side air bags, anti-lock brakes, daytime running lamps, air conditioning, power steering, tilt steering wheel, 60/40 custom cloth reclining front seat with center armrest and 4-way manual driver seat, seatback storage pocket, split fold-down rear seat, cupholder, AM/FM/cassette with automatic tone control, digital clock, power windows, power door locks, power mirrors, illuminated passenger-side visor mirror, reading lights, trip odometer, tachometer, intermittent wipers, floormats, chrome grille, Pass-Key theft-deterrent system, tinted glass, color-keyed grille, bodyside moldings, 205/70R15 touring tires, wheel covers.

Z34 adds: 3.8-liter V-6 engine, custom cloth front bucket seats with center console, cruise control, dual zone automatic air conditioning controls, steering-wheel radio controls, leather-wrapped steering wheel, power decklid release, remote keyless entry, cargo net, 4-wheel disc brakes, QNX 225/60R16 touring tires, alloy wheels.

OPTIONAL EQUIPMENT:
Major Packages

Preferred Equipment Group 1, LS	635	565

Cruise control, remote keyless entry, dual heater/air conditioner controls, power decklid release, trunk net.

Comfort and Convenience

OnStar System	895	761

Includes Global Positioning System, voice-activated cellular telephone, roadside assistance, emergency services. Requires dealer installation charge and monthly service charges.

Rear defogger	170	151
Cruise control, LS	225	200
Remote keyless entry, LS	220	196

Requires Preferred Equipment Group 1.

CD player	93	83

Includes automatic tone control.

Steering-wheel-mounted radio controls, LS	171	152

Includes leather-wrapped steering wheel.

Power driver seat	305	271
Front bucket seats w/center console, LS	200	178
Leather front bucket seats,		
LS	695	619
Z34	645	574
Power sunroof	700	623

LS requires a Preferred Equipment Group.

Appearance and Miscellaneous

Rear spoiler	175	156
Engine block heater	20	18
QNX 225/60R16 touring tires, LS	175	156

Requires alloy wheels.

Alloy wheels, LS	300	267

Requires QNX 225/60R16 touring tires.

CHEVROLET PRIZM

✓ BEST BUY

Chevrolet Prizm

Front-wheel-drive subcompact; similar to Toyota Corolla

Base price range: NA. Built in Fremont, Calif.

Also consider: Honda Civic, Mazda Protege, Nissan Sentra

FOR • Fuel economy • Ride • Optional anti-lock brakes • Optional side air bags

AGAINST • Rear seat room • Automatic transmission performance

Prizm is all-new for 1998, starting with its surname. Geo was coined in 1989 by Chevrolet as a global-sounding sub-brand to market Japanese-sourced or designed models. Along with the Metro and Tracker, Chevy brings these cars back into its bow tie fold for '98, though their Japanese sourcing and design hardly change.

Prizm, the best-selling neo Geo, is again based on Toyota's Corolla subcompact. Prizm and the similiarly redesigned Corolla are built on the same assembly line at a joint GM/Toyota plant in California and both are available this year with front side air bags, a rare feature in this class.

Prizm's appearance is similar to the 1993-96 generation, but all its sheetmetal is new. Wheelbase is virtually the same but overall length is up 2 inches and the car is slightly wider and taller. Interior room grows only fractionally. Base and LSi model levels return, both with 5-passenger seating.

Power again comes from a twin-cam 4-cylinder engine, but replacing 100- and 105-horsepower variants is a single new design with 120 horsepower. It has 122 pounds-feet of torque, 17 more than last year's top engine. Manual transmission is standard, with a 3-speed or 4-speed automatic optional.

Dual air bags, daytime running lights, and front seat belt pretensioners are standard. Anti-lock brakes and the front-seat-mounted side air bags are optional.

PERFORMANCE Familiar with the old Geo Prizm? You'll feel right at home in the new model. That's not at all a bad proposition. This is among the best small cars on the market.

Acceleration, while not sparkling, is much better then most rivals'. With the 5-speed manual, the car feels frisky and willing to move through traffic with authority. Performance with the automatic transmissions is less exciting. The 4-speed automatic in particular hunts between gears in stop and go traffic and saps a lot of life out of the engine.

Prizm's ride is controlled, but decidedly firm. You feel even small bumps, but the chassis does a good job filtering out most of the harshness. The standard suspension and tires quickly run out of grip on twisty roads and allow moderate body lean. The Handling Package optional on the LSi does a much better job of holding the road and exacts little penalty in ride quality.

Visibility is excellent to all directions, helped by large outside mirrors that fight blind spots to the rear quarters. Steering is direct and sharp, and the brakes, while mushy in feel on the cars we tested, do an adequate job in hauling the Prizm down from speed. Road noise is noticed in this car, but is no louder than most of the competition.

ACCOMMODATIONS Prizm's new interior is familiar, too, and is again roomy and comfortable for average-size adults. The front seats are especially supportive and head and leg room are ample.

Prices are accurate at time of publication; subject to manufacturer's changes.

Two adults fit comfortably in back, but only if the front seats are less than half-way back. Any more, and rear leg room is tight and foot room is almost nonexistent. Three across in the back seat means everyone will be scrunched for space.

Gauges are easy to see and the new dashboard hides no controls behind the steering wheel. Large rotary dials for the climate system are placed high on the dash where they're easy to use and understand. The stereo is mounted a bit low, but features generously sized buttons.

As in most subcompact sedans, entry and exit to the rear seats is a bit tight through the narrow door openings. Prizm's cargo area is about average for this class, but features a large opening and bumper-height access. The split-folding rear seats standard on the LSi (and unfortunately unavailable on the Base) incorporate a pass-through that accommodates long items while allowing use of the rear seats—another uncommon touch in this price class.

BUILD QUALITY Hard plastic dominates the interior but all models we drove were well assembled and free of squeaks and rattles.

VALUE FOR THE MONEY As before, Prizm comes across as a lower-cost Corolla. That makes it a solid small car that looks to stand up well to the punishment of daily driving. With its available side air bags, Toyota genes, and capable road manners, Prizm's a shopping-list topper.

RATINGS

	Base/LSi
Acceleration	3
Fuel economy	4
Ride quality	3
Steering/handling	4
Braking	4
Quietness	4
Driver seating	4
Instruments/controls	4
Room/comfort (front)	4
Room/comfort (rear)	3
Cargo room	3
Value for the money	5
Total	**45**

SPECIFICATIONS

	4-door sedan
Wheelbase, in.	97.0
Overall length, in.	174.2
Overall width, in.	66.7
Overall height, in.	53.7
Curb weight, lbs.	3330
Cargo vol., cu. ft.	NA
Fuel capacity, gals.	12.1
Seating capacity	5
Front head room, in.	39.3
Max. front leg room, in.	42.5
Rear head room, in.	36.9
Min. rear leg room, in.	33.2

ENGINES

	dohc I-4
Size, liters/cu. in.	1.8/110
Horsepower @ rpm	120@ 5600
Torque (lbs./ft.) @ rpm	122@ 4400
Availability	S

EPA city/highway mpg

5-speed OD manual	31/37
3-speed OD automatic	28/33
4-speed OD automatic	28/36

PRICES

Chevrolet Prizm	Retail Price	Dealer Invoice
Base 4-door sedan	$12043	$11465
LSi 4-door sedan	14614	13474
Destination charge	420	420

STANDARD EQUIPMENT:

Base: 1.8-liter DOHC engine, 5-speed manual transmission, driver- and passenger-side air bags, daytime running lights, power steering, cloth reclining front bucket seats, center console with storage tray and cupholders, intermittent wipers, dual trip odometer, automatic headlights, visor mirrors, remote fuel door and decklid release, rear heat ducts, left remote and right manual mirrors, tinted glass, body-side moldings, 175/65R14 tires.

LSi adds: power mirrors, air conditioning, power door locks, remote keyless entry, AM/FM/cassette, upgraded cloth upholstery, split folding rear seat, floormats, wheel covers.

OPTIONAL EQUIPMENT:

	Retail Price	Dealer Invoice
Major Packages		
Preferred Equipment Group 2,		
Base	$1222	$1051
Air conditioning, AM/FM radio with digital clock, floormats, wheel covers.		
Preferred Equipment Group 3,		
Base	1847	1588
Preferred Equipment Group 2 plus power door locks, cassette player, cruise control.		
Preferred Equipment Group 3, LSi	550	473
Power windows, cruise control, CD player, tilt steering wheel, Handling Pkg. (front stabilizer bar, 185/65R14 tires).		
Handling Pkg., LSi	70	60
Front stabilizer bar, 185/65R14 tires.		
Powertrains		
3-speed automatic transmission	495	426
4-speed automatic transmission	800	688
Safety Features		
Anti-lock brakes	645	555
Front side-impact air bags	295	254
Integrated child safety seat, LSi	125	108
Comfort and Convenience		
Air conditioning, Base	795	684
Cruise control	185	159
Tilt steering wheel	80	69
Rear defogger	180	155
Power door locks, Base	220	189
Power sunroof	675	581
Tachometer	70	60
Includes outside temperature gauge.		
AM/FM radio	335	288
Includes seek/scan, digital clock, and four speakers.		
AM/FM/cassette, Base	555	477
Includes seek/scan, digital clock, four speakers.		
AM/FM/CD player,		
Base	655	563
LSi	100	86
Includes seek/scan, digital clock, four speakers.		
Floormats, Base	40	34
Appearance and Miscellaneous		
Wheel covers, Base	52	45
Alloy wheels	335	288

CHEVROLET S-10 `RECOMMENDED`

Rear- or 4-wheel-drive compact pickup; similar to GMC Sonoma, and Isuzu Hombre

Base price range: $11,703-$19,603. Built in Linden, N.J., and Shreveport, La.

Also consider: Dodge Dakota, Ford Ranger, Toyota Tacoma

FOR • Standard anti-lock brakes • Acceleration (V-6) • Instruments/controls • Optional third door

AGAINST • Ride • Rear seat room (extended cab)

Chevy's compact pickups get a new look inside and out for 1998, highlighted by the addition of a passenger-side air bag.

Rating Scale: 5-Excellent; 4-Above average; 3-Average; 2-Below average; 1-Poor

CONSUMER GUIDE™

Chevrolet S-10 ZR2 extended cab

S-10s come in three forms: regular-cab short-bed, regular-cab long-bed, and extended-cab short bed. The short bed is 6-feet long, the long bed 7.5. There's an optional flared-fender short cargo-bed called Sportside. A driver-side rear door is optional on extended-cab models.

S-10s come with a 3-place bench seat. Extended-cab models add two rear jump seats, though the left-side jump seat is eliminated on models with the third door. Front buckets are optional.

The base engine is a 2.2-liter 4-cylinder. It's reworked for 1998 to improve fuel efficiency and lower noise levels, but sacrifices 10 horsepower. Four versions of GM's 4.3-liter V-6 are optional, ranging in horsepower from 175 to 190. Manual transmission is standard and automatic is optional.

GMC sells a similar truck as the Sonoma and it gets like changes for 1998, including the new nose appearance and revamped dashboard. The passenger-side air bag joins the already-standard driver-side air bag and includes a deactivation switch located on the dashboard. Four-wheel anti-lock brakes are standard, as are daytime running lights that this year automatically illuminate to full intensity at dusk.

Among S10's major options is the SS package for 2WD regular cab models; it adds a monochromatic exterior look, a 180-horsepower V-6, and sport suspension. The off-road-oriented ZR2 package for 4WD LS models includes unique front fenders and wheel flares, a 190-horsepower V-6, and heavy-duty chassis upgrades.

PERFORMANCE You won't notice much loss of power from the redesigned 4-cylinder, and though it does seem to run smoother, it still performs best with the manual transmission, providing adequate acceleration in light-duty chores. Want automatic transmission or plan even occasional hauling? Get a V-6. They have plenty of power.

Fuel economy isn't great with the V-6s, however. We averaged 18 mpg in our last test of an extended-cab 4WD. The 4-cylinder is more economical.

The base suspension takes most pavement imperfections with little harshness and minimal bounding. Different tire and suspension setups will produce different ride characteristics. The higher-payload and off-road suspensions are much firmer than the base arrangement, so drive them to see if you're willing to live with the compromises. Like any pickup with an empty cargo bed, the rear-end tends to hop over sharp bumps and ridges.

Though body lean is evident in turns, GM's compact pickups feel balanced and poised, with a natural feel to the power steering and good resistance to gusty crosswinds. Brake-pedal action is mushy, however.

ACCOMMODATIONS Front-seat comfort is good. The optional buckets are firmly padded, and the extended-cab versions benefit from generous rearward seat travel.

The extended-cab's small rear jump seats are best suited to children. The third door is easy to use and a real convenience and a feature shared by the GMC Sonoma but not offered on any other small pickup.

Gauges on the new dashboard are unobstructed and soft-touch rotary knobs for the climate system and large radio buttons enhance the simple control layout. The center console contains dual cupholders and several covered and open bins, and there are map pockets in the door panels.

BUILD QUALITY We have driven several iterations of these redesigned Chevy and GMC pickups. All were well assembled,

free from squeaks and rattles, and had a high-grade interior feel.

VALUE FOR THE MONEY We rate the new Ford Ranger slightly ahead of the S-10 and Sonoma in overall refinement, but most buyers will find plenty to like in both brands. The decision is likely to hinge on personal preference and the deal you can get.

RATINGS	Base reg. cab 2WD	LS ext. cab 4WD
Acceleration	3	4
Fuel economy	3	2
Ride quality	3	3
Steering/handling	3	3
Braking	3	4
Quietness	3	3
Driver seating	4	4
Instruments/controls	4	4
Room/comfort (front)	3	3
Room/comfort (rear)	—	2
Cargo room	1	2
Value for the money	4	3
Total	**34**	**37**

SPECIFICATIONS	Short bed	Long bed	Ext. cab short bed
Wheelbase, in.	108.3	117.9	122.9
Overall length, in.	190.1	206.1	204.8
Overall width, in.	67.9	67.9	67.9
Overall height, in.	62.0	62.9	62.7
Curb weight, lbs.	3003	3040	3222
Maximum payload, lbs.	1171	1509	1168
Fuel capacity, gals.	19.0	19.0	19.0
Seating capacity	3	3	5
Front head room, in.	39.5	39.5	39.6
Max. front leg room, in.	42.4	42.4	42.4
Rear head room, in.	—	—	NA
Min. rear leg room, in.	—	—	NA

ENGINES	ohv I-4	ohv V-6	ohv V-6	ohv V-6
Size, liters/cu. in.	2.2/134	4.3/262	4.3/262	4.3/262
Horsepower @ rpm	120@ 5000	175@ 4400	180@ 4400[1]	180@ 4400
Torque (lbs./ft.) @ rpm	140@ 3600	240@ 2800	240@ 2800[1]	245@ 2800
Availability	S[2]	O[2]	S[3]	S[4]
EPA city/highway mpg				
5-speed OD manual	23/30	18/25	18/25	18/25
4-speed OD automatic	20/27	17/23	17/23	17/23

1. ZR2, 190 @ 4400 and 250 @ 2800. 2. 2WD. 3. 4WD. 4. SS and ZR2.

PRICES

Chevrolet S-10	Retail Price	Dealer Invoice
Base 2WD regular cab, short bed	$11703	$11059
Base 2WD regular cab, long bed	12003	11343
LS 2WD regular cab, short bed	12553	11360
LS 2WD regular cab, long bed	12853	11632
LS 2WD regular cab, Sportside, short bed	13003	11768
LS 2WD extended cab	14553	13170
LS 2WD extended cab, Sportside	15003	13578
Base 4WD regular cab, short bed	16353	15454
Base 4WD regular cab, long bed	16685	15767
LS 4WD regular cab, short bed	17253	15614
LS 4WD regular cab, long bed	17680	16000
LS 4WD regular cab, Sportside, short bed	17703	16021
LS 4WD extended cab	19153	17333
LS 4WD extended cab, Sportside	19603	17741
Destination charge	510	510

STANDARD EQUIPMENT:

Base: 2.2-liter 4-cylinder engine, 5-speed manual transmission, 4-wheel anti-lock brakes, power steering, driver-side air bag, intermittent wipers, cloth or vinyl bench seat with head restraints, AM/FM radio, solar-control tinted glass, coolant-temperature and oil-pressure gauges, voltmeter, trip odometer, daytime running lights, dual outside mirrors, vinyl floor covering, rear step bumper, 5-lead trailer

Prices are accurate at time of publication; subject to manufacturer's changes.

wiring harness, 205/75R15 all-season tires.

LS adds: cloth 60/40 reclining split bench seat with storage armrest, vinyl rear jump seat (extended cab), upgraded door trim, reading lights, carpeting, illuminated visor mirrors, chrome grille, auxiliary power outlets, wheel trim rings.

4WD models include 4.3-liter V-6 engine, front tow hooks, 235/70R15 tires (long bed).

4WD Sportside requires Solid-Smooth Suspension, Increased Capacity Suspension or Off-Road Suspension.

OPTIONAL EQUIPMENT:

	Retail Price	Dealer Invoice
Powertrains		
Value Pkg., 2WD	($250)	($215)
2.2-liter 4-cylinder engine.		
4.3-liter V-6 engine, 2WD	990	851
Includes engine- and transmission-oil coolers.		
4.3-liter high output (HO) V-6 engine, 2WD	1249	1074
4WD	259	223
Includes tachometer, engine- and transmission-oil coolers.		
4-speed automatic transmission	1070	920

Major Packages

	Retail Price	Dealer Invoice
Preferred Equipment Group 1SA,		
base regular cab (credit)	(281)	(242)
Deletes AM/FM radio and rear step bumper.		
Preferred Equipment Group 1SH,		
LS 2WD regular cab short bed	(180)	(154)
Solid Smooth Suspension, AM/FM/cassette player, argent alloy wheels. Requires 2.2-liter engine, manual transmission.		
Preferred Equipment Group 1SJ,		
LS 2WD extended cab: w/bucket seats	1001	861
w/split bench seat	1101	947
4.3-liter V-6 engine, increased Capacity Suspension, reclining bucket seats with lumbar adjustment or 60/40 reclining split bench seat w/storage armrest, AM/FM/cassette player, argent alloy wheels.		
Preferred Equipment Group 1SM,		
LS 4WD extended cab: w/bucket seats	422	363
w/split bench seat	522	449
Electronic-shift transfer case, Increased Capacity Suspension, AM/FM/cassette player, reclining bucket seats with lumbar adjustment or 60/40 reclining split bench seat w/storage armrest, 235/70R15 tires, cast alloy wheels.		
Exterior Appearance Pkg., LS short bed 4WD	556	478
LS short bed 2WD	524	451
extended cab w/Preferred Equipment Group	276	237
Color-keyed bumpers, gray bodyside moldings with bright inserts, bright wheel opening moldings, cast alloy wheels (4WD), argent alloy wheels (2WD). NA with ZR2 Wide Stance Sport Performance.		
SS Pkg., LS 2WD regular cab short bed	629	541
Locking differential, front air dam with fog lights, color-keyed grille, rear-step-bumper delete, leather-wrapped steering wheel, SS badging, alloy wheels. Requires 4.3-liter HO engine; 4-speed automatic transmission; 3.42 axle ratio; Sport Suspension; red, black, or white solid paint. NA with Sportside.		
ZQ6 Convenience Group	535	460
Power windows, door locks, and mirrors. NA with Group 1SA.		
ZQ3 Convenience Group	395	340
Tilt steering wheel, cruise control.		

Comfort and Convenience

	Retail Price	Dealer Invoice
Air conditioning	805	692
Third door, extended cab	375	323
Remote keyless entry, LS	140	120
Requires ZQ6 Convenience Group.		
Reclining bucket seats	241	207
2WD with standard engine and transmission	96	83
Includes lumbar adjuster. Includes console w/optional engine or transmission.		
AM/FM radio, base with Group 1SA	226	194
AM/FM/cassette player, base with Group 1SA	348	299
LS	122	105

	Retail Price	Dealer Invoice
AM/FM/cassette player with equalizer, base with Group 1SA	$508	$437
LS	282	243
LS with preferred equipment group	160	138
CD player, LS	406	349
LS with preferred equipment group	284	244
Tachometer	59	51
Leather-wrapped steering wheel	54	46
NA with Group 1SA.		
Sliding rear window	113	97
Deep-tinted glass, regular cab	71	61
regular cab with sliding rear window	36	31
extended cab	107	92
extended cab with sliding rear window	72	62

Appearance and Miscellaneous

	Retail Price	Dealer Invoice
Front air dam with fog lights, 2WD	115	99
NA with Group 1SA.		
Rear step bumper, base with Group 1SA, LS with SS Pkg.	55	47
2-tone paint, LS	197	169
NA with Sportside.		
Cold Climate Pkg.	89	77
Heavy-duty battery, engine-block heater.		

Special Purpose, Wheels and Tires

	Retail Price	Dealer Invoice
Locking differential	252	217
Requires V-6 engine.		
Electronic shift transfer case, 4WD	123	106
NA base with Group 1SA.		
Sport Suspension, LS 2WD short bed, without SS Pkg.	703	605
with SS Pkg.	455	391
Heavy-duty rear springs and shock absorbers, 235/55R16 tires, cast alloy wheels. Requires V-6 engine.		
ZR2 Sport Performance Wide Stance, LS 4WD short bed	1745	1501
Includes Shield Pkg., Bilstein shock absorbers, heavy-duty springs, wheel opening flares, 31 x 10.5R15 on/off road tires, full-size spare tire, modified jack and spare-tire storage winch, chassis enhancements for increased height and width. Requires reclining bucket seats.		
Off-Road Suspension, 4WD short bed	651	560
Heavy-duty front springs, Bilstein shock absorbers, stabilizer bar, upsized torsion bar, jounce bumpers, 235/75R15 white-outline-letter tires, full-size spare tire.		
Shield Pkg., 4WD	126	108
Includes transfer-case and front-differential skid plates, fuel tank and steering-linkage shields.		
Argent alloy wheels, 2WD base with Group 1SA	340	292
LS	248	213
Cast alloy wheels, LS 4WD	280	241
Special alloy wheels, LS 4WD	280	241
base 4WD with Group 1SA	340	292
Silver-painted alloy wheels, LS 4WD	280	241
Bright alloy wheels, LS 4WD	280	241
LS with Group 1SM	NC	NC
205/75R15 white-letter all-season tires	121	104
Includes full-size spare tire.		
235/70R15 all-season tires, 4WD short bed	192	165
Includes full-size spare tire.		
235/75R15 white-outline-letter on/off-road tires, 4WD short bed	335	288
4WD long bed with Increased Capacity Suspension	143	123
Includes full-size spare tire.		
Full-size spare tire	75	65

CHEVROLET/GMC SUBURBAN

Rear- or 4-wheel-drive full-size sport-utility vehicle

Base price range: $25,065-$29,249. Built in Janesville, Wis., and Mexico.

Also consider: Chevrolet Tahoe, Ford Expedition, GMC Yukon, Lincoln Navigator

Rating Scale: 5-Excellent; 4-Above average; 3-Average; 2-Below average; 1-Poor

Chevrolet Suburban K1500 LT

FOR • Standard anti-lock brakes • Passenger and cargo room • Ride • Acceleration (7.4-liter) • Towing ability

AGAINST • Fuel economy • Rear seat entry/exit • Handling

This big sport-utility wagon is sold both by Chevrolet and GMC as the Suburban with only minor differences in equipment and trim. A new 4-wheel-drive system that can be used on dry pavement heads the list of changes for '98.

Suburban is the market's largest sport-utility vehicle and posted record-high sales in 1997, despite presence of its first real competitors, Ford's new Expedition and Lincoln Navigator.

Suburbans come with four side doors. Buyers can choose between two swing-open rear doors and a tailgate with a top-hinged rear window at no charge. Rear-drive Suburbans carry the "C" designation, 4-wheel-drive models use a "K" identifier. The 1500-series models have a half-ton payload rating and the 2500 series a three-quarter-ton rating. Dual air bags, anti-lock brakes, and daytime running lights are standard. Seating for up to nine on three rows of bench seats is available. The middle bench seat splits and folds, and the rear bench is removable. Front bucket seats are optional.

A 5.7-liter V-8 is the base engine. A 7.4-liter V-8 is optional on 2500s. A 6.5-liter turbocharged diesel V-8 is optional on all models. Automatic transmission is standard and GM says it's enhanced this year for increased durability and improved fuel economy.

Newly optional on Chevy 4x4s and standard on GMC 4x4s is AutoTrac full-time 4WD, which allows the 4WD system to remain engaged on any road surface. Standard on Chevy's 4x4 model is the Insta-Trac 4WD system, which allows shifting in and out of 4WD on the fly but is not for use on dry pavement.

GM's OnStar system is a new dealer-installed option. It links the vehicle by cellular phone and satellite with a 24-hour GM center from which operators can furnish directions and other serives and summon emergency help. OnStar's $895 cost includes a cell phone but does not cover installation and monthly service fees.

PERFORMANCE GM's strong, smooth 5.7 V-8 serves most Suburban needs adequately, though even with this base engine, fuel will be big cost of ownership. We averaged 14.8 mpg in our last test of a 4WD model. The 7.4-liter provides better acceleration but at the cost of even lower fuel economy. The diesel is more economical then either and well-suited to towing, but it adds almost $3000 to the price.

Suburban is a capable highway cruiser and 4WD models feel less jiggly over bad pavement than Ford counterparts. The long wheelbase disguises most bumps and there's only moderate floating over freeway dips. The steering is firmer and communicates more road feel than on the Expedition/Navigator, though turns at any speed are accompanied by noticeable body lean. Simulated panic stops induce pronounced nose dive, and in some Suburbans we've tested, rear-wheel locking.

ACCOMMODATIONS The driver enjoys good visibility and a car-like seating position. Suburban's dashboard design is shared with the Chevy Tahoe/GMC Yukon and the big GM pick-up trucks. It's a simple, attractive arrangement of gauges and controls.

Front seats have ample room and are comfortable on long drives. Suburban's 4x4 models ride lower than their Ford rivals, so step-in is not quite the chore it is on Expedition and Navigator. But

it's still not easy to get in or out of the rather narrow rear doors and it's really tough to wend your way to the rearmost seats.

There's not as much room for adults to stretch out in the rear seats as this vehicle's size would suggest and middle-row to middle-row, the Fords are more spacious. Suburban does have plenty of width for three abreast, and head room is generous even in the rear-most seats. The rear bench seat does not fold flat, and while it is removable, it's heavy and cumbersome.

BUILD QUALITY The last few Suburbans we have tested were well assembled and featured quality materials inside and out.

VALUE FOR THE MONEY There's still nothing quite like the Suburban, though the shorter, more "garageable" Tahoe/Yukon are more sensibile all-around choices in a full-size SUV. And if you're not a committed GM fan, also check out the highly competitent new Expedition and Navigator.

RATINGS	5.7-liter 2WD	7.4-liter 4WD
Acceleration	3	4
Fuel economy	1	1
Ride quality	4	3
Steering/handling	3	3
Braking	2	2
Quietness	4	4
Driver seating	4	4
Instruments/controls	4	4
Room/comfort (front)	5	5
Room/comfort (rear)	4	4
Cargo room	5	5
Value for the money	3	2
Total	**42**	**41**

SPECIFICATIONS

	4-door wagon
Wheelbase, in.	131.5
Overall length, in.	219.5
Overall width, in.	76.7
Overall height, in.	71.3
Curb weight, lbs.	4825
Cargo vol., cu. ft.	149.5
Fuel capacity, gals.	42.0
Seating capacity	9
Front head room, in.	39.9
Max. front leg room, in.	41.3
Rear head room, in.	38.9
Min. rear leg room, in.	36.2

ENGINES	ohv V-8	ohv V-8	Turbodiesel ohv V-8
Size, liters/cu. in.	5.7/350	7.4/454	6.5/400
Horsepower @ rpm	255@ 4600	290@ 4000	195@ 3400
Torque (lbs./ft.) @ rpm	330@ 2800	410@ 3200	430@ 1800
Availability	S	O¹	O
EPA city/highway mpg			
4-speed OD automatic	13/18	NA	NA

1. 2500 Series.

PRICES

Chevrolet Suburban	Retail Price	Dealer Invoice
C1500 4-door wagon	$25065	$21932
K1500 4-door wagon	27665	24207
C2500 4-door wagon	26649	23319
K2500 4-door wagon	29249	25594
Destination charge	675	675

C denotes 2WD; K denotes 4WD

STANDARD EQUIPMENT:

C models: 5.7-liter V-8 engine, 4-speed automatic transmission, anti-lock brakes, driver- and passenger-side air bags, daytime running lights, variable-assist power steering, vinyl front bench seat, power door locks, dual outside mirrors, tachometer, oil-pressure gauge, voltmeter, trip odometer, solar-control tinted glass, AM/FM radio, passenger-side visor mirror, auxiliary power outlets, reading lights, rear heat ducts, intermittent wipers, underhood storage, rear

Prices are accurate at time of publication; subject to manufacturer's changes.

tailgate or panel doors, Passlock theft-deterrent system, 7-lead trailer wiring harness, full-size sapre tire, 235/75R15X tires (C1500), P245/75R16 all-terrain tires (K1500), LT245/75R16E tires (2500).

K models add: part-time 4-wheel drive, transmission oil-cooler, front tow hooks.

OPTIONAL EQUIPMENT:
Major Packages (Chevrolet Suburban)

	Retail Price	Dealer Invoice
LS Preferred Equipment Group 1SB, 1500	$7418	$6379
2500, 1500 diesel	7168	6164

LS Decor (includes front and rear air conditioning, power windows and mirrors, tilt steering wheel, cruise control, leather-wrapped steering wheel, upgraded door trim, carpeting, rubber floormats, front door map pockets, cassette player with automatic tone control, 6-way power driver seat, cloth front 60/40 split bench seat, folding 3-passenger middle seat, 3-passenger rear seat, automatic day/night rearview mirror, illuminated visor mirrors, roof rack, chrome grille, dual-note horn, cargo net, spare tire cover, rally wheels [1500 with diesel engine, 2500], or alloy wheels [1500 with gasoline engine], deep-tinted glass, rear wiper/washer [with rear tailgate], rear defogger), remote keyless entry, rear heater.LT

Preferred Group 1SC, 1500	9168	7884
2500, 1500 diesel	8919	7669

Preferred Equipment Group 1SB plus LT Decor (LS Decor plus leather upholstery, front 60/40 split bench seat, power lumbar adjustment, storage armrest)

Comfort and Security Pkg.	1150	989

Heated front seats, power passsenger seat, carpeted floormats and cargo mat, Homelink universal garage door opener, Bilstein shock absorbers. Requires LT Group and bucket front seats.

Heavy-Duty Trailering Special Equipment,		
1500 w/5.7-liter engine and std. axle	455	383
1500 w/5.7-liter engine and 3/73 rear axle ratio	310	267
1500 with diesel engine, 2500	214	184

Includes platform hitch, engine-oil cooler, transmission-oil cooler.

Convenience Pkg. ZQ3	383	329

Cruise control and tilt steering column.

Major Packages (GMC Suburban)

SLE Marketing Option Pkg. 2,		
w/5.7-liter gasoline engine	7573	6513
w/6.5-liter Diesel engine, 2500	7323	6298

SLE Decor (front and rear air conditioning, rear heater, cruise control, tilt steering wheel, reclining front split bench seat with center armrest and power lumbar adjusters, 6-way power driver seat, seatback storage pockets, folding center and rear bench seats, custom cloth upholstery, leather-wrapped steering wheel, rear cupholders, deep tinted glass, power windows, power mirrors, deep-tinted glass, rear defogger, 8-speaker cassette player w/automatic tone control, automatic day/night inside mirror w/compass, carpeting, floormats, carpeted spare tire cover, illuminated visor mirrors, dual-note horn, color-keyed grille, roof rack, cargo net, electronic active transfer case [4WD], wheel trim rings [diesel, 2500], alloy wheels [1500 w/5.7-liter gasoline engine]), panel doors, cargo mat, remote keyless entry. Includes rear wiper/washer when ordered with rear tailgate.

SLT Marketing Option Pkg. 3,		
w/5.7-liter gasoline engine	9613	8267
w/6.5-liter diesel engine, 2500	9363	8052

SLE Marketing Option Pkg. 2 plus leather upholstery, reclining front bucket seats, storage armrest, cassette/CD player, seatback storage pockets, additional rear cupholders.

Convenience Pkg. ZQ3	383	329

Cruise control, tilt steering wheel.

Luxury Convenience Pkg.	995	856

Heated front seats, 6-way power passenger seat, heated driver-side mirror w/automatic day/night, Homelink universal garage door opener, Bilstein gas shock absorbers. Requires SLT Pkg.

Heavy-Duty Trailering Equipment	214	184

Platform hitch, heavy-duty flasher. Requires engine-oil cooler on 1500 when ordered with 5.7-liter V-8 engine and 3.42 rear axle. K1500 not available with skid plates when ordered with front bench seat or 60/40 split bench seat.

Powertrains

Autotrac Active transfer case, 4WD	400	344

Requires Convenience Pkg. ZQ3 or LS/LT Group.

	Retail Price	Dealer Invoice
7.4-liter V-8 engine, 2500	$600	$516
6.5-liter turbodiesel V-8 engine	2860	2460

Includes wheel-flare moldings when ordered with K1500. Deletes underhood storage compartment. 1500 requires optional tires.

Locking differential	252	217

Comfort and Convenience

Front and rear air conditioning	1395	1200

Includes cloth-covered rear quarter trim.

Front air conditioning	845	727
Rear heater	205	176
Rear defogger	154	132

Requires front air conditioning. NA with rear tailgate.

Rear defogger and wiper/washer	279	240

Requires rear tailgate, front air conditioning.

OnStar System	895	761

Includes Global Positioning System, voice-activated cellular telephone, roadside assistance, emergency services. Requires dealer installation charge and monthly service charges.

Cassette player	147	126
CD player w/automatic tone control, LS, LT	100	86
Cassette/CD player w/automatic tone control, LS, LT	200	172
Folding center seat	632	544
Folding center and rear seats	1182	1017

Includes cloth covered rear quarter trim.

Reclining front bucket seats,, LS	290	249

Includes power lumbar support. Requires LS/LT Group.

Carpeted floormats	155	133

Appearance and Miscellaneous

Deep-tinted glass	$305	$262

Includes cloth covered rear quarter trim.

Conventional 2-tone paint, LS, LT	200	172
Running boards	275	237
Wheel flare moldings, K1500	180	155

Special Purpose, Wheels and Tires

Engine-oil cooler, 1500	135	116
Heavy-duty transmission cooler, 1500	96	83
Skid Plate Pkg., 4WD models	225	194
Heavy-duty front springs, 4WD models	63	54

Requires std. 5.7-liter engine.

Rally wheels,	60	52
Alloy wheels, 1500	310	267

NA with diesel engine. 2WD requires 235/75R15 tires.

LT235/75R15 outline white letter tires	180	155

Requires std. 5.7-liter engine.

LT245/75R16E tires	459	396

Requires 6.5-liter V-8 engine.

LT245/75R16C on/off road outline white letter tires	182	155

Requires std. 5.7-liter engine.

LT245/75R16E	174	150

Requires deisel engine.

245/75R16C all-terrain outline white letter tires	140	120

Requires std. 5.7-liter engine.

CHEVROLET TAHOE
RECOMMENDED

Chevrolet Tahoe 2WD 2-door

Rear- or 4-wheel-drive full-size sport-utility vehicle; similar to GMC Yukon

Base price range: $23,585-$31,985. Built in Janesville, Wis.; Arlington, Tex.; and Mexico.

Rating Scale: 5-Excellent; 4-Above average; 3-Average; 2-Below average; 1-Poor

Also consider: Chevrolet/GMC Suburban, Ford Expedition, Isuzu Trooper, Lincoln Navigator

FOR • Acceleration (5.7-liter) • Standard anti-lock brakes • Passenger and cargo room • Towing ability

AGAINST • Fuel economy • Ride (2-door model) • Entry/exit (2-door and 4WD models)

General Motors lopped nearly two feet off its battleship-class Suburbans in 1995 to create the 4-door Chevy Tahoe and GMC Yukon. More maneuverable than the Suburban and roomier than compact SUVs like the Ford Explorer, they were immediate hits. But sales have cooled as buyers gravitate to the newest darlings of the growing full-size SUV market, the Ford Expedition and Lincoln Navigator.

GM fights back for '98, giving Tahoe and Yukon their first 4-wheel-drive systems that can be used on dry pavment, matching a feature of the Fords. And GM's OnStar navigation system also is newly available.

Tahoe offers two or four doors, the 4-doors with a longer wheelbase and body. Buyers can choose a bottom-hinged tailgate with a separately opening, top-hinged rear window or two side-hinged rear panel doors. Both body styles seat five, or six with the optional front bench. Dual air bags, anti-lock brakes, and daytime running lights are standard.

A 5.7-liter V-8 is standard and a 6.5-liter turbocharged diesel V-8 is optional on the 4WD 2-door. An automatic is the only transmission and Chevy says it's been modified for improved durability and fuel economy.

The standard 4WD system can be shifted on the fly between 2WD and 4WD High, but is not for use on dry pavement. The optional new Autotrac system allows the use of 4WD on any surface. Maximum towing capacity is 7000 pounds for 2WD models and 6500 pounds for 4x4s.

OnStar links the vehicle by cell phone and satellite to a 24-hour GM center from which operators can furnish directions and other services and summon emergency help. Its $895 cost includes a cell phone but doesn't cover monthly service fees.

PERFORMANCE A highly capable big wagon, the 4-door has the lion's share of Tahoe sales and is the match of the newer Expedition in most every area of performance. Blessed with a little more low-speed muscle than Expedition's smaller standard overhead-cam V-8, Tahoe's overhead-valve 5.7 furnishes good acceleration off the line and adequate power to pass or climb grades. It's linked to a transmission that provides unobtrusive gear changes and responds to the throttle with prompt downshifts. We averaged 14.3 mpg in our last last of a 4WD 4-door. That's about 1-2 mpg under what we average with V-8 Explorers and Jeep Grand Cherokees. The diesel engine is for heavy-duty use only.

Tahoe's suspension is tuned to maximize on-road comfort. The result is an absorbent ride worthy of a large domestic sedan. Body lean is the rule in turns, but it is not unnerving and grip in corners is reassuring. The steering feels firm and enables the Tahoe to cruise down the Interstate with a minimum of wandering. Two-door models ride more firmly, but have similar handling characteristics.

Tahoe muffles wind, road, and engine noise enough to qualify as an inviting cross-country cruiser.

ACCOMMODATIONS Access to the rear seat is vastly superior in 4-door models, but the rear door openings are narrow at the bottom, and step-in height is high.

Front-seat room is commodious, befitting a vehicle this size. The 4-door's back seat is in front of the rear wheels instead of even with them, so the rear bench has about six inches more rear hip room than in the 2-door, enough to easily seat three adults. Rear leg room is generous.

Cargo room in the 4-door is cavernous and benefits immensely from the under-carriage location of the spare tire. But it's a chore to stretch across the drop-down tailgate and reach into the cargo bay.

Tahoe has easy-to-read gauges and simple, handy controls. The 4-door model also has height-adjustable shoulder belts for all outboard seating positions. Visibility is unobstructed to all directions.

BUILD QUALITY Our test vehicles have been solidly assembled, with glossy paint and no squeaks or rattles. There were, however, unequal gaps in interior trim and the dashboard.

VALUE FOR THE MONEY Considering its room, comfort, and towing ability, Tahoe in 4-door 4WD form is an exceptional package, its only disadvantages being fuel economy and step-in height. Shop the new Fords, but don't overlook Tahoe.

RATINGS

	2-dr. 4WD	4-dr. 2WD
Acceleration	4	4
Fuel economy	1	1
Ride quality	2	4
Steering/handling	3	3
Braking	4	4
Quietness	4	4
Driver seating	4	4
Instruments/controls	4	4
Room/comfort (front)	5	5
Room/comfort (rear)	2	4
Cargo room	4	5
Value for the money	3	3
Total	**40**	**45**

SPECIFICATIONS

	2-door wagon	4-door wagon
Wheelbase, in.	111.5	117.5
Overall length, in.	188.0	199.6
Overall width, in.	77.1	76.8
Overall height, in.	71.4	72.8
Curb weight, lbs.	4632	4423
Cargo vol., cu. ft.	99.4	118.2
Fuel capacity, gals.	30.0	30.0
Seating capacity	6	6
Front head room, in.	39.9	39.9
Max. front leg room, in.	41.7	41.7
Rear head room, in.	37.8	38.9
Min. rear leg room, in.	36.4	36.2

ENGINES

	ohv V-8	Turbodiesel ohv V-8
Size, liters/cu. in.	5.7/350	6.5/395
Horsepower @ rpm	255@ 4600	180@ 3400
Torque (lbs./ft.) @ rpm	330@ 2800	360@ 1800
Availability	S	O[1]

EPA city/highway mpg
4-speed OD automatic 15/19

1. 4WD 2-door model.

PRICES

Chevrolet Tahoe	Retail Price	Dealer Invoice
2WD 2-door wagon	$23585	$20637
4WD 2-door wagon	26185	22912
LS 2WD 4-door wagon	29385	25712
LS 4WD 4-door wagon	31985	27987
Destination charge	640	640

STANDARD EQUIPMENT:

2-door: 5.7-liter V-8 engine, 4-speed automatic transmission, driver- and passenger-side air bags, anti-lock brakes, daytime running lights, variable-assist power steering, vinyl front reclining bucket seats, 3-passenger folding rear bench seat, AM/FM radio, tachometer, trip odometer, coolant-temperature gauge, voltmeter, oil-pressure gauge, dual outside mirrors, power door locks, intermittent wipers, auxiliary power outlets, reading lamps, passenger-side visor mirror, rear heat duct, Passlock theft-deterrent system, solar-control tinted glass, rear tailgate or liftgate, underhood storage box, front air dam, chrome bumpers, 7-lead trailer wiring harness, 235/75R15 all-season tires (2WD), full-size spare tire, 4WD models add part-time 4-wheel drive with 2-speed transfer case, automatic locking front hubs, front tow hooks, 245/75R16 all-terrain tires.

4-door adds: LS Decor (includes air conditioning, power windows,

Prices are accurate at time of publication; subject to manufacturer's changes.

power mirrors, tilt steering wheel, leather-wrapped steering wheel, cruise control, upgraded door trim, carpeting, rubber floormats, cassette player with automatic tone control, cloth upholstery, 60/40 front bench seat with storage armrest, 6-way power driver seat, power lumbar support adjuster, split folding rear bench seat with armrest, automatic day/night mirror, cargo cover, illuminated visor mirrors, rear wiper/washer [with tailgate], roof rack, chrome grille, deep-tinted glass, dual-note horn, cargo net, spare-tire cover, alloy wheels), remote keyless entry, 4WD models add part-time 4-wheel drive with 2-speed transfer case, automatic locking front hubs, front tow hooks, 245/75R16 all-terrain tires.

OPTIONAL EQUIPMENT:

	Retail Price	Dealer Invoice

Major Packages

LS Equipment Group 1SB, 2-door $4369 $3757
LS Decor (air conditioning, power windows and door locks, power mirrors, tilt steering wheel, cruise control, leather-wrapped steering wheel, 6-way power driver seat, upgraded door trim, carpeting, rubber floormats, cassette player with automatic tone control, cloth 60/40 front bench seat with storage armrest and power lumbar support adjuster, deep-tinted glass, automatic day/night mirror, illuminated visor mirrors, roof rack, chrome grille, dual-note horn, cargo net, spare-tire cover, rear defogger, rear wiper/washer [with tailgate], alloy wheels), remote keyless entry.

LT Equipment Group 1SC, 2-door	5719	4918
4-door	1350	1161

Group 1SB and remote keyless entry (2-door) plus LT Decor (LS Decor plus leather upholstery, cassette/CD player).

Off-Road Chassis Pkg., LS/LT 4WD 2-door	400	344

Bilstein shock absorbers, Skid Plate Pkg. Requires optional tires when ordered without Sport Pkg. Requires 265/75R16C all-terrain tires when ordered with Sport Pkg.

Comfort and Security Pkg., 2-door	755	649
4-door	1545	1329

Heated seats, 6-way power passenger-seat (4-door), heated power mirrors w/diver-side automatic day/night, rear air conditioning (4-door), Homelink universal garage door opener, Bilstein shock absorbers. Requires LT Pkg. and bucket seats. NA with Sport Pkg.

Comfort and Security Pkg. with carpeted floormats, 2-door	910	782
4-door	1700	1462

Comfort and Security Pkg. plus carpeted floormats. Requires LT pkg. and bucket seats. NA with Sport Pkg.

Sport Pkg., LS/LT 4WD 2-door	302	260

Dark argent grille, wheel flares, and bumpers; black front license bracket, front air dam, and mirrors; Sport decals. NA with turbodiesel engine, LT245/75R16C on-off-road white-outline tires, or 265/75R16 all-terrain white-outline-letter tires.

Convenience Group ZQ3	383	329

Cruise control, tilt steering wheel.

Heavy Duty Trailering Special Equipment,		
ordered w/6.5-liter engine	214	184
ordered w/5.7-liter engine and std. axle	349	300
ordered w/5.7-liter engine and 3.42 rear axle ratio	445	383
ordered w/5.7-liter engine and 3.73 rear axle ratio	310	267

Includes trailer hitch and platform, heavy-duty engine-oil and transmission coolers.

Powertrains

6.5-liter turbodiesel engine, 2-door 4WD	2860	2460

Includes heavy-duty automatic transmission, engine-oil cooler. NA with Sport Pkg. Deletes standard underhood storage box.

3.42 rear axle ratio, 2WD 2-door	NC	NC
3.73 rear axle ratio	135	116

Includes engine oil cooler. NA 2WD 2-door without LS or LT Pkg.

Locking differential	252	217

NA with turbodiesel engine. 2WD 2-door requires standard rear axle ratio.

Autotrac Active transfer case, 4WD	175	151

Requires Convenience Group ZQ3 or LS/LT Group.

Comfort and Convenience

OnStar System	895	761

Includes Global Positioning System, voice-activated cellular telephone, roadside assistance, emergency services. Requires dealer installation charge and monthly service charges.

	Retail Price	Dealer Invoice
Air conditioning, 2-door	$845	$727
Rear air conditioning, 4-door	550	473
High-back bucket seats, LS, LT	237	204
Includes center and overhead console.		
Rear defogger, 2-door with panel doors	154	132
Requires air conditioning.		
Rear Window Equipment, 2-door	279	240
Rear wiper/washer and defogger. Requires rear tailgate.		
Cassette player, 2-door	147	126
Cassette player w/automatic tone control, 2-door	202	174
CD player w/automatic tone control, 4-door, 2-door LS/LT	100	86
CD/cassette player with automatic tone control, 2-door LS/LT, 4-door	200	172
Carpeted floormats	155	133

Appearance and Miscellaneous

Wheel-flare moldings, 4WD 2-door	180	155
Running boards	275	237
2-tone paint, LS, LT	200	172
Deep-tinted glass	215	185
Cold Climate Pkg.	33	28
Includes engine-block heater. NA with turbodiesel engine.		
Stainless-steel camper-type mirrors, 2-door	53	46

Special Purpose, Wheels and Tires

Engine-oil cooler	135	116
NA with turbodiesel engine.		
Heavy-duty transmission-oil cooler	96	83
Requires 3.73 rear axle ratio. NA with turbodiesel engine.		
Heavy-duty front springs, 2-door	63	54
NA with 6.5-liter turbodiesel V-8 engine.		
Front tow hooks, 2WD 4-door	38	32
Skid Plate Pkg., 4WD 2-door	225	194
4WD 4-door	95	82
Rally wheels	60	52
NA with LS, LT.		
Alloy wheels	310	267
235/75R15 all-season white-letter tires, 2WD	125	108
245/75R16C all-terrain white-letter tires, 4WD 4-door	140	120
LT245/75R16C on-off road tires, 4WD	57	47
LT245/75R16C on-off road white-letter tires, 4WD 2-door	180	155
265/75R16C all-terrain tires, 4WD 2-door	190	163
Requires alloy wheels.		
265/75R16C all-terrain white-letter tires, 4WD 2-door	315	271
Requires alloy wheels.		

CHEVROLET TRACKER

Chevrolet Tracker 2WD 4-door

Rear- or 4-wheel-drive compact sport-utility vehicle; similar to Suzuki Sidekick
Base price range: $13,655-$15,605. Built in Canada.
Also consider: Honda CR-V, Jeep Wrangler, Toyota RAV4

FOR • Fuel economy • Optional anti-lock brakes
• Maneuverability

Rating Scale: 5-Excellent; 4-Above average; 3-Average; 2-Below average; 1-Poor

AGAINST • Ride • Noise • Rear seat room (convertible)

Since Chevrolet is adsorbing the Geo line, Tracker puts on a bow tie badge and loses its top LSi trim level, but gets no significant changes pending a scheduled redesign for 1999.

Tracker is based on the same design and mechanical components used by the Suzuki Sidekick, which also is slated for a '99 revamp. Both are built in Canada at a plant General Motors shares with Suzuki.

Tracker comes as a 2-door convertible and 4-door wagon with a 11-inch-longer wheelbase and a 15-inch-longer body. It has 15.3 cubic feet of cargo room, 8.4 more than the convertible. Shelving the LSi 4-door makes base the only trim level. Dual air bags and daytime running lights are standard. Anti-lock brakes are optional.

The available 4-wheel-drive system is not for use on dry pavement. Automatic locking hubs, which allow switching between 2WD and 4WD without leaving the vehicle, are optional. For 1998, the manual locking front hubs can remain locked, allowing shift on the fly at any speed.

The only engine is a 95-horsepower 1.6-liter 4-cylinder. Manual transmission is standard. A 3-speed automatic is optional on the convertible and a 4-speed automatic is optional on the wagon.

PERFORMANCE Tracker can muster only meager acceleration. Even with the manual transmission it's tough to stay with fast-moving traffic. With automatic, progress is downright slow.

On the upside, both tranmissions shift crisply, and fuel economy is good. We averaged 20.8 mpg in a test of a 4-door 4WD with automatic in mostly city driving. That's higher than we've seen with most other SUVs and is one advantage of Tracker's relatively light weight and small engine.

Unfortunately, the small engine emits a nasty growl under throttle and is never really quiet or refined. All Trackers also suffer lots of road noise and abundant wind noise at highway speeds.

On road or off road, modest length and width give Tracker outstanding maneuverability. The 4-door's longer wheelbase imparts a feeling of security absent from the convertibles. But no 4x4 should be driven as quickly as a passenger car in turns, and the Tracker feels tipsy in lane changes and on freeway ramps. Ride quality is best on the 4-door, but Tracker is not comfortable to ride in.

Braking power was more than adequate on our test vehicles, and the optional anti-lock feature works effectively on slippery surfaces.

ACCOMMODATIONS Four-doors have plenty of head room all around but mediocre rear leg room, and the narrow interior lacks shoulder room. Four adults fit, but it's cramped. Two-door models are best suited to transporting two people.

Luggage room in either model is poor unless you fold the rear seat. With it folded, there's less cargo space than in midsize SUVs but far more than in most passenger cars.

Gauges and controls are clearly marked and easy to use. There are new radio buttons and controls this year and they're an improvement over the old, being large and clearly marked.

Visibility to the rear is hampered by the outside-mount spare tire and rear head rests. The driver's view is otherwise unobstructed.

BUILD QUALITY Trackers we've tested have been generally rattle-free, though cost-cutting is apparent throughout the interior and in doors that close with a tinny clang.

VALUE FOR THE MONEY Aside from better fuel economy and lower prices, the Tracker is a questionable substitute for a more-substantial 4x4. Our nod for a compact SUV goes to Toyota's RAV4 or the Honda CR-V.

SPECIFICATIONS

	2-door convertible	4-door wagon
Wheelbase, in.	86.6	97.6
Overall length, in.	143.7	158.7
Overall width, in.	64.2	64.4
Overall height, in.	64.3	65.7
Curb weight, lbs.	2339	2747
Cargo vol., cu. ft.	6.9	15.3
Fuel capacity, gals.	11.1	14.5

	2-door convertible	4-door wagon
Seating capacity	4	4
Front head room, in.	39.5	40.6
Max. front leg room, in.	42.1	42.1
Rear head room, in.	39.0	40.0
Min. rear leg room, in.	31.7	32.7

ENGINES

	ohc I-4
Size, liters/cu. in.	1.6/97
Horsepower @ rpm	95 @ 5600
Torque (lbs./ft.) @ rpm	98 @ 4000
Availability	S

EPA city/highway mpg

3-speed automatic	23/24
4-speed OD automatic	22/26
5-speed OD manual	23/26

RATINGS

	2-dr. 5-speed	4-dr. automatic
Acceleration	2	1
Fuel economy	4	4
Ride quality	2	3
Steering/handling	2	2
Braking	4	4
Quietness	1	1
Driver seating	3	3
Instruments/controls	4	4
Room/comfort (front)	3	3
Room/comfort (rear)	2	3
Cargo room	3	4
Value for the money	3	3
Total	33	35

PRICES

Chevrolet Tracker	Retail Price	Dealer Invoice
2-door convertible, 2WD	$13655	$13000
2-door convertible, 4WD	14860	14147
4-door wagon, 2WD	14665	13952
4-door wagon, 4WD	15605	14856
Destination charge	340	340

STANDARD EQUIPMENT:

Base: 1.6-liter 4-cylinder engine, 5-speed manual transmission, driver- and passenger-side air bags, daytime running lights, power steering (wagon, 4WD convertible), rear defogger (wagon), cloth/vinyl reclining front bucket seats, folding rear bench seat (convertible), split folding rear bench seat (wagon), center console with storage tray and cupholders, tachometer, trip odometer, passenger-side visor mirror, intermittent wipers, dual outside mirrors, fuel-tank skid plate, full-size lockable spare tire, spare-tire cover, front and rear tow hooks, 195/75R15 tires (2WD) or 205/75R15 tires (4WD).

OPTIONAL EQUIPMENT:
Major Packages

Preferred Group 2, 2WD convertible	1644	1463
4WD convertible	1354	1205
wagon	1366	1216

Air conditioning, AM/FM radio with digital clock, power steering (2WD convertible), bodyside moldings, floormats.

Preferred Group 3,		
2WD wagon	2121	1888
4WD wagon	2321	2066

Group 2 plus automatic locking front hubs (4WD), Convenience Pkg. (power windows and door locks, power mirrors).

Expression color-appearance pkg., convertible	249	222
Expression Appearance Pkg.,		
convertible with Preferred Group	164	146

Adjustable rear bucket seats, custom upholstery, bodyside moldings, special tan exterior color treatments.

Convenience Pkg., wagon	580	516

Power windows and door locks, power mirrors.

Prices are accurate at time of publication; subject to manufacturer's changes.

Powertrains

	Retail Price	Dealer Invoice
3-speed automatic transmission, convertibles	$625	$556
4-speed automatic transmission, wagons	100	890
Automatic locking front hubs, 4WD	200	178

Safety Features

Anti-lock brakes..	595	530

Comfort and Convenience

Air conditioning..	935	832
Power steering, 2WD convertible............................	290	258
Cruise control...	175	156
AM/FM radio..	306	272
Includes digital clock.		
AM/FM/cassette	526	468
with Preferred Group	220	196
Includes digital clock.		
AM/FM/CD player..	626	557
AM/FM/cassette and CD players,		
with Preferred Group	320	284
Rear wiper/washer, wagon....................................	125	111
Floormats, convertible	28	25
wagon	40	36

Appearance and Miscellaneous

Bodyside moldings	85	76

Special Purpose, Wheels and Tires

Transfer-case and front-differential skid plates,		
4WD...	75	67
Alloy wheels	365	325

CHEVROLET VENTURE

RECOMMENDED

Chevrolet Venture

Front-wheel-drive minivan; similar to Oldsmobile Silhouette, and Pontiac Trans Sport

Base price range: $20,169-$22,259. Built in Doraville, Ga.

Also consider: Dodge Caravan, Ford Windstar, Mercury Villager, Toyota Sienna

FOR • Standard anti-lock brakes • Ride • Passenger and cargo room • Side air bags

AGAINST • Fuel economy

General Motors revamped its front-drive minivans for 1997, launching the Venture and companion Pontiac Trans Sport and Oldsmobile Silhouette, which differ only in styling and trim levels. For '98, front side air bags are standard, the regular-length Venture joins the longer model in offering an optional driver-side sliding door, and GM's OnStar navigation system is a new option.

Extended-length Ventures add 8 inches to the wheelbase and 14 inches to the body of the regular-length model. A right-side sliding door is standard and its power-opening-and-closing feature is optionally available on both bodies this year, not just on the extended model. The driver-side sliding door is manual. Also, a cargo version of the long wheelbase model has been added.

All Ventures have a 180-horsepower 3.4-liter V-6 and automatic transmission. The new side air bags are mounted to the front seats and join dual front air bags. Daytime running lights and anti-lock brakes also are standard. Traction control and built-in child safety seats are optional.

Standard 7-passenger seating in short-wheelbase models includes two front buckets, a 2-person middle bench, and a 3-person rear bench. Modular split bench seats, also with 7-passenger capacity, are standard on the extended models. Cargo models have two front buckets.

OnStar links the vehicle by cell phone and satellite to a 24-hour GM center from which operators can dispense travel advice, summon emergency help, and perform other services. Cost of the dealer-installed option includes a cell phone, but not installation or service fees.

PERFORMANCE Venture's V-6 provides adequate acceleration, helped by an automatic transmission that keeps unnecessary gear changes to a minimum and reacts quickly when asked to downshift in passing situations. In a mix of city and suburban commuting and freeway travel, we averaged 15.3 mpg, which is about par for this class.

Venture rides and handles much like a car—as do the Ford Windstar and Chrysler Corporation minivans—though the Chevy feels somewhat sportier. The steering is precise and accurately communicates what the front tires are doing. Turns are taken with good balance and moderate body lean. Most bumps are easily absorbed and the highway ride is comfortable and stable.

Our test vehicles stopped with good control and had a progressive pedal feel. At highway speeds wind noise was prominent around the mirrors, but road and engine sounds were well-muffled.

ACCOMMODATIONS GM does a commendable job of interior space utilization with these minivans. Modular seating allows easy removal and rearrangement of middle bucket seats that weigh just 39 pounds each, and even the 45-pound rear benches aren't overly cumbersome. To get seats this light, however, GM used cushions that aren't as substantial as those in the Chrysler and Ford rivals, and the seats are so low to the floor that adults find themselves sitting with their knees elevated.

There's a plethora of storage bins, cup/juice box holders, even a pencil and tissue holder in the glovebox and a handy storage net between the front seats. Cargo room is good on the long wheelbase model even with all seats in place. The tailgate is lightweight and easier than most to open and close.

Climbing aboard is simply a matter of stepping in, thanks to a low floor. The optional driver-side sliding door is a genuine convenience, as is the GM-exclusive power sliding passenger-side door. The driver-side sliding door opens wide enough to allow access to the third-row seats—a trick that even the vaunted Chrysler minivans can't match.

Visibility is excellent and large outside mirrors enhance the view over the shoulder.

BUILD QUALITY Our test Ventures have been well-built, feeling solid over bumps and exhibiting even panel gaps inside and out.

VALUE FOR THE MONEY GM's front-drive trio is among the most-desirable minivans. Base prices are higher than the rivals from Dodge, Plymouth, or Ford, but Venture comes with more standard features, including air conditioning, power locks, and anti-lock brakes. We're impressed and encourage you to take a look.

RATINGS	3-dr. reg. length	4-dr. ext. length
Acceleration	3	3
Fuel economy	2	2
Ride quality	3	4
Steering/handling	4	4
Braking	4	4
Quietness	4	4
Driver seating	4	4
Instruments/controls	4	4
Room/comfort (front)	4	4
Room/comfort (rear)	3	3
Cargo room	5	5
Value for the money	4	4
Total	44	45

SPECIFICATIONS	3-door van	3-door van
Wheelbase, in.	112.0	120.0
Overall length, in.	186.9	200.9
Overall width, in.	72.0	72.0
Overall height, in.	67.4	68.1

Rating Scale: 5-Excellent; 4-Above average; 3-Average; 2-Below average; 1-Poor

	3-door van	3-door van
Curb weight, lbs.	3699	3838
Cargo vol., cu. ft.	126.6	148.3
Maximum payload, lbs.	1658	1519
Fuel capacity, gals.	20.0	25.0
Seating capacity	7	7
Front head room, in.	39.9	39.9
Max. front leg room, in.	39.9	39.9
Rear head room, in.	39.3	39.3
Min. rear leg room, in.	36.9	39.0

ENGINES

	ohv V-6
Size, liters/cu. in.	3.4/207
Horsepower @ rpm	180@ 5200
Torque (lbs./ft.) @ rpm	205@ 4000
Availability	S

EPA city/highway mpg

4-speed OD automatic..	18/25

PRICES

Chevrolet Venture

	Retail Price	Dealer Invoice
Cargo Extended 3-door van	$20169	$18253
Cargo Extended 4-door van	20759	18787
Passenger SWB 3-door van	20249	18325
Passenger Extended 3-door van	21669	19610
Passenger LS SWB 4-door van	21429	19393
Passenger LS Extended 4-door	22259	20144
Destination charge	570	570

SWB denotes short wheelbase.

STANDARD EQUIPMENT:

Cargo: 3.4-liter V-6 engine, 4-speed automatic transmission, driver- and passenger-side air bags, anti-lock brakes, daytime running lamps, front air conditioning, power steering, tilt steering column, 2-passenger seating (vinyl front bucket seats), rubber floor covering, center storage console, overhead consolette, front cupholders, automatic headlights, interior air filter, intermittent wipers, rear wiper/washer, AM/FM radio, digital clock, power door locks, power mirrors, visor mirrors, front auxiliary power outlets, Passlock theft-deterrent, tinted glass, Sungate solar-coated windshield with integrated antenna, dual horn, 215/70R15 tires, wheel covers.

Passenger SWB 3-door adds: 7-passenger seating (cloth front bucket seats, center and rear solid bench seats), seatback tray, carpeting, floormats, cargo net, rear cupholders, rear power outlet, intermittent rear wiper/washer, 205/70R15 tires.

Passenger Extended 3-door adds: center and rear split folding bench seats, 215/70R15 tires.

Passenger LS SWB 4-door adds: driver-side sliding door, cruise control, LS trim (driver-side lumbar support, adjustable headrests, upgraded interior trim and upholstery), power windows, cassette player with automatic tone control, remote keyless entry, interior roof-rail lighting, additional sound insulation, liftgate cargo net.

Passenger LS Extended 4-door adds: 215/70R15 tires.

OPTIONAL EQUIPMENT:
Major Packages

	Retail	Dealer
Preferred Equipment Group 1	650	559

Power windows, cruise control, remote keyless entry.

LS Preferred Equipment Group 2, SWB 3-door......	1540	1324
Passenger Extended 3-door, 4-door....................	1205	1036

Group 1 plus power rear vent windows, custom cloth seats, center and rear split folding bench seats (SWB), front lumbar adjusters, adjusrable headrests, cassette player w/automatic tone control.

LS Preferred Equipment Group 3, Passenger Extended	2401	2065

Group 2 plus power driver seat, overhead console, rear defogger, deep-tinted glass, roof rack.

Safety and Security Pkg., Passenger	285	245
Passenger w/Touring Suspension	210	181

Theft-deterrent system including alarm, self-sealing tires.

	Retail Price	Dealer Invoice
Trailering Pkg.	$150	$129

Includes heavy-duty engine and transmission oil cooling.

Powertrains

Traction control..	195	159

Comfort and Convenience

OnStar System...	895	761

Includes Global Positioning System, voice-activated cellular telephone, roadside assistance, emergency services. Requires dealer installation charge and monthly serice charges.

Rear air conditioning, Passenger Extended	450	387

Requires deep-tinted glass and rear defogger. 3-door requires a preferred equipment group.

Rear heater, Cargo	205	176
Power passenger-side sliding door, SWB..............	435	374
Passenger Extended	385	331

Includes power rear vent windows. SWB requires Group 1. Extended requires Group 1 or 2.

6-way power driver seat, Passenger......................	270	232

3-door requires Group 2.

Cloth upholstery, Cargo	185	159
Center and rear split folding bench seats, SWB 3-door	335	288

Requires Group 1.

Center row captain's seats, Passenger...................	265	228
Rear bucket seats, Passenger...............................	115	99

Requires Group 2 or 3.

Integrated child seat, Passenger..........................	125	108

NA with captain's seats.

Dual integrated child seats, Passenger	225	194

NA with captain's seats.

Upgraded interior trim and upholstery, Passenger 3-door	NC	NC
Rear defogger	170	146
Cassette player, Cargo	165	141
Cassette player w/automatic tone control, SWB 3-door	232	220
CD player, Passenger	370	318
Passenger w/Group 2 or 3.	100	86

Includes automatic tone control, coaxial speakers, anti-theft feature.

Cassette/CD player, Passenger............................	470	404
Passenger w/Group 2 or 3	200	172

Includes automatic tone control, coaxial speakers, anti-theft feature.

Rear-seat audio controls, Passenger......................	120	103

Includes headphone jacks. 3-door requires Group 2 or 3.

Overhead console, Passenger...............................	271	233

Driver information center, illuminated visor mirrors.

Appearance and Miscellaneous

Touring Suspension, Cargo	195	167
Passenger SWB	285	245
Passenger Extended w/Group 2	245	211
Passenger Extended W/Group 3	210	181

Load-leveling suspension, auxiliary air inflator (passenger), 215/70R15 tires (SWB).

Roof rack...	175	151
Deep-tinted glass, Passenger...............................	275	237

Includes blackout center pillar w/most exterior colors. Requires rear defogger.

Deep-tinted glass w/rear defogger, Cargo	445	383
Engine-block heater	20	17
Theft-deterrent system, Cargo	60	51

Requires Preferred Equipment Group.

215/70R15 tires, SWB 3-door, LS SWB 4-door..	75	65
215/70R15 touring tires, Cargo Exended...............	35	30

3-door requires a Preferred Equipment Group.

Self-sealing tires, Cargo, Extended..	185	159
SWB..	225	194
Alloy wheels	295	254

Prices are accurate at time of publication; subject to manufacturer's changes.

CHRYSLER CIRRUS

Chrysler Cirrus LXi

Front-wheel-drive midsize; similar to Dodge Stratus and Plymouth Breeze.
Base price: $19,460. Built in Sterling Heights, Mich.
Also consider: Honda Accord, Mercury Sable, Toyota Camry

FOR • Standard anti-lock brakes • Ride • Steering/handling • Passenger and cargo room

AGAINST • Noise • Rear visibility • Automatic transmission performance

Cirrus is the Chrylser-badged version of a corporate trio that includes the Dodge Stratus and Plymouth Breeze. Chrysler aims to strengthen Cirrus's upscale image for '98 by dropping the 4-cylinder engine and making it the only one of the three to feature a V-6 exclusively. Further, the base LX-trim level is deep-sixed and the car is being marketed as the Cirrus LXi, adopting the name of last year's premium option package.

Gone is the 150-horsepower Chrysler-made 2.4-liter 4-cylinder, leaving last year's optional 168-horsepower Mitsubishi-made 2.5-liter V-6 as the sole engine. Automatic transmission is standard, as are dual air bags and anti-lock brakes.

Picked up from last year's $2335 LXi option package and included at no-cost are leather upholstery, an 8-way power driver's seat, and other luxury touches. One loss in the change is the integrated rear child seat, which had been optional on the LX.

PERFORMANCE Give Cirrus credit for some sporty moves. It corners with agility, good grip, and minimal body lean, and its precise steering centers easily after a turn. The suspension provides a stable, comfortable ride on most surfaces, though it does not absorb pock-marked pavement well.

Making the V-6 standard is an appropriate move given the car's more clearly defined mission. But while the overhead-cam engine has fairly lively acceleration, it doesn't generate much torque below 4000 rpm. As a result, it initially feels weak when called on for highway passing power or a quick burst of speed in the 40-50-mph range. The transmission generally shifts smoothly, though it usually pauses a frustrating moment before downshifting for passing. We averaged 21 mpg in a mix of rush-hour commuting and highway cruising.

Poor noise suppression is the car's biggest dynamic shortfall, and this is at odds with its upscale aspiration. Wind noise is managed, but there's a constant low rumble from the exhaust, even at idle. The V-6 is loud under hard throttle, and tire roar is prominent on the highway.

The brakes on our test car performed capably. Stopping distances were short and the anti-lock feature kicked in quickly and worked effectively.

ACCOMMODATIONS Chrysler puts an amazing amount of passenger space in a car that's just 187 inches long. The rear seat is almost as spacious as that of some full-size cars. Front or rear, there's enough head clearance for adults to sit upright and enough leg room to stretch out. Wide doors make it easy to climb in and out.

Large, round gauges are legible and brightly lit at night, and all controls are clearly labeled and easy to reach.

Visibility is great to the front and sides, but Cirrus's high rear parcel shelf renders the trunk invisible when backing up.

Interior storage is good: tiny map pockets on the front doors; cupholders at the base of the dashboard; coin slots and a small open bin between the front seats; and a useful center con-sole/armrest.

The trunk's flat floor goes well forward, but a small opening makes it hard to load bulky cargo. The one-piece rear seatback folds for additional cargo space and can be released from a handle in the trunk—a thoughtful touch.

BUILD QUALITY Our test car was free of squeaks and rattles and had smooth, glossy paint. Interior trim was of higher quality than some other Chrysler products, such as the Concorde, yet not as rich-feeling as the leather appointments available in the Toyota Camry.

VALUE FOR THE MONEY Cirrus is a capable family 4-door that delivers a touch of luxury at a reasonable price. It equals Japanese competitors in many areas, such as ride and handling, and soundly beats them for passenger and cargo space. And dealers should be willing to discount.

RATINGS

	LXi
Acceleration	3
Fuel economy	3
Ride quality	3
Steering/handling	4
Braking	3
Quietness	3
Driver seating	4
Instruments/controls	4
Room/comfort (front)	4
Room/comfort (rear)	4
Cargo room	4
Value for the money	3
Total	**42**

SPECIFICATIONS

	4-door sedan
Wheelbase, in.	108.0
Overall length, in.	187.0
Overall width, in.	71.7
Overall height, in.	52.5
Curb weight, lbs.	3181
Cargo vol., cu. ft.	15.7
Fuel capacity, gals.	16.0
Seating capacity	5
Front head room, in.	38.1
Max. front leg room, in.	42.3
Rear head room, in.	36.8
Min. rear leg room, in.	37.8

ENGINES

	ohc V-6
Size, liters/cu. in.	2.5/152
Horsepower @ rpm	168@ 5800
Torque (lbs./ft.) @ rpm	170@ 4350
Availability	S

EPA city/highway mpg

4-speed OD automatic	20/29

PRICES

Chrysler Cirrus	Retail Price	Dealer Invoice
LXi 4-door sedan	$19460	$17794
Destination charge	535	535

STANDARD EQUIPMENT:

LXi: 2.5-liter V-6 engine, 4-speed automatic transmission, anti-lock brakes, driver- and passenger-side air bags, variable-assist power steering, tilt steering column, leather-wrapped steering wheel, air conditioning, cloth reclining front bucket seats with driver-side manual height and lumbar adjusters, folding rear bench seat, console, AM/FM/cassette with six speakers, digital clock, trip odometer, oil-pressure and coolant-temperature gauges, voltmeter, tachometer, cruise control, rear defogger, power windows, speed-sensitive power door locks, heated power mirrors, speed-sensitive intermittent wipers, illuminated remote keyless entry, remote decklid release, universal garage-door opener, reading lights, auxiliary power outlet, color-keyed bodyside moldings, illuminated visor mirrors, floormats, tinted glass with solar-control windshield, fog lights, 195/65R15 tires, alloy wheels.

Rating Scale: 5-Excellent; 4-Above average; 3-Average; 2-Below average; 1-Poor

OPTIONAL EQUIPMENT:
Major Packages

	Retail Price	Dealer Invoice
Gold Pkg.	$500	$315

Gold trim and badging, chrome alloy wheels with gold accents.

Comfort and Convenience

Leather upholstery	1000	890
Manufacturer's discount price	NC	NC
Includes 8-way power diver seat.		
Premium cassette player	340	303
Includes eight speakers, power amplifier, CD changer controls.		
Premium cassette and 6-disc CD changer	550	490
Theft-deterrent system w/security alarm	150	134
Power sunroof	580	516
Smokers Pkg.	20	18

Appearance and Miscellaneous

Metallic candy-apple-red paint	200	178
Full-size spare tire	125	111

CHRYSLER CONCORDE

Chrysler Concorde LXi

Front-wheel-drive full size car; similar to Dodge Intrepid

Base price range: NA. Built in Canada.

Also consider: Buick LeSabre, Oldsmobile Eighty Eight/LSS/Regency, Pontiac Bonneville, Toyota Avalon

FOR • Passenger and cargo room • Ride • Steering/handling

AGAINST • Rear visibility • Trunk liftover

A redesigned Concorde goes on sale this fall with dramatic new styling and two new V-6 engines. The similar Dodge Intrepid also has been redesigned (see separate report), but there will not be a new Eagle Vision because the Eagle brand will be discontinued after 1998.

The new Concorde will spawn two other Chrysler models, the LHS luxury sedan and 300M sports sedan, both due during calendar 1998.

Concorde still rides a 113-inch wheelbase, but the front-drive chassis has been extensively modified and overall length has grown 7.5 inches with the new styling, highlighted by a Ferrari-like grille. Weight has dropped nearly 100 pounds through the use of aluminum for the rear suspension, the hood, and both new engines.

The base LX model uses a 2.7-liter V-6 with dual overhead camshafts and 200 horsepower. The upscale LXi comes with a 3.2-liter V-6 with a single overhead cam and 225. Both team with automatic transmission. Concord's only engine last year was 214-horsepower 3.5-liter V-6.

Dual front air bags are standard on both models. Anti-lock brakes are standard on the LXi and optional on the LX.

PERFORMANCE There isn't a world of difference between the two engines, but the 3.2-liter has stronger pull at low speeds, a deeper exhaust note, and more impressive passing ability. The 2.7-liter provides adequate acceleration, but has to work harder to deliver the same performance as the 3.2. With three people aboard, the 2.7 has just enough power to safely pass or merge with expressway traffic.

We have not had a chance to measure fuel economy, but Chrysler says both new engines are more efficient than last year's.

Both Concorde models have impressive handling ability. They carve tight turns with good grip and minimal body lean and respond instantly to steering changes. Ride quality also is impressive. The suspension soaks up rough roads and provides a stable, comfortable highway ride.

The old Concorde suffered too much road noise. The new model is markedly improved in this area, though still not in the Lexus class. Now that road noise is more subdued, wind noise is more noticeable at highway speeds yet still moderate.

ACCOMMODATIONS Like the previous Concorde, the new one has a generously sized interior. Wide, tall doorways make it easy to get in or out of the front or back, and there's ample room for five adults. The cabin is wide enough to hold three growups in the rear, and a taller roof shape gives slightly more rear headroom than in the Intrepid. A front bench seat is optional, but there isn't enough leg room in the center position except for children, who should sit in back, anyway.

While the driver's seat goes far enough back for tall people to find a comfortable reach to the wheel and pedals, the front passenger seat lacks enough leg room for 6-footers to stretch.

The driver's view to the rear is hampered by wide pillars, a sloping roof, and a narrow window that makes it impossible to see the trunk. The dashboard has clear white-on-black gauges and large, well-marked controls for the climate and audio systems.

Concorde's trunk opening is wider than the Intrepid's, and there's ample cargo room, but a high liftover. Concorde has a folding pass-through section in the rear seatback that allows storing long objects such as skis.

BUILD QUALITY Most interior materials are of good quality, though the door panels look plain and the roof pillars are trimmed with hard plastic that looks cut-rate. Models we drove had close-fitting body panels and smooth, lustrous paint.

VALUE FOR THE MONEY Prices weren't announced when this was written, but Chrysler was hinting the 1998 models will be only slightly more expensive than last year's. If that is the case, the new Concorde is an impressive value with stunning styling, loads of room, and exceptional handling.

RATINGS

	LX	LXi
Acceleration	3	4
Fuel economy	3	3
Ride quality	4	4
Steering/handling	4	4
Braking	3	3
Quietness	3	3
Driver seating	4	4
Instruments/controls	4	4
Room/comfort (front)	4	4
Room/comfort (rear)	4	4
Cargo room	4	4
Value for the money	4	4
Total	**44**	**45**

SPECIFICATIONS

	4-door sedan
Wheelbase, in.	113.0
Overall length, in.	209.1
Overall width, in.	74.4
Overall height, in.	55.9
Curb weight, lbs.	3430
Cargo vol., cu. ft.	18.7
Fuel capacity, gals.	17.0
Seating capacity	6
Front head room, in.	38.3
Max. front leg room, in.	42.2
Rear head room, in.	37.2
Min. rear leg room, in.	41.6

ENGINES

	dohc V-6	ohc V-6
Size, liters/cu. in.	2.7/167	3.2/197
Horsepower @ rpm	200@ 5800	225@ 6300
Torque (lbs./ft.) @ rpm	190@ 4850	225@ 3800
Availability	S[1]	S[2]

Prices are accurate at time of publication; subject to manufacturer's changes.

EPA city/highway mpg
4-speed OD automatic...................................... NA   NA

1. LX. 2. LXi.

PRICES

Chrysler Concorde	Retail Price	Dealer Invoice
LX 4-door sedan	$—	$—
LXi 4-door sedan	—	—
Destination charge	—	—

Prices not available at time of publication.

STANDARD EQUIPMENT:

LX: 2.7-liter DOHC V-6 engine, 4-speed automatic transmission, driver- and passenger-side air bags, 4-wheel disc brakes, power steering, tilt steering wheel, cruise control, cloth front bucket seats w/power driver seat, floor console, power windows, power door locks, remote keyless entry, power mirrors, tachometer, trip odometer, coolant-temperature gauge, AM/FM/cassette with four speakers, rear defogger, variable intermittent wipers, power decklid release, reading lights, floormats, tinted glass, 205/70R15 tires, wheel covers.

LXi adds: 3.2-liter DOHC V-6 engine, anti-lock brakes, leather upholstery, automatic temperature control, theft alarm, compass, trip computer, outside temperature display, universal garage-door opener, illuminated vanity mirrors, map lights, assist handles, automatic-dimming rearview mirror, CD changer controls, 225/60R16 tires.

OPTIONAL EQUIPMENT:
Major Packages
LX Pkg. 22D .... —   —
Eight speaker sound system, overhead trip computer, 8-way power passenger seat, 225/60R16 tires.

Powertrains
Traction control... —   —
Requires LX Pkg.

Safety Features
Anti-lock brakes... —   —

Comfort and Convenience
Power moonroof .... —   —
Requires LXi Pkg.
CD player .... —   —
Includes CD changer controls, eight speakers.
CD player w/Infinity speakers............................... —   —
Includes CD changer controls, nine speakers.
CD/cassette player .... —   —
Includes nine Infinity speakers. Requires LXi Pkg.
Universal garage door opener................................ —   —
Smokers group .... —   —
Includes ashtrays and lighter.

Appearance and Miscellaneous
Cold Weather Group .... —   —
Includes engine block and battery heater.
Metallic paint .... —   —
Full-size spare tire .... —   —
16-inch wheel and Tire Group .... —   —
Includes 225/60R16 tires.
Alloy wheels .... —   —
Requires LXi Pkg.

CHRYSLER SEBRING `RECOMMENDED`

Front-wheel-drive sports coupe; similar to Dodge Avenger

Base price range: $20,575-$25,040. Built in Normal, Ill., and Mexico.

Also consider: Chevrolet Monte Carlo, Honda Prelude, Mitsubishi Eclipse

FOR • Passenger and cargo room • Steering/handling • Anti-lock brakes

AGAINST • Acceleration (2.0-liter/automatic) • Road noise • Rear visibility

Chrysler Sebring JXi

The two cars that share the Sebring badge have less in common than their name suggests.

The Sebring coupe is built in Illinois by Mitsubishi and is based on the Japanese company's Galant sedan. It shares components with the Dodge Avenger. The Sebring convertible is built in Mexico by Chrysler and is based on the Chrysler Cirrus sedan. It does not have a corporate counterpart. The convertible is longer than the coupe and its power top includes a glass rear window with defroster. All Sebrings have dual front air bags that for '98 deploy with less force but still meet federal safety standards. Traction control is newly available on the convertibles.

The convertible outsells the coupe and is in fact the best-selling ragtop in the U.S., though about half its 40,000-plus annual sales are to rental fleets. Its big news for '98 is the addition of a top-line Limited version, set to debut shortly after the start of the model year. The Limited counts among its standard features leather upholstery with wood interior accents, chrome wheels, and the 168-horsepower V-6 that's optional on the base JX and mid-line JXi versions. It'll also include the traction control system that's a new option for the other convertibles.

The JX and JXi come with a 150-horsepower 4-cylinder engine. All the convertibles have automatic transmission, with Chrysler's Autostick (an automatic that can be shifted manually) standard on the Limited and optional on the others.

There's less news on the coupe side, where the addition of "Caffe Latte" to the color palette is the big change. LX coupes have a 140-horsepower 4-cylinder and manual or automatic transmission, LXi models a 163-horsepower V-6 and automatic, a combination that's optional on the LX. Anti-lock brakes are standard on all Sebrings except the JX convertible, where they're optional with the V-6.

PERFORMANCE The 4-cylinder/manual tranmission combination can be mildly entertaining, but the engine thrashes when worked hard and few Sebrings are built with this powertrain anyway. The vast majority are purchased with V-6s, and neither six really has enough muscle to sate the enthusiast driver, even with the shift-yourself Autostick. Our last test of a JXi convertible netted a 21-mpg fuel-economy average.

Handling, steering, and braking are far more satisfying, and blend with adequately damped suspensions to produce competent all-around road manners.

Too much road noise makes a long trip in either body style tiring, however.

ACCOMMODATIONS They may not share genes, but both the coupe and convertible stand out among their respective competitors by offering spacious interiors with rear seats that accommodate adults in reasonable comfort.

The dashboards are different and the convertible's design gets the edge for its more-accessible audio controls. The convertible also integrates its front safety belts into the seatbacks, so they move with the seat and always fit comfortably.

Both cars have visibility woes. The convertible top blocks the driver's over-the-shoulder view, while the coupe gets demerits for a high rear parcel shelf and generally bathtub-like seating.

Long doors on both body styles are a hinderance in parking lots. Rear entry and exit are better than on smaller cars in this class, but still require stooping.

BUILD QUALITY The structure of pre-1998 convertibles we tested wiggled more than most over bumps, but a '98 prototype Limited felt quite solid. Chrysler also seems to have shaved off some of the interior trim's annoying sharp edges, a problem the coupe never had,

---

Rating Scale: 5-Excellent; 4-Above average; 3-Average; 2-Below average; 1-Poor

though its cabin plastics suffer a low-budget feel.

VALUE FOR THE MONEY Pleasant manners and competitive pricing keep these cars interesting, but what sells them is their attractive styling. Both look racier than their sticker prices would suggest—just the quality a healthy segment of their buyers value most.

RATINGS

	LX 4-cylinder	LXi	JXi
Acceleration	3	3	3
Fuel economy	4	3	2
Ride quality	4	4	4
Steering/handling	3	4	4
Braking	3	4	4
Quietness	2	2	2
Driver seating	3	3	3
Instruments/controls	3	3	4
Room/comfort (front)	4	4	4
Room/comfort (rear)	3	3	3
Cargo room	3	3	3
Value for the money	3	4	4
Total	**38**	**40**	**40**

SPECIFICATIONS

	2-door coupe	2-door convertible
Wheelbase, in.	103.7	106.0
Overall length, in.	190.9	192.6
Overall width, in.	69.7	70.1
Overall height, in.	53.0	54.8
Curb weight, lbs.	2959	3344
Cargo vol., cu. ft.	13.1	11.3
Fuel capacity, gals.	16.9	16.0
Seating capacity	5	5
Front head room, in.	39.1	38.7
Max. front leg room, in.	43.3	42.4
Rear head room, in.	36.5	37.0
Min. rear leg room, in.	35.0	35.2

ENGINES

	dohc I-4	dohc I-4	ohc V-6	ohc V-6
Size, liters/cu. in.	2.0/122	2.4/148	2.5/152	2.5/152
Horsepower @ rpm	140@ 6000	150@ 5200	163@ 5500	168@ 5800
Torque (lbs./ft.) @ rpm	130@ 4800	167@ 4000	170@ 4350	170@ 4350
Availability	S[1]	S[2]	O[3]	O[4]

EPA city/highway mpg

4-speed OD automatic	21/30	20/28	20/27	18/27
5-speed OD manual	22/31			

1. LX. 2. JX, JXi. 3. Std. LXi, opt. LX. 4. JX, JXi.

PRICES

Chrysler Sebring Convertible

	Retail Price	Dealer Invoice
JX 2-door convertible	$20575	$18892
JXi 2-door convertible	25040	22866
Destination charge	535	535

STANDARD EQUIPMENT:

JX: 2.4-liter DOHC 4-cylinder engine, 4-speed automatic transmission, driver- and passenger-side air bags, variable-assist power steering, tilt steering column, air conditioning, front bucket seats, vinyl upholstery, console with storage armrest, visor mirrors, power windows, rear defogger, AM/FM radio, digital clock, trip odometer, oil-pressure gauge, coolant-temperature gauge, tachometer, variable intermittent wipers, map lights, vinyl convertible top with glass rear window, tinted glass, dual remote mirrors, 205/65R15 tires, wheel covers.

JXi adds: anti-lock brakes, cruise control, Firm Feel power steering, leather/vinyl seats, 6-way power front seats, programmable power door locks, heated power mirrors, leather-wrapped steering wheel and shifter, trip computer, cassette player with six Infinity speakers, power antenna, remote keyless entry, illuminated entry, illuminated visor mirrors, remote decklid release, floormats, touring suspension, cloth convertible top with glass rear window, theft-deterrent system, fog lamps, 215/55HR16 touring tires, alloy wheels.

OPTIONAL EQUIPMENT:

	Retail Price	Dealer Invoice

Major Packages

Pkg. 24B/26B, JX ... $1585 $1411
Power Convenience Group (programmable door locks, heated power mirrors), cassette player and CD control, 6-way power driver seat, cruise control, remote keyless entry, delay off headlamps, remote decklid release, illuminated entry, illuminated visor mirrors, additional trunk trim, floormats. Pkg. 26B requires 2.5-liter V-6 engine.

Pkg. 26C, JX ... 1780 1584
Pkg. 24B/26B plus Autostick 4-speed automatic transmission. Requires 2.5-liter V-6 engine.

Pkg. 26E, JXi ... 195 174
Autostick 4-speed automatic transmission.

Pkg. 28G, JXi ... 1550 1380
Includes 4-wheel disc brakes, traction control, autostick shifter, Limited Decor Group (leather seats, luxury floormats, color-keyed grille, chrome alloy wheels), Luxury Convenience Group (universal garage door opener, automatic day/night inside mirror, map light).

Luxury Convenience Group ... 175 156
Universal garage-door opener, automatic day/night rearview mirror, map light. JX requires option pkg.

Power Convenience Group, JX ... 360 320
Programmable power door locks, heated power mirrors.

Security Group, JX ... 175 156
Alarm system, programmable power door locks. Requires Pkg. 24B/26B.

Powertrains

2.5-liter V-6 engine, JX ... 1365 1215
JXi ... 800 712
Includes anti-lock brakes, bright exhaust outlets. Requires option pkg.

Traction control, JX ... 790 703
JX w/2.5-liter engine, JXi ... 225 200
Includes anti-lock 4-wheel disc brakes.

Safety Features

Anti-lock brakes, JX ... 565 503

Comfort and Convenience

Cruise control, JX ... 240 214
Premium cloth upholstery, JX ... 95 85
JXi (credit) ... (250) (223)
Cassette player, JX ... 275 245
Includes CD changer control.

Cassette player w/amplifier, JX ... 355 316
Includes six Infinity speakers, CD changer controls. Requires Pkg. 24B/26B.

CD player, JX ... 445 396
JX w/option pkg. ... 170 151
CD/cassette player w/amplifier, JX ... 695 619
JXi ... 340 303
Includes six Infinity speakers, power antenna. JX requires Pkg. 24B/26B.

6-disc CD changer ... 500 445
JX requires cassette player. NA with CD/cassette player.

Smoker's group ... 20 18

Appearance and Miscellaneous

Candy-apple-red metallic paint ... 200 178
16-inch Touring Group, JX ... 495 441
Firm Feel power steering, touring suspension, 215/55R16 touring tires, alloy wheels.

Chrysler Sebring Coupe

	Retail Price	Dealer Invoice
LX 2-door notchback	$16840	$15498
LXi 2-door notchback	20775	19000
Destination charge	535	535

STANDARD EQUIPMENT:

LX: 2.0-liter DOHC 4-cylinder engine, 5-speed manual transmission, driver- and passenger-side air bags, variable-assist power steering, tilt steering column, air conditioning, cloth front bucket seats, console with storage armrest and cupholders, rear defogger, split folding rear seat, rear headrests, AM/FM/cassette player, digital clock, trip odometer,

---

Prices are accurate at time of publication; subject to manufacturer's changes.

coolant-temperature gauges, tachometer, variable intermittent wipers, remote fuel-door and decklid releases, visor mirrors, map lights, color-keyed front and rear fascias, floormats, tinted glass, remote outside mirrors, fog lights, 195/70R14 tires, wheel covers.

LXi adds: 2.5-liter V-6 engine, 4-speed automatic transmission, 4-wheel disc brakes, power windows, power door locks, heated power mirrors, upgraded cloth upholstery and driver-seat lumbar support, leather-wrapped steering wheel, AM/FM/cassette/CD player, cruise control, remote keyless entry system w/security alarm, oil-pressure gauge, automatic day/night rear view mirror, compass, illuminated visor mirrors, Homelink universal garage-door opener, trunk net, rear spoiler, bright exhaust tips, 215/50HR17 tires, alloy wheels.

OPTIONAL EQUIPMENT:

	Retail Price	Dealer Invoice
Major Packages		
Pkg. 21H/24H, LX	$780	$694
Cruise control, power windows, door locks, and mirrors, illuminated visor mirrors, trunk net. Pkg. 21H requires 2.0-liter engine w/5-speed manual transmission. Pkg. 24H requires 2.5-liter V-6 engine and 4-speed automatic transmission.		
Pkg. 24K, LXi	626	557
Manufacturer's discount price	NC	NC
Leather upholstery, power driver seat.		
Powertrains		
2.5-liter V-6 engine, LX	830	739
Includes 4-wheel disc brakes, upgraded suspension, heavy-duty battery, oil pressure gauge, dual exhaust outlets, 205/55R16 tires. Requires 4-speed automatic transmission, Pkg. 24H.		
4-speed automatic transmission, LX	695	619
Safety Features		
Anti-lock brakes	600	534
LX requires Pkg. 21H/24H.		
Comfort and Convenience		
Power driver seat	205	182
LX requires Pkg. 21H/24H.		
Power sunroof	640	570
LX requires Pkg. 21H/24H.		
CD/cassette player, LX w/Pkg. 21H/24H	435	387
Includes graphic equalizer.		
CD/cassette player with Infinity speakers and equalizer, LX w/Pkg. 21H/24H	760	676
CD/cassette player with eight Infinity speakers and equalizer, LXi	325	289
Remote keyless entry w/security alarm, LX w/Pkg. 21H/24H	290	258
Appearance and Miscellaneous		
16-inch Wheel Group, LX	490	436
LX w/2.5-liter engine	335	298
Alloy wheels, 205/55HR16 tires.		

CHRYSLER TOWN & COUNTRY

Chrysler Town & Country LXi

Front- or all-wheel-drive minivan; similar to Dodge Caravan and Plymouth Voyager

Base price range: $27,135-$34,095. Built in St. Louis, Mo.

Also consider: Mercury Villager, Oldsmobile Silhouette, Toyota Sienna

---

FOR • Standard anti-lock brakes • Acceleration (3.8-liter) • Ride • Passenger and cargo room

AGAINST • Fuel economy • Wind noise

Chrysler's version of the minivan also sold as the Dodge Caravan and Plymouth Voyager is even more "Chrysler" for '98, adopting the open grille and winged emblem that's becoming a brand signature. There's also more power for the larger of the two V-6s.

Regular-length and 13-inch-longer extended-length bodies are available, both with rear sliding doors on both sides. Both seat seven but the longer model has more cargo space behind the rearmost seats.

Dual air bags and anti-lock brakes are standard and a permanent all-wheel-drive (AWD) system is available on extended models. It normally operates in front-wheel drive and automatically sends power to the wheels with the most traction when there is slip. AWD models also have 4-wheel disc brakes. Front-drive models have a traction-control system that works at low speeds to prevent wheel slip.

Two V-6s are available, a 158-horsepower 3.3-liter and a 3.8 that for '98 gains 12 horsepower for a total of 180. All engines link to an automatic transmssion.

The fresh grille is accompanied by new headlamps that automatically turn on and off based on ambient light levels; Chrysler says they're brighter than the old lights, too. Heated leather front seats are a new option, and the available left-side middle bucket seat gets the same fold-forward feature as the right one. Town & Country is popular among retirees shuttling grandchildren, and the integrated child seats optional on models with the middle bench seat now come with a 5-point safety harness.

PERFORMANCE Despite offering no mechanical features that aren't available on the less-expensive Dodge Caravan, Town & Country has managed to cultivate an identity as perhaps the only minivan untainted by the "soccer-mom" label. In some neighborhoods, it's even fashionable.

That's not to say it doesn't acquit itself very well on the road. Town & Country drives like a big car. The steering is precise and hard cornering brings out only modest body lean. The ride is supple yet well controlled at highway speeds.

The 3.3-liter V-6 has adequate power, even in the heavier extended model, but the 3.8's extra muscle makes a noticeable difference when merging onto expressways and going uphill. With either engine, fuel economy won't be great. We average 15-17 mpg in urban driving and barely into the low 20s on the highway. Tire noise is low, but wind noise is prominent at highway speeds.

The optional all-wheel-drive system works as advertised, but we aren't sure it's worth the added cost given that traction control is standard on front-drive models.

ACCOMMODATIONS Town & Country's tasteful exterior styling is a big factor in its successful upscale positioning, and one that should be even stronger with the snooty new snout. But an ergonomically sound interior is key, as well.

Entry/exit is especially easy for a minivan because the step-in height is among the lowest in the class. And the standard sliding side doors improve access to the middle and rear seats, though Chrysler still doesn't match General Motors with a power sliding door.

Seats are comfortable, supportive, and roomy at all poistions. There's ample cargo space at the rear in the extended-length body and adequate space in the short one. Cupholders and storage bins throughout provide plenty of places for stashing small stuff.

BUILD QUALITY Chrysler acknowledges it's fighting reliability gremlins that have cost it points on surveys of customer satisfaction. The T&Cs we've tested have been free of mechanical problems, with good fit and finish inside and out.

VALUE FOR THE MONEY Purely objectively, the Caravan and Plymouth Voyager are better values in a Chrysler minivan. And Ford's Windstar, the new GM entries, and Toyota's polished new Sienna should be considered. But if every minivan purchase was purely objective, Chrysler wouldn't be selling more than 50,000 T&Cs annually.

Rating Scale: 5-Excellent; 4-Above average; 3-Average; 2-Below average; 1-Poor

RATINGS

	SX	LXi
Acceleration	3	4
Fuel economy	3	2
Ride quality	4	4
Steering/handling	3	3
Braking	3	3
Quietness	3	3
Driver seating	4	4
Instruments/controls	4	4
Room/comfort (front)	4	4
Room/comfort (rear)	5	5
Cargo room	5	5
Value for the money	4	4
Total	45	45

SPECIFICATIONS

	4-door van	4-door van
Wheelbase, in.	113.3	119.3
Overall length, in.	186.4	199.7
Overall width, in.	76.8	76.8
Overall height, in.	68.7	68.7
Curb weight, lbs.	3958	4082
Cargo vol., cu. ft.	138.5	162.9
Fuel capacity, gals.	20.0	20.0
Seating capacity	7	7
Front head room, in.	39.8	39.8
Max. front leg room, in.	40.6	40.6
Rear head room, in.	40.5	39.6
Min. rear leg room, in.	35.0	37.2

ENGINES

	ohv V-6	ohv V-6
Size, liters/cu. in.	3.3/202	3.8/231
Horsepower @ rpm	158@	180@
	4850	4400
Torque (lbs./ft.) @ rpm	203@	240@
	3250	3200
Availability	S[1]	S[2]
EPA city/highway mpg		
4-speed OD automatic	17/24	17/24

1. SX and LX. 2. LXi; optional, SX and LX.

PRICES

Chrysler Town & Country

	Retail Price	Dealer Invoice
LX 4-door van, FWD	$27135	$24619
LX 4-door van, AWD	30135	27259
SX 4-door van, short wheelbase, FWD	26680	24218
LXi 4-door van, FWD	31720	28654
LXi 4-door van, AWD	34095	30744
Destination charge	580	580

LX AWD requires an option pkg. AWD denotes all-wheel drive. FWD denotes front-wheel drive.

STANDARD EQUIPMENT:

LX: 3.3-liter V-6 engine (FWD), 3.8-liter V-6 engine (AWD), 4-speed automatic transmission, traction control (FWD), driver- and passenger-side air bags, anti-lock brakes, power steering, tilt steering column, air conditioning with dual controls, dual sliding side doors, cruise control, seven passenger seating (cloth reclining front bucket seats with manual lumbar adjustment, reclining and folding middle bucket seats, rear-seat recliner and headrests), passenger-side underseat storage drawer, leather-wrapped steering wheel, overhead console with compass and trip computer, AM/FM/cassette, digital clock, tachometer, coolant-temperature gauge, trip odometer, power windows, power door locks, remote keyless entry, heated power mirrors, variable intermittent wipers, variable intermittent rear wiper/washer, windshield wiper de-icer, rear defogger, reading lights, front and rear auxiliary power outlets, illuminated visor mirrors, floormats, tinted glass, fog lights, load-leveling suspension (AWD), 215/65R16 tires.

SX adds: striping, alloy wheels.

LXi adds: 3.8-liter V-6 engine (FWD/AWD), rear air conditioning and heater, 8-way power front bucket seats with driver-side memory, leather upholstery, CD player with 10-speaker Infinity sound system

and equalizer, automatic day/night inside mirror and driver-side outside mirror, outside heated memory mirrors, automatic headlights, universal garage door opener, rear reading lights, load-leveling suspension (FWD and AWD), sunscreen/solar tinted windshield, rear privacy glass, security alarm, roof rack, full-size spare tire.

OPTIONAL EQUIPMENT:

	Retail Price	Dealer Invoice
Major Packages		
Pkg. 25R/28R/29R, LX	$1230	$1046
Manufacturer's discount price	85	73
Sunscreen/solar glass, 10-speaker Infinity sound system, equalizer, CD changer controls, 8-way power driver seat.		
Pkg. 25H/28H/29H, SX	1515	1288
Manufacturer's discount price	245	208
Sunscreen/solar glass, 10-speaker Infinity sound system, equalizer, CD changer control, 8-way power driver seat, roof rack, windshield wiper de-icer, full-size spare tire.		
Climate Control Group III, LX	405	344
Rear air conditioning and heater. Requires option pkg.		
Convenience Group VI, LX, SX	240	204
Universal garage door opener, theft-deterrent system. Requires option pkg.		
Loading and Towing Group II, LX	180	153
LX with Wheel/Handling Group II	145	123
Includes Heavy Load/Firm Ride Suspension and full-size spare. Requires option pkg. NA with AWD.		
Loading & Towing Group III, LX	380	323
LX with Wheel/Handling Group II	345	293
Heavy-duty battery, heavy-duty brakes, Heavy Load/Firm Ride Suspension, and full-size spare. Requires option pkg. NA with AWD.		
Trailer Tow Group, LXi	270	230
Heavy-duty battery, brakes, suspension, and radiator, heavy-duty transmission oil cooler; trailer wiring harness.		
Wheel/Handling Group II, LX	470	400
LX w/Loading & Towing Group III	435	370
Touring suspension, front and rear stabilizer bars, 16-inch alloy wheels.		
Powertrains		
3.8-liter V-6 engine, LX, SX	335	285
Requires option pkg.		
Safety Features		
Integrated child seats	NC	NC
Reclining and folding middle bench seat with two integrated child seats replaces middle bucket seats. LX and SX require option pkg. NA with leather upholstery on LX and SX.		
Comfort and Convenience		
Leather bucket seats, LX, SX	890	757
NA with integrated child seats. Requires option pkg.		
Heated front seats, LXi	250	213
Cassette/CD player with equalizer, LX, SX	310	264
Requires option pkg.		
Appearance and Miscellaneous		
Load-leveling suspension, LX	290	247
Requires option pkg. NA with AWD.		
Security alarm, LX, SX	150	128
Requires option pkg.		
Roof rack, LX, SX	175	149
Requires option pkg.		
Metallic paint	200	170
Full size spare tire, LX, SX	110	94
Requires option pkg.		
Alloy wheels, LX with option pkg	410	213

DODGE AVENGER `RECOMMENDED`

Front-wheel-drive sports coupe; similar to Chrysler Sebring

Base price range: $14,930-$17,310. Built in Normal, Ill.

Also consider: Chevrolet Monte Carlo, Honda Prelude, Mitsubishi Eclipse

FOR • Acceleration (V-6) • Steering/handling • Passenger and cargo room • Anti-lock brakes

Prices are accurate at time of publication; subject to manufacturer's changes.

Dodge Avenger ES

AGAINST • Acceleration (4-cylinder/automatic) • Road noise • Stereo location • Rear visibility

Avenger is the Dodge version of the sports coupe also sold as the Chrysler Sebring. Both are built at a Mitsubishi plant in Illinois and both are based on the platform of the Japanese company's Galant sedan.

Introduction of a new Sport appearance package for the base model tops Avenger's short list of '98 changes.

A Chrysler-built 2.0-liter 4-cylinder with either manual or automatic transmission is standard, with a Mitsubishi-made 2.5-liter V-6 optional. The V-6 comes only with automatic. Both base and ES Avengers come with dual air bags. The ES has 4-wheel disc brakes, but anti-lock brakes are optional for both models.

The new option package is available on V-6 base models and includes Sport nameplates, a body-colored rear spoiler, and 16-inch alloy-wheels. (ES versions use 17-inch wheels.) Four-cylinder ES models gain a rear sway bar, previously exclusive to the V-6 cars. And "Caffe Latte" is a new color.

PERFORMANCE The 4-cylinder is noisy and, with automatic transmission, slow. Hitched to manual tranmsission, acceleration is adequate. V-6 Avengers are fairly spunky, provided you floor the gas pedal and leave it there. Lack of low-speed torque combined with the automatic's hesitant downshifts can be frustrating. In hard acceleration, the transmission changes gears abruptly, but it shifts smoothly otherwise. Like the four, the V-6 is raucous at higher speeds, and, along with lots of tire thrum, betrays a stinginess with sound insulation in these cars. We averaged a laudable 25.6 mpg with the V-6, only slightly lower than the 4-cylinder delivers.

The optional 16-inch tires elevate handling from adequate to adept, while the ES's firmer suspension and 17-inch wheels and tires furnish tenacious grip. Body lean in corners is moderate, and the steering is precise and centers well after turns.

Avengers absorb lumpy pavement better than most sports coupes. Even the ES, which rides solidly on its firm suspension, becomes harsh only over the biggest bumps and potholes. Our ES test car stopped short and with good control with the optional anti-lock brakes.

ACCOMMODATIONS Avenger is roomier than nearly all other sports coupes, and nearly matches the spaciousness of midsizers like the Chevrolet Monte Carlo.

There's ample head room and leg room in front and enough space in the rear seat for two adults to sit comfortably. The driver's seat has a manual height adjustment, but the driving position still seems too low. Getting in or out of the rear seat requires some contortions, though it's easier than on most coupes.

Gauges and most controls are easy to use while driving, but the stereo is too low in the center of the dash and the unlit power window and lock switches on the driver's door are hard to find at night.

Cargo space is good. The trunk has a wide floor and the standard split rear seatback folds for additional space, though the modest trunk opening makes it hard to load bulky items.

As in many modern cars, an upward sweep of the tail results in a narrow rear window and a high parcel shelf that restrict rear visibility.

BUILD QUALITY All body panels lined up evenly and the paint was uniformly smooth and shiny on our ES test car. Some interior materials looked and felt chintzy and a stereo speaker kept cutting in and out.

VALUE FOR THE MONEY Avenger can't match the slick moves or tight construction of a Honda Prelude, but does deliver youthfully aggressive styling, better-than-average interior room, and entertaining handling at a reasonable price. A V-6 ES is the best choice here.

RATINGS

	Base	ES V-6
Acceleration	3	3
Fuel economy	4	3
Ride quality	4	3
Steering/handling	3	4
Braking	3	4
Quietness	2	2
Driver seating	3	3
Instruments/controls	3	3
Room/comfort (front)	4	4
Room/comfort (rear)	3	3
Cargo room	3	3
Value for the money	4	4
Total	39	39

SPECIFICATIONS

	2-door coupe
Wheelbase, in.	103.7
Overall length, in.	190.2
Overall width, in.	69.1
Overall height, in.	53.0
Curb weight, lbs.	2888
Cargo vol., cu. ft.	13.1
Fuel capacity, gals.	16.9
Seating capacity	5
Front head room, in.	39.1
Max. front leg room, in.	43.3
Rear head room, in.	36.5
Min. rear leg room, in.	35.0

ENGINES

	dohc I-4	ohc V-6
Size, liters/cu. in.	2.0/122	2.5/152
Horsepower @ rpm	140@ 6000	163@ 5500
Torque (lbs./ft.) @ rpm	130@ 4800	170@ 4350
Availability	S	O

EPA city/highway mpg
4-speed OD automatic	21/30	20/27
5-speed OD manual	22/32	

PRICES

Dodge Avenger	Retail Price	Dealer Invoice
Base 2-door notchback	$14930	$13738
ES 2-door notchback	17310	15856
Destination charge	535	535

STANDARD EQUIPMENT:

Base: 2.0-liter DOHC 4-cylinder engine, 5-speed manual transmission, driver- and passenger-side air bags, variable-assist power steering, cloth reclining front bucket seats, console with storage armrest and cupholders, split folding rear seat, rear headrests, rear defogger, tilt steering column, AM/FM radio w/four speakers, trip odometer, coolant-temperature gauges, tachometer, intermittent wipers, map lights, visor mirrors, tinted glass, dual remote mirrors, 195/70HR14 tires, wheel covers.

ES adds: 4-wheel disc brakes, air conditioning, upgraded cloth upholstery and driver-seat lumbar support, leather-wrapped steering wheel, cruise control, cassette player w/six speakers, floormats, cargo nets and hooks, handling suspension, decklid spoiler, fog lights, 215/50HR17 tires, alloy wheels.

OPTIONAL EQUIPMENT:
Major Packages

Pkg. 21C/22C, Base w/2.0-liter engine 1850 1647
Air conditioning, cruise control, cassette player w/six speakers, power windows and door locks, power mirrors, floormats, trunk net. Pkg. 22C requires 4-speed automatic transmission.

Pkg. 24S, Base w/2.5-liter engine 2265 1647
Pkg. 21C/22C plus 16-inch Wheel Group (alloy wheels, 205/55HR16 tires), sport badging, leather-wrapped steering wheel, rear spoiler.

Rating Scale: 5-Excellent; 4-Above average; 3-Average; 2-Below average; 1-Poor

	Retail Price	Dealer Invoice
Pkg. 21F/24F, ES	$1375	$1224

Power windows and door locks, power mirrors, illuminated passenger visor mirror, cassette/CD player, universal garage-door opener, remote keyless entry, theft-deterrent system. Pkg. 24F requires 2.5-liter engine.

Powertrains

2.5-liter V-6 engine, Base w/Pkg. 24S	675	601
ES	610	543

Includes 4-wheel disc brakes, upgraded suspension, oil pressure gauge, dual exhaust outlets, 205/55HR16 tires (base), 215/50HR17 tires (ES). Requires 4-speed automatic transmission.

4-speed automatic transmission	695	619

NA with ES 2.0-liter engine.

Safety Features

Anti-lock brakes...	600	534

Base requires option pkg.

Comfort and Convenience

Air conditioning, Base w/option pkg.	790	703
Leather upholstery, ES	630	561
Manufacturer's discount price	NC	NC
Includes power driver seat.		
Power driver seat, Base, ES	205	182
Base requires pkg. 24S. ES requires pkg. 21F/24F.		
Cassette player, Base	255	227
CD/cassette player,		
Base w/option pkg., ES w/Pkg. 21E/24E	435	387
CD/cassette player with eight Infinity speakers and equalizer,		
ES w/Pkg. 21F/24F	325	289
Remote keyless entry, Base.................................	290	258
Includes theft-deterrent system. Requires option pkg.		
Power sunroof	640	570
Requires option pkg.		

Appearance and Miscellaneous

16-inch Wheel Group, Base.................................	490	436

Alloy wheels, 205/55HR16 tires. Requires option pkg.

DODGE CARAVAN

✓ **BEST BUY**

Dodge Grand Caravan

Front- or all-wheel-drive minivan; similar to Chrysler Town & Country and Plymouth Voyager

Base price range: $17,415-$29,720. Built in St. Louis, Mo., and Canada.

Also consider: Ford Windstar, Pontiac Trans Sport, Toyota Sienna

FOR • Anti-lock brakes • Acceleration (3.8-liter) • Ride • Passenger and cargo room

AGAINST • Fuel economy • Wind noise

Caravan is America's best-selling minivan and with its sister vehicles, the Chrysler Town & Country and Plymouth Voyager, helps Chrysler Corporation account for nearly half of all minivan sales. More power for the top V-6 engine headlines 1998's brief list of changes.

Like its siblings, Caravan features a regular-length body and an extended-length variant, here called the Grand Caravan.

Base, SE, Sport, LE, and ES models are offered in both body lengths. All have seats for up to seven. Sliding rear doors on both sides are standard on all except the base-level regular-length model, where the driver-side slider costs extra. Front-wheel drive is standard, with traction control offered on LEs. All-wheel drive (AWD) is optional starting at the SE price level. It automatically transfers power from the front wheels to the wheels with the best traction.

All Caravans have dual air bags. Anti-lock brakes are standard except on base models, where they're optional. AWD models get 4-wheel disc brakes instead of rear drums. Integrated child safety seats are optional when a 3-passenger middle bench seat is installed.

A 2.4-liter 4-cylinder is the standard engine on the base regular-length Caravan, with V-6s of 3.0, 3.3, and 3.8 liters standard or optional on all other models. All Caravan engines use automatic transmissions. For '98, SEs with the 3.0 get a 4-speed instead of the previous 3-speed. And the 3.8 gains 14 horsepower, climbing to 180.

Among other changes, Caravans with middle-row bucket seats gain a tip-forward left-side bucket to match the right side. And this year, the middle bench gets seatback hooks for hanging plastic grocery bags. Finally, ESs gain headlights that turn on and off according to ambient light levels.

PERFORMANCE Like its Chrysler and Plymouth stablemates, Caravan handles more like a big sedan than a van. It's maneuverable in the city, responsive on curving roads, and a stable highway cruiser. The steering is nicely weighted and natural feeling.

Don't consider the 4-cylinder or the 3.0-liter V-6 unless you absolutely can't afford one of the larger engines. The 3.3 is fine in regular-length models and acceptible in the Grands, but the best overall choice and the most-sensible one in the Grands is the 3.8. It gives these minivans enough power to pass and merge with little drama. The downside is fuel economy. The last 3.8-liter Grand Caravan we tested averaged 17.7 mpg, with a high of 21.2 in one highway stint. The 3.3 isn't significantly more economical in the long run because it has to work that much harder. In any event, real-world averages of 17-20 mpg are about par for the minivan field.

Caravan is one of the quieter minivans, but wind and road noise can still build up at highway speeds, making long trips more tiring. Sudden stops cause the nose to dip sharply, but there's no loss of control and stopping power corresponds accurately to pressure on the brake pedal.

ACCOMMODATIONS No minivan is more comfortable or easier to live with. Entering and exiting a Caravan is simply a matter of stepping in and out, and the driver-side sliding door is so useful, we wonder how we got along without one.

Once aboard, accommodations are exceptional. Front and middle-row seats offer generous head and leg room; the third-row bench is more cramped in both areas, though it's not uncomfortable.

A user-friendly dashboard puts most controls within easy reach of the driver. A low dashboard and large windows contribute to outstanding outward visibility. However, the deep tint of the rear window is difficult to see through in dim light.

Cupholders (some adjustable for size) abound, as do assorted storage bins and nooks. Neat touches include lighted markers for power window switches and other controls; dual-zone climate control; and electric windshield wiper de-icers.

The middle and rear seats don't move fore and aft, but they recline, and their backrests tip forward to form a flat deck that will carry a 4x8-foot sheet of plywood with the tailgate closed. There's also space beneath the seats for stashing skis or 2x4s.

The middle and rear seats have built-in wheels, and once they're unlatched from their floor anchors, they can be rolled to a doorway. However, the bench seats weigh about 90 pounds each, so it takes two people to heft one in and out. Seats on the General Motors minivans weigh less, but don't offer the chair-like comfort of the more-solid Chrysler Corporation seats.

BUILD QUALITY Body pieces and interior panels were well assembled on our test Caravans. Some dull patches on the body detracted from the otherwise shiny paint finish.

Prices are accurate at time of publication; subject to manufacturer's changes.

VALUE FOR THE MONEY Chrysler's offerings are still at the head of the minivan class. But GM's new entries are formidable rivals in terms of driving ease, refinement, and price. The winner is the customer can use the competitive market to get a better deal.

RATINGS

	Base 4-cyl.	Grand 3.3-liter V-6	Grand 3.8-liter V-6
Acceleration	2	3	4
Fuel economy	3	2	2
Ride quality	3	4	4
Steering/handling	3	3	3
Braking	3	3	3
Quietness	3	3	3
Driver seating	4	4	4
Instruments/controls	4	4	4
Room/comfort (front)	4	4	4
Room/comfort (rear)	5	5	5
Cargo room	5	5	5
Value for the money	5	5	5
Total	44	45	46

SPECIFICATIONS

	3-door van	4-door van
Wheelbase, in.	113.3	119.3
Overall length, in.	186.3	199.6
Overall width, in.	76.8	76.8
Overall height, in.	68.5	68.5
Curb weight, lbs.	3517	3684
Cargo vol., cu. ft.	142.9	168.5
Fuel capacity, gals.	20.0	20.0
Seating capacity	7	7
Front head room, in.	39.8	39.8
Max. front leg room, in.	40.6	40.6
Rear head room, in.	41.0	40.0
Min. rear leg room, in.	42.3	36.6

ENGINES

	dohc I-4	ohc V-6	ohv V-6	ohv V-6
Size, liters/cu. in.	2.4/148	3.0/181	3.3/202	3.8/231
Horsepower @ rpm	150@ 5200	150@ 5200	158@ 4850	180@ 4400
Torque (lbs./ft.) @ rpm	167@ 4000	176@ 4000	203@ 3250	240@ 3200
Availability	S[1]	S[2]	S[3]	O[4]
EPA city/highway mpg				
3-speed automatic	20/25	19/24		
4-speed OD automatic	18/25		18/24	17/24

1. Base. 2. Sport and SE; opt. Base. 3. LE and ES; optional Base, Sport, and SE. 4. LE and ES.

PRICES

Dodge Caravan

	Retail Price	Dealer Invoice
Base 3-door van, SWB	$17415	$15845
Base Grand 4-door van	20125	18270
SE 4-door van, SWB	21290	19255
Grand SE 4-door van	22285	20171
Grand SE 4-door van, AWD	25650	23132
Sport 4-door van, SWB	21290	19255
Grand Sport 4-door van	22285	20171
LE 4-door van, SWB	25030	22546
Grand LE 4-door van	26025	23462
Grand LE 4-door van, AWD	29200	29256
Grand ES 4-door van	26605	23972
Grand ES 4-door van, AWD	29720	26714
Destination charge	580	580

Sport, FWD ES, and AWD models require option pkg. FWD denotes front-wheel drive. AWD denotes all-wheel drive. SWB denotes short wheelbase.

STANDARD EQUIPMENT:

Base: 2.4-liter DOHC 4-cylinder engine, 3-speed automatic transmission, 3.0-liter V-6 engine (Grand), 4-speed automatic transmission (Grand), driver- and passenger-side air bags, power steering, cloth reclining front bucket seats, 3-passenger rear bench seat (SWB), sliding driver-side door (Grand), 2-passenger middle bench seat (Grand), folding 3-passenger rear bench seat (Grand), cuphold-

ers, variable intermittent wipers, variable intermittent rear wiper/washer, coolant-temperature gauge, trip odometer, AM/FM radio, digital clock, front map/reading lights, visor mirrors, front and rear auxiliary power outlets, tinted glass, dual outside mirrors, 205/75R14 tires, wheel covers.

SE and Sport add: 3.0-liter V-6 engine, 4-speed automatic transmission, anti-lock brakes, sliding driver-side door, cruise control, tilt steering column, passenger-side underseat storage drawer, rear floor silencer, power mirrors, tachometer, cassette player, 215/65R15 tires.

AWD model adds: 3.8-liter V-6 engine, 4-wheel disc brakes, load-leveling suspension, air conditioning, power door locks.

LE and ES add: 3.3-liter V-6 engine, air conditioning, upgraded cloth upholstery, driver seat lumbar adjustment, heated power mirrors, computer with compass, outside temperature and travel displays, overhead storage console, CD/cassette storage, power windows, power door locks, oil-pressure gauge, voltmeter, windshield wiper de-icer, rear defogger, ignition-switch light, illuminated visor mirrors, remote keyless entry w/headlight-off delay and illuminated entry, deluxe sound insulation, floormats, striping, alloy wheels (ES).

AWD models add: 3.8-liter V-6 engine, 4-wheel disc brakes, load-leveling suspension.

OPTIONAL EQUIPMENT:
Major Packages

	Retail Price	Dealer Invoice
Pkg. 22T/24T/28T, Base SWB	$1235	$1050
Manufacturer's discount price	NC	NC

Air conditioning, 7-passenger seating, underseat storage drawer, rear floor silencer.

Pkg. 24T/28T, Grand Base	885	752
Manufacturer's discount price	25	21

Air conditioning, underseat storage drawer, rear floor silencer.

Pkg. 26B/25B/28B, SE	1205	1024
Manufacturer's discount price	195	165

Air conditioning, 7-passenger seating w/reclining and folding center and back seats, rear defogger, windshield wiper de-icer. NA SE AWD.

Pkg. 26D/25D/28D/29D, SE	2240	1904
Manufacturer's discount price	930	790

Pkg. 26B/25B/28B plus power windows and door locks, power rear quarter vent windows, illuminated visor mirrors, Light Group (interior courtesy lights, illuminated ignition), additional sound insulation, floormats.

Pkg. 25C/28C, Sport	2480	2108
Manufacturer's discount price	1195	1016

Pkg. 26B/25B/28B plus heavy-duty suspension, front and rear stabilizer bars, leather-wrapped steering wheel, sunscreen glass, fog lights, roof rack, bodyside moldings, 215/65R16 touring tires, sport wheel covers.

Pkg. 25E/28E, Sport	3515	2988
Manufacturer's discount price	1930	1641

Pkg. 25C/28C plus power windows and rear quarter vent windows, power door locks, deluxe sound insulation, Light Group (ignition and courtesy lights), illuminated vanity mirrors, floormats.

Pkg. 25K/28K/29K, LE	1275	1084
Manufacturer's discount price	85	72

Air conditioning with dual controls, 8-way power driver seat, sunscreen glass, 10-speaker cassette player.

Pkg 29M, ES AWD	1590	1352
Manufacturer's discount price	490	417

Air conditioning w/dual controls, AM/FM/cassette/CD changer controls w/ten Infinity speakers, 8-way power driver seat, leather-wrapped steering wheel, automatic headlights, automatic-dim inside mirror and driver-side exterior mirror, sunscreen glass, assist handles, fog lights, 215/65R16 touring tires, alloy wheels.

Pkg. 25M/28M/29M, ES	1765	1500
Manufacturer's discount price	575	488

Pkg. 29M (ES AWD) plus heavy-duty suspension, front and rear stabilizer bars, windshield wiper de-icer.

Convenience Group I, Base	435	370

Cruise control, tilt steering column, power mirrors. Requires option pkg.

Convenience Group II, Base	750	638
SE, Sport	315	268

Convenience Group I (Base) plus power door locks. Requires option pkg.

Rating Scale: 5-Excellent; 4-Above average; 3-Average; 2-Below average; 1-Poor

	Retail Price	Dealer Invoice

Convenience Group III, FWD SE, Sport $685 $582
Power door locks, power windows and rear quarter vent windows. Requires option pkg.
Convenience Group IV, SE, Sport 235 200
Remote keyless entry, illuminated entry, delay-off headlights. SE requires Pkg. 26D/25D/28D/29D. Sport requires Pkg. 25E/28E.
Convenience Group V, SE, Sport 385 327
LE, ES 150 128
Convenience Group IV (SE, Sport) plus security alarm. SE requires Pkg. 26D/25D/28D/29D. Sport requires Pkg. 25E/28E/29E. LE, ES require option pkg.
Climate Group II, Base, SE 450 383
Air conditioning, sunscreen glass. Requires option pkg.
Climate Group III,
FWD Grand SE w/Pkg.26B/25B/28B 1130 961
FWD Grand SE w/Pkg. 26D/25D/28D,
AWD Grand SE 1020 867
Grand Sport w/Pkg. 25C/28/C 615 523
Grand Sport w/Pkg. 25E/28/E 505 429
Grand LE w/option pkg. 470 400
Grand ES 405 344
Rear air conditioning and heater with dual zone controls, overhead console.
Loading & Towing Group II, FWD SE, FWD LE 180 153
FWD LE with Wheel/Handling Group 2,
FWD ES 145 123
Full-size spare tire, heavy load/firm ride suspension. Requires option pkg. NA with Pkg. 28C or 28E.
Loading & Towing Group III, Grand SE 445 378
Grand SE, Grand Sport, LE (All with
Climate Group III) 380 323
ES 345 293
Loading & Towing Group II plus heavy-duty alternator, battery, radiator, brakes, and transmission oil cooler. FWD Grand SE requires Pkg. 26D/25D/28D. Grand Sport Requires Pkg. 26E/28E. FWD LE Requires Pkg. 25K/28K/29K.
Wheel/Handling Group II, FWD LE 470 400
FWD LE w/Loading & Towing Group III 435 370
Front and rear stabilizer bars, heavy-duty suspension, 215/65R16 tires, alloy wheels. Requires Pkg. 25K/28K/29K.

Powertrains

3.0-liter V-6 engine, Base SWB 770 655
Requires 3-speed automatic transmission. Base requires option pkg. Not available with base in California, New York, and Massachusetts.
3.3-liter V-6 engine, Base 890 757
Grand Base, SE FWD, Sport, ... 200 170
Requires 4-speed automatic transmission. Base requires option pkg.
3.8-liter V-6 engine, FWD LE, FWD ES 335 285
Requires option pkg.
4-speed automatic transmission, Base 250 213
Requires 3.3-liter engine.
Traction control, FWD LE 175 149

Safety Features

Anti-lock brakes, Base 565 480

Comfort and Convenience

Air conditioning, Base, FWD SE 860 731
Sliding driver-side door, Base SWB 595 506
Requires option pkg.
Rear defogger, Base 195 166
Base w/Climate Group II or Convenience
Group I/II, FWD SE 230 196
Includes heated outside mirrors, windshield wiper de-icer.
Cassette player, Base 180 153
Requires option pkg.
CD player, Base 325 276
Requires option pkg.
AM/FM/cassette/CD w/equalizer, SE, Sport........... 325 276
LE, ES 310 264
Requires option pkg.
10-speaker Infinity sound system, SE, Sport......... 395 336
Requires AM/FM/cassette/CD w/amplifier.

7-passenger seating, Base SWB $350 $298
2-passenger middle bench seat, 3-passenger rear bench seat.
7-passenger seating w/integrated child seat, Base 285 242
2-passenger reclining middle bench seat with headrest and integrated child seats, 3-passenger rear bench seat. Requires option pkg.
Deluxe 7-passenger seating w/integrated child seats,
SE, Sport, LE, ES 225 191
Premium cloth 2-passenger reclining middle bench seat with headrests and integrated child seats, 3-passenger reclining rear bench seat. Requires option pkg.
Deluxe 7-passenger seating w/quad bucket seats,
SE, Sport, LE, ES 650 553
Premium cloth reclining middle bucket seats, 3-passenger reclining rear bench seat with headrests. SE requires Pkg. 26D/25D/29D/28D. Sport requires Pkg. 25E/28E. LE requires Pkg. 25K/28K.
Leather bucket seats, LE, ES 890 757
Requires option pkg. and deluxe 7-passenger seating w/quad bucket seats.
Smoker's Group 20 17
Cigarette lighter, ash trays.

Appearance and Miscellaneous

Load-leveling suspension,
FWD Grand SE w/Pkg. 26D/25D/28E, Grand
Sport w/Pkg. 25E/28E, FWD LE, FWD ES 290 247
Luggage rack.. 175 149
Requires option pkg.
Engine block heater 35 30
Candy-apple-red metallic paint, Sport, LE, ES 200 170
White-pearl paint, ES 200 170
Full-size spare tire, ... 110 94
16-inch alloy wheels, LE 410 349
Sport 265 225
LE requires Pkg. 25K/28K/29K. Sport requires option pkg.

DODGE DAKOTA

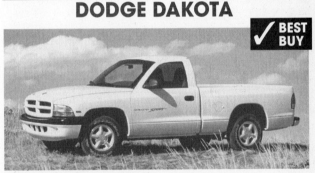

✓ BEST BUY

Dodge Dakota Sport regular cab

Rear- or 4-wheel-drive compact pickup
Base price range: $12,975-$19,755. Built in Warren, Mich.
Also consider: Chevrolet S-10, Ford Ranger, Toyota T100

FOR • Optional 4-wheel anti-lock brakes • Acceleration (V-8) • Quietness • Ride

AGAINST • No optional third door • Small rear seat on Club Cab • Fuel economy (V-8) • Acceleration (4-cylinder)

Dodge's full-size Ram pickup went from a blip on the sales charts to a formidable force with its bulldog-face redesign for 1994. For '97, Dodge transformed its junior pickup, the Dakota, into a virtual Ram lookalike, with similar results. Its sales were running 21 percent ahead of '96 levels.

A deactivation switch for the passenger-side air bag is the main change as the '98 model year gets underway, but Dodge promises the Springtime introduction of a high-performance model. Dubbed the Dakota R/T and available in 2-wheel-drive regular- and extended-cab body styles, it'll have a 250-horsepower 5.9-liter V-8 and automatic transmission, sport suspension, bucket seats, and distinct trim.

Meantime, Dakota features regular-cabs with 6.5- and 8-foot long cargo beds and an extended-cab, called the Club Cab, with

Prices are accurate at time of publication; subject to manufacturer's changes.

the 6.5-foot bed. Dual air bags are standard. The Club Cab adds 19 inches to the back of the regular cab and has a 3-place rear bench seat for 6-passenger capacity. It does not, however, offer a third door, which for now is a General Motors exclusive in the compact-pickup segment.

All Dakotas are available with rear-wheel drive or 4WD that can be shifted between 2WD and 4-High on the fly via a floor-mounted lever, but is not for use on dry pavement. Rear anti-lock brakes are standard, 4-wheel anti-lock brakes are optional.

There are three engines: a 4-cylinder with 120 horsepower; a V-6 with 175; and a V-8 with 230. Manual transmission is standard and automatic is optional with the V-6 and V-8.

Maximum towing weight is 6700 pounds.

PERFORMANCE The '97 redesign didn't include new power-trains, but it did put the revised sheetmetal over a frame that Dodge said was stiffened significantly. The more rigid chassis apparently pays big dividends. A 2WD Club Cab we tested was impressively solid on rough roads. Its suspension provided a comfortable, stable ride with only a little bouncing on wavy surfaces. A 4WD regular-cab felt more jiggly over bumps and wasn't as comfortable.

Dodge's decades-old 5.2-liter V-8 feels like a new engine in the latest Dakota. It still delivers strong acceleration and passing power, but it's smoother and quieter than ever. In fact, the Dakota Club Cab we tested was quieter overall than some of Dodge's passenger cars.

Now some bad news: We averaged just 13.3 mpg with the V-8 mainly from urban commuting.

The base 4-cylinder is too weak for a vehicle of this size and weight, so plan on paying extra for the V-8 or the V-6, which provides adequate acceleration in the Dakota.

ACCOMMODATIONS Contrary to previous practice, Dodge now markets Dakota as a compact pickup rather than a mid-size, even though it is larger in virtually every dimension than other compact trucks.

Though the Dakota is roomier than other compact pickups, the rear bench seat on Club Cab models doesn't have nearly enough leg room for adults. Because a third door is not available, getting to the rear seat is a squeeze, despite a front passenger's seat that automatically slides forward when the seat-back is released.

The dashboard holds no surprises and outward visibility is good.

BUILD QUALITY Exterior paint was glossy and panel gaps were even on our test models. The cabin's vinyls, plastics, and fabrics were a cut above those used in some Chrysler Corporation cars and fit was very good.

VALUE FOR THE MONEY Dakota retains a slight advantage in interior space and towing capacity over compact pickup rivals and a substantial advantage in payload. If you're struck by the styling, the rest of the truck most likely won't disappoint.

RATINGS

	Reg. Cab 4-cyl	Ext. Cab V-6	Ext. Cab V-8 4WD
Acceleration	2	3	4
Fuel economy	3	2	2
Ride quality	3	4	3
Steering/handling	3	4	3
Braking	2	3	3
Quietness	4	4	4
Driver seating	3	4	4
Instruments/controls	3	3	3
Room/comfort (front)	3	4	4
Room/comfort (rear)	—	1	4
Cargo room	—	3	3
Value for the money	4	4	4
Total	**30**	**39**	**41**

SPECIFICATIONS

	Short bed	Long bed	Ext. cab
Wheelbase, in.	111.9	123.9	131.0
Overall length, in.	195.8	215.1	214.8
Overall width, in.	71.5	71.5	71.5
Overall height, in.	65.6	65.3	65.6
Curb weight, lbs.	3481	3556	3723
Maximum payload, lbs.	2600	2600	2000

	Short bed	Long bed	Ext. cab
Fuel capacity, gals.	15.0[1]	15.0[1]	15.0[1]
Seating capacity	3	3	6
Front head room, in.	40.0	40.0	40.0
Max. front leg room, in.	41.9	41.9	41.9
Rear head room, in.	—	—	38.0
Min. rear leg room, in.	—	—	22.1

ENGINES

	ohv I-4	ohv V-6	ohv V-8
Size, liters/cu. in.	2.5/150	3.9/239	5.2/318
Horsepower @ rpm	120@ 5200	175@ 4800	230@ 4400
Torque (lbs./ft.) @ rpm	145@ 3250	225@ 3200	300@ 3200
Availability	S	O[2]	O
EPA city/highway mpg			
5-speed OD manual	20/25	17/22	14/20
4-speed OD automatic		16/21	14/18

1 22.0 gals. optional. 2. Standard, Club Cab, and 4WD models.

PRICES

Dodge Dakota	Retail Price	Dealer Invoice
2WD regular cab short bed	$12975	$11818
2WD regular cab long bed	13435	12223
4WD regular cab short bed	16955	15355
2WD Club Cab	16170	14665
4WD Club Cab	19755	17854
Destination charge	510	510

STANDARD EQUIPMENT:

Regular cab: 2.5-liter 4-cylinder engine (2WD), 3.9-liter V-6 engine (4WD), 5-speed manual transmission, driver- and passenger-side air bags, power steering, vinyl upholstery, 40/20/40 bench seat, cuphold-er, tinted glass, coolant-temperature and oil-pressure gauges, volt-meter, trip odometer, AM/FM/cassette, manual outside mirrors, inter-mittent wipers, rubber floormat, black front and rear bumpers, front stabilizer bar, 215/75R15 tires, full-size spare tire, 4WD models add part-time 4WD system with two-speed transfer case.

Club Cab adds: 3.9-liter V-6 engine, cloth upholstery, rear folding bench seat, carpeting, behind-seat storage compartments.

4WD models add: part-time 4WD system with two-speed transfer case.

OPTIONAL EQUIPMENT:

Major Packages

Quick Order Sport Pkg., 2WD regular cab	1635	1390
Manufacturer's discount price	985	837
Quick Order Sport Pkg., 4WD regular cab	1815	1543
Manufacturer's discount price	1165	990

Cloth/vinyl 40/20/40 split bench seat, passenger-side visor mirror, tachometer (NA w/2.5-liter engine), Sport Group (color-keyed grille, front and rear color-keyed fascia, colored-keyed grille, Sport badging, alloy wheels), upgraded door trim, carpeting, 215/75R15 white-letter tires (2WD), 235/75R15 outline-white-letter tires (4WD). 2WD requires optional engine.

Quick Order SLT Pkg., 2WD regular cab	2640	2244
Manufacturer's discount price	1990	1691
Quick Order SLT Pkg., 4WD regular cab	2820	2397
Manufacturer's discount price	2170	1844

Air conditioning, cloth/vinyl 40/20/40 split bench seat, carpeting, tachometer (NA w/2.5-liter engine), SLT Decor Group (passenger-side visor mirror, heavy-duty sound insulation, storage tray and jack cover, bright front and rear-step bumper, bright grille, seat-back covers, Dodge reflecto-flex lettering, SLT badging, alloy wheels), Light Group, upgraded door trim, carpeting, 22-gallon fuel tank, 215/75R15 white-letter tires (2WD), 235/75R15 outline-white-letter tires (4WD). 2WD requires optional engine.

Quick Order Sport Pkg., 2WD Club Cab	1035	880
Manufacturer's discount price	NC	NC
Quick Order SLT Plus Pkg., 2WD Club Cab	3310	2814
Manufacturer's discount price	1760	1496
Quick Order SLT Plus Pkg., 4WD Club Cab	3490	2967

Rating Scale: 5-Excellent; 4-Above average; 3-Average; 2-Below average; 1-Poor

CONSUMER GUIDE™

	Retail Price	Dealer Invoice
Manufacturer's discount price	$1940	$1649

SLT Pkg. plus cruise control, tilt steering column, power windows and door locks, power mirrors, theft-deterrent system, remote keyless entry, sliding rear window.

Quick Order Sport Pkg., 4WD Club Cab.................	1200	1020
Manufacturer's discount price	NC	NC

Tachometer, Sport Group (color-keyed grille, front and rear color-keyed fascia, Sport badging, alloy wheels), upgraded door trim, 22-gallon fuel tank, 215/75R15 white-letter tires (2WD), 235/75R15 outline-white-letter tires (4WD).

Quick Order Sport Plus Pkg., 4WD Club Cab.........	3485	2962
Manufacturer's discount price	1935	1644

Air conditioning, cruise control, cloth/vinyl front bucket seats, power mirrors, tilt steering column, tachometer, Sport Group (color-keyed grille, front and rear color-keyed fascia, Sport badging, alloy wheels), Light Group, upgraded door trim, sliding rear windows, fog lamps, 22-gallon fuel tank, 31x10.5R15 outline-white-letter tires. Requires 5.2-liter engine.

Quick Order SLT Pkg., 2WD Club Cab..................	1945	1653
Manufacturer's discount price	945	803
Quick Order SLT Pkg., 4WD Club Cab..................	2125	1806
Manufacturer's discount price	925	786

Air conditioning, tachometer, SLT Decor Group (passenger-side visor mirror, heavy-duty sound insulation, storage tray and jack cover, bright front and rear-step bumper, bright grille, seatback covers, Dodge reflecto-flex lettering, SLT badging, alloy wheels), Light Group, upgraded door trim, 22-gallon fuel tank, 215/75R15 white-letter tires (2WD), 235/75R15 outline-white-letter tires (4WD).

Deluxe Convenience Group	390	332

Cruise control, tilt steering column. 2WD regular cab requires 3.9- or 5.2-liter engine.

Power Convenience Group	570	485

Power windows and door locks, remote keyless entry. Requires Quick Order Pkg.

Power Overhead Convenience Group,

regular cab w/Quick Order Pkg., Club Cab w/Sport, Sport Plus, or SLT Pkg.	785	667
Club Cab w/SLT Plus Pkg.	215	183

Power windows and door locks, overhead storage console (includes compass, outside-temperature display, map/reading lights), remote keyless entry, automatic day/night inside mirror.

Light Group	125	106

Ignition-switch light w/time delay, instrument-panel courtesy light, ashtray and cigar-lighter light, glove-box and underhood lights, outside cargo lamp, auxiliary power outlet.

Trailer Tow Group	245	208

Class IV trailer-hitch receiver, 4-wire adapter. Requires Heavy Duty Service Group. NA w/rear valance panel. NA 2WD regular cab short bed. 2WD regular cab long bed requires 3.9- or 5.2-liter engine.

Powertrains

3.9-liter V-6 engine, 2WD regular cab.....................	500	425

Requires 22-gallon fuel tank when ordered without Quick Order Pkg.

5.2-liter V-8 engine, 2WD regular cab.....................	1090	927
4WD regular cab, Club Cab	590	502

Requires Quick Order Pkg.

Manual transmission, 2WD	NC	NC
Manufacturer's discount price, (credit)...................	(200)	(170)
4-speed automatic transmission	950	808

2WD regular cab requires 3.9- or 5.2-liter engine.

Optional axle ratio	40	34
Anti-slip differential	285	242

2WD requires optional axle ratio when ordered with V-8 engine. 4WD requires optional axle ratio ordered with standard V-6 engine.

Transfer case, 4WD	395	336

Safety Features

Anti-lock brakes...	500	425

Comfort and Convenience

Air conditioning..	800	680

	Retail Price	Dealer Invoice
Cloth/vinyl bucket seats, regular cab w/SLT or Sport Pkg.; Club Cab w/Sport, SLT, or SLT Plus Pkg...........................	$200	$170

Includes center console.

Power mirrors..	140	119

Requires Quick Order Pkg.

Power fold-away mirrors,

regular cab w/Quick Order Pkg., Club Cab w/Sport or SLT Pkg.	160	136
Club Cab w/Sport Plus or SLT Plus Pkg.	20	17
AM/FM/cassette w/equalizer	300	255

Includes Infinity Sound. Requires Quick Order Pkg.

AM/FM/cassette/CD player w/equalizer	660	561

Includes Infinity Sound. Requires Quick Order Pkg.

AM/FM/CD player w/equalizer	480	408

Includes Infinity Sound. Requires Quick Order Pkg.

Infinity Sound..	175	149

Requires Quick Order Pkg.

Tilt steering column	140	119
Tachometer..	60	51

2WD regular cab requires 3.9- or 5.2-liter engine.

Appearance and Miscellaneous

Fog lamps..	120	102

Requires Quick Order Pkg.

Sliding rear window	115	98
Theft-deterrent system	150	128

Requires Quick Order Pkg. and Power Convenience Group.

Special Purpose, Wheels and Tires

Maximum engine cooling,

ordered w/manual transmission........................	60	51
ordered w/automatic transmission.....................	120	102
Heavy Duty Electrical Group	120	102

Heavy-duty alternator and battery. 2WD regular cab requires 3.9- or 5.2-liter engine.

4x4 Protection Group, 4WD	130	111

Fuel-tank, front-axle, and transfer-case skid plates; front deflector shield.

Tire and Handling Pkg.,

2WD Club Cab w/Quick Order Pkg.	230	196

Rear stabilizer bar, 235/70R15 outline-white-letter tires, alloy wheels. Not available w/2000# GVWR.

235/70R15 tires,

2WD regular cab w/Sport or SLT Pkg.	65	55

235/70R15 outline-white-letter tires,

2WD regular cab w/Quick Order Pkg.	205	174

NA with standard 2.5-liter engine, 1800# GVWR, or 2600# GVWR.

31x10.5R15 outline-white-letter tires,

4WD w/Quick Order Pkg.	400	340

Includes rear stabilizer bar, wheel flares.

235/75R15 tires, 2WD Club Cab..........................	190	162
2WD Club Cab w/Quick Order Pkg., 4WD Club Cab without Quick Order Pkg.	65	55

DODGE DURANGO

Dodge Durango

Rear- or 4-wheel-drive midsize sport-utility vehicle
Base price: $25,810. Built in Newark, Del.

Prices are accurate at time of publication; subject to manufacturer's changes.

Also consider: Chevrolet Blazer, Ford Explorer, Jeep Grand Cherokee

FOR • Passenger and cargo room • Optional anti-lock brakes • Acceleration (5.9-liter V-8)

AGAINST • Fuel economy

Durango, which is based on the Dakota pickup, is a new entry in the booming sport-utility market. Dodge's last SUV was the Ramcharger, a full-size 2-door wagon dropped in 1993.

The 4-door Durango is positioned and priced against midsize SUVs like the Ford Explorer and Chevrolet Blazer. But it's considerably larger than those vehicles and rivals full-size SUVs in offering an optional third seat that gives it 8-passenger capacity. Dodge has priced the Durango below the more-upscale Jeep Grand Cherokee in an effort to keep if from stealing sales from its sister division at Chrysler Corporation.

The front styling and dashboard are the same as the Dakota's, but the Durango has different seats and other interior features.

Initially, Durango is available with standard 5.2-liter or optional 5.9-liter V-8 engines. A 3.9-liter V-6 will be added in the spring. All 1998 models have automatic transmission and 4-wheel drive. The standard 4WD system is the on-demand part-time type that's not for use on dry pavement. A full-time system that can be left engaged on dry pavement is optional. Two-wheel-drive models will be added next year.

Seats for five are standard (front buckets and a 3-place rear seat). Options include a 3-place front bench seat and a 2-place third bench. The middle and rear seats are not removable; instead, they fold flat to create 88 cubic feet of cargo space.

Maximum towing capacity is 7300 pounds with the 5.9-liter V-8, putting Durango in the same league as some full-size SUVs. Dual front air bags and anti-lock rear brakes are standard. Anti-lock brakes are optional.

PERFORMANCE Durango rides and handles more like a car than a truck. Body lean is moderate, and the Durango cruises down bumpy roads with good composure and little bouncing. The steering is vague around center, however, and requires a lot of corrections to maintain course at highway speeds.

Both V-8 engines are smooth and quiet. The 5.2-liter provides adequate vigor but lacks a strong punch at low speeds for quick getaways. The 5.9-liter has a huskier tone and feels stronger off the line and in passing situations. The transmission shifts smoothly and downshifts promptly for passing.

We haven't driven the V-6, but based on how it performs in the Dakota, we think it will be hard-pressed to provide adequate acceleration in the heavier Durango.

We have not measured fuel economy, though our experiences with the Dakota suggest both V-8s will be gas guzzlers. Expect less than 15 mpg except in straight highway cruising.

ACCOMMODATIONS Give Dodge credit for squeezing eight seats into a vehicle the size of a midsize car. However, the third seat is better for kids than adults. It has ample head room, but leg room is tight, the cushion is low, and adults find their knees pointed at the ceiling. The second-row seats have thin padding that isn't as supportive as the more-substantial cushions used by many rivals.

Otherwise, Durango has ample space for grownups, with generous head room at all seating positions. Entry/exit is easy, thanks to large doors and a modest step-in height for a 4WD vehicle.

The 18.8 cubic feet of cargo space behind the third seat is enough for a few small suitcases or a week's worth of groceries. The middle and rear seats fold flat in seconds, a handy alternative to removable seats. That opens up ample cargo room.

The dashboard is the same simple, convenient design as the Dakota's. All models have a floor-mounted transfer case lever that is a stretch for the driver.

BUILD QUALITY The body panels feel solid and the early production models we drove had smooth, lustrous paint. The black plastic trim over the gauge cluster and main dashboard controls feels cheap and flimsy, and the inside door panels look plain.

VALUE FOR THE MONEY A well-equipped Durango costs about $28,000, including the destination charge. Durango is a well-designed truck that deserves strong consideration.

RATINGS	SLT w/5.2 V-8	SLT Plus w/5.9 V-8
Acceleration	3	3
Fuel economy	2	2
Ride quality	3	3
Steering/handling	3	3
Braking	3	3
Quietness	3	3
Driver seating	4	4
Instruments/controls	4	4
Room/comfort (front)	4	4
Room/comfort (rear)	4	4
Cargo room	4	4
Value for the money	4	4
Total	**41**	**41**

SPECIFICATIONS

	4-door wagon
Wheelbase, in.	115.9
Overall length, in.	193.3
Overall width, in.	71.5
Overall height, in.	72.9
Curb weight, lbs.	4568
Cargo vol., cu. ft.	88.0
Fuel capacity, gals.	25.0
Seating capacity	8
Front head room, in.	39.8
Max. front leg room, in.	41.9
Rear head room, in.	40.6
Min. rear leg room, in.	35.4

ENGINES

	ohv V-8	ohv V-8
Size, liters/cu. in.	5.2/318	5.9/360
Horsepower @ rpm	230@ 4400	245@ 4000
Torque (lbs./ft.) @ rpm	300@ 3200	335@ 3200
Availability	S	O

EPA city/highway mpg

4-speed OD automatic	13/17	12/16

PRICES

Dodge Durango	Retail Price	Dealer Invoice
Base 4-door wagon	$25810	$23318
Destination charge	525	525

Requires a Quick Order Pkg.

STANDARD EQUIPMENT:

Base: 3.9-liter V-6 engine, 4-speed automatic transmission, part-time 4-wheel drive, driver- and passenger-side air bags, air conditioning, power steering, cloth/vinyl front bucket seats w/adjustable lumbar support, 40/20/40 split folding second row seat, cupholders, AM/FM/cassette w/four speakers, visor mirrors, intermittent wipers, trip odometer, tachometer, coolant-temperature gauge, oil-pressure gauge, rear defogger, rear wiper/washer, dual outside mirrors, tinted glass, roof rack, skid plates, 235/75R15 tires, alloy wheels.

OPTIONAL EQUIPMENT:

Major Packages

SLT Quick Order Pkg.	1800	1530
Manufacturer's discount price	1100	935

Floor console, upgraded door trim, map lights, underhood light, glove box light, auxiliary power outlet, cruise control, tilt steering wheel, power windows and door locks, remote keyless entry, white letter tires.

SLT Plus Quick Order Pkg.	3250	2763
Manufacturer's discount price	2250	1913

SLT Pkg. plus power driver seat, overhead console, trip computer, automatic day/night rearview mirror, illuminated visor mirrors, CD/cassette player, floormats, theft-deterrent system, color-keyed bodyside moldings, fog lights.

Rating Scale: 5-Excellent; 4-Above average; 3-Average; 2-Below average; 1-Poor

CONSUMER GUIDE™

	Retail Price	Dealer Invoice
Trailer Tow Prep Group	$245	$208

Includes 7-wire harness, platform hitch. Requires Heavy-Duty Service Group.

Powertrains

5.2-liter V-8 engine	590	502
5.9-liter V-8 engine	885	752

Requires SLT Plus Pkg.

Full-time 4WD	395	336
Limited slip differential..	285	242
3.92 axle ratio	40	34

Safety Features

Anti-lock brakes...	565	480

Comfort and Convenience

Air conditioning..	430	366

Requires Heavy-Duty Service Group.

Leather upholstery..	670	570

Requires SLT Plus Pkg.

Overhead Console Group	410	349

Includes illuminated visor mirrors, automatic day/night rearview mirror, compass, trip computer, outside temperature gauge.

Power mirrors	25	21
Front split bench seat...	NC	NC
Third row seat	550	468
Cassette/CD player	300	255

Includes graphic equalizer.

Infinity 8-speaker sound system.............................	330	281
Floormats	50	43

Appearance and Miscellaneous

Theft-deterrent system	150	128
Fog lights	240	204
Bodyside moldings	80	68

Special Purpose, Wheels and Tires

Skid Plate Group	90	70

Fuel tank and transfer case case skid plates.

Heavy-Duty Service Group	245	204

Heavy-duty alternator and battery, maximimum engine cooling.

31x10.5 all-terrain tires...	505	429

Includes body-colored wheel flares.

DODGE INTREPID

Dodge Intrepid ES

Front-wheel-drive full-size car; similar to Chrysler Concorde

Base price range: $19,545-$22,345. Built in Canada.

Also consider: Buick LeSabre, Oldsmobile Eighty Eight/LSS/Regency, Pontiac Bonneville

FOR • Passenger and cargo room • Ride • Steering/handling

AGAINST • Trunk liftover

Dodge's biggest sedan is redesigned for 1998, with new styling, new engines, and a substantially revised chassis. Intrepid uses the same basic mechanical design as the Chrysler Concorde, which also is redesigned this year (see separate report), but they no longer share any body panels.

There's no Eagle version of this car because Chrysler is discontinuing that division after the 1998 model year.

Intrepid comes two ways. The base model has a 200-horsepower 2.7-liter V-6 engine and a 4-speed automatic transmission. The sportier ES model has a 225-horsepower 3.2-liter V-6

and Chrysler's Autostick transmission, which can be used as a conventional 4-speed automatic or shifted manually. Both engines have aluminum blocks and cylinder heads and replace slightly larger V-6s of 161 and 214 horsepower.

Front bucket seats and a floor-mounted shift lever are standard. The shift lever moves to the steering column with the optional front bench seat available on the base model.

Dual front air bags are standard and anti-lock brakes are standard on the ES, optional on the base model.

PERFORMANCE Both Intrepids are agile and demonstrate commendable handling ability that belies their full-size dimensions. They tackle sweeping curves and tight turns with good grip and composure, and the steering is precise and centers promptly. The suspension is firm and stable at highway speeds without being harsh on rough pavement. The brakes provide short, straight stops from high speeds.

The 2.7-liter engine lacks neck-snapping acceleration but moves this full-size sedan with adequate quickness. With three or more adults aboard, however, there isn't enough power when you need to quickly pass other cars on two-lane roads. By contrast, the stronger 3.2-liter engine chirps the tires in quick takeoffs and delivers a quicker burst of power for passing and merging.

We have not had a chance to check mileage, but Dodge says the new engines will use less fuel than their predecessors.

The new engines are smooth and quiet and the new Intrepid has less road noise than the old one.

ACCOMMODATIONS Head room is generous in front, though the sloping roofline has taller rear-seaters brushing the headliner. There's enough leg room for 6-footers to be comfortable in all seats except the front passenger's, which doesn't have enough rearward travel to allow someone over 6-feet tall to stretch. The rear seat is wide enough for three adults, and all doors open wide for easy entry/exit.

Intrepid has black-on-white gauges (Concorde's are the opposite), but the dashboard design and control layout are the same, with the climate and audio switches easy to see and reach in the center. Intrepid has a much larger rear window than Concorde. It lets the driver see the trunk for parking and provides a better view of surrounding traffic.

Cargo room is ample, and the Intrepid has a split folding rear seatback that increases capacity; Concorde has only a center pass-through. However, the trunk liftover is high and the Intrepid's taillights make the trunk opening narrower than on the Chrysler version.

BUILD QUALITY The early production models we drove were nicely finished and generally well assembled, though the interior was trimmed with uninviting hard plastic moldings.

VALUE FOR THE MONEY The new Intrepid and Concorde make other full-size cars look and feel dated. Dodge indicated that prices on the new Intrepid will be slightly higher than last year, which would make these great buys among full-size cars. They look good, hold four or five passengers in comfort, and handle like European sports sedans.

RATINGS

	Base	ES
Acceleration	3	4
Fuel economy	3	3
Ride quality	4	4
Steering/handling	4	4
Braking	3	3
Quietness	3	3
Driver seating	4	4
Instruments/controls	4	4
Room/comfort (front)	4	4
Room/comfort (rear)	4	4
Cargo room	4	4
Value for the money	4	4
Total	**44**	**45**

SPECIFICATIONS

	4-door sedan
Wheelbase, in.	113.0
Overall length, in.	203.7
Overall width, in.	74.7

Prices are accurate at time of publication; subject to manufacturer's changes.

	4-door sedan
Overall height, in.	55.9
Curb weight, lbs.	3422
Cargo vol., cu. ft.	18.4
Fuel capacity, gals.	17.0
Seating capacity	6
Front head room, in.	38.3
Max. front leg room, in.	42.2
Rear head room, in.	37.5
Min. rear leg room, in.	39.1

ENGINES

	dohc V-6	ohc V-6
Size, liters/cu. in.	2.7/167	3.2/197
Horsepower @ rpm	200@	225@
	5800	6300
Torque (lbs./ft.) @ rpm	190@	225@
	4850	3800
Availability	S[1]	S[2]
EPA city/highway mpg		
4-speed OD automatic	NA	19/29

1. Base. 2. ES.

PRICES

Dodge Intrepid	Retail Price	Dealer Invoice
Base 4-door sedan	$19545	$17925
ES 4-door sedan	22345	20399
Destination charge	550	550

STANDARD EQUIPMENT:

Base: 2.7-liter DOHC V-6 engine, 4-speed automatic transmission, driver- and passenger-side air bags, 4-wheel disc brakes, air conditioning, power steering, tilt steering wheel, cloth front bucket seats, floor console, power mirrors, power windows, power door locks, rear defogger, intermittent wipers, AM/FM/cassette with four speakers, tachometer, power remote decklid release, floormats, 205/70R15 tires, wheel covers.

ES adds: 3.2-liter V-6 engine, Autostick 4-speed automatic transmission, anti-lock brakes, 8-way power driver seat, split folding rear seat, leather-wrapped steering wheel, 8-speaker sound system, Headliner Module (illuminated visor mirrors, rear reading lights), remote keyless entry system, fog lights, 225/60R16 tires, alloy wheels.

OPTIONAL EQUIPMENT:
Major Packages

	Retail	Dealer
Pkg. 22D, Base	1140	1015
Leather-wrapped steering wheel, 8-way power driver seat, 8-speaker sound system, remote keyless entry, Headliner Module (illuminated visor mirrors, rear reading lights).		
Pkg. 24M, ES	1130	1006
Traction control, automatic temperature control, overhead trip computer, 8-speaker Infinity sound system, CD changer controls, theft-deterrent system, full-size spare tire.		
Comfort and Security Group, ES	305	271
Automatic temperature control, theft-deterrent system.		

Safety Features

Anti-lock brakes, Base	600	534

Comfort and Convenience

Power moonroof, ES	795	708
Requires trip computer		
Trip computer, ES	310	275
Includes universal garage door opener.		
Automatic day/night mirror, ES	85	76
Requires Pkg. 24M.		
8-speaker sound system, Base	290	258
CD player, Base	435	387
Base w/option pkg., ES w/option pkg.	145	129
Includes eight Infinity speakers, CD changer controls.		
CD/cassette player, ES	515	458
ES w/opt. pkg.	300	267
Includes Infinity speakers.		
Cloth front split bench seat	NC	NC

	Retail Price	Dealer Invoice
Leather upholstery, ES	$1000	$890
Includes front bucket seats, 8-way power passenger seat. Requires Pkg. 24M.		
8-way power driver seat, Base	380	338
8-way power passenger seat, ES	380	338
Requires Pkg. 24M.		
Smoker's Group	20	18
Includes ashtrays and lighter.		

Appearance and Miscellaneous

Cold Weather Group	30	27
Includes engine block and battery heater.		
Metallic paint	200	178
Full-size spare tire	125	111
Wheel and Tire Group, Base	200	178
Includes alloy wheels, 225/60R16 tires.		

DODGE/PLYMOUTH NEON

BUDGET BUY

Dodge Neon R/T 2-door

Front-wheel-drive subcompact

Base price range: $10,900-$11,355. Built in Belvidere, Ill., and Mexico.

Also consider: Ford Escort/Escort ZX2, Honda Civic, Saturn Coupe, Saturn Sedan/Wagon

FOR • Optional anti-lock brakes • Fuel economy • Steering/handling • Passenger and cargo room

AGAINST • Engine noise • Automatic transmission performance

Sold in nearly identical form by Dodge and Plymouth dealers, Neon was Chrysler Corporation's first successful home-grown import fighter when it debuted in January 1994 as a 1995 model. Its spunky personality and low prices appealed to entry-level buyers, but in the last year or so the car has lost some sales steam to fresher new rivals.

A Neon by any other name is available as a 2-door coupe or 4-door sedan. Dual air bags are standard, anti-lock 4-wheel disc brakes are optional. For '98, the "base" trim level is dropped and last year's uplevel Highline takes over as the entry-level Neon. (The Competition version has a base price below that of the Highline, but it must be ordered with the $2060 package of performance items designed for Neons participating in organized road racing.) This year's Highline starts about $760 above last year's base model and $1300 below last year's Highline version. The biggest equipment change is that air conditioning, which was a Highline standard feature, is now a $1000 option.

The standard engine is a 132-horsepower 2.0-liter overhead-camshaft 4-cylinder. Optional is a dual-cam version of that engine with 150 horsepower. With either, a 5-speed manual transmission is standard and a 3-speed automatic is optional.

Dodge will emphasize its version's sporty nature with the planned Spring introduction of the Neon R/T. It draws equipment from the road-racing oriented Competition Package option and includes such features as special exterior graphics, a sport suspension, and a performance-tuned 150-horsepower twin-cam 2.0-liter engine and running gear.

PERFORMANCE Neon gives up a lot of refinement in the name of spry performance. It's lively even with the base engine,

Rating Scale: 5-Excellent; 4-Above average; 3-Average; 2-Below average; 1-Poor

CONSUMER GUIDE™

and 5-speed twin-cam versions are fun to drive. Most rivals offer a 4-speed automatic. Neon's 3-speed automatic keeps the engine near 3000 rpm at 60 mph; this hurts highway mileage and makes for noisy cruising. It also shifts abruptly in brisk acceleration.

Our automatic test car averaged 24.2 mpg. A 5-speed base-engine model topped 31 mpg in a mix of city and highway driving. It also cruised more quietly, turning a lazy 2250 rpm at 60 mph.

Despite Chrysler's efforts to quell engine noise, Neon's 4-cylinders growl loudly under hard throttle, and tire noise is prominent. Wind noise is noticeable but not intrusive, even at highway speeds.

Neon's standard suspension furnishes a taut, sporty ride. It feels stable at highway speeds but doesn't absorb bumps as well as the class-leading Toyota Corolla/Chevrolet Prizm or Honda Civic.

With the optional anti-lock brakes, our test car averaged 120 feet in 10 stops from 60 mph. However, the anti-lock system groans loudly when activated.

ACCOMMODATIONS Neon is similar in exterior size to the Saturn sedan, but it's roomier inside. Four 6-footers fit with only a little squeezing. The doors open wide to provide unusually easy entry and exit for a subcompact sedan.

A simple pull knob activates the headlamps, and large dials govern the climate system. The radio is mounted a little low, but big controls take the mystery out of tuning it. The floor console is located far forward, making for a long reach to the coin and cupholders.

A high rear parcel shelf restricts the view directly aft, but the dashboard allows a clear view forward.

There are no door map pockets. A good-sized glovebox and a small center console bin provide interior storage. Neon's trunk opens at bumper level to reveal a wide, flat cargo floor that provides adequate luggage space.

BUILD QUALITY Some manual-transmission Neons we've tested tended to bog and surge during gear shifts, but others have been free of mechanical glitches. There's lots of hard plastic interior trim, especially on the dashboard, but assembly quality is good.

VALUE FOR THE MONEY Roomy, fun to drive, and priced below most Japanese rivals, Neon is well worth considering. And good deals should be available.

RATINGS

	2-dr. dohc 5-speed	4-dr. ohc automatic
Acceleration	4	3
Fuel economy	5	4
Ride quality	3	3
Steering/handling	4	4
Braking	4	3
Quietness	2	2
Driver seating	3	3
Instruments/controls	3	3
Room/comfort (front)	4	4
Room/comfort (rear)	3	3
Cargo room	3	3
Value for the money	4	4
Total	**42**	**39**

SPECIFICATIONS

	2-door coupe	4-door sedan
Wheelbase, in.	104.0	104.0
Overall length, in.	171.8	171.8
Overall width, in.	67.4	67.2
Overall height, in.	54.9	54.9
Curb weight, lbs.	2470	2507
Cargo vol., cu. ft.	11.8	11.8
Fuel capacity, gals.	12.5	12.5
Seating capacity	5	5
Front head room, in.	39.6	39.6
Max. front leg room, in.	42.5	42.5
Rear head room, in.	36.5	36.5
Min. rear leg room, in.	35.1	35.1

ENGINES

	ohc I-4	dohc I-4
Size, liters/cu. in.	2.0/122	2.0/122
Horsepower @ rpm	132@ 6000	150@ 6500
Torque (lbs./ft.) @ rpm	129@ 5000	133@ 5500
Availability	S	O

EPA city/highway mpg

3-speed automatic	25/33	25/33
5-speed OD manual	29/38	29/38

PRICES

Dodge/Plymouth Neon

	Retail Price	Dealer Invoice
Competition 2-door coupe	$10900	$10313
Competition 4-door sedan	11100	10497
Highline 2-door coupe	11155	10325
Highline 4-door sedan	11355	10505

Competition requires Competition Pkg. Prices for R/T Pkg. not available at time of publication.

STANDARD EQUIPMENT:

5-speed manual transmission, driver- and passenger-side air bags, power steering, cloth/vinyl reclining bucket seats, storage armrest with cupholders, AM/FM radio with four speakers, trip odometer, variable intermittent wipers, passenger-side visor mirror, tinted glass, dual outside mirrors, 175/70R14 tires, wheel covers.

Highline adds: rear defogger, 60/40 split folding rear seat, remote decklid release, trunk light, 185/65R14 touring tires, bodyside moldings.

OPTIONAL EQUIPMENT:
Major Packages

Competition Pkg., Competition 4-door	2060	1895

2.0-liter DOHC 4-cylinder engine (2-door), unlimited speed engine controller, 4-wheel disc brakes, Firm Feel power steering, leather-wrapped steering and shift knob, competition suspension, sport bucket seats, tachometer with low fuel light, power bulge hood, 175/65HR14 tires (4-door), 185/60HR14 tires (2-door), alloy wheels.

Dodge Sport Pkg./Plymouth Expresso Pkg., Highline	1800	1602
Manufacturer's discount price	1300	1157

2.0-liter DOHC 4-cylinder engine, air conditioning, sport bucket seats, tachometer, interior assist handles, power bulge hood, rear spoiler, fog lamps, sport wheel covers.

R/T Pkg., Dodge Highline	—	—

Includes 2.0-liter DOHC 4-cylinder engine, 4-wheel disc brakes, sport suspension, sport bucket seats, leather-wrapped steering wheel, cassette player w/CD controls, tachometer, stripes, rear spoiler, fog lights, 185/65HR14 tires.

Value/Fun Group, Highline	1435	1277
Manufacturer's discount price	835	743

Power mirrors, power door locks, power front windows, Premium AM/FM/cassette w/CD changer controls, power sunroof.

Deluxe Convenience Group, Highline	350	312

Cruise control, tilt steering wheel.

Power Convenience Group, Highline 4-door	300	267
Highline 2-door	260	231

Power door locks, power mirrors.

Light Group, Highline	130	116

Illuminated visor mirrors, courtesy/reading lights.

Powertrains

2.0-liter DOHC 4-cylinder engine, Competition 2-door, Highline	150	134
Manufacturer's discount price	NC	NC
3-speed automatic transmission, Highline	600	534

Safety Features

Anti-lock 4-wheel disc brakes, Highline	565	503
Integrated child seat, Highline	100	89

Includes fixed rear seat back. NA with Sport Pkg, RT Pkg.

Comfort and Convenience

Air conditioning, Competition, Highline	1000	890
Power moonroof, Highline	595	530
Rear defogger, Competition	205	182
Remote keyless entry, Highline	155	138

Requires Power Convenience Group.

AM/FM/cassette w/eight speakers, Competition	595	530
Highline	260	231

Prices are accurate at time of publication; subject to manufacturer's changes.

	Retail Price	Dealer Invoice
Premium AM/FM/cassette w/eight speakers, Highline..........	$285	$254
Includes CD changer controls.		
Premium AM/FM/CD player w/eight speakers, Highline..........	395	352
Highline with Value/Fun Group..........	110	98
Power front door windows, Highline..........	265	236
Requires Power Convenience Group.		
Tachometer with low fuel light, Highline..........	100	89

Appearance and Miscellaneous

Alloy wheels, Highline..........	355	316

DODGE RAM 1500

RECOMMENDED

Dodge Ram 1500 SLT Quad Cab

Rear- or 4-wheel-drive pickup

Base price range: $14,485-$23,285. Built in Warren, Mich.; St. Louis, Mo.; and Mexico.

Also consider: Chevrolet C/K1500, Ford F-150, GMC Sierra 1500

FOR • Interior room • Acceleration (V-8s) • Cargo and towing ability • Optional 4-wheel anti-lock brakes

AGAINST • Fuel economy • Ride • Acceleration (V-6)

Dodge breaks new ground in the pickup market with the Quad Cab—rear doors for both sides of extended-cab models. The rear doors, which swing open to the rear, are a $750 option on the short- and long-bed versions of the Ram Club Cab.

Rival full-size pickups from Ford and General Motors are available with a passenger-side rear door, and the Toyota T100 doesn't offer a rear door for 1998.

The front doors must be open before the rear doors on the Quad Cab can be opened or closed. To make it easier to get in and out of the rear seat, the front seatbelts on Club Cabs are now integrated with the seats rather than anchored to a roof pillar.

All models have a new dashboard with a passenger-side air bag as a new standard feature. A key-operated dashboard switch allows disabling the passenger-side air bag to carry a rear-facing child seat in front. A driver-side air bag already was standard.

In addition to the extended-cab models, the Ram 1500 comes as a regular cab with short (6.5 feet) or long (8.0 feet) cargo beds. Both V-8 engines available in the Ram 1500 gain 10 horsepower this year from freer-flowing exhaust systems.

PERFORMANCE Either V-8 engine gives the Ram 1500 more-than-adequate acceleration, but the 5.9 liter is our favorite because the additional muscle it packs is worth the extra cost.

We averaged 14.4 mpg with a 5.2 liter over more than 700 miles of driving, reaching a high of 16 on the highway. The 5.9 liter won't use much more gas, and if you do any towing or haul anything that weighs more than a few hundred pounds, it's the better choice. For really big jobs, the 2500- and 3500-series are available with V-10 and diesel engines.

Forget the V-6 engine, which is in the lineup purely to keep the price down. It can't cut the mustard in this full-size truck.

The Ram pickups don't match the Ford F-150 in ride comfort, and the suspension allows more bouncing and banging over bumpy roads. As with other full-size pickups, the vague steering requires a lot of correction at highway speeds to stay on course.

ACCOMMODATIONS The Quad Cab is a success as far we're

concerned. Whether you use the rear seat for people or storage, it's much more convenient to have access from both sides. Moving the front seatbelts out of the way also makes rear entry/exit easier than in the F-150, which leaves the belt hanging in the doorway.

Dodge claims both its regular- and extended-cab models are the roomiest full-size pickups, and there is ample head room all around and plenty of leg space for the front seats. In the Club Cabs, however, the rear seat lacks leg room for adults to sit comfortably unless the front seats are pushed well forward.

Even the regular-cab models have adequate storage space behind the seats, with handy plastic bins, shelves, and a cargo net. Later this year, a divided storage bin that mounts under the rear seat of the Club Cabs will become available.

The new dashboard includes a larger glovebox and dual cupholders mounted lower so they no longer block the radio controls when in use. The overdrive off switch has been relocated from the dashboard to the end of the automatic transmission shift lever.

BUILD QUALITY Some of the interior trim is made of lightweight plastic and vinyl that doesn't feel durable, but the doors and other exterior panels feel sturdy.

VALUE FOR THE MONEY The Ram pickup initially grabbed a lot of attention with its "big rig" styling, but it also deserves consideration because it has a functional design, class-leading features like the 4-door Quad Cab, and competitive prices.

RATINGS	Reg. Cab V-6	Ext. Cab 5.2 V-8	Ext. Cab 5.9 V-8
Acceleration	2	3	4
Fuel economy	1	1	1
Ride quality	2	2	2
Steering/handling	3	3	3
Braking	3	3	3
Quietness	4	3	3
Driver seating	4	4	4
Instruments/controls	4	4	4
Room/comfort (front)	4	4	4
Room/comfort (rear)	—	2	2
Cargo room	2	4	4
Value for the money	4	4	4
Total	**33**	**37**	**38**

SPECIFICATIONS	Reg. cab short bed	Reg. cab long bed	Ext. cab short bed	Ext. cab long bed
Wheelbase, in.	118.7	134.7	138.7	154.7
Overall length, in.	204.1	224.1	224.0	244.0
Overall width, in.	79.4	79.4	79.4	79.4
Overall height, in.	71.9	71.8	71.6	71.5
Curb weight, lbs.	4024	4214	4640	4794
Maximum payload, lbs.	2307	2367	1760	1606
Fuel capacity, gals.	26.0	35.0	26.0	35.0
Seating capacity	3	3	6	6
Front head room, in.	40.2	40.2	40.2	40.2
Max. front leg room, in.	41.0	41.0	41.0	41.0
Rear head room, in.	—	—	39.4	39.4
Min. rear leg room, in.	—	—	31.6	31.6

ENGINES	ohv V-6	ohv V-8	ohv V-8
Size, liters/cu. in.	3.9/239	5.2/318	5.9/360
Horsepower @ rpm	175@ 4800	230@ 4400	245@ 4000[1]
Torque (lbs./ft.) @ rpm	230@ 3200	300@ 3200	335@ 3200[1]
Availability	S[2]	S[3]	O
EPA city/highway mpg			
4-speed OD automatic	14/18	13/18	13/17
5-speed OD manual	16/20	14/19	NA

1. Super Sport: 250 @ 4400 and 345 @ 3200. 2. Std. 2WD. 3. Std. 4WD.

PRICES

Dodge Ram 1500	Retail Price	Dealer Invoice
WS 2WD regular cab short bed	$14485	$13232
ST 2WD regular cab short bed	16260	14306
WS 2WD regular cab long bed	14755	13469
ST 2WD regular cab long bed	16545	14548
ST 4WD regular cab short bed	19815	17373
ST 4WD regular cab long bed	20155	17662

Rating Scale: 5-Excellent; 4-Above average; 3-Average; 2-Below average; 1-Poor

	Retail Price	Dealer Invoice
ST 2WD Club Cab short bed	$18975	$16649
ST 2WD Club Cab long bed	19255	16887
ST 4WD Club Cab short bed	22205	19434
ST 4WD Club Cab long bed	22535	19715
ST 2WD Quad Cab short bed	19725	17296
ST 2WD Quad Cab long bed	20005	17534
ST 4WD Quad Cab short bed	22955	20072
ST 4WD Quad Cab long bed	23285	20352
Destination charge	640	640

STANDARD EQUIPMENT:

Regular cab: 3.9-liter V-6 engine, 5-speed manual transmission, anti-lock rear brakes, driver- and passenger-side air bags, power steering, vinyl bench seat (WS), vinyl 40/20/40 split bench seat (ST), tinted glass, voltmeter, oil-pressure and coolant-temperature gauges, trip odometer, intermittent wipers, AM/FM/cassette (ST), digital clock, auxiliary power outlet, black-rubber floor covering, cargo lamp (ST), bright front and rear bumpers (ST), manual 6x9-inch outside mirrors, removable tailgate, bright grille, wheel trim rings, full-size spare tire, 225/75R16 tires.

4WD models add: part-time four-wheel drive, 5.2-liter V-8 engine.

Club Cab/Quad Cab adds to regular cab: 5.2-liter V-8 engine, rear folding bench seat.

Quad Cab models add: right- and left-side rear cab doors.

4WD models add: part-time four-wheel drive, 245/75R16 tires.

OPTIONAL EQUIPMENT:
Major Packages

SLT Pkg., ST 2WD, 4WD regular cab w/5.2- or 5.9-liter engine...	3105	2639
Manufacturer's discount price	2405	2044
SLT Pkg., 4WD Club Cab/Quad Cab	2975	2529
Manufacturer's discount price	2275	1934

Laramie SLT Decor Group (leather-wrapped steering wheel, power heated mirrors, passenger-side visor mirror, premium cloth upholstery, carpeting, bodyside moldings, front-bumper sight shields, dual horns, floormats), air conditioning, cruise control, tilt steering wheel, power windows and door locks, Light Group, tachometer, alloy wheels.

Deluxe Convenience Group	390	332

Tilt steering wheel, cruise control.

Sport Appearance Group, 2WD w/SLT Pkg.	385	327
4WD w/SLT Pkg.......................................	670	570

Tachometer, color-keyed front bumper and grille, front-bumper sight shields, color-keyed rear valence panel, Sport decal, fog lamps, dual horns, 245/75R16 outline-white-letter tires (2WD), 265/75R16 outline-white-letter tires (4WD), alloy wheels. NA with 3.9-liter engine.

Super Sport Truck Performance, 2WD regular cab short bed w/SLT Pkg.	1360	1156

Tachometer, sport-tuned exhaust w/bright outlets, color-keyed front bumper and grille, front-bumper sight shields, color-keyed rear valence panel, fog lamps, striping, 275/60R17 tires, alloy wheels. NA w/Sport Appearance Group or cab clearance lights. Requires 5.9-liter engine.

Travel Convenience Group, ordered w/SLT Pkg.....	295	251

Overhead console (includes compass, outside-temperature indicator, reading lights), automatic day/night inside mirror, lighted visor mirrors.

Leather Interior Group, regular cab w/SLT Pkg..	1400	1190
Club Cab/Quad Cab w/SLT Pkg.	1540	1309

Leather upholstery, 6-way power driver seat (regular cab) or 8-way power driver seat (Club Cab/Quad Cab), Travel Convenience Group, illuminated visor mirrors, wood interior trim.

Trailer Tow Group	245	208

Includes class IV trailer-hitch receiver, adapter plug, heavy-duty flasher. Requires Heavy Duty Service Group. NA with 3.9-liter engine.

Powertrains

5.2-liter V-8 engine, 2WD regular cab.....................	590	502
NA WS.		
5.9-liter V-8 engine, 2WD regular cab....................	$885	$752
4WD regular cab, Club Cab/Quad Cab	295	251
Requires 4-speed automatic transmission. NA WS.		
4-speed automatic transmission...........................	950	808
Anti-spin axle..	285	242

Safety Features

4-wheel anti-lock brakes	500	425
Fog lamps, ordered w/SLT Pkg............................	120	102

Comfort and Convenience

Air conditioning	800	680
Cloth 40/20/40 bench seat, ST	110	94
Cloth/vinyl bench seat, WS	110	94
6-way power driver seat, regular cab w/SLT Pkg.	320	272
8-way power driver seat, Club Cab /Quad Cab wSLT Pkg....................	360	306
Tachometer, ST	80	68
AM/FM/cassette, WS	400	340
AM/FM/cassette w/equalizer, ordered w/SLT Pkg.	335	285
AM/FM/CD player w/equalizer, ordered w/SLT Pkg.	510	434
AM/FM/cassette/CD w/equalizer, ordered w/SLT Pkg.	690	587
Remote keyless entry..	190	162
Requires SLT Pkg.		
Light Group, ST...	120	102

Overhead storage console with map/reading lights, passenger assist handle, cloth headliner, ignition light, glove-box light, under-hood light.

Appearance and Miscellaneous

Sliding rear window	140	119
Heated power 6x9-inch mirrors, ST	145	123
Security alarm, ordered w/SLT Pkg......................	150	128
Requires remote keyless entry.		
2-tone paint	195	166
NA WS.		
2-tone center-band paint	215	183
NA WS.		

Special Purpose, Wheels and Tires

Heavy Duty Service Group, 2WD w/3.9-liter engine or 5.2-liter engine and manual transmission.	215	183
2WD w/5.2- or 5.9-liter engine and automatic transmission.	345	293
4WD w/manual trans.	260	221
4WD w/automatic trans.	390	332

Heavy-duty alternator and battery, heavy-duty engine cooling (requires V-8 and auto. trans.), heavy-duty transmission-oil cooler (requires auto. trans.), skid plates (4WD).

Heavy-duty engine cooling, ordered w/automatic transmission......................	130	111
2WD regular cab requires 5.2- or 5.9-liter engine.		
245/75R16 tires, ST regular cab	130	111
245/75R16 all-terrain tires, 4WD..	280	238
265/75R16 all-terrain outline-white-letter tires, 4WD w/SLT Pkg.	415	353
Chrome wheels, ST...	345	293

DODGE STRATUS   `BUDGET BUY`

Front-wheel-drive midsize; similar to Chrysler Cirrus and Plymouth Breeze

Base price range: $14,840-$17,665. Built in Sterling Heights, Mich.

Also consider: Ford Taurus, Honda Accord, Toyota Camry

FOR • Optional anti-lock brakes • Acceleration (V-6) • Ride • Steering/handling • Passenger and cargo room

AGAINST • Noise • Rear visibility

Prices are accurate at time of publication; subject to manufacturer's changes.

Dodge Stratus

Stratus shares its design with the Chrysler Cirrus and Plymouth Breeze, residing in price and equipment between the entry-level Breeze and luxury-oriented Cirrus. An optional power sunroof, more standard power for the sporty ES Stratus, and some anti-noise measures are additions for the car's fourth season. On the debit side, anti-lock brakes are now optional, not standard, on the ES.

A 2.0-liter 4-cylinder engine and manual transmission are standard on the base Stratus. A 2.4-liter dual-camshaft 4-cylinder is optional on the base and, for '98, replaces the 2.0 as standard on the ES. A Mitsubishi-built V-6 is optional on the ES. The 2.4 and V-6 come only with automatic transmission, but the V-6's is Chrysler's Autostick, which allows manual control over gear changes by tilting the shift lever left or right. Last year, Autostick was an ES V-6 option. The new sunroof is optional on both Statuses.

Dual air bags are standard, but anti-lock brakes are now optional on both models. An integrated rear child safety seat also is optional on both models.

Sound-absorbing and noise-reflecting materials have been added to the body for '98.

PERFORMANCE Differing only in styling details and equipment availability, Stratus drives much like the Breeze and Cirrus. That means it has agile handling with little body lean and good grip. It's a family sedan that's at home on twisting roads. The price of this prowess is a suspension that does a poor job of absorbing bumpy pavement. Neither does Stratus filter out road noise as well as the class leaders.

Thanks to the manual transmission, the 2.0 4-cylinder feels as lively as the 2.4. Both furnish acceleration and passing power that's adequate for daily work. The 2.0 is noisier, however, and although new sound-deadening measures help some, neither 4-cylinder is quiet when put to the spur.

The V-6 furnishes the best overall performance, though it's not quiet either and has no abundance of torque. That means there's usually a frustrating pause before the automatic transmission downshifts for passing. We like Autostick's added degree of engine control, but it can't make up for the V-6's lack of low-end muscle.

Fuel economy is good for this class. Our Autostick Stratus averaged 21 mpg and a 2.0-liter 5-speed Breeze returned 21.2 mpg in a driving mix heavy on city commuting. The 2.0 is available with automatic in the Breeze and we averaged 27 mpg in mostly highway driving with one.

Improvements to the available anti-lock braking system have improved pedal feel and modulation.

ACCOMMODATIONS Chrysler doesn't shout about "cab forward" styling any more, but the design's benefits are evident here. Stratus makes the most of its compact-car-length body by efficiently distributing it over a midsize-class wheelbase. This helps create a cabin of uncommon roominess. There's ample leg space fore and aft, and sufficient rear-seat width for three medium-size adults to travel without feeling like sardines.

The dashboard design is among the best in this class, with instruments and controls placed for maximum visibility and accessibility.

The driver's outward view is great to all angles except the rear, where the high rear parcel shelf makes it hard to see out the back window. A large trunk with a flat floor and low liftover gives the Stratus good cargo-carrying ability.

BUILD QUALITY Our Stratus and Breeze test cars have generally been rattle-free, with good paint finishes and exterior panel fit. The grade of materials used in the cabins is below average for this class, and loose rubber trim around the rear door window was a problem on more than one test car.

VALUE FOR THE MONEY A loaded Stratus costs about as much as the mid-level models in some rival lineups. You'll give up a little refinement in the bargain, but this is a pleasingly competent midsize sedan for the money and deserves consideration.

RATINGS

	Base w/2.0	ES w/2.4	ES w/V-6
Acceleration	3	3	3
Fuel economy	4	4	3
Ride quality	3	3	3
Steering/handling	4	4	4
Braking	3	3	3
Quietness	2	3	3
Driver seating	4	4	4
Instruments/controls	4	4	4
Room/comfort (front)	4	4	4
Room/comfort (rear)	4	4	4
Cargo room	4	4	4
Value for the money	4	4	4
Total	**43**	**44**	**43**

SPECIFICATIONS

	4-door sedan
Wheelbase, in.	108.0
Overall length, in.	186.0
Overall width, in.	71.7
Overall height, in.	51.9
Curb weight, lbs.	2919
Cargo vol., cu. ft.	15.7
Fuel capacity, gals.	16.0
Seating capacity	5
Front head room, in.	38.1
Max. front leg room, in.	42.3
Rear head room, in.	36.8
Min. rear leg room, in.	37.8

ENGINES

	ohc I-4	dohc I-4	ohc V-6
Size, liters/cu. in.	2.0/122	2.4/148	2.5/152
Horsepower @ rpm	132@ 6000	150@ 5200	168@ 5800
Torque (lbs./ft.) @ rpm	128@ 5000	165@ 4000	170@ 4350
Availability	S[1]	S[2]	O[3]
EPA city/highway mpg			
4-speed OD automatic		20/30	20/29
5-speed OD manual	26/37		

1. Base. 2. ES; opt. Base. 3. ES.

PRICES

Dodge Stratus	Retail Price	Dealer Invoice
Base 4-door sedan	$14840	$13638
ES 4-door sedan	17665	16152
Destination charge	535	535

STANDARD EQUIPMENT:

Base: 2.0-liter 4-cylinder engine, 5-speed manual transmission, driver- and passenger-side air bags, air conditioning, power steering, cloth reclining front bucket seats, console, folding rear bench seat, AM/FM/cassette w/six speakers, digital clock, trip odometer, oil-pressure and coolant-temperature gauges, tachometer, voltmeter, tilt steering column, rear defogger, intermittent wipers, remote decklid release, visor mirrors, front floormats, tinted glass with solar-control windshield, dual remote mirrors, 195/70R14 tires, wheel covers.

ES adds: 2.4-liter DOHC 4-cylinder engine, 4-speed automatic transmission, cruise control, variable-assist power steering, leather-wrapped steering wheel and shift knob, 4-way manual driver seat with height and lumbar-support adjusters, power windows, power door locks, power door locks, heated power mirrors, reading lights, illuminated visor mirrors, rear floormats, assist handles, cruise control, touring suspension, fog lights, 195/65HR15 touring tires, alloy wheels.

Rating Scale: 5-Excellent; 4-Above average; 3-Average; 2-Below average; 1-Poor

OPTIONAL EQUIPMENT:
Major Packages

	Retail Price	Dealer Invoice
Pkg. 21B/24B, Base	$760	$676
Manufacturer's discount price	685	609

Power windows and door locks, heated power mirrors, 4-way manual driver seat with height adjuster, rear floormats. Pkg. 24B requires 2.4-liter DOHC 4-cylinder engine and 4-speed automatic transmission.

Pkg. 26R, ES	715	636
Manufacturer's discount price	345	307

Anti-lock brakes, autostick transmission. Requires 2.5-liter engine.

Pkg. 26S, ES	1995	1776
Manufacturer's discount price	995	886

Pkg. 26R plus leather upholstery, 8-way power driver seat, remote keyless entry, illuminated entry, cargo net. Requires 2.5-liter engine.

Remote/Illuminated Entry Group	170	151

Remote keyless entry, illuminated entry. Base requires Pkg. 21B/24B.

Powertrains

2.4-liter DOHC 4-cylinder engine, Base	450	401

Requires 4-speed automatic transmission.

2.5-liter V-6 engine, ES	800	712

Requires option pkg.

4-speed automatic transmission, Base	1050	935

Includes cruise control. Requires 2.4-liter engine.

Safety Features

Anti-lock brakes, Base, ES w/2.4-liter engine.	565	503
Integrated child safety seat, Base	100	89

Includes fixed rear seatback.

Comfort and Convenience

Power sunroof, Base	695	619
ES	580	519

Includes assist handles, map lights, illuminated visor mirrors (Base). Base requires option pkg. NA with integrated child seat.

Premium cassette player	340	303

Includes eight speakers, power amplifier, CD controls.

CD player, Base	200	178
6-disc CD changer and premium cassette player ...	550	490
Smoker's Group	20	18

Ashtray, lighter.

Appearance and Miscellaneous

Security alarm, ES	150	134

Requires Remote/Illuminated Entry Group.

Engine-block and battery heater	30	27
Candy apple red metallic paint	200	178
Full-size spare tire	125	111

DODGE VIPER

Dodge Viper GTS

Rear-wheel-drive Sports and GT
Base price: (1997 model) $66,000. Built in Detroit Mich.
Also consider: Chevrolet Corvette, Mitsubishi 3000GT

FOR • Acceleration • Steering/handling

AGAINST • No anti-lock brakes • Road and wind noise • Fuel economy

Chrysler hadn't yet introduced its LH sedans or Neon subcompact when it transformed the Viper from dream car to production reality in 1992. It was an outrageous move for a company in peaked financial health. Now Chrysler's a Wall-Street darling, and the Viper's still outrageous.

A GTS coupe joined the orignal RT/10 roadster in 1996. They share a 450-horsepower 8.0-liter V-10, America's largest and most-powerful production automobile engine. A version of this V-10 is used in Dodge's Ram pickup truck.

Dual air bags are standard on Viper, but anti-lock brakes and traction control are unavailable on these 2-seaters. A 6-speed manual is the sole transmission; its shifter is forced from first-gear to fourth-gear in light-throttle starts as a fuel-saving measure. Viper's clutch, brake, and gas pedals are adjustable for reach. The roadster comes with a removable hard top that, like the standard air conditioning, can be deleted for cash credit.

For '98, a cutoff switch is added for the passenger-side air bag, the interior is available in a black monochromatic color scheme, metallic silver is a new exterior color, and the exhaust system is constructed of lighter-weight materials.

PERFORMANCE Viper was built to deliver pure performance in the spirit of the 1960s Shelby Cobra. That it does. The V-10 loses 10 pounds-feet of torque for '98, but does a beach miss a thimble of sand? This car catapults ahead from virtually any speed and in any gear. The ultra-wide tires provide astonishing grip in turns and the taut suspension eliminates body lean. Steering response is immediate and the brakes are extraordinarily strong, though we'd like to see anti-locks available.

Fuel economy didn't surprise us. Our test GTS averaged 9.4 mpg, even with about half our miles on the freeway, where mileage benefits from fifth- and sixth-gear overdrive ratios.

Viper's plastic body panels are bonded to a rigid frame, and though the roadster's structure is virtually free of flex over railroad tracks and the like, its body panels flutter and vibrate over even mildly rough pavement. The coupe feels much more of a piece. It's quieter, too. Wind buffeting is intense with the roadster's top off, but the roar from tires, exhaust, and engine is prominent in either model.

ACCOMMODATIONS All original Vipers were roadsters that didn't have air bags or air conditioning, roll-up windows, even outside door handles. Introduction of the GTS introduced a degree of civilization and now both cars come with those features.

The easily adjusted pedals and tilt steering position the driver within a cockpit designed for the business of fast driving. Gauges and controls are simple and direct, and there's generous head and leg room for both occupants. The low seating position makes for less-than-ideal visibility, though well-positioned outside mirror take most of the fear out of lane changes.

Neither car has any interior storage to speak of and the roadster's tiny, ill-shaped trunk holds little more than a couple of gym bags. There's space enough for a weekend's worth of soft luggage beneath the coupe's rear hatch.

BUILD QUALITY Being virtually hand-built, there's latitude in Viper's fit, finish, and workmanship that isn't present in robot-assembled high-volume cars. To most buyers, that's part of the car's "special" character. Interior materials are solid but not fancy.

VALUE FOR THE MONEY There are more-civilized high-performance sports car that cost less, but few cars at any price match Viper's bold nature. Dodge builds just enough to keep demand ahead of supply, so don't expect a big discount.

RATINGS	RT/10	GTS
Acceleration	5	5
Fuel economy	1	1
Ride quality	2	2
Steering/handling	5	5
Braking	5	5
Quietness	1	2
Driver seating	3	3
Instruments/controls	4	4
Room/comfort (front)	4	4
Room/comfort (rear)	—	—
Cargo room	1	2
Value for the money	2	2
Total	**33**	**35**

Prices are accurate at time of publication; subject to manufacturer's changes.

SPECIFICATIONS

	2-door hatchback	2-door conv.
Wheelbase, in.	96.2	96.2
Overall length, in.	176.7	175.1
Overall width, in.	75.7	75.7
Overall height, in.	47.0	44.0
Curb weight, lbs.	3383	3319
Cargo vol., cu. ft.	9.1	6.8
Fuel capacity, gals.	19.0	19.0
Seating capacity	2	2
Front head room, in.	36.8	NA
Max. front leg room, in.	42.6	42.6
Rear head room, in.	—	—
Min. rear leg room, in.	—	—

ENGINES

	ohv V-10
Size, liters/cu. in.	8.0/488
Horsepower @ rpm	450@ 5200
Torque (lbs./ft.) @ rpm	490@ 3700
Availability	S

EPA city/highway mpg

6-speed OD manual	12/21

PRICES

1997 Dodge Viper	Retail Price	Dealer Invoice
RT/10 2-door convertible	$66000	$59280
GTS 2-door hatchback	66000	59280
Destination charge	700	700

Add $3000 Gas Guzzler Tax.

STANDARD EQUIPMENT:

RT/10: 8.0-liter V-10 415-horsepower engine, 6-speed manual transmission, limited-slip differential, driver- and passenger-side air bags, 4-wheel disc brakes, power steering, leather reclining front bucket seats with lumbar support adjuster, air conditioning, center console, power windows, remote keyless entry, tachometer, oil pressure and coolant temperature gauges, voltmeter, AM/FM/CD with dual power amplifiers and six speakers, tilt steering wheel, leather-wrapped steering wheel and shifter knob, map lights, 275/40ZR17 front and 335/35ZR17 rear tires, alloy wheels, fog lamps, theft-deterrent system, dual outside mirrors, tinted glass, removable hardtop and removable folding soft top with side curtains, tonneau cover.

GTS adds: V-10 450-horsepower engine, electronic door latching w/locks, adjustable pedals, and deletes removable hardtop and removable folding soft top with side curtains, tonneau cover.

OPTIONAL EQUIPMENT:

Comfort and Convenience

Air conditioning delete, RT/10 (credit)	(1000)	(850)

Appearance and Miscellaneous

Hardtop delete, RT/10 (credit)	(2500)	(2125)
Viper Blue exterior paint w/racing stripes	1200	1020
Polished alloy wheels	300	255

EAGLE TALON

Front- or all-wheel-drive sports coupe; similar to Mitsubishi Eclipse

Base price range: $14,505-$20,715. Built in Normal, Ill.

Also consider: Acura Integra, Honda Prelude, Toyota Celica

FOR • Anti-lock brakes • Acceleration (TSi, TSi AWD) • Steering/handling

AGAINST • Acceleration (base and ESi with automatic) • Rear seat room • Noise

The Eagle brand wings off into the sunset after the 1998 model year, making this Talon's swan-song season. Chrysler created Eagle in 1988 as its import-flavored division, but the idea never took off. Talon is outsold 5-1 by the Mitsubishi Eclipse, with

Eagle Talon TSi

which it shares its hatchback body, powertrains, overall styling, and Mitsubishi-run Illinois assembly plant. Talon finishes up with minimal changes after a 1997 facelift.

Base, ESi, and TSi models have front-wheel drive, the TSi AWD has permanent all-wheel drive. All have 2.0-liter 4-cylinder engines—a Chrysler-made unit in the base and ESi, a turbocharged Mitsubishi engine in the others. Manual transmission is standard, automatic is optional. Dual air bags are standard. Anti-lock brakes are optional on all but the base model.

New seat fabrics, a black-and-gray interior color scheme, silver-color exterior nameplates, and an optional CD player for the ESi are among this year's few changes.

Talon does not offer a convertible body style, as does the Eclipse, but otherwise performs the same as similarly equipped Mitsubishi counterparts.

See the Mitsubishi Eclipse report for an evaluation of the Talon.

SPECIFICATIONS

	2-door hatchback
Wheelbase, in.	98.8
Overall length, in.	174.8
Overall width, in.	69.9
Overall height, in.	51.6
Curb weight, lbs.	2729
Cargo vol., cu. ft.	16.6
Fuel capacity, gals.	16.9
Seating capacity	4
Front head room, in.	37.9
Max. front leg room, in.	43.3
Rear head room, in.	34.1
Min. rear leg room, in.	28.4

ENGINES

	dohc I-4	turbo dohc I-4
Size, liters/cu. in.	2.0/122	2.0/122
Horsepower @ rpm	140@ 6000	210@ 6000
Torque (lbs./ft.) @ rpm	130@ 4800	214@ 3000
Availability	S[1]	S[2]

EPA city/highway mpg

4-speed OD automatic	23/31	20/27
5-speed OD manual	22/32	23/31

1. Base, ESi. 2. TSi.

RATINGS

	Base/ ESi	TSi/TSi AWD
Acceleration	3	4
Fuel economy	3	3
Ride quality	3	2
Steering/handling	4	4
Braking	3	4
Quietness	3	2
Driver seating	3	3
Instruments/controls	4	4
Room/comfort (front)	2	2
Room/comfort (rear)	1	1
Cargo room	2	2
Value for the money	3	3
Total	34	34

Rating Scale: 5-Excellent; 4-Above average; 3-Average; 2-Below average; 1-Poor

CONSUMER GUIDE™

PRICES

Eagle Talon

	Retail Price	Dealer Invoice
Base 2-door hatchback	$14505	$13435
ESi 2-door hatchback	15275	14173
TSi 2-door hatchback	18460	17069
TSi AWD 2-door hatchback	20715	19119
Destination charge	535	535

AWD denotes all-wheel drive.

STANDARD EQUIPMENT:

Base 2.0-liter DOHC 4-cylinder engine, 5-speed manual transmission, driver- and passenger-side air bags, variable-assist power steering, cloth reclining front bucket seats, folding rear seat, front console with storage and armrest, tinted glass, tachometer, coolant temperature gauge, trip odometer, map lights, dual remote mirrors, visor mirrors, digital clock, remote fuel-door and hatch releases, tilt steering column, intermittent wipers, 195/70R14 tires, wheel covers.

ESi adds: AM/FM radio, variable intermittent wipers, color-keyed bodyside moldings, rear spoiler.

TSi adds: turbocharged engine, sport-tuned exhaust system, 4-wheel disc brakes, fog lamps, driver-seat lumbar support adjustment, split folding rear seat, leather-wrapped steering wheel and manual gearshift handle, power mirrors, turbo-boost and oil-pressure gauges, cassette player, rear wiper/washer, illuminated visor mirrors, rear defogger, cargo-area cover, upgraded suspension, 205/55R16 tires, painted alloy wheels.

TSi AWD adds: permanent 4-wheel drive, cruise control, power door locks and windows, 215/50VR17 tires, alloy wheels.

OPTIONAL EQUIPMENT:
Major Packages

	Retail	Dealer
Pkg. 21B/22B, ESi	1695	1441

Air conditioning, cruise control, rear defogger, power mirrors, cassette player, cargo area cover, front floormats.

Pkg. 21C/22C, ESi	2740	2329

Pkg. 21B/22B plus power windows and door locks, cargo net, upgraded interior trim, 205/55HR16 tires, alloy wheels.

Pkg. 23P/24P, TSi	2005	1704

Air conditioning, CD/cassette player, cruise control, power windows and door locks, front floormats.

Pkg. 25S/26S, TSi AWD	1225	1041

Air conditioning, remote keyless entry with security alarm, front floormats.

Pkg. 25L/26L, TSi AWD	4195	3566

Pkg. 25S/26S plus anti-lock brakes, power driver seat, leather/vinyl front upholstery, CD/cassette player with graphic equalizer and eight Infinity speakers, power sunroof.

Powertrains

4-speed automatic transmission, Base, ESi	745	633
TSi, TSi AWD	890	757
Limited-slip differential,		
TSi AWD w/option pkg.	265	225

Safety Features

Anti-lock brakes	650	553

Requires option pkg. NA base.

Comfort and Convenience

Air conditioning	860	731
Remote keyless entry with security alarm,		
ESi w/Pkg. 21C/22C, TSi w/option pkg.	335	285
Rear defogger, Base, ESi	165	140
AM/FM radio, Base	235	200
CD player, ESi	150	128
Cassette/CD player, ESi, TSi, TSi AWD	390	332

Includes graphic equalizer, CD changer controls. ESi requires Pkg. 21C/22C. TSi AWD requires pkg. 25S/26S.

Cassette/CD player w/graphic equalizer,		
TSi AWD	795	676
TSi w/option pkg.	405	344

Includes eight Infinity speakers. TSi requires pkg. 25S/26S.

Power sunroof	730	621

ESi requires Pkg. 21C/22C. TSi, TSi AWD requires option pkg. NA Base.

	Retail Price	Dealer Invoice
Leather/vinyl upholstery,		
TSi w/option pkg., TSi AWD w/Pkg. 25S/26S	$460	$391

TSi requires option pkg., TSi AWD requires 25L/26L.

Power driver seat, TSi, TSi AWD	335	285

Requires option pkg.

Appearance and Miscellaneous

Alloy wheels, ESi	510	434

Includes 205/55HR16 tires.

FORD CONTOUR

RECOMMENDED

Ford Contour LX

Front-wheel drive compact; similar to Mercury Mystique

Base price range: $14,460-$22,365. Built in Kansas City, Mo., and Mexico.

Also consider: Mazda 626, Mitsubishi Galant, Nissan Altima

FOR • Optional anti-lock brakes (LX, SE) • Acceleration (V-6) • Steering/handling

AGAINST • Road noise • Engine noise (4-cylinder) • Rear seat room

Contour is a "world car," based on a Ford of Europe design. It's been a big hit across the sea, but a sales disappointment in the U.S., alienating buyers who expected a low-cost Tempo replacement and frustrating others with its sparse rear-seat room.

The 1998 versions went on sale last March, and this fall, Ford condenses the lineup, dropping last year's bottom two models, the base and GL versions. That leaves LX, sporty SE, and a limited-edition, high-performance variant, the SVT. LX and SE come with a 125-horsepower 2.0-liter 4-cylinder engine, with a 170-horsepower 2.5-liter V-6 as a stand-alone option; the V-6 had been standard on the SE. The SVT's premium-fuel variant of the V-6 has 195 horsepower. Manual transmission is standard and automatic is optional on all but the SVT.

Last year, Ford recontoured the back of the front seats to allow for more rear leg room; this year, the rear seat has been repositioned to increase leg room by another half-inch. Other interior changes include a new center console with three cupholders, a driver's armrest, and a 3-point seatbelt for the center rear position.

Most '98 Fords have de-powered air bags that deploy with less force. However, the Contour and Mercury Mystique (basically a re-trimmed Contour sans the SVT model) won't begin getting the new air bags until later this year.

PERFORMANCE The 170-horsepower V-6 is smooth, responsive, and delivers lively acceleration. It works well with the automatic transmission, which shifts smoothly and downshifts promptly for passing. Our V-6 SE test car did 0-60 mph in 9.3 seconds. Manual-transmsision V-6 Countours feel brawnier at all speeds—especially the SVT. By contrast, the 4-cylinder becomes raucous at full throttle and feels sleepy with automatic transmission. We averaged 21.7 mpg in our test of an SE V-6 with automatic.

The SE's firm suspension and aggressive tires give it sporty road manners. Body lean is minimal and the firm steering is quick and precise. Some of the handling ability is achieved at the expense of ride quality; the SE doesn't ride harshly, but you feel nearly every bump. The LX trades some handling prowess for a more relaxed ride, and for most people, is probably the better

---

Prices are accurate at time of publication; subject to manufacturer's changes.

choice. Road noise can be intrusive, regardless of model.

The anti-lock brakes on our test SE performed well, stopping the car in an average of 124 feet in 10 stops from 60 mph.

ACCOMMODATIONS With the latest round of interior changes, rear leg room is now adequate for medium-size adults. Still, Contour remains mid-pack in passenger space, especially considering its wheelbase is longer than most other compact cars'. There's good head room and leg room for the front seats, but the rear seat is short of head clearance for anyone over 5-foot-10.

Some of our staff found the SE's front bucket seats too tight around the ribs and hips. Others said they were flat and too hard. LX seats are less sporty but more comfortable for a wider range of bodies. Detracting from the otherwise well-designed dashboard are pressure-sensitive audio-system buttons where simple knobs would do, and power mirror controls that are hidden to the left of the steering wheel. The new center console has handy cupholders and an open storage bin.

Visibility is clear to the front and sides, but it's hard for the driver to see the trunk even with a lot of neck stretching.

BUILD QUALITY Our Contour test cars have had only a few squeaks and rattles on rough roads. Body panels lined up well, and the glossy paint had a modest amount of bumpy orange-peel texture.

VALUE FOR THE MONEY We like Ford's simplification of the Contour lineup. Though smaller inside than some rivals, Contour and Mystique have polished road manners and reasonable prices. And discounts should be available on both.

SPECIFICATIONS

	4-door sedan
Wheelbase, in.	106.5
Overall length, in.	184.7
Overall width, in.	69.1
Overall height, in.	54.5
Curb weight, lbs.	2772
Cargo vol., cu. ft.	13.9
Fuel capacity, gals.	14.5
Seating capacity	5
Front head room, in.	39.0
Max. front leg room, in.	42.4
Rear head room, in.	36.7
Min. rear leg room, in.	34.4

ENGINES

	dohc I-4	dohc V-6	dohc V-6
Size, liters/cu. in.	2.0/121	2.5/155	2.5/155
Horsepower @ rpm	125@ 5500	170@ 6250	195@ 6625
Torque (lbs./ft.) @ rpm	130@ 4000	165@ 4250	165@ 5625
Availability	S[1]	S[2]	S[3]
EPA city/highway mpg			
4-speed OD automatic	23/32	21/30	
5-speed OD manual	24/33	20/30	20/29

1. GL and LX. 2. SE; optional GL and LX. 3. SVT.

RATINGS

	LX 4-cyl	SE V-6	SVT
Acceleration	3	4	4
Fuel economy	3	3	3
Ride quality	4	3	3
Steering/handling	3	4	4
Braking	3	4	4
Quietness	3	3	3
Driver seating	3	3	3
Instruments/controls	4	4	4
Room/comfort (front)	3	3	3
Room/comfort (rear)	3	3	3
Cargo room	2	2	2
Value for the money	4	4	4
Total	**38**	**40**	**40**

PRICES

Ford Contour

	Retail Price	Dealer Invoice
LX 4-door sedan	$14460	$13544
SE 4-door sedan	15785	14434
SVT 4-door sedan	22365	20270

	Retail Price	Dealer Invoice
Destination charge	$535	$535

Pricing and contents may vary in some regions.

STANDARD EQUIPMENT:

LX: 2.0-liter DOHC 4-cylinder engine, 5-speed manual transmission, driver- and passenger-side air bags, air conditioning, power steering, cloth reclining front bucket seats, cloth door-trim panel, power mirrors, tilt steering wheel, console w/cupholder, AM/FM radio, digital clock, trip odometer, coolant temperature gauge, rear passenger grab handles, intermittent wipers, visor mirrors, remote decklid release, interior air filter, solar-control tinted glass, 185/70R14 tires, wheel covers.

SE adds: power windows, power door locks, cruise control, cassette player, rear defogger.

SVT adds: 2.5-liter 195-horsepower DOHC V-6 engine, 4-wheel disc anti-lock brakes, 10-way power driver's seat, leather upholstery, split folding rear seat, tachometer, AM/FM/cassette player with Premium Sound, power antenna, remote keyless entry, floormats, fog lamps, sport suspension, 205/55ZR16 tires, 5-spoke alloy wheels.

OPTIONAL EQUIPMENT:
Major Packages

	Retail	Dealer
Comfort Group, SE	795	708

Leather-wrapped steering wheel, 10-way power driver seat, variable intermittent wipers, illuminated visor mirrors, power antenna, fog lights, 8-spoke alloy wheels. NA with Sport Group.

Sport Group, SE	1000	890

2.5-liter V-6 170-horsepower engine, tachometer, cloth sport bucket seats, leather-wrapped steering wheel, illuminated visor mirrors, sport floormats, variable intermittent wipers, rear spoiler, body cladding, badging, fog lights, 4-wheel disc brakes (w/manual transmission), performance suspension, 12-spoke alloy wheels, 205/60TR15 tires. NA with Comfort Group.

Powertrains

2.5-liter DOHC V-6 170-horsepower engine, LX, SE	495	441

Includes performance suspension, 4-wheel disc brakes (w/manual transmission), 195/65R14 tires, tachometer.

4-speed automatic transmission, LX, SE	815	725

Safety Features

Anti-lock brakes, LX, SE	500	445
Integrated child seat, SE	135	120

NA with leather upholstery.

Comfort and Convenience

Leather upholstery, SE	895	797

Requires split folding rear seat.

10-way power driver's seat, SE	350	312
Split folding rear seat, SE	205	182
Cassette player with Premium Sound, SE	135	120

Includes amplifier.

CD player with Premium Sound, SE	270	240
SVT	140	124
Power antenna, SE	95	85
Remote keyless entry, SE	190	169

Includes illuminated entry.

Power moonroof, SE, SVT	595	530
Rear defogger, LX	190	169

Appearance and Miscellaneous

Special wheel covers, SE	135	120

Includes 205/60TR15 tires.

8-spoke alloy wheels, SE	425	379

Includes 205/60TR15 tires.

FORD CROWN VICTORIA

Rear-wheel-drive full-size car; similar to Mercury Grand Marquis

Base price range: $20,935-$23,135. Built in Canada.

Also consider: Buick LeSabre, Dodge Intrepid, Toyota Avalon

Rating Scale: 5-Excellent; 4-Above average; 3-Average; 2-Below average; 1-Poor

Ford Crown Victoria

Since GM killed the Chevrolet Caprice, Buick Roadmaster, and Cadillac Fleetwood, Crown Victoria and its Mercury Grand Marquis sibling are the last remaining American full-size rear-drive sedans. Now the standard for police use, half of Crown Vic production goes to law enforcement agencies.

Revised front and rear styling grace the Crown Victoria for 1998, and it adopts the thicker rear roof-pillar treatment used on the Mercury Grand Marquis. There are also some noteworthy mechanical changes: The standard dual air bags are depowered units that deploy with less force; an altered rear suspension design is intended to increase resistance to crosswinds and add stability in turns; 16-inch wheels replace 15 inchers; Ford's SecuriLock anti-theft system is standard; brakes are larger; and the top-line LX gets an electronic compass, CD player, and 8-way power passenger seat with lumbar adjustment as optional equipment.

The Crown Victoria comes in base and LX price levels, both with a standard automatic transmission and 4.6-liter V-8 engine that gains 10 horsepower this year, now 200. Optional dual exhausts, part of the Handling and Performance package that also includes stiffer suspension, low-profile tires, and lower rear-axle ratio, boost output to 215. Four-wheel disc brakes are standard; anti-lock brakes are optional and are grouped with traction control.

The 1998 Crown Victoria is scheduled to go on sale just after Christmas. We have not yet driven the new model, so we cannot comment on its performance.

SPECIFICATIONS

	4-door sedan
Wheelbase, in.	114.4
Overall length, in.	212.0
Overall width, in.	78.2
Overall height, in.	56.8
Curb weight, lbs.	3917
Cargo vol., cu. ft.	20.6
Fuel capacity, gals.	19.0
Seating capacity	6
Front head room, in.	39.4
Max. front leg room, in.	42.5
Rear head room, in.	38.0
Min. rear leg room, in.	39.6

ENGINES

	ohc V-8	ohc V-8
Size, liters/cu. in.	4.6/281	4.6/281
Horsepower @ rpm	200@4250	215@4500
Torque (lbs./ft.) @ rpm	265@3000	275@3000
Availability	S	O
EPA city/highway mpg		
4-speed OD automatic	17/25	17/25

PRICES

Ford Crown Victoria	Retail Price	Dealer Invoice
Base 4-door notchback	$20935	$19566
LX 4-door notchback	23135	21568
Destination charge	605	605

STANDARD EQUIPMENT:

Base: 4.6-liter V-8 190 horsepower engine, 4-speed automatic transmission, driver- and passenger-side air bags, 4-wheel disc brakes, air conditioning, variable-assist power steering, tilt steering wheel, cruise control, cloth reclining split bench seat, cupholders, AM/FM radio with four speakers, digital clock, power mirrors, power windows, power door locks, power decklid release, voltmeter, oil-pressure and coolant-temperature gauges, trip odometer, rear defogger, intermittent wipers, automatic headlights, rear heat ducts, theft-deterrent system, 225/60SR16 all-season tires, wheel covers.

LX adds: upgraded interior trim, power driver seat with power recliner and power lumbar support, cassette player, Light/Decor Group (illuminated visor mirrors, map lights, body striping), remote keyless entry, carpeted spare tire cover.

OPTIONAL EQUIPMENT:	Retail Price	Dealer Invoice
Major Packages		
Comfort Group, LX	$900	$801
Automatic temperature control, power passenger seat with power lumbar support, leather-wrapped steering wheel, automatic day/night mirror with compass, alloy wheels.		
Comfort Plus Group, LX	2200	1958
Comfort Group plus anti-lock brakes, traction control, trip computer, digital instrumentation, Premium Audio System.		
Light/Decor Group, Base	—	—
Illuminated visor mirrors, map lights, body striping.		
Handling and Performance Pkg.	935	832
Includes 215 horsepower engine, dual exhaust, performance springs, shocks and stabilizer bars, rear air suspension, 3.27 axle ratio, 225/60TR16 touring tires, alloy wheels.		
Safety Features		
Anti-lock brakes with Traction Assist	775	690
Comfort and Convenience		
Remote keyless entry, Base	240	213
Leather upholstery, LX	735	654
Requires Comfort Group.		
6-way power driver seat, Base	360	321
Cassette player, Base	185	165
Premium Audio System, LX	360	321
Upgraded amplifier and six speakers. Requires Comfort Group.		
Universal garage door opener, LX	115	102
Floormats	55	50
Appearance and Miscellaneous		
Engine block heater	25	23
225/60SR16 whitewall tires	80	71
Full-size spare tire	120	107

FORD ESCORT/ESCORT ZX2

Ford Escort LX sedan

Front-wheel drive subcompact; similar to Mercury Tracer

Base price range: $11,280-$13,895. Built in Mexico.

Also consider: Chevrolet Prizm, Honda Civic, Toyota Corolla

FOR • Fuel economy • Optional anti-lock brakes

AGAINST • Rear seat room • Road noise

Escort is among America's ten best-selling vehicles, and the top-selling subcompact. Along with the nearly identical Mercury Tracer, Escort gets few equipment changes this year after undergoing a redesign for 1997.

Four-door sedans and wagons and a 2-door coupe are offered. Last year's base Escort sedan is rebadged SE. The better-eqiupped sedan and the wagon wear LX labels.

The sporty 2-door spinoff is called the Escort ZX2. It was added last spring in trim levels tagged "Cool" and "Hot." Though it shares the Escort's chassis, the ZX2 has unique interior and exterior styling, sportier suspension settings, and is aimed at a more youthful audience. Tracer doesn't offer a coupe.

All Escorts use a 2.0-liter 4-cylinder engine mated to manual or optional automatic transmission. Sedans and wagons have 110 horsepower, the ZX2 has 130. Sedans and wagons with automatic transmission are certified as low-emissions vehicles (LEV) in California.

Dual air bags are standard and, as on most Fords, are depowered on the sedans and wagons to deploy with less force. The ZX2 gets depowered bags later in the model year.

PERFORMANCE Sedans and wagons have adequate rather than inspiring acceleration, but they have good low-speed power, essential since 75 percent of these cars are sold with automatic transmission. The automatic shifts smoothly, though several Escorts we've tested with it had an annoying engine vibration at idle. Our last sedan averaged 23.9 mpg in primarily urban and suburban commuting; expect better fuel economy with more highway miles. Manual-transmission Escorts feel livelier and get better mileage than those with automatic.

Escort's well-tuned suspension helps it absorb bumps better than most subcompacts. Handling on sedans and wagons is competent rather that sporting, though the steering feels natural in turns and has an on-center sense that contributes to stable cruising.

Road and wind noise are noticed on the highway, but the sedans and wagons aren't much noisier than the class-leading Honda Civic. ZX2s we tested suffered much more road and engine noise—enough to annoy.

The ZX2 drives like the sportier Escort it is, aided by the extra punch of its stronger engine. Again, manual versions are quicker than automatics, but the 5-speed has the engine turning a buzzy 3000 rpm at 65 mph. We averaged a laudable 29.0 mpg with an automatic ZX2, 25 mpg in harder driving with the manual.

The ZX2 is at home on twisting roads, where grip and stability are good, and body roll is well-controlled.

ACCOMMODATIONS Interior space in sedans and wagons falls short of the standard set by the Dodge/Plymouth Neon but is adequate for a subcompact. Front-seat room is good, with a high ceiling that accommodates tall occupants. Rear knee room is tight with the front seats more than halfway back, but there's good toe space. Those over 5-foot-8 might brush the headliner in back.

Audio and climate controls are in an oval panel below normal sightlines but just a short reach from the steering wheel. The sedan's rear roof pillars are thick enough to block the over-the-shoulder view, but visibility is otherwise good. Interior storage space is good. The sedan's trunk is adequate for this class, the wagon is a versatile little hauler. Folding rear seatbacks are available, though they don't lie flat.

Being basically a 2-door subcompact, the ZX2 has more rear-seat space than the typical sport coupe, with adequate head and leg room for small adults. Rear entry and exit is worse than most, however. The front seatbacks flop forward, but neither front seat slides in the process. The standard steering wheel was too low for some of our test drivers, too high for others, but a tilt wheel is optional. ZX2 has a more closed-in feel than the sedan or wagon and the driver can't see the car's corners when parking.

There are three cupholders and numerous bins inside the ZX2, but no lockable storage. Trunk room is good for the class, but the opening is narrow at bumper level and the trunk lid struts cut into the load space.

BUILD QUALITY These Ford and Mercury subcompacts have padded interior surfaces where some rivals have hard plastic. Exterior workmanship was good on our test cars.

VALUE FOR THE MONEY The sedan and wagon, with their sensible designs, competent road manners, and reasonable prices, put Escort and Tracer at the top of our subcompact list. We're less impressed by the noiser ZX2. It doesn't have enough performance or personality to justify its higher price.

RATINGS

	Sedan	Wagon	ZX2
Acceleration	3	3	3
Fuel economy	3	3	4
Ride quality	4	4	3
Steering/handling	3	3	4
Braking	3	3	4
Quietness	3	3	3
Driver seating	4	4	4
Instruments/controls	4	4	4
Room/comfort (front)	3	3	3
Room/comfort (rear)	3	3	2
Cargo room	2	4	2
Value for the money	5	5	3
Total	**40**	**42**	**39**

SPECIFICATIONS

	4-door sedan	4-door wagon	2-door coupe
Wheelbase, in.	98.4	98.4	98.4
Overall length, in.	174.7	172.7	175.2
Overall width, in.	67.0	67.0	67.4
Overall height, in.	53.3	53.9	52.3
Curb weight, lbs.	2468	2531	2478
Cargo vol., cu. ft.	12.8	63.4	11.8
Fuel capacity, gals.	12.8	12.8	12.8
Seating capacity	5	5	4
Front head room, in.	39.0	38.7	38.0
Max. front leg room, in.	42.5	42.5	42.5
Rear head room, in.	36.7	39.1	35.1
Min. rear leg room, in.	34.0	34.0	33.4

ENGINES

	ohc I-4	dohc I-4
Size, liters/cu. in.	2.0/121	2.0/121
Horsepower @ rpm	110@ 5000	130@ 5750
Torque (lbs./ft.) @ rpm	125@ 3750	127@ 4250
Availability	S[1]	S[2]
EPA city/highway mpg		
5-speed OD manual	28/37	26/33
4-speed OD automatic	26/34	25/33

1. Sedan, wagon. 2. ZX2.

PRICES

Ford Escort/Escort ZX2

	Retail Price	Dealer Invoice
LX 4-door sedan	$11280	$10584
SE 4-door sedan	12580	11767
SE 4-door wagon	13780	12859
ZX2 Cool 2-door notchback	12580	11762
ZX2 Hot 2-door notchback	13895	12965
Destination charge	415	415

STANDARD EQUIPMENT:

LX: 2.0-liter 4-cylinder engine, 5-speed manual transmission, driver- and passenger-side air bags, power steering, cloth and vinyl reclining bucket seats, center console with cupholders, split folding rear seat, passenger-side visor mirror, coolant temperature gauge, trip odometer, AM/FM radio, digital clock, variable intermittent wipers, door pockets, tinted glass, dual outside mirrors, 185/65R14 tires, wheel covers.

ZX2 Cool adds: tachometer, driver seat memory recline.

SE adds to LX: upgraded upholstery, air conditioning, rear defogger, power mirrors, driver door remote keyless entry system, bodyside moldings, and deletes tachometer, driver seat memory recline.

ZX2 Hot adds: tachometer, driver seat memory recline.

OPTIONAL EQUIPMENT:
Major Packages

Sport Group, ZX2 Hot	595	530
SE sedan	495	441

Sport seats w/rear integrated headrests, passenger-side, rear map pocket, rear spoiler, bright exhaust outlets, fog lights (ZX2 Hot), alloy wheels, 185/60HR15 tires (ZX2 Hot). NA with Appearance Pkg.

Rating Scale: *5-Excellent; 4-Above average; 3-Average; 2-Below average; 1-Poor*

CONSUMER GUIDE™

	Retail Price	Dealer Invoice
Appearance Pkg., SE sedan, ZX2 Hot....................	$155	$138
SE wagon	120	107
Leather-wrapped steering wheel, bright exhaust outlets (SE sedan, ZX2 Hot), chrome wheel covers.		
Power Group, SE, ZX2 Hot......................................	395	352
Power windows, power door locks, all-door remote keyless entry.		
Comfort Group, SE, ZX2 Hot	345	307
Cruise control, tilt steering wheel, map lights, driver-side visor mirror.		
Wagon Group, SE Wagon......................................	295	263
Cargo cover, rear wiper/washer, roof rack.		

Powertrains

4-speed automatic transmission	815	725

Safety Features

Anti-lock brakes..	400	356
Integrated child seat, SE wagon	135	120
Downgrades split folding rear seat to folding rear seat. NA with Sport Group.		

Comfort and Convenience

Air conditioning, LX, ZX2 Cool	795	708
Rear defogger, LX, ZX2 Cool	190	169
AM/FM/cassette	185	165
LX, ZX2 Cool require rear defogger or air conditioning.		
Premium AM/FM/cassette, SE, ZX2 Hot................	255	221
AM/FM/cassette w/6-disc CD changer, SE, ZX2 Hot..	515	458
Includes premium sound system.		
Remote keyless entry, LX, ZX2 Cool	135	120
Driver door only.		
Power moonroof, ZX2 Hot....................................	595	530
Smoker's Pkg.	15	13
Includes ashtray, lighter.		
Floormats	55	49

Appearance and Miscellaneous

Engine block heater	20	18
Alloy wheels, SE, ZX2 Hot	265	236

FORD EXPEDITION

✓ **BEST BUY**

Ford Expedition

Rear- or 4-wheel-drive compact sport-utility vehicle; similar to Lincoln Navigator

Base price range: $27,985-$34,590. Built in Wayne, Mich.

Also consider: Chevrolet Tahoe, GMC Yukon

FOR • Acceleration (5.4-liter) • Standard anti-lock brakes • Passenger and cargo room • Visibility • Towing ability

AGAINST • Fuel economy • Entry/exit (4WD models)

It took less than a year on the market for Expedition to pass the Chevrolet Tahoe, GMC Yukon, and Chevrolet/GMC Suburban and become the new full-size sport-utility sales leader. Some new exterior colors and depowered air bags that deploy with less force are all that changes for '98.

Based on Ford's F-150 pickup, Expedition is available with 2- or 4-wheel drive in XLT and Eddie Bauer trim. Lincoln has a dressier version of the Expedition, the Navigator (see separate report).

Expedition, which is about 16 inches longer overall than Ford's Explorer, the best-selling SUV, slots between the Suburban and Tahoe/Yukon in overall size.

XLTs seat six, Eddie Bauers get front buckets and seat five. A 3-place third seat is optional on both.

Two overhead-cam V-8 engines are offered, a 4.6-liter and optional 5.4-liter, and both use automatic transmission. Four-wheel-drive models have Ford's Control Trac, which has four drive settings engaged by a dashboard switch: 2WD; automatic 4WD (which engages when there's wheel slip and can be used on dry pavement); 4WD High for slippery conditions; and 4WD Low for heavy-duty off-road conditions. Anti-lock brakes are standard.

Towing capacity is 4000 pounds standard, 8000 with the optional towing package.

PERFORMANCE The 4.6-liter V-8 furnishes brisk off-the-line acceleration in the 2WD models. Passing power is less than snappy and when called on to accelerate at highway speeds, the engine struggles to move two-and-a half tons of truck. If you want 4WD and/or plan on towing, especially in hilly areas, the 5.4-liter is the better choice. Both engines are smooth and fairly quiet.

We averaged 14.3 mpg in a mix of urban commuting and highway cruising with a 4.6 2WD, which matches our mileage with a 4WD 5.7-liter V-8 Chevy Tahoe. A 4WD Eddie Bauer with the 5.4 V-8 returned a sobering 12.0 mpg.

Expedition isn't agile, but it is light on its feet for a truck-based vehicle this size, and body lean is moderate as long as cornering speeds are modest.

Ride is stable and softer than some rivals on 2WD models. The 4x4s are stiffer and jiggle more, but neither is jarring.

Wind, road, and engine noise are well muffled, making Expedition an inviting cross-country cruiser.

ACCOMMODATIONS Expedition is longer, taller, and wider than Tahoe and Yukon, but its deep side glass helps it seem smaller when you're driving it. The interior is cavernous, with expansive shoulder room in front and enough width in back for three adults to ride in genuine comfort. And the floor is nearly flat, so no one straddles a hump. The optional third seat is crampsville for most adults, and cuts rear cargo space to a foot-long trench. Cargo room is expansive without the third seat, and both the second and third seats fold and can be removed.

Getting in or out of the 2WD model is easy, but the built-in grab handles are put to good use to hoist yourself into the higher-riding 4WD versions. The heavy rear liftgate is a chore to open or close.

There's nothing to criticize about the layout of the gauges and controls, and we found the power rear quarter windows innovative and worthwhile.

Expedition is without locking interior storage, but all four doors have map pockets and two cupholders pop out of the dashboard. Models with front buckets get a large center console, which includes open and covered compartments, two more cupholders, and handy storage slots on the outer walls.

BUILD QUALITY Our test Expeditions have been impressively solid and without visible flaws in fit or finish.

VALUE FOR THE MONEY Expedition gives up some low-speed muscle to the big General Motors SUVs, and Ford doesn't make a diesel engine available. But the new kid feels more modern and refined than its GM competition, offers a more versatile 4WD system, and is priced competitively. Ford seems to have hatched a trend-setter.

RATINGS	2WD 4.6 V-8	4WD 5.4 V-8
Acceleration	3	3
Fuel economy	1	1
Ride quality	4	3
Steering/handling	3	3
Braking	3	3
Quietness	4	4
Driver seating	4	4
Instruments/controls	4	4
Room/comfort (front)	5	5
Room/comfort (rear)	5	5
Cargo room	5	5
Value for the money	4	4
Total	**46**	**45**

Prices are accurate at time of publication; subject to manufacturer's changes.

SPECIFICATIONS

	4-door wagon
Wheelbase, in.	119.1
Overall length, in.	204.6
Overall width, in.	78.6
Overall height, in.	76.6
Curb weight, lbs.	4850
Cargo vol., cu. ft.	118.3
Fuel capacity, gals.	26.0
Seating capacity	9
Front head room, in.	39.8
Max. front leg room, in.	40.9
Rear head room, in.	39.8
Min. rear leg room, in.	38.9

ENGINES

	ohc V-8	ohc V-8
Size, liters/cu. in.	4.6/281	5.4/330
Horsepower @ rpm	215@	230@
	4400	4250
Torque (lbs./ft.) @ rpm	290@	325@
	3250	3000
Availability	S	O
EPA city/highway mpg		
4-speed OD automatic	14/18	13/17

PRICES

Ford Expedition	Retail Price	Dealer Invoice
XLT 4-door wagon, 2WD	$27985	$24533
XLT 4-door wagon, 4WD	30585	26743
Eddie Bauer 4-door wagon, 2WD	31955	27908
Eddie Bauer 4-door wagon, 4WD	34590	30148
Destination charge	640	640

STANDARD EQUIPMENT:

XLT: 4.6-liter V-8 engine, 4-speed automatic transmission, driver- and passenger-side air bags, anti-lock 4-wheel disc brakes, front cloth 40/60 split bench seat with manual driver-side lumbar support, variable-assist power steering, second-row cloth 60/40 split-folding-reclining bench seat, tilt steering wheel, front and rear cupholders, tinted glass, power mirrors, power windows, power door locks, AM/FM/cassette player, tachometer, voltmeter, coolant-temperature and oil-pressure gauge, remote keyless entry, front map lights, passenger-side illuminated visor mirror, rear defogger, speed-sensitive intermittent wipers, rear wiper/washer, front auxiliary power outlet, rear heat ducts, rear lift gate with flip-up glass, floormats, bright grille, 255/70R16 tires, full-size spare tire, styled steel wheels.

4WD adds: Control-Trac part-time 4WD, 2-speed transfer case, 30-gallon fuel tank.

Eddie Bauer adds: cruise control, leather upholstery, front captain's chairs with lumbar support and 6-way power driver seat, front storage console (rear radio controls, auxiliary rear power outlet, headphone jacks), overhead storage console with trip computer, leather-wrapped steering wheel, dual illuminated visor mirrors, rear map lights, power rear quarter windows, rear privacy glass, automatic headlights, roof rack, wheel-lip and rocker moldings, color-keyed grille and mirrors, fog lights, 255/70R16 all-terrain outline-white-letter tires, alloy wheels.

4WD adds: Control-Trac part-time 4WD, 2-speed transfer case, front tow hooks, 30-gallon fuel tank.

OPTIONAL EQUIPMENT:

Major Packages

Preferred Equipment Pkg. 685A, XLT	1770	1505
Manufacturer's discount price	1050	893

Front captain's chairs with lumbar support and 6-way power driver seat, front storage console (rear radio controls, auxiliary rear power outlet, headphone jacks), cruise control, rear privacy glass, dual illuminated visor mirrors, roof rack, alloy wheels.

Preferred Equipment Pkg. 687A, Eddie Bauer 2WD	1505	1279
Manufacturer's discount price	930	791
Preferred Equipment Pkg. 687A, Eddie Bauer 4WD	2155	1832
Manufacturer's discount price	1405	1194

5.4-liter V-8 engine, engine oil cooler, super engine cooling, Mach audio system with seven premium speakers, power signal mirrors, illuminated running boards, 265/70R17 all-terrain outline-white-letter tires (4WD), cast alloy wheels (4WD).

	Retail Price	Dealer Invoice
Extreme Weather Group, XLT	$190	$162
Eddie Bauer	80	68

Heated outside mirrors, fog lights (XLT), engine-block heater (XLT). XLT requires Pkg. 685A. NA Eddie Bauer w/Pkg. 687A.

Class III Trailer Tow Group, 2WD w/4.6-liter engine	880	748
4WD w/4.6-liter engine	390	332
2WD w/5.4-liter engine	940	799
4WD w/5.4-liter engine	450	383

7-pin trailer wiring harness, frame-mounted hitch, auxiliary transmission-oil cooler, super engine cooling, heavy-duty battery. 2WD models include rear load-leveling suspension and 30-gallon fuel tank. Includes engine-oil cooler when ordered with 5.4-liter engine.

Powertrains

5.4-liter V-8 engine	665	565
Limited-slip rear axle, ordered with 4.6-liter engine	255	217
ordered with 5.4-liter engine	315	267

Includes engine-oil cooler when ordered with 5.4-liter engine.

Comfort and Convenience

High-capacity front and rear air conditioning, XLT	755	642
Eddie Bauer	705	599

XLT includes overhead console. NA with power moonroof.

Power signal mirrors, Eddie Bauer	150	128
Power moonroof, Eddie Bauer	800	680
Cruise control, XLT	235	200
Leather captain's chairs, XLT w/Pkg. 685A	1300	1105
Cloth folding third-row seat, XLT	600	510

NA with leather captain's chairs.

Leather folding third-row seat, XLT	855	727

XLT requires leather captain's chairs.

Mach audio system, Eddie Bauer	355	302

Includes seven premium speakers.

6-disc CD changer	475	404

XLT requires Pkg. 685A.

Appearance and Miscellaneous

Illuminated running boards	435	370
Engine-block heater	35	30

NA XLT w/Pkg. 685A. Eddie Bauer requires Pkg. 687A.

Special Purpose, Wheels and Tires

Load-leveling suspension, 4WD	815	692

XLT requires Pkg. 685A.

Rear load-leveling suspension, 2WD	490	417

Includes 30-gallon fuel tank. XLT requires 685A.

Front tow hooks, XLT 4WD	40	34
Skid plates, 4WD	105	89
255/70R16 all-terrain outline-white-letter tires, XLT with Pkg. 685A	230	196
265/70R17 all-terrain outline-white-letter tires, XLT 4WD	380	323
Eddie Bauer 4WD	150	128

Requires cast alloy wheels. XLT requires Pkg. 685A.

17-inch alloy wheels, 4WD	185	158

Requires 265/70R17 all-terrain outline-white-letter tires. XLT requires Pkg. 685A.

Chrome steel wheels, 2WD	NC	NC

XLT requires Pkg. 685A.

FORD EXPLORER ✓ BEST BUY

Rear- or all-wheel drive compact sport-utility vehicle; similar to Mercury Mountaineer

Base price range: $21,485-$33,145. Built in Louisville, Ky., and St. Louis, Mo.

Also consider: Chevrolet Blazer, Jeep Grand Cherokee, Mercedes-Benz ML320, Toyota 4Runner

FOR • Standard anti-lock brakes • Acceleration (ohc V-6, V-8) • Passenger and cargo room • Visibility

AGAINST • Fuel economy • Engine noise (ohv V-6)

Explorer sales have slackened this year, a rare occurence that's prompted discounts unheard of in past years. Still, this is America's best-selling sport-utility vehicle overall, and one that

---

Ford Explorer Sport 2-door

accounts for one of every four sales in the midsize class.

An anti-theft system is standard for '98, steering wheel audio and climate controls are available on Limiteds and some Eddie Bauer models, and there's a new premium stereo with radio data system (RDS) capability. Taillamps and the rear bumper are new, as is the liftgate, which has larger glass. As on most Fords, the dual air bags are depowered to deploy with less force.

Two- and 4-door body styles are offered, all with standard anti-lock brakes. Engines consist of two V-6s, an overhead-valve with 160 horsepower and manual transmission, and an overhead-cam with 205 horsepower and a 5-speed automatic transmission, plus an optional V-8 with 215 horsepower and a 4-speed automatic transmission.

V-6 4WD models use Ford's Control Trac system, which employes rear-wheel drive and a selection of 4WD modes, including one that can be used on dry pavement. V-8 4WD models have permanently engaged 4WD.

The new available premium audio equipment plays both 3- and 5-inch CDs and, through RDS, displays information such as song titles and interrupts programming with emergency broadcasts.

Mercury sells a clone of the Explorer as the Mountaineer.

PERFORMANCE The overhead-cam V-6 is the best overall engine choice, being smoother than the gruff base V-6 and more powerful too. It can't match the V-8's muscle, but the 5-speed automatic does an admirable job of keeping the ohc six in its power band.

Expect mileage to average around 15-16 mpg with either V-6 and be thankful its not the abysmal 12.4 mpg we averaged with an AWD V-8 model.

Control Trac is more convenient than most rivals' 4WD systems. It can automatically send power to the wheels with the best traction so the driver doesn't constantly need to evaluate changing road conditions and decide whether the vehicle should be in 2WD or 4WD. The AWD system on V-8s offers similar freedom, a luxury unmatched by the Chevrolet Blazer or GMC Jimmy, but available on the Jeep Grand Cherokee and Oldsmobile Bravada.

Explorer corners confidently, with less body lean than the Blazer, but the Ford's ride is bouncy and more truck-like than that of the GM brands or Grand Cherokee.

The base V-6 and the V-8 roar in hard acceleration, but are otherwise unobtrusive. Road and wind noise at highway speeds are not exceptionally intrusive.

ACCOMMODATIONS Explorer scores with an interior that's roomier than its GM or Jeep rivals. There's ample room for four adults, and three abreast in the rear seat is possible for short distances. Unfortunately, the rear bench has a split seatback that's hard and short on shoulder support.

Explorer has a slightly higher step-in height than Blazer, so it's a little more work to get in or out.

Most switchgear is within easy reach, though it's a slight stretch to fiddle with the climate controls, which are low on the dashboard and recessed about two inches. Power window and headlight switches are illuminated for easy access in the dark.

Deep side and rear windows and well-placed outside mirrors give the driver a clear view of surrounding traffic.

Explorer's liftgate isn't light but it's less cumbersome than most rivals', and its rear glass opens separate. Storing the spare tire below the rear underbody creates good cargo room, and the split rear seatback folds in a single motion (without removing the headrest) to create a long, flat load floor.

BUILD QUALITY Explorer has a satisfyingly sold feel. There's smooth, glossy paint outside and materials of generally high quality inside.

VALUE FOR THE MONEY An array of engine and 4WD choices, sound ergonomics in a roomy cabin, and competitve pricing keeps Explorer and its Mountaineer cousin ahead of the pack. The desirable new Mercedes-Benz ML320 is priced against the top-trim Ford models, but is in far shorter supply.

SPECIFICATIONS

	2-door wagon	4-door wagon
Wheelbase, in.	101.7	111.5
Overall length, in.	178.6	188.5
Overall width, in.	70.2	70.2
Overall height, in.	67.9	67.7
Curb weight, lbs.	3692	3911
Cargo vol., cu. ft.	69.4	81.6
Fuel capacity, gals.	17.5	21.0
Seating capacity	4	6
Front head room, in.	39.9	39.9
Max. front leg room, in.	42.4	42.4
Rear head room, in.	39.1	39.3
Min. rear leg room, in.	36.5	37.7

ENGINES

	ohv V-6	ohc V-6	ohv V-8
Size, liters/cu. in.	4.0/245	4.0/245	5.0/302
Horsepower @ rpm	160@ 4200	205@ 5000	215@ 4200
Torque (lbs./ft.) @ rpm	225@ 2800	250@ 3000	288@ 3300
Availability	S[1]	S[2]	O[3]
EPA city/highway mpg			
5-speed OD manual	16/20		
4-speed OD automatic			14/18
5-speed OD automatic		15/19	

1. XL, XLT, Sport. 2. Eddie Bauer, Limited; opt. XL, XLT, Sport. 3. XLT, Eddie Bauer, Limited.

RATINGS

	XL 2-door ohv V-6	XLT 4-door ohc V-6	Limited V-8
Acceleration	3	4	4
Fuel economy	2	2	1
Ride quality	3	3	3
Steering/handling	3	3	3
Braking	4	4	4
Quietness	3	3	3
Driver seating	4	4	4
Instruments/controls	4	4	4
Room/comfort (front)	4	4	4
Room/comfort (rear)	3	3	3
Cargo room	5	5	5
Value for the money	4	4	4
Total	**42**	**43**	**42**

PRICES

Ford Explorer	Retail Price	Dealer Invoice
XL 4-door wagon, 2WD	$21485	$19532
XL 4-door wagon, 4WD	23405	21221
Sport 2-door wagon, 2WD	19880	18119
Sport 2-door wagon, 4WD	22650	20558
XLT 4-door wagon, 2WD	24615	22286
XLT 4-door wagon, 4WD	26620	24051
XLT 4-door wagon, AWD	26620	24051
Eddie Bauer 4-door wagon, 2WD	28785	25956
Eddie Bauer 4-door wagon, 4WD	30790	27721
Eddie Bauer 4-door wagon, AWD	30340	27324
Limited 4-door wagon, 2WD	31590	28425
Limited 4-door wagon, 4WD	33595	30189
Limited 4-door wagon, AWD	33145	29792
Destination charge	525	525

XL, Sport, XLT, Eddie Bauer require a Preferred Equipment Pkg. AWD denotes all-wheel drive. AWD models require 5.0-liter V-8 engine.

STANDARD EQUIPMENT:

XL: 4.0-liter V-6 engine, 5-speed manual transmission, 3.27 ratio axle, anti-lock 4-wheel disc brakes, driver- and passenger-side air bags, power steering, air conditioning, vinyl front bucket seats, split folding rear bench seat with headrests, solar-control tinted wind-

Prices are accurate at time of publication; subject to manufacturer's changes.

shield, intermittent wipers, auxiliary power outlet, illuminated entry, trip odometer, tachometer, AM/FM/cassette with digital clock, map light, cargo hooks, passenger-side visor mirror, chrome bumpers, 225/70R15 tires, full-size spare tire.

4WD adds: Control Trac part-time 4WD, transfer-case skid plate.

Sport and XLT add: cloth front captain's chairs (XLT), console (XLT), Power Equipment Group (power window, door and liftgate locks, power mirrors, upgraded door-panel trim, delayed-off accessory power), speed-sensitive intermittent wipers, rear privacy glass, rear wiper/washer and defogger, power rear-liftgate lock, leather-wrapped steering wheel, cruise control (XLT), tilt steering wheel (XLT), cargo cover (Sport), illuminated visor mirrors, color-keyed grille (Sport), color-keyed bodyside moldings, black painted bumpers (Sport), striping (XLT), alloy wheels.

4WD models add: Control Trac part-time 4WD, transfer-case skid plate.

AWD adds: permanent 4-wheel drive.

Eddie Bauer adds: 4.0-liter OHC V-6 engine, 5-speed automatic transmission, 4.10 ratio axle, 6-way power sport cloth front bucket seats with power lumbar adjusters, roof rack, CD player, cargo cover, floormats, 2-tone paint, 255/70R16 outline-white-letter all-terrain tires, chrome wheels, and deletes full-size spare tire.

4WD adds: Control Trac part-time 4WD, transfer-case skid plate.

AWD adds: permanent 4-wheel drive, Electronics Group (remote keyless entry, anti-theft system, automatic door locks, door keypad), fog lights.

Limited adds: automatic air conditioning, leather upholstery and door trim, Mach Audio System with CD/cassette player, power antenna, console with rear climate and radio controls, systems message center, overhead console with electronic compass and outside temperature indicator, heated power mirrors, automatic day/night rearview mirror, automatic headlights, running boards, color-keyed grille and bumpers, 235/75R15 outline-white-letter all-terrain tires, full-size spare tire (2WD, 4WD), and deletes 2-tone paint.

4WD adds: Control Trac part-time 4WD, transfer-case skid plate.

AWD adds: permanent 4-wheel drive.

OPTIONAL EQUIPMENT:

Major Packages

	Retail Price	Dealer Invoice
Preferred Equipment Pkg. 930A/940A, XL	$650	$553
Manufacturer's discount price	NC	NC
Preferred Equipment Pkg. 931A, Sport	NC	NC
Manufacturer's discount price (credit)	(410)	(349)
Cloth front captain's chairs, 235/75R15 all-terrain outline-white-letter tires.		
Preferred Equipment Pkg. 934A, Sport	3620	3086
Manufacturer's discount price	2290	1947
5-speed automatic transmission, 6-way power sport cloth bucket seats with power lumbar adjusters, Luxury Group (floor console with rear climate and radio controls, overhead console with electronic compass and outside-temperature indicator, Electronics Group [remote keyless entry, anti-theft system, automatic door locks, door keypad, puddle lights], fog lights), roof rack, cargo cover, floormats, 235/75R15 all-terrain outline-white-letter tires.		
Preferred Equipment Pkg. 941A, XLT	290	247
Manufacturer's discount price	NC	NC
Roof rack, CD player.		
Preferred Equipment Pkg. 945A, XLT	3255	2767
Manufacturer's discount price	1900	1615
Pkg. 941A plus 5-speed automatic transmission, 6-way power sport cloth bucket seats with power lumbar adjusters, Luxury Group, cargo cover, floormats.		
Preferred Equipment Pkg. 942A, Eddie Bauer	1050	893
Manufacturer's discount price	NC	NC
6-way power leather bucket seats with power lumbar adjusters, running boards.		
Preferred Equipment Pkg. 946A, Eddie Bauer	3375	2869
Manufacturer's discount price	1805	1535
Pkg. 942A plus Mach Audio System, automatic temperature control, systems message center, Luxury Group.		
Premium Sport Pkg., Sport	2000	1700
Manufacturer's discount price	1000	850
Includes 4.0-liter OHC V-6 engine, 5-speed automatic transmission, 4.10 ratio axle (4WD), 3.73 ratio axle (2WD), medium-graphite bumpers, moldings, and side-step bar, roof rack, rear tow hook, chrome wheels (2WD), alloy wheels (4WD), 235/75R15 white-letter tires (2WD), 255/70R16 all-terrain white-letter tires(4WD).		

	Retail Price	Dealer Invoice
Convenience Group, XL, Sport	$665	$565
Cruise control, leather-wrapped steering wheel, defogger, rear wiper/washer.		
Electronics Group, Eddie Bauer	415	357
Remote keyless entry, anti-theft system, puddle lights, automatic door locks, door keypad.		

Powertrains

	Retail Price	Dealer Invoice
4.0-liter OHC V-6 engine, XL, XLT, Sport	540	459
Requires 5-speed automatic transmission.		
5.0-liter V-8 engine, XLT w/Pkg. 941A	1125	956
XLT w/Pkg. 945A	1005	854
Eddie Bauer 2WD, Limited 2WD	430	366
Eddie Bauer AWD, Limited AWD	895	761
NA 4WD. Requires 4-speed automatic transmission. Includes limited-slip 3.73 ratio axle with Trailer Towing Pkg., 235/75R15 all-terrain white-letter tires (includes full-size spare on XLT 2WD only).		
4-speed automatic transmission, XLT w/Pkg. 941A	945	803
XLT w/Pkg. 945A, Eddie Bauer, Limited	NC	NC
NA 4WD. Requires 5.0-liter V-8 engine.		
5-speed automatic transmission, XL, XLT, Sport	1065	905
NA with 5.0-liter engine.		
Limited-slip axle (3.73 ratio) and Trailer Tow Pkg., 4.0-liter manual	355	302
NA Eddie Bauer or with Premium Sport Pkg.		
Limited-slip axle (4.10 ratio) and Trailer Tow Pkg., Sport w/Pkg. 934B, Eddie Bauer	310	263
Std. with AWD.		

Safety Features

	Retail Price	Dealer Invoice
Integrated rear child seat, 4-door	200	170
XL requires captain's chairs.		

Comfort and Convenience

	Retail Price	Dealer Invoice
Cloth captain's chairs, XL	280	238
Includes console.		
6-way power cloth bucket seats, Sport	1020	867
XLT w/Pkg. 941A	650	553
Includes power lumbar adjusters and console. Requires Premium Sound stereo.		
6-way power leather bucket seats, Sport w/Pkg. 934B, XLT w/Pkg. 945B	655	557
Includes floor console (XLT).		
High Series floor console, Eddie Bauer	380	323
Includes rear climate and radio controls. Requires Electronics Group.		
Automatic day/night mirror, Sport w/Pkg. 934B, XLT w/Pkg. 945A, Eddie Bauer w/Pkg. 946A	185	158
Includes automatic headlights.		
Power moonroof, Sport w/Pkg. 934A, XLT w/Pkg. 945B, Eddie Bauer w/Pkg. 946A, Limited	800	680
Includes front overhead console with rear reading lamps. Sport requires roof rack.		
CD player, XL	150	128
Requires Convenience Pkg.		
CD/cassette player, Sport	325	277
Sport w/Prem. Sport Pkg., Eddie Bauer	175	149
Mach Audio System, Sport w/Pkg. 934A, XLT w/Pkg. 945A, Eddie Bauer	650	553
Includes sub-woofer and power antenna. Eddie Bauer and XLT require console with rear climate and radio controls, Electronics Group.		
CD changer, Sport w/Pkg. 934A, XLT w/Pkg. 945A, Eddie Bauer, Limited	370	314
Eddie Bauer requires high series floor console.		
Cellular telephone, Eddie Bauer w/Pkg. 946A, Limited	690	587
Floormats/Cargo Cover Group, XLT	165	140

Appearance and Miscellaneous

	Retail Price	Dealer Invoice
Side-step bar, Sport	295	251
Running boards, XLT, Eddie Bauer	395	336
2-tone paint, XLT	120	102

Special Purpose, Wheels and Tires

	Retail Price	Dealer Invoice
Automatic Ride Control, Eddie Bauer w/Pkg. 946A, Limited	650	553
NA 2WD.		
235/75R15 all-terrain white-letter tires, XLT	230	196
Includes full-size spare on 2WD only.		

Rating Scale: 5-Excellent; 4-Above average; 3-Average; 2-Below average; 1-Poor

FORD F-150

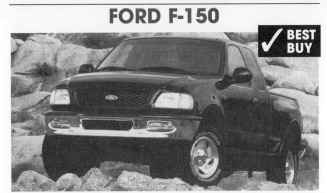

✓ BEST BUY

Ford F-150 XLT extended cab Flareside

Rear- or 4-wheel-drive full-size pickup

Base price range: $14,735-$27,295. Built in Kansas City, Mo.; Wayne, Mich.; Norfolk, Va.; Louisville, Ky.; and Canada.

Also consider: Chevrolet C/K1500, Dodge Ram 1500, Toyota T100

FOR • Acceleration (V-8s) • Anti-lock brakes • Interior room • Cargo and trailer towing capability

AGAINST • Acceleration (V-6) • Fuel economy • Noise (V-6)

Ford introduced a redesigned F-150 for 1997, and makes few changes to its full-size light-duty pickups for '98. The F-series has been the best-selling truck in the U.S. for the last 20 years, and the best-selling vehicle of any kind for 15 years.

Only the half-ton payload version, the F-150, is covered in this report, though the three-quarter-ton F-250 is similar. The F-250 Heavy-Duty and one-ton F-350 models are built from the previous F-Series design, but are to be updated with F-150-like styling during the '98 calendar year.

The F-150 is available with rear- or 4-wheel drive in regular-cab and extended-cab form. The latter, called the SuperCab, has a passenger-side third door and a 3-place rear seat that folds to create a flat, steel cargo floor. Short-bed models have a 6.5-foot-long cargo bed, long-bed models an 8-foot bed. Ford calls the flat-side cargo bed Styleside. The Flareside flared-fender box comes only as a short-bed.

A floor-mounted transfer case lever is standard on 4WD models, and an electric transfer case operated by a dashboard switch is optional. Both allow shifting in and out of 4WD High on the fly, though the 4WD system is not for use on dry pavement.

A 4.2-liter V-6 and overhead-cam V-8s of 4.6 and 5.4 liters are the available engines. The V-6 and 4.6 V-8 come with manual transmission. Automatic is optional and is required with the 5.4-liter V-8.

All models have standard depowered dual air bags and a key-operated dashboard switch that deactivates the passenger-side air bag to allow use of a rear-facing child seat. Rear-wheel anti-lock brakes are standard, with 4-wheel ABS standard on Lariats and optional on other F-150s.

Maximum payload is 2435 pounds, found on the regular cab-long bed. Maximum towing capacity is 8200 pounds.

PERFORMANCE The F-150 is quieter and rides more comfortably than the full-size trucks from General Motors and Dodge. The only area its rivals might the an advantage is under the hood.

The Ford's base V-6 is noisy at idle and becomes raucous under hard throttle. It provides adequate acceleration only in lighter models with little cargo aboard. The V-8s are smoother and more powerful, but don't have quite as much low-speed muscle as the larger overhead-valve V-8s offered by GM and Dodge. For most applications, we'd recommend getting one of the V-8s—the bigger the better.

No full-size pickup is going to deliver very good fuel economy. We've put nearly 10,000 miles on a long-term F-150 SuperCab 4x4 and averaged only 12.5 mpg in a mix of city and highway driving, though one highway trip netted 16.2 mpg.

On the highway, the F-150 has a stable, comfortable ride with little of the bouncing or pitching common to most pickups. On bumpy pavement, the suspension absorbs the worst of rough stuff and the rear axle resists juddering even when the cargo bed is empty. Wind and road noise are moderate for a pickup truck.

ACCOMMODATIONS Interior furnishings range from stark to luxurious, but all F-150s have a modern, convenient dashboard with handy controls. There are large door map pockets and cupholders pop from the dashboard.

There's generous head, leg, and shoulder room in front, but 4WD models sit high off the ground, so entry and exit require more effort than in the 2WD versions.

The SuperCab's standard passenger-side rear door makes life easier. There's loads of head room and adequate leg room for adults in the rear seat, but comfort levels are marginal, partly because the rear seatback is so stiff and upright.

BUILD QUALITY Exterior fit and finish and interior materials and workmanship on our long-term truck are hard to fault. A driveshaft yoke was replaced under warranty to cure some drivetrain slippage when getting away from a stop, but that was the only problem encountered.

VALUE FOR THE MONEY Other full-size pickups offer stronger engines, but none has a more-refined, car-like feel than the F-150. We agree with the marketplace: Overall, Ford's F-150 is the best of the bunch.

RATINGS

	2WD V-6 reg. cab	4WD V-8 SuperCab
Acceleration	3	3
Fuel economy	2	1
Ride quality	3	3
Steering/handling	3	3
Braking	3	3
Quietness	3	3
Driver seating	4	4
Instruments/controls	4	4
Room/comfort (front)	5	5
Room/comfort (rear)	—	2
Cargo room	1	3
Value for the money	4	4
Total	35	38

SPECIFICATIONS

	Reg. cab short bed	Reg. cab long bed	Ext. cab short bed	Ext. cab long bed
Wheelbase, in.	119.9	138.5	138.5	157.1
Overall length, in.	202.2	220.8	220.8	239.4
Overall width, in.	78.4	78.4	78.4	78.4
Overall height, in.	72.4	72.1	72.6	72.4
Curb weight, lbs.	4028	4339	4575	4658
Maximum payload, lbs.	2105	2390	1930	1780
Fuel capacity, gals.	25.0	30.0	25.0	30.0
Seating capacity	3	3	6	6
Front head room, in.	40.8	40.8	40.8	40.8
Max. front leg room, in.	40.9	40.9	40.9	40.9
Rear head room, in.	—	—	37.8	37.8
Min. rear leg room, in.	—	—	32.2	32.2

ENGINES

	ohv V-6	ohc V-8	ohc V-8
Size, liters/cu. in.	4.2/256	4.6/281	5.4/330
Horsepower @ rpm	210@ 4750	220@ 4500	235@ 4250
Torque (lbs./ft.) @ rpm	255@ 3000	290@ 3250	330@ 3000
Availability	S	S[1]	O

EPA city/highway mpg

4-speed OD automatic	17/22	16/21	14/18
5-speed OD manual	17/22	16/21	

1. Lariat; opt. other models.

PRICES

Ford F-150

	Retail Price	Dealer Invoice
Standard Styleside 2WD regular cab, short bed	$14735	$13477
Standard Styleside 2WD regular cab, long bed	15025	13732
XL Styleside 2WD regular cab, short bed	15765	13910
XL Styleside 2WD regular cab, long bed	16065	14165
XL Flareside 2WD regular cab, short bed	16775	14769
XLT Styleside 2WD regular cab, short bed	18415	16162
XLT Styleside 2WD regular cab, long bed	18715	16417

Prices are accurate at time of publication; subject to manufacturer's changes.

	Retail Price	Dealer Invoice
XLT Flareside 2WD regular cab, short bed	$19425	$17022
Lariat Styleside 2WD regular cab, short bed	20850	18233
Lariat Styleside 2WD regular cab, long bed	21150	18488
Lariat Styleside 2WD regular cab, long bed	21860	19091
Standard Styleside 4WD regular cab, short bed	18005	16354
Standard Styleside 4WD regular cab, long bed	18295	16610
XL Styleside 4WD regular cab, short bed	19155	16792
XL Styleside 4WD regular cab, long bed	19455	17047
XL Flareside 4WD regular cab, short bed	19920	17442
XLT Styleside 4WD regular cab, short bed	21465	18755
XLT Styleside 4WD regular cab, long bed	21765	19010
XLT Flareside 4WD regular cab, short bed	22230	19406
Lariat Styleside 4WD regular cab, short bed	23900	20825
Lariat Styleside 4WD regular cab, long bed	24200	21080
Lariat Flareside 4WD regular cab, short bed	24665	21475
Standard Styleside 2WD SuperCab, short bed	17090	15550
Standard Styleside 2WD SuperCab, long bed	17380	15804
XL Styleside 2WD SuperCab, short bed	18205	15984
XL Styleside 2WD SuperCab, long bed	18505	16239
XL Flareside 2WD SuperCab, short bed	19090	16737
XLT Styleside 2WD SuperCab, short bed	21095	18441
XLT Styleside 2WD SuperCab, long bed	21395	18696
XLT Flareside 2WD SuperCab, short bed	21860	19091
Lariat Styleside 2WD SuperCab, short bed	23530	20511
Lariat Flareside 2WD SuperCab, short bed	24295	21161
Lariat Styleside 2WD SuperCab, long bed	23830	20766
Standard Styleside 4WD SuperCab, short bed	20710	18735
Standard Styleside 4WD SuperCab, long bed	21000	18990
XL Styleside 4WD SuperCab, short bed	21955	19172
XL Styleside 4WD SuperCab, long bed	22255	19427
XL Flareside 4WD SuperCab, short bed	22720	19822
XLT Styleside 4WD SuperCab, short bed	24730	21531
XLT Styleside 4WD SuperCab, long bed	25030	21786
XLT Flareside 4WD SuperCab, short bed	25495	22181
Lariat Styleside 4WD SuperCab, short bed	26530	23061
Lariat Styleside 4WD SuperCab, long bed	26830	23316
Lariat Flareside 4WD SuperCab, short bed	27295	23711
Destination charge	640	640

STANDARD EQUIPMENT:

Standard: 4.2-liter V-6 engine, 4.6-liter V-8 engine (4WD SuperCab), 5-speed manual transmission, anti-lock rear brakes, driver- and passenger-side air bags, power steering, AM/FM radio, digital clock, vinyl bench seat, rear seat (SuperCab), cupholders, oil-pressure gauge, coolant-temperature gauge, voltmeter, headliner, black vinyl floormat, dual outside mirrors, intermittent wipers, argent grille and front bumper, argent steel wheel, 235/70R16 tires, full-size spare.

4WD models add: part-time 4-wheel drive.

XL adds: cloth bench seats, door map pockets, passenger-side visor mirror, map lights, underhood light, chrome grille, chrome front bumper.

4WD models add: part-time 4-wheel drive.

XLT adds: 40/60 split bench seat w/driver-side manual lumbar support, center storage console, power windows, power door locks, tachometer, speed-sensitive intermittent wipers, carpeting, side privacy glass, swing-out rear quarter windows (SuperCab), front tow hooks (4WD), color-keyed grille (4WD), chrome rear step bumper, styled steel wheels w/chrome hub.

4WD models add: part-time 4-wheel drive.

Lariat adds: 4.6-liter V-8 engine, 3.55 rear axle ratio, 4-wheel anti-lock brakes, leather upholstery, leather-wrapped steering wheel, front floormats, rear floormats (SuperCab), power mirrors, color-keyed grille, fog lamps (4WD), 255/70R16 outline-white-letter tires, alloy wheels.

4WD models add: part-time 4-wheel drive.

OPTIONAL EQUIPMENT:
Major Packages

	Retail Price	Dealer Invoice
XL Pkg. 502A, XL...	350	298
Manufacturer's discount price	NC	NC
Chrome rear step bumper, styled steel wheels.		
XLT Pkg. 507A, XLT...	1520	1293
Manufacturer's discount price	NC	NC
XL pkg. plus air conditioning, cruise control, tilt steering wheel, cassette player, alloy wheels.		

	Retail Price	Dealer Invoice
Lariat Pkg. 508A, Lariat	$1680	$1428
Manufacturer's discount price	NC	NC
XLT Pkg. plus power driver's seat.		
Class III Trailer Towing Group,		
Standard, XL, XLT w/auto. trans.	445	378
w/auto. trans. and engine block heater	390	331
w/man. trans.	375	319
w/man. trans. and engine block heater	320	272
Lariat w/auto. trans.	361	307
w/auto. trans. and engine block heater	305	259
w/man. trans.	293	249
w/man. trans. and engine block heater	237	201
Heavy Duty Electrical/Cooling Pkg., 7-wire trailer harness, trailer hitch, heavy-duty shock absorbers Requires rear step bumper.		
STX Pkg., 2WD XLT regular cab...........................	595	506
Body-color grille, grille surround, bumpers, and power mirrors, STX decal, 3.55 rear axle ratio, 275/60R17 tires, alloy wheels.		
Off-Road Equipment, 4WD, XLT	1145	973
Lariat	745	633
Skid plates, stabilizer bar, 3.55 rear axle, 4x4 off-road decal. NA SuperCab long bed, 2-tone paint, 4.2-liter V-6 engine, Payload Pkg. 3, or Snow Plow Prep Pkg.		
Payload Pkg. 2, 2WD regular cab...........................	50	43
Heavy-duty springs and shock absorbers. NA 3.08 rear axle ratio. NA w/long bed when ordered w/4.6-liter V-8 engine.		
Payload Pkg. 3,		
Standard 2WD regular cab long bed...................	470	399
XL and XLT 2WD regular cab long bed...............	270	229
Heavy-duty springs and shock absorbers, 245/75R16 tires, styled steel wheels Standard, XL) or chrome wheels (XLT). Requires 4.6-liter V-8 engine and automatic transmission. NA with 3.08 rear axle ratio.		
Heavy Duty Electrical/Cooling Pkg..........................	210	178
Heavy-duty battery, heavy-duty alternator (w/4.2-liter V-6 engine), super engine cooling, auxiliary transmission oil cooler (w/automatic transmission), engine oil cooler (w/5.4-liter V-8 engine)		
Pickup Box Security Group, Standard, XL..............	45	38
Tailgate lock, cargo bed light.		
Snow Plow Prep Pkg., 4WD regular cab long bed .	505	429

Powertrains

	Retail Price	Dealer Invoice
4.6-liter V-8 engine,		
regular cab Standard /XL/XLT	635	540
2WD Club Cub Standard/XL/XLT	385	316
5.4-liter V-8 engine,		
Standard 4WD regular cab long bed, XL, XLT	1300	1105
Lariat, 4WD SuperCab	665	565
Requires automatic transmission. Standard requires Snow Plow Prep Pkg.		
4-speed automatic transmission with overdrive	970	824
4WD modles include 3.55 rear axle ratio.		
Electric shift 4WD, 4WD XLT/Lariat	150	128
Requires 4.6-liter V-8 engine and 4-speed automatic transmission.		
3.55 rear axle ratio..	50	43
Limited slip differential......................................	260	221
Includes engine oil cooler. Requires 3.55 axle ratio.		

Safety Features

	Retail Price	Dealer Invoice
4-wheel anti-lock brakes, Standard, XL, XLT..........	500	425

Comfort and Convenience

	Retail Price	Dealer Invoice
Air conditioning, Standard, XL................................	805	684
with manual transmission	305	259
Remote keyless entry/theft-deterrent system,		
XLT, Lariat...	265	225
Requires air conditioning and cruise control.		
Cruise control and tilt steering column,		
Standard, XL..	385	328
40/60 split bench seat with driver-side lumbar support,		
XL	150	128
Cloth captain's chairs, XLT...................................	490	417
Includes floor console.		
Leather captain's chairs, Lariat SuperCab.............	490	417
Includes floor console.		
Cloth bench seat, Standard..................................	100	85

Rating Scale: 5-Excellent; 4-Above average; 3-Average; 2-Below average; 1-Poor

	Retail Price	Dealer Invoice
Power driver seat, XLT	$360	$306

Requires air conditioning, cruise control. Requires automatic transmission when ordered with captain's chairs.

Sliding rear window	115	97
Carpeting, XL	100	85
Front floormats, XLT	30	26
Front and rear floormats, XLT SuperCab	50	43
Rear storage bin	90	77

NA SuperCab.

AM/FM/cassette, Standard, XL	110	93
6-disc CD changer and cassette, XLT, Lariat	400	340

Requires air conditioning, cruise control.

Engine block heater	90	77
Power mirrors, XLT	100	85
Rear quarter window privacy glass, XL SuperCab	100	85
Flip-out rear quarter windows, Standard, XL	100	85

NA regular cab.

Appearance and Miscellaneous

Argent rear step bumper, Standard	100	85
2-tone paint, XLT, Lariat	190	162

NA XLT with Off-Road Equipment Group or Flareside.

Cab steps, regular cab	320	272
Fog lamps, Standard, XL, XLT	140	119

NA 2WD.

Special Purpose, Wheels and Tires

Skid plates, 4WD	160	136
4WD regular cab short bed	80	68
Tow hooks, Standard, XL	40	34

NA 2WD.

235/70R16 outline-white-letter tires, 2WD XLT	125	107
245/75R16 tires, Standard, XL, XLT	385	328
245/75R16 all-terrain outline-white-letter tires, 4WD Standard	715	607
255/70R16 all-terrain outline-white-letter tires, 4WD Standard/XL/XLT	400	340
255/70R16 outline-white-letter tires, 2WD XLT	295	251

Includes 3.55 axle ratio.

245/75R16 tires, Lariat, 2WD w/Payload Pkg. 3	90	77
2WD XL w/Appearance Pkg.	260	221

Includes 3.55 axle ratio with Standard, XL, and XLT; chrome wheels with XLT.

255/70R16 all-terrain outline-white-letter tires, 4WD Lariat	130	111

Includes 3.55 axle ratio with Standard, XL, and XLT.

245/75R16 all-terrain outline-white-letter tires, 4WD XL/XLT	515	437
4WD Lariat	345	293
4WD w/Snow Plow Prep Pkg.	240	204

Includes styled steel wheels with Standard, and XL, cast aluminum wheels with XLT, and 3.55 axle ratio with Standard, XL, and XLT.

Comfort and Convenience

Cloth bench seat, Standard	100	85

Appearance and Miscellaneous

Chrome rear bumper, XL	150	128
Cab steps, SuperCab	370	314

Major Packages

Snow Plow Prep Pkg., 4WD regular cab long bed ordered with Trailer Tow Pkg.	245	208

Heavy Duty Electrical/Cooling Pkg., 255/70R16 all-terrain outline-white-letter tires, styled steel wheels (Standard, XL) or chrome wheels (XLT), 3.55 rear axle ratio, heavy-duty shock absorbers. Requires 5.4-liter V-8 engine, automatic transmission, and rear bumper. NA Lariat.

FORD MUSTANG   **BUDGET BUY**

Rear-wheel-drive Sports and GT

Base price range: $15,970-$23,970. Built in Dearborn, Mich.

Ford Mustang GT convertible

Also consider: Chevrolet Camaro, Mitsubishi 3000GT, Pontiac Firebird

FOR • Acceleration (V-8s) • Handling • Anti-lock brakes

AGAINST • Fuel economy (V-8s) • Rear seat room • Ride (GT, Cobra)

While its perennial rivals, the Chevrolet Camaro and Pontiac Firebird, get facelifts and a new V-8 engine for '98, Mustang returns virtually unchanged except for 10 more horsepower in the GT version. Mustang outsells the Camaro and Firebird combined, and has been the most-popular sporty car in the U.S. for the past 12 years.

Coupes and convertibles are available in three levels of performance. The base model has a V-6 engine. The GT has a single-overhead cam V-8 with 225 horsepower. And the Cobra gets a twin-cam, 305-horsepower version of the GT's V-8. Manual transmission is standard. Automatic is optional on the base and GT, but is not offered on the Cobra. Anti-lock brakes are standard on the Cobra, optional on the others. Dual air bags are standard and as on most Fords for '98, are depowered to deploy with less force while still meeting federal regulations. Finally, Mustangs now have two front cupholders instead of a cupholder and an ashtray.

PERFORMANCE You'll have to look to the high-performance Cobra to uphold Mustang's honor against V-8 Camaros and Firebirds. While Mustang's GT is certainly more spirited than a V-6 version, it's little quicker than the V-6 Camaro/Firebird. A mix of city and highway driving has gotten us 20.3 mpg in a V-6 Mustang, 16.7 in a GT, and 14.4 in a Cobra. This is representative of cars in this class.

There are clear differences in ride and handling between Mustang models. Base cars have a relatively supple suspension that favors ride over handling. GTs are stiffer but offer a sporty balance between comfort and control. The Cobra is among the best-handling cars around, but its ride can be punishing on bad pavement.

Engine and exhaust noise in V-8 models is appropriately aggressive, but not as intrusive as that of the GM pony cars. Coupes have a moderate amount of road and wind noise, but the convertibles seem worse than most competitors at filtering out unpleasant sounds.

The rear-wheel-drive design that contributes to Mustang's sporty road manners also limits traction on slippery surfaces and unlike the GM rivals, Mustang does not offer traction control.

ACCOMMODATIONS Mustang has a more upright design than Camaro, so it has a slightly airier interior. The dashboard is tall and the seating position low, however, yet bigger drivers may wish for more head and leg room. The front seats are comfortable for everyone else. The tiny rear seat is best suited to those under 5-foot-6.

Mustang's slightly easier to get into and out of than most sports coupes, but rear-seat passengers still need to be limber to squeeze past the front seatbacks. Gauges are legible and most controls are handy and simple to operate. The driver also has a marginally better view to the sides and rear than in the Camaro. The convertible's power roof raises and lowers easily and includes a glass rear window but its thick rear "pillars" drastically restrict the over-the-shoulder view. Trunk space is meager, and the convertible lacks the coupe's split folding rear seatback.

Prices are accurate at time of publication; subject to manufacturer's changes.

BUILD QUALITY The last coupe we tested had a smooth paint finish and the exterior panels lined up evenly. Our convertible suffered no more body flexing than usual for a ragtop. Interior materials on both were attractive, though the center console has sharp plastic edges.

VALUE FOR THE MONEY Mustang is somewhat more user-friendly and easier to live with on a daily basis than Camaro or Firebird, but lags in the performance-per-dollar department. Insurance costs can be high on V-8 versions, and try to drive one in snow before laying down any money.

RATINGS

	Base coupe	GT conv.	Cobra
Acceleration	3	4	5
Fuel economy	3	2	2
Ride quality	3	3	2
Steering/handling	3	4	5
Braking	4	5	5
Quietness	3	2	2
Driver seating	3	3	3
Instruments/controls	4	4	4
Room/comfort (front)	3	3	3
Room/comfort (rear)	2	2	2
Cargo room	2	2	2
Value for the money	4	4	4
Total	**37**	**38**	**39**

SPECIFICATIONS

	2-door coupe	2-door conv.
Wheelbase, in.	101.3	101.3
Overall length, in.	181.5	181.5
Overall width, in.	71.8	71.8
Overall height, in.	53.4	53.3
Curb weight, lbs.	3393	3565
Cargo vol., cu. ft.	10.9	7.7
Fuel capacity, gals.	15.4	15.4
Seating capacity	4	4
Front head room, in.	38.2	38.1
Max. front leg room, in.	41.9	41.9
Rear head room, in.	35.9	35.7
Min. rear leg room, in.	30.3	30.3

ENGINES

	ohv V-6	ohc V-8	dohc V-8
Size, liters/cu. in.	3.8/232	4.6/282	4.6/282
Horsepower @ rpm	150@ 4000	225@ 4750	305@ 5800
Torque (lbs./ft.) @ rpm	215@ 2750	290@ 3500	300@ 4800
Availability	S[1]	S[2]	S[3]
EPA city/highway mpg			
5-speed OD manual	20/30	17/26	18/26
4-speed OD automatic	20/30	17/24	

1. Base. 2. GT. 3. Cobra.

PRICES

Ford Mustang

	Retail Price	Dealer Invoice
2-door notchback	$15970	$14658
2-door convertible	20470	18663
GT 2-door notchback	19970	18218
GT 2-door convertible	23970	21778
Cobra 2-door notchback	—	—
Cobra 2-door convertible	—	—
Destination charge	525	525

Cobra prices not available at time of publication.

STANDARD EQUIPMENT:

Base notchback: 3.8-liter V-6 engine, 5-speed manual transmission, driver- and passenger-side air bags, 4-wheel disc brakes, power steering, tilt steering wheel, air conditioning, reclining cloth bucket seats, split folding rear seat (notchback), storage console with armrest and cupholder, power mirrors, power windows, power door locks, remote keyless entry, AM/FM/CD/cassette, digital clock, tachometer, trip odometer, coolant-temperature and oil-pressure gauges, voltmeter, dual visor mirrors, intermittent wipers, auxiliary power outlet, power remote decklid release, theft-deterrent system,

tinted glass, 205/65R15 all-season tires, alloy wheels.

Base convertible adds: power convertible top, illuminated visor mirrors.

GT notchback adds to base notchback: 4.6-liter OHC V-8 engine, traction control, dual exhaust, GT bucket seats, power driver seat, leather-wrapped steering wheel, fog lamps, GT Suspension Pkg., 225/55ZR16 all-season tires.

GT adds to GT and base convertible: rear decklid spoiler.

Cobra adds: 4.6-liter DOHC V-8 engine, anti-lock 4-wheel disc brakes, sport bucket seats, cruise control, rear defogger, front floormats, performance suspension, 245/45ZR17 tires.

OPTIONAL EQUIPMENT:

	Retail Price	Dealer Invoice
Major Packages		
Convenience Group, Base	$495	$441
GT	295	263
Cruise control, power driver seat (Base), rear defogger, floormats.		
Powertrains		
4-speed automatic transmission	815	725
Optional axle ratio, GT	200	178
Safety Features		
Anti-lock brakes	500	445
Comfort and Convenience		
Leather upholstery	500	445
Mach 460 sound system	395	352
Includes 460 watts peak power, AM/FM stereo, 60-watt equalizer, CD-changer compatibility, soft-touch tape controls, ten speakers.		
Rear defogger	190	169
Iluminated visor mirrors, notchback	95	85
Engine block heater	20	18
Appearance and Miscellaneous		
Theft-deterrent system	145	129
Rear decklid spoiler, Base, GT notchback	195	174
17-inch alloy wheels, GT	500	445
Includes 245/45ZR17 tires		

FORD RANGER

Ford Ranger XLT regular cab

Rear- or 4-wheel-drive compact pickup; similar to Mazda B-Series Pickup

Base price range: $11,070-$20,325. Built in Louisville, Ky; St. Paul, Minn.; and Edison, N.J.

Also consider: Chevrolet S-10, Dodge Dakota, GMC Sonoma

FOR • Anti-lock brakes • Acceleration (4.0-liter V-6) • Ride • Handling

AGAINST • Acceleration (4-cylinder) • Interior room (regular cab)

Ranger has been the best-selling compact pickup for the past decade and is revised for '98 with a larger regular cab, a revamped 4-wheel-drive system, and a larger standard engine.

Regular-cabs come with 6- or 7-foot-long cargo beds, extended-cab SuperCabs come only with the 6-foot box. Both are offered with Flareside flare-fender short beds. Dual air bags are

Rating Scale: 5-Excellent; 4-Above average; 3-Average; 2-Below average; 1-Poor

standard and this year are depowered to deploy with less force. A dashboard cutoff switch can disable the passenger-side bag.

For '98, regular-cab passenger compartments are stretched three inches at the rear, allowing an extra inch of rearward seat travel, variable backrest adjustment, and more storage space behind the seat. Four-wheel-drive Rangers get a new and different grille than 2WD versions. And a new optional audio system accommodates cassettes as well as 3- and 5-inch CDs.

The standard 4-cylinder engine is enlarged from 2.3 to 2.5 liters and gains seven horsepower. Standard on 4x4s is a 3.0-liter V-6, which is optional on 4x2s. Optional for both is a 4.0-liter V-6. Manual transmission is standard. The optional automatic with the 2.5- and 3.0-liter engines is a 4-speed and with the 4.0 is a 5-speed. The 4WD system continues with shift-on-the-fly capability and still is not for use on dry pavement. But it no longer requires that the vehicle be stopped and backed up to unlock the front hubs after switching from 4WD to 2WD.

PERFORMANCE Four-cylinder Rangers labor to gain speed, especially with automatic transmission. Get the 4.0-liter V-6; it uses only slightly more fuel than the 3.0 V-6 and doesn't add much to the sticker price. The 4.0-liter is somewhat coarse and noisy, but it has plenty of low-speed torque and should perform most tasks with ease. It also works well with the automatic transmission and furnishes prompt passing power. We averaged 16.0 mpg in a long-term test of a 4WD SuperCab with the 4.0 and automatic.

Ranger has admirable ride and handling for a truck. The suspension absorbs most big bumps without jarring the occupants and provides stable cornering with moderate body lean.

No compact pickup offers 4WD that can be used on dry pavement, so Ranger's is as convenient as they come. It's controlled by a dashboard knob and can be switched between 2- and 4-wheel drive while on the move.

ACCOMMODATIONS Ranger's regular-cab interior is slightly roomier than before, but still not spacious. The longer cab allows the seatback to be tilted farther back than before, but taller drivers may find the SuperCab a necessity for comfort. Some of our shorter drivers said the bottoms of the Ranger's bucket seats were too long, catching them behind the knees.

Even with a bench seat, three adults would be a tight squeeze in front. SuperCabs have a pair of child-sized rear seats that flip down from the sidewalls.

The car-like interior puts controls within easy reach, though the climate panel is recessed too much for quick adjustment. We've criticized some of Ford's radios for their tiny buttons and lack of manual tuning capability, but this year's systems are much easier to use.

BUILD QUALITY Rangers we've tested have been solidly built, and the interior materials were of better quality than might be expected in a compact pickup. Our long-term tester experienced some electrical problems that were covered under warranty.

VALUE FOR THE MONEY Competitors offer some features Ranger doesn't, primarily a third door on extended-cab General Motors pickups and the Dodge Dakota's larger cab and V-8 option. However, the Ford is refined, well built, and priced competitively.

RATINGS

	Reg. cab 2WD 4-cyl	SuperCab 4WD 4.0 V-6
Acceleration	2	3
Fuel economy	3	2
Ride quality	3	3
Steering/handling	3	3
Braking	3	3
Quietness	3	3
Driver seating	3	3
Instruments/controls	4	4
Room/comfort (front)	3	3
Room/comfort (rear)	—	1
Cargo room	1	2
Value for the money	4	4
Total	**32**	**34**

SPECIFICATIONS

	Reg cab short bed	Reg cab long bed	Ext. cab
Wheelbase, in.	111.6	117.5	125.7
Overall length, in.	187.5	200.7	202.9
Overall width, in.	69.3	69.3	69.3
Overall height, in.	68.2	68.2	68.2
Curb weight, lbs.	3060	3100	3280
Maximum payload, lbs.	1660	1660	1620
Fuel capacity, gals.	17.0	20.0	20.0
Seating capacity	3	3	5
Front head room, in.	39.2	39.2	39.3
Max. front leg room, in.	42.2	42.2	42.2
Rear head room, in.	—	—	NA
Min. rear leg room, in.	—	—	NA

ENGINES

	ohc I-4	ohv V-6	ohv V-6
Size, liters/cu. in.	2.5/152	3.0/182	4.0/245
Horsepower @ rpm	117@ 4500	145@ 5000	158@ 4250
Torque (lbs./ft.) @ rpm	149@ 2500	178@ 3750	223@ 3000
Availability	S	S	O
EPA city/highway mpg			
5-speed OD manual	22/27	18/24	18/23
4-speed OD automatic	20/25	17/23	
5-speed OD automatic			16/22

PRICES

Ford Ranger	Retail Price	Dealer Invoice
XL 2WD regular cab, 108-inch WB	$11385	$10835
XL 2WD regular cab, 114-inch WB	11855	11267
XLT 2WD regular cab, 108-inch WB	13205	11981
XLT 2WD regular cab, 114-inch WB	13755	12465
XL 4WD regular cab, 108-inch WB	15765	14864
XL 4WD regular cab, 114-inch WB	16235	15296
XLT 4WD regular cab, 108-inch WB	17295	15580
XLT 4WD regular cab, 114-inch WB	17885	16099
XL 2WD SuperCab, 125-inch WB	14840	13419
XL 4WD SuperCab, 125-inch WB	17370	15646
XLT 2WD SuperCab, 125-inch WB	15345	13863
XLT 4WD SuperCab, 125-inch WB	18780	16886
Splash 2WD regular cab, 108-inch WB	14945	13511
Splash 4WD regular cab, 108-inch WB	18765	16873
Splash 2WD SuperCab, 125-inch WB	16575	14946
Splash 4WD SuperCab, 125-inch WB	19595	17604
Destination charge	510	510

XLT, STX, Splash require a Preferred Equipment Pkg.

STANDARD EQUIPMENT:

XL: 2.5-liter 4-cylinder engine (2WD), 3.0-liter V-6 engine (4WD), 5-speed manual transmission, anti-lock rear brakes, driver- and passenger-side air bags, power steering, 60/40 split vinyl bench seat, rear jump seats (SuperCab), AM/FM radio with digital clock (4WD), coolant-temperature and oil-pressure gauges, trip odometer, tachometer (4WD), tinted glass, floor consolette, black vinyl floormats, intermittent wipers, high-capacity fuel tank (SuperCab), auxiliary power outlets, front and rear mud flaps, painted bumpers, front black spoiler (2WD), black outside mirrors, wheel flares (4WD), heavy-duty gas shock absorbers (4WD), automatic locking front hubs (4WD), front and rear stabilizer bars (4WD), skid plates (4WD), front tow hooks (4WD), 205/75R14SL tires (2WD), 215/75R15SL outline-white-letter all-terrain tires (4WD), full-size spare tire, argent styled steel wheels.

XLT adds: cloth 60/40 split front bench seat, carpeting, AM/FM radio with digital clock (2WD), Light Group (cargo box and map lights), door map pockets, passenger-side visor mirror, cloth door trim panels, cargo-area cover (SuperCab), rear cupholders (SuperCab), behind-seat storage tray, bright bumpers and grille molding, trailer tow wire harness, full-face steel wheels.

Splash adds: 3.0-liter V-6 engine (2WD SuperCab), color-keyed bumpers, grille and power mirrors, bodyside moldings, 235/60R15SL tires (2WD), 235/75R15SL outline-white-letter all-terrain tires (4WD), chrome wheels (2WD), deep-dish alloy wheels (4WD).

Prices are accurate at time of publication; subject to manufacturer's changes.

OPTIONAL EQUIPMENT:

	Retail Price	Dealer Invoice

Major Packages

	Retail Price	Dealer Invoice
XLT Special Value Pkg. 864A, 2WD	$810	$688
Manufacturer's discount price	NC	NC
XLT Special Value Pkg. 864A, 4WD	640	554
Manufacturer's discount price	NC	NC

AM/FM/cassette, XLT Group (sliding rear window, striping, deep-dish alloy wheels), 225/70R14SL outline white-letter tires (2WD), 235/75R15SL outline-white-letter all-terrain tires (4WD).

XLT Luxury Pkg. 867A, 2WD	2975	2529
Manufacturer's discount price	1785	1517
XLT Luxury Pkg. 867A, 4WD	2745	2333
Manufacturer's discount price	1650	1402

Pkg. 864A plus Luxury Group (air conditioning, cruise control, tilt steering wheel, leather-wrapped steering wheel, tachometer [2WD], remote keyless entry, Power Equipment Group, AM/FM/CD player).

Splash Pkg. 866A	480	407
Manufacturer's discount price	240	204

AM/FM/CD player, sliding rear window, bodyside molding. NA regular cab long bed.

Optional Payload Pkg. 2	60	51
4x4 Value Discount, 4WD	(350)	(298)

Credit is applied to 4WD models.

4X4 Off-road Pkg., XLT 4WD	395	336
Manufacturer's discount price	195	166

Painted bumpers and grille, fog lamps, off-road shock absorbers, "4X4 Off-road" decal, 235/70R16SL outline-white-letter all-terrain tires, deep-dish alloy wheels

XLT Appearance Pkg., 2WD	425	362
Manufacturer's discount price	225	192
XLT Appearance Pkg., 4WD	515	438
Manufacturer's discount price	265	226

Two-tone paint, fog lamps (4WD), chrome wheels (2WD), 225/70R15 outline-white-letter tires (2WD), AM/FM/CD player.

Flareside Plus Pkg., XLT 2WD	705	599
Manufacturer's discount price	395	336
Flareside Plus Pkg., XLT 4WD	735	635
Manufacturer's discount price	395	336
Flareside Plus Pkg., XLT 4WD SuperCab with 3.0-liter V-6	735	636
Manufacturer's discount price	NC	NC

Flareside pickup body, fog lamps (4WD), chrome wheels (2WD), 225/70R15 outline-white-letter tires (2WD), AM/FM/CD player, tachometer (2WD).

Power Equipment Group, XLT	535	455
Splash	395	336

Power mirrors, windows, and door locks.

Power Security Group, XLT	810	688
Manufacturer's discount price	535	455
Power Security Group, Splash	670	569
Manufacturer's discount price	395	336

Power Equipment Group, remote keyless entry. XLT Requires Pkg. 864A.

Powertrains

2.5-liter 4-cylinder engine (credit)	(500)	(425)

Credit is applied to those models with the standard 2.5-liter 4-cylinder engine.

3.0-liter V-6, 2WD XL and XLT, 2WD Splash regular cab	450	383
4.0-liter V-6, 2WD XLT, 2WD Splash regular cab	900	765
4WD, 2WD Splash SuperCab	450	383

2WD SuperCab requires tachometer. NA XL.

4-speed automatic transmission	1070	909

Requires 2.5-liter or 3.0-liter engine. NA SuperCab with 2.5-liter 4-cylinder engine.

5-speed automatic transmission	1105	939

NA XL. Requires 4.0-liter engine.

Limited-slip rear axle	270	229

Requires V-6 engine. Includes auxiliary transmission oil cooler.

Safety Features

4-wheel anti-lock brakes, XLT, Splash	500	425

Appearance and Miscellaneous

	Retail Price	Dealer Invoice
Fog lights, XLT	$185	$158

Requires V-6 engine.

Comfort and Convenience

Air conditioning	805	684
Cruise control and tilt steering column, XLT, Splash	395	336

NA with 2.5-liter engine and automatic transmission.

Power mirrors, XLT	140	119
60/40 cloth split bench seat with consolette, XL	290	247

Consolette NA with automatic transmission.

Cloth sport bucket seats w/floor console, XLT, Splash	360	306

XLT requires Pkg. 867A.

6-way power seat, XLT SuperCab with Pkg. 856A, Splash SuperCab	210	178

Splash requires contents of Luxury Group.

Tachometer, XLT 2WD	60	51
Leather-wrapped steering wheel, XLT with Pkg. 867A	50	43

Requires cruise control and tilt steering column

Pivoting privacy quarter windows, SuperCab	60	51

NA XL.

AM/FM radio, XL 2WD	180	153
AM/FM/cassette, 2WD XL	320	273
4WD XL, XLT, Splash	140	119
AM/FM/CD player, XLT w/Pkg. 864A	95	81
AM/FM/cassette/CD player, XLT w/Pkg. 867A, Splash w/Pkg. 866A	135	115

Requires Power Equipment Group, cruise control and tilt steering column.

Remote keyless entry, XLT, Splash	275	233

Requires Power Equipment Group, tachometer.

Appearance and Miscellaneous

Flareside bed, XL, XLT	455	387

4WD requires 235/60R15 tires. 2WD requires 225/70R tires. NA regular cab long bed.

Bodyside moldings, XLT	120	102
Deluxe 2-tone paint, XLT	235	200
Narrow accent tape stripes, XLT	55	47

NA with 2-tone paint.

Special Purpose, Wheels and Tires

Full-face steel wheels, XL	100	85
Chrome wheels, XLT 2WD	290	247
XLT 2WD w/Pkg. 864A or 867A	40	34

Requires 225/70R15SL outline-white-letter tires.

225/70R14SL outline-white-letter-tires, XL 2WD	240	204

Includes temporary spare tire.

225/70R15SL outline-white-letter-tires, XLT 2WD	295	251
XLT 2WD Pkg. 864A or 867A	55	47

Requires chrome wheels

235/75R15SL outline-white-letter all-terrain tires, XL 4WD	70	59
265/75R15SL outline-white-letter all-terrain tires, XLT 4WD	180	153
265/75R15SL outline-white-letter all-terrain tires, XLT 4WD w/Pkg. 864A or 867A	110	93

Includes temporary spare tire. Requires 4.0-liter V-6 engine, 3.73 rear axle ratio. NA regular cab short bed.

FORD TAURUS ✓ BEST BUY

Front-wheel-drive midsize; similar to Mercury Sable

Base price range: $18,245-$28,920. Built in Atlanta, Ga., and Chicago, Ill.

Also consider: Chevrolet Lumina, Honda Accord, Pontiac Grand Prix, Toyota Camry

FOR • Anti-lock brakes • Acceleration (dohc V-6 and SHO) • Steering/handling • Passenger and cargo room

AGAINST • Rear visibility • Ride (SHO)

Taurus relinquished its title as America's best-selling car in 1997, a year after it was redesigned with unorthodox styling. It's now available with rebates and discounts as Ford scrambles to stay with the midsize-class sales-leading Honda Accord and Toyota Camry.

Rating Scale: 5-Excellent; 4-Above average; 3-Average; 2-Below average; 1-Poor

Ford Taurus LX sedan

As with most Fords, the model line is realigned for '98. Lower-rung G and GL models are gone and the line now consists of LX and SE sedans, the SE wagon, and the performance-oriented SHO sedan. All have depowered air bags that deploy with less force and minor appearance and mechanical updates.

All but the SHO come with an overhead-valve 3.0-liter V-6 as standard. The more-powerful double-overhead-cam version is now optional on either the LX or SE; it had been an SE exclusive. The SHO retains its V-8. All models come only with automatic transmission. Anti-lock brakes are standard on the SHO and optional on the others.

Taurus is built from the same design as the Mercury Sable, though they have different styling and Mercury has no V-8 model.

Taurus offers a bench seat or bucket seats up front. The front bench seat has a folding, flip-open center armrest with cupholders and storage space. Bucket seats come with a floor-mounted shift lever. A 2-place rear-facing third seat is optional on wagons.

PERFORMANCE The standard V-6 provides adequate acceleration off the line and acceptable passing power. But it's not a model of refinement, sounding coarse and loud at full throttle, and it doesn't get much help from the transmission. Gear changes are sometimes rough, and it's slow to downshift when called upon to respond in the 40-55 mph range.

The optional double-overhead-cam V-6 runs more smoothly than the base engine and provides more spirited acceleration. The SHO, with its V-8, is quicker still. Fuel economy is nothing special with any engine. We averaged 18.9 mpg with an ohv V-6, 17.1 mpg with a dohc V-6, and 14.3 mpg in an SHO.

All Tauruses take sharp turns with good grip and commendable composure, and the SHO handles like the sport sedan it is. All models are stable at highway speeds, but their suspensions don't absorb bumps well and feel too stiff on pockmarked roads, particularly the SHO. Wind and road noise are well muffled.

ACCOMMODATIONS Taurus has a roomy interior with some innovative features. Front-seat head and leg room are generous. The comfortable rear seat offers enough knee and foot room for 6-footers, but the sloping roof means there's only adequate rear head room.

Analog gauges are before the driver in a conventional instrument pod, but controls for the climate and audio systems are housed in a central dashboard panel. The oval panel is easy to see and reach, but it takes time to sort out all the buttons because so many look alike, and the confusion is worse with the automatic air conditioning option.

The front-bench seat's flip-open armrest is a clever idea, but deploying it blocks access to the power outlet, making it difficult to plug in a cellular phone or other device.

The driver has a clear view to the front and sides, but it's hard to see the trunk in the sedan, and the wagon's narrow rear windows make it hard to parallel park. The sedan's trunk is roomy, and the Taurus and Sable wagons are among the few still offered in the midsize class.

BUILD QUALITY Exterior panels lined up well, and the paint was smooth and glossy on our Taurus test cars. Materials and workmanship in the interior are good, though one test car suffered a chirping squeak from the front passenger door.

VALUE FOR THE MONEY Its styling is controversial, but the roomy, well-made, and enjoyable-to-drive Taurus and Sable are good values and excellent choices among midsize cars. Ford and Mercury are using incentives and discounted leases to promote sales, so there are good deals available.

RATINGS

	LX (ohv V-6)	SE (dohc V-6)	SHO (dohc V-8)
Acceleration	3	4	4
Fuel economy	2	2	2
Ride quality	4	4	3
Steering/handling	4	4	4
Braking	4	4	4
Quietness	4	4	3
Driver seating	4	4	4
Instruments/controls	4	4	4
Room/comfort (front)	4	4	4
Room/comfort (rear)	3	3	3
Cargo room	3	3	3
Value for the money	4	4	3
Total	**44**	**44**	**41**

SPECIFICATIONS

	4-door sedan	4-door wagon
Wheelbase, in.	108.5	108.5
Overall length, in.	197.5	199.6
Overall width, in.	73.0	73.0
Overall height, in.	55.1	57.6
Curb weight, lbs.	3329	3480
Cargo vol., cu. ft.	15.8	81.3
Fuel capacity, gals.	16.0	16.0
Seating capacity	6	8
Front head room, in.	39.2	39.3
Max. front leg room, in.	42.2	42.2
Rear head room, in.	36.2	38.9
Min. rear leg room, in.	38.9	38.5

ENGINES

	ohv V-6	dohc V-6	dohc V-8
Size, liters/cu. in.	3.0/182	3.0/181	3.4/207
Horsepower @ rpm	145@ 5250	200@ 5750	235@ 6100
Torque (lbs./ft.) @ rpm	170@ 3250	200@ 4500	230@ 4800
Availability	S[1]	O[1]	S[2]
EPA city/highway mpg			
4-speed OD automatic	20/28	19/28	17/26

1. LX, SE. 2. SHO.

PRICES

Ford Taurus	Retail Price	Dealer Invoice
LX 4-door sedan	$18245	$16875
SE 4-door sedan	19445	17761
SE 4-door wagon	21105	19239
SE Comfort 4-door sedan	19445	17761
SE Comfort 4-door wagon	21105	19239
SHO 4-door sedan	28920	26194
Destination charge	550	550

SE Comfort requires SE Comfort Group.

STANDARD EQUIPMENT:

LX: 3.0-liter V-6 engine, 4-speed automatic transmission, driver- and passenger-side air bags, air conditioning, variable-assist power steering, tilt steering wheel, 6-passenger seating with dual recliners, front center seating console and cupholders, power windows, power mirrors, visor mirrors, intermittent wipers, rear defogger, AM/FM radio, digital clock, tachometer, coolant-temperature gauge, trip odometer, remote decklid release, tinted glass, 205/65R15 tires, wheel covers.

SE adds: cassette player with six speakers, power antenna (wagon), power door locks, remote keyless entry, 60/40 split/folding rear seat, cruise control, interior air filter, rear wiper/washer (wagon), 4-wheel disc brakes (wagon), luggage rack (wagon).

SHO adds: 3.4-liter DOHC V-8 engine, anti-lock 4-wheel disc brakes, automatic air conditioning, heated power mirrors, leather upholstery, 5-passenger seating with reclining front bucket seats and floor console, 6-way power front seats with driver-side power lumbar support, map pockets, floor shifter, rear air conditioning ducts, illuminated visor mirrors, low fuel warning light, Mach audio system, 6-disc CD changer, power antenna, power moonroof, leather-wrapped steering wheel, Light Group (map lights, courtesy lights), grab handles, automatic headlights, floormats, bodyside cladding, dual exhaust outlets, aerodynamic wipers, theft-deterrent system, rear spoiler, semi-active han-

Prices are accurate at time of publication; subject to manufacturer's changes.

dling suspension, sport variable-assist power steering, overdrive lock-out switch, 225/55ZR16 tires, chrome alloy wheels.

OPTIONAL EQUIPMENT:

	Retail Price	Dealer Invoice
Major Packages		
SE Sport Group, SE sedan	$695	$619
SE Comfort sedan	550	489
Includes 3.0-liter DOHC V-6 engine, 5-passenger seating w/center console and floor shifter, rear spoiler, chrome wheel covers (SE), chrome alloy wheels (SE Comfort).		
SE Comfort Group, SE Comfort sedan	1450	1291
SE Comfort wagon	1285	1144
Includes 3.0-liter DOHC V-6 engine, 5-passenger seating w/center console and floor shifter, power driver seat w/power lumbar support, leather-wrapped steering wheel, automatic air conditioning, power antenna, Light Group (map and courtesy lights), delay-off headlight control, theft-deterrent system, illuminated visor mirrors, alloy wheels.		
Powertrains		
3.0-liter DOHC engine, LX, SE	495	441
Safety Features		
Anti-lock 4-wheel disc brakes, LX, SE, SE Comfort	600	534
Daytime running lights	40	35
Includes heavy-duty battery.		
Comfort and Convenience		
Power door locks, LX	275	245
Heated mirrors, SE, SE Comfort	55	49
Leather upholstery, SE, SE Comfort	895	797
6-passenger seating, SE Comfort	NC	NC
6-way power driver seat, SE	350	312
6-way power passenger seat, SE Comfort	350	312
Rear-facing third seat, wagon	200	178
Integrated child seat, wagon	135	120
NA with leather upholstery.		
Cassette player, LX	185	165
Mach Audio System, SE, SE Comfort	400	356
Includes power antenna.		
6-disc CD changer, SE, SE Comfort	350	312
Voice-activated cellular telephone	725	646
Requires 6-passenger seating. NA SHO, SE Sport Group or with leather upholstery.		
Remote keyless entry, LX	190	169
Power moonroof, SE, SE Comfort	740	658
Includes overhead map lights.		
Light Group, SE	45	40
Map and courtesy lights.		
Wagon Group, wagon	140	124
Cargo area cover and net.		
Floormats, LX, SE, SE Comfort	55	49
Appearance and Miscellaneous		
Engine block heater	35	31
Heavy-duty suspension, wagon	25	23
Full-size spare tire, SE, SE Comfort	125	112
NA on wagon.		
Alloy wheels, LX, SE	315	280
Chrome alloy wheels, SE Comfort, SHO	725	646

FORD WINDSTAR `RECOMMENDED`

Front-wheel-drive minivan

Base price range: $18,010–$29,505. Built in Canada.

Also consider: Chevrolet Venture, Dodge Caravan, Toyota Sienna

FOR • Standard anti-lock brakes • Passenger and cargo room • Ride • Handling

AGAINST • Fuel economy

Ford is playing catch-up after failing to foresee how well the public would take to the dual sliding doors offered on Chrysler Corporation and General Motors minivans. Windstar was designed with only a right-side sliding door, but Ford rushed the 1998 model into showrooms last spring with a wider driver's door to ease rear-seat access. The early '98s also got revised front styling and a new top-line Limited model.

Ford Windstar GL

That one joins base, GL, and LX models, as well as a cargo version that isn't covered in this report. The base and GL come with a 3.0-liter V-6. LX and Limited use a 3.8-liter V-6 that's optional on the GL. Traction control is optional with the 3.8. Both engines use automatic transmission. Maximum towing capacity is 3500 pounds.

Seats for seven are standard; optional configurations include four bucket seats, bench seats that convert to beds, and integrated rear child safety seats. Anti-lock brakes are standard, as are dual air bags; depowered bags that deploy with less force are due later in the model year.

Minivans from Chevrolet, Pontiac, Oldsmobile, Chrysler, Dodge, Plymouth, and now Toyota offer dual sliding side doors. Windstar's wider driver's door is a stopgap measure until the body can be altered to accept a left-side sliding door, which will probably be next year. The new driver's door, standard on all '98s, is six inches longer than the left door. A driver's seat that slides forward when the backrest is tipped is standard on Limited and LX models and optional on the others. The wider door allows passengers to enter from the driver's side and walk to the middle seats.

PERFORMANCE The 3.0-liter V-6 struggles to provide adequate acceleration, making the 3.8 the logical choice. It's got the most horsepower of any minivan engine and furnishes adequate power even with a full load of passengers. It's quieter and smoother than the 3.0, to boot.

Our most-recent LX test vehicle averaged 16.6 mpg in a mix of city and highway driving. That's about par for this class and not significantly thirstier than Windstar's 3.0 V-6.

The longest wheelbase of any minivan combines with an absorbent suspension to deliver a stable, car-like ride at highway speeds and to soak up most bumps without disturbing the occupants. Body lean is moderate and the tires grip well in cornering.

ACCOMMODATIONS A 16-inch step-in height makes it almost as easy to get in or out of Windstar's front seats as in most passenger cars. The tip-slide seat delivers what it promises and the wider driver's door is not so long as to be cumbersome to open. Still, it is less convenient than a driver-side sliding door.

Head room is generous in the front and middle seats and adequate in the rear. There's adult-size leg room in all three rows, though only with the rear seat pushed all the way back on its 7-inch track.

Windstar's audio-system buttons are small and hard to decipher, and the climate controls are a bit low and hard to reach.

A variety of bins, pockets, and cupholders provide ample interior storage. Our test vehicle had the optional floor console, which is roomy but blocks passage to the rear seats.

The middle seats and 3-place rear bench have quick-release latches but are heavy and awkward to maneuver. The rear and middle seatbacks fold flat so cargo can be stored on top of them.

BUILD QUALITY Our test Windstars have been nicely finished inside and out, with neatly applied trim and glass-smooth paint.

VALUE FOR THE MONEY Chrysler's minivans are our Best Buys in this category, but the easy-driving Windstar also is a good choice. Ford has been offering rebates and attractive leases, and dealers should be discounting prices.

Rating Scale: 5-Excellent; 4-Above average; 3-Average; 2-Below average; 1-Poor

CONSUMER GUIDE™

RATINGS

	Base	LX
Acceleration	3	4
Fuel economy	2	2
Ride quality	4	4
Steering/handling	3	3
Braking	4	4
Quietness	4	4
Driver seating	3	3
Instruments/controls	3	3
Room/comfort (front)	4	4
Room/comfort (rear)	5	5
Cargo room	5	5
Value for the money	4	4
Total	**44**	**45**

SPECIFICATIONS

	3-door van
Wheelbase, in.	120.7
Overall length, in.	201.2
Overall width, in.	75.4
Overall height, in.	68.0
Curb weight, lbs.	3762
Cargo vol., cu. ft.	144.0
Fuel capacity, gals.	20.0
Seating capacity	7
Front head room, in.	39.3
Max. front leg room, in.	40.7
Rear head room, in.	38.9
Min. rear leg room, in.	39.2

ENGINES

	ohv V-6	ohv V-6
Size, liters/cu. in.	3.0/182	3.8/232
Horsepower @ rpm	150@ 5000	200@ 5000
Torque (lbs./ft.) @ rpm	172@ 3300	225@ 3000
Availability	S[1]	S[2]
EPA city/highway mpg		
4-speed OD automatic	18/25	17/24

1. Base, GL. 2. LX, Limited; optional, GL.

PRICES

Ford Windstar

	Retail Price	Dealer Invoice
Cargo 3-door van	$18010	$16384
Base 3-door van	19380	17977
GL 3-door van	20960	18980
LX 3-door van	26205	23595
Limited 3-door van	29505	26499
Destination charge	580	580

STANDARD EQUIPMENT:

Cargo: 3.0-liter V-6 engine, 4-speed automatic transmission, driver- and passenger-side air bags, anti-lock brakes, power steering, 2-passenger seating (vinyl high-back front buckets), front passenger area carpeting and cloth headliner, solar-tinted windshield and front door glass, AM/FM radio, intermittent wipers, rear wiper/washer, cupholders, coolant-temperature gauge, front-door map pockets, storage bins, visor mirrors, dual outside mirrors, 20-gallon fuel tank, 215/70R15 tires, full wheel covers.

Base adds: 7-passenger seating (cloth high back bucket seats, 2-place middle seat and 3-place bench seats), rear passenger area carpeting and cloth headliner, 205/70R15 tires.

GL adds: reclining middle bench seat, adjustable rear-seat track.

LX adds: Power Convenience Group (power windows, door locks, and mirrors), Light Group (front map/dome light and glovebox, instrument-panel and engine-compartment lights), 3.8-liter V-6 engine, front air conditioning, low-back front bucket seats with power lumbar adjustment, 6-way power tip-slide driver seat, AM/FM/cassette, tilt steering wheel, cruise control, tachometer, illuminated entry, illuminated visor vanity mirrors, closed cargo bins, map pockets on front seatbacks, cargo net, bodyside molding, 25-gallon fuel tank, 215/70R15 tires, alloy wheels.

Limited adds: rear air conditioning, rear defogger, quad bucket seats, leather upholstery, premium AM/FM/cassette, automatic headlights, remote entry system, electrochromatic rearview mirror, overhead console (includes rear seat radio controls, compass, thermometer, conversation mirror, coin holder, and garage door opener/sunglasses holder), storage drawer under front passenger seat, fog lights, 225/60R16 tires, polished alloy wheels.

OPTIONAL EQUIPMENT:
Major Packages

	Retail Price	Dealer Invoice
Preferred Pkg. 481B, Cargo	$2730	$2320
Manufacturer's discount price	1880	1597

Front air conditioning, cloth reclining high back bucket seats w/underseat storage drawer, cruise control, tilt steering wheel, Power Convenience Group (power windows and door locks, power mirrors), AM/FM/cassette, rear defogger.

Preferred Pkg. 470B, Base	1535	1305
Manufacturer's discount price	1010	859

Front air conditioning, Power Convenience Group (power windows, door locks, and mirrors).

Preferred Pkg. 472B, GL	2480	2108
Manufacturer's discount price	1800	1530

Front air conditioning, tip-slide driver seat, cassette player, cruise control, tilt steering wheel, tachometer, Power Convenience Group (power windows and door locks, power mirrors), rear defogger, bodyside moldings.

Preferred Pkg. 473B, GL	4405	3745
Manufacturer's discount price	3075	2614

Pkg. 472B plus 3.8-liter V-6 engine, rear air conditioning, Light Group (front map/dome light, glovebox light), overhead console, privacy glass, luggage rack.

Preferred Pkg. 477B, LX	2545	2161
Manufacturer's discount price	1580	1340

Rear air conditioning, rear defogger, quad bucket seats, overhead console, privacy glass, front and rear floormats, luggage rack, 2-tone paint, remote entry system.

Preferred Pkg. 479B, Limited	680	578
Manufacturer's discount price	NC	NC

Privacy glass, roof rack, floormats.

Northwoods Appearance Pkg., GL	795	676
LX	285	243

Tan roof rack, green grille and door handles, badging and graphics, special floormats, alloy wheels with tan accents.

Gold Appearance Pkg., LX	235	200
Manufacturer's discount price	NC	NC

Gold-tone badging, gold-tone grille surround and bodyside molding inserts, two-tone paint delete, alloy wheels with gold accents. Requires Pkg. 477B.

Light Group, Base, GL	75	63

Front map/dome light and glovebox light.

Premium Light Group, LX	295	251

Includes fog lamps, automatic headlamps, electrochromatic mirror.

Interior Convenience Group, GL	50	43

Left rear storage bin, covered center bin, cargo net.

Trailer Towing Pkg., GL, LX	435	370
GL or LX with front and rear air conditioning, Limited	410	347

Includes heavy-duty battery, engine-oil and power-steering coolers, auxiliary transmission-oil cooler, trailer wiring-harness, full-size spare tire. NA base.

Security Group, LX, Limited	200	171

Includes programmable garage door opener, theft-deterrent system.

Family Security Pkg., GL	1050	893
Manufacturer's discount price	655	557
Family Security Pkg., LX	875	744
Manufacturer's discount price	480	408

Security Group plus remote keyless entry, self-sealing tires, sport wheel covers.

Powertrains

3.8-liter V-6 engine, Cargo, GL	685	583
Includes tachometer.		
Traction Control, GL, LX, Limited	395	336

Comfort and Convenience

Rear air conditioning, GL	475	404
Includes rear heater. Requires Light Group.		
Rear defogger, Cargo, Base	170	144
Cruise control/tilt steering wheel, Base	375	319

Prices are accurate at time of publication; subject to manufacturer's changes.

	Retail Price	Dealer Invoice
Floor console, GL, LX, Limited	$155	$132
Includes cupholders and covered storage bin. Requires rear air conditioning. GL requires Pkg. 473B.		
Overhead console, GL	100	85
Includes rear seat radio controls, conversation mirror, coin holder, and garage door opener/sunglasses holder). Requires Light Group.		
Remote keyless entry, GL	175	149
Remote entry system and illuminated entry. Requires Power Convenience Group.		
Premium AM/FM/cassette, LX	155	132
Premium AM/FM/CD player, GL, LX	325	276
Limited	170	144
Requires cruise control/tilt steering wheel, Light Group.		
JBL Audio System, LX	665	565
Limited	510	433
LX requires Premium radio.		
Cloth high back bucket seats, GL	615	522
Includes tip-slide driver seat, rear seat bed.		
Low back bucket seats, GL	550	468
Includes two integrated child seats.		
Quad bucket seats, GL	745	633
Quad bucket seats delete, LX (credit)	(625)	(532)
Quad buckets seats included in Pkg. 477B.		
Low back quad bucket seats, GL	1040	884
Includes power driver seat. Requires Pkg. 473B		
Power driver seat, GL	325	277
Requires Pkg. 473B.		
Tip-slide driver seat, Base	150	128
Leather upholstery, LX	865	735
Requires quad bucket seats.		
Integrated child seats (two), Base	285	242
GL	225	191
LX, replacing quad bucket seats (credit)	(285)	(242)

Appearance and Miscellaneous

Luggage rack, GL	175	149
Load-levelling air suspension, LX, Limited	290	247
Requires Power Convenience Group.		
Privacy glass, Cargo, Base, GL	415	352
Cargo requires Preferred Pkg. 481A.		
Alloy wheels, GL	415	352
Includes 215/70R15 tires.		
215/70R15 self-sealing tires, GL, LX	280	238
GL requires alloy wheels.		
Full-size spare tire	110	93

GMC JIMMY

RECOMMENDED

GMC Jimmy SLT 4-Door

Rear- or 4-wheel-drive midsize sport-utility vehicle; similar to Chevrolet Blazer and Oldsmobile Bravada

Base price range: $21,786-$25,855. Built in Moraine, Ohio, and Linden, N.J.

Also consider: Ford Explorer, Jeep Grand Cherokee, Toyota 4Runner

FOR • Standard anti-lock brakes • Acceleration • Passenger and cargo room • Ride

AGAINST • Rear seat comfort • Fuel economy

GMC's trucks are not functionally different from Chevrolet's counterparts, but GMC's goal is to cast them as upscale alter-

natives to their bow-tie brethren. Thus, it will unveil in the Spring a high-zoot luxury Jimmy called the Envoy.

For fall, '98 Jimmys get a revised instrument panel, a restyled front end, and standard 4-wheel anti-lock disc brakes. A passenger-side air bag joins the previously standard driver-side bag and both are depowered to deploy with less force.

Jimmy comes as a 2- or 4-door wagon with a drop-down tailgate with a separate top-hinged window; 4-door models can be equipped with a one-piece liftgate with independently opening window.

Both body styles offer SL and SLS trim, and the 4-door adds SLE and SLT price levels. Exclusive to the Envoy will be a two-tone leather interior, load-leveling suspension, high-intensity headlamps, and GM's OnStar communications system. OnStar links the vehicle by satellite and cellular phone to a 24-hour GM center where advisors provide directions and can notify local authorities in an emergency.

The 4-wheel-drive system is not for use on dry pavement but can be engaged on the fly via a dashboard button. The midsize GMC and Chevy SUVs have been shorn of the previously available permanently engaged 4WD systems, relinquishing that feature to the third member of the family, the Oldsmobile Bravada.

Jimmy's only engine is a 4.3-liter V-6. Automatic transmission is standard, manual is available on 2-door models.

Also new for '98 are available heated mirrors and heated leather seats, audio systems with speed-compensated volume, and an electrochromatic rearview mirror.

PERFORMANCE Ford Explorer and Jeep Grand Cherokee offer V-8 engines, but Jimmy's V-6 is more than adequate for all but the heaviest towing chores. Fuel economy is no bargain. We averaged 16.4 mpg with a 4WD Jimmy in 725 miles of driving, about half of which was on expressways. That's about average for this class.

Jimmy and Blazer do lose ground to Ford and Jeep by no longer offering 4WD that can be used on dry pavement, a convenience available on Explorer and on both the Grand Cherokee and Cherokee.

None of these can match Jimmy and Blazer's overall ride softness, however. The standard suspension easily cushions most bumps, but allows too much bouncing at highway speeds. The "luxury ride" setup available on the 4-door offers the best blend of comfort and control.

ACCOMMODATIONS Jimmys have ample room for four adults, though the front footwells are rather narrow. The rear seatback is short, hard, and uncomfortable. The standard split rear seat folds easily to increase cargo space, but overall cargo room is not as large as an Explorer's. We prefer the liftgate to the tailgate because it makes it easier to reach items in the forward end of the cargo area.

The restyled dashboard has easier-to-use climate controls than the old. Envoy's accommodations are plusher but no more functional than other Jimmys'. Its OnStar system is a good safety plus, but its electronics eat up lots of center-console space.

Step-in height is low, but getting into the rear seat of the 4-door model demands some twisting to negotiate the narrow doorway, and getting in or out of the 2-door's rear seat is a chore.

BUILD QUALITY The 1998 models we've driven were all prototypes, but even they were nicely finished. Earlier versions had too much cheap-looking plastic interior trim; the restyled interiors of the '98s feel richer.

VALUE FOR THE MONEY Jimmy and Envoy earn our recommendation for their ride comfort, strong V-6, and competitive pricing.

RATINGS	2-dr. 4WD	4-dr. 4WD
Acceleration	4	4
Fuel economy	2	2
Ride quality	3	4
Steering/handling	3	3
Braking	3	3
Quietness	3	3
Driver seating	4	4
Instruments/controls	4	4
Room/comfort (front)	4	4
Room/comfort (rear)	2	3
Cargo room	4	5
Value for the money	4	4
Total	**40**	**43**

Rating Scale: 5-Excellent; 4-Above average; 3-Average; 2-Below average; 1-Poor

CONSUMER GUIDE™

SPECIFICATIONS

	2-door wagon	4-door wagon
Wheelbase, in.	100.5	107.0
Overall length, in.	177.3	183.8
Overall width, in.	67.8	67.8
Overall height, in.	64.9	64.2
Curb weight, lbs.	3848	3999
Cargo vol., cu. ft.	66.9	74.1
Maximum payload, lbs.	1002	1329
Fuel capacity, gals.	19.0	18.0
Seating capacity	4	6
Front head room, in.	39.6	39.6
Max. front leg room, in.	42.4	42.4
Rear head room, in.	38.3	38.2
Min. rear leg room, in.	35.6	36.3

ENGINES

	ohv V-6
Size, liters/cu. in.	4.3/262
Horsepower @ rpm	190@ 4400
Torque (lbs./ft.) @ rpm	250@ 2800
Availability	S
EPA city/highway mpg	
4-speed OD automatic	16/21
5-speed OD manual	17/23

PRICES

GMC Jimmy

	Retail Price	Dealer Invoice
2-door wagon, 2WD	$21786	$19716
2-door wagon, 4WD	23774	21515
4-door wagon, 2WD	23867	21600
4-door wagon, 4WD	25855	23399
Destination charge	515	515

STANDARD EQUIPMENT:

2-door: 4.3-liter V-6 engine, 4-speed automatic transmission, 4-wheel disc anti-lock brakes, driver-side air bag, daytime running lights, air conditioning, power steering, reclining cloth front bucket seats with lumbar adjusters, storage console with cupholders, split folding rear 3-passenger bench seat, coolant-temperature and oil-pressure gauges, tachometer, voltmeter, trip odometer, AM/FM radio, digital clock, illuminated entry, intermittent wipers, passenger-side visor mirror, floormats, Passlock theft-deterrent system, dual outside manual mirrors, rear tailgate, tinted glass, 205/75R15 tires, wheel trim rings.

4WD models add: part-time 4WD with electronic transfer case, front tow hooks.

4-door adds: full-size spare tire, 6-wire tailering harness, deletes console with storage and cupholders.

4WD models add: part-time 4WD with electronic transfer case, front tow hooks.

OPTIONAL EQUIPMENT:

Major Packages

	Retail Price	Dealer Invoice
SLS Sport Pkg. 2, 2-door	2776	2387
Manufacturer's discount price	1376	1183

Includes cassette player, power windows and door locks, power mirrors, cruise control, tilt steering wheel, leather-wrapped steering wheel, cloth door-trim panels, reading lamps, cargo net, auxiliary power outlets, illuminated visor mirrors, power remote tailgate release, rear defogger, intermittent rear wiper/washer, striping, deep-tinted tailgate glass, roof rack, alloy wheels, Euro-Ride Suspension Pkg., 235/70R15 tires.

SLS Pkg. 4, 4-door	2645	2275
Manufacturer's discount price	1245	1071

SLS Sport Pkg. 2 plus floor console, cupholders, cargo cover, rear liftgate, Luxury Ride Suspension

SLE Pkg. 5, 4-door	3679	3164
Manufacturer's discount price	2279	1960

SLS Pkg. 4 plus remote keyless entry, 6-way power driver seat, cassette player with automatic tone control, floor shift, overhead console, bodyside moldings.

SLT Pkg. 6, 4-door 4WD	4877	4194
Manufacturer's discount price	3477	2990

SLE Pkg. 5 plus automatic temperature control, leather upholstery, bucket seats, automatic day/night rearview mirror, fog lights.

	Retail Price	Dealer Invoice
Convenience Pkg. ZQ3	$395	$340

Cruise control, tilt steering wheel.

Convenience Pkg. ZQ6, 2-door	535	460
4-door	710	611

Power windows, mirrors, and door locks.

Rear Window Convenience Pkg. ZM8	322	277

Power remote tailgate/liftgate release, rear defogger, rear wiper/washer.

Heavy-duty trailering equipment	210	181

Weight distributing hitch platform, 8-lead wiring harness, heavy-duty flasher.

Powertrains

5-speed manual transmission, 2-door (credit)	(890)	(765)
Optional axle ratio	NC	NC
Locking differential	252	217

Comfort and Convenience

Power glass sunroof	695	598

Requires overhead console.

6-way power driver seat and remote keyless entry, SLS, SLE	390	335
Heated front seats, 4-door	225	194

Requires SLT Pkg.

Overhead console	147	126

Includes reading lights, outside-temperature gauge, compass. Requires SLS Pkg.

Cassette player	122	105
Cassette player with automatic tone control	80	69

Requires SLS Pkg.

Cassette player with equalizer, SLS, SLE	205	176
CD player, SLS, SLE, SLT	180	155
CD/cassette player, 2-door	280	241

Requires SLS Pkg.

Homelink universal garage-door opener	130	112

Includes trip computer. Requires overhead console.

Cargo cover, 4WD 2-door	69	59

Requires SLS Pkg., exterior spare-tire carrier.

Heated power mirrors	115	99

Includes automatic day/night rearview mirror.

Appearance and Miscellaneous

Roof rack	126	108
Fog lights w/air deflector, 2WD 2-door, 4-door	115	99

Requires option pkg.

Two-tone paint, 4-door	172	148

Requires SLE or SLT Pkgs.

Heavy-duty battery	56	48
Cold Climate Pkg.	89	77

Heavy-duty battery, engine-block heater.

Special Purpose, Wheels and Tires

Shield Pkg., 4WD	126	108

Front differential skid plates, transfer-case, steering-linkage and fuel-tank shields.

Smooth Ride Suspension Pkg., 4-door with option pkg.	114	98

Gas shock absorbers, front and rear stabilizer bars. Requires 205/75R15 tires.

Luxury Ride Suspension Pkg., 4-door	197	169

Gas shock absorbers, urethane jounce bumpers, front and rear stabilizer bars. Requires 235/75R15 tires.

Solid Smooth Ride Suspension Pkg., 2-door with Pkg. 2	114	98

Gas shock absorbers, urethane jounce bumpers, front and rear stabilizer bars, upgraded rear springs. Requires 205/75R15 tires.

Euro-Ride Suspension Pkg.	197	169

Gas shock absorbers, front and rear stabilizer bars, heavy-duty springs. Requires 235/70R15 tires.

Off-Road Suspension Pkg., 2-door 4WD	244	210

Gas shock absorbers, urethane jounce bumpers, front and rear stabilizer bars, upgraded torsion bars. Requires 235/75R15 on/off-road white-letter tires.

205/75R15 all-season white-letter tires	121	104
235/70R15 all-season tires	192	165
235/70R15 all-season white-letter tires	325	280

Prices are accurate at time of publication; subject to manufacturer's changes.

	Retail Price	Dealer Invoice
235/75R15 on/off-road white-letter tires,		
2-door 4WD	$335	$288
4-door 4WD	410	353
2-door includes full-size spare tire. 2-door requires exterior spare-tire carrier. Requires Euro-Ride or Off-Road Suspension Pkg.		
Exterior spare-tire carrier,		
2-door 4WD	159	137
Alloy wheels, 4WD	280	241

GMC SAFARI

GMC Safari SLE

Rear- or 4-wheel-drive minivan; similar to Chevrolet Astro

Base price range: $19,404-$22,438. Built in Baltimore, Md.

Also consider: Chevrolet Venture, Ford Windstar, Plymouth Voyager

FOR • Standard anti-lock brakes • Passenger and cargo room • Trailer towing capability

AGAINST • Fuel economy • Entry/exit • Ride

With the demise of Ford's Aerostar for 1998, Safari and its Chevrolet Astro twin are the only domestic rear-drive truck-based minivans. Safari and Astro are larger inside than front-drive minivan rivals, and their big V-6 engines allow more towing capacity. Both come in passenger and cargo versions.

Safari changes little for '98. It's available with rear-wheel drive or permanently engaged all-wheel drive. It comes in a single body length with a passenger-side sliding door and a choice of two side-hinged rear doors or swing-out rear "Dutch" doors with a separate liftgate that swings up.

Dual air bags, anti-lock brakes, and daytime running lights are standard. Unlike most GM products, Safari doesn't get depowered air bags this year; they're expected for 1999.

Five-passenger seating is standard. Seats for up to eight are optional. Child safety seats that fold from the middle-row seats are optional, and leather upholstery is a new option with the top-line Safari SLT package.

The sole powertrain consists of a 4.3-liter V-6 and automatic transmission.

Safari performance and accommodations match those of similarly equipped Astros.

See the Chevrolet Astro for an evaluation of the Safari.

RATINGS

	SLX 2WD
Acceleration	4
Fuel economy	1
Ride quality	3
Steering/handling	3
Braking	3
Quietness	3
Driver seating	3
Instruments/controls	4
Room/comfort (front)	3
Room/comfort (rear)	4
Cargo room	5
Value for the money	3
Total	39

SPECIFICATIONS

	3-door van
Wheelbase, in.	111.2
Overall length, in.	189.8
Overall width, in.	77.5
Overall height, in.	75.0
Curb weight, lbs.	4185
Cargo vol., cu. ft.	170.4
Maximum payload, lbs.	1764
Fuel capacity, gals.	25.0
Seating capacity	8
Front head room, in.	39.2
Max. front leg room, in.	41.6
Rear head room, in.	37.9
Min. rear leg room, in.	36.5

ENGINES

	ohv V-6
Size, liters/cu. in.	4.3/262
Horsepower @ rpm	190@ 4400
Torque (lbs./ft.) @ rpm	250@ 2800
Availability	S
EPA city/highway mpg	
4-speed OD automatic	16/21

PRICES

GMC Safari	Retail Price	Dealer Invoice
SL 3-door Cargo van	$19404	$17561
SL AWD 3-door Cargo van	21804	19733
SLX 3-door van	20138	18225
SLX AWD 3-door van	22438	20306
Destination charge	585	585

AWD denotes all-wheel drive.

STANDARD EQUIPMENT:

SL cargo: 4.3-liter V-6 engine, 4-speed automatic transmission, anti-lock brakes, driver- and passenger-side air bags, daytime running lights, power steering, air conditioning, 2-passenger seating (front reclining vinyl bucket seats), rubber floor covering, front cloth headliner, trip odometer, voltmeter, coolant-temperature and oil-pressure gauges, intermittent wipers, remote fuel-door release, auxiliary power outlets, Passlock theft-deterrent system, rear cargo doors, 6-wire trailering harness, tinted glass, dual outside mirrors, 215/75R15 tires, hub caps.

AWD adds permanent 4-wheel drive.

SLX adds: 5-passenger seating (3-passenger center bench seat), front and rear cupholders, carpeting, full cloth headliner, AM/FM radio, digital clock, visor mirrors, storage bin.

AWD adds: permanent 4-wheel drive.

OPTIONAL EQUIPMENT:
Major Packages

	Retail	Dealer
SLX Option Pkg. 2, SLX	2136	1837
Manufacturer's discount price	1536	1321

Tilt steering wheel, cruise control, 8-passenger seating, (Seat Pkg. front inboard/outboard armrests, manual lumbar support, map pocket), power door locks, power windows, reading lights, cargo net, chrome accent grille, bodyside moldings, panel doors, deep-tinted glass, silver styled wheels.

SLE Option Pkg. 3, SLX	3395	2920
Manufacturer's discount price	2695	2318

SLX Option Pkg. 2 plus custom cloth trim, cassette player with automatic tone control, floormats, swing-out rear door glass, lower bodyside cladding.

SLE Option Pkg. 4, SLX	4184	3598
Manufacturer's discount price	3484	2996

SLE Option Pkg. 3 plus remote-keyless entry, 6-way power driver seat, overhead console, illuminated visor mirrors, under passenger seat storage compartment, roof rack, alloy wheels.

SLT Option Pkg. 5, SLX	5799	4987
Manufacturer's discount price	4999	4299

SLE Option Pkg. 4 plus special cloth upholstery, leather-wrapped steering wheel, CD player with automatic tone control, fold-down center console, additional cupholders, power mirrors.

Rating Scale: 5-Excellent; 4-Above average; 3-Average; 2-Below average; 1-Poor

	Retail Price	Dealer Invoice
Convenience Pkg. ZQ2, SL	$474	$408
Power door locks, power windows.		
Convenience Pkg. ZQ3, SL	383	329
Tilt steering wheel, cruise control.		
Trailer towing equipment	309	266
Platform hitch, 8-lead wiring harness.		

Powertrains

Locking differential	252	217

Safety Features

Dual integrated child seats.................................	240	206
NA with 7-passenger seating or SLT Option Pkg.		

Comfort and Convenience

Rear air conditioning, SLX	523	450
Rear heater	205	176
Rear defogger	154	132
Requires rear liftgate.		
7-passenger seating, SLX	969	833
w/SLE Pkg.	318	273
Front reclining bucket seats w/lumbar support and armrests, middle bucket seats, split folding reclining rear bench seat w/armrests, rear headrests. SLX includes Seat Pkg.		
8-passenger seating, SLX	395	340
Cloth upholstery, front reclining bucket seats w/lumbar support and armrests, center and rear bench seats.		
6-way power driver seat, SLX	240	206
Requires Option Pkg. 2 or 3. NA with vinyl upholstery.		
Power passenger seat, SLX	240	206
Requires 6-way power driver seat. NA with vinyl upholstery. Deletes storage compartment under passenger seat.		
Seat Pkg.	168	144
Front armrests, front lumbar support, map pocket. Requires Option Pkg. 2. NA with vinyl upholstery.		
Cloth upholstery	NC	NC
Leather upholstery, w/SLT Pkg...........................	950	817
Power door locks..	223	192
Remote keyless entry...	150	129
Requires power door locks.		
Power mirrors, SLX	98	84
Requires Option Pkg. 2.		
AM/FM cassette	147	126
Upgraded AM/FM/cassette..................................	307	264
Includes anti-theft feature, speed volume control, auto tone control. SL requires Convenience Pkg. ZQ2. SLX requires option pkg.		
AM/FM/CD player..	407	350
Includes anti-theft feature, speed volume control, auto tone control. SL requires Convenience Pkg. ZQ2. SLX requires option pkg.		
AM/FM/cassette/CD player	507	436
Includes anti-theft feature, speed volume control, auto tone control. SL requires Convenience Pkg. ZQ2. SLX requires option pkg.		
Rear headphone jacks/radio controls, SLX............	125	108
Requires SLE or SLT Pkg.		
Universal garage-door opener	115	99
Requires option pkg. 4 or 5.		
Leather-wrapped steering wheel, w/SLE Pkg.	54	46

Appearance and Miscellaneous

Rear liftgate...	364	313
w/SLE/SLT Pkg.	305	262
Includes dutch doors, rear wiper/washer and remote liftgate release. Requires power door locks.		
Bodyside moldings	121	104
Luggage rack...	126	108
Deep-tinted glass, SLX	290	249
SL	262	225
Complete body glass, SL	368	316
Ride/Handling Suspension, SLX 2WD	306	263
Gas shocks, rear stabilizer bar, 235/65R15 white outlined tires.		
Alloy wheels, SLX	365	314
w/SLE Pkg.	273	235
Chrome-appearance styled wheels........................	340	292
w/SLE Pkg.	248	213
NA with upgraded suspension on SLT.		

GMC SIERRA 1500

RECOMMENDED

GMC Sierra K1500 SLT extended cab

Rear- or 4-wheel-drive pickup; similar to Chevrolet C/K1500

Base price range: $15,000-$26,169. Built in Ft. Wayne, Ind; Pontiac, Mich.; and Canada.

Also consider: Dodge Ram 1500, Ford F-150, Toyota T100

FOR • Standard anti-lock brakes • Acceleration (V-8 engines) • Cargo and towing ability

AGAINST • Fuel economy (V-8 engines) • Ride quality

There are only minor changes to the Sierra, GMC's full-size pickup and a twin of the Chevrolet C/K pickup. For 1998, the standard dual air bags are depowered units that deploy with less force.

Sierra comes in regular-cab form or as an extended cab that can be ordered with a passenger-side third door. Cargo beds come in 6.5- and 8-foot lengths. The slab-side box is called Wideside, the flared-fender bed is the Sportside and comes only in the shorter length.

Three series are offered, with designations based on payload capacity: 1500 for a half-ton rating, 2500 for a three-quarter-ton rating, and 3500 for a one-ton rating. This report covers only the 1500 series.

SL, SLE, and SLT are the trim levels. All come with a 3-place front bench seat. Cloth front buckets are optional on the SLE, with leather buckets optional on the SLT. Extended-cab models have a standard 3-place rear bench for 6-passenger capacity.

Anti-lock brakes and daytime running lights are standard. Four engines are offered: a 4.3-liter V-6; 5.0- and 5.7-liter V 8s; and a 6.5-liter turbocharged diesel V-8 that's offered only with 4WD.

The 4WD models have General Motors' Insta-Trac on-demand 4WD, a part-time system (not for use on dry pavement) with shift-on-the-fly. An electronic transfer case operated by dashboard buttons is optional in place of the standard floor-mounted transfer-case lever.

Manual transmission is standard with all engines and automatic is optional. Maximum towing weight on the 1500 series is 7000 pounds.

Sierra duplicates the performance and accommodations of the Chevrolet C/K series pickup trucks.

See the Chevrolet C/K report for an evaluation of the Sierra 1500.

RATINGS	Reg. cab V-6	Ext. cab 5.7 V-8
Acceleration	3	4
Fuel economy	2	1
Ride quality	2	2
Steering/handling	2	2
Braking	3	3
Quietness	3	3
Driver seating	4	4
Instruments/controls	4	4
Room/comfort (front)	5	5
Room/comfort (rear)	—	2
Cargo room	1	3
Value for the money	4	4
Total	33	37

SPECIFICATIONS	Reg. cab short bed	Reg. cab long bed	Ext. cab short bed	Ext. cab long bed
Wheelbase, in.	117.5	131.5	141.5	155.5
Overall length, in.	194.5	213.4	218.5	237.4
Overall width, in.	76.8	76.8	76.8	76.8
Overall height, in.	70.8	70.0	70.8	70.1
Curb weight, lbs.	3869	4021	4160	4407
Maximum payload, lbs. ...	2231	2079	2040	1793
Fuel capacity, gals.	25.0	34.0	25.0	34.0

Prices are accurate at time of publication; subject to manufacturer's changes.

	Reg. cab short bed	Reg. cab long bed	Ext. cab short bed	Ext. cab long bed
Seating capacity	3	3	6	6
Front head room, in.	40.0	40.0	40.0	40.0
Max. front leg room, in. ...	41.5	41.5	41.5	41.5
Rear head room, in.	—	—	38.0	40.0
Min. rear leg room, in.	—	—	28.7	28.7

ENGINES

	ohv V-6	ohv V-8	ohv V-8	Turbodiesel ohv V-8
Size, liters/cu. in.	4.3/262	5.0/306	5.7/350	6.5/400
Horsepower @ rpm	200@ 4400	230@ 4600	255@ 4600	180@ 3400
Torque (lbs./ft.) @ rpm	255@ 2800	285@ 2800	330@ 2800	360@ 1800
Availability	S	O	O	O

EPA city/highway mpg

4-speed OD automatic.....	16/20	15/20	14/19	15/19
5-speed OD manual	17/23	15/20	14/19	NA

PRICES

GMC Sierra 1500

	Retail Price	Dealer Invoice
C Special Wideside regular cab, short bed	$15000	$13575
C Special Wideside regular cab, long bed	15320	13865
C SL Wideside regular cab, short bed	16425	14372
C SL Wideside regular cab, long bed	16725	14634
C SL Sportside regular cab, short bed	17000	14875
K Special regular cab, short bed	18700	16924
K Special regular cab, long bed	19020	17213
K SL Wideside regular cab, short bed	19425	16997
K SL Wideside regular cab, long bed	19725	17259
K SL Sportside regular cab, short bed	20000	17500
C SL Wideside extended cab, short bed	18425	16122
C SL Wideside extended cab, long bed	19220	16818
C SLE Sportside extended cab, short bed	23169	20272
K SL Wideside extended cab, short bed	21425	18747
K SL Wideside extended cab, long bed	22220	19443
K SL Sportside extended cab, short bed	26169	22898
Destination charge	625	625

C denotes 2WD; K denotes 4WD.

STANDARD EQUIPMENT:

Special: 4.3-liter V-6 engine (regular cab, extended cab short bed), 5.0-liter V-8 engine (extended cab long bed), 5-speed manual transmission, anti-lock brakes, driver- and passenger-side air bags, daytime running lamps, variable-assist power steering, folding 3-passenger vinyl bench seat (regular cab), 60/40 split-folding 3-passenger vinyl front bench seat (extended cab), folding 3-passenger vinyl rear bench seat (extended cab), cupholders, tachometer, coolant-temperature and oil-pressure gauges, voltmeter, trip odometer, AM/FM radio, digital clock, swing-out rear quarter windows (extended cab), rear heater ducts (extended cab), intermittent wipers, passenger-side visor mirror, reading lamps, auxiliary power outlets, black vinyl floor covering, underhood storage compartment, chrome front bumper, Passlock theft-deterrent system, dual outside mirrors, tinted glass, 8-lead trailer wiring harness, full-size spare tire, 235/75R15 tires.

K models add: 4-wheel drive w/2-speed transfer case, front tow hooks, 245/75R16 tires.

SL adds: color-keyed vinyl floor covering, color-keyed cloth headliner, passenger assist handle.

K models add: 4-wheel drive w/2-speed transfer case, front tow hooks, 245/75R16 tires.

SLE Sportside extended cab adds: 5.0-liter V-8 engine, 4-speed automatic transmission, SLE Decor (air conditioning, tilt steering wheel, cruise control, power windows, power door locks, power mirrors, cassette player, leather-wrapped steering wheel, storage tray, carpeting, front bumper rub strip, chrome rear step bumper, color-keyed grille, dual note horn, black bodyside moldings, bright wheel opening moldings, floormats, wheel trim rings).

K models add: 4-wheel drive w/2-speed transfer case, front tow hooks, 245/75R16 tires.

OPTIONAL EQUIPMENT:
Major Packages

	Retail Price	Dealer Invoice
SL Marketing Option Pkg. 2, SL..............................	1337	1150
Manufacturer's discount price, w/manual transmission	$337	$290
w/automatic transmission	837	720
Air conditioning, cassette player, cruise control, tilt steering wheel.		
SLE Marketing Option Pkg. 3, SL.............................	3036	2611
Manufacturer's discount price, w/manual transmission	1786	1536
w/automatic transmission	2286	1966

SLE Decor (air conditioning, tilt steering wheel, cruise control, power windows and door locks, cassette player, leather-wrapped steering wheel, power mirrors, storage tray, carpeting, front-bumper rub strip, chrome rear step bumper, color-keyed grille, dual-note horn, black body-side moldings, bright wheel-opening moldings, front floormats [regular cab], front and rear floormats [extended cab], wheel trim rings).

SLT Marketing Option Pkg. 4, SL regular cab.........	4970	4119
Manufacturer's discount price	4040	3474
SLT Marketing Option Pkg. 4, SL extended cab	4856	4176
Manufacturer's discount price	4106	3531

SLT Decor (SLE Decor plus 60/40 split bench seat, power lumbar support adjusters, 6-speaker cassette with automatic tone control, floor console, leather upholstery), remote keyless entry, 6-way power driver seat (extended cab), alloy wheels.

Image Max Pkg. and SLE Decor, SL extended cab short bed.................................	5541	4765
Manufacturer's discount price	4791	4121

5.7-liter V-8 engine, 4-speed automatic transmission, alloy wheels, SLE Decor (air conditioning, tilt steering wheel, cruise control, power windows and door locks, cassette player, leather-wrapped steering wheel, power mirrors, storage tray, carpeting, front-bumper rub strip, chrome rear step bumper, color-keyed grille, dual-note horn, black bodyside moldings, bright wheel-opening moldings, front and rear floormats, wheel trim rings).

Image Max Pkg. and SLT Decor, SL extended cab short bed.................................	7021	6038
Manufacturer's discount price	6271	5393

5.7-liter V-8 engine, 4-speed automatic transmission, alloy wheels, SLT Decor (SLE Decor plus 60/40 split bench seat, power lumbar support adjusters, 6-speaker cassette player with automatic tone control, floor console, leather upholstery), remote keyless entry, 6-way power driver seat, alloy wheels.

Value Max Pkg., SL Wideside regular cab..............	1875	1613
Manufacturer's discount price, w/manual transmission	675	581
w/automatic transmission	1175	1011
Value Max Pkg., SL Sportside regular cab	1844	1586
Manufacturer's discount price, w/manual transmission	644	554
w/automatic transmission	1144	984

Air conditioning, cruise control, cassette player, tilt steering, Bright Appearance Group, color-keyed carpeting. NA w/5.7-liter engine. 5.0-liter engine requires automatic transmission.

Deluxe Front Appearance Pkg.	191	164

Color-keyed grille, composite halogen headlights, dual horns. NA Special.

Bright Appearance Group, Wideside.......................	413	355
Manufacturer's discount price	283	243
Bright Appearance Group, Sportside......................	452	389
Manufacturer's discount price	252	217

Deluxe Front Appearance Pkg., front-bumper rub strip, chrome rear step bumper, bodyside and wheel opening moldings, rally wheel trim. NA Special, SLE, or SLT Decor.

Convenience Group ZQ3	385	331

Cruise control, tilt steering column.

Off-Road Chassis Pkg., K......................................	270	232

Bilstein gas shock absorbers, skid plates. NA with 5.0-liter engine when ordered w/4-speed automatic transmission, Heavy-Duty Trailering Equipment, and std. 3.42 rear-axle ratio. NA with 245/75R16 all-terrain tires, 245/75R16 all-terrain outline-white-letter tires. Requires SLE or SLT Decor.

Heavy Duty Trailering Equipment............................	204	175
ordered w/Snow Plow Prep Pkg. or Off-Road Chassis Pkg.	164	141

Trailer hitch, wiring harness, Bilstein shock absorbers (except with Snow Plow or Off-Road Pkgs). Long bed models require rear step bumper. Requires automatic transmission. Requires engine-oil cooler when ordered with 4.3-, 5.0-, and 5.7-liter engines and standard axle ratio. NA Special, GT Pkg. NA with 5.0-liter engine when ordered w/4-speed automatic transmission, Off-Road Chassis, and std. 3.42 rear-axle ratio.

Rating Scale: 5-Excellent; 4-Above average; 3-Average; 2-Below average; 1-Poor

CONSUMER GUIDE™

Powertrains

	Retail Price	Dealer Invoice
5.0-liter V-8 engine (std. extended cab long bed, extended cab Sportside)	$495	$426
NA Special.		
5.7-liter V-8 engine	1195	1028
extended cab long bed	700	602
NA Special.		
6.5-liter V-8 turbodiesel engine,		
K Wideside extended cab short bed	4055	3487
K extended cab long bed	3560	3062
Includes heavy-duty chassis. Deletes underhood storage compartment.		
4-speed automatic transmission	970	834
Std. Sportside extended cab.		
Heavy-duty 4-speed automatic transmission, K	970	834
Includes heavy-duty transmission oil cooler. Requires 6.5-liter V-8 turbodiesel engine. NA regular cab short bed.		
Heavy-duty 5-speed manual transmission	NC	NC
Manufacturer's discount price, (credit)	(500)	(430)
NA Sportside extended cab.		
3.08 rear-axle ratio, C	NC	NC
Electronic transfer case, K	150	129
Requires automatic transmission, Convenience Group ZQ3.		
Locking differential	252	217
NA with 3.08 rear-axle ratio.		

Comfort and Convenience

	Retail Price	Dealer Invoice
OnStar System	895	761
Includes Global Positioning System, voice-activated cellular telephone, roadside assistance, emergency services. Requires dealer installation charge, and monthly service charges.		
Air conditioning	805	692
Power driver seat, extended cab	240	206
Requires SLE Decor, and 60/40 split bench seat or front highback reclining buckets seats.		
Custom cloth 60/40 split bench seat,		
regular cab w/SLE Decor	174	150
extended cab w/SLE Decor	NC	NC
Includes center armrest, power lumbar adjusters, seatback storage pockets.		
Front reclining highback bucket seats,		
extended cab w/SLE or SLT Decor	270	232
regular cab w/SLE Decor	386	332
Includes center console, inboard armrests, power lumbar support, seatback storage pockets. Requires cloth upholstery. NA regular cab with SLT Marketing Option Pkg. 4.		
Automatic day/night rearview mirror, SLT	145	125
Includes compass.		
Power door locks	156	134
Cassette player	147	126
Cassette player w/automatic tone control	90	77
Requires SLE Decor.		
CD player w/automatic tone control	190	163
Requires SLE or SLT Decor.		
CD/cassette player w/automatic tone control	290	249
Requires SLE or SLT Decor. Requires 4-speed automatic transmission.		
Rear defogger, extended cab	154	132
Requires SLE or SLT Decor.		
Remote keyless entry	150	129
Requires SLE Decor.		

Appearance and Miscellaneous

	Retail Price	Dealer Invoice
Third door, extended cab short bed, SLE, SLT	420	361
Requires automatic transmission and 5.0- or 5.7-liter V-8 engine.		
2-tone paint	190	163
Requires SLE or SLT Decor.		
Chrome rear step bumper	99	85
Requires front-bumper rub strip. NA Special.		
Deep-tinted glass, regular cab	35	30
extended cab	107	92
extended cab w/rear defogger	72	62
Regular cab requires sliding rear window.		
Sliding rear window	115	99
NA with rear defogger.		
Bedliner	225	194
NA Sportside.		

Special Purpose Wheels and Tires

	Retail Price	Dealer Invoice
Auxiliary heavy-duty battery	$134	$115
Requires 5.0- or 5.7-liter engine.		
Engine-oil cooler	135	116
Requires gasoline engine and 3.08 or 3.42 rear axle ratio.		
Heavy-duty transmission-oil cooler	96	83
Requires 4-speed automatic transmission and 5.7- or 6.5-liter engine.		
Heavy-duty chassis, K extended cab	230	198
Skid plates, K	95	82
Heavy-duty shock absorbers	40	34
NA with Off-Road Chassis Pkg.		
Bilstein gas shock absorbers, C	225	194
Alloy wheels, SL	400	344
Chrome wheels, C	310	267
ordered w/SLE or SLT Decor, ordered w/ Bright Appearance Group	250	215
NA Special.		
235/75R15 white-letter tires, C, each axle	50	43
NA Special.		
245/75R16 all-terrain outline-white-letter tires, K each axle	50	43
265/75R16 all-terrain tires, K	54	46
Requires alloy wheels.		
245/75R16 on/off-road outline-white-letter tires, K extended cab each axle	72	62
Alloy wheels, ordered w/SLE Decor, ordered w/Bright Appearance Group	340	292
NA Special.		

GMC Sonoma SLS Sportside extended cab

Rear- or 4-wheel-drive pickup; similar to Chevrolet S-10 and Isuzu Hombre

Base price range: (1997 model) $11,617-$19,864. Built in Linden, N.J., and Shreveport, La.

Also consider: Dodge Dakota, Ford Ranger

FOR • Standard anti-lock brakes • Acceleration (V-6) • Handling • Optional third door

AGAINST • Rear seat room (extended cab)

Sonoma gets a mild facelift, a restyled dashboard, and several minor refinements for 1998, many intended to support GMC's efforts to project a sportier, more upscale impage for its vehicles. The new dashboard adds a passenger-side air bag to the already-standard driver-side bag. Both are depowered units that deploy with less force. The Sonoma is mechanical twin of the Chevrolet S10, while Isuzu sells a version of these trucks as the Hombre.

Regular- and extended-cab Sonomas are available, with a driver-side rear door optional on extended-cabs. Cargo beds measuring 6- and 7.5-feet long are offered. The short bed comes in both Wideside and flare-fendered Sportside styling; the long bed is a Wideside only.

A 3-place bench seat is standard and front buckets are optional. Extended-cab models add two rear jump seats; the left-side jump seat is eliminated on models with the third door.

The base engine is a 2.2-liter 4-cylinder. A 4.3-liter V-6 is standard on 4WD models and optional on 2WD models. Manual transmission is standard, automatic is optional. Maximum towing capacity is 6000 pounds.

Sonoma 4x4s use GM's Insta-Trac, a 4WD system that's not for use on dry pavement but can be shifted between 2WD and

Prices are accurate at time of publication; subject to manufacturer's changes.

4-High at any speed via a dashboard switch.

Sonoma's performance and accommodations mirror those of similiarly equipped Chevy S-10s.

See the Chevrolet S-10 report for an evaluation of the Sonoma.

RATINGS

	Reg. cab 4-cyl. 2WD	Ext. cab V-6 4WD
Acceleration	3	4
Fuel economy	3	2
Ride quality	3	3
Steering/handling	3	3
Braking	3	4
Quietness	3	3
Driver seating	4	4
Instruments/controls	4	4
Room/comfort (front)	3	5
Room/comfort (rear)	—	2
Cargo room	1	2
Value for the money	4	3
Total	**34**	**39**

SPECIFICATIONS

	Short bed	Long bed	Ext. cab short bed
Wheelbase, in.	108.3	117.9	122.9
Overall length, in.	189.0	205.0	203.7
Overall width, in.	67.9	67.9	67.9
Overall height, in.	63.2	62.1	63.9
Curb weight, lbs.	3029	3091	3232
Cargo vol., cu. ft.	—	—	—
Maximum payload, lbs.	1171	1509	1168
Fuel capacity, gals.	19.0	19.0	19.0
Seating capacity	3	3	5
Front head room, in.	39.5	39.5	39.5
Max. front leg room, in.	42.4	42.4	42.4
Rear head room, in.	—	—	NA
Min. rear leg room, in.	—	—	NA

ENGINES

	ohv I-4	ohv V-6	ohv V-6
Size, liters/cu. in.	2.2/134	4.3/262	4.3/262
Horsepower @ rpm	120@ 5000	175@ 4400[1]	180@ 4400[2]
Torque (lbs./ft.) @ rpm	140@ 3600	240@ 2800	245@ 2800
Availability	S	O[3]	O
EPA city/highway mpg			
4-speed OD automatic	20/27	17/22	17/22
5-speed OD manual	23/30	17/23	17/23

1. 180 with 4WD. 2. 190 with 4WD. 3. Standard on 4WD models.

PRICES

1997 GMC Sonoma

	Retail Price	Dealer Invoice
2WD SL Wideside regular cab, short bed	$11617	$10978
2WD SLS Wideside regular cab, short bed	12714	11506
2WD SLS Sportside regular cab, short bed	13164	11913
2WD SL Wideside regular cab, long bed	11917	11262
2WD SLS Wideside regular cab, long bed	13014	11778
4WD SL Wideside regular cab, short bed	16367	15467
4WD SLS Wideside regular cab, short bed	17514	15850
4WD SLS Sportside regular cab, short bed	17964	16257
4WD SL Wideside regular cab, long bed	16699	15781
4WD SLS Wideside regular cab, long bed	17941	16237
2WD SLS Wideside extended cab, short bed	14714	13316
2WD SLS Sportside extended cab extended cab, short bed	15164	13723
4WD SLS Wideside extended cab extended cab, short bed	19414	17570
4WD SLS Sportside extended cab extended cab, short bed	19864	17977
Destination charge	510	510

STANDARD EQUIPMENT:

SL: 2.2-liter 4-cylinder engine (2WD), 5-speed manual transmission, anti-lock brakes, driver-side air bag, power steering, vinyl or cloth folding bench seat, tinted glass, manual outside mirrors, oil-pressure and coolant-temperature gauges, voltmeter, trip odometer, AM/FM radio, digital clock, passenger-side visor mirror, intermittent wipers, black vinyl floor covering, color-keyed bumpers, daytime running lights, 6-lead trailer wiring harness, Smooth Ride Suspension Pkg. (regular cab short bed, 4WD extended cab), Heavy-Duty Suspension Pkg. (regular cab long bed, 2WD extended cab), 205/75R15 tires.

SLS adds: cloth reclining 60/40 split bench seat w/storage armrest, rear jump seats (extended cab), floor console, upgraded door trim, carpeting, illuminated entry system, reading lights, illuminated visor mirrors, auxiliary power outlets, floormats, striping, color-keyed grille, wheel trim rings.

4WD models add: 4.3-liter V-6 engine (180-horsepower), 4-wheel drive w/2-speed transfer case, tow hooks, Smooth Ride Suspension Pkg. (extended cab), 235/75R15 tires (regular cab long bed).

OPTIONAL EQUIPMENT:

	Retail Price	Dealer Invoice

Major Packages

1SQ Marketing Option Pkg. 3,
2WD SLS extended cab ... $2987 $2569
4.3-liter V-6 engine, 4-speed automatic transmission, air conditioning, cruise control, tilt steering wheel, cassette player, alloy wheels.

1SR Marketing Option Pkg. 3, 4WD SLS extended cab ... 1200 1032
4.3-liter V-6 engine, air conditioning, cruise control, front reclining bucket seats (requires electronic-shift transfer case when ordered w/automatic transmission), tilt steering wheel, cassette player, alloy wheels.

1SS Marketing Option Pkg. 5,
2WD SLS regular cab short bed ... 1815 1561
4.3-liter V-6 engine, Sport Suspension Pkg. (heavy-duty shock absorbers, special coil springs, heavy-duty front and rear stabilizer bars, urethane jounce bumpers, 235/55R16 tires), cloth reclining front bucket seats, cassette player, air deflector, fog lamps, alloy wheels.

1ST Marketing Option Pkg. 4, 2WD SLS extended cab 2620 2253
4.3-liter V-6 engine, air conditioning, Sport Suspension Pkg., cruise control, front reclining bucket seats (requires electronic-shift transfer case when ordered w/automatic transmission), tilt steering wheel, cassette player, air deflector, fog lamps, alloy wheels, 235/55R16 tires.

SLE Decor Pkg.,
2WD regular cab short bed, 2WD extended cab. 822 707
4WD regular cab short bed, 4WD extended cab. 854 734
Painted gray bumpers with rub strips, bright-trimmed gray grille, gray bodyside moldings, 2-tone paint, alloy wheels. NA SL. Deletes SLS striping.

Smooth Ride Suspension Pkg.,
2WD extended cab (credit) ... (64) (55)
Heavy-duty shock absorbers.

Heavy Duty Suspension Pkg.,
2WD regular cab short bed ... 64 55
4WD short bed ... 256 220
Heavy-duty shock absorbers and rear springs, 235/70R15 tires (4WD).

Highrider Suspension Pkg.,
4WD SLS Wideside regular cab short bed, 4WD SLS Wideside extended cab ... 1725 1484
Includes Shield Pkg., Bilstein shock absorbers, heavy-duty springs, wheel-opening flares, 31x10.5R15 on/off-road tires, chassis enhancements for increased height and width. Requires 3.73 rear-axle ratio, bucket seats.

Sport Suspension Pkg.,
2WD SLS short bed ... 703 605
Heavy-duty shock absorbers, special coil springs, heavy-duty front and rear stabilizer bars, urethane jounce bumpers, 235/55R16 tires.

Off-Road Suspension Pkg.,
4WD regular cab short bed and extended cab.... 651 560
Bilstein gas shock absorbers, upsized torsion bar, jounce bumpers, stabilizer bar, heavy-duty springs, full-size spare tire, 235//75R15 on-off-road white-letter tires.

Underbody Shield Pkg., 4WD ... 126 108
Transfer case, front differential, fuel tank, and steering linkage skid plates.

Cold Climate Pkg. ... 89 77
Engine-block heater, heavy-duty battery.

Convenience Pkg. ZQ6, SLS ... 535 460
Power windows and door locks, power mirrors. Requires SLS or SLE Decor.

Rating Scale: 5-Excellent; 4-Above average; 3-Average; 2-Below average; 1-Poor

	Retail Price	Dealer Invoice
Convenience Pkg. ZQ3	$395	$340

Tilt steering wheel, cruise control.

Powertrains

4.3-liter V-6 engine (175-horsepower), 2WD	990	851

Includes engine- and transmission-oil cooler when ordered with automatic transmission.

4.3-liter V-6 engine (2WD: 180-horsepower;		
4WD: 190-horsepower), 2WD	1249	1074
4WD	259	223

Includes tachometer, engine- and transmission-oil cooler (automatic transmission).

4-speed automatic transmission	1070	920

4WD extended cab w/reclining bucket seats requires electronic-shift transfer case.

Locking differential	252	217
Electronic-shift transfer case, SLS 4WD	123	106

Comfort and Convenience

Air conditioning...	805	692
Third door, extended cab	375	323

Deletes driver-side jump seat.

Cloth reclining front bucket seats,		
2WD SLS w/std. 2.2-liter engine and		
manual transmission	96	83
2WD SLS w/optional engine or automatic		
transmission, 4WD..	241	207

Includes manual lumbar adjuster. Requires SLS or SLE decor. 2WD extended cab w/automatic transmission requires electronic-shift transfer case.

Leather-wrapped steering wheel, SLS	54	46

Requires SLS or SLE Decor.

CD player	406	349

Requires SLS or SLE Decor.

Remote keyless entry..	140	120

Requires Convenience Pkg. ZQ6.

Appearance and Miscellaneous

Carpeting, SL regular cab	40	34
Sliding rear window	113	97
Deep-tinted rear glass, regular cab......................	71	61
regular cab w/sliding rear window	36	31
extended cab	107	92
extended cab w/sliding rear window....................	72	62
Air deflector and fog lamps, 2WD SLS	115	99

Requires SLS or SLE Decor.

Rear bumper delete, SL Wideside (credit)..............	(55)	(47)
Special two-tone paint, SLS Wideside	297	255

NA with 1SN Marketing Option Pkg. 4.

Special Purpose, Wheels and Tires

Alloy wheels, 2WD	340	292
2WD SLS...	248	213
4WD SLS...	280	241
205/75R15 outline-white-letter tires	121	104

NA 4WD regular cab long bed.

235/75R15 on/off-road outline-white-letter tires, 4WD	163	154

Requires Heavy Duty Suspension Pkg.

GMC YUKON   `RECOMMENDED`

Rear- or 4-wheel-drive full-size sport-utility vehicle; similar to Chevrolet Tahoe

Base price range: $29,604-$32,604. Built in Janesville, Wis., and Mexico.

Also consider: Ford Expedition, Lincoln Navigator, Toyota Land Cruiser

FOR • Acceleration (5.7-liter) • Standard anti-lock brakes • Passenger and cargo room • Towing ability

AGAINST • Fuel economy • Entry/exit (4WD models)

Yukon gains an upmarket edition and a more-sophisticated 4-wheel-drive system, but loses its 2-door body style as GMC accelerates its cultivation of an upscale image.

GMC Yukon SLT 4-door

Witht the 2-door and its available diesel V-8 history, Yukon is now a 4-door wagon that comes only with 5.7-liter V-8 and automatic transmission. Both the 2-door body and the diesel are still offered in Chevrolet's similar Tahoe.

Two- and four-wheel drive are offered, the latter General Motors' Autotrac system, which for the first time allows Yukon to use 4WD on dry pavement. Its Auto 4WD mode detects slip at the rear wheels and transfers power to the front to restore traction. Locked-in 4WD High and Low ranges can also be selected, as can Neutral, which allows Yukon to be towed by a motorhome. Four-wheel anti-lock brakes are standard.

Like most GM vehicles, Tahoe's standard dual air bags are depowered to deploy with less force. Also newly standard are a 6-way power driver's seat and electrochromatic rear-view mirror. New options include heated front seats and mirrors.

Joining returning SLE and SLT trim levels is the Denali. It bows in early calendar '98 and features unique front styling, tail trim, and body-side cladding and it comes just one way: loaded, with no options.

Standard equipment includes chromed aluminum wheels, wood-accented two-tone leather interior, Autotrac 4WD, premium audio with rear-seat controls, heated front and rear seats, and GM's OnStar communication and navigation system. OnStar links the vehicle by cell phone and satellite to a 24-hour GM center where operators can furnish directions and other services and summon emergency help.

PERFORMANCE Four-door Yukons and 4-door Tahoes have nearly identical performance, so see the Tahoe report for more details. However, the new Denali doesn't have a twin in the Chevrolet line.

Denali is aimed at luxury competitors like the new Lincoln Navigator. With added sound insulation and unique tires, it rides a bit smoother and quieter than a Yukon, which already has refinement on par with a large sedan. And equipped with GM's fine 5.7-liter V-8 and smooth automatic transmission, plus the versatile new Autotrac 4WD, its on-road behavior is, if anything, better than the new Lincoln's.

ACCOMMODATIONS Again, Yukon mimics the 4-door Tahoe, so see that report for an evaluation of its accommodations.

Denali goes Yukon and Tahoe one better, with more-luxurious furnishings and unique, specially constructed seats that are among the most-comfortable available in any SUV. OnStar, which is standard on Denali but unavailable on Yukon, is a worthwhile security and convenience feature.

BUILD QUALITY The Denali we tested had glossy paint and the interior was well assembled and rattle-free.

VALUE FOR THE MONEY Yukon prices aren't much higher than upper-level compact SUVs, yet interior room is far greater. At around $40,000, the Denali is pricey, but matches luxury features with any rival, and beats most in power and refinement.

RATINGS	4WD	2WD	Denali
Acceleration	4	4	4
Fuel economy	1	1	1
Ride quality	3	4	4
Steering/handling	3	3	3
Braking	4	4	4
Quietness	4	4	4
Driver seating	4	4	5
Instruments/controls	4	4	4
Room/comfort (front)	4	4	4
Room/comfort (rear)	4	4	4
Cargo room	5	5	5
Value for the money	3	3	3
Total	**43**	**44**	**45**

Prices are accurate at time of publication; subject to manufacturer's changes.

SPECIFICATIONS

	4-door wagon
Wheelbase, in.	117.5
Overall length, in.	199.6
Overall width, in.	76.8
Overall height, in.	74.2
Curb weight, lbs.	4911
Cargo vol., cu. ft.	118.2
Maximum payload, lbs.	1469
Fuel capacity, gals.	29.5
Seating capacity	6
Front head room, in.	39.9
Max. front leg room, in.	41.7
Rear head room, in.	38.9
Min. rear leg room, in.	36.4

ENGINES

	ohv V-8
Size, liters/cu. in.	5.7/350
Horsepower @ rpm	255@ 4600
Torque (lbs./ft.) @ rpm	330@ 2800
Availability	S

EPA city/highway mpg

4-speed OD automatic	15/19

PRICES

GMC Yukon

	Retail Price	Dealer Invoice
SLE 2WD 4-door wagon	$29604	$25904
SLE 4WD 4-door wagon	32604	28529
Destination charge	640	640

Denali prices unavailable at time of publication.

STANDARD EQUIPMENT:

2WD: 5.7-liter V-8 engine, 4-speed automatic transmission, driver- and passenger-side air bags, anti-lock brakes, daytime running lamps, power steering, tilt steering wheel, leather-wrapped steering wheel, cruise control, cloth 60/40 reclining split front bench seat, power driver seat, 3-passenger split folding rear bench seat, power mirrors, power windows, power door locks, remote keyless entry, air conditioning, digital clock, AM/FM/cassette player w/automatic tone control and eight speakers, illuminated visor mirrors, trip odometer, tachometer, oil-pressure and coolant-temperature gauges, voltmeter, intermittent wipers, reading lamps, rear heat ducts, auxiliary power outlets, rear defogger, rear wiper/washer (when ordered with rear tailgate), automatic day/night inside mirror, floormats, cargo cover, cargo net, Passlock theft-deterrent system, heavy-duty battery, rear panel doors, dual horns, underhood storage compartment, deep-tinted glass, roof rack, 7-lead trailer wiring harness, 235/75R15 tires, alloy wheels.

4WD adds: part-time 4-wheel drive w/electronic 2-speed transfer case, automatic locking front hubs, front tow hooks, 245/75R16 all-terrain tires.

OPTIONAL EQUIPMENT:

Major Packages

SLT Pkg. 5, 4-door	2137	1838

SLT Decor includes rear air conditioning leather upholstery, highback reclining front bucket seats with armrests, cassette/CD player, roof and floor consoles.

Luxury Convenience Group	995	856

Heated front seats, heated driver-side mirror w/automatic day/night, Homelink universal garage door opener, Bilstein gas shock absorbers.

Trailer Towing Pkg.	164	141

Platform hitch, heavy-duty flasher. Requires engine-oil cooler with out 3.73 rear-axle ratio.

Powertrains

3.73 rear-axle ratio	135	116
Locking differential	252	217

Comfort and Convenience

OnStar System	895	761

Includes Global Positioning System, voice-activated cellular telephone, roadside assistance, emergency services. Requires dealer installation charge, and monthly service charges.

	Retail Price	Dealer Invoice
Rear air conditioning	$550	$473
Cloth reclining highback front bucket seats	237	204
Includes floor and roof consoles.		
CD player w/automatic tone control	100	86
CD/cassette player w/automatic tone control	200	172

Appearance and Miscellaneous

	Retail	Dealer
Rear tailgate	NC	NC
Replaces rear panel doors.		
2-tone paint	200	172
Running boards	225	194
Cold Climate Pkg.	33	28
Includes engine-block heater.		

Special Purpose, Wheels and Tires

Engine-oil cooler	135	116
NA 3.73 rear-axle ratio.		
Heavy-duty transmission-oil cooler	96	83
Heavy-duty air cleaner	25	22
Skid Plate Pkg., 4WD	95	82
Differential and transfer-case shields.		
Front tow hooks, 2WD	38	33
245/75R16 all-terrain white-letter tires,4WD 4-door	140	120

HONDA ACCORD ✓ BEST BUY

Honda Accord LX V-6 sedan

Front-wheel-drive midsize car

Base price range: $15,100-$24,150. Built in Marysville, Ohio.

Also consider: Ford Taurus, Nissan Maxima, Toyota Camry

FOR • Acceleration (V-6 models) • Quietness • Instruments/controls • Steering/handling

AGAINST • No front side air bags available

A perennial top-seller since its 1976 debut, the Accord is fully redesigned for '98, getting marginally larger in the process. The wagon body style is gone, but the mainstay sedan wears new styling penned in Japan, while the coupe gets its own look for the first time, thanks to Honda's California designers. Both body styles come in LX and EX trim levels with 4-cylinder or V-6 power—the latter a first for Accord coupes; there's also a price-leader 4-cylinder DX sedan.

That base 4-door uses a 2.3-liter 4-cylinder with 5 more horsepower than the previous 2.2. The LX/EX use a more-powerful version with Honda's VTEC variable valve timing; this is also the first gasoline engine to meet California's strict ULEV (Ultra Low Emissions Vehicle) standards. V-6 models exchange last year's 2.7-liter engine for the new 3.0-liter unit (also with VTEC) introduced in the upscale Acura CL coupe. All Accords come with manual transmission and offer an automatic option.

Dimensionally, sedans have an unchanged wheelbase but are slightly longer, taller and stride wider tracks (width between wheels on the same axle). Coupes span a 1.8-inch shorter wheelbase and are a bit lower and shorter than before.

Anti-lock brakes are standard on V-6 and 4-cylinder EX models, optional on the 4-cylinder LX sedan with automatic transmission. Leather interior trim is standard on EX V-6s and optional on the 4-cylinder versions. Pricewise, 4-cylinder models are up fractionally from '97, while V-6s have been cut by about $1000.

Rating Scale: 5-Excellent; 4-Above average; 3-Average; 2-Below average; 1-Poor

CONSUMER GUIDE™

PERFORMANCE Though we've had only brief preview drives so far, the new Accord seems the best one yet. For starters, all engines are silky, revvy, and quiet, and there's little wind noise in any model, though some tire hum is audible on coarse pavement. The V-6 provides quick getaways, ample passing power and, says Honda, a 0-60 mph run of 8.2 seconds. The 4-cylinder makes that dash in a claimed 9.6 seconds with manual shift, also more than adequate. Four or V-6, the automatic transmission makes near-seamless upshifts even in hard acceleration; it's also pretty smooth and responsive in "kickdown" changes.

Accords have always absorbed bumps well, and the new one does too. What has changed is handling, which is noticeably more precise, with less body lean and better grip in tight corners thanks to the wider stance. Quick steering adds to driving fun, though we'd like more road feel at highway speeds.

ACCOMMODATIONS The 4-door is every bit as roomy inside as a Toyota Camry or Ford Taurus sedan. And like those cars, both Accord body styles are more comfortable for four adults than five; none is quite wide enough for a middle rear-seat grownup. But Accord's gains in hip and shoulder room are visible and welcome, and seat comfort is first-rate, especially up front. Wider doors ease entry/exit on sedans, but rear access in coupes remains crouch-and-crawl.

Honda dashboards are usually models of functional simplicity, and the '98 Accord hews to tradition. Airy outward vision is another Honda hallmark, but the new-style Accords have high rear package shelves that slightly inhibit sightlines directly astern.

Sedans have a deep, wide flat-floor trunk with a larger lid that again opens to bumper level. Liftover is a bit higher in coupes, which also have slightly less trunk volume. All models come with a handy split-fold rear seat.

BUILD QUALITY The new Accord should maintain its predecessors' record of exemplary workmanship. Though we've seen only pre-production models, their fit and finish were uniformly excellent. Interior materials are particularly attractive and classy.

VALUE FOR THE MONEY The old Accord had fallen behind its competition, but the new one catches up decisively, especially in the "space race." As one of our testers put it, the '98 represents "more Accord for the money"—reason enough to make it a must-see if you're looking for a top-notch family midsize.

RATINGS

	LX/EX sedan	LX/EX coupe	V-6 sedan	V-6 coupe
Acceleration	3	3	4	4
Fuel economy	4	4	3	3
Ride quality	4	4	4	4
Steering/handling	4	4	4	4
Braking	4	4	4	4
Quietness	3	3	4	3
Driver seating	4	4	4	4
Instruments/controls	4	4	4	4
Room/comfort (front)	4	4	3	4
Room/comfort (rear)	3	3	3	3
Cargo room	4	3	4	3
Value for the money	5	4	5	4
Total	**46**	**44**	**46**	**44**

SPECIFICATIONS

	2-door coupe	4-door sedan
Wheelbase, in.	105.1	106.9
Overall length, in.	186.8	188.8
Overall width, in.	70.3	70.3
Overall height, in.	55.1	56.9
Curb weight, lbs.	2943	2888
Cargo vol., cu. ft.	13.6	14.1
Fuel capacity, gals.	17.1	17.1
Seating capacity	5	5
Front head room, in.	39.7	40.0
Max. front leg room, in.	42.6	42.1
Rear head room, in.	36.5	37.6
Min. rear leg room, in.	32.4	37.9

ENGINES

	ohc I-4	ohc I-4	ohc V-6
Size, liters/cu. in.	2.3/137	2.3/137	3.0/183
Horsepower @ rpm	135@ 5400	150@ 5700	200@ 5500
Torque (lbs./ft.) @ RPM	145@ 4700	152@ 4900	195@ 4700
Availability	S[1]	S[2]	S[3]
EPA city/highway mpg			
4-speed OD automatic	22/29	23/30	21/28
5-speed OD manual	25/31	25/31	

1. DX, LX, SE. 2. EX. 3. V-6 models.

PRICES

Honda Accord	Retail Price	Dealer Invoice
DX 4-door sedan, 5-speed	$15100	$13343
DX 4-door sedan, automatic	15900	14050
LX 2-door notchback, 5-speed	18290	16162
LX 2-door notchback, automatic	19090	16869
LX 4-door sedan, 5-speed	18290	16162
LX 4-door sedan, automatic	19090	16869
LX 4-door sedan w/ABS, automatic	19690	17399
LX V-6 2-door notchback, automatic	21550	19042
LX V-6 4-door sedan, automatic	21550	19042
EX 2-door notchback, 5-speed	20800	18380
EX 2-door notchback, automatic	21600	19086
EX 2-door notchback w/leather, 5-speed	21950	19396
EX 2-door notchback w/leather, automatic	22750	20103
EX 4-door sedan, 5-speed	20800	18380
EX 4-door sedan, automatic	21600	19086
EX 4-door sedan w/leather, 5-speed	21950	19396
EX 4-door sedan w/leather, automatic	22750	20103
EX V-6 2-door notchback, automatic	24150	21340
EX V-6 4-door sedan, automatic	24150	21340
Destination charge	395	395

ABS denotes anti-lock 4-wheel disc brakes.

STANDARD EQUIPMENT:

DX: 2.3-liter 4-cylinder 135-horsepower engine, 5-speed manual or 4-speed automatic transmission, driver- and passenger-side air bags, variable-assist power steering, cloth reclining front bucket seats, folding rear seat, storage console with armrest, tachometer, coolant-temperature gauge, trip odometer, maintainance interval indicator, AM/FM/cassette w/two speakers, integrated antenna, digital clock, tilt steering column, cupholder, intermittent wipers, rear defogger, remote fuel-door and decklid releases, visor mirrors, rear heat ducts, tinted glass, dual remote outside mirrors, 195/70R14 tires, wheel covers.

LX adds: 2.3-liter 4-cylinder VTEC 150-horsepower engine, cruise control, air conditioning, power windows, power door locks, power mirrors, illuminated visor mirrors, power seat manual height adjustment, map lights, rear armrest w/trunk pass-through (4-door), split folding rear seat (2-door), variable intermittent wipers, 4-speaker sound system, 195/65HR15 tires.

LX V-6 adds: 3.0-liter V-6 engine, 4-speed automatic transmission, anti-lock 4-wheel disc brakes, 6-way power driver seat, 205/65R15 tires.

EX adds to LX: anti-lock 4-wheel disc brakes, power sunroof, driver seat power height adjustment, driver seat adjustable lumbar support, CD player with six speakers, automatic-off headlights, power decklid release, alloy wheels.

EX w/leather adds: leather upholstery, leather-wrapped steering wheel, 8-way power driver seat.

EX V-6 adds: 3.0-liter V-6-cylinder engine, 4-speed automatic transmission, automatic temperature control, Homelink universal garage door opener, 205/65R15 tires (4-door), 205/60R16 tires (2-door).

Options are available as dealer-installed accessories.

HONDA CIVIC

Front-wheel-drive subcompact

Base price range: $10,650-$17,280. Built in East Liberty, Ohio; Canada; and Japan.

FOR	• Fuel economy • Visibility
AGAINST	• Road noise

Prices are accurate at time of publication; subject to manufacturer's changes.

Honda Civic EX 2-door notchback

Honda's popular subcompact is little changed for a second year following its major 1996 redesign. The only alterations are new-design wheel covers for some models and deletion of the remote tailgate release on hatchbacks in favor of an exterior handle.

The lineup again comprises DX, HX, and EX coupes; CX and DX 2-door hatchbacks; and DX, LX, and EX 4-door sedans. All carry a 1.6-liter 4-cylinder engine and standard manual transmission. CX, DX, and LX Civics muster 106 horsepower, EX models 127; all can be ordered with extra-cost automatic transmission. A 115-horsepower engine is exclusive to the high-mileage HX coupe, where the automatic option is Honda's CVT transmission. Unlike conventional automatics, which have three or four forward gears, the CVT uses a belt-and-pulley system to provide an infinite number of gear ratios.

PERFORMANCE All Civics have at least adequate acceleration. An automatic DX hatchback ran 0-60 mph in 10.2 seconds—good going for a small automatic-transmission car—while averaging a thrifty 29.1 mpg despite those gas-eating performance tests. EX models border on lively with extra power, yet are hardly less frugal. An automatic sedan gave us 36 mpg on the highway and 29 mpg in suburban commuting.

Civic's regular automatic transmission upshifts smoothly, it also downshifts fairly readily for passing with a healthy prod on the gas pedal. The CVT works well too, delivering a steady flow of power. Engine noise is not intrusive in any Civic, but road noise is prominent at highway speeds.

Eager, agile handling remains a Civic virtue. It's no sports car, but body lean is a bother only in hard, fast turns. Light steering and a tight turning circle make for easy parking and friendly close-quarters maneuvering. The latest Civics have a slightly smoother ride than earlier models, but there's still some short-wheelbase chop on freeways, and broken pavement induces some wheel patter.

ACCOMMODATIONS Civic's 1996 redesign gave all models more passenger and cargo room. Hatchbacks gained the most space, but the sedans added enough room to qualify as compact-class cars based on interior volume (hatchbacks and coupes remain subcompacts). All models have adequate rear space for people about 6-feet tall to ride without feeling like sardines. Still, leg space is limited without the front seats moved up, and rear entry/exit is nothing special, even on sedans.

Per Civic custom, thin roof pillars and large windows make for fine all-round visibility. The driving position remains low but comfortable, the dash a model of good design. All Civics have a split-fold rear seatback to expand cargo capacity.

BUILD QUALITY No Civic is really luxurious, but workmanship is solid and thorough, regardless of model.

VALUE FOR THE MONEY Honda's small car is far from the cheapest, but it tops the list for all-around practicality and offers a healthy dose of driving fun. A proven record of reliability, durability, and high resale value continue to make Civic a must-see for small-car shoppers.

RATINGS

	CX	DX	HX	LX	EX
Acceleration	3	3	3	3	4
Fuel economy	4	4	4	4	4
Ride quality	3	3	3	3	3
Steering/handling	4	4	4	4	4
Braking	4	4	4	4	4
Quietness	4	4	4	4	4
Driver seating	4	4	4	4	4
Instruments/controls	4	4	4	4	4
Room/comfort (front)	4	4	4	4	4
Room/comfort (rear)	2	2	2	2	2
Cargo room	3	3	3	3	3
Value for the money	5	5	5	5	5
Total	44	44	44	44	45

SPECIFICATIONS

	2-door coupe	2-door hatchback	4-door sedan
Wheelbase, in.	103.2	103.2	103.2
Overall length, in.	175.1	175.1	175.1
Overall width, in.	67.1	67.1	67.1
Overall height, in.	54.1	54.1	54.1
Curb weight, lbs.	2262	2222	2319
Cargo vol., cu. ft.	11.9	13.4	11.9
Fuel capacity, gals.	11.9	11.9	11.9
Seating capacity	5	5	5
Front head room, in.	38.8	38.8	39.8
Max. front leg room, in.	42.7	42.7	42.7
Rear head room, in.	36.2	37.2	37.6
Min. rear leg room, in.	34.1	34.1	34.1

ENGINES

	ohc I-4	ohc I-4	ohc I-4
Size, liters/cu. in.	1.6/97	1.6/97	1.6/97
Horsepower @ rpm	106@ 6200	115@ 6300	127@ 6600
Torque (lbs./ft.) @ rpm	103@ 4600	104@ 5400	107@ 5500
Availability	S[1]	S[2]	S[3]

EPA city/highway mpg

4-speed OD automatic	29/35		28/35
5-speed OD manual	32/38	37/44	30/36

1. CX, DX, LX. 2. HX. 3. EX.

PRICES

Honda Civic	Retail Price	Dealer Invoice
CX 2-door hatchback, 5-speed	$10650	$9990
CX 2-door hatchback, automatic	11650	10928
DX 2-door hatchback, 5-speed	12100	10856
DX 2-door hatchback, automatic	12900	11574
DX 2-door notchback, 5-speed	12580	11287
DX 2-door notchback, automatic	13380	12005
DX 4-door sedan, 5-speed	12735	11426
DX 4-door sedan, automatic	13535	12144
HX 2-door notchback, 5-speed	13400	12022
HX 2-door notchback, CVT	14400	12920
LX 4-door sedan, 5-speed	14750	12988
LX 4-door sedan, automatic	15550	13706
EX 2-door notchback, 5-speed	15250	13682
EX 2-door notchback, automatic	16050	14400
EX 2-door notchback w/ABS, automatic	16650	14938
EX 4-door sedan, 5-speed	16480	14786
EX 4-door sedan, automatic	17280	15504
Destination charge	395	395

ABS denotes anti-lock brakes.

STANDARD EQUIPMENT:

CX: 1.6-liter 4-cylinder 106-horsepower engine, 5-speed manual or 4-speed automatic transmission, driver- and passenger-side air bags, power steering (requires automatic transmission), reclining cloth front bucket seats, 50/50 split folding rear seats, remote fuel-door and hatch releases, rear defogger, dual remote outside mirrors, cupholder, intermittent wipers, visor mirrors, tinted glass, 185/65R14 tires.

DX hatchback adds: rear wiper/washer, AM/FM stereo w/clock, rear map pocket, cargo cover, cargo room.

DX sedan/notchback adds to CX: power steering (2-door requires automatic transmission), lockable 60/40 fold-down rear seat, AM/FM stereo w/clock, tilt steering column, rear heat ducts, remote trunk release, rear map pocket, full wheel covers.

HX adds to DX sedan/notchback: 1.6-liter 4-cylinder VTEC 115-horsepower engine, 5-speed manual or Continuously Variable Transmission (CVT), power steering, power windows, power mirrors, power door locks, console, tachometer, cargo-area light, alloy wheel covers.

LX adds to DX sedan/notchback: air conditioning, power steering, power mirrors, power windows, cruise control, power door locks, tachometer, front storage console with armrest, cargo-area light.

EX adds to LX: 1.6-liter 4-cylinder VTEC 127-horsepower engine, anti-lock brakes (4-door), power moonroof, six-speakers (2-door), remote keyless entry, color-keyed bodyside molding.

Options are available as dealer-installed accessories.

Rating Scale: 5-Excellent; 4-Above average; 3-Average; 2-Below average; 1-Poor

CONSUMER GUIDE™

HONDA CR-V

✔ BEST BUY

Honda CR-V

Front- or Four-wheel-drive compact sport-utility vehicle

Base price range: (1997 model) $19,400-$20,400. Built in Japan.

Also consider: Kia Sportage, Subaru Forester, Toyota RAV4

FOR • Steering/handling • Passenger and cargo room • Entry/exit • Ride

AGAINST • Aceleration

A sales success since its U.S. debut last January, Honda's first in-house SUV is sized and priced between compacts like the Toyota RAV4 and midsizers like Honda's own Passport (which is designed and built by Isuzu). CR-V ("Comfortable, Run-about Vehicle") is unchanged going into 1998. Come February, Honda will add a front-wheel-drive model and switch the standard transmission to a manual.

Until then, CR-V continues with standard automatic, 4-cylinder power, and "Real-Time 4WD." The last normally sends most engine torque to the front wheels, but diverts it to the rear when sensors detect the front tires losing traction. The CR-V isn't intended for hard off-road use and lacks separate low-range gearing.

Based on a Japanese-market 4WD Civic subcompact car, the CR-V has unibody construction instead of truck-type body-on-frame, and all-independent suspension instead of a solid rear axle. The RAV4 shares these features, being based on a Toyota car platform.

PERFORMANCE That manual transmission will be welcome when it arrives, because the CR-V is none too quick with automatic. We timed a '97 at a lengthy 11.3 seconds 0-60 mph—and that with just the driver aboard. Add any kind of load and you're in the slow lane, especially on steep upgrades. All this suggests the 2.0-liter four just doesn't have the muscle for the CR-V's weight. So does our overall mileage of 19.7 mpg; we expected closer to 25 even in hard city/freeway work.

Still, the CR-V doesn't feel dramatically underpowered around town, and it's pleasantly car-like to drive. Wind noise is unusually well suppressed at cruise, tire thrum is low, and though the engine becomes boomy above 4000 rpm, it's never throbby or irritating. The transmission provides smooth, quick upshifts even at full-throttle, but can downshift with a hefty jerk. The steering is a bit inert on-center, but positive and precise for a "truck." Body lean is modest in tight turns, so the CR-V can be tossed around much like any small wagon. Ride comfort is generally good, but some undulations cause annoying hop.

ACCOMMODATIONS The CR-V has ample head and leg room, but the interior isn't wide enough for three adults in back. Step-in is low despite an 8-inch ground clearance, so entry/exit is easy, though the rear doors are narrow for larger folk.

The driving stance is bus-like but accommodating, thanks to a standard tilt steering wheel and manual seat-height adjuster. The column-mount shifter sits awkwardly behind the wiper stalk. Otherwise, the driving environment is simple and convenient—much like that of a Civic.

As for utility, CR-V's 50/50 split rear seat can be folded to form a flat load floor; with the seat in use, there's space behind for about 10 grocery bags. Cargo bay access is less than ideal, however, as you must get past an external spare-tire carrier, glass liftgate, and swing-out tailgate. A nice touch is the plastic cargo-floor panel that transforms into a free-standing picnic table via fold-down legs.

BUILD QUALITY Our test CR-V was solid and rattle-free on the roughest surfaces we could find. Fit and finish were excellent inside and out.

VALUE FOR THE MONEY With more power, the CR-V would be just about perfect. As it is, it's a handy, well-built compact wagon with car-like manners and no-brainer 4WD. While it can't match the space or brawn of bigger SUVs, the CR-V is the nicest baby 4x4 by far.

RATINGS

	CR-V
Acceleration	3
Fuel economy	3
Ride quality	3
Steering/handling	4
Braking	4
Quietness	3
Driver seating	3
Instruments/controls	4
Room/comfort (front)	4
Room/comfort (rear)	3
Cargo room	4
Value for the money	4
Total	42

SPECIFICATIONS

	4-door wagon
Wheelbase, in.	103.1
Overall length, in.	176.4
Overall width, in.	68.9
Overall height, in.	65.9
Curb weight, lbs.	3150
Cargo vol., cu. ft.	34.3
Fuel capacity, gals.	15.3
Seating capacity	5
Front head room, in.	40.5
Max. front leg room, in.	41.5
Rear head room, in.	39.2
Min. rear leg room, in.	36.7

ENGINES

	dohc I-4
Size, liters/cu. in.	2.0/122
Horsepower @ rpm	126@ 5400
Torque (lbs./ft.) @ rpm	126@ 4300
Availability	S

EPA city/highway mpg

4-speed OD automatic	22/25

PRICES

1997 Honda CR-V	Retail Price	Dealer Invoice
4-door wagon	$19400	$17604
4-door wagon w/ABS	20400	18511
Destination charge	395	395

STANDARD EQUIPMENT:

2.0-liter DOHC 4-cylinder engine, 4-speed automatic transmission, variable-assist power steering, Real-Time 4-wheel drive, air conditioning, driver- and passenger-side air bags, cruise control, reclining front bucket seats w/driver-seat height adjustment, split folding and reclining 50/50 rear bench seat, cupholders, power windows, power door locks, power mirrors, tilt steering column, tachometer, solar-control tinted glass, AM/FM radio w/clock, rear defogger, intermittent rear wiper/washer, visor mirrors, interior air filter, map lights, remote hatch release, lift-out folding picnic table, auxiliary power outlet, rear mud guards, outside spare-tire carrier w/cover, 205/70R15 tires.

ABS adds: 4-wheel anti-lock brakes, alloy wheels.

Options are available as dealer-installed accessories.

Prices are accurate at time of publication; subject to manufacturer's changes.

HONDA ODYSSEY

Honda Odyssey LX

Front-wheel-drive minivan; similar to Isuzu Oasis
Base price range: (1997 model) $23,560-$25,550. Built in Japan.
Also consider: Dodge Caravan, Plymouth Voyager, Toyota Sienna

FOR • Ride • Steering/handling • Entry/exit
AGAINST • Engine and road noise • Acceleration

Odyssey bowed in 1995 as Honda's first minivan and the last to be introduced by a major manufacturer. Built on a stretched version of the Accord passenger-car platform, it's offered in a single body length with four swing-open side doors (like Mazda's MPV). Honda furnishes Isuzu a near-identical version sold as the Isuzu Oasis.

For '98, Odyssey exchanges a 2.2-liter 4-cylinder engine for the new 2.3-liter VTEC unit developed for the new 1998 Accord. Horsepower goes up by 10, torque increases by 7 pounds/feet, and automatic transmission remains standard. Outside are a mildly restyled grille and bumpers, and inside is a revised instrument panel with a tachometer for the first time, plus a new-design steering wheel. Also borrowed from the '98 Accord is a standard anti-theft immobilizer that prevents "hot wiring" the engine.

Odyssey continues in 6- and 7-passenger LX models and in ritzier 6-passenger EX trim. The 6-seaters have removable middle "captain's chair" buckets instead of a 3-place bench. All Odysseys have a 2-place third-row seat that folds flush with the cargo floor.

PERFORMANCE Pleasant and competent on the road, Odyssey drives much like the "tall Accord" it is. It suffers little wind noise for a minivan and, in hard cornering, little body lean, but tire roar is higher than it should be on coarse pavement. Ride is steady and firm at highway speeds, absorbent and comfortable on bumpy urban streets.

Previous Odysseys felt slightly underpowered in both standing starts and passing maneuvers. Though an EX model ran 0-60 mph in a decent 10 seconds or so with just a driver aboard, it wasn't nearly so frisky with four or five passengers, and the engine was loud under hard throttle. We don't expect any of this to change much with the modestly more-potent new 2.3-liter engine. However, Odyssey should remain one of the thriftiest minivans; last year's model averaged 21.3 mpg in our usual city/expressway driving.

ACCOMMODATIONS How large should a minivan be? Odyssey is smaller than most. Though it's about as long as the Mercury Villager/Nissan Quest twins, it stands some three inches lower, which pays off in a shorter step-in that eases entry/exit. However, Odyssey also is three to five inches narrower than other minivans, which limits what size cargo you can carry. It also leaves a tight front-to-rear walk-through space and makes for cramped 3-across seating on the middle bench in 7-passenger models. Six adults fit more comfortably, though third-row occupants should be on the small side, as leg room there is tight.

The driving position is car-like, the dashboard attractive and well organized, and visibility good to all corners. Cupholders and storage cubbies abound, and the flush-fold rear seat is handy for making extra cargo space. The captain's chairs are light enough to be removed or reinstalled with no sweat.

BUILD QUALITY Odyssey is tight and solid over rough roads without feeling heavy or "trucky." Like Accord, it's put together with care, and the interior bespeaks quality in an understated way.

VALUE FOR THE MONEY Modest size and lack of 6-cylinder muscle limit Odyssey's appeal against domestic minivans for many buyers. It also starts out at higher prices than most competitors, though it's well built, well equipped, and likely to be reliable. It's worth a look if you aren't seeking maximum space for the buck.

RATINGS

	LX/EX
Acceleration	3
Fuel economy	3
Ride quality	4
Steering/handling	3
Braking	4
Quietness	3
Driver seating	4
Instruments/controls	4
Room/comfort (front)	4
Room/comfort (rear)	4
Cargo room	4
Value for the money	4
Total	**44**

SPECIFICATIONS

	4-door van
Wheelbase, in.	111.4
Overall length, in.	187.2
Overall width, in.	70.6
Overall height, in.	64.6
Curb weight, lbs.	3450
Cargo vol., cu. ft.	102.5
Fuel capacity, gals.	17.2
Seating capacity	7/8
Front head room, in.	40.1
Max. front leg room, in.	40.7
Rear head room, in.	39.3
Min. rear leg room, in.	40.2

ENGINES

	dohc I-4
Size, liters/cu. in.	2.3/140
Horsepower @ rpm	150@5700
Torque (lbs./ft.) @ rpm	152@4900
Availability	S

EPA city/highway mpg

4-speed OD automatic	NA

PRICES

1997 Honda Odyssey	Retail Price	Dealer Invoice
LX 5-door van, 7-passenger	$23560	$20818
LX 5-door van, 6-passenger	23970	21180
EX 5-door van	25550	22577
Destination charge	395	395

STANDARD EQUIPMENT:

LX: 2.2-liter 4-cylinder engine, 4-speed automatic transmission, anti-lock 4-wheel disc brakes, driver- and passenger-side air bags, variable-assist power steering, front and rear air conditioning, cloth front bucket seats, split folding middle bench seat (7-passenger seating) or removable captain's chairs (6-passenger seating), folding third bench seat, AM/FM/cassette, digital clock, power windows and door locks, power mirrors, cruise control, remote fuel-door release, rear defogger, intermittent wipers, tilt steering column, visor mirrors, cupholders, rear wiper/washer, bodyside moldings, 205/65R15 tires.

EX adds: power sunroof, 6-passenger seating, driver's seat with power height adjustment, remote keyless entry system, 6-speaker sound system, map lights, color-keyed bodyside moldings, alloy wheels.

Options are available as dealer-installed accessories.

Rating Scale: 5-Excellent; 4-Above average; 3-Average; 2-Below average; 1-Poor

CONSUMER GUIDE™

HONDA PASSPORT

1997 Honda Passport LX

Rear- or 4-wheel-drive midsize sport-utility vehicle; similar to Isuzu Rodeo

Base price range: $22,700-$29,950. Built in Lafayette, Ind.

Also consider: Ford Explorer, GMC Jimmy, Toyota 4Runner

FOR • 4-wheel anti-lock brakes (EX 4WD) • Passenger and cargo room • Acceleration

AGAINST • Road and wind noise • Fuel economy

Like sister Acura division with the SLX, Honda got into the sport-utility market by putting its badge on an Isuzu—in this case, the Rodeo. Honda called its version Passport and put it on sale in 1994.

This year, Honda and Isuzu have redesigned their midsize SUV, making it slightly larger and giving its V-6 a bit more power. Passport remains very similar to Rodeo, differing mainly in model choices, cosmetic details, and available features. Both versions are again built at the Subaru-Isuzu plant in Indiana.

As in '97, Passport offers LX and ritzier EX models with either rear drive or on-demand 4-wheel drive. All carry an improved version of Isuzu's 3.2-liter twin-cam V-6 with 15 additional horsepower and 26 more pounds/feet of torque. EX models again have a standard automatic transmission, which is optional on LXs in lieu of a 5-speed manual. The 4x4s retain a 2-speed transfer case with separate low-range gearing, but 4WD is now engaged electrically by a dashboard button instead of mechanically with a lever. As before, 4WD is not for use on dry pavement, though the vehicle can be shifted between 4-High and 2WD at any speed up to 60 mph.

Against its predecessor, the '98 Passport is, somewhat surprisingly, 2.1 inches shorter in wheelbase, but about an inch longer overall, almost 4 inches taller and 1.4 inches wider. Base-model curb weight is up by a scant 44 pounds.

Engineering changes include standard anti-lock brakes (previously available only on the EX 4WD), rack-and-pinion steering (ousting less-precise recirculating-ball), coil-spring rear suspension (replacing leaf springs), and a sturdier new-design frame.

Besides evolutionary styling, the tailgate is now left-hinged (formerly bottom-hinged) below a separate glass liftgate. LXs stow their spare tires under the rear cargo floor; EXs have a swing-away external tire carrier. Regardless of model, rated towing capacity is 4500 pounds with electric trailer brakes.

Passport's performance and accommodations mirror those of similarly equipped Isuzu Rodeo.

See the Isuzu Rodeo report for an evaluation of the Passport.

SPECIFICATIONS

	4-door wagon
Wheelbase, in.	106.4
Overall length, in.	177.4
Overall width, in.	70.4
Overall height, in.	67.9
Curb weight, lbs.	3589
Cargo vol., cu. ft.	81.1
Fuel capacity, gals.	21.1
Seating capacity	5
Front head room, in.	38.9
Max. front leg room, in.	42.1
Rear head room, in.	38.3
Min. rear leg room, in.	35.0

ENGINES

	dohc V-6
Size, liters/cu. in.	3.2/193
Horsepower @ rpm	205@ 5400
Torque (lbs./ft.) @ rpm	214@ 3000
Availability	S

EPA city/highway mpg

5-speed OD manual	NA
4-speed OD automatic	NA

RATINGS

	LX 2WD	EX 4WD
Acceleration	3	3
Fuel economy	3	2
Ride quality	3	3
Steering/handling	3	3
Braking	3	3
Quietness	3	3
Driver seating	4	4
Instruments/controls	3	3
Room/comfort (front)	4	4
Room/comfort (rear)	3	3
Cargo room	4	4
Value for the money	3	3
Total	**38**	**37**

PRICES

Honda Passport	Retail Price	Dealer Invoice
LX 2WD 4-door wagon, 5-speed	$22700	$20135
LX 2WD 4-door wagon, automatic	23850	21155
LX 4WD 4-door wagon, 5-speed	25450	22574
LX 4WD 4-door wagon with 16-inch Wheel Pkg., 5-speed	25850	22929
LX 4WD 4-door wagon, automatic	26600	23594
LX 4WD 4-door wagon with 16-inch Wheel Pkg., automatic	27000	23949
EX 2WD 4-door wagon, automatic	26500	23506
EX 2WD 4-door wagon w/leather, automatic	27500	24393
EX 4WD 4-door wagon, automatic	28950	25679
EX 4WD 4-door wagon w/leather, automatic	29950	26566
Destination charge	395	395

STANDARD EQUIPMENT:

LX 2WD: 3.2-liter V-6 engine, 5-speed manual or 4-speed automatic transmission, driver- and passenger-side air bags, anti-lock brakes, variable-assist power steering, tilt steering column, cruise control, reclining front bucket seats, center storage console, cupholders, 60/40 split folding rear bench seat, power windows, power door locks, tachometer, rear defogger, AM/FM/cassette, visor mirrors, remote tailgate release, tinted glass, dual outside mirrors, skid plates, full-size spare tire, 225/75R16 mud and snow tires.

LX 4WD adds: part-time 4-wheel drive, automatic locking front hubs, 2-speed transfer case, 4-wheel disc brakes, air conditioning, transfer case skid plate, alloy wheels.

LX 4WD w/16-inch Wheel Pkg. adds to LX 4WD: flared wheel opening moldings, splash guards, 245/70R16 tires, 16-inch alloy wheels.

EX 2WD adds to LX 2WD: removable tilt-up moonroof, leather upholstery (w/leather models), heated power mirrors, rear wiper/washer, leather-wrapped steering wheel, intermittent wipers, cargo net, map lights, chrome bumpers, rear privacy glass, 16-inch Wheel Pkg. (16-inch alloy wheels, 245/70R16 tires, flared wheel openings, splash guards).

EX 4WD adds: part-time 4-wheel drive, limited-slip differential, automatic locking front hubs, 2-speed transfer case, 4-wheel disc brakes, transfer-case skid plate.

Options are available as dealer-installed accessories.

✓ BEST BUY

HONDA PRELUDE

Front-wheel-drive sports coupe

Base price range: $23,300-$25,800. Built in Japan.

FOR • Acceleration • Steering/handling

Prices are accurate at time of publication; subject to manufacturer's changes.

Honda Prelude SH

AGAINST • Rear seat room • Cargo room

Honda redesigned its sport coupe last year, giving it more-conservative styling and a conventional dashboard design, but adding some high-tech features. A new paint color is the only change for '98.

The fifth-generation Prelude continues in base and Type SH models. Both use a 2.2-liter 4-cylinder engine with dual overhead camshafts and Honda's VTEC variable-valve-timing system. A manual transmission is standard and automatic is optional only on the base model. It reduces horsepower by 5 to 190.

That automatic, called Sequential SportShift, mimics other "automanual" transmissions with a secondary shift gate allowing full manual gear selection. The lever can also be left in Drive as usual. Exclusive to the SH is the Active Torque Steer System, designed to counter the tendency of front-drive cars to plow, or understeer, when accelerating through a turn. Controlled by computer, ATSS automatically redirects up to 80 percent of engine torque to the outside front wheel when accelerating in a turn, enabling the wheel to rotate up to 15 percent faster than normal. The SH front suspension differs slightly from the base Prelude's.

PERFORMANCE Prelude's revvy engine produces more torque at low rpm than most small twin-cam fours, so acceleration is lively with either transmission. We went 0-60 mph in 8.5 seconds with a SportShift base model; our test SH took just 7.6 seconds. Hard driving exacts a toll at the pumps, though: a 19.4 mpg average for our SH, a more likable 23.2 for the automatic model, with premium fuel mandatory for both. Typical of Hondas, Prelude's 5-speed manual is a slick-shifting delight. The SportShift's do-it-yourself changes are crisp and immediate, but high-rpm downshifts usually occur with a jerky lunge.

In hard cornering the torque-transfer system makes the SH feel like it's being "pulled" toward the inside. But ATSS doesn't work in a straight line, so it's no substitute for genuine traction-control, which isn't available. Otherwise, handling is almost go-kart sporty. The power steering is quick and natural-feeling, and though the suspension allows mild body lean in turns, there's ample grip and stability.

Ride is reasonably supple for a sports coupe, but uneven surfaces induce marked jiggle. Engine, wind, and road ruckus are pretty low at cruising speeds, but "tire slap" is heard from the rear even in town driving.

ACCOMMODATIONS Despite being larger outside than its predecessors, the latest Prelude is not usefully bigger inside, so rear-seat space remains tight, though the Honda is no worse in this regard than most rivals. The trunk is none too capacious, and a relatively small opening limits the size of what you can load there.

As ever, Prelude drivers sit low to the ground in a well-bolstered seat. A legs-out stance is mandatory, but not uncomfortable for long drives, and visibility is uncluttered all around. The redesign brought a new dashboard that returns Prelude to the Honda fold with clear analog gauges and a convenient layout. The one downer is the use of old-fashioned sliders instead of rotary knobs for the climate system.

BUILD QUALITY Our test Preludes were taut and rattle-free over railroad tracks and other big disturbances. Overall workmanship was equally pleasing. Interior decor is more economy-car than suave sports machine, however.

VALUE FOR THE MONEY Prelude is at the top of the sports coupe price scale, but it's worth considering if you appreciate polished road manners and sophisticated engineering.

RATINGS

	Base w/auto. trans.	SH
Acceleration	4	5
Fuel economy	3	2
Ride quality	3	3
Steering/handling	4	4
Braking	4	4
Quietness	3	3
Driver seating	4	4
Instruments/controls	4	4
Room/comfort (front)	3	3
Room/comfort (rear)	2	2
Cargo room	2	2
Value for the money	4	4
Total	**40**	**40**

SPECIFICATIONS

	2-door coupe
Wheelbase, in.	101.8
Overall length, in.	178.0
Overall width, in.	69.0
Overall height, in.	51.8
Curb weight, lbs.	2954
Cargo vol., cu. ft.	8.7
Fuel capacity, gals.	15.9
Seating capacity	5
Front head room, in.	37.9
Max. front leg room, in.	43.0
Rear head room, in.	35.3
Min. rear leg room, in.	28.1

ENGINES

	dohc I-4
Size, liters/cu. in.	2.2/132
Horsepower @ rpm	195@ 7000
Torque (lbs./ft.) @ rpm	156@ 5250
Availability	S

EPA city/highway mpg

4-speed OD automatic	21/26
5-speed OD manual	22/26

PRICES

Honda Prelude	Retail Price	Dealer Invoice
Base 2-door coupe, 5-speed	$23300	$20667
Base 2-door coupe, automatic	24300	21554
SH 2-door coupe, 5-speed	25800	22885
Destination charge	395	395

STANDARD EQUIPMENT:

Base: 2.2-liter 4-cylinder VTEC engine, 5-speed manual or 4-speed Sequential SportShift automatic transmission, driver- and passenger-side air bags, anti-lock 4-wheel disc brakes, air conditioning, variable-assist power steering, tilt steering wheel, leather-wrapped steering wheel, cruise control, cloth upholstery, reclining front bucket seats w/driver-seat height adjustment, folding rear seat, storage console w/armrest, front and rear cupholders, power windows, power door locks, power outside mirrors, power moonroof, AM/FM/CD player w/Acoustic Feedback Control, integrated rear-window antenna, digital clock, tachometer, visor mirrors, map lights, rear defogger, remote fuel-door and decklid release, variable intermittent wipers, auxiliary power outlet, dual exhaust outlets, theft-deterrent system, 205/50R16 tires, alloy wheels.

SH adds: 5-speed manual transmission, Active Torque Transfer System, leather-wrapped shifter, rear spoiler.

Options are available as dealer-installed accessories.

HYUNDAI ACCENT

Front-wheel-drive subcompact

Base range: (1997 model) $8599-$10,954. Built in South Korea.

Also consider: Chevrolet Metro, Nissan Sentra, Suzuki Swift/Esteem, Toyota Tercel

FOR • Fuel economy • Visibility • Optional anti-lock brakes • Maneuverability

Rating Scale: 5-Excellent; 4-Above average; 3-Average; 2-Below average; 1-Poor

CONSUMER GUIDE™

Hyundai Accent GSi hatchback

RATINGS

	2-dr. 5-spd.	4-dr. auto.
Acceleration	3	2
Fuel economy	5	4
Ride quality	3	3
Steering/handling	3	3
Braking	3	3
Quietness	2	2
Driver seating	2	2
Instruments/controls	4	4
Room/comfort (front)	3	3
Room/comfort (rear)	3	3
Cargo room	3	3
Value for the money	3	3
Total	**37**	**35**

SPECIFICATIONS

	2-door hatchback	4-door sedan
Wheelbase, in.	94.5	94.5
Overall length, in.	161.5	162.1
Overall width, in.	63.8	63.8
Overall height, in.	54.9	54.9
Curb weight, lbs.	2101	2105
Cargo vol., cu. ft.	16.1	10.7
Fuel capacity, gals.	11.9	11.9
Seating capacity	5	5
Front head room, in.	38.7	38.7
Max. front leg room, in.	42.6	42.6
Rear head room, in.	37.8	38.0
Min. rear leg room, in.	32.7	32.7

ENGINES

	ohc I-4
Size, liters/cu. in.	1.5/91
Horsepower @ rpm	92 @ 5500
Torque (lbs./ft.) @ rpm	97 @ 4000
Availability	S

EPA city/highway mpg
4-speed OD automatic	27/35
5-speed OD manual	28/36

PRICES

1997 Hyundai Accent

	Retail Price	Dealer Invoice
L 2-door hatchback, 5-speed	$8599	$8104
GS 2-door hatchback, 5-speed	9399	8664
GS 2-door hatchback, automatic	10154	9348
GL 4-door notchback, 5-speed	9799	9033
GL 4-door notchback, automatic	10554	9717
GT 2-door hatchback, 5-speed	10199	9402
GT 2-door hatchback, automatic	10954	10086
Destination charge	415	415

STANDARD EQUIPMENT:

L: 1.5-liter 4-cylinder engine, 5-speed manual transmission, driver- and passenger-side air bags, cloth reclining front bucket seats, folding rear seat, front and rear center consoles, remote outside mirrors, coolant-temperature gauge, trip odometer, rear defogger, remote fuel-door release, passenger-side visor mirror, intermittent wipers, cargo-area cover, 155/80R13 tires.

GS and GL add: 5-speed manual or 4-speed automatic transmission, adjustable driver seat w/lumbar support, 60/40 split folding rear seat (GS), fixed rear seat (GL), tinted glass, tachometer, digital clock, remote hatch/decklid release, rear wiper/washer (GS), cargo-area cover (GS), bodyside moldings, 175/70R13 tires, wheel covers.

GT adds to GS: 1.5-liter DOHC 4-cylinder engine, power steering, sports-tuned suspension, AM/FM radio, leather-wrapped steering wheel and shifter, rear spoiler, lower bodyside cladding, fog lamps, 175/70R14 performance tires, alloy wheels.

OPTIONAL EQUIPMENT:
Major Packages
Option Pkg. 2, GS, GL	710	582
Power steering, AM/FM/cassette.

AGAINST • Noise • Driving position • Passing power

Accent is the entry-level subcompact from Hyundai, South Korea's largest automaker. This is one of the smallest, lightest, and least-expensive cars sold in America and it gets some appearance tweaks while losing its "performance" model.

Two-door hatchbacks in L, GS, and GSi form are offered, the last replacing a GT model. The 4-door comes only in GL trim.

A 92-horsepower 4-cylinder is the only engine; the GT had used a 105-horsepower version. Manual transmission is standard and automatic is optional on all models except the L hatchback. Dual air bags are standard and anti-lock brakes are an option on all but the price-leader L.

For 1998, the hatchback's front and rear fascias are revised, and the sedan gets a revised hood, headlights, and trunklid.

PERFORMANCE High noise levels are the price of Accent's lightweight build. There's substantial roar from the road at highway speeds and the engine makes a lot of racket in hard acceleration.

Acceleration is adequate around town with either transmission, but highway passing requires a long stretch of open road, and the engine strains going up even small hills. We tested a 5-speed sedan that took nearly 11 seconds to reach 60 mph. We estimate it takes a second or two more with the smooth shifting automatic transmission.

The payoff comes in good fuel economy. In exclusively urban driving, we averaged 30 mpg with a manual transmission Accent and 23.7 mpg with an automatic.

Accent is stable at highway speeds, and while its suspension allows large bumps to come through with a loud "thump," most smaller ones are taken in stride. Handling ability is adequate, but the narrow tires quickly relinquish their grip as cornering speed exceeds a modest pace.

Steering effort is light but the steering isn't sloppy. However there is some torque steer—the front end pulls to the side—in hard acceleration. Accent's brakes feel strong enough, but our test cars pulled to one side in hard stops.

ACCOMMODATIONS Front head room is ample for 6-footers and the rear seat is big enough for occupants up to about 5-foot-10. We were surprised by how roomy the rear seat is. Usually in cars in this price class, the rear seat is an afterthought. Still, getting into and out of the rear seat on 2-door models was a contortionistic excercise.

Some test drivers found the fixed steering wheel position too high for a comfortable driving position, and a tilt feature isn't offered. Also, longer stints behind the wheel exposed the front seats' lack of back and thigh support. The dashboard has easy-to-read gauges. Radio and climate controls are close at hand. The door-lock buttons are at the rear of the door panel, not by the door handle as in most cars. Outward visibility is good.

BUILD QUALITY We've tested several Accents and all were free of squeaks and rattles. The quality of the exterior paint and interior trim was impressive for the car's price level.

VALUE FOR THE MONEY The jury is still out on Hyundai's long-term reliability, but we're pleasantly surprised by the Accent. It's more satisfying to drive than most entry-level cars.

Prices are accurate at time of publication; subject to manufacturer's changes.

	Retail Price	Dealer Invoice
Option Pkg. 3, GS, GL	$1605	$1352
Air conditioning, power steering, AM/FM/cassette.		
Option Pkg. 4, GS, GL	2080	1739
Air conditioning, power steering, pop-up sunroof, AM/FM/CD player.		
Option Pkg. 5, GS, GL	2630	2249
Anti-lock brakes, air conditioning, power steering, pop-up sunroof, AM/FM/CD player.		
Option Pkg. 6, GS, GL	2005	1682
Air conditioning, power steering, AM/FM/cassette, pop-up sunroof.		
Option Pkg. 7, GS, GL	2555	2192
Anti-lock brakes, air conditioning, power steering, AM/FM/cassette, pop-up sunroof.		
Option Pkg. 15, GT	1525	1278
Air conditioning, cassette player, pop-up sunroof.		
Option Pkg. 16, GT	2075	1788
Anti-lock brakes, air conditioning, cassette player, pop-up sunroof.		
Option Pkg. 17, GT	1600	1335
Air conditioning, CD player, pop-up sunroof.		
Option Pkg. 18, GT	2150	1845
Anti-lock brakes, air conditioning, CD player, pop-up sunroof.		
Special Edition Pkg. 19, GS, GL	2205	1846
Air conditioning, AM/FM/cassette, power steering, rear spoiler, leather-wrapped steering wheel, floormats, cargo net, badging, alloy wheels, upgraded tires.		
Special Edition Pkg. 20, GS, GL	2605	2176
Special Edition Pkg. 19 plus sunroof w/removable sun shade.		

Comfort and Convenience

AM/FM/CD player	525	405
Remote keyless entry	349	215
Includes theft-deterrent system.		
Floormats	60	38

Appearance and Miscellaneous

Theft-deterrent system	249	155
Rear spoiler	395	261
Mud guards	55	35

HYUNDAI ELANTRA

Hyundai Elantra GLS sedan

Front-wheel-drive subcompact

Base price range: (1997 model) $11,099-$13,999. Built in South Korea.

Also consider: Chevrolet Cavalier, Dodge/Plymouth Neon, Ford Escort, Mitsubishi Mirage

FOR • Fuel economy • Optional anti-lock brakes • Interior room

AGAINST • Passing power (automatic transmission) • Small trunk opening • Automatic transmission performance

Elantra is a subcompact on paper, but it's nearly a foot longer than Hyundai's entry-level Accent subcompact, besides being roomier and more expensive. Elantra is, in fact, near the top of the subcompact class is both interior and exterior dimensions.

The '98 version is unchanged after a 1996 redesign that included fresh, rounded styling and a new station wagon body style. Base and upscale GLS trim are offered. Dual air bags are standard and anti-lock brakes are optional on GLS versions.

The sole engine is a 1.8-liter 4-cylinder called the "Beta" engine by Hyundai because it's the second to be wholly designed and built by South Korea's largest automaker. Transmission choices are manual or optional automatic.

PERFORMANCE Few subcompacts have as much as Elantra's 130 horsepower, but there's little low-end torque, so acceleration is slow off the line with the automatic transmission. It picks up as the engine climbs into its power range until 60 mph or so, over which there's not much passing power even with the throttle floored.

Making matters worse, the automatic often shifts to a higher gear too early in around-town driving and hesitates before downshifting. The engine feels stronger with the manual transmission.

We put 13,690 miles in a long-term test of an automatic-transmission GLS wagon and averaged 23.4 mpg, with a best of 26.4 on a highway trip.

Elantra is not a quiet car, even by subcompact standards. The engine is raucous in hard acceleration and there's lots of road noise, particularly in the wagon with its open cargo area.

Ride quality is on the stiff side but is never harsh, though bumps cause a lot of thumping from the tires and suspension. The taut suspension delivers cornering ability that's impressive—sporty even—and on curvy roads, Elantra feels more competent than most subcompacts. Stopping power in routine driving is more than adequate, but the rear wheels of models without anti-lock brakes tend to lock quickly on slippery road surfaces.

ACCOMMODATIONS Head room is generous in front, and the firm, well-shaped front bucket seats have enough travel to accommodate people with long legs. Elantra's rear seat provides surprisingly good head and leg room, too, though it's not wide enough to fit three people without squeezing. Is is fairly easy to get in or out of the back, despite rather narrow doors.

The driver's view is clear to all directions. The gauge cluster is unobstructed (GLS models include a tachometer) and simple rotary climate controls are in the center of the dashboard. The poorly designed audio system is mounted below the climate controls and is slightly recessed, making it awkward to reach. Worse, it has tiny buttons with ambiguous markings.

A roomy glovebox, front-door map pockets, and small bins between the front seats provide ample interior storage. Room in the low-liftover trunk is good for the class, and wagons have a split rear seat that folds to increase cargo space.

BUILD QUALITY Interior materials look richer than in some cars in this price range. The only problems we experienced with our long-term test GLS were a burned-out windshield wiper motor at 8200 miles (repaired under warranty) and an annoying rattle from the tailgate area that came and went.

VALUE FOR THE MONEY Elantra isn't as refined as subcompact-class leaders such as the Honda Civic and Toyota Corolla, but it's roomier and offers more features for the money. Value-conscious shoppers should give it a look.

RATINGS

	Sedan, 5-spd	Wagon, auto.
Acceleration	3	2
Fuel economy	5	4
Ride quality	3	3
Steering/handling	4	4
Braking	3	3
Quietness	2	2
Driver seating	4	4
Instruments/controls	3	3
Room/comfort (front)	4	4
Room/comfort (rear)	3	3
Cargo room	3	4
Value for the money	4	4
Total	41	40

SPECIFICATIONS

	4-door sedan	4-door wagon
Wheelbase, in.	100.4	100.4
Overall length, in.	174.0	175.2
Overall width, in.	66.9	66.9
Overall height, in.	54.9	58.8
Curb weight, lbs.	2458	2619
Cargo vol., cu. ft.	11.4	32.3
Fuel capacity, gals.	14.5	14.5
Seating capacity	5	5
Front head room, in.	38.6	38.6
Max. front leg room, in.	43.2	43.2
Rear head room, in.	37.6	38.9
Min. rear leg room, in.	34.6	34.8

Rating Scale: 5-Excellent; 4-Above average; 3-Average; 2-Below average; 1-Poor

CONSUMER GUIDE™

ENGINES

	dohc I-4
Size, liters/cu. in.	1.8/110
Horsepower @ rpm	130@
	6000
Torque (lbs./ft.) @ rpm	122@
	5000
Availability	S

EPA city/highway mpg
4-speed OD automatic.................................	23/31
5-speed OD manual......................................	24/32

PRICES

1997 Hyundai Elantra

	Retail Price	Dealer Invoice
Base 4-door notchback, 5-speed	$11099	$10117
Base 4-door notchback, automatic	11899	10842
Base 4-door wagon, 5-speed	11999	10938
Base 4-door wagon, automatic	12799	11663
GLS 4-door notchback, 5-speed	12549	11181
GLS 4-door notchback, automatic	13349	11906
GLS 4-door wagon, automatic	13999	12472
Destination charge	415	415

STANDARD EQUIPMENT:

Base: 1.8-liter DOHC 4-cylinder engine, 5-speed manual transmission or 4-speed automatic transmission, driver- and passenger-side air bags, variable-assist power steering, cloth reclining front bucket seats, 60/40 split folding rear seat (wagon), front storage console, tilt steering column, remote outside mirrors, digital clock, trip odometer, coolant-temperature gauge, passenger-side visor mirror, tinted glass, variable intermittent wipers, rear defogger, remote fuel-door and decklid release, rear heat ducts, roof rack (wagon), cargo-area cover (wagon), 175/65R14 tires, wheel covers.

GLS adds: 4-wheel disc brakes, upgraded cloth upholstery, 6-way adjustable driver seat, 60/40 split folding rear seat, deluxe front storage console w/armrest, power windows, power door locks, power mirrors, tachometer, AM/FM/cassette, rear wiper/washer (wagon), driver-side visor mirror, map lights, full cargo-area trim, 194/60HR14 tires, deluxe wheel covers.

OPTIONAL EQUIPMENT:
Major Packages

Option Pkg. 2, base...................................	450	348
AM/FM/cassette.		
Option Pkg. 3, base...................................	1345	1085
Air conditioning, AM/FM/cassette.		
Option Pkg. 4, base...................................	1565	1266
Air conditioning, cruise control, AM/FM/cassette.		
Option Pkg. 5, base...................................	1640	1323
Air conditioning, cruise control, CD player.		
Option Pkg. 13, GLS	2320	1895
Pkg. 14 plus rear spoiler, alloy wheels.		
Option Pkg. 14, GLS	1840	1507
Air conditioning, cruise control, power moonroof, AM/FM/CD player.		
Option Pkg. 15, GLS	1590	1301
Air conditioning, cruise control, AM/FM/CD player, alloy wheels.		
Option Pkg. 19, GLS	1115	918
Air conditioning, cruise control.		
Option Pkg. 20, GLS	1890	1636
Air conditioning, cruise control, anti-lock brakes.		
Option Pkg. 21, GLS	1595	1306
Air conditioning, cruise control, rear spoiler, alloy wheels.		
Special Edition Pkg. 22, base notchback...............	2145	1744
Includes air conditioning, AM/FM/cassette, tachometer, leather-wrapped steering wheel, deluxe console, cargo net, fog lamps, rear spoiler, badging, upgraded tires, alloy wheels.		
Special Edition Pkg. 23, base notchback...............	2735	2230
Special Edition Pkg. 22 plus power sunroof.		

Comfort and Convenience

AM/FM/CD player.....................................	525	405
Remote keyless entry.................................	365	230
Includes theft-deterrent system.		
Console armrest.......................................	125	78
Wind deflector...	55	36
Requires moonroof.		

	Retail Price	Dealer Invoice
Cargo net..	$38	$23
Floormats...	70	40

Appearance and Miscellaneous

Theft-deterrent system	260	160
Rear spoiler	395	261
NA wagon.		
Bodyside moldings	75	45
Mud guards	60	38

HYUNDAI SONATA

Hyundai Sonata GLS

Front-wheel-drive midsize car
Base price range: (1997 model) 14,749-$18,549. Built in Korea.
Also consider: Chevrolet Malibu, Dodge Stratus, Honda Accord, Toyota Camry

FOR • Optional anti-lock brakes • Passenger and cargo room • Acceleration (V-6) • Ride

AGAINST • Automatic transmission performance • Wind noise

Hyundai's largest and most-expensive car carries on unchanged for '98. In size and equipment, Sonata goes head-to-head with such midsize mainstays as the Chevrolet Malibu, Dodge Stratus, Honda Accord, and Toyota Camry, but it costs considerably less when comparably equipped.

A 2.0-liter 4-cylinder engine is standard in base and GL models. A 3.0-liter V-6 is optional for the GL and standard on the top-line GLS. The base Sonata comes with a manual transmission. Automatic is optional on the base model and standard on the others.

Dual air bags are standard and anti lock brakes are optional on the GL and GLS. Other standard equipment includes air conditioning, AM/FM cassette, rear defogger, and tilt steering wheel.

PERFORMANCE This is a highly competent sedan, with a driving feel rivaling that of any number of better-known competitors.

Sonata's 4-cylinder engine feels sluggish with the automatic transmission in standing-start acceleration but provides adequate passing power. We averaged 23.8 mpg in a 4-cylinder test car, reaching 28 mpg on the highway and dropping to 19 in the city. The V-6 furnishes stronger acceleration (9.2 seconds 0-60 mph in our test) and better passing response. Our current long-term-test Sonata GLS has averaged 22.7 mpg over 2600 miles. That's quite good for a midsize V-6 sedan.

Hyundai's automatic transmission is of the adaptive variety, that is, it's designed to program shifts according to individual driving styles. The automatic on our test car seems slow to adapt to the different styles of our crew of test drivers. Some testers have few complaints, but others say the transmission is slow to downshift for passing, shifts harshly during hard acceleration, and often is in too high or too low a gear around town.

We're in agreement about ride quality: It's impressive. The suspension is firm enough to provide a stable, comfortable highway ride and absorbent enough to soak up most bumps.

The steering is light and direct, and the brakes have good stopping power. However, as the miles have piled up on our long-term tester, the brake pedal has lost some feel and travel has increased.

Wind noise is prominent around the side windows at highway

speeds, which makes long drives more tiring than usual, but road and engine noise are very well muffled.

ACCOMMODATIONS Sonata has a spacious-feeling interior. There's adequate front-seat head room—even with the optional sunroof—and excellent leg room. Some of our taller drivers find the front buckets slightly deficient in upper-back and thigh support. The roomy rear seat accepts three adults without scrunching them too uncomfortably—a rare feat among today's midsize cars.

A trunk that opens at bumper level and has a wide, flat floor gives the Sonata generous cargo space. A 60/40 split-folding rear bench seat is standard and increases cargo versatility.

The design of the gauges and controls for the climate system and power accessories is outstanding, but the radio is mounted too low and its controls are too small to operate easily while driving.

BUILD QUALITY Our long-term Sonata GLS has required no unscheduled maintenance and has shown little wear and tear. Other Sonatas we've tested were similarly free of squeaks and rattles and used quality materials throughout.

VALUE FOR THE MONEY Sonata doesn't match midsize class leaders such as the Accord or Camry in overall refinement and Hyundai certainly can't boast levels of owner-satisfaction near Honda's or Toyota's. But this is a polished sedan, priced well below those rivals, and worth considering.

RATINGS

	Base	GL, GLS (V-6)
Acceleration	2	4
Fuel economy	4	3
Ride quality	4	4
Steering/handling	2	3
Braking	3	4
Quietness	3	3
Driver seating	3	3
Instruments/controls	3	3
Room/comfort (front)	4	4
Room/comfort (rear)	4	4
Cargo room	4	4
Value for the money	4	4
Total	**40**	**43**

SPECIFICATIONS

	4-door sedan
Wheelbase, in.	106.3
Overall length, in.	185.0
Overall width, in.	69.7
Overall height, in.	55.3
Curb weight, lbs.	2935
Cargo vol., cu. ft.	13.2
Fuel capacity, gals.	17.2
Seating capacity	5
Front head room, in.	38.5
Max. front leg room, in.	43.3
Rear head room, in.	37.7
Min. rear leg room, in.	36.6

ENGINES

	dohc I-4	ohc V-6
Size, liters/cu. in.	2.0/122	3.0/181
Horsepower @ rpm	137@ 6000	142@ 5000
Torque (lbs./ft.) @ rpm	129@ 4000	168@ 2400
Availability	S[1]	S[2]
EPA city/highway mpg		
5-speed OD manual	21/28	
4-speed OD automatic	20/27	18/24

1. Base model, GL. 2. GLS; optional, GL.

PRICES

1997 Hyundai Sonata

	Retail Price	Dealer Invoice
Base 4-door notchback, 5-speed	$14749	$15549
Base 4-door notchback, automatic	15549	14159
GL 4-door notchback, automatic	16349	14650
GL 4-door notchback, V-6 automatic	17349	15546
GLS 4-door notchback, V-6 automatic	18549	16240
Destination charge	415	415

STANDARD EQUIPMENT:

Base: 2.0-liter DOHC 4-cylinder engine, 5-speed manual or 4-speed automatic transmission, air conditioning, power steering, driver- and passenger-side air bags, cloth reclining front bucket seats w/4-way adjustable driver seat, 60/40 split-folding rear seat, front storage console, cupholders, tilt steering wheel, remote outside mirrors, tinted glass, tachometer, coolant-temperature gauge, trip odometer, digital clock, AM/FM/cassette w/6-speakers, remote fuel-door and decklid releases, rear defogger, rear heat ducts, variable intermittent wipers, visor mirrors, 195/70R14 tires, wheel covers.

GL adds: 2.0-liter DOHC 4-cylinder or 3.0-liter V-6 engine, 4-speed automatic transmission, power windows and door locks, power mirrors, deluxe wheel covers.

GLS adds to GL: 3.0-liter V-6 engine, 4-wheel disc brakes, cruise control, upgraded cloth upholstery, 6-way adjustable driver seat, console armrest, rear armrest, upgraded audio system w/6-speakers, power antenna, passenger-side visor mirror, seatback pockets, map lights, 205/60HR15 tires, alloy wheels.

OPTIONAL EQUIPMENT:
Major Packages

	Retail Price	Dealer Invoice
Option Pkg. 3, GL	$965	$767
Cruise control, console armrest, power moonroof, reading lights.		
Option Pkg. 4, GL	1245	1107
Anti-lock 4-wheel disc brakes, cruise control, console armrest.		
Option Pkg. 6, GL	365	273
Cruise control, console armrest.		
Option Pkg. 10, GLS	600	494
Power moonroof, reading lights.		
Option Pkg. 11, GLS	1350	1112
Power moonroof, AM/FM/cassette/CD player.		
Option Pkg. 12, GLS	1400	1226
AM/FM/cassette/CD player, Leather Pkg. (leather upholstery, leather-wrapped steering wheel).		
Option Pkg. 13, GLS	2000	1720
Power moonroof, AM/FM/cassette/CD player, Leather Pkg. (leather upholstery, leather-wrapped steering wheel), reading lights.		
Option Pkg. 14, GLS	2880	2554
Anti-lock brakes, power moonroof, AM/FM/cassette/CD player, Leather Pkg. (leather upholstery, leather-wrapped steering wheel), reading lights.		
Option Pkg. 15, GLS	880	834
Anti-lock brakes.		
Special Edition Pkg. 16, GL V-6	850	700
Leather-wrapped steering wheel, cargo net, floormats, rear spoiler, fog lamps, badging, alloy wheels.		
Special Edition Pkg.17, GL V-6	1450	1194
Special Edition Pkg. plus power moonroof.		

Comfort and Convenience

Wind deflector, GL, GLS	55	36
Requires moonroof.		
Cargo net	38	23
Console armrest, base, GL	135	85
Floormats	78	45

Appearance and Miscellaneous

Theft-deterrent system, GL, GLS	365	225
Includes remote keyless entry.		
Mud guards	75	43

HYUNDAI TIBURON

Front-wheel-drive sports coupe

Base price range: (1997 model) $13,499-$15,699. Built in South Korea.

Also consider: Ford Escort ZX2, Nissan 200SX, Saturn Coupe, Toyota Paseo

FOR • Optional anti-lock brakes (FX) • Steering/handling • Ride

AGAINST • Passing power (automatic transmission) • Rear seat room • Entry/exit

Replacing the Scoupe last year as the sports coupe from South Korea's largest automaker, Tiburon returns for 1998 without the weaker of its two original engines. Though based loose-

Rating Scale: 5-Excellent; 4-Above average; 3-Average; 2-Below average; 1-Poor

Hyundai Tiburon FX

ly on Hyundai's Elantra subcompact, Tiburon rides a 3-inch-shorter wheelbase and has a hatchback instead of Scoupe's coupe format.

Last year base models had a 130-horsepower 1.8-liter 4-cylinder and FX models a 140-horsepower 2.0; both now use the 2.0. Manual transmission is standard, an automatic (with Normal and Power shift modes) is optional.

Dual air bags are standard. Anti-lock brakes with rear discs are optional on the FX.

Both models come with a longer list of standard features than most other lower-priced sports coupes, including power windows, air conditioning, and a tilt steering wheel. The FX adds wider tires on alloy wheels and is available with leather upholstery and a CD player.

PERFORMANCE Tiburon plays the sports-coupe role well in terms of handling, but its engine disappoints. The 2.0 generates a loud, crude growl in even moderate acceleration and is no smoother when cruising. Add copious amounts of road noise and suspension thumping, and this is one unpleasant car on a long trip.

The 2.0 doesn't balance all that commotion with good performance, feeling especially sluggish with the automatic transmission. Passing power is adequate, and the automatic downshifts fairly promptly with the transmission in the Power shift mode. Manual-transmission Tiburons are livelier, but not enough to satisfy serious drivers.

Our automatic-transmission test car averaged 25 mpg in a mix of urban commuting and rush-hour expressway driving. We didn't have a chance to measure fuel economy with our 5-speed car, but it should be slightly higher.

Handling is sporty and secure, with well-managed body lean and good grip in corners. The firm steering has plenty of road feel and centers quickly after turns. The suspension provides a taut ride, but it isn't uncomfortably stiff even on bumpy streets

Our test cars lacked the optional anti-lock brakes, but stopping power felt more than adequate.

ACCOMMODATIONS Tiburon has a low, snug driving position, a well arranged dashboard, laughable back seat space for anyone over toddler size, and entry/exit that's none too easy even in front.

Visibility is better than average for a sports coupe and the FX's large rear spoiler helps mark the back of the car when parallel parking.

With its hatchback design and standard split-folding rear seatback, Tiburon exceeds the cargo capacity and practicality of many sports coupes, and FX models get a handy cargo cover. Unfortunately, the liftover is high enough to be a real back strainer if you're heaving heavy items around.

Map pockets on the doors, a small glovebox, tiny covered and open bins in the center console, and two cupholders that pop from the dashboard provide adequate interior storage.

BUILD QUALITY Tiburon is impressively solid. Even with frameless windows, the doors close with a "thunk." One of our test cars had a minor rattle in the folding rear seatback, but interior fit and finish was otherwise very good.

VALUE FOR THE MONEY Overriding Tiburon's distinctive styling, enticing base prices, and good road manners is its lack of powertrain refinement. That's a big negative for a sports coupe.

RATINGS

	Base w/auto. trans	FX w/man. trans
Acceleration	2	3
Fuel economy	4	4
Ride quality	3	3
Steering/handling	4	4
Braking	3	3
Quietness	2	2
Driver seating	3	3
Instruments/controls	4	4
Room/comfort (front)	2	2
Room/comfort (rear)	1	1
Cargo room	3	3
Value for the money	3	3
Total	**34**	**35**

SPECIFICATIONS

	2-door hatchback
Wheelbase, in.	97.4
Overall length, in.	170.9
Overall width, in.	68.1
Overall height, in.	51.7
Curb weight, lbs.	2570
Cargo vol., cu. ft.	12.8
Fuel capacity, gals.	14.5
Seating capacity	4
Front head room, in.	38.0
Max. front leg room, in.	43.1
Rear head room, in.	34.4
Min. rear leg room, in.	29.9

ENGINES

	dohc I-4
Size, liters/cu. in.	2.0/122
Horsepower @ rpm	140@ 6000
Torque (lbs./ft.) @ rpm	133@ 4800
Availability	S

EPA city/highway mpg

5-speed OD manual	22/29
4-speed OD automatic	21/28

PRICES

1997 Hyundai Tiburon	Retail Price	Dealer Invoice
2-door hatchback, 5-speed	$13499	$12166
2-door hatchback, automatic	14299	12891
FX 2-door hatchback, 5-speed	14899	13121
FX 2-door hatchback, automatic	15699	13846
Destination charge	415	415

STANDARD EQUIPMENT:

1.8-liter 4-cylinder engine, 5-speed manual or 4-speed automatic transmission, driver- and passenger-side air bags, power steering, cloth reclining front bucket seats, split-folding rear seat, front storage console, cupholders, tilt steering column, power windows, remote outside mirrors, tinted glass, coolant-temperature gauge, trip odometer, tachometer, digital clock, AM/FM/cassette, rear defogger, remote hatch and fuel-door releases, variable intermittent wipers, map lights, rear heat ducts, cargo-area cover, bright exhaust outlets, 195/60R14 performance tires, wheel covers.

FX adds: 2.0-liter 4-cylinder engine, 4-wheel disc brakes, upgraded seat trim, 6-way adjustable driver seat, deluxe front storage console, power door locks, power mirrors, passenger-side visor mirror, fog lights, rear spoiler, rear wiper/washer, alloy wheels.

OPTIONAL EQUIPMENT:

Option Pkg. 2, base	895	737
Air conditioning.		
Option Pkg. 3, base	1245	1025
Air conditioning, upgraded audio system.		
Option Pkg. 4, base	1745	1419
Air conditioning, upgraded audio system, rear spoiler, fog lights.		
Option Pkg. 5, base	2140	1735
Air conditioning, upgraded audio system, rear spoiler, fog lights, 195/HR15 performance tires, alloy wheels.		

Prices are accurate at time of publication; subject to manufacturer's changes.

	Retail Price	Dealer Invoice
Option Pkg. 6, FX	$1425	$1174

Air conditioning, cruise control, upgraded audio system.

Option Pkg. 7, FX 2050 1689
Air conditioning, cruise control, power sunroof, upgraded audio system.

Option Pkg. 8, FX 2425 1998
Air conditioning, cruise control, power sunroof, AM/FM/cassette/CD player.

Option Pkg. 9, FX 3125 2647
Anti-lock brakes, air conditioning, cruise control, power sunroof, AM/FM/cassette/CD player.

Option Pkg. 10, FX 3910 3364
Anti-lock brakes, air conditioning, cruise control, leather upholstery, leather-wrapped steering wheel, power sunroof, AM/FM/cassette/CD player, 195/55HR15 performance tires.

Option Pkg. 11, FX 3210 2715
Air conditioning, cruise control, leather upholstery, leather-wrapped steering wheel, power sunroof, AM/FM/cassette/CD player, 195/55HR15 performance tires.

Option Pkg. 12, FX 1885 1551
Air conditioning, cruise control, AM/FM/cassette/CD player, 195/55HR15 performance tires.

Option Pkg. 13, FX 2510 2066
Air conditioning, cruise control, power sunroof, AM/FM/cassette/CD player, 195/55HR15 performance tires.

Option Pkg. 14, FX 1510 1242
Air conditioning, cruise control, upgraded audio system, 195/55HR15 performance tires.

Option Pkg. 15, FX 2135 1757
Air conditioning, cruise control, power sunroof, upgraded audio system, 195/55HR15 performance tires.

Option Pkg. 16, FX 3210 2715
Anti-lock brakes, air conditioning, cruise control, power sunroof, AM/FM/cassette/CD player, 195/55HR15 performance tires

INFINITI I30

✓ BEST BUY

Infiniti I30t

Front-wheel-drive near-luxury car; similar to Nissan Maxima

Base price range: $28,900-$32,500. Built in Japan.

Also consider: BMW 3-Series, Lexus ES 300, Mazda Millenia

FOR • Standard anti-lock brakes • Acceleration • Steering/handling • Ride • Side air bags

AGAINST • Rear seat comfort • Rear visibility • Fuel economy

With the rear-drive J30 being dropped for lack of sales, the front-drive I30 becomes the only V-6 sedan from Nissan's upscale division for 1998. Introduced two years ago as a bucks-up clone of the Nissan Maxima, the I30 differs mainly from Maxima in having more standard features, plus a more formal exterior look.

The big news for '98 is the arrival of standard front side air bags, a supplemental safety feature that's optional on this year's top-line Maxima SE and GLE models. Other I30 changes involve restyled headlamps and taillamps and an outside temperature indicator in the climate-control panel. Finally, last year's "Leather-Appointed" model is replaced by a Leather and

Convenience Package option that upgrades the base I30 with hide upholstery, a tilt/slide power moonroof, and integrated Homelink garage-door opener. A sportier Touring model, badged I30t, continues with a firmer suspension, traction control, and new 16-inch wheels (instead of 15s) with wider tires among its features. Automatic transmission is again standard on the base I30 and optional for the Touring.

PERFORMANCE The I30 has strong, refined performance and capable handling. Nissan's smooth V-6 produces enough torque at low rpm to give quick launches—0-60 mph takes about 8 seconds—and brisk passing sprints. Fuel economy disappoints, averaging under 19 mpg in our tests; highway cruising can average in the mid-20s, though. Premium gas is recommended. Not surprisingly, all this is true for the Maxima, but the I30 may be a tad quieter owing to some extra insulation and other noise-dampening measures.

Suspension is relatively firm even on the standard I30, yet it easily soaks up most bumps. Rear passengers, however, feel expansion joints and tar strips more than those in front. Steering is precise and has good feedback. In high-speed corners the I30 has stable front-drive moves, little body lean, and ample grip. The Touring's firmer suspension and higher-performance tires provide more responsive handling, but also a stiffer ride and more road noise at highway speeds, so don't buy that model without driving it. Braking is short, straight, and true in any I30.

ACCOMMODATIONS If you've been in a Maxima, you've been in an I30. Gauges and controls are all in the same locations here, and are as well-marked and easily reached. Visibility is good to the front and sides, but the rear headrests block the view directly aft.

Though passenger room is ample for four adults, rear-seat comfort is compromised by a backrest that's too reclined for some tastes. The spacious trunk is augmented by a pass-through slot that allows carrying long items, such as skis, and the interior provides good small-items stowage.

BUILD QUALITY I30s we've driven have been uniformly well built inside and out. Most interior surfaces look and feel rich, but the pseudo-woodgrain console trim is strictly 1970s Detroit.

VALUE FOR THE MONEY If you don't need so much luxury, a Maxima will give you all the I30's basic virtues for less money. However, Infiniti offers a more comprehensive warranty and the promise of better customer service. Overall, the I30 is a fine choice in an entry-level luxury sedan.

RATINGS

	I30
Acceleration	4
Fuel economy	2
Ride quality	4
Steering/handling	4
Braking	4
Quietness	4
Driver seating	4
Instruments/controls	4
Room/comfort (front)	4
Room/comfort (rear)	3
Cargo room	4
Value for the money	4
Total	**45**

SPECIFICATIONS

	4-door sedan
Wheelbase, in.	106.3
Overall length, in.	189.6
Overall width, in.	69.7
Overall height, in.	55.7
Curb weight, lbs.	3090
Cargo vol., cu. ft.	14.1
Fuel capacity, gals.	18.5
Seating capacity	5
Front head room, in.	40.1
Max. front leg room, in.	43.9
Rear head room, in.	37.4
Min. rear leg room, in.	34.3

Rating Scale: 5-Excellent; 4-Above average; 3-Average; 2-Below average; 1-Poor

CONSUMER GUIDE™

ENGINES

	dohc V-6
Size, liters/cu. in.	3.0/181
Horsepower @ rpm	190@
	5600
Torque (lbs./ft.) @ rpm	205@
	4000
Availability	S

EPA city/highway mpg

4-speed OD automatic................................	21/28
5-speed OD manual....................................	21/26

PRICES

Infiniti I30	Retail Price	Dealer Invoice
I30 4-door sedan	$28900	$25683
I30t Touring 4-door sedan, 5-speed	31500	27676
I30t Touring 4-door sedan, automatic	32500	28555
Destination charge	495	495

STANDARD EQUIPMENT:

I30 3.0-liter DOHC V-6 engine, 4-speed automatic transmission, anti-lock 4-wheel disc brakes, driver- and passenger-side air bags, automatic climate control, air conditioning, variable-assist power steering, tilt steering column, leather-wrapped steering wheel, shifter knob, and parking brake handle, illuminated remote keyless entry, cruise control, power cloth front bucket seats, console with armrest, AM/FM/cassette and CD player with six speakers, power antenna, power windows, power door locks, power mirrors, rear defogger, remote fuel-door and decklid releases, intermittent wipers, tachometer, coolant-temperature gauge, trip odometer, digital clock, rear folding armrest, illuminated visor mirrors, map lights, cargo net, floormats, tinted glass, anti-theft alarm, fog lights, 205/65R15 tires, cast alloy wheels.

I30t adds: Leather and Convenience Pkg. (leather upholstery, power sunroof, Homelink universal garage door opener, automatic day/night inside mirror), Heated Seat Pkg. (heated front seats, heated mirrors, low-windshield-washer-fluid warning light, heavy-duty battery), 5-speed manual or 4-speed automatic transmission, limited-slip differential, sport suspension, decklid spoiler, 215/60HR15 touring tires, forged alloy wheels.

OPTIONAL EQUIPMENT:
Major Packages

Leather and Convenience Pkg., I30.........................	1300	985

   Leather upholstery, power sunroof, automatic day/night inside mirror, Homelink universal garage door opener.

Heated Seat Pkg., I30.............................	400	351

   Heated front seats and mirrors, low-windshield-washer-fluid warning light, heavy-duty battery. Requires Leather and Convenience Pkg.

Traction Enhancement Pkg., I30..............................	830	729

   Heated Seat Pkg. plus limited slip differential. Requires Leather and Convenience Pkg.

Safe and Sound Pkg.	990	771

   6-disc CD changer, mud guards, wheel locks, trunk mat.

Comfort and Convenience

Power sunroof, I30	950	835
6-disc CD changer	680	527

INFINITI Q45

Rear-wheel-drive luxury car

Base price range: (1997 model) $48,395-$50,395. Built in Japan.

Also consider: Cadillac Seville, Lexus LS 400, Mercedes-Benz E-Class

FOR • Acceleration • Quietness • Side air bags

AGAINST • Fuel economy • Cargo room

The flagship sedan of Nissan's luxury division was fully redesigned last year, emerging trimmer, more fuel efficient, and no more expensive. The Q45 then gained standard front side air bags for "1997½."

Predictably, the '98 model is a '97 rerun apart from two minor

Infiniti Q45

refinements: front safety belt pretensioners and a liquid crystal display odometer (replacing mechanical). As in some other cars, the pretensioners employ a small "firing" device that automatically cinches the belt in a crash to more tightly secure an occupant.

The Q45 continues in standard and Touring models, both fully equipped. Heated seats are the only factory option for the base version and are standard on the Q45t, which also gets a firmer suspension, specific-design alloy wheels, rear spoiler and black grille. The sole powertrain again comprises a 4.1-liter V-8 and automatic transmission.

PERFORMANCE Infiniti's latest image leader is quick, smooth, and quiet on most any road. It may have "less engine" than earlier Q45s, but it also has less weight, so it goes just as well. We clocked 0-60 mph in a brisk 7.2 seconds. Mid-range power is equally ample, aided by a velvety, responsive automatic transmission. Fuel economy isn't so nice. We averaged 15.4 mpg in 600 miles of mostly rush-hour commuting; a second test Q45 returned 17.6 in easier driving.

Against the old Q, the new standard model is less agile and more roly-poly on tight twisty roads—more Lexus LS than BMW 5-Series. Slightly numb on-center steering feel doesn't help. Damping is soft enough to allow fair nosedive in hard braking—which is otherwise excellent—but it does provide an almost "magic carpet" ride with outstanding impact absorption. Cruising is hushed, with little noise from road, wind, or engine.

ACCOMMODATIONS Though smaller than the old Q outside, the new one is a bit roomier inside. Even so, lanky rear-seaters must ride knees-up behind a tall front passenger, and aft head room is only adequate. The trunk is wide but not very long, with room for about four medium suitcases and a few odds and ends.

No complaints about front-cabin room or comfort, and there are enough adjustments to accommodate most any size occupant. The dashboard looks uninspired but is orderly and convenient. Driver visibility is good except over-the-shoulder, where the wide rear roof pillars interfere.

BUILD QUALITY Our test cars had smooth, lustrous paint and a generally solid feel over railroad tracks and other hazards. One car, though, had several interior rattles and a dashboard creak. Another had a loose, flimsy-feeling center console.

VALUE FOR THE MONEY Though quick, quiet, and pleasantly undemanding to drive, the new Q45 is as bland as its "Japanese Buick" looks, and it literally comes up short in cargo room. It's far from a bad car; it's just not as compelling as most competitors, which you'd be well advised to check out too.

RATINGS	Q45t
Acceleration	4
Fuel economy	2
Ride quality	4
Steering/handling	3
Braking	4
Quietness	5
Driver seating	4
Instruments/controls	4
Room/comfort (front)	4
Room/comfort (rear)	3
Cargo room	3
Value for the money	3
Total	**43**

Prices are accurate at time of publication; subject to manufacturer's changes.

SPECIFICATIONS

	4-door sedan
Wheelbase, in.	111.4
Overall length, in.	199.2
Overall width, in.	71.7
Overall height, in.	56.9
Curb weight, lbs.	3879
Cargo vol., cu. ft.	12.6
Fuel capacity, gals.	21.1
Seating capacity	5
Front head room, in.	37.6
Max. front leg room, in.	43.6
Rear head room, in.	36.9
Min. rear leg room, in.	35.9

ENGINES

	dohc V-8
Size, liters/cu. in.	4.1/252
Horsepower @ rpm	266@ 5600
Torque (lbs./ft.) @ rpm	278@ 4000
Availability	S

EPA city/highway mpg

4-speed OD automatic	18/23

PRICES

1997 Infiniti Q45

	Retail Price	Dealer Invoice
Q45 4-door notchback	$48395	$43064
Q45t 4-door notchback	50395	44841
Destination charge	495	495

STANDARD EQUIPMENT:

Q45: 4.1-liter DOHC V-8 engine, 4-speed automatic transmission, anti-lock 4-wheel disc brakes, variable-assist power steering, traction control system, limited-slip differential, driver- and passenger-side air bags, cruise control, automatic climate control, leather upholstery, 10-way power front bucket seats, memory driver seat, folding rear seat with armrest, front storage console with auxiliary power outlet, cupholders, wood interior trim, leather-wrapped steering wheel and shifter, tilt/telescopic steering wheel w/memory, Nissan/Bose AM/FM/CD/cassette player, power antenna, integrated diversity antenna, power sunroof, green tinted glass, power windows, power door locks, remote keyless entry, heated power mirrors, tachometer, coolant-temperature gauge, digital clock, outside temperature indicator, automatic day/night inside mirror, interior air filter, rear air ducts, rear defogger, remote fuel-door and decklid releases, illuminated visor mirrors, map lights, variable intermittent wipers, theft-deterrent system, automatic headlamps, Homelink universal garage-door opener, floormats, fog lights, cargo net, 215/60R16 tires, alloy wheels.

Q45t adds: sport-tuned suspension, leather-wrapped sport steering wheel, heated front seats, 6-disc CD changer, rear spoiler, performance alloy wheels.

OPTIONAL EQUIPMENT:

Heated front seats, Q45	400	355

INFINITI QX4

Infiniti QX4

Rear- or 4-wheel-drive midsize sport-utility vehicle; similar to Nissan Pathfinder

Base price: $35,550. Built in Japan.

Also consider: Lexus RX 300, Mercedes-Benz ML320, Mercury Mountaineer

FOR • Standard anti-lock brakes • Steering/handling • Ride

AGAINST • Rear seat entry/exit • Rear leg room • Engine noise • Fuel economy

Nissan's luxury division sauntered into the booming sport-utility market last year with a high-end SUV based on the Nissan Pathfinder. Infiniti makes no changes to the 1998 QX4 other than shuffling content on a couple of option packages.

The QX4 shares Pathfinder's V-6 engine, though here it's offered only with automatic transmission. The higher-priced Infiniti differs in front and rear styling and includes full-house luxury equipment and a more-sophisticated 4-wheel-drive system.

Called "All-Mode 4WD," the QX4's system has three settings selected by a rotary switch: 2WD routes power only to the rear wheels; Auto distributes up to 50 percent power to the front wheels when the rear wheels begin to slip; and Lock splits power 50/50 under all conditions. A separate console lever activates low-range 4WD gearing. Auto can be used on smooth, dry pavement; Pathfinder, by contrast, offers only part-time 4WD that can't be used on dry pavement.

PERFORMANCE Infiniti isn't alone in claiming its SUV "drives like a car, not like a truck." The QX4 is indeed quite car-like, with a firm suspension that absorbs bumps better than many SUVs do, plus relatively low noise levels and confident cornering ability with good grip and little body lean. Still, the QX4 doesn't ride like a luxury sedan, and the V-6 sounds and feels rough when worked hard—as it must be to provide decent passing power. Acceleration is at least adequate nevertheless, aided by an automatic transmission that shifts smoothly but sometimes hesitates to kick down.

Like most SUVs, the QX4 guzzles gas. We averaged just 12.5 mpg, in a mix of city and freeway driving, with a high of 15.2 mph on the highway.

ACCOMMODATIONS Apart from a more upscale, leather-upholstered ambience, the QX4 interior is the same as Pathfinder's. That means a high step-in even with the standard running boards. Rear access is complicated by rear doors that are narrow at the bottom and don't open close to 90 degrees. All-around head and leg room are adequate for four adults, though rear passengers have virtually no underseat foot space.

Cargo room is plentiful even with the 60/40 rear seat in place. Converting it requires swinging the cushion forward and removing the headrests, but the seatbacks then lie flat to create a long, wide deck. There's also a rear under-floor compartment big enough to hide a laptop computer.

Drivers enjoy good visibility and a convenient, guess-free dash layout. Standard dual power front seats combine with a tilt steering wheel for easy tailoring of the driver's position.

BUILD QUALITY The QX4 gives little cause for complaint about workmanship. Indeed, it has topped independent surveys of customer satisfaction and our examples have been free from flaws in fit and finish.

VALUE FOR THE MONEY In a class that includes the impressive new Mercedes ML320, the QX4 doesn't look very competitive. Unless you crave Infiniti's red-carpet customer service, a carefully optioned Pathfinder will give you most of what the QX4 does at a far friendlier price.

RATINGS

	QX4
Acceleration	3
Fuel economy	1
Ride quality	3
Steering/handling	4
Braking	4
Quietness	3
Driver seating	4
Instruments/controls	4
Room/comfort (front)	4
Room/comfort (rear)	3
Cargo room	5
Value for the money	3
Total	**41**

Rating Scale: 5-Excellent; 4-Above average; 3-Average; 2-Below average; 1-Poor

SPECIFICATIONS

	4-door wagon
Wheelbase, in.	106.3
Overall length, in.	178.3
Overall width, in.	68.7
Overall height, in.	67.1
Curb weight, lbs.	4275
Cargo vol., cu. ft.	85.0
Fuel capacity, gals.	21.1
Seating capacity	5
Front head room, in.	39.5
Max. front leg room, in.	41.7
Rear head room, in.	37.5
Min. rear leg room, in.	31.8

ENGINES

	ohc V-6
Size, liters/cu. in.	3.3/201
Horsepower @ rpm	168@ 4800
Torque (lbs./ft.) @ rpm	196@ 2800
Availability	S
EPA city/highway mpg	
4-speed OD automatic	15/19

PRICES

Infiniti QX4

	Retail Price	Dealer Invoice
4-door wagon	$35550	$31666
Destination charge	495	495

STANDARD EQUIPMENT:

Base: 3.3-liter V-6 engine, 4-speed automatic transmission, All-Mode 4-wheel drive, driver- and passenger-side air bags, anti-lock brakes, air conditioning w/automatic climate control, variable-assist power steering, tilt steering column, leather-wrapped steering wheel and shifter, cruise control, leather upholstery, power front bucket seats, reclining 60/40 split-folding rear seat, rear armrest, center storage console w/armrest, over-head storage console (includes outside-temperature indicator, compass, map lights), cupholders, heated power mirrors, power windows, power door locks, remote keyless entry, tachometer, trip odometer, 6-speaker Bose audio system with AM/FM/cassette/CD player, integrated diversity antenna, variable intermittent wipers, intermittent rear wiper, rear defogger, remote fuel-door and hatch releases, auxiliary power outlet, illuminated visor mirrors, wood interior trim, cargo net and cover, rear storage bin, floormats, fog lights, theft-deterrent system, tinted glass, step rail, roof rack, mud guards, fuel-tank skid plates, 245/70R16 tires, alloy wheels.

OPTIONAL EQUIPMENT:
Major Packages

Premium Sport Pkg.	700	622

Limited-slip rear differential, heated front seats. Requires Sunroof Pkg.

Sunroof Preferred Pkg.	1250	1112

Sunroof, 6-disc CD changer, rear window wind deflector.

Comfort and Convenience

Heated front seats	400	355

Requires sunroof.

Power sunroof	950	845

Special Purpose, Wheels and Tires

Tow hitch	390	289

ISUZU HOMBRE

Rear- or 4-wheel-drive compact pickup; similar to Chevrolet S-10 and GMC Sonoma

Base price range: (1997 model) $11,272-$16,413. Built in Shreveport, La.

Also consider: Dodge Dakota, Ford Ranger, Toyota Tacoma

FOR • Standard anti-lock brakes • Acceleration (V-6)

1997 Isuzu Hombre XS Spacecab

AGAINST • Rear seat comfort (extended cab) • Ride

General Motors sells Isuzu rights to its Chevrolet S-10/GMC Sonoma compact pickup trucks, and the Japanese company designs some distinct sheetmetal and markets the result as the Hombre. All three are assembled at a GM plant in Louisiana. American assembly allows Isuzu to skirt the 25-percent tariff on imported trucks. GM owns a minor interest in Isuzu.

For '98, Hombre adds a staple of the genre: 4-wheel-drive capability. Last year, only 2-wheel-drive models were offered.

Still, Hombre's model mix is not as comprehensive as that of the GM twins. For instance, there's no 2WD standard-cab V-6, and you can't get a manual transmission with the V-6 Spacecab. However, most of the popular combinations are available. What is still not offered in the Hombre is GM's nifty third door for extended-cab models.

Hombre, like its GM twins, has a redesigned dashboard for 1998 that adds a passenger-side air bag to the carried-over driver-side air bag. A passenger air bag deactivation switch is furnished for use when a child seat is in place.

Base S models are available in regular-cab bodies, while uplevel LS models come in regular- and extended-cab (Spacecab) styles. GM's 120-horsepower (down 10 from last year) 2.2-liter 4-cylinder is offered on 2WD models with a 5-speed manual or 4-speed automatic transmission. Two-wheel-drive Spacecabs come with a 175-horsepower 4.3-liter V-6 mated only to an automatic transmission. Four-wheel-drive models get a 180-horsepower version of the V-6, and it can be backed by either the manual or automatic transmission.

The 4WD is GM's shift-on-the-fly, slippery-surfaces-only system. Anti-lock brakes are standard and 4WD models add rear disc brakes.

Hombre's performance and accommodations mirror those of similarly equipped S10s and Sonomas.

See the Chevrolet S-10 report of an evaluation of the Hombre.

RATINGS

	Reg. cab 2WD 4 cyl.	Spacecab 4WD V-6
Acceleration	3	4
Fuel economy	3	2
Ride quality	3	3
Steering/handling	3	3
Braking	3	4
Quietness	3	3
Driver seating	4	4
Instruments/controls	4	4
Room/comfort (front)	3	2
Room/comfort (rear)	—	2
Cargo room	1	2
Value for the money	4	3
Total	**34**	**37**

Prices are accurate at time of publication; subject to manufacturer's changes.

SPECIFICATIONS

	Reg. cab	Ext. cab
Wheelbase, in.	108.3	122.9
Overall length, in.	187.1	201.7
Overall width, in.	67.9	67.9
Overall height, in.	63.9	63.9
Curb weight, lbs.	3125	3305
Maximum payload, lbs.	1138	1154
Fuel capacity, gals.	18.5	18.5
Seating capacity	3	5
Front head room, in.	39.5	39.6
Max. front leg room, in.	42.4	42.4
Rear head room, in.	—	NA
Min. rear leg room, in.	—	NA

ENGINES

	dohc I-4	ohv V-6
Size, liters/cu. in.	2.2/133	4.3/262
Horsepower @ rpm	120@ 5000	175[1]@ 4400
Torque (lbs./ft.) @ rpm	140@ 3600	240@ 2800
Availability	S	S[2]

EPA city/highway mpg
5-speed OD manual	22/29	

1. 180 horsepower with 4WD. 2. 2WD V-6 Spacecab and 4WD.

PRICES

1997 Isuzu Hombre

	Retail Price	Dealer Invoice
S regular cab, 5-speed	$11272	$10821
S regular cab, automatic	12247	11757
XS regular cab, 5-speed	11699	11114
XS regular cab, automatic	12674	12040
XS Spacecab 4-cylinder, 5-speed	14289	13246
XS Spacecab 4-cylinder, automatic	15264	14150
XS Spacecab V-6	16413	15070
Destination charge	485	485

STANDARD EQUIPMENT:

S: 2.2-liter 4-cylinder engine, 5-speed manual transmission or 4-speed automatic transmission, anti-lock brakes, driver-side air bag, variable assist power steering, 3-passenger cloth bench seat, dual outside mirrors, front storage console, tinted glass, trip odometer, coolant temperature gauge, voltmeter, cupholders, detachable tailgate, daytime running lights, 205/75R15 tires, wheel covers.

XS adds: Custom cloth 60/40 split bench seat, AM/FM radio, tachometer, carpeting, rear bumper w/end caps.

Spacecab 4-cylinder adds: dual vinyl rear jump seats, walk-in device for front passenger seat, cloth door trim panels, dual illuminated visor mirrors, AM/FM radio, rear bumper.

Spacecab V-6 adds: 4.3-liter V-6 engine, 4-speed automatic transmission, center armrest.

OPTIONAL EQUIPMENT:
Major Packages

	Retail	Dealer
Preferred Equipment Pkg., XS regular cab	1131	1074
Air conditioning, sliding rear window, AM/FM radio, tachometer, floormats.		
Spacecab	896	851
Air conditioning, sliding rear window, AM/FM/cassette, tachometer, floormats.		
Spacecab V-6	1151	1093
Air conditioning, sliding rear window, AM/FM/CD player, premium speakers, tachometer, floormats.		
Convenience Pkg., Spacecab	425	404
Tilt steering wheel, cruise control.		
Power Pkg., Spacecab V-6	530	503
Power windows, locks, and mirrors.		
Performance Pkg., 4-cylinder models	65	58
Heavy-duty suspension, 4.10 axle ratio.		

Comfort and Convenience

Air conditioning	835	743
Sliding rear window, XS	125	111
AM/FM radio, S	235	209
AM/FM/cassette, XS regular cab	380	338

	Retail Price	Dealer Invoice
Spacecab V-6	$145	$129

Appearance and Miscellaneous

Tachometer, XS	65	58
Rear bumper, regular cabs	60	53

ISUZU OASIS

Isuzu Oasis LS

Front-wheel-drive minivan; similar to Honda Odyssey
Base price range: (1997 model) $23,730-$25,990. Built in Japan.
Also consider: Chevrolet Venture, Dodge Caravan, Toyota Sienna

FOR • Standard anti-lock brakes • Ride • Steering/handling • Entry/exit

AGAINST • Engine noise • Road noise

Isuzu supplies Honda with a version of its Rodeo sport-utility vehicle for sale as the Honda Passport. Honda, in turn, furnishes Isuzu with its Odyssey minivan and Isuzu sells it as the Oasis.

Like Odyssey, Oasis has four conventional swing-open side doors and a rear liftgate. And like its Honda twin, Oasis gets slightly more power for '98, trading a 140-horsepower 2.2-liter 4-cylinder for a 150-horsepower 2.3-liter version. Automatic transmission is standard. Also new is a restyled dashboard shared with the Odyssey; it includes the vehicle's first tachometer. The horn is now activated by a steering-wheel-hub pad rather than steering-wheel spoke buttons. Dual air bags and 4-wheel anti-lock disc brakes are standard.

Oasis' base S model seats seven with two front bucket seats, a 3-place middle bench, and a 2-place rear bench. The LS model seats six, replacing the middle bench with two captain's-chair buckets. Both models' middle seats are removable and the 2-place rear seat folds flush into the floor for additional cargo space.

Oasis and Odyssey are built in Japan by Honda. The Isuzu version's performance and accommodations are identical to those of the Odyssey.

PERFORMANCE Because the Oasis is a clone of the Odyssey, see the report on the Honda version as well.

Oasis has a firm and stable ride, exhibiting little body lean in turns. It's more agile and surefooted than most competitors and feels more like a sedan than a minivan.

The 4-cylinder engine becomes loud in hard acceleration, and there's too much road noise at highway speeds. Acceleration is fairly brisk, however, and fuel economy is higher than usual for a minivan. We've averaged in the low 20s in city/highway driving with the Oasis and Odyssey, better than we usually achieve in straight highway driving with larger, V-6 powered rivals.

Where Oasis and Odyssey come up short—literally—is in interior room. Competitors such as the Dodge Grand Caravan and Ford Windstar are longer and wider, providing more space for passengers and cargo.

There's still ample room for six people in the Oasis and Odyssey and more than enough cargo space for most needs. The rear seat that folds flush to the floor is a clever alternative to removable seats.

If you don't need the interior space of a larger minivan or if you prefer swing-out rear doors to sliding doors, the Oasis and

Rating Scale: 5-Excellent; 4-Above average; 3-Average; 2-Below average; 1-Poor

CONSUMER GUIDE™

Odyssey are good choices. Since the two are virtually identical and Honda has a more recognized name than Isuzu, the Oasis is a better choice only if the Isuzu dealer is more convenient or offers a lower price.

See the Honda Odyssey report for an evaluation of the Oasis.

RATINGS

	S/LS
Acceleration	3
Fuel economy	3
Ride quality	4
Steering/handling	3
Braking	4
Quietness	3
Driver seating	4
Instruments/controls	4
Room/comfort (front)	4
Room/comfort (rear)	4
Cargo room	4
Value for the money	4
Total	**44**

SPECIFICATIONS

	4-door van
Wheelbase, in.	111.4
Overall length, in.	187.2
Overall width, in.	70.6
Overall height, in.	64.6
Curb weight, lbs.	3473
Cargo vol., cu. ft.	102.5
Fuel capacity, gals.	17.2
Seating capacity	7
Front head room, in.	40.1
Max. front leg room, in.	40.7
Rear head room, in.	39.3
Min. rear leg room, in.	40.2

ENGINES

	dohc I-4
Size, liters/cu. in.	2.3/137
Horsepower @ rpm	150@ 5600
Torque (lbs./ft.) @ rpm	152@ 4700
Availability	S
EPA city/highway mpg	
4-speed OD automatic	NA

PRICES

1997 Isuzu Oasis

	Retail Price	Dealer Invoice
S 4-door van	$23730	$21831
LS 4-door van	25990	23911
Destination charge	445	445

STANDARD EQUIPMENT:

S: 2.2-liter 4-cylinder engine, 4-speed automatic transmission, driver- and passenger-side air bags, variable assist power steering, anti-lock brakes 4-wheel disc brakes, dual air conditioning, power mirrors, power windows, power door locks, cruise control, tilt steering column, 4-speaker AM/FM/cassette player, rear defogger, rear wiper/washer, theft-deterrent system, intermittent wipers, dual visor mirrors with passenger-side illumination, reclining cloth front bucket seats, 3-passenger center bench seat, folding retractable rear bench seat, front and center storage console w/cupholders, door pockets, carpeting, remote fuel door and tailgate releases, rear seat heat ducts, coolant temperature gauge, trip odometer, digital clock, tinted glass, dual exhaust, tool kit, bodyside molding, mud guards, 205/65R15 tires, wheel covers.

LS adds: power driver's seat height adjustment, center captain's chairs, luggage rack, power sunroof, remote entry system, 6-speaker sound system w/theft-deterrent system, map lights, alloy wheels.

OPTIONAL EQUIPMENT:
Comfort and Convenience

	Retail Price	Dealer Invoice
CD player, S	470	369
LS	470	369
Rear seat tray, LS	70	55

Appearance and Miscellaneous	Retail Price	Dealer Invoice
Luggage rack, S	$230	$181

ISUZU RODEO

Isuzu Rodeo LS V-6

Rear- or 4-wheel-drive midsize sport-utility vehicle; similar to Honda Passport

Base price range: $17,995-$28,910. Built in Lafayette, Ind.

Also consider: Chevrolet Blazer, Ford Explorer, Jeep Grand Cherokee, Toyota 4Runner

FOR • Standard 4-wheel anti-lock brakes • Passenger and cargo room • Acceleration (V-6)

AGAINST • Road and engine noise • Fuel economy

Isuzu redesigns its U.S.-built sport-utility vehicle, giving it rounded styling and more power. A similarly redesigned Honda version, the Passport, is again based on the Rodeo and the two share an Indiana assembly plant.

Rodeo's new body is fractions of an inch longer than its old one, but it's four inches wider. The wheelbase (distance between wheels on the same side of the vehicle) is shorter by 2.3 inches, a move Isuzu credits with helping reduce curb weight by 285 pounds. A flip-up rear window is retained, but a side-hinged tailgate replaces a drop-down gate. The spare tire mounts under the cargo area, but an outside-mounted spare that swings with the tailgate is optional.

Both the S and better-equipped LS models are offered with 2- or 4-wheel drive. The 4WD system still is not for use on dry pavement, but a dashboard switch replaces a floor lever to activate the shift-on-the-fly transfer case.

Two-wheel-drive S models use a twin-cam 2.2-liter 4-cylinder engine of 129 horsepower, nine more than last year's base 2.6-liter four. Returning as standard on all other Rodeos is a 3.2-liter V-6, now with dual overhead cams and 200 horsepower, 10 more than before. Manual transmission is standard, and automatic is optional only with the V-6. Towing capacity is 4500 pounds.

Dual air bags returns as standard in a redesigned dashboard. Four-wheel anti-lock brakes are now standard instead of optional.

A two-door version of the Rodeo, reviving the Amigo name, is expected later in the 1998 model year.

PERFORMANCE A shorter wheelbase, lighter weight, and more power helps Rodeo feel more nimble than before, though it sets no new SUV standard in the handling department. There's plenty of body lean and tire squeal in tight turns, but that's typical of the class.

Rodeo's suspension provides a stable ride without pitching or bouncing. Small bumps and imperfections register but don't intrude, while larger bumps are not absorbed nearly as well as they should be.

Isuzu's smart to confine the 4-cylinder engine to 2WD and manual transmission, where its lack of power is not a huge drawback. V-6 Rodeos feel considerably livelier than before, with brisk acceleration and good passing power. The automatic transmission shifts smoothly and downshifts quickly. We tested an LS 4WD and averaged 15.8 mpg in a mix of driving.

Push-button 4WD is an improvement over a floor-mounted lever, but Rodeo doesn't offer the convenience of the 4WD setups in the rival Ford Explorer and Grand Cherokee, which

Prices are accurate at time of publication; subject to manufacturer's changes.

can be used on dry pavement.

ACCOMMODATIONS Despite the tighter wheelbase, interior room is greater than before. There's good passenger space all around and the driver enjoys a commanding position, even though the seat isn't height-adjustable. Controls for the climate and audio systems are recessed and just a bit too far for no-distraction use by the driver.

Step-in height is a little lower than the compact-SUV norm, making getting in and out no great chore. The rear doors allow passengers to slip through easily, though we wish they'd open a bit wider.

Forward visibility is high point thanks to a low cowl and hood line, but the optional outside spare interfers with the driver's view to the rear.

We're not sold on the new side-opening tailgate. You have to open the window before it can be used, and when the door is opened fully, you have to reach into the hinge area and release a bare-metal lever to free the door for closing.

BUILD QUALITY Paintwork is smooth and lustrous and body panels fit nicely. There's an abundance of hard plastic trim on the dashboard and doors, but its grain and lack of sheen keeps it from looking cheap.

VALUE FOR THE MONEY V-6 Rodeos furnish better acceleration than most Japanese rivals and lean toward the "sport" side of "sport-utility." However, prices are not bargain-rate, and overall, there's no one outstanding feature that sets Rodeo apart from the competition.

RATINGS

	S 2WD	LS 4WD
Acceleration	2	3
Fuel economy	3	2
Ride quality	3	3
Steering/handling	3	3
Braking	3	3
Quietness	3	3
Driver seating	4	4
Instruments/controls	3	3
Room/comfort (front)	4	4
Room/comfort (rear)	3	3
Cargo room	4	4
Value for the money	3	3
Total	**38**	**38**

SPECIFICATIONS

	4-door wagon
Wheelbase, in.	106.4
Overall length, in.	176.7
Overall width, in.	70.4
Overall height, in.	68.8
Curb weight, lbs.	3260
Cargo vol., cu. ft.	81.1
Fuel capacity, gals.	21.9
Seating capacity	5
Front head room, in.	38.9
Max. front leg room, in.	42.1
Rear head room, in.	38.3
Min. rear leg room, in.	35.0

ENGINES

	dohc I-4	dohc V-6
Size, liters/cu. in.	2.2/134	3.2/193
Horsepower @ rpm	129@ 5200	205@ 5400
Torque (lbs./ft.) @ rpm	144@ 4000	214@ 3000
Availability	S[1]	S[2]

EPA city/highway mpg
5-speed OD manual	21/24	16/20
4-speed OD automatic		16/20

1. 2WD S. 2. S V-6, LS.

PRICES

Isuzu Rodeo

	Retail Price	Dealer Invoice
S 4-cylinder 2WD 4-door wagon, 5-speed	$17995	$16916
S V-6 2WD 4-door wagon, 5-speed	20950	18750
S V-6 2WD 4-door wagon, automatic	$21950	$19645
S V-6 4WD 4-door wagon, 5-speed	23240	20684
S V-6 4WD 4-door wagon, automatic	24240	21574
LS V-6 2WD 4-door wagon, automatic	26390	23488
LS V-6 4WD 4-door wagon, 5-speed	27910	24700
LS V-6 4WD 4-door wagon, automatic	28910	25585
Destination charge	445	445

STANDARD EQUIPMENT:

S: 2.6-liter 4-cylinder engine, 5-speed manual transmission, driver- and passenger-side air bags, anti-lock rear brakes, variable-assist power steering, cloth reclining front bucket seats with folding armrest, folding rear seat, center storage console, 4-speaker AM/FM/cassette, rear defogger, coolant-temperature gauge, trip odometer, visor mirrors, cargo rope hooks, rear wiper/washer, dual outside mirrors, tinted glass, fuel-tank skid plate, full-size spare tire, 225/75R16 all-season tires, alloy wheels.

S V-6 adds: 3.2-liter V-6 engine, 5-speed manual or 4-speed automatic transmission, 4-wheel disc brakes, tachometer, voltmeter, oil-pressure gauge, radiator skid plate, floormats, outside spare-tire carrier.

4WD adds: part-time 4WD, automatic locking hubs, tow hooks, transfer-case skid plate.

LS adds: air conditioning, moquette upholstery, tilt steering wheel, leather-wrapped steering wheel, cruise control, split folding rear seat, power windows, power door locks, remote keyless entry, heated power mirrors, 6-speaker premium audio system, illuminated visor mirrors, intermittent front wipers, power hatchgate release, front-door map pockets, map and courtesy lights, cargo net and cover, theft-deterrent system, fog lamps, roof rack, privacy rear quarter and rear side glass, bright exterior trim, dual note horn, mud guards, 245/70R16 tires.

4WD adds: part-time 4WD, automatic locking hubs, tow hooks, transfer-case skid plate.

OPTIONAL EQUIPMENT:

Major Packages

	Retail	Dealer
Preferred Equipment Pkg. 1, S	1010	899

Air conditioning, cargo net and cover.

Preferred Equipment Pkg. 2, S V-6	2350	2092

Preferred Equipment Pkg. 1 plus tilt steering wheel, cruise control, heated power mirrors, power windows, power door locks, remote keyless entry, power tailgate release, center armrest pad, 6-speaker sound system, theft-deterrent system.

Sport Pkg. 2WD, S V-6	520	256

Fog lights, 235/75R15 tires, wheel locks.

Sport Pkg. 4WD, S V-6	970	864

Fog lights, 245/75R16 tires, wheel locks.

Sport Pkg. limited slip 4WD, S V-6	770	686

Fog lights, limited slip differential, 235/75R15 tires, wheel locks.

Powertrains

Limited-slip differential, S 4WD, LS 4WD	250	224

Safety Features

4-wheel anti-lock brakes	800	712

Comfort and Convenience

Air conditioning, S	950	845
Leather upholstery, LS	995	886
Power sunroof, S V-6, LS	700	623
CD player, S V-6, LS	550	434

S V-6 requires Preferred Equipment Pkg. 2.

6-disc CD changer, S V-6, LS	650	513

S V-6 requires Preferred Equipment Pkg. 2.

Appearance and Miscellaneous

Color-keyed bumpers, S V-6	100	89
Running boards	360	283
Side steps	355	281

Special Purpose, Wheels and Tires

Trailer hitch	253	200

Other options available as port-installed items.

Rating Scale: 5-Excellent; 4-Above average; 3-Average; 2-Below average; 1-Poor

CONSUMER GUIDE™

ISUZU TROOPER

1997 Isuzu Trooper LS

4-wheel-drive full-size sport-utility vehicle; similar to Acura SLX

Base price range: (1997 model) $26,550-$37,990. Built in Japan.

Also consider: Chevrolet Tahoe, Ford Expedition, Toyota Land Cruiser

FOR • Standard anti-lock brakes • Passenger and cargo room

AGAINST • Fuel economy • Ride • Entry/exit

Isuzu's flagship sport-utility vehicle gets a more powerful engine for '98. Isuzu supplies Honda's Acura luxury division with a nearly identical vehicle, which Acura sells as the SLX.

Sales of the Trooper and SLX fell in the wake of allegations last summer that they were more prone than other SUVs to tipping in turns. However, the National Highway Traffic Safety Administration (NHTSA) found no merit to the charges and has found no safety defect in the design.

Trooper is a 4-door wagon with swing-out rear doors that are split 70/30. For '98 it comes in three levels of trim: S; S with Performance Package; and S with Luxury Package. All have part-time 4-wheel drive that can be engaged on the fly but is for use on slippery surfaces only. The transfer case is operated by a console-mounted lever in base S models and by a dashboard button on Performance and Luxury Package models.

Trooper again uses a V-6, but it replaces a single-overhead cam 3.2-liter with a double overhead-cam 3.5-liter. The new engine has 25 more horsepower and 42 more pounds/feet of torque than last year's. The base S model comes with manual transmission. Automatic is optional on the base S and standard on Performance and Luxury Package Troopers. Dual air bags are standard along with 4-wheel anti-lock disc brakes. Maximum towing capacity is 5000 pounds.

PERFORMANCE This year's increase in power is immediately evident and most welcome. Trooper and its SLX twin now step away from a stop with a quickness the 3.2-liter versions couldn't muster. They've lost their slightly ponderous feeling in around-town driving and the infusion of torque coaxes pompter, more effective downshifts out of the automatic transmission in highway passing. EPA fuel-economy estimates haven't changed, so mileage will likely be about the same as in the previous models, which was nothing to brag about: In a recent test we averaged 15.8 mpg even with a lot of highway driving, where our best was 17.4.

Trooper's suspension provides a stable highway ride, though it still doesn't soak up big bumps well and feels harsh on rough pavement. Body roll is quite evident in tight turns, and the power steering is both slow and numb. Stopping is good, thanks to standard anti-lock brakes, but distances aren't exceptionally short. Again, less weight would help.

ACCOMMODATIONS This is one of the roomiest SUVs, with loads of head clearance front and rear, plus enough width in the back seat for three adults to fit without squeezing. However, getting in and out of the Trooper can be a chore because there's such a high step-up into the interior.

The tall build combines with large windows for fine visibility,

but the steering wheel sits at a bus-like angle that takes getting used to, and some minor controls seem haphazardly placed.

Trooper's trademark 70/30 rear cargo door (something like an upright refrigerator/freezer) opens onto a tall, long cargo area that holds mounds of luggage. However, the larger left door is held open by a catch in the hinge area, and we're not comfortable reaching in amongst the metal brackets to flip the release that frees it.

BUILD QUALITY Trooper has a hefty, rugged feel and displays thorough detail workmanship.

VALUE FOR THE MONEY Trooper's pricing pits it against rivals such as the Chevrolet Tahoe and Ford Expedition, both of which come with V-8 engines and more-convenient 4WD systems; Expedition also offers seats for nine. We don't rate the Trooper or SLX as highly as those vehicles, but they do have abundant passenger and cargo room and are solidly built, and this year's additional engine power helps them feel more competitive.

RATINGS

	S w/ Luxury Pkg.
Acceleration	3
Fuel economy	2
Ride quality	3
Steering/handling	3
Braking	3
Quietness	3
Driver seating	4
Instruments/controls	3
Room/comfort (front)	4
Room/comfort (rear)	4
Cargo room	5
Value for the money	2
Total	**39**

SPECIFICATIONS

	4-door wagon
Wheelbase, in.	108.7
Overall length, in.	185.5
Overall width, in.	72.2
Overall height, in.	72.2
Curb weight, lbs.	4530
Cargo vol., cu. ft.	90.2
Fuel capacity, gals.	22.5
Seating capacity	5
Front head room, in.	39.8
Max. front leg room, in.	40.8
Rear head room, in.	39.8
Min. rear leg room, in.	39.1

ENGINES

	dohc V-6
Size, liters/cu. in.	3.5/213
Horsepower @ rpm	215@ 5400
Torque (lbs./ft.) @ rpm	230@ 3000
Availability	S

EPA city/highway mpg

4-speed OD automatic	15/19
5-speed OD manual	16/19

PRICES

1997 Isuzu Trooper

	Retail Price	Dealer Invoice
S 4-door 4WD wagon, 5-speed	$26550	$24161
S 4-door 4WD wagon, automatic	27800	25298
LS 4-door 4WD wagon, automatic	32270	28882
Limited 4-door 4WD wagon, automatic	37990	34001
Destination charge	445	445

STANDARD EQUIPMENT:

S: 3.2-liter V-6 engine, 5-speed manual or 4-speed automatic transmission, variable-assist power steering, driver- and passenger-side air bags, anti-lock 4-wheel disc brakes, part-time 4WD system with automatic locking front hubs, cloth reclining front bucket seats, full door trim, AM/FM/cassette, front and center storage console, dual

---

Prices are accurate at time of publication; subject to manufacturer's changes.

outside mirrors, rear defogger, tilt steering column, intermittent wipers, rear wiper/washer, anti-theft alarm, remote fuel door release, skid plates, tachometer, voltmeter, coolant temperature and oil pressure gauges, trip odometer, visor mirrors, door map pockets, tinted glass, rear step pad, rear air deflector, front and rear tow hooks, cargo tie down hooks, cover and net, 245/70R16 tires, full-size spare tire.

LS adds: 4-speed automatic transmission, air conditioning, cruise control, 4-way manual driver's seat, split folding and reclining rear seat, power windows, power door locks, bright grille, overfenders with formed mud flap, rocker panel molding, leather-wrapped steering wheel, upgraded cloth upholstery, 60/40 split reclining rear seat, heated power mirrors, premium 6-speaker sound system, passenger-side illuminated visor mirror, variable intermittent wipers, bronze-tint windshield, rear privacy glass, map light, 2-tone paint, striping, alloy wheels.

Limited adds: limited-slip differential, leather upholstery, power front seats, heated front seats, 12-disc CD changer, power sunroof, keyless remote entry system, multi-meter gauge, headlamp wiper/washer, leather-wrapped shifter and parking brake, wood interior trim, fog lights.

OPTIONAL EQUIPMENT:
Major Packages
Preferred Equipment Pkg., S 2190 2059
Air conditioning, cruise control, power windows and door locks, premium 6-speaker audio system, 60/40 split reclining rear seat, heated power mirrors, passenger-side illuminated visor mirror, alloy wheels.

Comfort and Convenience
Power sunroof, LS..	1100	979
Leather power/heated front seats, LS.....................	2250	2002
Keyless remote entry system, S, LS	250	198
CD player, S, LS..	550	434
12-disc CD changer, S, LS...................................	650	513

Special Purpose, Wheels and Tires
Limited-slip differential, L, LS	290	258
Multi-meter gauge, LS	200	178

JAGUAR XJ SEDAN

Jaguar XJ8

Rear-wheel-drive luxury car
Base price range: $54,750–$67,400. Built in England.
Also consider: Cadillac Seville, Infiniti Q45, Lexus LS 400

FOR • Ride • Acceleration • Quietness • Side air bags

AGAINST • Fuel economy • Cargo space

Jaguar's bread-and-butter models, the XJ sedans, drop their 6-cylinder engine for a new powertrain featuring V-8s and also gain side air bags for 1998.

The four XJ6 models become XJ8s by switching from a 245-horsepower 4.0-liter inline-six to the 290-horsepower 4.0-liter V-8 introduced with last year's new XK8 coupe and convertible. Also on hand are 5-speed automatic transmissions to replace 4-speed units.

Seat-mounted front side air bags, standard Automatic Stability Control (ASC) traction assist, larger front brakes, variable-assist power steering (replacing fixed-rate assist), a redesigned dashboard and center console, and body strengthening at several points are additional new features.

The XJ8 and XJR ride a 113-inch wheelbase. The XJ8L and ritzy Vanden Plas have a 117.9-inch chassis. The XJR again carries a supercharged engine and this year it packs 80 more horsepower and 87 more pounds/feet of torque than the other models. XJR also has a stronger transmission (built by Mercedes-Benz instead of ZF) and full traction control (engine and brake intervention versus engine only with ASC), which is optional elsewhere.

PERFORMANCE We haven't driven the V-8-powered XJ sedans, but the 8-cylinder engine has impressed us in Jaguar's XK8 coupe and convertible and promises to be just as smooth and muscular-feeling here. We found the 6-cylinder engines provided brisk acceleration in this car, and the 1998 models have shed about 100 pounds of curb weight while adding power and a more-sophisticated transmission, so performance ought to be even more spirited.

The precise, responsive steering and athletic handling shouldn't change, and neither should the suspension's ability to easily soak up bumps and provide a stable ride.

ACCOMMODATIONS Part of the XJ sedan's charm is its intimate cabin. The car does cosset in supple leather and wood surroundings, but it is also quite cozy. Room is adequate in front, but rear-seat passengers in regular-wheelbase versions must scrunch up because of limited knee space. There's ample leg room in the back seat of the stretched editions, but the seat cushion remains low to the floor so even the Vanden Plas can't furnish the sofa-like comfort of most rivals. Rear doors are wider on the stretched models but the roof is just as low, requiring some ducking and bending upon entry and exit.

Jaguar has added steering-wheel switches for cruise control, audio functions and optional telephone, plus one-touch-down operation for all door windows. Still, controls are not nearly as logically arrayed as they should be. Visibility is hampered to the rear by back-seat headrests. The car's trim tail makes for limited trunk height and cargo space that rates as subpar for the class.

BUILD QUALITY Jaguar was acquired by Ford Motor Company in 1990 and has improved its customer-satisfaction ratings ever since. The XJ sedans we're tested recently have had top-notch fit and finish.

VALUE FOR THE MONEY More than just a stylish Rodeo Drive trinket, the XJ sedans have the power, suspension, and steering to satisfy a demanding driver. If you're unfazed by the problematical rear-seat accommodations and limited cargo space, it's an attractive alternative to more staid rivals such as the Lexus LS 400 and Mercedes-Benz E-Class.

RATINGS	XJ8	XJ8L/ Vanden Plas	XJR
Acceleration	4	4	5
Fuel economy	2	2	2
Ride quality	5	5	4
Steering/handling	4	4	4
Braking	5	5	5
Quietness	5	5	5
Driver seating	3	3	3
Instruments/controls	3	3	3
Room/comfort (front)	4	4	4
Room/comfort (rear)	3	4	3
Cargo room	2	2	2
Value for the money	3	3	3
Total	43	44	43

SPECIFICATIONS
	4-door sedan	4-door sedan
Wheelbase, in.	113.0	117.9
Overall length, in.	197.8	202.7
Overall width, in.	70.8	70.8
Overall height, in.	52.7	53.2
Curb weight, lbs.	3996	4048
Cargo vol., cu. ft.	12.7	12.7
Fuel capacity, gals.	21.4	21.4
Seating capacity....................................	5	5
Front head room, in.	37.2	37.8
Max. front leg room, in.	41.2	41.2
Rear head room, in.	36.3	37.0
Min. rear leg room, in.	34.3	39.2

Rating Scale: 5-Excellent; 4-Above average; 3-Average; 2-Below average; 1-Poor

ENGINES

	dohc V-8	Supercharged dohc V-8
Size, liters/cu. in.	4.0/244	4.0/244
Horsepower @ rpm	290@ 6100	370@ 6150
Torque (lbs./ft.) @ rpm	290@ 4250	387@ 3600
Availability	S[1]	S[2]
EPA city/highway mpg		
4-speed OD automatic	NA	NA

1. XJ6, XJ6-L, Vanden Plas. 2. XJR.

PRICES

Jaguar XJ Sedan

	Retail Price	Dealer Invoice
XJ8 4-door sedan	$54750	$47830
XJ8 L 4-door sedan	59750	52198
Vanden Plas 4-door sedan	63800	55736
XJR 4-door sedan	67400	55881
Destination charge	580	580

XJR includes retail price includes $2100 Gas Guzzler tax.

STANDARD EQUIPMENT:

XJ8: 4.0-liter DOHC V-8 engine, 5-speed automatic transmission, traction control, driver- and passenger-side side air bags, front side-impact air bags, anti-lock 4-wheel disc brakes, variable-assist power steering, power tilt/telescopic steering wheel, cruise control, air conditioning w/automatic climate control, leather upholstery, walnut interior trim, 12-way power front bucket seats with power lumbar adjusters, contoured rear bench seat, front storage console, overhead console, cupholders, driver memory system (seat, steering wheel, outside mirrors), automatic headlights, power sunroof, power heated mirrors w/memory feature, power windows, automatic power door locks, remote keyless entry, trip computer, outside-temperature indicator, automatic day/night inside mirror, AM/FM/cassette, rear defogger, remote fuel-door and decklid releases, illuminated visor mirrors, universal garage-door opener, map lights, variable intermittent wipers, carpeted floormats, theft-deterrent system, chrome hood ornament, front and rear fog lamps, 225/60ZR16 tires, full-size spare tire, alloy wheels.

XJ8 L adds: 5-inch longer wheelbase.

Vanden Plas adds: wood and leather-wrapped steering wheel, wood shift knob, walnut picnic trays on front seatbacks, upgraded leather upholstery and wood interior trim, lambswool floormats.

XJR adds to XJ8: supercharged 4.0-liter DOHC V-8 engine, traction control, limited-slip differential, Harman/Kardon audio system w/CD changer, heated front and rear seats, wood and leather-wrapped steering wheel, maple interior trim and shifter, sport suspension, 255/45ZR17 tires.

OPTIONAL EQUIPMENT:
Major Packages

All-Weather Pkg., XJ8, XJ8 L, Vanden Plas	2000	1680
Full traction control, heated front and rear seats.		

Comfort and Convenience

6-disc CD changer	800	672
Harman/Kardon audio system w/CD changer, XJ8, XJ8 L, Vanden Plas	1800	1512

Appearance and Miscellaneous

Extra-cost paint	1000	840

JAGUAR XK8

Rear-wheel-drive luxury coupe
Base price range: $64,900-$69,900. Built in England.
Also consider: Cadillac Eldorado, Lexus SC 300/400, Mercedes-Benz SL-Class

FOR • Acceleration • Ride • Quietness

AGAINST • Passenger and cargo room • Entry/exit • Rear visibility

Jaguar unveiled the XK8 coupe and convertible for 1997 to replace the 21-year-old XJS design. In name and appearance,

Jaguar XK8 convertible

the new models hark to the E-type or "XKE," yet have some kinship to the XJS, using part of its platform, the same basic suspension, and a near identical wheelbase. Significantly, the XK8 introduced Jaguar's first V-8, a 4.0-liter aluminum engine with twin overhead camshafts and four valves per cylinder.

For '98, the XK8 adds only a few features: automatic on/off headlamps; a security system with engine immobilizer to prevent "hot wiring"; steering-wheel controls for cruise, audio, and optional telephone functions; and a more-ergonomic audio unit with integrated phone keypad.

The convertible retains a fully lined power soft top with glass rear window and electric defroster, and both models again have Automatic Stability Control (ASC), which throttles back engine power to maintain traction in low-grip conditions. Full traction control, which also applies the brakes as needed, is part of an optional All-Weather Package that includes heated seats and headlight washers.

PERFORMANCE It's billed as a "sports car," but the XK8 is too plush and heavy for that, and its soft suspension allows more body roll in tight corners than the sports-car norm. Still, it shows fair agility over twisty roads and provides excellent ride comfort anywhere—firm yet absorbent, with little impact harshness. Happily, the brakes are up to the heft, quickly scrubbing off speed without drama.

Jaguar's new V-8 is a gem. Silky and nearly silent at idle, it rises only to a muted, expensive-sounding growl when worked hard. Not that you need to do that much, for there's enough low-speed torque to vault the coupe to 60 mph in a claimed 6.5 seconds. The mandatory 5-speed automatic transmission is silky and responsive too. Fuel economy is almost a moot point in the luxury class, but we averaged a not-objectionable 15 mpg in a mix of city-highway work with our ragtop test car.

ACCOMMODATIONS As was the XJS, the XK8 is quite snug inside. A bulky center console, narrow footwells, shallow side glass, and huge over-the-shoulder blind spots with the convertible roof up conspire to make even medium-size adults feel hemmed-in—and that's in front. The back seat is too small even for some dogs. Use it for cargo instead—as you may need to, though the trunk will take about a week's worth of gear for two if they pack light with soft luggage. Entry/exit is no picnic because the XK8 inherits the XJS's awkwardly wide door sills and, on the driver's side, an outboard handbrake lever with odd double-jointed action.

Things are better once you've wriggled in. The seats hug your body just enough to inhibit sliding around in exuberant driving, while the attractive, well-designed dashboard has simple switches and large, legible gauges.

BUILD QUALITY Evidence suggests Ford's influence has lessened Jaguar's assembly-quality woes. The XK8s we've driven have had a solid, all-of-a-piece feel; the only craftsmanship shortfall was a loose instrument-panel surround on one test car. The convertible seems unusually rigid for an open car, and its top works like a charm.

VALUE FOR THE MONEY Though demand for personal luxury cars is waning, the XK8 stands out for refined performance in an elegant, luxurious package brimming with traditional Jaguar charm. It also seems to be the best-built Jag ever, and it's attractively priced, all things considered. Sales were strong in '97, and we expect a repeat performance this year.

Prices are accurate at time of publication; subject to manufacturer's changes.

RATINGS

	Conv.	Coupe
Acceleration	5	5
Fuel economy	2	2
Ride quality	4	4
Steering/handling	4	4
Braking	4	4
Quietness	4	4
Driver seating	3	3
Instruments/controls	4	4
Room/comfort (front)	3	3
Room/comfort (rear)	1	1
Cargo room	2	2
Value for the money	1	3
Total	**42**	**43**

SPECIFICATIONS

	2-door coupe	2-door conv.
Wheelbase, in.	101.9	101.9
Overall length, in.	187.4	187.4
Overall width, in.	72.0	72.0
Overall height, in.	51.0	51.4
Curb weight, lbs.	3673	3867
Cargo vol., cu. ft.	11.1	9.5
Fuel capacity, gals.	19.9	19.9
Seating capacity	4	4
Front head room, in.	37.4	37.0
Max. front leg room, in.	43.0	43.0
Rear head room, in.	33.3	33.1
Min. rear leg room, in.	NA	NA

ENGINES

	dohc V-8
Size, liters/cu. in.	4.0/244
Horsepower @ rpm	290@ 6100
Torque (lbs./ft.) @ rpm	290@ 4200
Availability	S

EPA city/highway mpg

5-speed OD automatic	17/25

PRICES

Jaguar XK8	Retail Price	Dealer Invoice
2-door notchback	$64900	$57104
2-door convertible	69900	61472
Destination charge	580	580

STANDARD EQUIPMENT:

Base: 4.0-liter DOHC V-8 engine, 5-speed automatic transmission, traction control, driver- and passenger-side air bags, anti-lock 4-wheel disc brakes, air conditioning w/automatic climate control, variable-assist power steering, power tilt/telescopic steering wheel, leather-wrapped steering wheel, cruise control, power top (convertible), leather upholstery, 4-way power front bucket seats w/power lumbar support, memory driver seat, cupholders, walnut interior trim and shifter, tachometer, voltmeter, oil-pressure gauge, trip computer, outside-temperature indicator, automatic headlights, AM/FM/cassette, heated power mirrors w/memory feature, power windows, automatic power door locks, remote keyless entry, universal garage-door opener, illuminated visor mirrors, automatic day/night rearview mirror, rear defogger, remote fuel-door and decklid release, variable intermittent windshield wipers, map lights, theft-deterrent system, front and rear fog lights, full-size spare tire, 245/50ZR17 tires, alloy wheels.

OPTIONAL EQUIPMENT:

Major Packages

All-Weather Pkg.	2000	1680

Full traction Control, heated front seats, headlamp washers.

Comfort and Convenience

6-disc CD changer	800	672
Harmon-Kardon sound system w/CD changer	1800	1512

Appearance and Miscellaneous

Extra-cost paint	1000	840
Chrome wheels	1000	840

JEEP CHEROKEE `BUDGET BUY`

Jeep Cherokee Classic 4-door

Rear- or 4-wheel-drive midsize sport-utility vehicle
Base price range: $15,440-$21,995. Built in Toledo, Ohio.
Also consider: Chevrolet Blazer, Honda Passport, Isuzu Rodeo

FOR • Acceleration (6-cylinder) • Optional anti-lock brakes • Passenger and cargo room

AGAINST • Fuel economy • Acceleration (4-cylinder)

Careful not to disturb its well-established character, Jeep updated the Cherokee last year with subtle styling revisions, including a new grille, and a revamped interior that added a passenger-side air bag.

For '98, the lineup gets a new model and two new badges, and the 4-cylinder engine gets an automatic transmission.

SE, Sport, and Classic are the model names. All come in 2- or 4-wheel drive, but only the SE and Sport offer a 2-door body style in addition to the 4-door. The Classic is new and slots above the Sport in price and features. The Limited badge replaces last year's top-line tag, Country, and is an option package on Classics.

A 4-cylinder engine comes in the base SE model and this year adds an optional 3-speed automatic to go along with its standard manual transmission. Optional on the SE and standard on the others is a 6-cylinder with either a manual or a 4-speed automatic transmission.

Cherokee offers two 4WD systems. Both can shift on the fly between 2WD and 4WD, but Command Trac is not for use on dry pavement, while Selec-Trac (available on 6-cylinder models) can. All Cherokees have dual air bags and this year they're depowered to open with less force while still meeting federal standards. Anti-lock brakes are optional on 6-cylinder models.

A quicker steering gear, aluminum radiators, and Chili Pepper Red paint are among other changes for '98.

PERFORMANCE The current Cherokee traces its roots to the 1984 model year, when it debuted as the first SUV in its class with four doors. Chrysler has done an admirable job keeping a basically solid design fresh enough to warrant consideration in today's tough market.

The 4-cylinder just qualifies as adequate with manual transmission. With automatic, it feels overmatched in anything but light cruising. Most Cherokees are sold with the six, and they have solid acceleration throughout the speed range. We average about 15 mpg with automatic, 17 with manual—close to the average for all midsize SUVs.

Good balance and tailored dimensions help Cherokee feel highly maneuverable in most any situation. The firm suspension provides a solid ride that absorbs all but the worst bumps without jarring. The optional anti-lock brakes feel strong and natural.

Jeep's been adding sound insulation to the Cherokee, but there still are powertrain and road resonances heard and felt hear that aren't present in younger midsize SUVs. Wind noise also is prominent at highway speeds.

ACCOMMODATIONS This is where Cherokee really shows its age. There's no surplus of shoulder room in front and a shortage of knee clearance in back. Entry/exit to the rear seat is made difficult by extremely narrow lower doorways.

No gauges are obstructed from view, and no controls are difficult to reach. Outward visibility is good, though larger outside

---

Rating Scale: 5-Excellent; 4-Above average; 3-Average; 2-Below average; 1-Poor

mirrors would help lane changing.

The inside-mounted spare tire eats up a chunk of cargo room, but there's still decent space with the rear seatback in place and a long load floor with it lowered.

BUILD QUALITY Cherokees we've tested have exhibited the ocassional rattle and wider-than-usual panel gaps around the hood and tailgate. But we've experienced no mechanical problems.

VALUE FOR THE MONEY Can't afford a Grand Cherokee or Explorer? Try a Cherokee on for size. Convenient 4WD systems, commendable off-road capabilities, civilized on-road manners, and attractive pricing are the high notes here.

RATINGS

	SE 4-cyl.	Sport
Acceleration	2	4
Fuel economy	3	3
Ride quality	3	3
Steering/handling	4	4
Braking	3	4
Quietness	3	3
Driver seating	3	3
Instruments/controls	4	4
Room/comfort (front)	3	3
Room/comfort (rear)	3	3
Cargo room	4	4
Value for the money	3	4
Total	**38**	**42**

SPECIFICATIONS

	2-door wagon	4-door wagon
Wheelbase, in.	101.4	101.4
Overall length, in.	167.5	167.5
Overall width, in.	69.4	69.4
Overall height, in.	64.0	64.0
Curb weight, lbs.	2979	3032
Cargo vol., cu. ft.	6.0	69.0
Fuel capacity, gals.	20.0	20.0
Seating capacity	5	5
Front head room, in.	37.8	37.8
Max. front leg room, in.	41.4	41.4
Rear head room, in.	37.8	38.0
Min. rear leg room, in.	41.4	35.0

ENGINES

	ohv I-4	ohv I-6
Size, liters/cu. in.	2.5/150	4.0/242
Horsepower @ rpm	125@ 5400	190@ 4600
Torque (lbs./ft.) @ rpm	150@ 3250	225@ 3000
Availability	S[1]	S[2]
EPA city/highway mpg		
5-speed OD manual	19/23	17/20

1. SE. 2. Sport and Country; optional, SE.

PRICES

Jeep Cherokee

	Retail Price	Dealer Invoice
SE 2-door wagon 2WD	$15440	$14510
SE 2-door wagon 4WD	16955	15909
SE 4-door wagon 2WD	16480	15477
SE 4-door wagon 4WD	17990	16871
Sport 2-door wagon 2WD	18055	16348
Sport 2-door wagon 4WD	19565	17697
Sport 4-door wagon 2WD	19090	17279
Sport 4-door wagon 4WD	20600	18628
Classic 4-door wagon 2WD	20480	18502
Classic 4-door wagon 4WD	21995	19856
Destination charge	525	525

STANDARD EQUIPMENT:

SE: 2.5-liter 4-cylinder engine, 5-speed manual transmission, driver- and passenger-side air bags, power steering, vinyl upholstery, front bucket seats, folding rear seat, floor console, AM/FM radio w/two speakers, intermittent wipers, remote outside mirrors, tinted glass, 215/75R15 tires.

4WD adds: Command-Trac part-time 4-wheel drive.

Sport adds: 4.0-liter 6-cylinder engine, cloth/vinyl upholstery, tachometer, cassette player w/four speakers, Sport Decor Group, lower bodyside molding, spare-tire cover, 225/75R15 outlined-white-letter all-terrain tires.

4WD adds: Command-Trac part-time 4-wheel drive.

Classic adds: 4-speed automatic transmission, upgraded cloth upholstery, tilt steering wheel, leather-wrapped steering wheel, power mirrors, courtesy lights, map/dome lights, cargo-area light), intermittent rear wiper/washer, cloth door trim and map pockets, floormats, striping, roof rack, 225/70R15 outline-white-letter tires, alloy wheels.

4WD adds: Command-Trac part-time 4-wheel drive.

OPTIONAL EQUIPMENT:

Major Packages

	Retail Price	Dealer Invoice
Quick Order Pkg. 22B/23B/25B/26B, SE	$1275	$1084
Manufacturer's discount price	NC	NC

Air conditioning, cloth and vinyl high back bucket seats, power mirrors, intermittent rear wiper/washer.

Quick Order Pkg. 25J/26J, Sport 2-door	2170	1845
Sport 4-door	2345	1993
Manufacturer's discount price	NC	NC

Air conditioning, Light Group (On Time Delay headlights, illuminated visor mirrors, map lights, underhood light), Power Equipment Group (power windows and door locks, remote keyless entry, power mirrors), intermittent rear wiper/washer, leather-wrapped tilt steering wheel, floormats, roof rack.

Quick Order Pkg. 26S, Classic	1825	1551
Manufacturer's discount price	NC	NC

Air conditioning, Light Group (On Time Delay headlights, illuminated visor mirrors, map lights, underhood light), Power Equipment Group (power windows and door locks, remote keyless entry), tilt steering wheel.

Limited Quick Order Pkg. 26H, Classic 4WD	4345	3693
Manufacturer's discount price	2365	2010
Limited Quick Order Pkg. 26H, Classic 2WD	3950	3358
Manufacturer's discount price	1970	1675

Quick Order Group 26S plus Limited Group (rear defogger, leather upholstery, front low back bucket seats, overhead console, cruise control, deep-tinted glass, body striping, Selec-Trac transfer case full-time 4WD (4WD), 225/70R15 white-letter tires), 6-way power driver seat.

Power Equipment Group, Sport 2-door	630	536
Sport 4-door	805	684

Includes remote keyless entry, power windows and door locks, power mirrors. Requires Light Group, rear wiper/washer.

Light Group, SE, Sport	160	136

On Time Delay headlights, illuminated visor mirrors, underhood light, courtesy lights, map/dome lights, cargo-area light.

Trailer Tow Group	365	310
4WD w/Up Country Suspension Group	245	208

Equalizer hitch, 7-wire receptacle, 4-wire trailer adapter, maximum engine cooling. SE and Sport require automatic transmission and full-size spare tire. Classic requires full-size spare tire.

Up Country Suspension Group,		
SE 4WD w/4.0-liter engine	1070	910
SE 4WD w/2.5-liter engine	1030	876
Sport 4WD w/alloy wheels, automatic, Classic	845	718
Sport 4WD w/alloy wheels, manual	805	684
Sport 4WD w/automatic	780	663
Sport 4WD w/manual	740	629
Classic w/Limited Pkg.	760	646

Trac-Lok rear differential, maximum engine cooling, off-road suspension, tow hooks, Skid Plate Group, rear stabilizer bar delete, 225/75R15 outline-white-letter all-terrain tires, full-size spare tire.

Powertrains

4.0-liter 6-cylinder engine, SE	995	846
3-speed automatic transmission, SE 2WD	665	565

Requires 2.5-liter engine.

4-speed automatic transmission, SE, Sport	945	803

SE requires 4.0-liter 6-cylinder engine.

Selec-Trac full-time 4-wheel drive,		
Sport 4WD, Classic 4WD	395	336

Sport requires automatic transmission.

Trac-Lok rear differential	285	242

Requires full-size spare tire.

Prices are accurate at time of publication; subject to manufacturer's changes.

Safety Feature

	Retail Price	Dealer Invoice
Anti-lock brakes..	$600	$510

SE requires 4.0-liter 6-cylinder engine.

Comfort and Convenience

Air conditioning..	850	723
Cloth upholstery, SE..................................	145	123
6-way power driver seat, Sport, Classic............	300	255
Sport requires Power Equipment Group.		
Overhead console, Sport, Classic..........................	235	200
Sport requires Power Equipment Group, Light Group, rear wiper/washer.		
Tilt steering column.....................................	140	119
Leather-wrapped steering wheel, SE, Sport	50	43
Cruise control	250	213
SE and Sport require leather-wrapped steering wheel.		
Power mirrors, SE, Sport	130	111
Heated power mirrors, SE...........................	175	149
SE/Sport w/Quick Order Pkg., Classic	45	38
Requires rear defogger.		
Cassette player, SE....................................	300	255
Includes four speakers.		
Cassette/CD player, SE..............................	710	604
Sport, Classic..	410	349
SE includes four speakers.		
Infinity speakers	350	298
Includes power amplifier, eight speakers, cargo-area light. Requires cassette/CD player.		
Rear defogger	165	140
SE and Sport require rear wiper/washer.		
Intermittent rear wiper/washer, SE, Sport	150	128
Cargo-area cover	75	64
Floormats, SE, Sport..................................	50	43

Appearance and Miscellaneous

Sunscreen glass, Sport 2-door................................	375	319
Sport 4-door, Classic	270	230
Requires rear defogger.		
Fog lights, Sport, Classic	110	94
Sport requires rear defogger and rear wiper/washer.		
Roof rack, SE, Sport..................................	140	119

Special Purpose, Wheels and Tires

Skid Plate Group, 4WD...............................	145	123
Fuel-tank, transfer-case, and front-suspension skid plates.		
Maximum engine cooling, SE, Sport....................	120	102
Requires Quick Order Pkg.		
Alloy wheels, SE	440	374
Sport	245	208
Requires full-size spare tire.		
225/75R15 white-letter tires, SE....................	315	268
Requires full-size spare tire.		
Full-size spare tire, SE w/std. 215/75R15 tires.......	75	64
SE w/225/75R16 tires................................	120	102
Includes spare wheel.		
Sport	145	123
Sport w/alloy wheels..................................	210	179
Includes spare wheel.		
Classic	280	238
Includes spare wheel.		

JEEP GRAND CHEROKEE

RECOMMENDED

Rear- or 4-wheel-drive compact sport-utility vehicle

Base price range: $25,845-$38,175. Built in Detroit, Mich.

Also consider: Ford Explorer, Mercedes-Benz ML320, Mercury Mountaineer, Oldsmobile Bravada

FOR • Standard anti-lock brakes • Acceleration • Passenger and cargo room

AGAINST • Fuel economy • Engine noise

Grand Cherokee has been a consistently strong seller, trailing only the Ford Explorer among midsize SUVs. But 1998 will be an interesting year for it, as Dodge introduces its new Durango, a

Jeep Grand Cherokee 5.9 Limited

larger sport-utility wagon than Grand Cherokee and capable of seating seven to the Jeep's five.

At least Grand Cherokee won't trail Durango in the power department. For '98, it's available with Chrysler's 245-horsepower 5.9-liter V-8; that's also Durango's top engine. The 5.9 is exclusive in the Grand Cherokee line to a new premium model, the 5.9 Limited. That model has its own mesh grille, hood louvers, and spoke alloy wheels. Inside it has exclusive "calf's nap" grain leather, Birdseye Maple trim, and other luxury touches.

Laredo, TSi, and Limited models return, but the Orvis trim level goes back in the tackle box. All have dual air bags (depowered this year), anti-lock brakes, and a choice of two 4-wheel-drive systems: on-demand Selec-Trac, which can be used on dry pavement; or permanently engaged Quadra-Trac that apportions power between axles as needed for best traction.

Base engine is a 4.0-liter 6-cylinder with 185 horsepower; optional on all but the 5.9 Limited is a 5.2-liter V-8 with 220. Automatic is the sole transmission.

PERFORMANCE Jeep says the new 5.9 Limited is the fastest Jeep vehicle ever, able to do 0-60 mph in 7.3 seconds. Judging by our initial test drives, in which the roaring 5.9 shoved us back in our seat and shifted gears with a wallop, it is indeed a new breed: the muscle SUV.

Either of the other engines will serve as well for most duty, both furnishing strong acceleration and brisk passing response. The 5.2 V-8 has the edge in towing ability, 6700-pounds, which is 1700 pounds more than either the 6-cylinder or the 5.9. But none of these engines is quiet enough under hard throttle to suit Grand Cherokee's upscale image. An even mix of city and highway driving got us 16.5 mph with the six and 13.3 with a 5.2 V-8; we've yet to measure the 5.9.

The coil suspension that makes Grand Cherokee so capable off-road also gives it responsive, predictable on-road manners and a controlled ride that's softer than Explorer's. Improved steering response for '98 increases its top-drawer handling ability.

ACCOMMODATIONS Grand Cherokee is smaller inside than Explorer, but head and leg room are generous all around and three adults can ride in the rear cross-town, if not cross-country. All outboard seats have height-adjustable shoulder belts. The control layout is convenient and sporty.

With the rear seatback up, there's not much more luggage room than in a midsize car, partly because the spare tire's mounted inside rather than below or outside, as on many competitors. The split rear seat folds to create a long load floor.

BUILD QUALITY Grand Cherokee's quality feel is undercut a little by some hard interior surfaces, but our bigger concern is its overall mechanical reliability based on what owners have told us.

VALUE FOR THE MONEY Impressive performance in most any circumstance earns Grand Cherokee our recommendation, but it's one among several fine midsize SUV choices, starting with the new Mercedes-Benz ML320 and the proven Explorer.

SPECIFICATIONS

	4-door wagon
Wheelbase, in.	105.9
Overall length, in.	177.2
Overall width, in.	70.7
Overall height, in.	64.9
Curb weight, lbs.	3800
Cargo vol., cu. ft.	79.3
Fuel capacity, gals.	23.0
Seating capacity	5
Front head room, in.	38.9
Max. front leg room, in.	40.9
Rear head room, in.	39.1

Rating Scale: 5-Excellent; 4-Above average; 3-Average; 2-Below average; 1-Poor

	4-door wagon
Min. rear leg room, in.	35.7

ENGINES

	ohv I-6	ohv V-8	ohv V-8
Size, liters/cu. in.	4.0/242	5.2/318	5.9/360
Horsepower @ rpm	185@ 4600	220@ 4400	245@ 4000
Torque (lbs./ft.) @ rpm..................	220@ 2400	300@ 2800	345@ 3200
Availability	S	O	S¹
EPA city/highway mpg			
4-speed OD automatic..................	15/20	14/17	13/16

1. 5.9 Limited.

RATINGS

	Laredo 6-cyl.	TSi/ Limited 5.2 V-8
Acceleration	3	4
Fuel economy	2	1
Ride quality	3	3
Steering/handling	4	4
Braking	4	4
Quietness	3	3
Driver seating	3	3
Instruments/controls	4	4
Room/comfort (front)	4	4
Room/comfort (rear)	4	4
Cargo room	4	4
Value for the money	4	4
Total	42	42

PRICES

Jeep Grand Cherokee	Retail Price	Dealer Invoice
Laredo 4-door wagon 2WD	$25845	$23419
Laredo 4-door wagon 4WD	27815	25187
TSi 4-door wagon 2WD	27995	25311
TSi 4-door wagon 4WD	29965	27079
Limited 4-door wagon 2WD	31360	28272
Limited 4-door wagon 4WD	33790	30445
5.9 Limited 4-door wagon 4WD	38175	34304
Destination charge	525	525

TSi requires Pkg. 26S/28S.

STANDARD EQUIPMENT:

Laredo: 4.0-liter 6-cylinder engine, 4-speed automatic transmission, driver- and passenger-side air bags, anti-lock 4-wheel disc brakes, power steering, leather-wrapped tilt steering wheel, cruise control, cloth reclining front bucket seats, split folding rear seat, air conditioning, power mirrors, power windows, power door locks, remote keyless entry, tachometer, voltage and temperature gauges, trip odometer, illuminated entry system, storage console with armrest and cupholders, AM/FM/cassette w/four speakers, rear defogger, intermittent front and rear wiper/washer, illuminated visor mirrors, floormats, cargo cover, net and tiedown hooks, tinted glass, roof rack, 215/75R15 tires, alloy wheels.

4WD adds: Selec-Trac full-time 4WD.

TSi adds: eight Infinity speakers, leather reclining front bucket seats, cruise control, steering wheel with radio controls and cruise control buttons, body-color grille.

4WD adds: Quadra-Trac permanent 4WD.

Limited adds: automatic temperature control, Luxury Group (power front seats w/memory, automatic day/night mirror, automatic headlights, vehicle information system), remote keyless entry w/memory feature, heated memory outside mirrors, universal garage-door opener, overhead console (compass, trip computer, map/reading lights), Infinity Gold speakers, fog lights, deep-tinted side and rear glass, theft-deterrent system, gold or silver badging and graphics, 225/70R16 outlined white-letter tires, gold- or silver-accented alloy wheels.

4WD adds: Quadra-Trac permanent 4WD.

5.9 Limited adds: 5.9-liter V-8 engine, Quadra-Trac permanent 4WD, heated front seats, CD/cassette player, ten Infinity speakers, power sunroof.

OPTIONAL EQUIPMENT:

Major Packages

	Retail Price	Dealer Invoice
Pkg. 26X/28X, Laredo	755	642
Manufacturer's discount price	$55	$47

Deep-tinted glass, overhead console (except w/sunroof), 225/75R15 tires.

	Retail Price	Dealer Invoice
Pkg. 26Y/28Y, Laredo	3287	2248
Manufacturer's discount price	1495	1270

Pkg. 26X/28X plus 8-speaker Infinity sound system, Luxury Group (automatic headlights, automatic day/night rearview mirror, power driver seat w/memory, leather-wrapped steering wheel w/radio controls, driver's information center), heated power mirrors, theft-deterrent system, fog lights.

Pkg. 26S/28S, 2WD TSi	2700	2295
Manufacturer's discount price	1300	1105
Pkg. 26S/28S, 4WD TSi	3305	2809
Manufacturer's discount price	1905	1619

Overhead console, fog lights, deep tinted glass, Luxury Group (power driver seat w/memory, leather-wrapped steering wheel w/radio controls, automatic day/night rearview mirror, automatic headlights, vehicle information system), heated mirrors, Infinity Gold speakers, theft-deterrent system, Quadra-Trac transfer case (4WD), full-size spare tire (4WD), P225/70R16 white-letter tires.

Pkg. 26K/28K, Limited..	1290	1097
Manufacturer's discount price	790	672

Power sunroof, mini overhead console, heated front seats, CD/cassette player.

Trailer Tow Prep Group	105	89

Includes 3.73 axle ratio, auxiliary transmission-oil cooler, special fan drive, special power steering pump.

Trailer Tow Group III, Laredo, TSi, Limited	360	306

Includes Trailer Tow Prep Group, frame mounted equalizing hitch receptacle. NA 5.9 Limited or with 5.2 liter V-8 engine.

Trailer Tow Group IV	245	208

Includes Trailer Tow Prep Group, frame mounted equalizing trailer hitch receptacle. Requires 5.2-liter or 5.9-liter V-8 engine.

Up Country Suspension Group (4WD only),		
Laredo..	825	701
Laredo w/option pkg.	575	489
TSi, Limited...	230	196

Skid Plate Group, tow hooks, high-pressure gas shocks, 245/70R15 outlined-white-letter all-terrain tires (Laredo), 225/70R16 Wrangler outlined-white-letter all-terrain tires (TSi, Limited), conventional spare tire, matching fifth wheel.

Powertrains

5.2-liter V-8 engine,		
2WD Laredo w/option pkg., TSi, Limited	880	748
4WD Laredo w/option pkg.	1485	1262

Includes Trailer Tow Prep Group. 4WD includes Quadra-Trac permanent 4WD.

Quadra-Trac permanent 4WD, 4WD Laredo	605	514
4WD Laredo w/Up Country Group	445	378

Requires full-size spare tire.

Trac-Lok rear differential, Laredo, TSi, Limited.......	285	242

Includes 3.73 axle ratio. Std. 5.9 Limited.

Select-Trac full-time 4WD, 4WD TSi, 4WD Limited	NC	NC

NA with 5.2-liter V-8 engine.

Comfort and Convenience

Power sunroof, Laredo w/Pkg. 26X/28X	845	718
Laredo w/Pkg. 26Y/28Y, Limited, TSi	760	646

Includes mini overhead console, reading lights, automatic day/night mirror, trip computer.

Leather seats, Laredo	580	493

Requires Pkg. 26Y/28Y.

Heated front seats, Laredo,		
Tsi, Limited..	250	213

Laredo requires Pkg. 26Y/28Y, leather seats.

AM/FM/cassette/CD player, Laredo	560	476

Requires option pkg.

AM/FM/cassette with Infinity Gold speakers,		
Laredo	660	561

AM/FM/cassette/CD with Infinity Gold speakers,		
Laredo	940	799
Laredo Pkg. 26Y/28Y, Limited, TSi	280	238

Appearance and Miscellaneous

Theft-deterrent system, Laredo...............................	150	128

Prices are accurate at time of publication; subject to manufacturer's changes.

	Retail Price	Dealer Invoice
Deep-tinted glass, Laredo	$270	$230
Fog lights, Laredo	120	102

Special Purpose, Wheels and Tires

	Retail Price	Dealer Invoice
Skid Plate/Tow Hook Group, 4WD	$200	$170
Full-size spare tire, Laredo..........................	160	136
225/75R15 white-letter tires, Laredo	250	213
225/75R15 white-letter all-terrain tires,		
Laredo	315	268
Laredo with option pkg.	65	55
NA with Skid Plate/Tow Hook Group.		

JEEP WRANGLER

BUDGET BUY

Jeep Wrangler Sahara

Four-wheel-drive compact sport-utility vehicle

Base price range: $14,090-$19,615. Built in Toledo, Ohio.

Also consider: Honda CR-V, Kia Sportage, Toyota RAV4

FOR • Optional anti-lock brakes • Versatility

AGAINST • Fuel economy • Acceleration (4-cylinder w/automatic) • Noise

Jeep considers Wrangler the "icon of the brand" and so its 1997 redesign kept what loyalist liked about the old and what engineers knew would improve it. The result was traditional styling (with a return to round headlamps) and a new coil suspension drawn from the Grand Cherokee, plus an interior redone with dual air bags. Wrangler responded with record sales, despite higher prices. Details are all that change for '98.

Cruise control is a first-time option, as is an engine-immobilizing anti-theft system. The driver's seat gets the tilt-forward entry that the front passenger seat already had. There's a revised steering gear designed for quicker response. And off-roaders will note that a 3.73:1 axle ratio replaces a 3.55:1 as a no cost option with the 6-cylinder engine.

All models come with a soft top and plastic side windows; a hardtop with roll-up side windows is optional.

The base SE comes with a 4-cylinder engine, the Sport and Sahara models with the same 6-cylinder used in the Cherokee and Grand Cherokee. Manual transmission is standard, a 3-speed automatic optional. All models have 4-wheel drive that can be shifted on the fly but isn't for use on dry pavement. Anti-lock brakes are optional on 6-cylinder Wranglers.

PERFORMANCE Wrangler isn't the ox cart it once was, but an off-road-ready suspension and short wheelbase still have it reacting abruptly to dips and bumps. Nonetheless, it isn't jarring unless the pavement is really bad. Its manners are sporty, it's maneuverable, and accurate steering helps it feel stable in turns and at highway speeds.

The 4-cylinder/manual transmission combination handles everything in stride except merging with or overtaking fast-moving freeway traffic. The automatic relegates Wrangler to the slow lane. There's fine power with the six and either transmission, though it's not the hot rod one might expect because 6-cylinder Wranglers weigh more than 3257 pounds. We averaged 19.3 mpg in our last test of a Sahara, more than we've gotten in previous 6-cylinder Wranglers and only slightly less than we've gotten with base models.

Braking is undramatic, and the optional anti-lock control works as advertised. Top up or down, wind noise is brutally loud in the convertible. It's somewhat less in the hardtop, but that only allows the copious road noise to drum through.

ACCOMMODATIONS Head room is terrific front or rear and the front seats are chair-height comfortable. Two adults fit in back without touching shoulders, but knee room is tight and the seat cushion is short on thigh and back support.

Gauges and controls are logically grouped and there are no serious impediments to outward visibility. A single row of grocery bags fits behind the back seat; folding the rear bench forward or removing it creates a steamer-trunk sized load space. Putting the soft top up or down means a choreographed sequence of zippers, fabric fasteners, and struts that seems harder than it ought to be.

BUILD QUALITY Compared to most other vehicles, Wrangler still has a para-military feel. Within this context, materials and workmanship are good.

VALUE FOR THE MONEY It's neither refined nor comfortable in any traditional sense, but few modern vehicles have more personality or are more at home off-road. Six-cylinder models quickly top $20,000, but Wranglers hold their value well as used cars.

RATINGS

	SE 4-cyl.	Sport/ Sahara
Acceleration	2	3
Fuel economy	3	3
Ride quality	2	2
Steering/handling	3	3
Braking	3	4
Quietness	2	2
Driver seating	3	3
Instruments/controls	4	4
Room/comfort (front)	3	3
Room/comfort (rear)	2	2
Cargo room	4	4
Value for the money	4	4
Total	**35**	**37**

SPECIFICATIONS

	2-door conv.
Wheelbase, in.	93.4
Overall length, in.	151.8
Overall width, in.	66.7
Overall height, in.	70.2
Curb weight, lbs.	3092
Cargo vol., cu. ft.	55.7
Fuel capacity, gals.	15.0
Seating capacity	4
Front head room, in.	42.3
Max. front leg room, in.	41.1
Rear head room, in.	40.6
Min. rear leg room, in.	34.9

ENGINES

	ohv I-4	ohv I-6
Size, liters/cu. in.	2.5/150	4.0/242
Horsepower @ rpm	120@ 5400	181@ 4600
Torque (lbs./ft.) @ rpm	140@ 3500	222@ 2800
Availability	S[2]	S[2]
EPA city/highway mpg		
3-speed automatic	17/19	15/17
5-speed OD manual	19/21	15/18

1. SE. 2. Sport, Sahara.

PRICES

Jeep Wrangler	Retail Price	Dealer Invoice
SE 2-door convertible	$14090	$13504
Sport 2-door convertible	17505	15804
Sahara 2-door convertible	19615	17661
Destination charge	525	525

STANDARD EQUIPMENT:

SE: 2.5-liter 4-cylinder engine, 5-speed manual transmission,

Command-Trac part-time 4WD, driver- and passenger-side air bags, power steering, reclining front vinyl bucket seats, tachometer, voltmeter, trip odometer, oil pressure and coolant temperature gauge, front carpeting, mini floor console w/cupholder, dual outside mirrors, dual horn, fender flares, rear bumper, front and rear stabilizer bars, 205/75R15 all-terrain tires, styled steel wheels.

Sport adds: 4.0-liter 6-cylinder engine, folding rear bench seat, 2-speaker AM/FM radio, clock, rear carpeting, cargo net, front and rear bumper extensions, 215/75R15 all-terrain tires.

Sahara adds: tilt steering wheel, cloth upholstery, Convenience Group, 4-speaker cassette player with rear sound bar and lamp, intermittent wiper, leather-wrapped steering wheel, map pockets, front floormats, fog lights, bodyside steps, upgraded fender flares, extra-capacity fuel tank, spare-tire cover, heavy-duty suspension, Heavy Duty Electrical Group, front tow hooks, 225/75R15 outline white-letter tires, alloy wheels.

OPTIONAL EQUIPMENT:

	Retail Price	Dealer Invoice
Major Packages		
Pkg. 22N/23N, SE	$865	$735
AM/FM radio, high back bucket seats, back seat.		
Pkg. 25D/24D, Sport	540	459
Tilt steering wheel, intermittent wipers, Convenience Group, extra-capacity fuel tank, full-size spare tire.		
Convenience Group, SE, Sport	165	140
Full storage console w/cupholders, courtesy lights.		
Powertrains		
3-speed automatic transmission	625	531
Trac-Loc rear differential	285	242
Requires full-size spare tire. SE and Sport require anti-lock brakes. NA with SE when ordered with 3-speed automatic transmission.		
Dana 44 rear axle, Sport, Sahara	595	506
Requires full-size spare. NA with anti-lock brakes. Includes Trac-Loc rear differential.		
Safety Features		
Anti-lock brakes, Sport, Sahara	600	510
Comfort and Convenience		
Hard top, SE, Sport	755	642
Sahara	1160	986
Includes full metal doors with roll-up windows, rear wiper/washer, deep-tinted glass (Sahara), cargo light.		
Soft and hard tops, SE, Sport	1395	1186
Sahara	1800	1560
Includes hard doors.		
Full metal doors w/roll-up windows	125	106
Air conditioning	895	761
Vinyl rear seat, SE	595	506
Includes rear carpeting.		
Cloth/vinyl reclining front bucket seats with rear seat,		
SE	735	625
SE w/22N/23N, Sport	150	128
SE includes rear carpeting.		
Tilt steering wheel, SE, Sport	195	166
Includes intermittent wipers.		
Leather-wrapped steering wheel, SE, Sport	50	43
Cruise control, Sahara	250	213
Rear defogger for hardtop	165	140
Requires Heavy Duty Electrical Group or air conditioning.		
AM/FM radio with 2 speakers, SE	270	230
AM/FM/cassette, SE	715	608
SE w/22N/23N	445	378
Sport	425	361
SE includes Sound Group. Sport includes rear sound bar and lamp.		
Sound Group, SE	535	455
SE w/22N/23N	245	208
AM/FM radio, four speakers with rear sound bar and lamp.		
Four speakers w/rear sound bar and lamp, Sport	243	207
Appearance and Miscellaneous		
Theft-deterrent system	75	64
Add-A-Trunk lockable storage	125	106
SE requires rear seat.		
Deep-tinted rear-quarter and liftgate glass, SE, Sport	405	344
Includes rear defogger. Requires hardtop.		

	Retail Price	Dealer Invoice
Bodyside steps, SE, Sport	$75	$64
Fog lights, Sport	120	102
Requires Heavy Duty Electrical Group or air conditioning.		
Extra-capacity fuel tank, SE, Sport	65	55
Engine block heater	35	30
Spare-tire cover, SE, Sport	50	43
NA with full-size spare tire. NA with SE when ordered with optional tires.		
Special Purpose, Wheels and Tires		
Heavy-duty suspension, SE, Sport	90	77
SE requires optional tires.		
Heavy-Duty Electrical Group, SE, Sport	135	115
with A/C or rear defogger	NC	NC
Heavy-duty battery and alternator.		
Front tow hooks, SE, Sport	40	34
Five 215/75R15 outline white-letter all-terrain tires,		
SE	280	238
Sport	235	200
Sport w/Pkg. 25D/24D	120	102
SE requires 5-spoke steel wheels.		
Five 225/75R15 outline white-letter all-terrain tires,		
SE	470	400
Sport	425	361
Sport w/Pkg. 25D/24D	310	264
SE requires 5-spoke steel or alloy wheels.		
Full-size spare tire, SE, Sport	115	98
Sahara	215	183
Tire and Wheel Pkg., Sport	785	667
Sport w/Pkg. 25D/24D	670	570
Sahara	360	306
Five alloy wheels, full-size spare, 30x9.5R15 outline white-letter tires. Sport includes heavy-duty suspension. NA with optional tires or 5-spoke alloy wheels. Deletes spare-tire cover on Sahara.		
Five 5-spoke steel wheels, SE	235	196
Requires optional tires.		
15x7 alloy wheels, Sport	265	225
Requires full-size spare or optional tires.		

KIA SPORTAGE

1997 Kia Sportage

Rear- or 4-wheel-drive compact sport-utility vehicle
Base price range: (1997 model) $14,495-$16,615. Built in South Korea.
Also consider: Honda CR-V, Subaru Forester, Toyota RAV4

FOR • Handling/maneuverability • Visibility

AGAINST • Acceleration (4-door) • Limited shift-on-the-fly 4WD • Rear anti-lock brakes only

Sportage arrived four years ago as the second product offered in the U.S. by Kia, South Korea's second-largest vehicle maker, after Hyundai. As a compact SUV, Sportage had a head start on the Honda CR-V and Toyota RAV4, but sales have been modest so far, partly because of Kia's go-slow approach to building its U.S. dealer network.

Kia picks up the pace for 1998, mildly facelifting the Sportage 4-door wagon and adding a new 2-door convertible model. Both body styles are available with rear drive or on-demand 4-wheel

Prices are accurate at time of publication; subject to manufacturer's changes.

drive. They share front sheetmetal and a 2.0-liter 4-cylinder engine, but the convertible is shorter in wheelbase and overall, and seats four instead of five. Like Isuzu's larger Amigo (newly resurrected this year), the Sportage convertible has a manual-fold soft top over the rear seat and a metal roof ahead. Though final plans hadn't been made at presstime, Kia says the convertible will likely go on sale in spring 1998 at prices below those of comparable wagons. Wagons are offered in 2WD and 4WD base and EX models.

PERFORMANCE Sportage is as capable off-road as most other small SUVs. However, most rivals have full shift-on-the-fly 4WD or permanently engaged 4WD. Sportage's 4WD can't be used on dry pavement, and although you can shift into 4-wheel High at up to 15 mph, returning to 2WD requires a stop, then backing up a few feet. The Kia also lags in braking technology, with anti-lock control only at the rear versus 4-wheel ABS.

Granted, SUVs are used mostly on pavement, but even the manual-shift Sportage wagon feels sluggish in routine driving, especially up steep grades. Acceleration is even worse with the optional automatic transmission. We haven't driven the new convertible yet, but its performance should be more acceptable, owing to less weight.

Wagon handling is a nice surprise, not unlike that of a good small sedan. For its size, Sportage has a fairly wide track (width between wheels on the same axle), so stability in tight turns is good, body lean modest. Springing is tight, though, so ride is more "trucky" than car-like, with moderate bounce and pitch on patchy pavement. Noise levels are fairly high from all sources, even in gentle highway cruising.

ACCOMMODATIONS The Sportage wagon is shorter than most compact SUVs yet provides adequate room for four adults. Head clearance is particularly good, even for 6-footers. Easy entry/exit is another plus, thanks to largish doors and relatively low step-in height.

Drivers enjoy a well-arranged dash with car-like instruments and controls, plus a clear view to all quarters, although the available outside spare tire gets in the way directly aft.

At least the outside spare frees up useful cargo room inside, and the wagon's rear seat easily folds to increase the space.

BUILD QUALITY Sportage is one of the cheaper SUVs but doesn't look or feel so cheap. Still, materials and workmanship are not up to Honda CR-V standards, and Kia is near the bottom of the list in consumer surveys of reliability and customer satisfaction.

VALUE FOR THE MONEY We like the Sportage because it's small enough to cope with the urban jungle yet large enough to be a practical family vehicle. Even so, a Honda CR-V or Toyota RAV4 offers better long-term value, especially at trade-in time. They're also more pleasant to drive and better built.

RATINGS

	Wagon
Acceleration	3
Fuel economy	4
Ride quality	3
Steering/handling	4
Braking	3
Quietness	3
Driver seating	4
Instruments/controls	4
Room/comfort (front)	4
Room/comfort (rear)	3
Cargo room	3
Value for the money	3
Total	**41**

SPECIFICATIONS

	4-door wagon	2-door conv.
Wheelbase, in.	104.4	92.9
Overall length, in.	159.4	148.0
Overall width, in.	68.1	68.1
Overall height, in.	65.2	65.0
Curb weight, lbs.	3280	NA
Cargo vol., cu. ft.	55.4	NA
Fuel capacity, gals.	15.8	14.0
Seating capacity	5	4

	4-door wagon	2-door conv.
Front head room, in.	39.6	39.6
Max. front leg room, in.	44.5	44.5
Rear head room, in.	37.8	NA
Min. rear leg room, in.	31.1	NA

ENGINES

	dohc I-4
Size, liters/cu. in.	2.0/122
Horsepower @ rpm	130@ 5500
Torque (lbs./ft.) @ rpm	127@ 4000
Availability	S
EPA city/highway mpg	
4-speed OD automatic	19/22
5-speed OD manual	19/23

PRICES

1997 Kia Sportage	Retail Price	Dealer Invoice
Base 4-door wagon, 2WD	$14495	$13177
Base 4-door wagon, 4WD	15995	14410
EX 4-door wagon 2WD	15390	13865
EX 4-door wagon 4WD	16615	14835
Destination charge	425	425

STANDARD EQUIPMENT:

2.0-liter DOHC 4-cylinder engine, 5-speed manual transmission, anti-lock rear brakes, driver-side air bag, power steering, cloth reclining front bucket seats w/driver-side lumbar adjuster, split folding rear bench seat, cupholders, tinted glass, power windows, power door locks, power mirrors, digital clock, tachometer, rear defogger, remote fuel-door release, passenger-side visor mirror, intermittent wipers, full-size spare with cover, rear spare-tire carrier, 205/75R15 tires, alloy wheels.

4WD adds: part-time 4WD, automatic locking hubs, alloy wheels.

EX adds: cruise control, rear wiper/washer, bright door handles, color-keyed outside mirrors, roof rack.

OPTIONAL EQUIPMENT:

Powertrains

4-speed automatic transmission	1000	910

Comfort and Convenience

Air conditioning	900	763
AM/FM/cassette	400	305
AM/FM/CD	545	430
Leather upholstery, EX	1000	865

Includes leather door-panel inserts, leather-wrapped steering wheel.

Appearance and Miscellaneous

Sport appearance graphics	95	60
Rear spoiler	189	143
Roof rack, base	185	142

Special Purpose, Wheels and Tires

Alloy wheels, base 2WD	340	274

LAND ROVER DISCOVERY

Four-wheel-drive midsize sport-utility vehicle

Base price range: (1997 model) $32,000-$38,500. Built in England.

Also consider: Infiniti QX4, Mercedes-Benz ML320, Oldsmobile Bravada

FOR • Standard anti-lock brakes • Ride

AGAINST • Fuel economy • Noise • Entry/exit

Discovery is the less-expensive of the two sport-utility vehicles offered by Britian's Land Rover North America. Not imported for '98 is the Defender 90—a para-military-style 2-door 4x4.

Discovery for '98 comes in LE and LSE trim, both with a V-8 engine,

---

Rating Scale: 5-Excellent; 4-Above average; 3-Average; 2-Below average; 1-Poor

CONSUMER GUIDE™

Land Rover Discovery LSE

automatic transmission, permanently engaged 4-wheel drive, and anti-lock 4-wheel disc brakes. The manual transmission offered last year is no longer available. Dual air bags are standard, but there are no side air bags.

Discovery has aluminum body panels and standard leather upholstery, dual sunroofs, and a split folding rear seat. Optional on both models is a package that includes two folding center-facing rear seats (for 7-passenger capacity), rear air conditioning, plus a hydraulic rear step that deploys when the swing-out tailgate is opened.

The LSE's standard equipment includes a wood-trimmed center console, a Harmon-Kardon audio system, and color-keyed exterior trim with stainless steel door handles and chrome bumpers. The base model makes do with only minor trim adjustments and map lights that have been integrated into the rearview mirror.

Land Rovers are built in England by the Rover Group, which is owned by BMW of Germany.

PERFORMANCE Acceleration is fairly lively, but even with a V-8, Discover's no quicker than a 6-cylinder Jeep Grand Cherokee. There's more road and mechanical noise, too, including some gear whine. Fuel economy is no bargain, either: just 13 mpg in our mix of expressway and suburban driving.

On the upside, the suspension manages to absorb most bumps well and does an admirable job controlling body lean in turns, considering this vehicle is nearly 6.5 feet tall. Discovery's grip on the road is unquestioned, but there's still a more tipsy feeling in changes of direction than in the usual midsize SUV. Some of our testers say the firm power steering requires too much muscle at low speeds. Stopping power is good, but there's more nose dive than we like in hard stops. Off-road performance is exceptional and the tall ground clearance lets you go where other vehicles fear to tread.

ACCOMMODATIONS Ground clearance is an off-road advantage but a hinderance to getting in or out because there's such a high step up to the interior. Head room and leg room are generous for the front buckets and middle-row bench seats. The steering wheel is mounted more horizontally than in conventional SUVs, and there's little shoulder room to the driver's left, so you're smack against the door. The middle seat is wide enough to hold three adults and the center position is as comfortable as the outboard positions. The optional rear jump seats are large enough only for kids.

Discovery's gauges are easy to see and are well lit at night, and the climate controls are simple to use, though the steering wheel hides the rear wiper/washer switch. The dealer-installed CD changer is under the driver's seat; you have to squat outside the vehicle to load it.

Cargo room is generous and the cargo bay is about as tall as it is wide. Interior storage is abundant, with unusual touches such as cargo nets on the ceiling and small cargo bins above the sunvisors.

BUILD QUALITY The nicely-finished body panels lined up evenly and our recent test vehicles felt rock solid.

VALUE FOR THE MONEY Though this Land Rover is extremely capable off-road, few people buy it for that reason. Similarly priced rivals such as the Infiniti QX4 and Mercedes-Benz ML320

are more accommodating as everyday transportation. In its favor, Discovery comes loaded with features and is a sort of out-doorsy fashion statement.

RATINGS

	LE/LSE
Acceleration	4
Fuel economy	1
Ride quality	4
Steering/handling	3
Braking	5
Quietness	2
Driver seating	3
Instruments/controls	4
Room/comfort (front)	4
Room/comfort (rear)	4
Cargo room	5
Value for the money	3
Total	**42**

SPECIFICATIONS

	4-door wagon
Wheelbase, in.	100.0
Overall length, in.	178.7
Overall width, in.	70.6
Overall height, in.	77.4
Curb weight, lbs.	4465
Cargo vol., cu. ft.	69.8
Fuel capacity, gals.	23.4
Seating capacity	7
Front head room, in.	37.4
Max. front leg room, in.	38.5
Rear head room, in.	39.2
Min. rear leg room, in.	36.3

ENGINES

	ohv V-8
Size, liters/cu. in.	4.0/241
Horsepower @ rpm	182@ 4750
Torque (lbs./ft.) @ rpm	233@ 3000
Availability	S

EPA city/highway mpg

4-speed OD automatic	14/17

PRICES

1997 Land Rover Discovery	Retail Price	Dealer Invoice
SD 4-door wagon, 5-speed	$32000	$28480
SD 4-door wagon, automatic	32000	28480
SD 4-door wagon w/leather interior, automatic	34000	30260
SE 4-door wagon, automatic	36000	32040
SE7 4-door wagon, 5-speed	38500	34265
SE7 4-door wagon, automatic	38500	34265
Destination charge	625	625

STANDARD EQUIPMENT:

SD: 4.0-liter V-8 engine, 5-speed manual or 4-speed automatic transmission, permanent 4-wheel drive, anti-lock 4-wheel disc brakes, driver- and passenger-side air bags, dual-zone climate control, power steering, cruise control, cloth upholstery, front bucket seats w/adjustable lumbar support, 60/40 split folding rear seat, front storage console, cupholders, leather-wrapped tilt steering wheel, power windows, power door locks, heated power mirrors, tachometer, coolant-temperature gauge, AM/FM/cassette/CD player with amplifier, power diversity antenna, rear defogger, remote keyless entry, illuminated visor mirrors, automatic day/night inside mirror, variable intermittent wipers, rear wiper/washer, headlamp washers, theft-deterrent system, burled-walnut interior trim, cargo cover, Class III towing hitch receiver, rear-mounted full-size spare tire, 235/70HR16 mud and snow tires, Freestyle alloy wheels.

SD w/leather interior adds: leather upholstery, heated power front seats.

SE adds: 4-speed automatic transmission, dual power sunroofs, Homelink universal garage-door opener, additional wood interior trim, front fog lights, dished alloy wheels.

SE7 adds: 5-speed manual or 4-speed automatic transmission, rear

---

Prices are accurate at time of publication; subject to manufacturer's changes.

air conditioning, rear jump seats, hydraulic rear step.

OPTIONAL EQUIPMENT:

	Retail Price	Dealer Invoice
Comfort and Convenience		
Rear jump seats, SD w/cloth upholstery	$875	$735
SD w/leather upholstery, SE	975	825
6-disc CD changer	625	525
Appearance and Miscellaneous		
Beluga black paint...	300	250

LAND ROVER RANGE ROVER

Land Rover Range Rover 4.0 SE

Four-wheel-drive full-size sport-utility vehicle

Base price range: (1997 model) $55,500-$63,000. Built in England.

Also consider: Acura SLX, Lexus LX 450, Lincoln Navigator

FOR • Standard anti-lock brakes • Ride • Passenger and cargo room • Trailer towing

AGAINST • Price • Fuel economy • Entry/exit

Ranger Rover no longer has the luxury sport-utility field to itself, and competition from newcomers such as Lexus, Lincoln, and Infiniti have helped reduce sales of these high-zoot 4x4s.

Nonetheless, changes are minimal for the two Range Rover models, similar except for engines and some features. Both are built in England by Rover Group, which is owned by Germany's BMW. The same company also markets the midsize Land Rover Discovery.

The 4.0 SE and 4.6 HSE are powered by aluminum overhead-valve V-8 engines. The SE uses a 4.0-liter version with 190 horsepower, the HSE a 4.6-liter with 225. Automatic transmission is standard, as is permanently engaged 4-wheel drive with a two-speed transfer case and traction control. Anti-lock 4-wheel disc brakes and dual air bags are standard. Side air bags are unavailable.

Leather upholstery, wood interior trim, and and a driver-adjustable electronic suspension with air springs and automatic self leveling come on both models. Equipment exclusive to the 4.6 HSE includes special 18-inch wheels. Changes for 1998 are minimal. The HSE gets a 12-speaker Harmon-Kardon audio system and new seat and door trim patterns. And both models offer a few new exterior colors. Towing capacity is 6500 pounds.

PERFORMANCE Off-road, Range Rovers are extremely capable and highly accommodating. On-road, they perform well, but aren't as spry as some domestic SUVs that cost thousands less. Ride quality is excellent. The suspension easily absorbs bumps and ruts and allows only a little bouncing on wavy surfaces. There's noticeable body lean in turns, but corners are taken with good grip and reassuring stability.

The 4.0-liter V-8 is smooth and quiet, even at full throttle, but feels lethargic with the transmission in the Normal shift mode. Push a button to change to the Sport mode and it feels like you've added 20 horsepower, yet 0-60 mph still took a long 11.4 seconds in our test.

The 4.6 HSE's V-8 feels a little stronger in all situations, but the larger, lower-profile tires hurt ride quality, so it suffers some harshness on bumpy pavement. We averaged just 14.3 mpg in a test of a 4.0 SE, despite lots of highway driving. The 4.6 HSE is no better.

ACCOMMODATIONS A tall step up into the interior makes getting in or out more work than in most SUVs. Inside, though, there's ample room for five on richly padded seats. An expansive cargo area is augmented by an array of cupholders and bins. Nifty touches abound. The rear seatbelt buckles are incorporated into the seat cushion, so they don't have to be fed through the seat after it has been folded down for load-carrying. And when the tailgate's down, a reinforced plastic panel bridges the gap between the tailgate opening and the load floor, to make it easier to slide objects in and out.

Some testers find the gauges a bit small for easy reading, but no instrument is obstructed. Controls are generally easy to reach, though there are lots of them and you have to study the owner's manual to decipher some of the identifying icons. The windows and sunroof conveniently open and close at a single touch of a button.

BUILD QUALITY Our test Range Rovers have had deep, blemish-free paint jobs and leather-and-wood interior appointments that befit their high price. However, they have also suffered a number of electrical glitches, including in the power seats, mirrors, and radios.

VALUE FOR THE MONEY Ranger Rovers are marvelous off-road, and well-suited to their role as transport for the foxes-and-hounds set. But they offer nothing of tangible value you can't get in rival SUVs for thousands less.

RATINGS

	4.0 SE	4.6 HSE
Acceleration	3	4
Fuel economy	1	1
Ride quality	4	3
Steering/handling	3	4
Braking	5	5
Quietness	3	3
Driver seating	4	4
Instruments/controls	3	3
Room/comfort (front)	5	5
Room/comfort (rear)	5	5
Cargo room	5	5
Value for the money	2	1
Total	43	43

SPECIFICATIONS

	4-door wagon
Wheelbase, in.	108.1
Overall length, in.	185.6
Overall width, in.	74.4
Overall height, in.	71.6
Curb weight, lbs.	4960
Cargo vol., cu. ft.	58.0
Fuel capacity, gals.	24.6
Seating capacity	5
Front head room, in.	38.1
Max. front leg room, in.	42.6
Rear head room, in.	38.2
Min. rear leg room, in.	36.5

ENGINES

	ohv V-8	ohv V-8
Size, liters/cu. in.	4.0/241	4.6/278
Horsepower @ rpm............................	190@ 4750	225@ 4750
Torque (lbs./ft.) @ rpm.......................	236@ 3000	280@ 3000
Availability	S[1]	S[2]
EPA city/highway mpg		
4-speed OD automatic........................	13/17	12/16

1. 4.0 SE. 2. 4.6 HSE.

PRICES

1997 Land Rover Range Rover

	Retail Price	Dealer Invoice
4.0 SE 4-door wagon	$55500	$49125
4.6 HSE 4-door wagon	63000	55750
Destination charge	625	625

STANDARD EQUIPMENT:

4.0 SE: 4.0-liter V-8 engine, 4-speed automatic transmission, permanent 4-wheel drive, electronic 2-speed transfer case, electronic trac-

Rating Scale: 5-Excellent; 4-Above average; 3-Average; 2-Below average; 1-Poor

tion control, anti-lock 4-wheel disc brakes, driver- and passenger-side air bags, variable-assist power steering, automatic load-leveling suspension, dual-zone automatic climate control w/interior air filter, cruise control, leather upholstery, heated 10-way power front bucket seats w/memory feature, split folding rear bench seat, front storage console w/cupholders, leather-wrapped tilt/telescopic steering wheel, power windows, power door locks, heated power mirror w/memory, power sunroof, trip computer, computer message center, 11-speaker AM/FM/cassette w/6-disc CD changer and weather band, integrated diversity antenna, steering-wheel radio controls, tinted glass, remote keyless entry, automatic day/night rearview mirror, Homelink garage-door opener, theft-deterrent system, remote fuel-door release, heated windshield and rear window, variable intermittent wipers w/heated washer nozzles, rear wiper/washer, heated headlight wiper/washers, illuminated visor mirrors, map lights, trailer hitch and wiring harness, burl walnut interior trim, cargo cover, front spoiler, front and rear fog lights, 225/65HR16 tires, full-size spare tire, alloy wheels.

4.6 HSE adds: 4.6-liter V-8 engine, leather-wrapped shifter, chrome exhaust outlet, mud guards, Pirelli 225/55HR18 tires.

OPTIONAL EQUIPMENT:

	Retail Price	Dealer Invoice
Major Packages		
Kensington Interior Pkg., 4.6 HSE	$3000	$2675

Light Stone leather upholstery w/Ash Black piping, leather interior trim, storage box, burled walnut interior trim, Harmon Kardon sound system, cellular-phone prewiring.

Appearance and Miscellaneous

Beluga black clearcoat paint, 4.0 SE	300	250
Extra-cost paint, 4.6 HSE	1000	—

LEXUS ES 300

Lexus ES 300

✓ BEST BUY

Near-luxury car; similar to Toyota Camry
Base price: $30,790. Built in Japan.
Also consider: Audi A4, Infiniti I30, Mazda Millenia

FOR • Side air bags • Acceleration • Ride • Quietness • Passenger and cargo room

AGAINST • Rear visibility • Steering feel

Widely regarded as the benchmark for near-luxury sedans, the Lexus ES 300 is little changed following its 1997 redesign. This is the entry-level model from Toyota's luxury division and it uses the same basic design as the Toyota Camry. Camry was also redesigned last year, but the two models are visually distinct, and the Lexus has more standard features.

For 1998, standard equipment expands with the addition of front side air bags and an engine immobilizer. The former are mounted on the seat sides instead of in the doors, as on some other '98 cars. The immobilizer prevents engine "hot wiring" by potential thieves. Also new are a higher-power Nakamichi premium audio option and an integrated pocket-size cell phone as a dealer-installed option.

The ES 300's 3.0-liter V-6 makes 200 horsepower, six more than the Camry version. Traction control is optional, as is a "semi-active" Adaptive Variable Suspension that monitors vehi-

cle speed, acceleration, braking and other conditions to continuously adjust shock damping within "soft, normal, or sport" firmness ranges as set by the driver. It also detects rapid steering movements and stiffens outboard shock damping to reduce body lean in hard cornering.

PERFORMANCE Quietness is a major asset of the ES 300. Wind rush is barely a whisper at highway speeds, road noise rarely more than a muted hum, and the V-6 is silent at idle, silken under power. Power it has—enough for 0-60 mph sprints of just 7.6 seconds by our stopwatch. Though premium fuel is required, even hard driving failed to push our overall mpg below 20. Braking is swift and vice-free except for marked nosedive in "panic" stops.

That implies the ES 300 is more "little limo" than sports sedan, and it is. Its steering is quick but lacking some in road feel, and though a capable handler, the Lexus isn't as nimble or precise as the admittedly less-isolated BMW 3-Series or Mercedes C-Class. We don't recommend the Adaptive Variable Suspension option. It works best in its middle setting, where it gives a comfortable ride on most surfaces—just like the standard chassis. We also found it made little difference in body lean through fast turns, so why bother?

ACCOMMODATIONS The ES 300 interior is an inviting place for four adults. Six-footers can sit comfortably in tandem, although those in back must ride knees-up and have little toe room beneath the front seats. Cargo space isn't vast, but the trunk is roomy enough, usefully shaped, and blessed with a low liftover.

Last year's redesign gave the ES 300 such appreciated features as one-touch-open operation for the optional power moonroof and a convenient glovebox mounting for the available CD changer. The driving position is a model of considered design, with a good range of seat and steering wheel adjustments, clear gauges, and handy switchgear, including an audio unit that sits above the less frequently used climate controls. Outward visibility is fine except for invisible rear corners, a penalty of the high-tail styling.

BUILD QUALITY Like Toyota with the Camry, clever simplifying of some components allowed Lexus to shave costs and list price without compromising quality. ES300 workmanship thus remains first-rate, the car's luxury character undiminished.

VALUE FOR THE MONEY It's hard to fault the ES 300. It does most everything a near-luxury sedan should, and very well. If you value comfort and elegance over sporty road manners, there's no better buy in this class. Toyota reliability and Lexus customer service ice a tempting cake.

RATINGS

	ES 300
Acceleration	4
Fuel economy	3
Ride quality	4
Steering/handling	3
Braking	4
Quietness	5
Driver seating	5
Instruments/controls	5
Room/comfort (front)	4
Room/comfort (rear)	3
Cargo room	3
Value for the money	5
Total	**48**

SPECIFICATIONS

	4-door sedan
Wheelbase, in.	105.1
Overall length, in.	190.2
Overall width, in.	70.5
Overall height, in.	54.9
Curb weight, lbs.	3296
Cargo vol., cu. ft.	13.0

Prices are accurate at time of publication; subject to manufacturer's changes.

	4-door sedan
Fuel capacity, gals.	18.5
Seating capacity	5
Front head room, in.	38.0
Max. front leg room, in.	43.5
Rear head room, in.	36.2
Min. rear leg room, in.	34.4

ENGINES

	dohc V-6
Size, liters/cu. in.	3.0/181
Horsepower @ rpm	200@ 5200
Torque (lbs./ft.) @ rpm	214@ 4400
Availability	S
EPA city/highway mpg	
4-speed OD automatic	19/26

PRICES

Lexus ES 300	Retail Price	Dealer Invoice
Base 4-door sedan	$30790	$26745
Destination charge	495	495

STANDARD EQUIPMENT:

Base: 3.0-liter DOHC V-6, 4-speed automatic transmission, driver- and passenger-side air bags, front side-impact air bags, anti-lock 4-wheel disc brakes, variable-assist power steering, tilt steering wheel, cruise control, air conditioning w/automatic climate control, cloth upholstery, power front bucket seats, driver-side power lumbar support, split folding rear seat with trunk pass-through, walnut interior trim, front console with auxiliary power outlet, overhead console, rear cupholder, power windows, power door locks, remote keyless entry, heated power mirrors, AM/FM cassette, tachometer, outside-temperature indicator, rear defogger, variable intermittent wipers, illuminated visor mirrors, remote fuel-door and decklid releases, first-aid kit, automatic headlamps, solar-control tinted glass, theft-deterrent system, fog lights, full-size spare tire, 205/65VR15 tires, alloy wheels.

OPTIONAL EQUIPMENT:

Major Packages

Leather Trim Pkg.	1650	1320
Leather upholstery, memory driver seat.		

Powertrains

Traction control	300	240
Requires Leather Trim Pkg. and all-season tires.		

Comfort and Convenience

Power moonroof	1000	800
Heated front seats	420	336
Requires Leather Trim Pkg.		
Nakamichi premium audio system	1600	1253
Includes 6-disc CD changer.		
6-disc CD changer	1050	840

Appearance and Miscellaneous

Adaptive Variable Suspension	600	480
Requires Leather Trim Pkg.		
Chrome alloy wheels	1700	850
205/65VR15 all-season tires	NC	NC

Other **options** are available as port installed items.

LEXUS GS 300/400

Rear-wheel-drive luxury car
Base price range: $36,800-$44,800. Built in Japan.
Also consider: Acura RL, BMW 5-Series, Mercedes-Benz E-Class

Lexus GS 400

FOR • Standard front and side air bags • Acceleration • Steering/handling • Quietness

AGAINST • Rear entry/exit

Lexus's entry-level ES 300 and flagship LS 400 have been strong sellers, while the in-between GS 300 went largely ignored since its 1993 debut. Toyota's luxury division hopes to change that with a redesigned GS 300 and a new V-8 GS 400.

As before, the 300 uses a 3.0-liter inline-6; its stablemate gets the LS 400's 4.0-liter V-8. Both engines become more potent for '98 thanks to Lexus's Variable Valve Timing/Intelligence (VVT-I).

Both GS models come with 5-speed automatic transmission. Exclusive to the 400 is "E-shift," a quartet of steering-wheel buttons allowing sequential manual gear selection once the shift lever is slotted into "M." Upshifts are made with either of two buttons on the wheel's face, downshifts by "mirror" buttons on the backside. Against its predecessor, the '98 GS is about a half-inch shorter in wheelbase but a whopping 6 inches trimmer overall, yet Lexus claims more passenger and cargo room.

Like this year's LS 400 (see report), both GS models come with Lexus's new Vehicle Stability Control anti-skid system, which is integrated with standard anti-lock brakes and traction control. Also like the LS, there's an optional in-dash navigation system with touch-screen display. Seat-mounted front side air bags are standard.

PERFORMANCE With German sports sedans boasting Lexus-like refinement, the new GS tilts Lexus toward BMW/Mercedes for handling and performance. That's especially true of the 400, which storms to 60 mph in only 6.0 seconds, a claim that our preview drives seemed to confirm. The 300 isn't much slower at a quoted 7.6, bit it doesn't feel quite so strong on take-off.

V-8 or six, these cars have silky powertrains, ultra-low noise levels, ample mid-range punch, and powerful, undramatic braking. What's new—and welcome—for a Lexus sedan is their higher level of control. Both GS models arrow with iron stability at high speed and corner with grippy precision, aided by firm, responsive steering. There's a trifle more body lean than with, say, a 5-Series BMW, and the GS isn't quite as "tossable" on curvy roads, but it invites enthusiastic driving like no other Lexus sedan. Even so, ride is comfortably supple on most any surface.

ACCOMMODATIONS Despite its bobbed nose and tail, the new GS beats the old one for passenger and cargo room, though that's not saying much. Rear entry/exit isn't the best, and aft head room remains tight for 6-footers, but space is otherwise ample for four adults, five if you must. The trunk isn't outstandingly roomy, but it's enough.

Drivers face another well-arranged Lexus dash presenting big gauges (with self-adjusting high-tech lighting on the 400) and large, simple minor controls. The optional in-dash navigator gives you a busier layout, with audio and climate functions controlled from its touch-screen display; it's like Buick used to do and we still don't like it. The 400's "E-shift" buttons do the job, but take time to learn and aren't really needed in a road car. Seat and steering-wheel adjustments cater to any size driver, but over-the-shoulder vision is hindered some by the roof and tail styling.

BUILD QUALITY We expect a Lexus to be solid, carefully finished and crafted of top-quality materials. Though we've only driven pre-production models so far, the GS seems to qualify on all counts.

VALUE FOR THE MONEY Lexus calls the new GS a luxury car for "drivers in a hurry." We say it's the only real Japanese alternative to taut-handling German sports sedans, yet it's still every inch a posh, smooth-riding, feature-laden Lexus. As a Lexus it

---

Rating Scale: 5-Excellent; 4-Above average; 3-Average; 2-Below average; 1-Poor

CONSUMER GUIDE™

merits strong consideration, though it's far from bargain-priced.

RATINGS

	GS 300	GS 400
Acceleration	4	5
Fuel economy	3	3
Ride quality	4	4
Steering/handling	4	4
Braking	4	4
Quietness	4	4
Driver seating	4	4
Instruments/controls	3	3
Room/comfort (front)	4	4
Room/comfort (rear)	3	3
Cargo room	3	3
Value for the money	3	3
Total	43	44

SPECIFICATIONS

	4-door sedan
Wheelbase, in.	110.2
Overall length, in.	189.0
Overall width, in.	70.9
Overall height, in.	56.7
Curb weight, lbs.	3690
Cargo vol., cu. ft.	14.8
Fuel capacity, gals.	19.8
Seating capacity	5
Front head room, in.	39.2
Max. front leg room, in.	44.5
Rear head room, in.	37.0
Min. rear leg room, in.	34.3

ENGINES

	dohc I-6	dohc V-8
Size, liters/cu. in.	3.0/183	4.0/242
Horsepower @ rpm	225@ 6000	300@ 6000
Torque (lbs./ft.) @ rpm	220@ 4000	310@ 4000
Availability	S[1]	S[2]
EPA city/highway mpg 5-speed OD automatic	NA	NA

1. GS 300. 2. GS 400.

PRICES

Lexus GS 300/400

	Retail Price	Dealer Invoice
GS 300 4-door sedan	$36800	$31964
GS 400 4-door sedan	44800	38461
Destination charge	495	495

STANDARD EQUIPMENT:

GS 300: 3.0-liter DOHC 6-cylinder engine, 5-speed automatic transmission, traction control, dual exhaust, driver- and passenger-side air bags, front side-impact air bags, anti-lock 4-wheel disc brakes, air conditioning w/automatic dual-zone climate control, variable-assist power steering, power tilt/telescopic steering column, cruise control, cloth upholstery, power front bucket seats with power lumbar support, front storage console, rear folding armrest, cupholder, walnut wood trim, power heated outside mirrors, automatic day/night rearview mirror, power windows, power door locks, remote keyless entry, Lexus/Pioneer Audio System with AM/FM/cassette and seven speakers, diversity antenna, rear defogger, digital clock, variable intermittent wipers, two trip odometers, outside-temperature indicator, illuminated visor mirrors, universal garage door opener, remote fuel-door and trunk releases, front and rear reading lights, automatic headlamps, first-aid kit, color-keyed tinted glass, theft-deterrent system, fog lights, tool kit, 215/60VR16 tires, alloy wheels.

GS 400 adds: 4.0-liter DOHC V-8 engine, leather upholstery, leather-wrapped steering wheel, memory system (driver seat, steering wheel, outside mirrors), automatic day/night outside mirrors, 225/55VR16 tires.

OPTIONAL EQUIPMENT:
Major Packages

	Retail	Dealer
Leather Trim Pkg., GS 300	1710	1368

Leather upholstery, leather-wrapped steering wheel and shifter, memory system (driver seat, steering wheel, outside mirrors).

Comfort and Convenience

	Retail Price	Dealer Invoice
Navigation system	$2250	$1913

Requires 6-disc CD changer.

Heated front seats	420	336

GS requires Leather Trim Pkg.

Lexus/Nakamichi Premium Audio System	2250	1740

GS requires Leather Trim Pkg. Includes 6-disc CD changer.

6-disc CD changer	1050	840
Power moonroof	1020	816

Appearance and Miscellaneous

High intensity headlights	500	400
Rear spoiler, GS 400	420	336
Chrome alloy wheels	1700	850

Other options are available as port installed items.

LEXUS LS 400

Lexus LS 400

Rear-wheel-drive luxury car
Base price: $52,900. Built in Japan.
Also consider: Cadillac Seville, Infiniti Q45, Mercedes-Benz E-Class

FOR • Standard front side air bags • Acceleration • Ride • Quietness

AGAINST • Fuel economy

The flagship sedan from Toyota's luxury division was updated two years ago, and a more radically redesigned successor is two years away. Even so, the LS 400 sees a number of changes for 1998.

Dimensions don't change, but the nose and taillamps are subtly altered, and the body gets thicker glass and more sound insulation. Mechanically, the LS's 4.0-liter V-8 adds 30 horsepower and 30 pounds/feet of torque via a new Variable Valve Timing/Intelligence system (VVT-i). Matching this extra muscle is a 5-speed automatic transmission (with Mercedes-style slotted shift gate), replacing the previous 4-speeder.

Yet another new standard wrinkle is Vehicle Stability Control. This uses input from the anti-lock brake and traction-control sensors to brake individual wheels so as to avoid or minimize "fishtailing" and front-end "plowing," thus keeping the rear-wheel-drive sedan on course through a curve, emergency lane-change, and such. Other new features include front-safety belt pretensioners, a remote-entry control built into the master key, an automatic air-recirculation function for smoggy days, standard 15-function trip computer, optional HID (high intensity discharge) headlamps, and an extra-cost satellite-based navigation system with dashboard touch-screen display.

PERFORMANCE The LS 400 was already smooth, quick, and quiet. The '98 is more so, though the differences aren't startling. Acceleration and passing punch do seem improved. Our preview drives suggest the '98 should do 0-60 mph in about 6.3 seconds, versus the 6.9 we clocked last year. Fuel economy, however, may be somewhat worse than our '97 model's overall average of 19.5 mpg.

As ever, Lexus's creamy twin-cam V-8 emits but a muted growl at high rpm, and this year's extra noise dampening measures make one of the world's quietest cars even more isolated from wind and road ruckus. But the LS also isolates its driver too much. Though ride comfort is excellent and the damping

Prices are accurate at time of publication; subject to manufacturer's changes.

doesn't feel that soft initially, higher-speed driving brings out marked vertical bounce over big humps and dips, while the power steering, already light to the touch, becomes numb and a bit twitchy. There's also distinct body lean through fast, tight turns.

By contrast, the new Vehicle Stability Control does an admirable job keeping you safely on track when the road gets slippery. Lexus set up a special slick-surface handling road to prove the point, so we know VSC really works.

ACCOMMODATIONS Front seat head and leg room are ample, and the seats are wide enough for larger occupants. The rear seat has good leg room but only adequate head room. Access to the rear seats is hampered by tall door sills, and the driveshaft hump of this rear-drive car limits practical seating in the rear to two.

Large, easy-to-read gauges appear to be analog but actually are electroluminescent. Unlike some similar systems, the LS 400's gauges are easy to see even in direct sunlight. The climate system has large buttons and individual left-right temperature settings, and controls for the stereo are simple and intuitive, even with the optional premium audio system.

Visibility is generally good, but thick rear roof pillars can make lane changes challenging.

At 13.9 cubic feet, cargo space is at the low end of the luxury sedan class, but it's more than adequate for a weekend's worth of stuff. All doors have map pockets and there are cupholders for both the front and rear seats.

BUILD QUALITY Lexus workmanship vies with the world's best, especially on the LS 400. The interior decor may be Japanese, but door closings, paint finish, detail assembly, and overall solidity say "German."

VALUE FOR THE MONEY The LS 400 can easily top $60,000 with options—a lot of money, but then, this is a lot of car. Fine materials and workmanship, exceptional refinement and durability, and high resale value should ease the cost of ownership over the long run.

RATINGS

	Lexus LS 400
Acceleration	5
Fuel economy	3
Ride quality	4
Steering/handling	3
Braking	4
Quietness	5
Driver seating	5
Instruments/controls	5
Room/comfort (front)	5
Room/comfort (rear)	4
Cargo room	3
Value for the money	5
Total	**50**

SPECIFICATIONS

	4-door sedan
Wheelbase, in.	112.2
Overall length, in.	196.7
Overall width, in.	72.0
Overall height, in.	56.5
Curb weight, lbs.	3890
Cargo vol., cu. ft.	13.9
Fuel capacity, gals.	22.5
Seating capacity	5
Front head room, in.	38.9
Max. front leg room, in.	43.7
Rear head room, in.	36.9
Min. rear leg room, in.	36.9

ENGINES

	dohc V-8
Size, liters/cu. in.	4.0/242
Horsepower @ rpm	290@ 6000
Torque (lbs./ft.) @ rpm	300@ 4000
Availability	S
EPA city/highway mpg	
5-speed OD automatic	NA

PRICES

Lexus LS 400	Retail Price	Dealer Invoice
Base 4-door sedan	$52900	$44880
Destination charge	495	495

STANDARD EQUIPMENT:

Base: 4.0-liter DOHC V-8 engine, 5-speed automatic transmission, traction control, dual exhaust outlets, driver- and passenger-side air bags, front side-impact air bags, anti-lock 4-wheel disc brakes, variable-assist power steering, power tilt/telescopic steering wheel, leather-wrapped steering wheel and shifter, cruise control, air conditioning w/automatic dual-zone climate control, interior air filter, leather upholstery, power front bucket seats with power lumbar support, rear folding armrest, memory system (driver seat, steering wheel, outside mirrors), front storage console with auxiliary power outlet, cupholders, walnut interior trim, heated power mirrors w/passenger-side back-up aid, automatic day/night inside and outside mirrors, power windows, power door locks, remote keyless entry, Lexus/Pioneer AM/FM/cassette with seven speakers, diversity antenna, digital clock, tachometer, two trip odometers, coolant-temperature gauge, outside-temperature indicator, trip computer, rear defogger, remote fuel-door and decklid releases, illuminated visor mirrors, universal garage door opener, front and rear reading lights, speed-sensitive variable intermittent wipers, automatic headlamps, first-aid kit, color-keyed tinted glass, theft-deterrent system, fog lights, tool kit, full-size spare tire, 225/60VR16 tires, alloy wheels.

OPTIONAL EQUIPMENT:
Comfort and Convenience

Navigation system	3300	2753
Includes 6-disc CD changer.		
Power moonroof	1120	896
Heated front seats	420	336
Lexus/Nakamichi Premium Audio System	2250	1740
Includes 6-CD auto changer. NA with Navigation sytem.		
6-disc CD changer	1050	840
Woodgrain steering wheel	330	264

Appearance and Miscellaneous

High intensity headlights	500	400
Electronic air suspension	2970	2376
Includes power moonroof. Requires Lexus/Nakamichi Premium Audio System, or Navigation system.		
Chrome alloy wheels	1700	850

Other options are available as port installed items.

1997 LEXUS LX 450

Lexus LX 450

Four-wheel-drive full-size sport-utility vehicle; similar to Toyota Land Cruiser

Base price: (1997 model) $48,450. Built in Japan.
Also consider: GMC Yukon, Land Rover Range Rover, Lincoln Navigator

FOR • Passenger and cargo room

AGAINST • Fuel economy • Ride • Entry/exit

Toyota's luxury division is prepping a new full-size SUV for a spring debut. Details were slim at presstime, but the '98 model will be badged LX 470 to denote a new 4.7-liter V-8 engine that's also destined for Toyota's T100 pickup. Expect more rounded styling on a longer wheelbase than the outgoing 6-cylinder LX 450. The 470's basic design will be used for the new Toyota Land Cruiser due about the same time.

Meanwhile, Lexus will sell '97 LX 450s until inventory runs out. Introduced for 1996 to cash in on the booming market for upscale SUVs, the 450 is a more-expensive version of the 1991-vintage Land Cruiser, with slightly different styling, more standard features, and a longer warranty.

PERFORMANCE Like Land Cruiser, the LX 450 is heavy for its 6-cylinder engine, so acceleration is adequate at best. Fuel economy is dismal, just 11 mpg in our last test.

With slightly softer damping than the Cruiser, the LX 450 smoothes out bumpy roads a bit better, but it's still a big rig that feels rather ponderous. Braking is stable, but all the weight makes for longish stops.

The LX 450 has more sound insulation than the Land Cruiser, so it suffers less road noise, but you'll never mistake it for a Lexus sedan. Wind rush is prominent even at modest speeds in this high, bluff vehicle, and the engine fan whirs loudly too much of the time.

ACCOMMODATIONS With the same huge interior as the Land Cruiser, the LX 450 offers bountiful room for five and cramped seating behind for two more—preferably kids. At least those third-row seats fold up easily to leave a tall, fairly long load space.

Simulated wood trim and aromatic leather give the LX 450 a posh ambience, but the upright driving position is utilitarian 4x4. So is the high ground clearance, which makes getting in or out a real chore. Visibility is good apart from some headrest clutter. A few minor controls are placed like afterthoughts, but gauges and most switches are simple and handy.

BUILD QUALITY As you'd expect, the LX 450 has a robust feel that implies good long-term durability and resistance to squeaks and rattles. Detail workmanship is neat and thorough.

VALUE FOR THE MONEY Lexus says its customers want a prestige sport-utility backed by excellent dealer service. The LX 450 delivers on both counts, but is it worth several thousand more than the basically similar Land Cruiser? We say no, but a fair number of folks have said yes with their wallets, and that's why a new LX is on the way.

RATINGS

	LX 450
Acceleration	3
Fuel economy	1
Ride quality	3
Steering/handling	3
Braking	3
Quietness	3
Driver seating	4
Instruments/controls	3
Room/comfort (front)	5
Room/comfort (rear)	5
Cargo room	5
Value for the money	2
Total	**40**

SPECIFICATIONS

	4-door wagon
Wheelbase, in.	112.2
Overall length, in.	189.8
Overall width, in.	76.0
Overall height, in.	73.6
Curb weight, lbs.	4971
Cargo vol., cu. ft.	90.9
Fuel capacity, gals.	25.1
Seating capacity	7
Front head room, in.	40.3
Max. front leg room, in.	41.7
Rear head room, in.	39.7
Min. rear leg room, in.	28.5

ENGINES

	dohc I-6
Size, liters/cu. in.	4.5/275
Horsepower @ rpm	212@ 4600
Torque (lbs./ft.) @ rpm	275@ 3200
Availability	S
EPA city/highway mpg	
4-speed OD automatic	13/15

PRICES

1997 Lexus LX 450	Retail Price	Dealer Invoice
4-door wagon	$48450	$41595
Destination charge	495	495

STANDARD EQUIPMENT:

4.5-liter DOHC 6-cylinder engine, 4-speed automatic transmission, full-time 4-wheel drive, anti-lock 4-wheel disc brakes, automatic climate control, driver- and passenger-side air bags, variable-assist power steering, cruise control, leather upholstery, power front bucket seats with driver-side lumbar support, split folding middle bench seat, retractable rear seats, rear folding armrests, front storage console with cupholders, tilt steering wheel, leather-wrapped steering wheel and shifter, Lexus/Pioneer AM/FM/cassette with seven speakers, power antenna, front green-tinted glass, rear privacy glass, sliding rear-quarter windows, remote outside mirrors, power windows, rear defogger, theft-deterrent system, tachometer, voltmeter, coolant-temperature and oil-pressure gauge, digital clock, illuminated visor mirrors, map lights, wood interior trim, variable intermittent wipers, automatic headlamps, rear heat duct, remote fuel-door release, first-aid and tool kits, 275/70HR16 tires, full-size spare tire, alloy wheels, power door locks.

OPTIONAL EQUIPMENT:
Major Packages

Convenience Pkg.	1039	646
Cargo mat, running boards, roof rack, tow hitch assembly.		

Comfort and Convenience

Power moonroof	1300	1040
6-disc CD changer	1050	840
Floormats	112	68

Special Purpose, Wheels and Tires

Differential locks	900	720
Wheel locks	50	35

1999 LEXUS RX 300

1999 Lexus RX 300

Four-wheel-drive midsize sport-utility vehicle
Base price range: NA. Built in Japan.

Toyota's luxury division joins the midsize sport-utility ranks with the 1999 RX 300. Based on the platform used for the 1992-96 Toyota Camry and Lexus ES 300 sedans, the RX is all but identical to the 1997 Lexus SLV concept vehicle.

Lexus says the RX 300 will combine "the comfort, convenience and performance of a luxury sport sedan with the recreational character and ruggedness expected of an SUV."

This 4-door wagon is sized close to the Jeep Grand Cherokee and features front-wheel drive or permanent all-wheel drive. As on the smaller Toyota RAV4 and Honda's CR-V, construction is unitized, not truck-type body-on-frame. Mimicking Mercedes' new M-Class, suspension is all-independent.

Powering the RX 300 is the 3.0-liter Camry/ES 300 V-6, but uprated with Toyota's Variable Valve Timing/Intelligence system (VVT-i) as on the '98 Lexus V-8 engine. A 4-speed automatic will be the only transmission.

Other standard features include seat-mounted front side air bags, all-disc anti-lock brakes, 16-inch alloy wheels, a 60/40 split-fold rear seat, and an LCD touch screen for operating audio and climate controls.

Expect to see the RX 300 at auto shows, with sales commencing by spring. We have not driven the RX 300 and so cannot comment on its performance. Specifications, standard equipment, options, and prices were unavailable at presstime.

LEXUS SC 300/400

✓ BEST BUY

Lexus SC 400

Rear-wheel-drive luxury coupe
Base price range: $40,900-$52,700. Built in Japan.
Also consider: Cadillac Eldorado, Jaguar XK8, Lincoln Mark VIII

FOR • Quietness • Acceleration • Steering/handling

AGAINST • Fuel economy • Rear seat room • Cargo room

Luxury coupes are withering on the sales vine, yet Toyota's upscale division keeps fine-tuning its sporty SC models. The highlights are revised engines—the same ones found in Lexus's redesigned GS sedans.

The V-8 SC 400 adds 40 horsepower and 30 pounds/feet of torque thanks to Variable Valve Timing/Intelligence (VVT-i), claimed to be the first system that adjusts intake-valve timing continuously. The inline-6 of the junior SC 300 gains 10 pounds/feet but no more horsepower.

Additionally, the SC 400 replaces its 4-speed automatic transmission with a 5-speed automatic. Like Mercedes and some other cars, there's a slotted "wiggle worm" gate allowing manual gear selection almost like a stick shift. The SC 300 is now sold only with 4-speed automatic, the previous standard 5-speed manual dying of slow sales.

Both SCs add an engine immobilizer (to prevent "hot wiring"), integrated garage-door opener, a remote entry control built into the master key, and more wood interior trim. Dual front air bags and optional traction control continue, but front side air bags are unavailable.

PERFORMANCE We haven't yet driven the '98 SCs, but the new VVT-i engines promise to make a pair of suave performers even more so. Quicker too, and they weren't laggards before. Lexus claims 0-60 mph in 6.6 seconds for the SC 400 and 7.9 for the SC 300. We do hope for better economy than last year's 17.2 mpg average with the V-8 model and 18 with the six—not bad given the these cars' heft, but not great since both need premium gas.

The SCs used to have a sportier on-road personality than any other Lexus, but the redesigned GS sedans may tilt even more toward enthusiasts. Still, the coupes are agile for their size and weight, corner with precision, and feel solidly planted on the highway. Ride is much firmer than that of Lexus's big LS 400 sedan, but is not harsh, though the V-8 coupe becomes a tad choppy on washboard surfaces. The SCs are also a bit noisier than their sedan sisters, but very quiet by absolute standards.

ACCOMMODATIONS The term "2+2" aptly describes these cars. They carry two adults comfortably in front and maybe two small children behind. Rear head room is skimpy at best, and aft leg room vanishes if the front seats are set more than halfway back. Tall front-seaters have limited head room, especially beneath the optional power moonroof. Entry/exit isn't the best either, what with the low-slung styling and long, heavyish doors.

Coupes don't typically shine for cargo space, and while there's enough for two on a long weekend, the high, small trunk opening complicates loading.

Drivers sit relatively low, and some might feel a bit hemmed-in by the broad center console, but most should get easily situated with the wide range of seat and steering-wheel adjustments. Gauges and controls are large, well placed, and intuitive. Visibility is clear even to the rear corners, and the optional spoiler eases parking in tight spots.

BUILD QUALITY Though not endowed with the latest in high-strength body engineering, SCs feel solid and substantial on the road. Detail finish is exemplary most everywhere you look.

VALUE FOR THE MONEY Luxury cars don't have to be practical and the Lexus coupes aren't, but they make few compromises in comfort, convenience, or performance while ranking at the top in quality and customer satisfaction. A few good alternatives sell for less, but none are more satisfying to drive or to own.

RATINGS

	SC 300	SC 400
Acceleration	4	5
Fuel economy	3	3
Ride quality	4	4
Steering/handling	4	4
Braking	4	4
Quietness	4	4
Driver seating	3	3
Instruments/controls	4	4
Room/comfort (front)	3	3
Room/comfort (rear)	1	1
Cargo room	2	2
Value for the money	4	4
Total	**40**	**41**

SPECIFICATIONS

	2-door coupe
Wheelbase, in.	105.9
Overall length, in.	192.5
Overall width, in.	70.9
Overall height, in.	53.2
Curb weight, lbs.	3655
Cargo vol., cu. ft.	9.3
Fuel capacity, gals.	20.6
Seating capacity	4
Front head room, in.	38.3
Max. front leg room, in.	44.1
Rear head room, in.	36.1
Min. rear leg room, in.	27.2

ENGINES

	dohc I-6	dohc V-8
Size, liters/cu. in.	3.0/183	4.0/242
Horsepower @ rpm	225@ 6000	300@ 6000
Torque (lbs./ft.) @ rpm	220@ 4000	310@ 4000
Availability	S[1]	S[2]

EPA city/highway mpg

4-speed OD automatic	NA	NA
5-speed OD automatic	NA	NA

1. SC 300. 2. SC 400.

PRICES

Lexus SC 300/400	Retail Price	Dealer Invoice
SC 300 2-door notchback	$40900	$35526
SC 400 2-door notchback	52700	45243
Destination charge	495	495

STANDARD EQUIPMENT:

SC 300: 3.0-liter DOHC 6-cylinder engine, 5-speed automatic transmis-

Rating Scale: 5-Excellent; 4-Above average; 3-Average; 2-Below average; 1-Poor

CONSUMER GUIDE™

sion, driver- and passenger-side air bags, anti-lock 4-wheel disc brakes, air conditioning w/automatic climate control, variable-assist power steering, tilt/telescoping steering column, leather-wrapped steering wheel, cruise control, cloth upholstery, power front bucket seats, maple wood interior trim, heated power mirrors, power windows, tachometer, power door locks, remote keyless entry, Pioneer Audio System with AM/FM/cassette and seven speakers, diversity antennas, trip computer w/outside-temperature indicator, rear defogger, illuminated visor mirrors, universal garage door opener, remote fuel-door and decklid releases, variable intermittent wipers, automatic day/night inside mirror, cellular phone pre-wiring, automatic on/off headlamps, first aid kit, solar-control tinted glass, theft-deterrent system, fog lights, tool kit, 225/55VR16 performance tires, alloy wheels.

SC 400 adds: 4.0-liter DOHC V-8 engine, leather upholstery and trim, memory driver seat, power tilt/telescoping steering column w/memory, automatic day/night outside mirrors w/memory.

OPTIONAL EQUIPMENT:

	Retail Price	Dealer Invoice

Major Packages

	Retail Price	Dealer Invoice
Leather Trim Pkg., SC 300	2050	1640

Leather upholstery and trim, automatic day/night outside mirrors w/memory, power tilt/telescoping steering column w/memory, memory driver seat.

Powertrains

	Retail Price	Dealer Invoice
Traction control system w/heated front seats	1220	976

Requires 225/55VR16 all-season tires. SC 300 requires Leather Trim Pkg.

Comfort and Convenience

	Retail Price	Dealer Invoice
Power glass moonroof	1120	896
Remote 12-disc CD changer	1050	840
Lexus/Nakamichi Premium Sound System	2250	1740

Includes remote 12-disc CD changer. SC 300 requires Leather Trim Pkg.

Appearance and Miscellaneous

	Retail Price	Dealer Invoice
Rear spoiler, SC 400	420	336
Chrome alloy wheels	1700	850
225/55VR16 all-season tires	NC	NC

Other options are available as port installed items.

LINCOLN CONTINENTAL

Lincoln Continental

Front-wheel-drive luxury car

Base price: $37,830. Built in Wixom, Mich.

Also consider: Acura RL, Buick Park Avenue, Cadillac Seville

FOR • Acceleration • Passenger and cargo room • Standard anti-lock brakes

AGAINST • Fuel economy

Lincoln redesigned its Continental for 1995, loading it with high-tech features and giving it sports-sedan airs. But sales languished, running barely half those of the Buick Park Avenue. So the Continental gets a major revamp for '98, with new styling, a carried-over powertrain, and a less-complicated standard suspension.

It's almost exactly the same size as the model it replaces, but new proportions give the '98 Continental a shorter nose and longer tail. The restyled cabin features bird's-eye maple trim. An inch less rear leg room is the only change of note in interior dimensions. The dual air

bags are depowered units that deploy with less force, but side air bags are not offered. Four-wheel anti-lock disc brakes are again standard.

Last year's standard driver-adjustable electronic suspension hardware has been relegated to the options list. The standard setup now consists of regular shock absorbers with automatic rear leveling via air springs. Returning as standard is power steering that can be adjusted by the driver to provide low, "normal," and high levels of assist.

A dual overhead-cam 4.6-liter V-8 returns with its 260-horsepower rating, though this year, premium fuel is recommended, rather than required, for best performance. Automatic transmission and traction control are again standard.

A tire-pressure alert system and run-flat tires are again optional, as is RESCU—Remote Emergency Satellite Cellular Unit. It links the car via cellular telephone and a global positioning satellite to a Ford-staffed response center from which emergency help can be summoned.

PERFORMANCE We've always appreciated Continental's strong V-8 power, but were unimpressed with the variable suspension and steering systems. Making the electronic suspension an option was a good idea; it seemed incapabale of delivering the blend of comfort and control that cars of this class should have.

This year's base suspension feels slightly more absorbent over bumps than the optional system, though both are smooth enough with just a trace more bounding after high-speed dips than most import rivals allow. Both systems furnished confident cornering ability, though the electronic suspension seem to react more sharply to steering inputs.

We timed last year's Continental at 7.4 seconds 0-60 mph—a commendable performance that the '98 should at least duplicate. In mostly urban commuting, our 1998 test car averaged 16.0 mpg, nearly identical to our most-recent test of the previous model.

Continental is very quiet on the road, bothered only by some tire noise on concrete surfaces. The engine goes about its business almost silently.

ACCOMMODATIONS Continental has adequate room for those under six-feet tall both front and rear, but leg room in back is only adequate and passengers will find the foot space under the front seats to be narrow. Buyers have their choice of a front bench seat with fold-down center console or front buckets. The buckets are comfortable but don't have enough lateral support to hold occupants fast in hard turns. And the interior isn't wide enough for 3-across seating front or rear without rubbing shoulders.

The instrument panel projects sharply defined gauge markings that are striking at night and bright enough to read in direct sunlight. Radio and climate controls are fairly easy to reach, but the buttons could be larger. Optional steering-wheel-mounted climate and radio controls come in a package with the adjustable suspension and steering.

Visibility is fine to the front and sides, but the headrests and hefty rear roof pillars block the view to the rear corners.

BUILD QUALITY Fit and finish are good inside and out, with the optional tri-coat metallic paint looking particularly satiny. Trimmed in wood, suede, and leather, the interior has a rich look.

VALUE FOR THE MONEY Continental doesn't feel as roomy as a Park Avenue, nor as sporty as a Cadillac Seville. We'd like to see side air bags among its equipment, but at a base price of about $38,000, this Lincoln offers a bundle of features for the money.

RATINGS

	Continental
Acceleration	4
Fuel economy	2
Ride quality	4
Steering/handling	3
Braking	4
Quietness	4
Driver seating	4
Instruments/controls	4
Room/comfort (front)	4
Room/comfort (rear)	3
Cargo room	4
Value for the money	4
Total	44

Prices are accurate at time of publication; subject to manufacturer's changes.

SPECIFICATIONS

	4-door sedan
Wheelbase, in.	109.0
Overall length, in.	207.0
Overall width, in.	73.6
Overall height, in.	56.0
Curb weight, lbs.	3868
Cargo vol., cu. ft.	18.9
Fuel capacity, gals.	20.0
Seating capacity	6
Front head room, in.	39.2
Max. front leg room, in.	41.9
Rear head room, in.	38.0
Min. rear leg room, in.	38.0

ENGINES

	dohc V-8
Size, liters/cu. in.	4.6/281
Horsepower @ rpm	260@ 5750
Torque (lbs./ft.) @ rpm	270@ 3000
Availability	S
EPA city/highway mpg	
4-speed OD automatic	17/25

PRICES

Lincoln Continental	Retail Price	Dealer Invoice
Base 4-door sedan	$37830	$34524
Destination charge	670	670

STANDARD EQUIPMENT:

Base: 4.6-liter DOHC V-8 engine, 4-speed automatic transmission, traction control, driver- and passenger-side air bags, anti-lock 4-wheel disc brakes, programmable variable-assist power steering, leather-wrapped tilt steering wheel, cruise control, air conditioning w/automatic climate control, interior air-filtration system, leather upholstery, reclining front bucket seats with power lumbar adjusters, 6-way power front seats, center console, burl walnut interior trim, heated power mirrors w/tilt-down back-up aid, power windows, automatic power door locks, 2-driver memory system, rear defogger, automatic day/night rearview mirror w/compass, variable intermittent wipers, tachometer, coolant temperature gauge, AM/FM/cassette, analog clock, remote keyless entry, remote fuel-door and decklid releases, overhead console, systems message center, reading lights, illuminated visor mirrors, automatic headlights, floormats, cargo net, adjustable suspension system, automatic load leveling, solar-control tinted glass, anti-theft alarm system, 225/60R16 tires, alloy wheels.

OPTIONAL EQUIPMENT:

Major Packages

	Retail	Dealer
Personal Security Pkg.	925	796
Manufacturer's discount price	750	646

Securitire with pressure alert, programmable garage-door opener. NA with chrome wheels.

Driver Select System	595	512

Semi-active suspension, selectable ride control, Memory Profile System, steering wheel with touch controls, automatic day/night outside mirrors.

Comfort and Convenience

RESCU Pkg.	2970	2554
Manufacturer's discount price	2345	2016
RESCU Pkg., ordered w/Personal Security Pkg.	2850	2452
Manufacturer's discount price	2225	1914

Global-positioning satellite, JBL Audio System, programmable garage-door opener, and voice-activated cellular telephone.

Power moonroof	1515	1302

Requires programmable garage-door opener.

Front split bench seat	NC	NC
Heated seats	290	250
Voice-activated cellular telephone	790	680

Requires JBL Audio System.

JBL Audio System	565	486

Digital signal processing, subwoofer amplifier, additional speakers.

	Retail Price	Dealer Invoice
CD changer	$595	$512

Requires JBL Audio System.

Programmable garage-door opener	120	104

Appearance and Miscellaneous

Tri-coat paint	365	314
Engine block heater	60	52
Double-window chrome wheels	845	726

NA with Personal Security Pkg.

Polished alloy wheels	350	302

LINCOLN MARK VIII

Lincoln Mark VIII LSC

Rear-wheel-drive luxury coupe

Base price range: $37,830-$39,320. Built in Wixom, Mich.

Also consider: Buick Riviera, Cadillac Eldorado, Lexus SC 300/400

FOR • Standard anti-lock brakes • Acceleration • Steering/handling • Traction control

AGAINST • Fuel economy • Rear seat room

Mark VIII got a host of updates for '97, but changes little for '98 as Ford Motor Company contemplates the big coupe's future. Sales are slow and some industry analysts predict Lincoln's line-up won't include this car in its present form much beyond 1999.

The '97 revamp included a restyled front end incorporating high-intensity discharge headlamps that cast a bright blue-white light. For '98, the previously standard CD player moves to the options list and is replaced by a cassette player. And as is most Ford-company cars, the standard dual air bags are depowered units that deploy with less force; side air bags are unavailable.

Two versions are offered: base and LSC. The LSC has a sportier flavor with body-colored trim in place of chrome, special chrome wheels, tauter suspension settings, a lower rear axle ratio, and a slightly more-powerful version of the Mark VIII's 4.6-liter V-8. Automatic transmission, anti-lock 4-wheel disc brakes, and traction control are standard.

PERFORMANCE Mark VIII is quick off the line and once above 15 mph it really flies. We clocked it at 6.8 seconds 0-60 mph. The twin-cam V-8 is silky smooth, has a sporty growl in hard acceleration, and delivers outstanding passing power at highway speeds. We averaged 15.3 mpg from mostly urban commuting in a test of a '97 LSC.

Even though traction control is standard, don't think the rear-wheel-drive Mark VIII is going to plow through snow as well as a front-drive car. There's just not enough weight over the rear wheels, and the tire tread favors grip in dry corners over going in the snow.

Lincoln's luxury coupe is as agile as the rival front-drive Cadillac Eldorado, but has a more supple suspension. The rear-drive Lexus SC 400 is just as fast, and is more nimble than either, but has the firmest ride of the three.

ACCOMMODATIONS Mark VIII has more interior space than the Lexus coupe and is on a par with the Eldorado, but roominess isn't a strong point. Tall passengers don't have an excess of head room front or rear. Back-seat leg space is limited, and two adults is the comfortable maximum in back.

The rounded, cocoon-like dashboard has clearly marked gauges, and the stereo and climate controls are intuitive and

Rating Scale: 5-Excellent; 4-Above average; 3-Average; 2-Below average; 1-Poor

angled toward the driver.

BUILD QUALITY Lincoln upgraded Mark VIII's interior materials a few years ago and they're now appropriately luxurious for its price. Exterior panel fit and paint are first rate.

VALUE FOR THE MONEY Mark VIII is priced about the same as the Cadillac Eldorado and significantly less than the Lexus SC 400. It gives up nothing in performance to either, but lacks the wet-weather traction of the Eldo and the overall refinement of the Lexus. Still, check it out if your shopping this market, but also consider the Buick Riviera.

RATINGS

	Base/LSC
Acceleration	5
Fuel economy	2
Ride quality	3
Steering/handling	4
Braking	4
Quietness	4
Driver seating	4
Instruments/controls	4
Room/comfort (front)	3
Room/comfort (rear)	3
Cargo room	3
Value for the money	3
Total	**42**

SPECIFICATIONS

	2-door coupe
Wheelbase, in.	113.0
Overall length, in.	207.2
Overall width, in.	74.8
Overall height, in.	53.6
Curb weight, lbs.	3765
Cargo vol., cu. ft.	14.4
Fuel capacity, gals.	18.0
Seating capacity	5
Front head room, in.	38.1
Max. front leg room, in.	42.6
Rear head room, in.	37.5
Min. rear leg room, in.	35.7

ENGINES

	dohc V-8	dohc V-8
Size, liters/cu. in.	4.6/281	4.6/281
Horsepower @ rpm	280@ 5500	290@ 5750
Torque (lbs./ft.) @ rpm	285@ 4500	290@ 4500
Availability	S[1]	S[2]

EPA city/highway mpg

4-speed OD automatic	18/26	18/26

1. Base model. 2. LSC.

PRICES

Lincoln Mark VIII	Retail Price	Dealer Invoice
Base 2-door notchback	$37830	$34524
LSC 2-door notchback	39320	35850
Destination charge	670	670

STANDARD EQUIPMENT:

Base: 4.6-liter DOHC V-8 280-horsepower engine, traction control, dual exhaust, driver- and passenger-side air bags, anti-lock 4-wheel disc brakes, 4-speed automatic transmission (3.07 final drive ratio), air conditioning w/automatic climate control, variable-assist power steering, tilt/telescopic steering wheel, leather-wrapped steering wheel, cruise control, leather upholstery, reclining 6-way power front seats with power lumbar supports and driver-side memory, rear armrest, console with cupholder and storage bin, analog instrumentation with message center and programmable trip functions, tachometer, service interval reminder, heated power mirrors with remote 3-position memory, automatic day/night inside/outside mirrors, power windows, power locks, remote keyless entry, illuminated visor mirrors, rear defogger, remote decklid and fuel-door releases, JBL audio system with AM/FM/cassette, integrated antenna, intermittent wipers,

automatic headlamps, solar-control tinted glass, theft-deterrent system, bright grille, bright exterior trim, 225/60VR16 tires, lacy-spoke alloy wheels.

LSC adds: 4.6-liter DOHC V-8 290-horsepower engine, 4-speed automatic transmission (3.27 final drive ratio), perforated-leather upholstery, upgraded suspension, color-keyed grille, color-keyed exterior trim, chrome directional wheels with locking lug nuts.

OPTIONAL EQUIPMENT:	Retail Price	Dealer Invoice
Safety Features		
Child restraint tether	NC	NC
Comfort and Convenience		
Power moonroof	$1515	$1302
Heated seats	290	250
Premium CD player	NC	NC
Replaces standard cassette player.		
CD changer	670	576
Portable voice-activated cellular telephone	790	680
Universal garage door opener	120	103
Floormats	NC	NC
Appearance and Miscellaneous		
Tri-coat paint	365	314
Engine block heater	60	52
Chrome octastar wheels, Base	845	726
LSC	NC	NC

LINCOLN NAVIGATOR

Lincoln Navigator

Rear- or 4-wheel-drive full-size sport-utility vehicle; similar to Ford Expedition

Base price range: $39,310-$42,660. Built in Wayne, Mich.
Also consider: GMC Yukon, Land Rover Range Rover, Toyota Land Cruiser

FOR • Standard anti-lock brakes • Ride • Passenger and cargo room • Instruments/controls

AGAINST • Fuel economy • Entry/exit • Maneuverability

Lincoln takes a Ford Expedition, ladles on luxury appointments and extroverted exterior trim, and creates its first sport-utility vehicle. Navigator was a sales success in its first year and, important for Lincoln, draws buyers in their mid-to-late 40s, significantly younger than the brand's usual crowd. Moreover, 40 percent of Navigator buyers pay cash, compared to about 15 percent of other Lincoln buyers.

Differentiating Navigator from Expedition are front and rear styling, extra sound deadening, special suspension tuning, and a host of standard features. It has depowered front air bags but side air bags are unavailable. Anti-lock 4-wheel disc brakes are standard.

Navigator's only engine is the larger of Expedition's two available V-8s, a 5.4-liter. It mates with automatic transmission and rear-wheel drive or Ford's Control Trac 4WD, which can be left engaged on dry pavement. Automatic self-levelling via air-ride shock absorbers (front and rear on the 4x4, rear only with 2WD) is included. Seven-passenger seating is standard: bucket seats with center consoles front and rear and a three-place third-row seat; a middle bench is a no-cost substitute for the rear buckets. The standard leather interior features walnut trim. Towing capacity is 8000 pounds.

Prices are accurate at time of publication; subject to manufacturer's changes.

Navigator carries Lincoln's 4-year/50,000-mile warranty, versus Ford's 3/36,000 guarantee. Navigators get a special post-assembly inspection and 25-mile pre-shipment road test that Expeditions don't. Further, Lincoln is mandating special dealer treatment for Navigator owners, including free use of a loaner vehicle.

PERFORMANCE While it doesn't drive like a car—it's too big and heavy for that—Navigator does have good scoot for a large SUV and handles with surprising poise on twisty roads. However, the steering feels too light and divorced from the road, especially on 4x4s. They also have a jiggly ride that's absent on 2WD models, which ride nearly as smoothly as some cars. Both are quiet in highway driving.

Navigator inherits Expedition's towing brawn and the convenient Control Trac 4WD option, which provides a simple dashboard switch from which the driver can select 2WD, automatic 4WD (shifts automatically between 2- and 4-wheel drive), locked-in 4WD High, or 4WD Low.

Vices include dismal fuel economy: just over 12 mpg for us in tests of both 2WD and 4WD models. The vehicle's sheer size makes it difficult to park, and its height, especially in 4WD form, may prevent it from fitting in some garages.

ACCOMMODATIONS Navigator provides every luxury the reasonable hedonist could desire, along with real stretch-out space front and rear. It's difficult to access the third-row seat, which is best left to pre-teens anyway. And it's a tall step-up into the interior even on 2WD models. It's worse on the 4x4s, despite their air suspension that lowers the vehicle an inch when the ignition is turned off.

Some of our test drivers find the driver's seat too hard, too low, and lacking in lumbar support. Instruments and switchgear are well laid-out, and the steering wheel holds a nice array of duplicate radio and climate controls. Cargo space is skimpy with the third seat in place, immense with it removed. With two gym-bag sized center consoles and bins and pockets galore, interior storage is unmatched, though none of it locks.

Visibility is good to the front and sides, but is hindered to the rear by the forest of large headrests.

BUILD QUALITY Our test vehicles exhibited no squeaks or rattles and had a nice paint finish. Inside, touches of wood trim highlighted rich-looking materials.

VALUE FOR THE MONEY If you crave Navigator's amenities, its price premium over Expedition isn't that staggering. If you can do without the extra Lincoln fluff, Expedition ends up the better dollar buy—and a good one, at that.

RATINGS

	2WD	4WD
Acceleration	3	3
Fuel economy	1	1
Ride quality	4	3
Steering/handling	3	3
Braking	3	3
Quietness	4	4
Driver seating	4	4
Instruments/controls	4	4
Room/comfort (front)	5	5
Room/comfort (rear)	5	5
Cargo room	5	5
Value for the money	3	3
Total	**44**	**43**

SPECIFICATIONS

	4-door wagon
Wheelbase, in.	119.1
Overall length, in.	204.8
Overall width, in.	79.9
Overall height, in.	76.7
Curb weight, lbs.	5150
Cargo vol., cu. ft.	116.4
Fuel capacity, gals.	30.0
Seating capacity	8
Front head room, in.	39.8
Max. front leg room, in.	41.0
Rear head room, in.	39.8
Min. rear leg room, in.	39.7

ENGINES

	ohc V-8
Size, liters/cu. in.	5.4/330
Horsepower @ rpm	230@ 4250
Torque (lbs./ft.) @ rpm	325@ 3000
Availability	S
EPA city/highway mpg	
4-speed OD automatic	14/18

PRICES

Lincoln Navigator	Retail Price	Dealer Invoice
4-door wagon, 2WD	$39310	$34333
4-door wagon, 4WD	42660	37181
Destination charge	640	640

STANDARD EQUIPMENT:

2WD: 5.4-liter V-8 engine, 4-speed automatic transmission w/overdrive, anti-lock power 4-wheel disc brakes, driver- and passenger-side air bags, automatic air conditioning, variable-assist power steering, leather-wrapped steering wheel w/radio and climate controls, tilt steering column, cruise control, quad bucket seats, 6-way power front seats w/driver-side memory, third row bench seat, leather upholstery, walnut trim, cupholders, dual heated power mirrors, power windows, power door locks, trip odometer, tachometer, oil-pressure gauge, voltmeter, automatic-on headlights, AM/FM/cassette, digital clock, dual illuminated visor mirrors, floormats, cargo net, intermittent wipers, rear defogger, rear washer/intermittent wiper, remote keyless entry, fog lamps, roof rack, running boards, rear self-leveling suspension, Trailer Towing Group (7-wire harness, hitch, heavy-duty flasher, engine-oil cooler, auxiliary transmission-oil cooler), full-size spare tire, 245/75R16 tires, alloy wheels.

4WD adds: Control Trac on-demand 4WD, limited slip differential, front and rear self-leveling suspension, front tow hooks.

OPTIONAL EQUIPMENT:

Powertrains

Limited slip differential, 2WD	255	217
Includes 3.73 axle ratio.		

Comfort and Convenience

Auxiliary air conditioning	705	599
NA with moonroof.		
Power moonroof	1655	1407
Includes mini overhead console and universal garage door opener. NA with auxiliary air conditioning.		
Mach AM/FM/cassette	355	302
Includes 290 watts with seven speakers.		
6-disc CD changer	595	506
Automatic day/night mirror	110	94

Appearance and Miscellaneous

Engine block heater	35	30

Special Purpose, Wheels and Tires

Skid plates, 4WD	105	89
17-inch alloy wheels, 4WD	235	200
Requires 255/75R17 tires.		
17-inch chrome alloy wheels, 4WD	950	808
Requires 255/75R17 tires.		
245/75R16 outline white-letter tires	130	111
255/75R17 outline white-letter tires, 4WD	305	259
Requires 17-inch wheels.		

LINCOLN TOWN CAR `BUDGET BUY`

Rear-wheel-drive luxury car

Base price range: $37,830-$41,830. Built in Wixom, Mich.

Also consider: Cadillac DeVille, Jaguar XJ Sedan, Lexus LS 400

FOR • Standard anti-lock brakes • Passenger and cargo room

AGAINST • Fuel economy • Rear visibility

Rating Scale: 5-Excellent; 4-Above average; 3-Average; 2-Below average; 1-Poor

LINCOLN

Lincoln Town Car

Lincoln redesigns its automotive flagship for '98, trimming it by three inches in length and 200 pounds in heft. It's still a very large vessel, however, and the only full-size, rear-wheel-drive American luxury car.

Three models are offered, each increasingly opulent: base Executive, mid-level Signature, and line-topping Cartier. All come with a 4.6-liter V-8 that makes 200 horsepower in the Executive and Signature, 220 (with dual exhausts) in the Cartier. In addition, a Touring Sedan package for the Signature includes the 220-horsepower engine and firmer suspension. Automatic is the only transmission. Anti-lock 4-wheel disc brakes are standard, as are depowered front air bags; side air bags are unavailable.

New standard features include leather upholstery, a 40/20/40 front bench seat design with folding center armrest, traction control, and electrochromatic rearview mirror with compass.

PERFORMANCE With a tad more horsepower and a little less weight, Town Car moves off the line in a fairly spirited manner. The transmission has been reworked, and while it still upshifts seamlessly, it now downshifts more quickly for passing.

Town Car's ride remains smooth, but it's now less floaty and more controlled than before thanks to a revised suspension. Likewise, handling is improved. Town Car is no longer as wallowing and boat-like as it used to be. Less body roll in turns and sharper steering response helps it tolerate spirited driving, if not encourage it.

ACCOMMODATIONS Town Car always offered spacious accommodations, and though the new one is a bit trimmer, interior room hasn't suffered. Doors are large, making it easy to get in and out of the front and rear seats. Head room is generous all around and leg room is good. The car isn't wide enough to fit six adults without real squeezing.

Another Town Car tradion is quietness. If anything, the new version is even more serene inside than the old model, with almost no road or wind noise, and just a muted roar from the engine.

Gauges are now analog (needle-type) rather than digital, and climate and radio controls are easy to see, reach, and use. Ourward visibility is compromised by thick side and rear roof pillars and a high rear deck.

Trunk room is down about 10 percent. That still leaves a lot of luggage space, though much of the volume is again in a deep center well from which it is a strain to lift heavy objects.

BUILD QUALITY So far, we've driven only pre-production models at a press preview. They seemed well built, but we'll need to see production versions before making a judgment.

VALUE FOR THE MONEY Its road manners are less aquatic and its styling is more contemporary, but Town Car's traditional roominess, soft ride, and isolation from unpleasant noises is intact. At thousands less than import luxury cars, this new Lincoln is worth considering.

RATINGS

	Town Car
Acceleration	3
Fuel economy	2
Ride quality	5
Steering/handling	3
Braking	4
Quietness	5
Driver seating	4
Instruments/controls	4
Room/comfort (front)	5
Room/comfort (rear)	4
Cargo room	4
Value for the money	4
Total	**47**

SPECIFICATIONS

	4-door sedan
Wheelbase, in.	117.7
Overall length, in.	215.3
Overall width, in.	78.2
Overall height, in.	58.0
Curb weight, lbs.	3860
Cargo vol., cu. ft.	20.6
Fuel capacity, gals.	20.0
Seating capacity	6
Front head room, in.	39.2
Max. front leg room, in.	42.6
Rear head room, in.	37.5
Min. rear leg room, in.	41.1

ENGINES

	ohc V-8	ohc V-8
Size, liters/cu. in.	4.6/281	4.6/281
Horsepower @ rpm	200@ 4500	220@ 4500
Torque (lbs./ft.) @ rpm	265@ 3500	275@ 3500
Availability	S[1]	S[2]

EPA city/highway mpg

4-speed OD automatic	17/25	17/25

1. Executive, Signature. 2. Cartier and Signature Touring Pkg.

PRICES

Lincoln Town Car	Retail Price	Dealer Invoice
Executive 4-door sedan	$37830	$34524
Signature 4-door sedan	39480	35992
Cartier 4-door sedan	41830	38084
Destination charge	670	670

STANDARD EQUIPMENT:

Executive: 4.6-liter V-8, 4-speed automatic transmission, traction assist, driver- and passenger-side air bags, anti-lock 4-wheel disc brakes, variable-assist power steering, tilt steering wheel, leather-wrapped steering wheel, cruise control, air conditioning w/automatic climate control, leather upholstery, 6-way power twin-comfort lounge seats with 2-way front headrests, front and rear armrests, power windows, power door locks, remote keyless entry, heated power mirrors, auxiliary power outlet, automatic headlights, automatic day/night inside and driver-side mirrors, compass, rear defogger, AM/FM/cassette, diversity antenna, coolant-temperature gauge, remote fuel-door and decklid releases, power decklid pulldown, intermittent wipers, digital clock, illuminated visor mirrors, floormats, trunk net, solar-control tinted glass, theft-deterrent system, cornering lamps, 225/60SR16 tires, alloy wheels.

Signature adds: memory driver-seat, power lumbar support, power front recliners, memory mirrors, dual footwell lights, front-seat storage with cupholders, steering-wheel radio and climate controls, rear cupholders, programmable garage-door opener.

Cartier adds: upgraded leather upholstery, heated front seat, analog clock, 4-way front-seat headrests, Ford JBL Audio System, upgraded door trim panels, gold pkg., dual exhaust.

OPTIONAL EQUIPMENT:
Major Packages

Touring Pkg., Signature	500	430

Upgraded suspension, performance axle ratio and torque converter, perforated leather upholstery, 225/60TR16 tires, chrome alloy wheels.

Entertainment Pkg., Signature	2675	2300
Manufacturer's discount price	2100	1814

JBL Audio system w/CD changer, power moonroof.

Comfort and Convenience

Power moonroof	1515	1302

NA Executive.

Cloth upholstery, Executive (credit)	(770)	(662)
Heated front seats, Signature	290	250
JBL Audio System w/CD changer, Signature	1160	998
Manufacturer's discount price	845	728
Trunk-mounted CD changer	585	512
Voice-activated cellular telephone	790	680

NA on Executive.

Prices are accurate at time of publication; subject to manufacturer's changes.

Appearance and Miscellaneous

	Retail Price	Dealer Invoice
Tri-coat paint, Signature	$365	$314
Engine block heater	60	52
Full-size spare tire	120	104
Chrome alloy wheels, Cartier	845	726

MAZDA B-SERIES PICKUP

RECOMMENDED

1997 Mazda B4000 extended cab

Rear- or 4-wheel-drive compact pickup; similar to Ford Ranger

Base price range: $10,470-$19,585. Built in Edison, N.J.

Also consider: Chevrolet S-10, Dodge Dakota, GMC Sonoma

FOR • Acceleration (B4000) • Regular cab passenger room • 4WD system

AGAINST • Engine noise

For several years now, Mazda's compact pickup has been a cousin of the Ford Ranger, built in the same New Jersey plant but with different styling. Ranger is overhauled for 1998, so the B-Series is too. Though Mazda still has no flare-fender model like Ranger's Splash, the B-Series retains its own appearance, with a swept-back look said to be favored by import-brand truck buyers.

The new B-Series naturally shares improvements made to the '98 Ranger. These include a stiffer, fully boxed frame; independent front suspension (versus solid axle); rack-and-pinion steering (ousting recirculating-ball); a standard cab lengthened 3 inches; "depowered" dual air bags; and an on/off switch for the passenger-side air bag. In addition, 4x4s can now be shifted between 2WD and 4-wheel High at up to 70 mph, and changed between 4-wheel High and Low at up to 35 mph.

As before, Mazda offers regular and extended Cab Plus pickups in SX or upscale SE trim. The base 4-cylinder engine has been upsized to 2.5 liters, making the B2500 model. A 3.0-liter V-6 option (B3000) is reinstated below the carryover 4.0 V-6 (B4000). Automatic transmission is optional in lieu of manual for SE models and regular-cab SXs; B4000s use a new 5-speed automatic instead of the 4-speed employed elsewhere.

See the Ford Ranger for an evaluation of the B-Series.

RATINGS

	B2500 Reg cab	B3000 Cab Plus	B4000 Cab Plus
Acceleration	2	3	3
Fuel economy	3	3	2
Ride quality	3	3	3
Steering/handling	3	3	3
Braking	3	3	3
Quietness	3	3	3
Driver seating	3	3	3
Instruments/controls	4	4	4
Room/comfort (front)	3	3	3
Room/comfort (rear)	—	1	1
Cargo room	1	2	2
Value for the money	4	4	4
Total	**32**	**35**	**34**

SPECIFICATIONS

	Reg. cab	Ext. cab
Wheelbase, in.	111.6	125.7
Overall length, in.	187.5	202.9
Overall width, in.	69.4	69.4
Overall height, in.	64.9	64.7
Curb weight, lbs.	3242	3497
Maximum payload, lbs.	1660	1620
Fuel capacity, gals.	17.0	20.5
Seating capacity	3	5
Front head room, in.	39.2	39.2
Max. front leg room, in.	42.4	42.2
Rear head room, in.	—	35.6
Min. rear leg room, in.	—	NA

ENGINES

	ohc I-4	ohv V-6	ohv V-6
Size, liters/cu. in.	2.5/152	3.0/182	4.0/245
Horsepower @ rpm	119@ 5000	150@ 5000	160@ 4200
Torque (lbs./ft.) @ rpm	146@ 3000	185@ 3750	225@ 3000
Availability	S[1]	S[2]	S[3]
EPA city/highway mpg			
5-speed OD manual	NA	NA	NA
4-speed OD automatic	NA	NA	
5-speed OD automatic			NA

1. B2500. 2. B3000. 3. B4000.

PRICES

Mazda B-Series Pickup	Retail Price	Dealer Invoice
B2300 Base 2WD regular cab	$10470	$9718
B2300 SE 2WD regular cab	12350	11060
B2300 SE 2WD Cab Plus	14670	13131
B4000 SE 2WD Cab Plus	15995	14276
B4000 Base 4WD regular cab	16365	15263
B4000 Base 4WD Cab Plus	18250	16285
B4000 SE 4WD Cab Plus	19585	17474
Destination charge	510	510

Prices are for vehicles distributed by Mazda Motor of America, Inc. Prices may be higher in areas served by independent distributors. SE requires SE Group.

STANDARD EQUIPMENT:

Base: 2.3-liter 4-cylinder engine (B2300), 4.0-liter V-6 engine (B4000), 5-speed manual transmission, rear anti-lock brakes, driver-side air bag, power steering (4WD, Cab Plus), vinyl 3-passenger bench seat, upgraded door trim panels, rear jump seat (Cab Plus), dual outside mirrors, coolant-temperature gauge, oil-pressure gauge, voltmeter, tachometer (4WD), trip odometer, tinted glass, intermittent wipers, auxiliary power outlet, passenger-side visor mirror (Cab Plus), black vinyl floor covering, additional insulation (Cab Plus), black rear step bumper and grille, fender flares (4WD), front spoiler, front and rear mud guards, rear tow hook (4WD), skid plates (4WD), 195/70R14 tires (2WD), 215/75R15 tires (4WD).

SE adds: cloth/vinyl 60/40 split bench seat (regular Cab), cloth/vinyl reclining 60/40 split bench seat w/storage armrest (Cab Plus), floor consolette w/cupholders, tachometer, AM/FM radio, passenger-side visor mirror (regular Cab), map light, carpeting, additional insulation, cargo light, cargo net (Cab Plus), striping, chrome bumpers, silver-painted grille, dual-note horn, 225/70R14 tires (2WD), 235/75R15 tires (4WD).

OPTIONAL EQUIPMENT:
Major Packages

Appearance Group, SE regular cab	1100	902
Manufacturer's discount price	150	123

AM/FM/cassette, digital clock, chrome bumpers and grille, sliding rear window, bedliner, alloy wheels, 225/70R15 tires (2WD), Payload Performance Pkg. (heavy-duty suspension, 1500 lb. payload, limited slip differential) (4WD).

Power Pkg., SE 2WD	3245	2661
Manufacturer's discount price	2100	1722
Power Pkg., B3000/4000 SE	3515	2882
Manufacturer's discount price	2250	1845

Appearance Pkg. plus air conditioning, power windows and door locks, power mirrors, cruise control, tilt leather-wrapped steering wheel, CD player.

Appearance Group, B2500 SE Cab Plus	1275	1144

Rating Scale: 5-Excellent; 4-Above average; 3-Average; 2-Below average; 1-Poor

CONSUMER GUIDE™

	Retail Price	Dealer Invoice
Manufacturer's discount price	$250	$205
Appearance Pkg., B3000/4000 SE Cab Plus	1495	1226
Manufacturer's discount price	400	328

Appearance Pkg. regular cab plus swing-out rear quarter windows, rear privacy glass, cargo cover.

Powertrains
4-speed automatic transmission, B2300 regular cab	1070	877
5-speed automatic transmission, B4000 SE	1105	906

Major Packages
SE Group,
B2300 SE, B4000 Cab Plus, B4000 SE Cab Plus	125	103

Power steering (B2300 regular cab), AM/FM/cassette player, sliding rear window, 225/70R14 outline white-letter tires (2WD), 235/75R15 outline white-letter tires (4WD), alloy wheels. Cab Plus also includes pivoting rear quarter windows, privacy glass, cargo cover.

SE-5 Group,
B2300 SE, B4000 Cab Plus, B4000 SE Cab Plus	895	734

SE Group plus air conditioning, bedliner.

SE-5 Plus Group, B4000 SE 2WD..........................	2995	2456
B4000 SE 4WD	2765	2267

SE-5 Group plus 4-wheel anti-lock brakes, passenger-side air bag, cruise control, tilt steering wheel, power windows and door locks, power mirrors, premium AM/FM/cassette player, remote keyless entry w/theft-deterrent system.

Comfort and Convenience
Air conditioning, Base	805	660
Power steering, B2300 Base.................................	275	226
AM/FM radio, B2300 Base	180	148

Includes digital clock. Requires automatic transmission.

AM/FM/CD player, SE	85	70

Requires SE-5 Group.

CD changer, B4000 SE...	445	365

2WD w/manual transmission and 4WD require SE-5 Plus Group.

Sport bucket seats, B4000 2WD............................	360	295

Requires SE-5 Plus Group when ordered w/manual transmission. Deletes floor consolette.

Appearance and Miscellaneous
Bedliner, B2300 Base...	275	165

Special Purpose, Wheels and Tires
Towing/Payload Pkg., B4000 SE 2WD	330	271
B4000 SE 4WD	440	361

Handling Pkg., performance axle ratio, limited slip differential, Payload Pkg. #2, 265/75R15 all-terrain tires (4WD).

1999 MAZDA MIATA

✓ BEST BUY

1999 Mazda Miata

Rear-wheel-drive sports and GT car
Base price range: $19,125–$24,485. Built in Japan.
Also consider: BMW Z3, Chevrolet Camaro, Ford Mustang, Pontiac Firebird

FOR • Acceleration • Steering/handling • Optional anti-lock brakes • Fuel economy

AGAINST • Cargo room • Noise

Mazda's popular roadster sits out 1998, but only because a thoroughly revised '99 model will be on sale by early spring.

Miata revived the market for small low-cost sports cars on its 1990 debut.

The '99 amounts to an upgrade of the well-liked current design and will retain the classic front-engine/rear-drive chassis and soft-top 2-seat body configuration. Dimensions are within fractions of an inch of the current car.

Though recognizably Miata, all outer sheetmetal is new, with exposed headlamps (versus flip-up) and a larger "mouth" grille. There's also a reshaped trunklid with a more prominent lip spoiler. Inside are a new instrument panel, 3-spoke steering wheel, and standard CD audio; a Bose sound system is a new option.

The engine remains a 1.8-liter twin-cam 16-valve 4-cylinder with manual or automatic transmission, though horsepower increases by seven and torque by five pounds/feet.

Increased structural rigidity and suspension changes are aimed at improved handling. The soft top still folds manually, but the rear window switches from plastic to glass, complete with electric defroster.

Option groups will mirror the current packages, including the R Package, oriented to weekend racers. Anti-lock brakes are again available, as is a removable hardtop. Prices are expected to be close to '97 levels.

Note: Some 1997 Miatas will be available at dealerships through the early months of 1998. The following evaluation, specifications, ratings, and prices are for 1997 Miatas.

PERFORMANCE The 1.8-liter engine in the '97 model doesn't have much kick at low speed, but it revs quickly into its power band to provide brisk acceleration. We clocked one with the 5-speed at 8.3 seconds to 60 mph. A Miata with automatic transmission is not nearly as frisky.

Because there's little low-end power, you have to frequently shift to a lower gear in urban traffic, though that's never a chore with the Miata's precise shifter and light-effort clutch. Fuel economy is good with the 5-speed manual. We averaged 24.3 mpg in mostly city driving. We've reached nearly 30 mpg on the highway in previous models.

The engine has a deep, growling exhaust note that's appropriate for an open sports car, though it combines with lots of tire and wind noise for raucous highway cruising.

Miata corners with confidence and agility. The power steering is quick and precise. Body lean is minimal, reflecting the low center of gravity and a taut suspension that notices nearly every bump in the road. The ride is firm and stable on smooth roads, and active—sometimes even harsh—on rough pavement.

ACCOMMODATIONS Small though it is, Miata is adequately roomy inside. Head room with the top up is sufficient for 6-footers. To get sufficient leg room, however, tall drivers may have to move their seats all the way back to the rear bulkhead, forcing the backrest bolt-upright. Some drivers may also find the non-adjustable steering wheel leaves too little room for their thighs.

The neat, convenient dashboard includes large round gauges and simple controls that are easy to reach and use while driving. Visibility is good for a low-slung car, though there are large blind spots to the rear corners with the top up. Miata's manual top, which can be raised or lowered from the driver's seat in seconds, is a model of simplicity.

Two medium-size soft gym bags are about all you can squeeze into the short, shallow trunk—even less if the tonneau cover is stowed there too. You can carry a few small things on the shelf behind the seats, but there's no barrier to keep them from sliding forward. You learn to travel light in the Miata.

BUILD QUALITY Our test car was nicely finished, with only a slight orange-peel texture to the paint. The Miata has little body shake compared to most convertibles, but it's not as solid as a hardtop.

VALUE FOR THE MONEY Lively, agile, and fun, Miata has all the requisites for a true sports car. Though its price has crept up over the years—'97 base prices started at more than $19,000—Miata is still the least expensive of its kind. However, it's no longer the only one of its kind. BMW's Z3, the Mercedes SLK, and the Porsche Boxster all offer similar attributes, though they cost considerably more.

SPECIFICATIONS (1997 model)

	2-door conv.
Wheelbase, in.	89.2
Overall length, in.	155.4

Prices are accurate at time of publication; subject to manufacturer's changes.

MAZDA

Overall width, in. 65.9
Overall height, in. 48.2

	2-door conv.
Curb weight, lbs.	2293
Cargo vol., cu. ft.	3.6
Fuel capacity, gals.	12.7
Seating capacity	2
Front head room, in.	37.1
Max. front leg room, in.	42.7
Rear head room, in.	—
Min. rear leg room, in.	—

ENGINES

	dohc I-4
Size, liters/cu. in.	1.8/112
Horsepower @ rpm	133@ 6500
Torque (lbs./ft.) @ rpm	114@ 5500
Availability	S

EPA city/highway mpg
5-speed OD manual 22/29
4-speed OD automatic 22/28

PRICES

1997 Mazda Miata	Retail Price	Dealer Invoice
2-door convertible	$19125	$17248
M-Edition 2-door convertible	24485	22077
Destination charge	450	450

Prices are for vehicles distributed by Mazda Motor of America, Inc. Prices may be higher in areas served by independent distributors.

STANDARD EQUIPMENT:

1.8-liter DOHC 4-cylinder engine, 5-speed manual transmission, 4-wheel disc brakes, driver- and passenger-side air bags, cloth reclining bucket seats, front storage console w/cupholder, tachometer, coolant-temperature gauge, trip odometer, AM/FM/cassette, digital clock, dual outside mirrors, remote fuel-door and decklid releases, intermittent wipers, cargo light, 185/60HR14 tires, bright center caps.

M-Edition adds: Popular Equipment Pkg. (includes variable-assist power steering, power windows, power mirrors, leather-wrapped steering wheel, door map pockets, alloy wheels, limited-slip differential [5-speed], cruise control, headrest speakers, power antenna), Leather Pkg. (includes tan interior with leather seating surfaces, tan vinyl top), air conditioning, premium AM/FM/cassette/CD, floormats.

OPTIONAL EQUIPMENT:
Powertrains
4-speed automatic transmission	850	739

Requires Popular Equipment Pkg., Leather Pkg., or Touring Pkg.

Safety Features
Anti-lock brakes	900	765

Requires Popular Equipment Pkg. or Leather Pkg.

Major Packages
Touring Pkg., base	1100	924

Power steering, power windows and mirrors, leather-wrapped steering wheel, door map pockets, alloy wheels. NA w/premium sound system, anti-lock brakes, detachable hardtop.

Popular Equipment Pkg., base,		
ordered w/5-speed	2090	1756
ordered w/automatic	1700	1428

Touring Pkg. plus limited-slip differential (5-speed) cruise control, headrest speakers, power antenna.

Leather Pkg., base, ordered w/5-speed	2985	2507
ordered w/automatic	2595	2180

Popular Equipment Pkg. plus tan interior with leather seating surfaces, tan vinyl top.

R Pkg., base, ordered w/5-speed	1500	1260

Limited-slip differential, sport suspension, Bilstein shock absorbers, front and rear spoilers, alloy wheels. NA with Popular Equipment Pkg., Power Steering Pkg., or Leather Pkg.

Comfort and Convenience
Power Steering Pkg., base	300	252

Variable-assist power steering, wheel trim rings.

	Retail Price	Dealer Invoice
Air conditioning, base	$900	$720
CD player, base	350	298
Premium sound system w/AM/FM/cassette/CD player, base	675	540

Requires Popular Equipment or Leather Pkg.

Floormats, base	80	56

Appearance and Miscellaneous
Detachable hardtop	1500	1215

Includes rear defogger. Base requires Popular Equipment Pkg. or Leather Pkg.

MAZDA MILLENIA

Mazda Millenia S

Front-wheel-drive near-luxury car
Base price range: $28,995-$36,595. Built in Japan.
Also consider: Infiniti I30, Lexus ES 300, Mitsubishi Diamante

FOR • Acceleration (S model) • Steering/handling • Braking

AGAINST • Transmission performance • Rear visibility

Introduced three years ago as Mazda's "near-luxury" sedan, the Millenia is a virtual rerun for 1998. The one visual tip-off is the new "winged M" logo now seen on all Mazda products. Millenia's lack of change partly reflects the financial and sales difficulties that have plagued Mazda in recent years. Indeed, Ford Motor Company, which now controls the Japanese automaker, recently installed a new management team at Mazda while providing cash infusions.

Millenia continues in three V-6 models, all with automatic transmission. The top-line S carries a supercharged 2.3-liter twin-cam engine. Base and L versions use a normally aspirated 2.5-liter that also powers some of Mazda's 626 sedans. While the 626 is fully overhauled for '98, Millenia is still loosely based on the previous 626 design. The L model upgrades base-level equipment with leather upholstery (versus cloth), power passenger seat (versus manual), power moonroof and remote keyless entry, all of which are standard on the S.

PERFORMANCE Millenia still impresses us with top-notch refinement. All models have little wind or engine noise, and tire drone is reasonably low. Braking is excellent: a short, true 125 feet from 60 mph in our "panic stop" tests. Handling is responsive and surefooted, with little body lean and safe, predictable front-drive cornering behavior abetted by firm steering with ample feedback.

Performance and fuel economy depend on model. The base and L feel rather "sleepy," though 0-60 mph acceleration isn't bad at 9.4 seconds. The S needs just 7.8 seconds by our clocking and feels much stronger in mid-range passing sprints. Alas, the S engine exhibits some annoying throttle lag, a delay between stepping on the gas and getting more power. The automatic transmission is generally smooth and responsive in all Millenias, but flooring the throttle can result in harsh, abrupt downshifts.

ACCOMMODATIONS Like most in its class, the Millenia seats four adults comfortably, five in a pinch. All-round head room is good even in models with the power moonroof, and rear leg room is fit for grownups up to about 5-foot-10. Entry/exit is easy to all quarters.

Rating Scale: 5-Excellent; 4-Above average; 3-Average; 2-Below average; 1-Poor

CONSUMER GUIDE™

There's adequate cargo space in the fairly wide, deep trunk and a lid that opens almost vertically helps it swallow large boxes.

Millenia's straightforward driving position should suit most people, aided by a power-tilt steering wheel that can be set to rise out of the way on opening the driver's door. Gauges and switches hold no mysteries, but the LCD climate-control display tends to wash out in bright light, and power window/door lock/mirror switches have no night lighting. Wide roof pillars inhibit over-the-shoulder visibility, and the high-tail styling makes the rear corners invisible when parallel parking.

BUILD QUALITY Here's another area where Millenia impresses. It feels reassuringly solid on rough roads, and work-manship is first-rate, with minimal body panel gaps, above-par paint, and generally high-class cabin furnishings.

VALUE FOR THE MONEY Base and L Millenias deliver lots of luxury for less money than most rivals, but can't match their performance. The S is a sporty alternative to the similarly priced ES 300, though the Lexus rates higher for overall quality and customer service. Still, Millenia is a fine choice among near-luxury sedans, especially for those who don't like following the crowd.

RATINGS

	Base/L	S
Acceleration	3	4
Fuel economy	3	3
Ride quality	4	4
Steering/handling	4	4
Braking	5	5
Quietness	4	4
Driver seating	4	4
Instruments/controls	4	4
Room/comfort (front)	4	4
Room/comfort (rear)	3	3
Cargo room	3	3
Value for the money	3	3
Total	**44**	**45**

SPECIFICATIONS

	4-door sedan
Wheelbase, in.	108.3
Overall length, in.	189.8
Overall width, in.	69.7
Overall height, in.	54.9
Curb weight, lbs.	3220
Cargo vol., cu. ft.	13.3
Fuel capacity, gals.	18.0
Seating capacity	5
Front head room, in.	39.3
Max. front leg room, in.	43.3
Rear head room, in.	37.0
Min. rear leg room, in.	34.1

ENGINES

	dohc V-6	Super dohc V-6
Size, liters/cu. in.	2.5/152	2.3/138
Horsepower @ rpm	170@ 5800	210@ 4800
Torque (lbs./ft.) @ rpm	160@ 4800	210@ 3500
Availability	S	S[1]
EPA city/highway mpg		
4-speed OD automatic	20/27	20/28

1. S model.

PRICES

Mazda Millenia

	Retail Price	Dealer Invoice
Base 4-door sedan	$28995	$25562
S 4-door notchback	36595	31514
Destination charge	450	450

Prices are for vehicles distributed by Mazda Motor America, Inc. Prices may be higher in areas served by independent distributors.

STANDARD EQUIPMENT:

Base: 2.5-liter DOHC V-6 engine, 4-speed automatic transmission, dual exhaust outlets, driver- and passenger-side air bags, anti-lock 4-wheel disc brakes, air conditioning w/automatic climate control, variable-assist power steering, leather-wrapped power tilt steering wheel, cruise control, cloth reclining front bucket seats, 8-way power driver seat, front storage console w/cupholder, folding rear armrest, tachometer, trip odometer, outside-temperature indicator, heated power mirrors, power windows, power door locks, variable intermittent wipers, AM/FM/cassette/CD player, digital clock, integrated diversity antenna, illuminated visor mirrors, rear defogger, auxiliary power outlet, remote fuel-door and decklid releases, floormats, rear heat ducts, theft-deterrent system, tinted glass, fog lights, 205/65HR15 tires, alloy wheels w/locks.

S adds: 2.3-liter DOHC supercharged V-6 engine, traction control, leather upholstery, 8-way power front passenger seat, remote keyless entry, power moonroof, Bose audio system, heavy-duty starter, 215/55VR16 tires.

OPTIONAL EQUIPMENT:

	Retail Price	Dealer Invoice
Major Packages		
Premium Pkg., Base	$4000	$3189

Leather upholstery, power passenger seat, power moonroof, remote keyless entry.

4-Seasons Package, Base	600	504
S	300	252

Traction control (Base), heated front seats, heavy-duty wipers, heavy-duty battery, extra-capacity windshield-washer tank.

Comfort and Convenience		
Bose audio system, Base	700	560

Appearance and Miscellaneous		
White pearl metallic paint	350	294
Polished alloy wheels	500	300

MAZDA MPV

Mazda MPV All-Sport

Rear- or all-wheel-drive minivan

Base price range: $23,095-$28,895. Built in Japan.

Also consider: Dodge Caravan, Ford Windstar, Plymouth Voyager

FOR • Passenger and cargo room

AGAINST • Acceleration • Fuel economy • Ride

Like several other Mazdas, the MPV returns from 1997 with almost no change, though a new "winged M" corporate logo is a small exception. Mazda was one of the first imports to answer Chrysler's pioneering minivans, but the MPV ("Multi-Purpose Vehicle") has seen little change since its 1988 debut and is now by far the oldest minivan design on the market.

Last year, Mazda tried to boost MPV sales with the All-Sport, a dress-up package with the style of a sport-utility vehicle. It wasn't enough to pull the MPV out of the sales doldrums, however. MPV continues with a V-6 engine and automatic transmission in LX and nicer ES trim with choice of rear drive or on-demand 4-wheel drive. The All-Sport package is standard on all MPVs except the 2WD LX.

PERFORMANCE Though the MPV was competitive a few years ago, it's way behind current minivan standards in many respects. For one, it's piled on weight without adding power, so acceleration is less than sparkling and fuel economy is mediocre at best. We managed just 14.4 mpg with a 4WD ES over three days and 570 miles of admittedly hard city/freeway driving.

Equally disappointing is the MPV's "trucky" driving feel. Where newer minivans are pleasantly car-like, the Mazda still serves up slow-witted steering, pronounced cornering lean, marked wind and road noise, and a lumpy ride. All this makes the MPV rather tiring in the daily stop-and-go. The veteran 3.0-liter V-6 is tolerably smooth but audibly thrashy when worked hard, and the transmission is reluctant to kick down for passing.

On the plus side, MPV's 4WD can be used on dry pavement and engages easily "on the fly" via a button on the column-mounted shift lever. Another button activates a center-differential lock for max traction in severe conditions.

ACCOMMODATIONS Like the Honda Odyssey/Isuzu Oasis, MPV has four swing-open passenger doors. LX models seat eight on twin front buckets and a pair of bench seats behind. The ES versions hold seven by substituting a pair of middle-row buckets, which are optionally available on LS models. Second- and third-row seats have folding backrests for utility, but only the rearmost bench is removable (via quick-release clamps).

MPV is on the small side for a minivan, with less people and package space than Chrysler's models or a Ford Windstar, plus a higher step-in that complicates entry/exit. At least head room is generous all around. The driving position is rather bus-like but comfortable, with commanding visibility and clear, well-placed gauges and controls.

BUILD QUALITY MPVs are well screwed together, with pleasant interior decor matching that of most rivals. Still, some molded plastic looks low-budget, and marked body drumming on rough roads betrays this vehicle's elderly body engineering.

VALUE FOR THE MONEY MPV has its points, but not enough for us to recommend it, especially since similar money buys more zoom, room, and refinement in a Windstar or Caravan/Voyager, even a Chevrolet Venture. As for the All-Sport trimmings, they're a masquerade, the only thing Mazda can offer a market gone mad for SUVs.

RATINGS

	2WD	4WD
Acceleration	3	3
Fuel economy	2	2
Ride quality	3	3
Steering/handling	3	3
Braking	4	4
Quietness	3	3
Driver seating	3	3
Instruments/controls	3	3
Room/comfort (front)	4	4
Room/comfort (rear)	4	4
Cargo room	4	4
Value for the money	3	3
Total	**39**	**39**

SPECIFICATIONS

	4-door van	4-door van
Wheelbase, in.	110.4	110.4
Overall length, in.	183.5	183.5
Overall width, in.	71.9	71.9
Overall height, in.	68.9	71.5
Curb weight, lbs.	3790	3790[1]
Cargo vol., cu. ft.	42.1	42.1
Fuel capacity, gals.	19.6	19.8
Seating capacity	8	8
Front head room, in.	40.0	40.0
Max. front leg room, in.	40.4	40.4
Rear head room, in.	39.7	36.9
Min. rear leg room, in.	33.4	34.2

ENGINES

	ohc V-6
Size, liters/cu. in.	3.0/180
Horsepower @ rpm	155@ 5000
Torque (lbs./ft.) @ rpm	169@ 4000
Availability	S

EPA city/highway mpg

4-speed OD automatic	16/21

1. 4WD, 4045 lbs.

PRICES

Mazda MPV

	Retail Price	Dealer Invoice
LX 2WD 3-door van	$23095	$20834

	Retail Price	Dealer Invoice
ES 2WD 3-door van	$26395	$23807
LX 4WD 3-door van	26895	24258
ES 4WD 3-door van	28895	26060
Destination charge	480	480

All models require a Preferred Equipment Pkg. Prices are for vehicles distributed by Mazda Motor of America, Inc. Prices may be higher in areas served by independent distributors.

STANDARD EQUIPMENT:

LX 2WD: 3.0-liter V-6 engine, 4-speed automatic transmission, driver- and passenger-side air bags, anti-lock 4-wheel disc brakes, variable-assist power steering, tilt steering wheel, cruise control, velour upholstery, 8-passenger seating (reclining front bucket seats, 3-passenger reclining and folding middle bench seat, 3-passenger rear bench seat), power mirrors, power windows, power door locks, tachometer, AM/FM/CD, digital clock, variable intermittent wipers, intermittent rear wiper/washer, rear defogger, remote fuel-door release, rear heat ducts, tinted glass, wheel covers, 195/75R15 tires.

LX 4WD adds: part-time 4-wheel drive, 4-Seasons Pkg. (rear heater, large-capacity washer tank, heavy-duty battery), high-capacity cooling fan, All-Sport Pkg. (grille guard, stone guard, eyebrow fender flares, rear bumper guard, roof rack, All-Sport graphics, alloy wheels, 225/70R15 mud and snow tires), special 2-tone paint, full-size spare tire.

ES 2WD adds to LX 2WD: leather upholstery, 7-passenger seating (quad captain's chairs, 3-passenger rear bench seat), leather-wrapped steering wheel, Load Leveling Pkg. (automatic load leveling, transmission-oil cooler, high-capacity cooling fan, full-size spare), All-Sport Pkg. (includes 215/65R15 tires), special 2-tone paint, deletes middle bench seat.

ES 4WD adds: part-time 4-wheel drive, 4-Seasons Pkg., All-Sport Pkg. (includes 225/70R15 mud and snow tires).

OPTIONAL EQUIPMENT:
Major Packages

LX Preferred Equipment Group 1, LX	1550	1318
Manufacturer's discount price	795	676
Front air conditioning, remote keyless entry, rear privacy glass, floormats.		
LX Preferred Equipment Group 2, LX	2250	1913
Manufacturer's discount price	1495	1271
Front and rear air conditioning, remote keyless entry, rear privacy glass, floormats.		
ES Preferred Equipment Group 1, ES	2250	1913
Manufacturer's discount price	1395	1186
Front and rear air conditioning, remote keyless entry, rear privacy glass, floormats.		
Load Leveling Pkg., LX 2WD	595	506
LX 4WD	495	421
Automatic load leveling, transmission-oil cooler, high-capacity cooling fan (2WD), full-size spare tire (2WD).		
All-Sport Pkg., LX 2WD	880	748
Grille guard, stone guard, eyebrow fender flares, rear bumper guard, roof rack, All-Sport graphics, alloy wheels, 215/65R15 tires.		

Comfort and Convenience

Quad captain's chairs, LX	400	340
Power moonroof, ES	1200	1020
Cassette player	250	213

Appearance and Miscellaneous

Special 2-tone paint, LX 2WD	350	298
Alloy Wheel Pkg., LX 2WD	495	421
215/65R15 tires, alloy wheels.		

MAZDA PROTEGE   `RECOMMENDED`
Front-wheel-drive subcompact

Rating Scale: *5-Excellent; 4-Above average; 3-Average; 2-Below average; 1-Poor*

Mazda Protege ES

RATINGS

	DX/LX	ES
Acceleration	3	4
Fuel economy	5	4
Ride quality	4	4
Steering/handling	4	4
Braking	3	3
Quietness	3	3
Driver seating	3	3
Instruments/controls	4	4
Room/comfort (front)	4	4
Room/comfort (rear)	3	3
Cargo room	3	3
Value for the money	4	4
Total	**43**	**43**

SPECIFICATIONS

	4-door sedan
Wheelbase, in.	102.6
Overall length, in.	174.5
Overall width, in.	67.3
Overall height, in.	55.9
Curb weight, lbs.	2385
Cargo vol., cu. ft.	13.1
Fuel capacity, gals.	14.5
Seating capacity	5
Front head room, in.	39.2
Max. front leg room, in.	42.2
Rear head room, in.	37.4
Min. rear leg room, in.	35.6

ENGINES

	dohc I-4	dohc I-4
Size, liters/cu. in.	1.5/91	1.8/110
Horsepower @ rpm	92 @ 5500	122 @ 6000
Torque (lbs./ft.) @ rpm	96 @ 4000	117 @ 4000
Availability	S[1]	S[2]

EPA city/highway mpg

4-speed OD automatic	25/33	23/30
5-speed OD manual	30/37	26/32

1. DX, LX. 2. ES.

PRICES

Mazda Protege	Retail Price	Dealer Invoice
DX 4-door sedan	$12145	$11455
LX 4-door sedan	13545	12498
ES 4-door sedan	15295	13956
Destination charge	450	450

Prices are for vehicles distributed by Mazda Motor of America, Inc. Prices may be higher in areas served by independent distributors.

STANDARD EQUIPMENT:

DX: 1.5-liter DOHC 4-cylinder engine, 5-speed manual transmission, driver- and passenger-side air bags, variable-assist power steering, tilt steering wheel, cloth/vinyl reclining front bucket seats, cupholders, storage console, rear defogger, remote fuel-door release, coolant-temperature gauge, trip odometer, intermittent wipers, auxiliary power outlet, remote outside mirrors, green tinted glass, 175/70R13 tires.

LX adds: cruise control, AM/FM/CD, digital clock, velour upholstery, split folding rear seat, remote decklid release, tachometer, power windows, power door locks, power mirrors, map lights, passenger-side vanity mirror, front side storage trays, full wheel covers, 185/65R14 tires.

ES adds: 1.8-liter DOHC 4-cylinder engine, 4-wheel disc brakes, air conditioning, sport front bucket seats with thigh-support and height adjustment, rear stabilizer bar.

OPTIONAL EQUIPMENT:
Major Packages

Convenience Pkg., DX	1575	1292
Air conditioning, AM/FM/cassette, floormats.		
Luxury Pkg., LX	1145	939
Air conditioning, raised console armrest (automatic transmission-equipped models), floormats.		

AGAINST • Rear entry/exit

Protege is another Mazda that marks time for '98, with almost no change apart from new "winged M" badges in place of last year's "flame" logos. Introduced for 1995 and modestly facelifted last season, the current Protege is a distant structural cousin of the latest Ford Escort and Mercury Tracer, but is built in Japan with Mazda-designed 4-cylinder engines.

Ford now owns a controlling interest in Mazda, which is struggling to recover from several years of steep sales and revenue losses. One result is longer "product cycles," which for Protege means a design life extended from the usual four years to six; that takes it to 2001, when the next version should appear.

Base DX and mid-range LX versions have 1.5-liter engines and the top-shelf ES has a 1.8-liter. Dual air bags are standard. Anti-lock brakes are optional except on the DX.

PERFORMANCE If it's going to be around a while, it's a good thing Protege's willing engines and nimble chassis make it more fun to drive than most economy cars. The 1.5-liter DX/LX engine gives passable acceleration with manual shift—we timed 0-60 mph in 10.6 seconds—but feels sluggish with automatic (which stretches the time to more like 12 seconds). The 1.8-liter ES doesn't seem much stronger around town, but highway merging and passing are noticeably easier. Fuel thrift is a strong point in any Protege. Our manual LX returned a satisfying 30.2 mpg over 230 miles of mostly hard rush-hour commuting.

Protege's suspension is supple without being mushy, so most bumps are nicely absorbed, though with a curious loud "thump" on occasion. Hard cornering induces fair body lean, and the DX's narrow 13-inch tires start squealing early in turns, but front-end "plowing" is well checked, and the steering is quick and informative. The LX and ES are even grippier and more nimble on their standard 14-inch tires. Noise levels are modest by class standards, but both engines become a bit coarse at high rpm.

ACCOMMODATIONS Mazda offers one of the roomier subcompact sedans, with relatively abundant front head room and rear leg room. Still, it shares with most in this class rear doors that are narrow at the bottom, making it awkward to get in or out, and a cabin width that precludes three adults from riding in back without rubbing shoulders. Trunk space is good but not exceptional.

Protege's dashboard is generally well designed, with clear gauges and handy headlight and wiper control stalks. All models come with a tilt steering column, but tall drivers may find the wheel sits too low even at its top setting. Visibility is all but unobstructed, thanks to a low waistline and large windows.

BUILD QUALITY Though not luxurious even in top-line ES trim, the Protege is a tight, solid little car with workmanship to equal anything in its class. Door and trunk closings remain a bit tinny, however.

VALUE FOR THE MONEY Protege tends to be overlooked by many buyers, and that's a shame, for in many ways it's the equal of the class-leading Honda Civic and Chevrolet Prizm/Toyota Corolla twins. It's certainly a good value now that Mazda dealers are really bargaining to win new customers, so put Protege on your list of must-see small cars.

Prices are accurate at time of publication; subject to manufacturer's changes.

	Retail Price	Dealer Invoice
Premium Pkg., ES...............................	$1195	$956
Alloy wheels with locks, power sunroof.		
Touring Pkg., ES	105	84
Floormats, raised console armrest. Requires automatic transmission.		

Powertrains
4-speed automatic transmission	800	720

Safety Features
Anti-lock brakes, LX, ES	800	680

Comfort and Convenience
Power sunroof, LX................................	700	560
Cassette player	250	213
DX requires Convenience Pkg.		
Remote keyless entry, LX, ES..............	200	160
Includes theft-deterrent system.		
Floormats	80	64

MAZDA 626

✓ BEST BUY

Mazda 626

Front-wheel-drive compact

Base price range: $15,695-$23,995. Built in Flat Rock, Mich.

Also consider: Ford Contour, Mercury Mystique, Nissan Altima

FOR • Acceleration (V-6) • Standard traction control (V-6 models) • Steering/handling

AGAINST • Automatic transmission performance • Road noise

Long the best-seller in Mazda's U.S. line, the family-oriented 626 is redesigned this year. Like its predecessor, it's built at the joint Ford-Mazda plant in Michigan, but this is the first 626 to share nothing with a coupe, as Mazda's MX-6 and the related Ford Probe are no more.

Four models continue; DX, LX, LX-V6, and ES-V6 in ascending order of features and price. DX and LX retain a 2.0-liter 4-cylinder engine, but with 9 more horsepower; "V6" models carry a 2.5-liter V-6 with an extra 6 horsepower. All come with manual transmission or optional automatic.

Dimensionally, the 626 is 2 inches longer in wheelbase, 2.4 inches longer overall, and about a half-inch wider. Base-model curb weight increases about 50 pounds.

V-6 models include traction control and an engine immobilizer, both new for 626. All-disc brakes with anti-lock control are optional on V-6 models.

PERFORMANCE Though our experience with the new 626s has so far been limited to brief preview drives, the '98s improve on the old models in several important ways. For one thing, they're quieter, with a noticeable reduction in engine noise and wind rustle. Tire roar seems lower too, if still a bit too audible over coarse pavement.

Ride remains firm but absorbent. The longer wheelbase helps reduce pitch and hop on scalloped freeways, yet cornering is still decisive and sporty, with only mild apparent body lean and stable front-wheel-drive responses. Quick, precise steering helps. Braking is good, with little nosedive and steady tracking in hard stops.

As for performance, 4-cylinder models are at least adequate

with manual shift but a bit sluggish with automatic. V-6 models are lively with either transmission. However, V-6 or four, the automatic can still downshift with a jerk sometimes.

ACCOMMODATIONS If bigger on the outside, the '98 626 should be usefully roomier inside, right? It is. Six-footers can sit in tandem without the rear rider's knees digging into the front seats. There's also good underseat foot room and about ¾-inch of rear head clearance even with the available power moonroof. The cabin is still a bit narrow for uncrowded three-abreast grownup travel in back, but larger doorways make for easy entry/exit all-around.

When it comes to visibility, driver seating, and dash layout, the new 626 is competitive, though not brilliant. Tall drivers, in fact, might want a little more rearward seat travel to get further from the steering wheel. Small-items stowage is better than average, with roomy compartments in the dash and console, plus map pockets on front doors and seatbacks.

BUILD QUALITY Previous 626s were far from tinny, but the new one feels reassuringly stout on rough roads. Detail finish on our preview cars was equally satisfying, and LX/ES interior decor has a tasteful, understated look.

VALUE FOR THE MONEY The 626 is a competent family car with more of a sporting flair than most rivals, especially with the V-6 engine. LX versions offer the best combination of features and value. There's lots of competition, so you shouldn't have to pay full retail price.

RATINGS
	DX/LX	LX-V6/ES-V6
Acceleration	3	4
Fuel economy	4	3
Ride quality	4	4
Steering/handling	4	4
Braking	3	4
Quietness	4	4
Driver seating	4	4
Instruments/controls	4	3
Room/comfort (front)	4	4
Room/comfort (rear)	1	4
Cargo room	4	3
Value for the money	4	4
Total	**43**	**45**

SPECIFICATIONS
	4-door sedan
Wheelbase, in.	105.1
Overall length, in.	186.8
Overall width, in.	69.3
Overall height, in.	55.1
Curb weight, lbs.	2798
Cargo vol., cu. ft.	14.2
Fuel capacity, gals.	16.9
Seating capacity	5
Front head room, in.	39.2
Max. front leg room, in.	43.6
Rear head room, in.	37.0
Min. rear leg room, in.	34.6

ENGINES
	dohc I-4	dohc V-6
Size, liters/cu. in.	2.0/122	2.5/152
Horsepower @ rpm	125@ 5500	170@ 5000
Torque (lbs./ft.) @ rpm	127@ 3000	163@ 5000
Availability	S[1]	S[2]
EPA city/highway mpg		
5-speed OD manual.............................	NA	NA
4-speed OD automatic..........................	NA	NA

1. DX, LX. 2. LX V-6, ES.

PRICES
Mazda 626	Retail Price	Dealer Invoice
DX 4-door sedan	$15695	$14130
LX 4-cylinder 4-door sedan	17895	16108
LX V-6 4-door sedan	20795	18715
ES V-6 4-door sedan	23995	21592

Rating Scale: *5-Excellent; 4-Above average; 3-Average; 2-Below average; 1-Poor*

	Retail Price	Dealer Invoice
Destination charge	$450	$450

Prices are for vehicles distributed by Mazda Motor of America, Inc. Prices may be higher in areas served by independent distributors.

STANDARD EQUIPMENT:

DX: 2.0-liter DOHC 4-cylinder engine, 5-speed manual transmission, driver- and passenger-side air bags, variable-assist power steering, tilt steering wheel, velour upholstery, reclining front bucket seats w/adjustable thigh support, 60/40 folding rear seat w/folding armrest, storage console with armrest, cupholders, tachometer, coolant-temperature gauge, trip odometer, intermittent wipers, power mirrors, remote fuel-door and decklid releases, rear defogger, passenger-side visor mirror, rear heat ducts, green tinted glass, front mud guards, 185/70SR14 tires, full wheel covers.

LX adds: air conditioning, upgraded velour upholstery, power windows, power door locks, cruise control, power mirrors, AM/FM/CD, digital clock, dual visor mirrors w/illuminated passenger-side mirror.

LX V-6 adds: 2.5-liter DOHC V-6 engine, anti-lock 4-wheel disc brakes, variable intermittent wipers, remote keyless entry, illuminated visor mirrors, theft-deterrent system, rear stabilizer bar, dual bright exhaust outlets, 205/60HR15 tires.

ES adds: leather upholstery, 8-way power driver seat, leather-wrapped steering wheel and shifter, Bose sound system, power antenna, power moonroof, map lights, floormats, fog lights, alloy wheels.

OPTIONAL EQUIPMENT:
Major Packages
Convenience Pkg., DX	1495	1196
Air conditioning, AM/FM/CD, floormats.		
Luxury Pkg., LX 4-cylinder	1695	1356
Power moonroof, theft-deterrent system, remote keyless entry, floormats, 205/60HR15 tires, alloy wheels.		

Powertrains
4-speed automatic transmission	800	696
Deletes leather-wrapped shifter on ES.		
Anti-lock brakes, LX 4-cylinder.................................	550	468

Major Packages
Premium Pkg., LX V-6...	1895	1516
Power driver seat, power moonroof, Bose sound system, power antenna, floormats, alloy wheels.		

Comfort and Convenience
Cassette player	250	213
DX requires Convenience Pkg.		
Floormats, DX, LX..	80	56

MERCEDES-BENZ C-CLASS AND CLK

Mercedes-Benz C280

Rear-wheel-drive near-luxury car
Base price range: $30,450-$39,850. Built in Germany.
Also consider: Audi A4, BMW 3-Series, Volvo C70, Volvo S70/V70

FOR • Standard front side air bags • Steering/handling • Acceleration (C280, CLK)

AGAINST • Road noise (C-Class) • Rear seat and cargo room

Picking up the pace in their chase of the better-selling BMW 3-Series, Mercedes' entry-level sedans get several new features for 1998, plus a new companion coupe. The latter, called CLK320, shares the C-Class platform and wheelbase, but is slightly longer and lower, and has its own styling marked by an oval-lamp nose like that on the larger E-Class sedans. Powering the CLK is Mercedes' first V-6, a 3.2-liter engine with single overhead camshaft and three valves per cylinder. A 2.8-liter version of this V-6 replaces last year's 2.8-liter inline-6 in the C280 sedan. The C230's twin-cam 4-cylinder is unchanged.

All three come with door-mounted front side air bags, plus two safety features new to most other 1998 Mercedes. One is "BabySmart," which deactivates the passenger-side air bags when a special Mercedes-designed child seat is in place. The second is "Brake Assist," which interprets certain rapid brake-pedal movement as a panic-stop situation and automatically applies full braking force. In the same vein, Mercedes' anti-skid Electronic Stability Program is optional for the C280 and CLK. Those models also have ASR traction control as standard; it's optional on the C230.

Another new shared option is rain-sensing wipers that vary the speed of the intermittent sweep. Standard for all three models is a new "SmartKey" anti-theft ignition system that uses a coded electronic data link instead of a conventional key; Mercedes says it's virtually impossible to duplicate.

In addition, sedans get minor styling revisions to nose, side sills, and tail, and last year's C280 "C6" Sport Package has been upgraded to 16-inch wheels and tires (standard on CLK), plus gauges and interior trim inspired by those of the SLK roadster. Exclusive to the CLK are a standard 60/40 split-fold rear seat and dual power-forward front seats.

PERFORMANCE We have yet to test the new V-6 editions, but the 3.2-liter should make the CLK quite lively. Likewise, the 2.8 should be as smooth and quiet as last year's inline-6, but with extra mid-range torque that promises to give the C280 stronger all-around performance. The C230 engine is pretty refined for a 4-cylinder, but provides only adequate punch. Regardless of model, Mercedes' 5-speed automatic transmission has a gear for most every situation, and shifts with smooth authority.

All these cars have a firm ride that lets you feel most bumps but not really harsh impacts. Road roar is noticeable, especially from the rear tires, but wind and mechanical ruckus is well checked. Braking is superb, and handling remains responsive and stable, though not quite as agile as that of a BMW 3-Series.

ACCOMMODATIONS All these Mercedes suffer skimpy back-seat leg room and tight rear entry/exit as far as adults are concerned. Note, too, that the CLK's rear seat is configured for two only. All-around head room is just adequate for 6-footers. Cargo space isn't good either, but what's there is quite usable.

On the plus side, sufficient seat and steering-wheel adjustments allow most drivers to get comfortable. Controls are handy and user-friendly once you've deciphered a few markings, and visibility is generally good.

BUILD QUALITY Per Mercedes tradition, the C-Class sedans are rock-solid and well engineered, and we'd expect no less of the CLK. Fit, finish, and materials are in line with the sticker prices, though some molded interior plastic doesn't look really top-notch.

VALUE FOR THE MONEY Performance and engineering earn the C-Class sedans our respect, but small interiors for the price keep them from earning our recommendation. The CLK offers Mercedes prestige and greater refinement for about the same money as Volvo's new C70 coupe. High resale value is a plus for any Mercedes, whether you plan to buy or lease.

Prices are accurate at time of publication; subject to manufacturer's changes.

RATINGS

	C230	C280	CLK
Acceleration	3	4	4
Fuel economy	3	3	3
Ride quality	3	3	3
Steering/handling	4	4	4
Braking	5	5	5
Quietness	3	4	4
Driver seating	4	4	4
Instruments/controls	3	3	3
Room/comfort (front)	3	3	3
Room/comfort (rear)	2	2	2
Cargo room	3	3	2
Value for the money	3	4	3
Total	**39**	**42**	**40**

SPECIFICATIONS

	4-door sedan	2-door coupe
Wheelbase, in.	105.9	105.9
Overall length, in.	177.4	180.2
Overall width, in.	67.7	67.8
Overall height, in.	56.1	53.0
Curb weight, lbs.	3250	3240
Cargo vol., cu. ft.	12.9	11.0
Fuel capacity, gals.	16.4	16.4
Seating capacity	5	4
Front head room, in.	37.2	36.9
Max. front leg room, in.	41.5	41.9
Rear head room, in.	37.0	35.6
Min. rear leg room, in.	32.8	31.1

ENGINES

	dohc I-4	ohc V-6	ohc V-6
Size, liters/cu. in.	2.3/140	2.8/171	3.2/195
Horsepower @ rpm	148@ 5500	194@ 5800	215@ 5500
Torque (lbs./ft.) @ rpm	162@ 4000	195@ 3000	229@ 3000
Availability	S[1]	S[2]	S[3]

EPA city/highway mpg

5-speed OD automatic	23/30	21/27	20/27

1. C230. 2. C280. 3. CLK.

PRICES

Mercedes-Benz C-Class and CLK	Retail Price	Dealer Invoice
C230 4-door sedan	$30450	$26490
C280 4-door sedan	35400	30800
CLK 2-door notchback	39850	34670
Destination charge	595	595

STANDARD EQUIPMENT:

C230: 2.3-liter DOHC 4-cylinder engine, 5-speed automatic transmission, driver- and passenger-side air bags w/automatic child seat recognition system, side-impact air bags, anti-lock 4-wheel disc brakes, power steering, leather-wrapped steering wheel and shifter, cruise control, air conditioning w/automatic climate control, cloth 10-way power driver seat, 10-way manual adjustable passenger seat, center storage console, folding rear armrest, cupholders, heated power mirrors w/automatic day/night, burl walnut interior trim, power windows, power door locks, remote keyless entry, remote AM/FM/cassette, digital clock, tachometer, coolant-temperature gauge, trip odometer, outside-temperature indicator, remote decklid release, illuminated visor mirrors, rear defogger, Homelink universal garage-door opener, first-aid kit, floormats, theft-deterrent system, tinted glass, fog lights, 195/65HR15 all-season tires, alloy wheels.

C280 adds: 2.8-liter ohc V-6 engine, traction control, 10-way power passenger seat, Bose sound system.

CLK adds: 3.2-liter ohc V-6 engine, leather upholstery, memory system, dual-zone automatic climate control, interior air filter, 205/55R16 tires.

OPTIONAL EQUIPMENT:
Major Packages

	Retail Price	Dealer Invoice
Option Pkg. C1, C280	1890	1644
Electronic Stability Program, heated front seats, headlight washer/wiper.		
Option Pkg. C2, C230, C280	$350	$304
Split folding rear seat. w/pass-through and ski sack.		
Option Pkg. C3, C230	2190	1905
C280	1990	1731
Leather upholstery, 10-way power passenger seat, power sunroof, rain-sensing wipers (C280).		
Option Pkg. C6, C280	890	774
Leather upholstery, bucket front seats, sport interior trim, telescoping steering wheel, bodyside moldings, sport suspension, 205/55HR16 tires.		
Option Pkg. K1	1495	1087
Integrated mobile cellular telephone, 6-disc CD changer.		
Option Pkg. K2	1895	1445
Integrated portable cellular telephone, 6-disc CD changer.		
Option Pkg. K3, CLK	1290	1122
Power glass sunroof, power rear sun shade, automatic day/night rearview and driver side mirrors.		
Option Pkg. K4, CLK	1950	1696
Electronic Stability Program, Xenon headlights, rain-sensing wipers.		

Powertrains

	Retail Price	Dealer Invoice
Automatic slip control, C230	990	861

Comfort and Convenience

	Retail Price	Dealer Invoice
Headlamp washer/wipers	340	296
Power glass sunroof	1100	966
Telescopic steering wheel, C230, C280	125	109
Multi-contour driver seat	390	339
NA with Option Pkg. C6.		
Multi-contour power passenger seat	390	339
NA with Option Pkg. C6.		
Heated front seats	595	518
Rear seat pass-through, CLK	175	152
Includes ski sack.		
Bose sound system, C230	570	496
Rain-sensing wipers, C230, C280	170	148

Appearance and Miscellaneous

	Retail Price	Dealer Invoice
Xenon headlights, C230, C280	960	835
Metallic paint	600	522

MERCEDES-BENZ E-CLASS

Mercedes-Benz E320 sedan

BEST BUY

Rear- or all-wheel-drive luxury car

Base price range: $41,800-$49,900. Built in Germany.

Also consider: BMW 5-Series, Lexus GS 300/400, Volvo S90/V90

FOR • Standard front and side air bags • Acceleration (E320 and E420) • Steering/handling • Ride • Available all-wheel drive (E320)

AGAINST • Fuel economy (E420)

Mercedes' mid-range series gets a number of changes for '98, headlined by the addition of a station wagon body style and optional all-wheel drive (AWD).

The E-Class sedans kick off with the diesel 6-cylinder E300, which adds a turbocharger and intercooler to deliver 30 percent more horsepower and 57 percent more torque than the previous non-turbo model. One step up is the mainstay gas-powered E320 sedan, which switches from a 3.2-liter inline 6-cylinder engine to a new Mercedes V-6 with similar displacement but a

Rating Scale: 5-Excellent; 4-Above average; 3-Average; 2-Below average; 1-Poor

much broader torque band. The V-6 also powers a new E320 wagon, which seats seven via a fold-down 2-place third seat. The line-topping V-8 E420 sedan continues in 1997 form until '98 models are ready.

The new AWD is a $2750 option for E320s. The same basic system used in Mercedes' new ML320 sport-utility vehicle, it employs the anti-lock brake and traction-control sensors to direct power to the wheels with greatest grip—even just one wheel, if needed. Mercedes' anti-skid Electronic Stability Program is optional on E320s with or without AWD.

All E-Class models now come with Mercedes' "BabySmart" child-seat recognition system, "Brake Assist" feature, and electronic "Smart Key" ignition/locking system (see C-Class report). New options for this line include rain-sensing intermittent wipers and, from the big S-class, the Parktronic vehicle maneuvering aid that signals the presence of nearby objects that might go unseen.

PERFORMANCE We have yet to test a '98 E-Class, but Mercedes says the Turbodiesel runs 0-60 mph in under 9 seconds, more than 3 seconds ahead of the old E300; the V-6 E320 sedan needs 7.5 seconds with AWD, 7.1 without. All three claims may be conservative, as we timed an inline-6 E320 at 7 seconds flat. Fuel economy remains a diesel strength, and we hope the new V-6 does better than the so-so 21.1 mpg we averaged with its inline predecessor. The V-8 E420 is a Teutonic hot rod, but quite thirsty.

E-Class sedans are more athletic than most luxury 4-doors, if not so nimble as a 5-Series BMW or Lexus's new GS. Steering is firm and precise, body lean modest in hard cornering. The taut suspension provides a comfortable highway ride and smothers most bumps and ruts around town. Quietness remains another virtue. All this should apply to the E320 wagon, which weighs little more than the sedan. The same goes for the AWD option, which adds less than 200 pounds to E320 curb weight.

ACCOMMODATIONS There's ample room for four adults in any E-Class, though a bulky transmission tunnel precludes real long-distance comfort for a rear center-seater. All models have good cargo capacity, flat load floors, and low liftovers. The wagon's third seat easily folds flush with the cargo deck, but it's sized more for kids than grownups.

As ever, the E-Class offers good visibility from a comfortable, easily tailored driver's post. Gauges and controls are also well designed, though markings on some switches aren't obvious.

BUILD QUALITY Mercedes usually shines here, and the E-Class is no exception. From lustrous paint to top-drawer interior furnishings to a vault-solid driving feel, workmanship is all one could want.

VALUE FOR THE MONEY With its exceptional quality, high resale value and improved performance, the E-Class merits even stronger consideration among premium sedans in 1998. The new wagon and AWD option are added attractions for those upscale buyers who want superior traction in something other than a sport-utility.

RATINGS

	E300 TD	E320	E420
Acceleration	3	4	5
Fuel economy	4	3	2
Ride quality	4	4	4
Steering/handling	4	4	4
Braking	5	5	5
Quietness	4	4	4
Driver seating	4	4	4
Instruments/controls	3	3	3
Room/comfort (front)	4	4	4
Room/comfort (rear)	4	4	4
Cargo room	4	4	4
Value for the money	3	4	4
Total	**46**	**47**	**47**

SPECIFICATIONS

	4-door sedan	4-door wagon
Wheelbase, in.	111.5	111.5
Overall length, in.	189.4	190.4
Overall width, in.	70.8	70.8
Overall height, in.	56.7	59.3
Curb weight, lbs.	3460	3670

	4-door sedan	4-door wagon
Cargo vol., cu. ft.	15.3	82.6
Fuel capacity, gals.	21.1	18.5
Seating capacity	5	7
Front head room, in.	37.6	38.6
Max. front leg room, in.	41.3	41.3
Rear head room, in.	37.2	37.0
Min. rear leg room, in.	36.1	36.1

ENGINES

	turbo dohc I-6	ohc V-6	diesel dohc V-8
Size, liters/cu. in.	3.0/183	3.2/195	4.2/256
Horsepower @ rpm	174@ 5000	221@ 5500	275@ 5700
Torque (lbs./ft.) @ rpm	244@ 1600	232@ 3000	295@ 3900
Availability	S[1]	S[2]	S[3]
EPA city/highway mpg 5-speed OD automatic	26/34	21/29	18/25

1. E300 Diesel. 2. E320. 3. E420.

PRICES

Mercedes-Benz E-Class	Retail Price	Dealer Invoice
E300TD 4-door sedan	$41800	$36370
E320 4-door sedan	45500	39580
E320 4-door wagon	46500	40450
1997 E420 4-door sedan	49900	43410
Destination charge	595	595

STANDARD EQUIPMENT:

E300TD 3.0-liter DOHC 6-cylinder turbocharged diesel engine, 5-speed automatic transmission, ASR (acceleration slip control), front and side air bags, anti-lock 4-wheel disc brakes, variable-assist power steering, cloth upholstery, 10-way power front bucket seats with memory feature, split folding rear seats, cupholders, power tilt/telescopic steering wheel with memory feature, leather-wrapped steering wheel, power windows, power door locks, tachometer, outside-temperature indicator, AM/FM/cassette, power heated outside mirrors with memory feature, automatic day/night inside and driver-side outside mirrors, tinted glass, rear defogger, illuminated visor mirrors, remote keyless entry, remote decklid release, Homelink universal garage-door opener, variable intermittent wipers, reading lights, walnut interior trim, interior air filter, first-aid kit, fog lamps, floormats, alloy wheels, full-size spare tire, automatic climate control, cruise control, theft-deterrent system, 215/55R16 tires.

E320 adds to E300TD: 3.2-liter OHC V-6 engine, leather upholstery.

E320 wagon deletes: leather upholstery and adds to sedan: folding third seat, cargo net, cargo cover, rear power outlet, intermittent rear wiper and heated washer, automatic rear load levelling.

E420 adds to E320 sedan: 4.2-liter DOHC V-8 engine, Bose sound system.

OPTIONAL EQUIPMENT:
Major Packages

E1 Option Pkg., E300TD, E320	1950	1696

Electronic Stability Program, Xenon headlamps, rain-sensing windshield wipers, heated headlamp washers.

E420	760	661

Heated front seats, headlamp washers.

E2 Option Pkg., E300TD, E320	1350	1174

Bose sound system, power glass sunroof.

K2 Option Pkg., E300TD, E320	1895	1445

Integrated portable cellular telephone, 6-disc CD changer.

E4 Option Pkg., E420	1630	1418

Dual multicontour power seats, headlamp washers, Xenon headlamps.

E5 Option Pkg. (E420)/K2 Option Pkg. (E300TD, E320)	1495	1087

Integrated cellular telephone , 6-disc CD changer.

E6 Sport Pkg., E420	3900	3393

Ground effects, 235/45ZR17 performance tires, monoblock alloy wheels.

E7 Option Pkg., E420	1950	1696

Electronic Stability Program, headlamp washers, Xenon headlamps.

Prices are accurate at time of publication; subject to manufacturer's changes.

Powertrains

	Retail Price	Dealer Invoice
All-wheel-drive system, E320	$2750	$2400

Safety Features

Parktronic system, E300TD, E320	975	848
Electronic Stability Program, E300TD, E320	990	861

Comfort and Convenience

Power glass sunroof, E300TD, E320	1110	966
Power glass moonroof, E420	1090	948
Leather upholstery, E300TD, E320 wagon	1695	1475
Multicontour power driver seat, E300TD, E320	390	339
E420	380	331
Multicontour power passenger seat, E300TD, E320	390	339
E420	380	331
Heated front seats	595	518
Bose Premium Sound System, E300TD, E320	570	496
Heated headlamp washers, E300TD, E320............	340	296
Headlamp washers, E420	335	291
Power rear window sunshade	395	344
NA station wagon.		
Xenon headlamps, E300TD, E320........................	960	835
Requires heated headlamp washers.		
E420	950	826
Requires headlamp washers or E1 Option Pkg.		
Rain-sensing windshield wipers, E300TD, E320	170	148

Appearance and Miscellaneous

Metallic paint, E300D, E320	695	605
E420	NC	NC
Luggage rack, E320 wagon	390	339

MERCEDES-BENZ ML320

✓ BEST BUY

Mercedes-Benz ML320

Four-wheel-drive midsize sport-utility vehicle
Base price: $33,950. Built in Tuscaloosa, Ala.
Also consider: Ford Explorer, Jeep Grand Cherokee, Mercury Mountaineer, Toyota 4Runner

FOR • Side air bags • Steering/handling • Ride

AGAINST • Fuel economy

Mercedes calls it an "All-Activity Vehicle," but the new ML320 is really a sport-utility, the German automaker's first. It's also the first Mercedes built in America—at a new Alabama plant that can turn out up to 65,000 annually for worldwide sale. Of those, about half are earmarked for the U.S.

Designed from scratch, the ML320 uses body-on frame-construction, but stands apart from truck-based SUVs with all-independent suspension.

Power comes from Mercedes' first V-6, which mates with a 5-speed automatic transmission to drive all wheels through front, center, and rear differentials. Unlike the couplings or locking differentials of most SUVs, Mercedes' "4ETS" system uses anti-lock brake and traction-control sensors to direct power to the wheels with greatest grip. Power normally divides 50/50 front/rear, but can be automatically directed to any combination of wheels to maintain traction—even one if needed. Separate low-range gearing is engaged via a dashboard button.

The ML320 comes as a single well-equipped model that includes door-mounted front side air bags. Options include power moonroof, a Class III 5000-pound trailer hitch, and an "M1" package with leather-and-wood interior trim. Mercedes

promises a V-8 ML430 for 1999, as well as an optional 2-place third-row seat.

PERFORMANCE In the seemingly universal quest to create an SUV that drives like a car, Mercedes has taken a clear lead with the ML320. Though it doesn't feel that snappy getting away from a stop (Mercedes quotes a so-so 9.0-second 0-60 mph time), the smooth, responsive automatic helps get the best from the overhead-cam V-6. Noise levels are low for an SUV, though the engine sounds coarse when pushed, and wind rush at highway speeds can't quiet match that of a family sedan. Mileage is a typical SUV weakness, but the Mercedes shouldn't be unduly thirsty.

A few tours of a special handling course revealed the ML320 as poised and stable in tight turns, with far less body lean and faster, more precise steering than most every other SUV. Likewise, the smooth and supple on-road ride is head-of-the-class. The effective, transparent nature of the 4ETS system is evident in light-duty off-pavement work. It's not as effective in severe back-trail conditions as more-traditional 4WD systems, but few ML320s will see that sort of use.

ACCOMMODATIONS The ML320 has ample room for four adults, but isn't wide enough for three grownups in back. The rear seat can be slid forward some 3 inches for extra cargo space, but aft leg room then becomes tight for 6-footers. Step-in height is much lower than the SUV norm. Unusually wide doors also ease entry/exit.

Drivers face a dash that mimics those of Mercedes cars. Some controls are deployed differently, but they're easy to find and operate. Outward vision is fine forward and laterally, but a bit cluttered by headrests directly aft and over-the-shoulder.

Mercedes claims more cargo space than a Ford Explorer or Jeep Grand Cherokee. Load volume is certainly ample—and easy to use with the low, flat load floor. The spare tire mounts beneath it.

BUILD QUALITY It may be American-made, but the ML320 is every inch a Mercedes in its sturdy driving feel and careful detail workmanship. Some molded interior plastic looks slightly low-buck, though.

VALUE FOR THE MONEY With the Mercedes badge and a competitive $33,950 base price, the ML320 would be a hit even if it were mediocre. In fact, though, we think it leads the SUV pack for refinement, handling, and car-like convenience. That new Alabama plant won't be able to build 'em fast enough.

RATINGS

	ML320
Acceleration	3
Fuel economy	3
Ride quality	3
Steering/handling	4
Braking	3
Quietness	4
Driver seating	4
Instruments/controls	4
Room/comfort (front)	4
Room/comfort (rear)	3
Cargo room	4
Value for the money	4
Total	**43**

SPECIFICATIONS

	4-door wagon
Wheelbase, in.	111.0
Overall length, in.	180.6
Overall width, in.	73.2
Overall height, in.	69.9
Curb weight, lbs.	4200
Cargo vol., cu. ft.	85.4
Fuel capacity, gals.	19.0
Seating capacity	5
Front head room, in.	39.8
Max. front leg room, in.	40.3
Rear head room, in.	39.7
Min. rear leg room, in.	38.0

Rating Scale: 5-Excellent; 4-Above average; 3-Average; 2-Below average; 1-Poor

CONSUMER GUIDE™

ENGINES

	ohc V-6
Size, liters/cu. in.	3.2/195
Horsepower @ rpm..	215@ 5500
Torque (lbs./ft.) @ rpm......................................	233@ 3000
Availability	S
EPA city/highway mpg 5-speed OD automatic..	17/21

PRICES

Mercedes-Benz ML320	Retail Price	Dealer Invoice
Base 4-door wagon	$33950	$29540

STANDARD EQUIPMENT:

Base: 3.2-liter V-6 engine, 5-speed automatic transmission, full-time 4WD, anti-lock 4-wheel disc brakes, driver- and passenger-side air bags, front side-impact air bags, air conditioning, power windows, power door locks, heated power mirrors, rear window defogger, rear wiper/washer, power steering, tilt steering wheel, cruise control, AM/FM/cassette/weatherband with 4 speakers, remote keyless entry, tachometer, temperature gauge, oil pressure gauge, trip odometer, 6-way manual front seats, split folding rear seat, front and rear cupholders, front center armrest with storage, illuminated visor mirrors, cargo cover, illuminated entry, floormats, theft-deterrent system, rear fog lamp, 255/65R16 tires, alloy wheels.

OPTIONAL EQUIPMENT:
Major Packages

M1 Pkg.	2950	2570

Leather-trimmed seats, leather-wrapped steering wheel and shift knob, walnut interior trim, heated 8-way power front seats, automatic inside rear view mirror, trip computer, outside temperature indicator, lockable safebox, rear privacy glass.

M4 Pkg.	1595	1390

Includes running boards, mud guards, outside-mounted full size spare tire. Requires sunroof.

M7 Pkg., w/cloth upholstery	900	780
w/leather upholstery...	1050	910

Includes two third-row bucket seats, power rear quarter windows. Requires sunroof.

Comfort and Convenience

Power sunroof	1095	950
Bose sound system with 6-disc CD changer...	1050	910

Includes 6 speakers and subwoofer.

Appearance and Miscellaneous

Metallic paint	475	410

MERCEDES-BENZ S-CLASS/ CL-CLASS

Mercedes-Benz S-Class

Rear-wheel-drive luxury car
Base price range: $64,000-$135,300. Built in Germany.
Also consider: BMW 7-Series, Jaguar XJ Sedan, Lexus LS 400

FOR • Side air bags • Acceleration (except S320) • Ride • Passenger and cargo room (S-Class) • Steering/handling

AGAINST • Price • Fuel economy • Rear seat room (CL-Class)

Mercedes' largest, most opulent cars enter their eighth season with few changes as the German automaker readies redesigned smaller, lighter versions for a model-year 2000 debut in the U.S.

One change applies to the S500 and S600 coupes, which are rebadged CL500 and CL600 to avoid confusion with the S500 and S600 sedans. (Don't confuse the CLs with this year's new CLK320, a much smaller coupe based on Mercedes' compact C-Class sedan.)

As before, the S-Class starts with the 6-cylinder S320, which is available in standard- and longer-wheelbase form. It continues with the V-8 S420 and S500, and culminates with the V-12 S600, all on the longer wheelbase. Model numbers denote engine displacement: 3.2, 4.2, 5.0, and 6.0 liters.

The CL500/600 use a third, shorter wheelbase and differ in some dimensions. They are "pillarless hardtops" with no fixed center roof post.

For 1998, all these cars get Mercedes' new "Brake Assist" and "BabySmart" features as standard. The former applies full braking force in response to rapid brake-pedal movement to minimize "panic" stopping distances. BabySmart automatically deactivates the right front and side air bags when a special Mercedes-designed child seat is in place.

Pricewise, the S420, S500, and CL500 are unchanged from '97. V-12 models go up 1.5 percent, the two S320s by 1.1 percent. Also, Mercedes has cut $300 from the option price of its Electronic Stability Program anti-skid system for all S and CL models bar the V-12s, where it remains standard.

PERFORMANCE Acceleration runs from tepid on S320s to forceful on 600s (which do 0-60 mph in a claimed 6.3 seconds). Fuel economy also varies greatly, but it's not good in any case. The S320s have too little power for their weight, while other models simply have big, thirsty engines.

And make no mistake: These are some of the largest, heaviest cars around. Yet handling is surprisingly agile, all things considered, with steering, stopping, and cornering poise that inspire confidence. These are also some of the quietest cars around (helped on sedans by double-pane side windows), and all deliver a smooth, controlled ride on just about any surface.

ACCOMMODATIONS S-Class sedans boast limousine-like passenger and cargo space in keeping with their expansive exterior size.

The CL coupes come up a bit short in rear leg room, and aft entry/exit demands stooping past relatively long, heavy doors. Sedan access is no-sweat.

All these cars comfortably accommodate any size driver before a typical Mercedes dash with convenient if not always self-evident controls. Visibility is uniformly good.

BUILD QUALITY These are also some of the costliest cars around, so it's just as well they have tank-solid structures and superb detail finish. This is, after all, what you expect for such lofty prices.

VALUE FOR THE MONEY The S-Class sedans and CL coupes are among the world's finest automobiles, but plenty of alternatives cost thousands less yet don't lack for luxury and performance. More than most cars, if you're concerned about price, you can't afford one of these Mercedes-Benzes.

RATINGS	S320	S420	S500/ S600	CL500
Acceleration	3	4	5	5
Fuel economy	2	1	1	1
Ride quality	5	5	5	5
Steering/handling	4	4	4	4
Braking	5	5	5	5
Quietness	5	5	5	4
Driver seating	4	4	4	4
Instruments/controls	3	3	3	3
Room/comfort (front)	5	5	5	5
Room/comfort (rear)	4	5	5	3
Cargo room	4	4	4	3
Value for the money	3	3	3	3
Total	47	48	49	45

Prices are accurate at time of publication; subject to manufacturer's changes.

SPECIFICATIONS

	2-door coupe	4-door sedan	4-door sedan
Wheelbase, in.	115.9	119.7	123.6
Overall length, in.	199.4	201.3	205.2
Overall width, in.	75.3	74.3	74.3
Overall height, in.	56.9	58.5	58.5
Curb weight, lbs.	4700	4480	4700
Cargo vol., cu. ft.	14.2	15.6	15.6
Fuel capacity, gals.	26.4	26.4	26.4
Seating capacity	5	5	5
Front head room, in.	36.5	38.0	38.0
Max. front leg room, in.	41.7	41.3	41.3
Rear head room, in.	37.2	37.8	38.5
Min. rear leg room, in.	31.5	36.1	39.6

ENGINES

	dohc I-6	dohc V-8	dohc V-8	dohc V-12
Size, liters/cu. in.	3.2/195	4.2/256	5.0/303	6.0/365
Horsepower @ rpm	228@	275@	315@	389@
	5600	5700	5600	5200
Torque (lbs./ft.) @ rpm	232@	295@	347@	420@
	3750	3900	3900	3800
Availability	S[1]	S[2]	S[3]	S[4]
EPA city/highway mpg				
5-speed OD automatic	17/23	15/22	15/21	13/19

1. S320. 2. S420. 3. S500, CL500. 4. S600, CL600.

PRICES

Mercedes-Benz S-Class/CL-Class

	Retail Price	Dealer Invoice
S320 4-door sedan (119.7-inch wheelbase)	$64000	$55680
S320 4-door sedan (123.6-inch wheelbase)	67300	58550
S420 4-door sedan	73900	64290
S500 4-door sedan	87500	76120
CL500 2-door notchback	91900	79950
S600 4-door sedan	132250	115060
CL600 2-door notchback	135300	117710
Destination charge	595	595

S420/CL500 add Gas Guzzler Tax $1300. S500 add Gas Guzzler Tax $1700. CL600 add Gas Guzzler Tax $2600. S600 add Gas Guzzler Tax $3000.

STANDARD EQUIPMENT:

S320: 3.2-liter DOHC 6-cylinder engine, 5-speed automatic transmission, ASR traction control, driver- and passenger-side air bags w/automatic child seat recognition sytem, front side-impact air bags, anti-lock 4-wheel disc brakes, air conditioning w/dual-zone automatic climate control, variable-assist power steering, power tilt/telescopic steering column w/memory feature, leather-wrapped steering wheel and shift knob, cruise control, power memory mirrors, automatic day/night inside and driver-side outside mirror, power windows, power door locks, leather upholstery, remote keyless entry and decklid release, 12-way power front bucket seats w/memory feature, front storage console, power glass sunroof, Bose AM/FM/cassette, power antenna, tachometer, oil-pressure gauge, trip odometer, rear defogger, headlamp wipers/washers (123.6-inch wheelbase), rain-sensing windshield wipers, Homelink universal garage-door opener, front reading lights, rear reading lights, illuminated front and rear visor mirrors, floormats, cargo net, theft-deterrent system, front and rear fog lights, full-size spare tire, 225/60HR16 tires, alloy wheels.

S420 adds: 4.2-liter DOHC V-8 engine, 235/60HR16 tires.

S500/CL500 adds: 5.0-liter DOHC V-8 engine, automatic rear leveling system, upgraded leather upholstery (CL), heated front seats, heated rear seats (S), Parktronic system (CL), rear storage console (CL), Xenon headlamps.

S600/CL600 adds: 6.0-liter DOHC V-12 engine, upgraded leather upholstery, multicontour power front seats, power rear seats (S), rear dual-zone air conditioner, 6-disc CD changer, portable cellular telephone, power rear-window sunshade, Adaptive Damping System, Electronic Stability Program.

OPTIONAL EQUIPMENT:
Comfort and Convenience

	Retail Price	Dealer Invoice
Dual zone rear air conditioner, S320, S420, S500	1980	1723
Parktronic system, S320, S420, S500, S600	$975	$848
Power rear-window sunshade	495	431
Std. S600, CL600.		
Multicontour power front seats, each	390	339
Std. S600, CL600.		
4-place power seating, S500 4-door, S600 4-door	5540	4820
Power rear seat, S500	1750	1522
Heated front seats, S320, S420	595	518
Headlamp washers, S320 (119.7-inch wheelbase)	340	296

Appearance and Miscellaneous

	Retail Price	Dealer Invoice
Adaptive Damping System, S500, CL500	2270	1975
Includes automatic rear leveling system.		
Automatic rear leveling system, S320, S420	940	818
Electronic Stability Program, S320, S420, S500	990	861
Xenon headlamps, S320, S420	960	835

MERCEDES-BENZ SL-CLASS

Mercedes-Benz SL-Class

Rear-wheel-drive luxury coupe

Base price range: (1997 model) $79,600-$123,200. Built in Germany.

Also consider: Jaguar XK8, Lexus SC 300/400, Lincoln Mark VIII

FOR • Acceleration • Standard side air bags • Steering/handling • Braking

AGAINST • Fuel economy • Price • Cargo space

With introduction of the compact SLK230 roadster, the SL-Class becomes Mercedes-Benz's "senior" 2-seat convertible. SL is an abbreviation of "very light" in German, but there's nothing dainty about these two-ton cars, which come with a power soft top and a removable aluminum hardtop.

The entry-level 6-cylinder SL320 is dropped for '98, but Mercedes cuts the sticker price of the V-8 SL500 by $10,000, an 11-percent reduction. The cost of the SL500's anti-skid Electronic Stability Program (ESP) option also has been cut, by $300. The V-12 SL600 continues as a $125,000 limited edition with ESP standard.

Equipment on both SLs, already generous, expands with addition of Mercedes' "Brake Assist" and "BabySmart" features (described in the S-Class/CL-Class report). Also new are trunk-release and "panic" functions for the remote central-locking system.

Like other Mercedes cars, SLs come with door-mounted side air bags and an occupant detection sensor that deactivates both right-side air bags without a weight of at least 26 pounds on the passenger seat. Options include a glass-roof "Panorama" hardtop and a Sport Package with uprated suspension damping and 17-inch wheels.

PERFORMANCE Think of either SL as a German Corvette: less flashy, perhaps, but fast and quite complex. Engines have bags of torque, so the 500 does 0-60 mph in a swift 6 seconds, says Mercedes; the 600 is quicker still. Fuel economy is grim (both SLs carry a Gas Guzzler Tax), but if that's a concern, you're reading the wrong report.

Though too weighty and bulky to be genuine sports cars, the SLs are willing and capable on twisty roads, with enough muscle to power safely through corners without much body lean, tempered by standard traction control and/or the anti-skid ESP. Ride is always firm, becoming a bit jiggly on broken pavement, but it's quite comfortable for a short-wheelbase car. Brakes, powerful and fade-free, are well up to the heft. Engine noise is muted even in hard acceleration, but some wind rush

---

Rating Scale: 5-Excellent; 4-Above average; 3-Average; 2-Below average; 1-Poor

intrudes with the hardtop attached, and tire roar can annoy on coarse surfaces.

ACCOMMODATIONS The cockpit accommodates two adults of most any size, both of whom enjoy a multitude of seat adjustments. The driver also benefits from a power tilt/telescope steering wheel, which is linked with mirror and seat positions in the standard memory system. Cargo space usually is scarce in convertibles, and so it is here, but the trunk is usefully shaped and luxuriously finished. The low-built body hampers entry/exit somewhat.

Visibility is good with the hardtop in place, but it's big and heavy enough that two people are needed to remove or install it. The power soft top raises and lowers in an entertaining mechanical pirouette bested only by the metal roof on the little SLK. The SL dash generally works well, though deciphering some control icons may require consulting the owner's manual.

BUILD QUALITY Weight implies substance, and the SLs do feel substantial from behind the wheel. Materials and workmanship are appropriate for the prices, but there's more body shake over bumps than we think appropriate for convertibles this costly.

VALUE FOR THE MONEY No one needs a lush high-priced ragtop. If you've got the money, though, an SL delivers the pleasures of open-air driving with lots of comfort, safety, and style—not to mention speed. Of course, the SLK offers all this for far less money, but then, there's a long waiting list for that one.

RATINGS

	SL500	SL600
Acceleration	5	5
Fuel economy	2	1
Ride quality	3	3
Steering/handling	4	4
Braking	5	5
Quietness	4	4
Driver seating	4	4
Instruments/controls	3	3
Room/comfort (front)	4	4
Room/comfort (rear)	—	—
Cargo room	2	2
Value for the money	2	2
Total	**38**	**37**

SPECIFICATIONS

	2-door conv.
Wheelbase, in.	99.0
Overall length, in.	177.1
Overall width, in.	71.3
Overall height, in.	51.3
Curb weight, lbs.	4165
Cargo vol., cu. ft.	7.9
Fuel capacity, gals.	21.1
Seating capacity	2
Front head room, in.	37.1
Max. front leg room, in.	42.4
Rear head room, in.	—
Min. rear leg room, in.	—

ENGINES

	dohc V-8	dohc V-12
Size, liters/cu. in.	5.0/303	6.0/365
Horsepower @ rpm	315@ 5600	389@ 5200
Torque (lbs./ft.) @ rpm	343@ 3900	420@ 3800
Availability	S[1]	S[2]
EPA city/highway mpg 5-speed OD automatic	16/23	14/20

1. SL500. 2. SL600.

PRICES

1997 Mercedes-Benz SL-Class

	Retail Price	Dealer Invoice
SL320 2-door convertible	$79600	$69250
SL500 2-door convertible	89900	78210
SL600 2-door convertible	123200	107180
Destination charge	595	595
Gas Guzzler Tax, SL500	1300	1300
Gas Guzzler Tax, SL600	2100	2100

STANDARD EQUIPMENT:

SL320: 3.2-liter DOHC 6-cylinder engine, 5-speed automatic transmission, ASR traction control, anti-lock 4-wheel disc brakes, front air bags, side air bags, power steering, automatic climate control, cruise control, leather upholstery, 10-way power front seats w/memory feature, front storage console, power convertible top, power tilt/telescopic steering column w/memory feature, leather-wrapped steering wheel and shifter, Bose AM/FM/cassette, power antenna, power windows, power door locks, tachometer, oil-pressure gauges, trip odometer, illuminated visor mirrors, remote decklid and fuel-door release, power mirrors w/memory feature, rear defogger, remote keyless entry, Homelink universal garage-door opener, automatic variable intermittent wipers, theft-deterrent system, automatic day/night inside and driver-side outside mirrors, reading lights, heated headlamp wipers/washers, pop-up roll bar, front and rear fog lights, floormats, 225/55ZR16 tires, alloy wheels.

SL500 adds: 5.0-liter DOHC V-8 engine.

SL600 deletes headlight washer nozzles and adds: 6.0-liter DOHC V-12 engine, Adaptive Damping System, Electronic Stability Program, upgraded leather upholstery, 6-disc CD changer, portable cellular telephone, heated front seats, Xenon headlights.

OPTIONAL EQUIPMENT:

	Retail Price	Dealer Invoice
Major Packages		
40th Anniversary Edition, SL320, SL500	NC	NC

Includes unique leather interior and floormats, heated seats, CD changer, 245/45ZR17 tires (SL500), 6-spoke alloy wheels (SL500). Deletes all exterior badging except Mercedes logo.

Comfort and Convenience		
Heated front seats, SL320, SL500	$595	$518
Multicontour power front seats, each	380	331

Appearance and Miscellaneous		
Removable panorama roof	3500	3045
Xenon headlights, SL320, SL500	950	826

Deletes headlight washer nozzles.

Special Purpose, Wheels and Tires		
Adaptive Damping System, SL320, SL500	4325	3763

Includes automatic rear leveling system.

Electronic Stability Program, SL500	1290	1122
Sport Pkg.	4900	4263

Ground effects, 245/40ZR18 front tires, 275/35ZR18 rear tires, monoblock alloy wheels.

MERCEDES-BENZ SLK230

RECOMMENDED

Mercedes-Benz SLK

Rear-wheel-drive Sports and GT car
Base price: $39,700. Built in Germany.
Also consider: BMW Z3, Chevrolet Corvette, Mazda Miata, Mercedes-Benz SL-Class

FOR • Acceleration • Steering/handling • Side air bags

AGAINST • Cargo room

Here's Mercedes' answer to the "retro roadster" craze begun by the Mazda Miata and picked up by the BMW Z3 and Porsche Boxster.

Prices are accurate at time of publication; subject to manufacturer's changes.

SLK, which takes its name from German words meaning sporty, light, and compact, was voted the 1997 North American Car of the Year by journalists.

Mercedes-Benz's compact C-Class sedan was the starting point for this novel 2-seat hardtop-convertible, which has a metal roof that folds into the trunk at the touch of a button. The trunk lid opens forward for cargo and tilts from the rear to raise or lower the top—an operation that takes just 25 seconds.

The SLK has a 2.3-liter 4-cylinder engine with supercharger (hence the "Kompressor" badge on front fenders) and 5-speed automatic transmission. Standard equipment includes dash and door air bags, traction control, and Mercedes' "BabySmart" feature that automatically deactivates the right-side air bags with a special Mercedes child seat installed.

PERFORMANCE Though more luxury tourer than pure sports car, the SLK is a fun drive, with precise steering, grippy cornering, and adroit overall balance. Acceleration off the line is a bit leisurely, but speed gathers quickly once the supercharger hits full puff at about 3000 rpm. Mid-range power is strong, but in some situations there's a lag between flooring the throttle and feeling extra thrust, a delay that can be frustrating in city driving.

The transmission furnishes the right gear for most occasions and smooth, generally prompt shift action. It also helps fuel economy. We averaged nearly 24 mpg for 600 miles of fast highway driving. Expect 17-18 mpg in city/suburban work with a light right foot.

Though smooth for a four, the engine emits an unbecoming growl when worked hard. The exhaust is audible too, but things settle down to a low hum at cruising speeds, and wind noise is modest with the top and windows raised. Road rumble is prominent except on glassy asphalt, a penalty of the aggressive tires. Those tires also make for a thumpy ride over expansion joints and broken pavement, but big ruts and bumps are smothered quite well.

ACCOMMODATIONS Entry/exit is tricky with the low-slung build, and the driving position is snug, but 6-footers won't complain in either seat, both of which are firm and comfortable for long drives. The haute-couture gauges and control layout are informative and entertaining. But we're dismayed by door windows that don't quite lower all the way, leaving a half-inch ridge of glass.

The hardtop lowers in a trice, but cuts trunk space by two-thirds, to little more than three cubic feet below a pull-out vinyl cover. That cover must be deployed to operate the top, because it's really a safety switch to prevent the roof from accidentally crushing stuff. Top up, the trunk's 9.5 cubic feet will carry soft baggage for two on a long weekend, but the space is very oddly shaped.

BUILD QUALITY SLK has that carved-from-granite solidity expected of a Mercedes. There are some minor body tremors with the top down, but only on very rough roads. Too bad the dashboard's pop-out cupholder is so cheap and the radio reception is surprisingly mediocre.

VALUE FOR THE MONEY It's a coupe, it's a convertible, it's a Mercedes, and it's fun, and that's why there's a waiting list for SLKs. Discounts? Not anytime soon. Though a V-8 Corvette and 6-cylinder Z3 go for similar money, there's nothing else quite like the SLK.

RATINGS

	SLK
Acceleration	4
Fuel economy	2
Ride quality	3
Steering/handling	4
Braking	5
Quietness	3
Driver seating	4
Instruments/controls	4
Room/comfort (front)	4
Room/comfort (rear)	—
Cargo room	2
Value for the money	2
Total	**37**

Rating Scale: 5-Excellent; 4-Above average; 3-Average; 2-Below average; 1-Poor

SPECIFICATIONS

	2-door conv.
Wheelbase, in.	94.5
Overall length, in.	157.3
Overall width, in.	67.5
Overall height, in.	50.7
Curb weight, lbs.	3036
Cargo vol., cu. ft.	9.5
Fuel capacity, gals.	14.0
Seating capacity	2
Front head room, in.	37.4
Max. front leg room, in.	42.7
Rear head room, in.	—
Min. rear leg room, in.	—

ENGINES

	Super dohc I-4
Size, liters/cu. in.	2.3/140
Horsepower @ rpm	185@ 5300
Torque (lbs./ft.) @ rpm	200@ 2500
Availability	S

EPA city/highway mpg

5-speed OD automatic	22/30

PRICES

Mercedes-Benz SLK230	Retail Price	Dealer Invoice
SLK 2-door convertible	$39700	$34540
Destination charge	600	600

STANDARD EQUIPMENT:

SLK: 2.3-liter supercharged DOHC 4-cylinder engine, 5-speed automatic transmission, ASR Traction System, driver- and passenger-side air bags with BabySmart automatic child recognition system, door mounted side-impact air bags, anti-lock 4-wheel disc brakes, power steering, air conditioning and dual-zone climate control with dust/pollen filter, cruise control, leather upholstery, cupholders and coinholders, rear window defroster, manually telescoping steering wheel, leather-wrapped steering wheel, power locks, power windows, power heated mirrors, outside temperature readout, integrated garage door opener, AM/FM/cassette, remote keyless entry, remote trunk release, tachometer, power retractable steel hardtop, tinted glass, theft-deterrent system, heated headlight washers, fog lamps, 205/55R16 tires (front), 225/50R16 tires (rear), alloy wheels.

OPTIONAL EQUIPMENT:
Comfort and Convenience

Heated seats	595	518
K1 Pkg.	1495	1087
Includes integrated mobile phone and 6-disc CD changer.		
K2 Pkg.	1895	1445
Includes integrated portable phone and 6-disc CD changer.		

Appearance and Miscellaneous

Metallic paint	600	522

MERCURY GRAND MARQUIS

Mercury Grand Marquis LS

Rear-wheel-drive full-size car; similar to Ford Crown Victoria

Base price range: (1997 model) $22,495-$23,930. Built in Canada.

Also consider: Buick LeSabre, Chrysler Concorde, Toyota Avalon

FOR • Passenger and cargo room • Optional anti-lock brakes and traction control

AGAINST • Fuel economy

Mercury revises its biggest car for 1998, giving it new front and rear styling along with a revamped suspension, larger brakes, and a standard anti-theft system. Grand Marquis is near twin of the Ford Crown Victoria and, with General Motors discontinuing its full-size rear-drive cars, they're the only surviving American offerings of their type.

Grand Marquis comes in GS and LS price levels, both with a 4.6-liter V-8 engine of 200 horsepower, up 10 from last year, and automatic transmission. An optional Handling Package includes dual exhausts that adding 15 more horsepower, a lower rear axle ratio for faster getaways, performance tires and suspension, and rear load-leveling air springs.

Four-wheel disc brakes are standard on Grand Marquis; anti-lock brakes and traction control are optional. Maximum trailer weight is 2000 pounds.,

We have not driven the 1998 Grand Marquis and so cannot comment on its performance.

SPECIFICATIONS

	4-door sedan
Wheelbase, in.	114.4
Overall length, in.	212.0
Overall width, in.	77.9
Overall height, in.	56.8
Curb weight, lbs.	3917
Cargo vol., cu. ft.	20.6
Fuel capacity, gals.	19.0
Seating capacity	6
Front head room, in.	39.4
Max. front leg room, in.	42.5
Rear head room, in.	38.0
Min. rear leg room, in.	39.6

ENGINES

	ohc V-8	ohc V-8
Size, liters/cu. in.	4.6/281	4.6/281
Horsepower @ rpm	200@ 4250	215@ 4500
Torque (lbs./ft.) @ rpm	265@ 3000	275@ 3000
Availability	S	O
EPA city/highway mpg		
4-speed OD automatic	17/25	17/25

PRICES

1997 Mercury Grand Marquis	Retail Price	Dealer Invoice
GS 4-door notchback	$22495	$21001
LS 4-door notchback	23930	22294
Destination charge	605	605

All models require a Preferred Equipment Pkg.

STANDARD EQUIPMENT:

GS: 4.6-liter V-8 engine, 4-speed automatic transmission, 4-wheel disc brakes, variable-assist power steering, driver- and passenger-side air bags, air conditioning, cloth bench seats, 6-way power driver seat, front and rear folding armrests, power windows, power mirrors, solar-control tinted glass, tilt steering wheel, oil-pressure and coolant-temperature gauges, voltmeter, trip odometer, digital clock, AM/FM/cassette, integrated rear-window antenna, intermittent wipers, rear defogger, passenger-side visor mirror, automatic headlamps, rear heat ducts, 215/70R15 whitewall tires, wheel covers.

LS adds: upgraded upholstery, rear-seat headrests, power driver-seat lumbar adjuster.

OPTIONAL EQUIPMENT:	Retail Price	Dealer Invoice
Major Packages		
Preferred Pkg. 157A, GS (credit)	($860)	($764)

Group 1 (cruise control, floormats, radial-spoke wheel covers), Group 2 (Power Lock Group [power door locks, remote decklid release], illuminated entry).

Preferred Pkg. 172A, LS (credit)	(80)	(71)

Group 1 (cruise control, floormats), Group 2, Group 3 (Luxury Light Group [includes underhood light, dual dome/map lights, rear reading lights, dual secondary sun visors, illuminated visor mirrors], striping, leather-wrapped steering wheel, remote keyless entry, cornering lamps, alloy wheels).

Preferred Pkg. 173A, LS	1755	1559

Pkg. 172A plus Group 4 (anti-lock brakes with Traction-Assist, Electronic Group [includes digital instrumentation, tripminder computer, heavy-duty battery], automatic climate control, outside-temperature indicator, automatic day/night mirror, premium cassette player w/upgraded speakers and amplifier, power passenger seat).

Luxury Light Group, GS	190	169

Includes dual dome/map lights, rear reading lights, dual secondary sun visors, illuminated visor mirrors.

Electronic Group, LS	455	405

Digital instrumentation, tripminder computer. Requires Automatic climate control, premium cassette player w/upgraded speakers and amplifier.

Handling Pkg., GS	1020	908
LS	600	534

Includes rear air suspension, tuned suspension, larger stabilizer bars, power steering fluid cooler, dual exhaust, 3.27 axle ratio, 225/60R16 handling whitewall tires, alloy wheels.

Safety Features

Anti-lock brakes w/Traction-Assist	695	619

Comfort and Convenience

Automatic climate control, LS	175	156

Includes outside-temperature indicator.

Keyless entry system, GS	240	213
Power front passenger seat, LS	360	321
Leather upholstery, LS	735	654

Requires power front passenger seat.

Premium cassette player, LS	360	321

Includes upgraded speakers, amplifier. Requires automatic climate control.

Full-size spare tire, LS	185	165
LS w/Handling Pkg.	240	213

Appearance and Miscellaneous

Cast alloy wheels, LS	NC	NC
Striping, GS	60	54
Engine-block heater	25	23

MERCURY MOUNTAINEER

✓ BEST BUY

Mercury Mountaineer

Rear- or 4-wheel-drive midsize sport-utility vehicle; similar to Ford Explorer

Base price range: (1997 model) $27,240-$29,240. Built in Louisville, Ky.

Also consider: Chevrolet Blazer, Jeep Grand Cherokee, Mercedes-Benz ML320, Toyota 4Runner

FOR • Standard anti-lock brakes • Acceleration • Passenger and cargo room • Visibility

Prices are accurate at time of publication; subject to manufacturer's changes.

AGAINST • Fuel economy

Mountaineer, a clone of the highly successful Ford Explorer, was introduced last year as Mercury's first sport-utility vehicle. Changes for '98 include the adoption of an overhead-cam V-6 with 5-speed automatic as the standard powertrain, and styling refinements, such as a new grille and standard two-tone paint.

Explorer comes in 2- and 4-door body styles, but all Mountaineers are 4-door wagons with a choice of rear-wheel drive or 4-wheel drive. With the V-6, the 4WD system is Ford's Control Trac, which offers 2WD and three 4WD modes, one of which can be left engaged on dry pavement. Last year's only powertrain was a 5.0-liter V-8, 4-speed automatic transmission, and permanently-engaged 4WD. That powertrain is optional for '98.

There's a wider choice of audio systems this year, including one that plays both CDs and cassettes and raises its volume as vehicle speed increases.

Mountaineer doesn't offer Explorer's base 4.0-liter overhead-valve V-6, but is otherwise mechanically identical to similarly equipped Explorers and provides the same performance and accommodations.

See the Ford Explorer report for an evaluation of the Mountaineer.

RATINGS

	4WD V-6	AWD V-8
Acceleration	4	4
Fuel economy	2	1
Ride quality	3	3
Steering/handling	3	3
Braking	4	4
Quietness	3	3
Driver seating	4	4
Instruments/controls	4	4
Room/comfort (front)	4	4
Room/comfort (rear)	3	3
Cargo room	5	5
Value for the money	4	4
Total	**43**	**42**

SPECIFICATIONS

	4-door wagon
Wheelbase, in.	111.5
Overall length, in.	188.5
Overall width, in.	70.2
Overall height, in.	67.6
Curb weight, lbs.	4139
Cargo vol., cu. ft.	81.6
Fuel capacity, gals.	21.0
Seating capacity	5
Front head room, in.	39.9
Max. front leg room, in.	42.4
Rear head room, in.	39.3
Min. rear leg room, in.	37.7

ENGINES

	ohc V-6	ohv V-8
Size, liters/cu. in.	4.0/245	5.0/302
Horsepower @ rpm	205@5000	215@4200
Torque (lbs./ft.) @ rpm	250@3000	288@3300
Availability	S	O

EPA city/highway mpg

4-speed OD automatic		14/18
5-speed OD automatic	15/19	

PRICES

1997 Mercury Mountaineer

	Retail Price	Dealer Invoice
4-door wagon, 2WD	$27240	$24591
4-door wagon, AWD	29240	26351
Destination charge	525	525

All models require a Preferred Equipment Pkg.

STANDARD EQUIPMENT:

5.0-liter V-8 engine, 4-speed automatic transmission, limited-slip differential, anti-lock 4-wheel disc brakes, driver- and passenger-side air bags, air conditioning, power steering, cruise control, cloth front bucket seats w/leather headrests, split folding rear seat, floor console, tilt leather-wrapped steering wheel, power mirrors, power windows, power door locks, tachometer, trip odometer, front solar-tinted glass, rear privacy glass, rear wiper/washer, rear defogger, AM/FM/cassette, digital clock, visor mirrors, speed-sensitive intermittent wipers, auxiliary power outlets, dual-note horn, door map pockets, map lights, bright grille, scuff plates, skid plate (AWD), fog lamps, 235/75R15 all-terrain outline white-letter tires, full-size spare, alloy wheels.

OPTIONAL EQUIPMENT:

	Retail Price	Dealer Invoice
Major Packages		
Preferred Equipment Pkg. 650A	$230	$195
Running boards, roof rack, floormats		
Preferred Equipment Pkg. 655A	1415	1203
Pkg. 650A plus 6-way power front seats w/power lumbar support, upgraded floor console (includes rear climate and radio controls, cupholders), overhead console (includes outside temperature gauge, compass, reading lamps, storage), Electronics Group, cargo cover.		
Electronics Group	370	314
Includes remote keyless entry, anti-theft system, auto-locking. Requires 6-way power seats.		
Comfort and Convenience		
6-way power front seats	955	812
Includes power lumbar support.		
Leather upholstery	655	557
Requires Pkg. 655A.		
Integrated child seats	200	170
Requires Pkg. 655A and leather upholstery.		
Automatic day/night rearview mirror	185	158
Includes automatic on/off headlamps. Requires Pkg. 655A.		
High Series floor console	390	332
Includes rear climate controls, cupholders.		
Overhead storage console	175	149
Includes outside temperature gauge, compass, reading lamps, storage.		
Power moonroof	800	680
Requires Pkg. 655A.		
JBL Sound System w/Luxury Cassette	830	706
Requires Pkg. 655A.		
CD player	65	55
6-disc CD changer	370	314
Requires Pkg. 655A.		
Appearance and Miscellaneous		
Running boards	395	336
Roof rack	140	119
Cargo cover	80	68
Engine block heater	35	30
Floormats	45	38

MERCURY MYSTIQUE

RECOMMENDED

Mercury Mystique LS

Front-wheel-drive compact; similar to Ford Contour

Base price range: $16,235-$17,645. Built in Kansas City, Mo., and Mexico.

Also consider: Mazda 626, Mitsubishi Galant, Nissan Altima

Rating Scale: 5-Excellent; 4-Above average; 3-Average; 2-Below average; 1-Poor

FOR • Optional anti-lock brakes • Acceleration (V-6) • Steering/handling

AGAINST • Road noise • Engine noise (4-cylinder) • Rear seat room

Like its Contour sibling at Ford, the 1998 edition of the Mystique went on sale last March. Both are derived from the European Ford Mondeo, but have different styling. This fall, as part of Ford Motor Company's model streamlining, Mercury drops the base Mystique, leaving GS and LS models.

The '98 Mystique got a redesigned grille, headlamps, and hood. A built-in rear child-safety seat joined the options list. The new center console has three cupholders—two in front and one in back—and there's a new folding armrest for the driver's seat. The center rear seat gains a 3-point lap-shoulder belt in place of instead of just a lap belt. Re-contoured cushions provided an additional half-inch of rear leg room.

GS models come only with a 2.0-liter 4-cylinder engine, while the LS comes only with a 2.5-liter V-6. Manual transmission is standard, automatic is optional, as are anti-lock brakes.

Mystique's performance and accommodations mirror those of similarly equipped Contours.

See the Ford Contour for an evaluation of the Mystique.

RATINGS

	LS	GS
Acceleration	4	3
Fuel economy	3	3
Ride quality	3	4
Steering/handling	4	3
Braking	4	3
Quietness	3	3
Driver seating	3	3
Instruments/controls	4	4
Room/comfort (front)	3	3
Room/comfort (rear)	3	3
Cargo room	2	2
Value for the money	4	4
Total	40	38

SPECIFICATIONS

	4-door sedan
Wheelbase, in.	106.5
Overall length, in.	184.8
Overall width, in.	69.1
Overall height, in.	54.5
Curb weight, lbs.	2808
Cargo vol., cu. ft.	13.9
Fuel capacity, gals.	14.5
Seating capacity	5
Front head room, in.	39.0
Max. front leg room, in.	42.4
Rear head room, in.	36.8
Min. rear leg room, in.	34.4

ENGINES

	dohc I-4	dohc V-6
Size, liters/cu. in.	2.0/121	2.5/155
Horsepower @ rpm	125@ 5500	170@ 6250
Torque (lbs./ft.) @ rpm	130@ 4000	165@ 4250
Availability	S[1]	S[2]
EPA city/highway mpg		
5-speed OD manual	24/35	18/28
4-speed OD automatic	24/32	21/30

1. GS. 2. LS.

PRICES

Mercury Mystique	Retail Price	Dealer Invoice
GS 4-door sedan	$16235	$14844
LS 4-door sedan	17645	16099
Destination charge	535	535

STANDARD EQUIPMENT:

GS: 2.0-liter DOHC 4-cylinder engine, 5-speed manual transmission, driver- and passenger-side air bags, air conditioning, cruise control, power mirrors, power windows, power door locks, rear defogger, power steering, tilt steering wheel, cloth reclining front bucket seats, front storage console, tachometer, coolant-temperature gauge, trip odometer, AM/FM/cassette, digital clock, intermittent wipers, remote decklid release, interior air filter, visor mirrors, solar-control tinted glass, 185/70R14 tires, wheel covers.

LS adds: 2.5-liter V-6 engine, 4-wheel disc brakes (w/manual transmission), 10-way power driver seat, remote keyless entry, leather upholstery, leather-wrapped steering wheel, 60/40 split folding rear seat, variable intermittent wipers, illuminated passenger-side visor mirror, floormats, fog lights, performance suspension and steering, 205/60R15 tires, polished Mach alloy wheels.

OPTIONAL EQUIPMENT:

	Retail Price	Dealer Invoice
Major Packages		
Sport Group, GS	$395	$352
Leather-wrapped steering wheel, sport floormats, rear spoiler, fog lights, sport badging.		
Powertrains		
4-speed automatic transmission	815	725
Safety Features		
Anti-lock brakes	500	445
Integrated child seat, GS	135	120
LS	NC	NC
NA w/leather upholstery.		
Comfort and Convenience		
Split folding rear seat, GS	205	182
10-way power driver seat, GS	350	312
Power moonroof	595	530
Remote keyless entry, GS	190	169
Premium cassette player	135	120
CD player	275	245
Includes premium sound.		
Power antenna	95	85
Smokers Pkg.	15	13
Includes ashtray, cigarette lighter.		
Floormats, GS	55	49
Appearance and Miscellaneous		
Rear spoiler, GS, LS	245	218
Engine-block heater	20	18
Mach alloy wheels, GS	475	423
Includes 205/60R15 tires.		
Polished Mach alloy wheels, GS	475	423
Includes 205/60R15 tires.		

MERCURY SABLE

Mercury Sable GS wagon

Front-wheel-drive midsize; similar to Ford Taurus

Base price range: $19,445-$22,285. Built in Atlanta, Ga., and Chicago, Ill.

Also consider: Honda Accord, Toyota Camry

FOR • Optional anti-lock brakes • Acceleration (LS) • Steering/handling • Passenger and cargo room

AGAINST • Rear visibility

Sable is functionally identical to the Ford Taurus but has different styling, which this year is altered by a new grille. Ford also offers a high-performance V-8 model that isn't available as a Mercury.

Prices are accurate at time of publication; subject to manufacturer's changes.

Sable comes as a sedan or wagon in GS and LS price levels. Both have a 3.0-liter V-6 engine and automatic transmission, but the GS engine is an overhead-valve design with 145 horsepower and the LS's is a double-overhead-cam with 200.

For '98, the LS gets a numerically higher axle ratio designed to provide better off-the-line punch. The dual air bags are depowered this year to deploy with less force. Anti-lock brakes are optional.

Seating for five is available with front bucket seats and for six with a front bench. A 2-passenger rear-facing third seat is optional on wagons.

Sable's performance and accommodations duplicate those of similarly equipped Taurus models.

See the Ford Taurus for an evaluation of the Sable.

RATINGS

	GS (ohv V-6)	LS (dohc V-6)
Acceleration	3	4
Fuel economy	2	2
Ride quality	4	4
Steering/handling	4	4
Braking	4	4
Quietness	4	4
Driver seating	4	4
Instruments/controls	4	4
Room/comfort (front)	4	4
Room/comfort (rear)	4	3
Cargo room	3	3
Value for the money	4	4
Total	**44**	**44**

SPECIFICATIONS

	4-door sedan	4-door wagon
Wheelbase, in.	108.5	108.5
Overall length, in.	199.7	199.1
Overall width, in.	73.0	73.0
Overall height, in.	55.4	57.6
Curb weight, lbs.	3388	3536
Cargo vol., cu. ft.	16.0	81.3
Fuel capacity, gals.	16.0	16.0
Seating capacity	6	8
Front head room, in.	39.4	39.3
Max. front leg room, in.	42.2	42.2
Rear head room, in.	36.6	38.9
Min. rear leg room, in.	38.9	38.5

ENGINES

	ohv V-6	dohc V-6
Size, liters/cu. in.	3.0/182	3.0/181
Horsepower @ rpm	145@ 5250	200@ 5750
Torque (lbs./ft.) @ rpm	170@ 3250	200@ 4500
Availability	S[1]	S[2]

EPA city/highway mpg

4-speed OD automatic	20/28	19/28

1. GS. 2. LS.

PRICES

Mercury Sable	Retail Price	Dealer Invoice
GS 4-door sedan	$19445	$17781
LS 4-door sedan	20445	18761
LS 4-door wagon	22285	20309
LS Premium 4-door sedan	20445	18761
LS Premium 4-door wagon	22285	20309
Destination charge	550	550

LS Premium models require Premium Pkg.

STANDARD EQUIPMENT:

GS: 3.0-liter V-6 engine, 4-speed automatic transmission, driver- and passenger-side air bags, air conditioning, variable-assist power steering, cruise control, tilt steering wheel, 6-passenger seating (cloth upholstery, reclining front bucket seats w/center seating console, 60/40 split folding rear seat), cupholders, front armrest, tachometer, coolant temperature gauge, trip odometer, AM/FM/cassette player w/six speakers, digital clock, power mirrors, power windows, power door locks, variable intermittent wipers, rear defogger,

remote decklid release, visor mirrors, rear heat ducts, solar-control tinted glass, 205/65R15 tires, wheel covers.

LS/LS Premium sedan adds: rear air conditioning, interior air filter, 5-passenger seating (cloth/leather upholstery, reclining front bucket seats w/6-way power driver seat, 60/40 split folding rear seat), rear armrest, floor console, leather-wrapped steering wheel and shifter, remote keyless entry, remote fuel-door release, Light Group (courtesy, reading, map and dome lights), alloy wheels.

LS/LS Premium wagon adds: 4-wheel disc brakes, rear wiper/washer, power antenna, cargo tie-downs, cargo-area light, luggage rack, deletes remote rear decklid release.

OPTIONAL EQUIPMENT:

	Retail Price	Dealer Invoice
Major Packages		
Premium Pkg., LS Premium sedan	$825	$735
LS Premium wagon	675	601
Duratec 3.0-liter dohc V-6 engine, automatic air conditioning, automatic headlights, illuminated visor mirrors, power antenna (sedan), key pad entry system, theft-deterrent system.		
Powertrains		
Duratec 3.0-liter dohc V-6 engine, GS, LS	495	441
Safety Features		
Anti-lock 4-wheel disc brakes, GS	600	534
Includes 4-wheel disc brakes.		
Daytime running lights	40	36
Includes heavy-duty battery.		
Integrated child seat, wagon	135	120
Comfort and Convenience		
Remote keyless entry, GS	190	169
Light Group, GS	45	41
Courtesy, reading, map, and dome lights.		
Power moonroof, LS, LS Premium	740	658
Ford Mach audio system, LS	400	357
LS Premium	320	286
Sedan includes power antenna.		
6-disc CD changer	350	312
Leather upholstery, LS, LS Premium	895	797
Bucket seats with center console, GS	NC	NC
Front split bench seat, LS, LS Premium	NC	NC
Rear-facing third seat, wagon	200	178
Interior air filter, GS	30	27
Heated mirrors	35	31
Floormats	55	49
Wagon Group, wagon	140	124
Cargo-area cover, cargo net.		
Appearance and Miscellaneous		
Engine-block heater	35	31
Full-size spare tire	125	112
Alloy wheels, GS	315	280
Chrome alloy wheels, LS, LS Premium	580	516

MERCURY TRACER

Front-wheel-drive subcompact; similar to Ford Escort

Base price range: (1997 models) $11,145-$12,660. Built in Wayne, Mich., and Mexico.

Also consider: Chevrolet Prizm, Honda Civic, Toyota Corolla

FOR • Optional anti-lock brakes • Fuel economy

AGAINST • Road noise • Rear seat room

Rating Scale: 5-Excellent; 4-Above average; 3-Average; 2-Below average; 1-Poor

Mercury Tracer Trio sedan

Mercury's smallest model is a clone of the Ford Escort save for some distinctive styling touches, though Tracer doesn't offer a version of the sporty 2-door Escort ZX2. Tracer registers only minor changes for '98.

It comes as a 4-door sedan in GS and LS trim, and as an LS wagon. A sporty Trio package with fog lamps, alloy wheels, a spoiler, and other interior and exterior features is available on the LS sedan.

The only engine is a 2.0-liter 4-cylinder with manual transmission or optional automatic. Anti-lock brakes are optional, and like Escort, Tracer's dual air bags are depowered for '98 to deploy with less force.

The center console is larger this year, and the premium sound system is now a stand-alone option available on all models; it had been available only on the LS.

Tracer's performance and accommodations are the same as those of like-equipped Escorts.

See the Ford Escort/ZX2 report for an evaluation of the Tracer.

RATINGS

	Sedan	Wagon
Acceleration	3	3
Fuel economy	3	3
Ride quality	4	4
Steering/handling	3	3
Braking	3	3
Quietness	3	3
Driver seating	4	4
Instruments/controls	4	4
Room/comfort (front)	3	3
Room/comfort (rear)	3	3
Cargo room	2	4
Value for the money	5	5
Total	40	42

SPECIFICATIONS

	4-door sedan	4-door wagon
Wheelbase, in.	98.4	98.4
Overall length, in.	174.7	172.7
Overall width, in.	67.0	67.0
Overall height, in.	53.3	53.9
Curb weight, lbs.	2469	2532
Cargo vol., cu. ft.	12.8	63.4
Fuel capacity, gals.	12.8	12.8
Seating capacity	5	5
Front head room, in.	39.0	38.7
Max. front leg room, in.	42.5	42.5
Rear head room, in.	36.7	39.1
Min. rear leg room, in.	34.0	34.0

ENGINES

	ohc I-4
Size, liters/cu. in.	2.0/121
Horsepower @ rpm	110@ 5000
Torque (lbs./ft.) @ rpm	125@ 3750
Availability	S
EPA city/highway mpg	
4-speed OD automatic	26/34
5-speed OD manual	28/37

PRICES

1997 Mercury Tracer	Retail Price	Dealer Invoice
GS 4-door notchback	$11145	$10442

	Retail Price	Dealer Invoice
LS 4-door notchback	$11950	$11175
LS 4-door wagon	12660	11821
Destination charge	415	415

LS requires Preferred Pkg.

STANDARD EQUIPMENT:

GS: 2.0-liter 4-cylinder engine, 5-speed manual transmission, driver- and passenger-side air bags, power steering, cloth and vinyl reclining bucket seats, folding rear seat, center console with cupholders, tinted glass, dual mirrors, coolant temperature gauge, trip odometer, AM/FM radio, digital clock, variable intermittent wipers, door pockets, 185/65R14 tires, wheel covers.

LS adds: upgraded upholstery, 60/40 split rear seatback, tachometer, passenger-side visor mirror, color-keyed bodyside moldings, bolt-on full wheel covers.

Wagon adds: cargo cover.

OPTIONAL EQUIPMENT:
Major Packages

	Retail	Dealer
Preferred Pkg. 541A, LS	835	743
Air conditioning, rear defogger, power mirrors, driver-side remote keyless entry.		
Preferred Pkg. 542A, LS	1530	1361
Pkg. 541A plus power windows, power door locks w/anti-theft system, cassette player.		
Convenience Group, LS	355	316
Cruise control, tilt steering wheel, dual visor mirrors, map lights, floormats.		
Trio Pkg., LS notchback	495	441
Fog lamps, decklid spoiler, bright exhaust outlets, alloy wheels.		
Wagon Group, wagon	240	213
Rear wiper/washer, roof rack.		

Safety Features

Integrated child seat, LS	135	120
Anti-lock 4-wheel disc brakes	570	507

Powertrains

4-speed automatic transmission	815	725

Comfort and Convenience

Air conditioning, GS	795	708
Rear defogger, GS	190	169
AM/FM/cassette	165	147
Requires rear defroster or air conditioning.		
AM/FM/cassette w/6-disc CD changer, LS	515	458
LS w/Preferred Equipment Pkg. 542A	350	312
Includes premium sound system.		

Appearance and Miscellaneous

Floormats	45	40

Special Purpose, Wheels and Tires

Alloy wheels, LS	265	236

MERCURY VILLAGER

Mercury Villager Nautica

Front-wheel-drive minivan; similar to Nissan Quest
Base price range: (1997 model) $20,215-$26,915. Built in Avon Lake, Ohio.

Prices are accurate at time of publication; subject to manufacturer's changes.

Also consider: Chevrolet Venture, Dodge Caravan, Toyota Sienna

FOR • Passenger and cargo room • Steering/handling
• Standard anti-lock brakes

AGAINST • Passing power • Control layout • Fuel economy

Villager is built from the same design and uses the same powertrain as the Nissan Quest. The two are built at a Ford plant in Ohio, and differ in styling details and available features. Both come in a single body length, and are equivalent in size to a regular-length Dodge Caravan. They have a single sliding passenger-side door and a one-piece rear liftgate, which can be ordered with an optional flip-up window.

GS, LS, and first-cabin Nautica models are offered, all with seven-passenger seating. For '98, the GS comes with the four captain's-chair setup that's standard on the LS and Nautica. Optional on GS and LS in place of the second row of buckets is a two-passenger bench seat that can be fitted with two integrated child safety seats. A three-passenger rear bench is standard on all models. This seat can slide fore-and-aft on tracks in the floor.

Nissan supplies the only powertrain, a 3.0-liter V-6 mated to an automatic transmission. Depowered dual air bags that deploy with less force are standard. Traction control is optional. Anti-lock brakes are optional on the GS and standard on the others.

PERFORMANCE Because it has much in common with Nissan's Maxima sedan, the Villager, as well as the Quest, is a quite, car-like minivan. The engine is smooth, generally hushed, and strong enough for routine errand-running, but steep hills or any sizable load slow acceleration noticeably. We timed one at 11.9 seconds to 60 mph, which is adequate, but that was with just the driver and no cargo aboard. Fuel economy is so-so at best. We averaged 17-18 mpg in urban driving, low 20s on the highway.

Villager handles with more poise than some cars thanks to quick, responsive steering and only moderate body lean in hard cornering. The rear axle tends to react abruptly over some pavement flaws, but the suspension is generally absorbent, the ride stable and comfortable. Wind and road noise are well tamed in town, but rise appreciably at highway speeds, especially for those in the rear seats.

ACCOMMODATIONS The car-like nature of these vans shows up in a low step-in that allows easy entry/exit. Other plus-points include a comfortable driving posture, good visibility, and an ample supply of cupholders and cubbies. On the debit side are low-mounted controls for stereo and climate system that make a long reach for the driver. In addition, the buttons are hard to operate with gloves on.

Modest minivan dimensions limit what Villager and Quest can haul. Passenger room is generous in front and adequate at other positions, but there's scant cargo space with all seats in use. The handy sliding third-row seat provides lots of options for dividing the available space between people and packages, but the middle bench is heavy and thus clumsy to remove or install.

BUILD QUALITY We've tested a number of Villagers in the last couple of years, and nearly all exhibited a few squeaks and rattles, but were otherwise well assembled. One had some orange-peel texture to the paint, but the others looked fine.

VALUE FOR THE MONEY Villager and Quest are pleasant minivans with some clever features but need more power to be a practical all-round proposition for larger families. Lack of a left-side rear passenger door is another demerit. But if you value family-car finesse over cargo space and towing ability, Villager and Quest earn a look.

RATINGS

	GS	LS/ Nautica
Acceleration	3	3
Fuel economy	2	2
Ride quality	3	3
Steering/handling	3	3
Braking	3	4
Quietness	3	3
Driver seating	4	4
Instruments/controls	3	3
Room/comfort (front)	4	4
Room/comfort (rear)	3	3
Cargo room	5	5
Value for the money	3	3
Total	**39**	**40**

SPECIFICATIONS

	3-door van
Wheelbase, in.	112.2
Overall length, in.	189.9
Overall width, in.	73.8
Overall height, in.	65.6
Curb weight, lbs.	3815
Cargo vol., cu. ft.	120.0
Maximum payload, lbs.	1200
Fuel capacity, gals.	20.0
Seating capacity	7
Front head room, in.	39.4
Max. front leg room, in.	39.9
Rear head room, in.	39.7
Min. rear leg room, in.	36.3

ENGINES

	ohc V-6
Size, liters/cu. in.	3.0/181
Horsepower @ epm	151@ 4800
Torque (lbs./ft.) @ rpm	174@ 4400
Availability	S

EPA city/highway mpg

4-speed OD automatic	17/23

PRICES

1997 Mercury Villager	Retail Price	Dealer Invoice
GS 3-door van	$20215	$18299
LS 3-door van	25085	22585
Nautica 3-door van	26915	24174
Destination charge	580	580

All models require a Preferred Equipment Pkg.

STANDARD EQUIPMENT:

GS: 3.0-liter V-6 engine, 4-speed automatic transmission, driver- and passenger-side air bags, power steering, cloth upholstery, 5-passenger seating (reclining front bucket seats, 3-passenger second-row bench seat), front and rear cupholders, tilt steering column, AM/FM/cassette, tachometer, coolant-temperature gauge, trip odometer, solar-tinted glass, dual outside mirrors, visor mirrors, variable-intermittent wipers, rear wiper/washer, cornering lamps, rear auxiliary power outlet, rear storage bin, color-keyed bodyside molding, floormats, 205/75R15 tires, wheel covers.

LS adds: front air conditioning, anti-lock brakes, 7-passenger seating (reclining front bucket seats, 3-passenger second-row bench seat, 2-passenger rear bench seat), cruise control, power windows, power door locks, power mirrors, Light Group (overhead dual map lights, dual liftgate lights, front door step lights, power rear vent windows, under instrument panel lights with time delay), privacy glass, rear defogger, luggage rack, illuminated visor mirrors, seatback map pockets, automatic headlamps, lockable underseat storage bin, 2-tone paint, color-keyed bodyside molding w/chrome strip.

Nautica adds: leather quad captain's chairs, unique exterior paint, color-keyed bodyside molding w/yellow Mylar insert, unique grille, white alloy wheels.

OPTIONAL EQUIPMENT:
Major Packages

Preferred Equipment Pkg. 691A, GS	1600	1359

Front air conditioning, cruise control, quad captain's chairs, power windows and door locks, power mirrors, rear defogger.

Preferred Equipment Pkg. 692A, GS	3400	2891

Pkg. 691A plus anti-lock brakes, 8-way power driver seat, rear air conditioning and heater, remote keyless entry, flip-open liftgate window, privacy glass, luggage rack, underseat storage bin, alloy wheels.

Preferred Equipment Pkg. 696A, LS	1930	1639

Rear air conditioning and heater, cruise control, leather quad captain's chairs, 8-way power driver seat, 4-way power front passenger seat, leather-wrapped steering wheel w/radio controls, heated power mirrors, Premium Sound cassette player (rear radio controls with front-seat lockout, dual mini headphone jacks, cassette/CD storage console), remote keyless entry, illuminated visor mirrors, flip-open liftgate window, deluxe alloy wheels.

Rating Scale: 5-Excellent; 4-Above average; 3-Average; 2-Below average; 1-Poor

	Retail Price	Dealer Invoice
Preferred Equipment Pkg. 697A, Nautica	$1500	$1275

Automatic front and rear air conditioning and heater, cruise control, 8-way power driver seat, 4-way power front passenger seat, Premium Sound cassette player (rear radio controls with front-seat lockout, dual mini headphone jacks, cassette/CD storage console), leather-wrapped steering wheel w/radio controls, flip-open liftgate window, heated power mirrors, electronic instrumentation, remote keyless entry, illuminated visor mirrors.

Light Group, GS w/Pkg. 692A	165	140

Overhead dual map lights, dual liftgate lights, front-door step lights, power rear vent windows, under instrument panel lights with time delay.

Trailer Towing Pkg.	250	213

Includes heavy-duty battery, full-size spare tire, 3500-pound trailer rating.

Handling suspension	85	73

Includes 215/70R15 performance tires, firm-ride suspension, rear stabilizer bar. GS requires deluxe alloy wheels. NA GS w/Pkg. 691A.

Safety Features

Anti-lock brakes, GS w/Pkg. 691A	590	503
Integrated child seats, GS, LS	240	204

Requires 7-passenger seating.

Comfort and Convenience

Rear air conditioning and heater, GS w/Pkg. 691A	465	395
Automatic temperature control, LS..........................	180	153

Includes front and rear air conditioning and heater.

Power moonroof, LS, Nautica	775	659
7-passenger seating, GS, LS	NC	NC

Cloth upholstery, reclining front bucket seats, 3-passenger second-row bench seat, 2-passenger rear bench seat.

Cloth quad captain's chairs, LS............................	NC	NC
8-way power driver seat, GS w/Pkg. 691A	395	336
Premium Sound cassette player, GS w/Pkg. 692A.	310	263

Includes rear radio controls with front seat lockout, dual mini headphone jacks, cassette/CD storage console.

Premium Sound cassette/6-disc CD changer, GS w/Pkg. 692A	680	578
LS, Nautica	370	314

Includes rear radio controls with front seat lockout, dual mini headphone jacks, cassette/CD storage console.

Supersound CD/cassette player, LS, Nautica.........	865	735

Premium Sound cassette/6-disc CD changer plus subwoofer speaker.

Electronic instrumentation, LS	245	208

Requires automatic temperature control.

Remote keyless entry, GS w/Pkg. 691A	175	149

Appearance and Miscellaneous

Flip-open liftgate window, GS w/Pkg. 691A	115	97

Requires rear defogger.

Privacy glass, GS w/Pkg. 691A	415	352

Requires rear defogger.

Theft-deterrent system	100	85

Requires remote keyless entry. GS w/Pkg. 691A requires anti-lock brakes.

Luggage rack, GS w/Pkg. 691A	175	149
2-tone paint, GS	295	251

Special Purpose, Wheels and Tires

Deluxe alloy wheels, GS w/Pkg. 692A....................	40	34

MITSUBISHI DIAMANTE

Front-wheel-drive near-luxury car

Base price range: (1997 model) $25,900-$29,990. Built in Australia.

Also consider: Infiniti I30, Lexus ES 300

FOR • Acceleration • Quietness • Ride

AGAINST • Interior room

This is the U.S. flagship of Japan's Mitsubishi Motors Corporation. The company is part of the giant Mitsubishi con-

Mitsubishi Diamante ES

glomerate that has manufacturing interests the world over, so it's no surprise that U.S. Diamantes are built in Australia, where wage rates are lower than in Japan.

Diamante was redesigned last year with a larger V-6 engine, a bigger interior, and crisper styling versus the original 1992-96 series. While the '98 edition is predictably little changed, anti-lock brakes (ABS) and keyless entry do move from the options list to the standard equipment roster on both the ES and upscale LS models. A power moonroof and Homelink remote-control transmitter, also formerly optional on the LS, are now standard. As before, the ES is sold mainly to corporate fleets, while the LS is the mainstream "consumer" model.

PERFORMANCE All due credit to Mitsubishi for finally making ABS standard instead of optional on the Diamante. Most rivals already had standard ABS anyway, and buyers deserve the best brakes they can get. Diamante now does just fine in panic stops, aside from an excess of queasy nosedive.

Diamante's 3.5-liter V-6 is one of the largest engines in the near-luxury class and provides satisfying go in most any situation. It's also a smooth, quiet operator, if a little coarse-sounding. There's torque enough for the mandatory automatic transmission to provide clean, quick shifts up and down the gears. Wind and road noise are low too, though some tire roar can be heard on pebbled pavement.

Diamante is quietly billed as a sports sedan, but it's biased quite strongly toward ride comfort. Most bumps are easily absorbed, but the body floats over humpbacks and sharp crests taken quickly, and the soft suspension detracts from handling, allowing marked body roll in tight turns. Diamante is thus nowhere near as athletic as, say, a Mazda Millenia. Still, most buyers will like Mitsubishi's choice of spring and shock-absorber settings.

ACCOMMODATIONS Though last year's redesign added nearly 4 inches to overall length, the passenger package didn't grow proportionally. Diamante thus compares more with the low-slung Acura TL than the Lexus ES 300 for useable interior room. Nevertheless, four adults won't lack for leg or foot space, though head clearance is marginal for 6-footers beneath the power moonroof. The trunk is usefully roomy and easy to load, but outright volume isn't top-of-the-class.

Neither is the dash layout, which is simpler and more convenient than earlier Diamantes had, but rather busy next to many rival instrument panels. At least the dash top is reasonably low, which benefits visibility, but there's still a mild over-the-shoulder blind spot to contend with.

BUILD QUALITY Diamante's driving feel is weighty but not substantial in the way of the European competition. Detail assembly is thorough and materials generally look good, but door closings are a bit tinny, and the car doesn't feel quite as solid or well screwed together as it might on rough roads.

VALUE FOR THE MONEY The attractively priced Diamante certainly merits consideration, but not the level interest com-

Prices are accurate at time of publication; subject to manufacturer's changes.

manded by some rivals, especially the stand-out ES 300. The Mitsu also lags some in prestige, which has financial implications at trade-in time whether you buy or lease.

RATINGS

	LS	ES
Acceleration	4	4
Fuel economy	3	3
Ride quality	4	4
Steering/handling	3	3
Braking	4	4
Quietness	4	4
Driver seating	4	4
Instruments/controls	3	3
Room/comfort (front)	4	4
Room/comfort (rear)	3	3
Cargo room	3	3
Value for the money	4	4
Total	43	43

SPECIFICATIONS

	4-door sedan
Wheelbase, in.	107.1
Overall length, in.	194.1
Overall width, in.	70.3
Overall height, in.	53.9
Curb weight, lbs.	3494
Cargo vol., cu. ft.	14.2
Fuel capacity, gals.	19.0
Seating capacity	5
Front head room, in.	37.6
Max. front leg room, in.	43.6
Rear head room, in.	36.3
Min. rear leg room, in.	36.6

ENGINES

	ohc V-6
Size, liters/cu. in.	3.5/213
Horsepower @ rpm	210@ 5000
Torque (lbs./ft.) @ rpm	231@ 4000
Availability	S

EPA city/highway mpg

4-speed OD automatic	18/26

PRICES

1997 Mitsubishi Diamante

	Retail Price	Dealer Invoice
ES 4-door notchback	$25900	$22274
LS 4-door notchback	29990	25492
Destination charge	470	470

STANDARD EQUIPMENT:

ES: 3.5-liter V-6 engine, 4-speed automatic transmission, 4-wheel disc brakes, power steering, driver- and passenger-side air bags, automatic climate control, cruise control, velour upholstery, 7-way adjustable front bucket seats, front console with armrest, cupholders, folding rear armrest, power windows, power door locks, power mirrors, tilt steering column, tinted glass, remote fuel-door and decklid releases, tachometer, coolant-temperature gauge, trip odometer, variable intermittent wipers, AM/FM/cassette, power and diversity antenna, digital clock, rear defogger, theft-deterrent system, front map light, rear heat ducts, 205/65VR15 tires, wheel covers, full-size spare tire.

LS adds: power driver seat, leather upholstery, leather-wrapped steering wheel, AM/FM/cassette/CD player, rear map light, wood interior trim, 215/60VR16 tires, alloy wheels.

OPTIONAL EQUIPMENT:
Safety Features

Anti-lock brakes, ES, LS	732	600
Integrated child seat, ES, LS	195	160

Major Packages

Premium Leather Pkg., ES	2000	1640

Leather upholstery, power driver seat, leather-wrapped steering wheel, remote keyless entry, cargo net, fog lights, 215/60R16 tires, alloy wheels.

	Retail Price	Dealer Invoice
Luxury Group, LS	$2287	$1875

Power sunroof Homelink universal garage-door opener, high contrast instrument panel w/two trip odometers.

Luxury Convenience Group, LS	2561	2100

Anti-lock brakes, power passenger seat, integrated child seat, Infinity AM/FM/cassette/CD player, remote keyless entry, automatic day/night inside mirror, steering wheel controls, power fuel door release.

Comfort and Convenience

Power sunroof, ES, LS	963	790

Includes Homelink universal garage door opener.

10-disc CD changer, LS	758	522

Includes trunk mat.

CD player, ES	399	299
Remote keyless entry, LS	216	150
Floormats, LS	90	58
Trunk mat, LS	71	46
Cargo net, LS	36	23

Appearance and Miscellaneous

Mud guards	125	87
Wheel locks, LS	39	27

MITSUBISHI ECLIPSE

Mitsubishi Eclipse Spyder GS-T

Front- or all-wheel-drive sports coupe; similar to Eagle Talon

Base price range: (1997 model) $13,830-$26,630. Built in Normal, Ill.

Also consider: Chrysler Sebring Coupe, Dodge Avenger, Honda Prelude

FOR • Acceleration (GS-T, GSX) • Steering/handling

AGAINST • Acceleration (RS, GS w/automatic) • Rear seat room • Road noise • Cargo room (convertibles)

This line of American-built sporty compacts is a virtual rerun following last year's styling update. Eclipse continues in four hatchback coupe and two Spyder convertible models, all with twincam 4-cylinder power. The base RS and step-up GS coupes use a 2.0-liter engine, the GS Spyder a 2.4-liter. A slightly different turbocharged 2.0 powers the GS-T coupe and GS-T Spyder and the all-wheel-drive GSX coupe. Other Eclipses have front drive. Convertibles come with a power top and glass rear window.

Among the few changes for '98 are standard wheel locks on GS models, chrome-plated 16-inch wheels for GS-Ts, and the addition of power moonroof, leather upholstery, power driver's seat and remote entry/security system to GSX equipment. All Eclipses come with manual transmission and offer an automatic option. Anti-lock brakes are available for all models except the base RS coupe. Eclipse and its near-relation, the Eagle Talon coupe sold by Chrysler Corporation, are built at a Mitsubishi-run plant in Illinois.

PERFORMANCE Eclipse's base 2.0-liter four is the same Chrysler-designed engine used in the Dodge/Plymouth Neon, so it runs smoothly but none too quietly. It's also short on torque below 3500 rpm, so pickup with automatic transmission is marginal for passing sprints and freeway on-ramps. Progress is livelier with the slick-shifting 5-speed; we timed a manual GS coupe at a decent 9.2 seconds to 60 mph.

Turbo models are decidedly faster: 6.9 seconds to 60 mph in

our tests. Sadly, Mitsubishi hasn't eliminated "turbo lag," which is especially noticed with automatic. Floor the throttle and you wait a second or two before extra power arrives, which can upset balance when you're pushing hard on a twisty road.

All models have nimble handling, good grip, and quick, accurate steering. Ride, however, becomes choppy on freeways and rough secondary roads, especially on the GS-T and GSX with their stiffer suspensions and higher-performance tires. Road noise is marked in any model, and wind rush is a problem at highway speeds in convertibles with the top up.

ACCOMMODATIONS As in most every car like this, Eclipse's tiny back seat is strictly for pre-teens. The front cabin is adult-size, though, with adequate head room and sufficient seat travel for 6-footers. Cargo space is minuscule in Spyders but adequate in coupes with their folding rear seats. All models suffer a tall cargo liftover for loading and unloading, and the ragtop's small trunk opening further limits what size luggage you can carry.

Eclipse's driving position is slightly "bathtub," but visibility is pretty good except in convertibles, where the soft top's wide rear quarters leave a large blind spot. The dashboard is well laid out except the stereo is too low in the center and thus tricky to adjust while driving.

BUILD QUALITY Eclipse convertibles we've driven had serious shakes even on smooth roads—enough for us to think that squeaks and rattles will set in long before the "new" wears off. Coupes are much tighter, but interior plastics don't impress on any model.

VALUE FOR THE MONEY Except for the AWD GSX, Eclipse coupes offer nothing the competition doesn't, and they're short on both cabin room and general polish. The Spyders are pleasant and practical small convertibles, but we question their long-term structural stamina.

RATINGS

	RS/GS	GS-T/ GSX	GS conv.	GS-T conv.
Acceleration	3	4	3	4
Fuel economy	4	3	3	3
Ride quality	3	3	3	3
Steering/handling	3	4	4	4
Braking	4	4	4	4
Quietness	3	3	3	3
Driver seating	4	4	4	4
Instruments/controls	3	3	3	3
Room/comfort (front)	3	3	3	3
Room/comfort (rear)	1	1	1	1
Cargo room	4	4	2	2
Value for the money	4	4	3	3
Total	**39**	**40**	**36**	**37**

SPECIFICATIONS

	2-door coupe	2-door conv.
Wheelbase, in.	98.8	98.8
Overall length, in.	172.4	172.4
Overall width, in.	68.5	68.5
Overall height, in.	49.8	52.8
Curb weight, lbs.	2754	2888
Cargo vol., cu. ft.	16.6	5.1
Fuel capacity, gals.	15.9	15.9
Seating capacity	4	4
Front head room, in.	37.9	38.8
Max. front leg room, in.	43.3	43.3
Rear head room, in.	34.3	34.9
Min. rear leg room, in.	28.4	28.4

ENGINES

	dohc I-4	ohc I-4	Turbo dohc I-4
Size, liters/cu. in.	2.0/122	2.4/143	2.0/122
Horsepower @ rpm	140@ 6000	141@ 5000	210@ 6000
Torque (lbs./ft.) @ rpm	130@ 4800	148@ 3000	214@ 3000
Availability	S[1]	S[2]	S[3]
EPA city/highway mpg			
5-speed OD manual	22/33	22/30	23/31
4-speed OD automatic	21/30	21/28	20/27

1. Base, RS, GS. 2. Spyder GS. 3. GS-T, GSX.

PRICES

1997 Mitsubishi Eclipse

	Retail Price	Dealer Invoice
Base 2-door hatchback, 5-speed	$13830	$12440
Base 2-door hatchback, automatic	$14510	$13051
RS 2-door hatchback, 5-speed	15140	13156
RS 2-door hatchback, automatic	15830	13768
GS 2-door hatchback, 5-speed	17550	15255
GS 2-door hatchback, automatic	18240	15866
Spyder GS 2-door convertible, 5-speed	19940	17340
Spyder GS 2-door convertible, automatic	20650	17957
GS-T 2-door hatchback, 5-speed	21190	18424
GS-T 2-door hatchback, automatic	22020	19154
Spyder GS-T 2-door convertible, 5-speed	25780	22422
Spyder GS-T 2-door convertible, automatic	26630	23160
GSX 2-door hatchback, 5-speed	23220	19963
GSX 2-door hatchback, automatic	24070	20694
Destination charge	420	420

STANDARD EQUIPMENT:

Base: 2.0-liter DOHC 4-cylinder engine, 5-speed manual transmission or 4-speed automatic transmission, driver- and passenger-side air bags, power steering, cloth upholstery, reclining front bucket seats, folding rear seat, 5-way adjustable driver seat w/memory feature, front storage console w/cupholders, tilt steering column, coolant-temperature gauge, trip odometer, digital clock, tinted glass, dual outside mirrors, map lights, remote fuel-door release, 185/70HR14 tires.

RS adds: tachometer, AM/FM radio w/4-speakers, rear defogger, remote hatch release, cargo light, 195/70HR14 tires, wheel covers.

GS adds: 4-wheel disc brakes, 6-way adjustable driver seat w/memory feature, split folding rear seat, cassette player w/6-speakers, power mirrors, Homelink universal garage-door opener, rear wiper/washer, low rear spoiler, fog lights, cargo cover and net, 205/55HR16 tires.

Spyder GS adds to RS: 2.4-liter 4-cylinder engine, variable-assist power steering, power insulated soft top with glass rear window, vinyl tonneau cover, 6-way adjustable driver seat w/memory feature, power windows, power door locks, power mirrors, CD player, alloy wheels.

GS-T adds to GS: 2.0-liter DOHC 4-cylinder tubocharged and intercooled engine, air conditioning, sport suspension, cruise control, oil-pressure gauge, turbo-boost gauge, Infinity 8-speaker AM/FM/cassette/CD player w/amplifier, power windows, power door locks, dual bright exhaust outlets, high rear spoiler, 205/55HR16 tires, alloy wheels.

Spyder GS-T adds to GS-T: variable-assist power steering, sport suspension, power insulated soft top with glass rear window, vinyl tonneau cover, leather upholstery, remote keyless entry, theft-deterrent system, leather-wrapped steering wheel and shifter, 205/55VR16 tires.

GSX adds to GS-T: all-wheel drive, leather upholstery, 215/50VR17 tires.

OPTIONAL EQUIPMENT:

Safety Features

Anti-lock brakes,		
Spyder GS, GS-T, Spyder GS-T, GSX	716	587

Major Packages

Preferred Value Pkg. P1, GS	1963	1930

Air conditioning, power moonroof, power windows and door locks, cruise control, alloy wheels.

Premium Value Pkg. P2, GS	3031	2889

Pkg. P1 plus Infinity AM/FM/cassette, leather upholstery, theft-deterrent system, remote keyless entry.

Premium Plus Value Pkg. P3, GS	3747	3476

Pkg. P2 plus anti-lock brakes.

Preferred Equipment Pkg. PM, RS	1529	1254

Air conditioning, rear spoiler, cargo cover, alloy wheels.

Preferred Equipment Pkg. PU, GSX	789	647

Leather upholstery, power driver seat.

Appearance Pkg., Spyder GS	924	758

Rear spoiler, lower bodyside cladding, fog lamps, alloy wheels.

Convenience Pkg., Spyder GS	1551	1272

Air conditioning, cruise control, remote keyless entry, theft-deterrent system, Homelink universal garage-door opener.

Prices are accurate at time of publication; subject to manufacturer's changes.

	Retail Price	Dealer Invoice
Power Pkg., RS	$755	$619

Power windows and door locks, cruise control.

Comfort and Convenience

Power moonroof, RS, GS-T, GSX	731	599
Air conditioning, base, RS, GS, Spyder GS...........	891	731
Leather upholstery, GS-T	457	375
Spyder GS	567	465
AM/FM radio, base	234	192
Cassette player, RS	323	265
Infinity 8-speaker AM/FM/cassette with amplifier, Spyder GS,		
Spyder GS	720	590
CD player, base, RS, GS, Spyder GS	399	299
Base requires AM/FM radio.		
Remote keyless entry,		
RS, GS, Spyder GS, GS-T, GSX.......................	136	89
RS requires Power Pkg. GS requires Preferred Value Pkg. 1.		
Remote keyless entry/theft-deterrent system,		
GS, GS-T, GSX	334	274
Rear defogger, base....................................	162	133
Floormats	49	32

Appearance and Miscellaneous

Mud guards	93	61

Special Purpose, Wheels and Tires

Limited-slip differential, GSX	266	218
Chrome alloy wheels, Spyder GS-T	488	400
Wheel locks, RS, GS, Spyder GS	33	23

MITSUBISHI GALANT

Mitsubishi Galant ES

Front-wheel-drive compact car

Base price range: (1997 model) $15,420-$23,980. Built in Normal, Ill.

Also consider: Ford Contour, Mazda 626, Nissan Altima

FOR • Passenger and cargo room • Ride

AGAINST • Engine noise • Rear visibility

Mitsubishi's compact-sized family 4-door is in the final year of its current design. The new Galant scheduled for 1999 will reportedly have more angular styling in the image of the larger Diamante, plus slightly larger dimensions and—finally—available V-6 power. A V-6 Galant has been promised for the past three years, but for a variety of reasons it hasn't happened.

Meantime, the vintage-1994 series closes out with a few equipment changes. The base DE model is unaffected, but the mid-line ES switches from standard automatic transmission to manual (as on the DE). Automatic remains standard on the top-shelf LS, which now comes with anti-lock brakes and alloy wheels as standard. Both features are ES options. A 2.4-liter 4-cylinder is again the only engine available for Galant, which is assembled at the same Illinois plant that builds the sporty Mitsubishi Eclipse and Eagle Talon.

PERFORMANCE Galant is a capable all-around performer, but doesn't excel in any particular area. Standing-start acceleration is more than acceptable, though. We timed a 4-cylinder automatic at 9.4 seconds to 60 mph, which beats a like-equipped '98 Nissan Altima by more than a half-second—a noticeable difference despite similar engines. Fuel economy, on the other hand, is ordinary at best. Though we've managed 21.6 mpg with auto-

matic in city/highway driving, sustained high-speed freeway work can bring that down below 20.

Galant's automatic changes gears smoothly most of the time, but full-throttle downshifts can be sudden and harsh. The engine is also generally smooth, but becomes vocal when worked hard. Wind and tire noise aren't excessive, but they're not unusually low, either.

The suspension absorbs bumps well and provides a stable ride at highway speeds. Hard cornering induces considerable body lean, but grip is good and handling responses are front-drive safe and predictable. Quick, precise steering helps, though it could use more road feel. Galant handles 60-mph "panic" stops with no-sweat directional control, but stopping distances are strictly average.

ACCOMMODATIONS Galant's chief advantage over rivals such as the Altima and Mazda 626 was more cabin room, but those competitors are redesigned for '98 and narrow the space-gap considerably. Even so, the Mitsubishi remains quite roomy for a compact, particularly in overall head room, which borders on generous in the rear. Aft leg space is very good too. Cargo room is just okay, though the trunk is wide and has a large, convenient bumper-height opening. ES and LS models get a one-piece fold-down back seat, which is useful but not as versatile as the split backrests on many rivals.

Galant's dash presents an attractive gauge cluster and climate controls are stacked above the stereo in the center. In a welcome change from past Mitsubishi practice, the stereo sits high enough to easily see and reach while driving. Visibility is good, though wide rear roof pillars force drivers to do some neck-stretching for lane changes.

BUILD QUALITY Though workmanship is generally up to class standards, Galant's paint lacks a certain richness and a few interior materials look budget-grade even on the top-line LS. By contrast, the commendably solid driving feel is reminiscent of some German cars.

VALUE FOR THE MONEY Galant is a pleasant and competent family compact that's worth a look, though we'd also check into the Altima, 626, and Ford Contour. The one real problem here is forgettable blandness, the reason Galant has yet to make much of an impression on the market.

RATINGS

	DE	ES/LS
Acceleration	3	3
Fuel economy	4	4
Ride quality	4	4
Steering/handling	3	3
Braking	3	4
Quietness	3	3
Driver seating	4	4
Instruments/controls	3	3
Room/comfort (front)	4	4
Room/comfort (rear)	4	4
Cargo room	3	3
Value for the money	3	3
Total	**41**	**42**

SPECIFICATIONS

	4-door sedan
Wheelbase, in.	103.7
Overall length, in.	187.6
Overall width, in.	68.1
Overall height, in.	53.1
Curb weight, lbs.	2778
Cargo vol., cu. ft.	12.5
Fuel capacity, gals.	16.9
Seating capacity	5
Front head room, in.	39.4
Max. front leg room, in.	43.3
Rear head room, in.	37.5
Min. rear leg room, in.	35.0

ENGINES

	ohc I-4
Size, liters/cu. in.	2.4/143
Horsepower @ rpm..................................	141@ 5000

Rating Scale: 5-Excellent; 4-Above average; 3-Average; 2-Below average; 1-Poor

	ohc I-4
Torque (lbs./ft.) @ rpm..	148@ 3000
Availability	S
EPA city/highway mpg	
5-speed OD manual..	23/30
4-speed OD automatic...	22/28

PRICES

1997 Mitsubishi Galant	Retail Price	Dealer Invoice
DE 4-door notchback, 5-speed	$15420	$13717
DE 4-door notchback, automatic	16290	14493
ES 4-door notchback, automatic	18115	15958
LS 4-door notchback, automatic	23980	20380
Destination charge	420	420

STANDARD EQUIPMENT:

DE: 2.4-liter 4-cylinder engine, 5-speed manual or 4-speed automatic transmission, driver- and passenger-side air bags, power steering, cloth upholstery, 5-way adjustable driver seat, front storage console w/armrest, tilt steering column, cupholders, radio prep pkg., digital clock, tinted glass, driver-side visor mirror, tachometer, coolant-temperature gauge, remote fuel-door and decklid releases, rear defogger, intermittent wipers, remote outside mirrors, 185/70HR14 tires, wheel covers.

ES adds: 4-speed automatic transmission, air conditioning, cruise control, upgraded cloth upholstery, folding rear seat with center armrest, power windows, power door locks, AM/FM/cassette, power diversity antenna, power mirrors, variable intermittent wipers, passenger-side visor mirror, door map pockets, woodgrain interior trim, floormats, cargo net.

LS adds: automatic climate control, power driver seat, leather upholstery, power sunroof, Infinity audio system w/amplifier, Homelink universal garage-door opener, fog lamps, illuminated visor mirrors, seatback map pockets, 195/60HR15 tires, alloy wheels.

OPTIONAL EQUIPMENT:
Major Packages

Premium Pkg., ES..	1787	1465

Power sunroof, Homelink universal garage door opener, illuminated visor mirrors, remote keyless entry, fog lamps, 195/60R15 tires, alloy wheels.

Safety Features

Anti-lock brakes, ES, LS	965	791

Comfort and Convenience

Air conditioning, DE...	902	740

MITSUBISHI MIRAGE

Mitsubishi Mirage LS Sedan

Front-wheel-drive subcompact car

Base price range: (1997 model) $10,520-$14,020. Built in Japan.

Also consider: Ford Escort/Escort ZX2, Honda Civic, Toyota Corolla

FOR • Fuel economy • Steering/handling

AGAINST • Acceleration (DE) • Rear seat room (coupes)

Chrysler used to sell the Mirage as the near-identical Eagle Summit and Dodge/Plymouth Colt, but that was before it brought out the Neon to fight its small-car battles. Chrysler has lately been loosening its 25-year-old ties with the Japanese automaker. One result is that the Mirage became a Mitsubishi exclusive for 1997.

Mirage was also redesigned for '97, so the '98s are virtual reruns. Offerings comprise 2- and 4-doors in DE ("Deluxe") and LS trim. DEs have a 1.5-liter 4-cylinder engine with three valves per cylinder. LS models use a 1.8-liter four-valve version. Anti-lock brakes are optional for LS models only.

Among the few changes for '98 are a heavy-duty starter and battery. The DE coupe gets standard power steering (it was optional), and the LS coupe gains no-cost air conditioning, wheel locks, and AM/FM/CD audio, plus a new power moonroof option.

PERFORMANCE The latest Mirage is like old wine in a new bottle, with proven engines in stiffer, more-modern bodies. The result is decidedly quieter and more substantial-feeling than earlier models—almost a match for the stellar Honda Civic, in fact.

Still, engine noise is relatively high, and acceleration is pokey on DE models even with manual shift. Last year's redesign included an improved automatic transmission that's more responsive than the old one, but DEs don't have the power to pull it with any gusto. There's not much real-world difference between the two engines, but we recommend avoiding either DE model unless your budget won't stretch to an LS. We haven't had a chance to measure fuel economy, but all Mirages earn high EPA ratings.

As for ride, handling, and braking, all Mirages are acceptable though not outstanding. Cornering is nimble, predictable, front-drive secure, and even fun, but other small cars can claim that too. Ride comfort is okay, but things turn a bit hoppy on broken surfaces and freeway expansion joins. Tire thrum annoys more than it should on coarse pavement, though wind rush isn't excessive at highway speeds.

ACCOMMODATIONS As with most coupe/sedan siblings, the 4-door Mirage affords much easier entry/exit than the 2-door, plus more usable rear passenger space. Even so, aft leg and foot room are necessarily tight behind a tall front-seater, so adults won't want to ride there for long. All models have a flat-floor trunk and competitive cargo volume for the class, but only the LS coupe comes with the extra versatility of a split-fold back seat, though that's available in a package option for sedans.

Like most rivals, Mirage provides its driver with clear all-around visibility and a tidy, easily mastered dash. Long-legged folks may wish for more rearward seat travel, however, as well as the tilt steering wheel that's standard on LS and optional on the DE.

BUILD QUALITY Where earlier Mirages had a somewhat tinny, bargain-basement air, the newest models compare well with the class-leading Civic and Toyota's Corolla. Still, interior materials are more "economy" than "business class," and detail finish is nothing special.

VALUE FOR THE MONEY Mirage isn't lavishly equipped even for a subcompact, and though sticker prices are attractive, they climb fast once you start adding extras. Still, the smallest Mitsubishis are good enough to merit a look, particularly if you're considering a Civic or Corolla.

RATINGS	DE 2-door	LS 4-door
Acceleration	2	3
Fuel economy	4	4
Ride quality	3	3
Steering/handling	4	4
Braking	3	3
Quietness	3	3
Driver seating	3	3
Instruments/controls	3	3
Room/comfort (front)	4	4
Room/comfort (rear)	2	3
Cargo room	3	3
Value for the money	4	4
Total	38	40

SPECIFICATIONS	2-door coupe	4-door sedan
Wheelbase, in.	95.1	98.4
Overall length, in.	168.1	173.6

Prices are accurate at time of publication; subject to manufacturer's changes.

	2-door coupe	4-door sedan
Overall width, in.	66.5	66.5
Overall height, in.	51.4	52.6
Curb weight, lbs.	2127	2227
Cargo vol., cu. ft.	11.5	11.5
Fuel capacity, gals.	13.2	13.2
Seating capacity	5	5
Front head room, in.	38.6	39.8
Max. front leg room, in.	43.0	43.0
Rear head room, in.	35.8	37.4
Min. rear leg room, in.	31.1	33.5

ENGINES

	ohc I-4	ohc I-4
Size, liters/cu. in.	1.5/90	1.8/112
Horsepower @ rpm	92 @ 5500	113 @ 5500
Torque (lbs./ft.) @ rpm	93 @ 3000	116 @ 4500
Availability	S[1]	S[2]

EPA city/highway mpg

5-speed OD manual	33/40	28/37
4-speed OD automatic	29/36	26/33

1. DE models. 2. LS models.

PRICES

1997 Mitsubishi Mirage

	Retail Price	Dealer Invoice
DE 2-door notchback, 5-speed	$10520	$9566
DE 2-door notchback, automatic	11230	10178
DE 4-door notchback, 5-speed	12220	10878
DE 4-door notchback, automatic	12920	11490
LS 2-door notchback, 5-speed	13350	11857
LS 2-door notchback, automatic	14020	12469
LS 4-door notchback, 5-speed	13150	11707
LS 4-door notchback, automatic	13830	12319
Destination charge	420	420

STANDARD EQUIPMENT:

DE: 1.5-liter 4-cylinder engine, 5-speed manual or 4-speed automatic transmission, driver- and passenger-side air bags, power steering (4-door), vinyl/cloth upholstery (2-door), cloth upholstery (4-door), highback front bucket seats (2-door), sport front bucket seats (4-door), front and rear armrests, front storage console, coolant-temperature gauge, tachometer (4-door w/5-speed), rear defogger, dual outside mirrors, tinted glass, remote fuel-door and decklid release, 175/70R13 tires, wheel covers (4-door).

LS adds: 1.8-liter 4-cylinder engine, air conditioning (4-door), power steering, cloth upholstery, sport front bucket seats, height-adjustable driver seat, split folding rear seat (2-door), tilt steering column, tachometer (5-speed), digital clock, AM/FM/cassette with CD controls (2-door), intermittent wipers, cloth door-trim panels, rear spoiler (2-door), 175/70R13 tires (4-door), 185/65R14 tires (2-door), alloy wheels (2-door).

OPTIONAL EQUIPMENT:
Safety Features

Anti-lock brakes, LS	732	600

Major Packages

Preferred Equipment Pkg. PE, DE 2-door	166	136
Tilt steering wheel, intermittent wipers, wheel covers.		
Value Pkg. VM, LS 2-door	1017	901
Air conditioning, CD player, cargo net, floormats, wheel locks.		
Appearance Pkg., LS 2-door	207	170
Fog lamps, air dam.		
Convenience Pkg., LS 2-door	744	610
Cruise control, power windows and door locks, power mirrors, variable intermittent wipers, visor mirrors.		
Premium Pkg. PR, LS 4-door	1190	976
Power sunroof, alloy wheels, wheel locks.		
Value Pkg. VL, LS 4-door	1637	1477
Air conditioning, cruise control, split folding rear seat, power windows and power door locks, AM/FM/cassette with CD controls, power mirrors, variable intermittent wipers, 185/65R14 tires, floormats.		

	Retail Price	Dealer Invoice
Value Pkg. VE, DE 4-door	$1070	$960

Air conditioning, split folding rear seat, tilt steering wheel, AM/FM/cassette, remote outside mirrors, visor mirrors, cargo-area light, intermittent wipers, cloth door-trim panels, floormats.

Comfort and Convenience

Power steering, DE 2-door	262	215
Air conditioning, DE	880	720
AM/FM/cassette, DE	352	247
AM/FM/cassette with CD controls, DE 2-door	470	330
CD player, DE 2-door, LS 4-door	399	299
DE 2-door requires AM/FM/cassette. LS 4-door requires Value Pkg. VL.		
Remote keyless entry, LS	254	165
Requires Convenience Pkg.		
Cargo net	36	23
NA LS 2-door		
Floormats, DE	65	43

Appearance and Miscellaneous

Mud guards	71	46

MITSUBISHI MONTERO

Mitsubishi Montero

Four-wheel-drive full-size sport-utility vehicle

Base price range: (1997 model) $29,290-$36,460. Built in Japan.

Also consider: Ford Expedition, Isuzu Trooper, Toyota Land Cruiser

FOR • Passenger/cargo room

AGAINST • Fuel economy • Entry/exit • Ride

Mitsubishi last year introduced the Montero Sport, a midsize sport-utility vehicle built on the same chassis as this "big" Montero. Mitsubishi continues to emphasize its "junior" SUV at the expense of the taller, costlier, regular Montero, whose sales remain meager—partly, we suspect, because of an elderly 7-year-old design.

As a result, Montero now comes in one model instead of two. Equipped about halfway between last year's LS and upscale SR, the '98 wears a fresh grille, bumpers, and quarter panels. Inside, the center console, door trim, and steering wheel are new, plus rear jump seats are standard, giving 7-passenger capacity.

As before, a 3.5-liter V-6 couples to automatic transmission. Mitsubishi's "Active Trac" on-demand 4-wheel drive can be used on dry pavement and has a locking center differential and separate low-range gearing. Anti-lock brakes are now standard rather than optional, as are air conditioning and dark-tint rear privacy glass. Four option packages are offered: Value, Luxury, Premium, and Cold Weather.

PERFORMANCE Though some V-8 SUVs can easily outsprint it, the big Montero has good grunt for most situations—enough to do 0-60 mph in about 10 seconds. But the big V-6 is no miser and has lots of weight to move, so fuel economy is sorry—below 15 mpg for us in urban driving.

Montero's 4WD is switchable between 2WD and 4WD on the fly and can be driven in either mode on dry pavement. The automatic transmission is less likable: Full-throttle downshifts sometimes occur with a lurchy jolt.

Montero is relatively narrow for its height, so it feels ponder-

Rating Scale: 5-Excellent; 4-Above average; 3-Average; 2-Below average; 1-Poor

ous yet tippy on twisty roads, much more so than lower-built SUVs. It also tends to get blown around quite easily by stiff crosswinds at highway speeds. Curiously, the steering is almost too quick for best control. The stiff suspension transmits most every pavement imperfection, yet allows copious body lean in corners. All this makes Montero seem nervous, old-fashioned and truck-like except in gentle driving. The anti-lock brakes deliver straight, secure "panic" stops, but distances are on the long side, another penalty of the hefty 4400-pound curb weight.

ACCOMMODATIONS Montero's high-profile design pays off in abundant passenger and cargo space, as well as tall-in-the-saddle seating with excellent all-around visibility. Still, this "big-tire" rig stands way off the ground, so entry/exit means stepping lively, particularly through the rear doors that narrow appreciably at the bottom. Montero's dashboard remains dated and messy, though controls are clearly marked. Some drivers may find the steering wheel raked too far forward for comfort.

The jump seats have room enough only for small children and are difficult for adults to reach because there's little space for crawling past the middle bench. Even with the jump seats deployed there's room for several grocery bags behind. Stowing the jump seats against the sidewalls creates a spacious load area that can be further enlarged by folding the split second-row seat.

BUILD QUALITY Despite a heavyweight driving feel, Montero suffers some irritating body drumming on very rough pavement and washboard trails, plus so-so paint finish. The interior is generally well executed, but the available real-wood trim somehow manages to look fake.

VALUE FOR THE MONEY Monteros may have finished 1-2-3 in the taxing 1997 Dakar Rally, but this is an old-fashioned SUV that lags way behind newer rivals in most areas except interior space. It's also no bargain on price. You'll do better by looking elsewhere.

RATINGS

	Montero
Acceleration	3
Fuel economy	1
Ride quality	3
Steering/handling	3
Braking	3
Quietness	3
Driver seating	4
Instruments/controls	3
Room/comfort (front)	4
Room/comfort (rear)	4
Cargo room	4
Value for the money	3
Total	**38**

SPECIFICATIONS

	4-door wagon
Wheelbase, in.	107.3
Overall length, in.	186.6
Overall width, in.	69.9
Overall height, in.	74.8
Curb weight, lbs.	4431
Cargo vol., cu. ft.	67.1
Fuel capacity, gals.	24.3
Seating capacity	7
Front head room, in.	40.9
Max. front leg room, in.	40.3
Rear head room, in.	40.0
Min. rear leg room, in.	37.6

ENGINES

	ohc V-6
Size, liters/cu. in.	3.5/213
Horsepower @ rpm	200@ 5000
Torque (lbs./ft.) @ rpm	228@ 3500
Availability	S
EPA city/highway mpg	
4-speed OD automatic	16/19

PRICES

1997 Mitsubishi Montero	Retail Price	Dealer Invoice
LS 4-door wagon	$29290	$25028
SR 4-door wagon	36460	30436
Destination charge	445	445

STANDARD EQUIPMENT:

LS: 3.5-liter V-6 engine, 4-speed automatic transmission, Active-Trac 4-wheel drive, 4-wheel disc brakes, driver- and passenger-side air bags, power steering, engine oil cooler, cruise control, cloth reclining front bucket seats, split folding second-row seat with headrests, tilt steering column, front storage console w/cupholders, leather-wrapped steering wheel, power windows and door locks, power mirrors, digital clock, trip odometer, tachometer, coolant-temperature gauge, AM/FM/cassette, power diversity antenna, rear defogger, variable intermittent wipers, intermittent rear wiper/washer, remote fuel-door release, auxiliary power outlets, map/spot lights, visor mirrors w/illuminated passenger-side mirror, cargo tie-down hooks, tool kit, rear heat ducts, front and rear tow hooks, skid plates, mud guards, full-size spare tire, 235/75R15 tires.

SR adds: rear differential lock, leather upholstery, power driver seat, split folding third-row seat, Infinity AM/FM/cassette/CD player w/amplifier, power sunroof, multi-meter (oil-pressure gauge, compass, outside-temperature indicator, voltmeter), illuminated driver-side visor mirror, rear privacy glass, sliding rear quarter window, headlamp washers, 265/70R15 tires, alloy wheels.

OPTIONAL EQUIPMENT:
Major Packages

	Retail	Invoice
Preferred Equipment Pkg. #1, LS	1422	1166

Includes split folding third row seat, power moonroof, multi-meter (oil-pressure gauge, compass, outside-temperture inducator, volt-meter), sliding rear quarter windows. NA with luggage rack.

Preferred Equipment Pkg. #2, LS	1654	1356

Preferred Equipment Pkg. #1 plus rear privacy glass. NA with luggage rack.

Value Pkg., LS	1955	1887

Air conditioning, alloy wheels, 10-disc CD changer, theft-deterrent system, remote keyless entry, luggage rack, side steps, spare tire cover, cargo mat, cargo net, cargo cover, floormats, wheel locks. requires a Preferred Equipment Pkg. #1 or #2.

Value Pkg., SR	1922	1856

Air conditioning, 10-disc CD changer, theft-deterrent system, remote keyless entry, wood trim, luggage rack, side steps, spare tire cover, cargo mat, cargo net, cargo cover, floormats, wheel locks.

All-Weather Pkg., LS	1402	1150
SR	1585	1300

Anti-lock brakes, heated front seats. SR also includes adjustable shock absorbers.

Luxury Pkg., LS	1933	1585

Leather upholstery, power driver seat, Infinity sound system w/amplifier.

Air conditioning/alloy wheels, LS	1305	1070

Comfort and Convenience

CD player, LS	399	299
10-disc CD changer, LS	675	465
Remote keyless entry, LS	216	150
Remote keyless entry w/theft-deterrent system, LS	345	224
Fog lights	230	152
Cargo Kit, LS	235	153

Includes cargo mat, cargo net, cargo cover.

Floormats, LS	70	40

Appearance and Miscellaneous

Luggage rack, LS	246	160

NA with Preferred Pkg. #1 or #2.

Side steps, LS	367	247
Spare tire cover, LS	189	123

Special Purpose, Wheels and Tires

Trailer hitch w/harness	252	164
Wheel locks	48	33
Chrome wheels, SR	927	760

Prices are accurate at time of publication; subject to manufacturer's changes.

MITSUBISHI MONTERO SPORT

Mitsubishi Montero Sport LS

Rear- or 4-wheel-drive midsize sport-utility vehicle
Base price range: (1997 model) $17,620-$31,110. Built in Japan.

Also consider: Ford Explorer, Jeep Grand Cherokee, Mercedes-Benz ML320

FOR • Standard anti-lock brakes (XLS, 4WD LS)
• Instruments/controls • Visibility

AGAINST • Fuel economy • Entry/exit • Ride

The Montero Sport bowed for 1997 as Mitsubishi's belated entry in the midsize sport-utility market. It's built on the same chassis as the regular Montero, but has a shorter, lighter, much lower body. It also comes with smaller engines and a less sophisticated 4-wheel-drive system.

A few features and a 2WD model in top XLS trim (sold only with 4WD last year) are added for '98. Rounding out the line are 2WD and 4WD LS models and an entry-level 2WD ES. Mitsubishi's veteran 3.0-liter V-6 powers all Sports save the ES, which uses a 2.4-liter 4-cylinder. The ES and 4WD LS have standard manual transmission, other models automatic.

Feature-wise, anti-lock brakes go from optional to standard status on XLSs and the LS 4x4. The 4WD XLS also adds heated seats and door mirrors, plus a locking rear differential that's useful in tough off-road situations. The locking differential is available in a package option for all other models but the ES. Finally, a new Luxury option for LS/XLS models delivers power moonroof and premium audio. Two other new packages upgrade the 4WD LS with some XLS features, including two-tone paint, fender flares, chrome grille, and larger wheels and tires.

PERFORMANCE Montero Sport needs more power—especially the ES model, whose 4-cylinder engine just can't handle the weight. The V-6 versions' movement off the line is only a bit less sluggish even with a light load, and modest upgrades slow progress noticeably—worrisome if that slope is a freeway on-ramp. Because the Sport demands a heavy right foot to achieve just middling performance, you pay a price at the pump. We managed about 17 mpg in city/highway work with one test model, but another couldn't break 15 in somewhat harder driving.

Riding that big Montero chassis gives the Sport a stiff, lively on-road ride and overlight power steering that's also rather vague. It's far more stable than the Montero in cornering thanks to its lower stance, but body lean is still noticed in tight turns on-road, accompanied by marked tire squeal.

Montero Sport's 4WD is a part-time type that can't be used on dry pavement, though it permits on-the-fly shifting between 2WD and 4-wheel High.

Noise levels are higher than today's SUV norm. The big door mirrors generate copious turbulence on the highway, the engine fan whines loudly at higher rpm, and tire noise is prominent.

ACCOMMODATIONS Ample ground clearance for off-road work gives the Sport a lofty interior step-in that makes entry/exit a chore, especially to the rear, plus a high cargo floor. In passenger room, the Sport is more like a Jeep Cherokee than a Ford Explorer. The low-roof cabin architecture limits head room for 6-footers, and rear leg space is adequate rather than generous. Still, there's room enough for four adults not to feel claustrophobic, plus all the cargo they're likely to carry. On some

models, the spare tire mounts under the load deck so it doesn't eat into space.

Drivers have a commanding view from a high perch, though the thick rear roof posts hinder lane-changes or parking. Gauges are large and legible, and most minor controls are within easy reach.

BUILD QUALITY Whether on trails or turnpikes, Sport has a truck-like solidity that implies top-flight engineering and assembly. Backing up this impression are tidy detail finish throughout, good-quality interior materials, and nice paint.

VALUE FOR THE MONEY Montero Sport is too slow, noisy, and stiff-riding to be a satisfying suburban utility vehicle, which is how most people really use SUVs. It's happier off-road, where high ground clearance and low-speed lugging ability count more than power or running refinement. Give it a look, but look harder at the "Also Consider" alternatives.

RATINGS

	ES	LS/XLS
Acceleration	2	3
Fuel economy	3	2
Ride quality	3	3
Steering/handling	3	3
Braking	4	4
Quietness	3	3
Driver seating	3	3
Instruments/controls	3	3
Room/comfort (front)	4	4
Room/comfort (rear)	3	3
Cargo room	4	4
Value for the money	3	3
Total	**38**	**38**

SPECIFICATIONS

	4-door wagon
Wheelbase, in.	107.3
Overall length, in.	178.3
Overall width, in.	66.7
Overall height, in.	65.6
Curb weight, lbs.	3980
Cargo vol., cu. ft.	79.3
Fuel capacity, gals.	19.5
Seating capacity	5
Front head room, in.	38.9
Max. front leg room, in.	42.8
Rear head room, in.	37.3
Min. rear leg room, in.	33.5

ENGINES

	ohc I-4	ohc V-6
Size, liters/cu. in.	2.4/143	3.0/181
Horsepower @ rpm	132@ 5500	173@ 5250
Torque (lbs./ft.) @ rpm	148@ 2750	188@ 4000
Availability	S[1]	S[2]

EPA city/highway mpg

5-speed OD manual	22/25	17/20
4-speed OD automatic		19/22

1. ES. 2. LS, XLS.

PRICES

1997 Mitsubishi Montero Sport	Retail Price	Dealer Invoice
ES 2WD 4-door wagon, 5-speed	$17620	$15858
LS 2WD 4-door wagon, automatic	21820	18983
LS 4WD 4-door wagon, 5-speed	23130	20123
LS 4WD 4-door wagon, automatic	23970	20854
XLS 4WD 4-door wagon, automatic	31110	27064
Destination charge	445	445

STANDARD EQUIPMENT:

ES: 2.4-liter 4-cylinder engine, 5-speed manual transmission, driver- and passenger-side air bags, power steering, cloth upholstery, front bucket seats, reclining folding rear seat, front cupholders, tilt steering column, trip odometer, coolant-temperature gauge, tinted glass, dual outside mirrors, AM/FM/CD player w/four speakers, digital

Rating Scale: 5-Excellent; 4-Above average; 3-Average; 2-Below average; 1-Poor

clock, rear defogger, intermittent wipers, visor mirrors, map lights, auxiliary power outlet, carpeting, mud guards, front and rear tow hooks, front-end and fuel-tank skid plates, 225/75R15 mud and snow tires.

LS 2WD adds: 3.0-liter V-6 engine, 4-speed automatic transmission, split folding rear seat, rear cupholders, rear privacy glass, AM/FM/cassette w/six speakers, power antenna, variable intermittent wipers, rear wiper/washer, chrome grille accent.

LS 4WD adds: 4-speed automatic or 5-speed manual transmission, 4-wheel disc brakes, part-time 4-wheel drive, automatic locking front hubs, transfer-case skid plates.

XLS adds: 4-speed automatic transmission, air conditioning, cruise control, leather upholstery, power windows, power door locks, power outside mirrors, power sunroof, Infinity AM/FM/cassette player w/eight speakers, fender flares, side steps, 2-tone paint, 265/70R15 mud and snow tires.

OPTIONAL EQUIPMENT:
Safety Features
Anti-lock brakes, LS, XLS	$610	$500

Major Packages
Preferred Pkg. 3, ES, LS	1037	825
Air conditioning, cargo net, floormats.		
Preferred Pkg. 4, ES, LS	755	505
Roof rack, rear wind deflector, side steps. NA w/Premium Pkg., Appearance Pkg., or power sunroof.		
Convenience Pkg., LS	829	680
Cruise control, power windows and door locks, power mirrors.		
All-Weather Pkg., LS 4WD, XLS	744	610
Limited-slip differential, rear heater, multi-meter (includes compass, outside-temperature indicator, voltmeter, oil-pressure gauge).		
Off-Road Pkg., LS 4WD	1037	850
All-Weather Pkg. plus rear-mounted spare-tire cover.		
Appearance Pkg., LS	1793	1470
Leather-wrappped steering wheel, side steps, bright grille, fender flares, 265/70R15 tires, alloy wheels.		
Premium Pkg., LS	3070	2517
Appearance Pkg. plus power sunroof, Infinity AM/FM/cassette.		

Comfort and Convenience
Air conditioning, ES, LS	915	750
Leather upholstery, LS 2WD	1220	1000
Power sunroof, LS	793	650
CD player, LS, XLS	399	299
10-disc CD changer, LS, XLS	675	465
Rear wiper/washer, ES	195	160
Floormats	85	51

Appearance and Miscellaneous
Rear wind deflector	145	95
Side steps, ES, LS	350	245
Roof rack, ES, LS w/o sunroof	260	165
Spare tire carrier, LS 4WD	75	50
Requires Off-Road Pkg.		

Special Purpose, Wheels and Tires
Trailer hitch w/harness	252	164
Wheel trim rings, ES, LS	70	45
Four wheel locks, LS, XLS	50	33
Five wheel locks, LS 4WD	60	40
Requires Off-Road Pkg.		
Alloy wheels, LS	427	350

NISSAN ALTIMA

✓ BEST BUY

Front-wheel-drive compact
Base price range: $14,990–$19,890. Built in Smyrna, Tenn.
Also consider: Ford Contour, Mazda 626, Mitsubishi Galant

FOR • Quietness • Ride • Passenger room

AGAINST • Automatic transmission performance

Altima is Nissan's entry in the hard-fought compact family sedan market and the company's best-selling U.S. model. It's

Nissan Altima GLE

also made in the U.S. and only in the U.S., being designed expressly for this market.

For 1998, Altima gets a heavy makeover of the original 1993-97 design, with harder-edged styling on a slightly larger package, plus mildly revised powertrains and suspension. Wheelbase is unchanged, but overall length increases 2.6 inches, while overall width and track (width between wheels on the same axle) swell about 2 inches. The '98 also has a bit more rear head and leg room.

Altima's sole engine, a 2.4-liter 4-cylinder, receives internal alterations designed to improve low-speed power delivery. Nissan also says the automatic transmission, an option in place of manual shift, has been reprogrammed for smoother operation. The car's structure is claimed to be 20 percent stiffer than before.

Altima continues in four models: base XE, volume-selling GXE, sporty SE, and luxury GLE. The SE has a firmer suspension, alloy wheels, wider tires, rear disc brakes (versus drums), and a body-color rear spoiler. The GLE boasts leather upholstery and power driver's seat. Anti-lock brakes are optional on all models.

PERFORMANCE From the driver's seat, the new Altima feels like the old model with most of the rough edges smoothed out. Though not measurably quieter, our test GLE sounded far more mechanically pleasant than earlier Altimas. A mild engine "boom" still occurs around 4000-4500 rpm, but cruising revs are well below that, so it's not a big problem. Overall low noise levels had us thinking "junior Buick." Tires thump gently over bumps but seldom roar, and wind rush is low even at highway speeds.

Acceleration is little changed. Our test GLE ran 0-60 mph in a so-so 10 seconds with automatic transmission. There's also little change in the transmission's reluctance to downshift promptly or in its smoothness when it does. Our test GXE returned a somewhat disappointing 20.3 mpg, while our GLE averaged 23.4 mpg despite hard city driving and performance testing.

We haven't driven an SE yet, but other Altimas again had us thinking Buick, with a smooth, absorbent ride except on washboard surfaces, where minor wheel pattering disturbs the calm. Alas, the ride exacts a tradeoff in wimpy body control over big humps and dips, plus more body lean in tight turns than we prefer. Even so, Altima handling is competently agile, aided by quick steering with good feedback. Braking with our test car's ABS option was safe and undramatic, but also unexceptional by today's standards.

ACCOMMODATIONS Unlike previous Altimas, the new one allows 6-footers to sit comfortably in tandem. The cabin still isn't wide enough for three adults aft, but leg, knee, and foot space are all good, as is overall head room even with a power moonroof. Entry/exit to the front earns no complaints, though the rear entryways are fairly narrow at floor level and the doors don't open exceptionally wide.

The new dash is nicely laid out, with clean gauges and convenient, guess-free controls that complement a comfortable driver's post. Commuters should welcome the new console-mount dual cupholders, much more useful than the rickety pull-out contraption of old. Visibility is good except over the shoulder, due to the high-tail styling and wide rear roof posts.

Trunk space is good if not great. A wide rear bumper shelf makes for some back-straining reaches and the lid hinges intrude into the cargo area. The cabin has plenty of places for bric-a-brac, though none accessible to rear-seaters.

Prices are accurate at time of publication; subject to manufacturer's changes.

BUILD QUALITY The '98 Altima is acceptably solid and well finished. Still, one of our early-production test cars suffered a visible hood flutter and a rattly dashboard vibration, plus mild body drumming over railroad tracks. The other had a flimsy feeling trunk lid.

VALUE FOR THE MONEY Like some other '98 cars, Altima has been reduced in price from last year. For example, the mainline GXE with automatic lists for $1500 lower. Combine that with the new model's improvements, especially its low noise levels and soft ride, and Altima remains a must-see for value-minded buyers.

RATINGS

	XE/GXE	SE	GLE
Acceleration	3	3	3
Fuel economy	4	4	4
Ride quality	4	4	4
Steering/handling	3	4	3
Braking	4	4	4
Quietness	4	4	4
Driver seating	3	3	3
Instruments/controls	3	3	3
Room/comfort (front)	4	4	4
Room/comfort (rear)	3	3	3
Cargo room	3	3	3
Value for the money	5	5	5
Total	**43**	**44**	**43**

SPECIFICATIONS

	4-door sedan
Wheelbase, in.	103.1
Overall length, in.	183.1
Overall width, in.	69.1
Overall height, in.	55.9
Curb weight, lbs.	2859
Cargo vol., cu. ft.	13.8
Fuel capacity, gals.	15.9
Seating capacity	5
Front head room, in.	39.4
Max. front leg room, in.	42.0
Rear head room, in.	37.7
Min. rear leg room, in.	33.9

ENGINES

	dohc I-4
Size, liters/cu. in.	2.4/146
Horsepower @ rpm	150@ 5600
Torque (lbs./ft.) @ rpm	154@ 4400
Availability	S
EPA city/highway mpg	
5-speed OD manual	24/31
4-speed OD automatic	22/30

PRICES

Nissan Altima	Retail Price	Dealer Invoice
XE 4-door sedan, 5-speed	$14990	$14265
XE 4-door sedan, automatic	15790	15025
GXE 4-door sedan, 5-speed	17190	15646
GXE 4-door sedan, automatic	17990	16373
SE 4-door sedan, 5-speed	18490	16638
SE 4-door sedan, automatic	19290	17358
GLE 4-door sedan, automatic	19890	17897
Destination charge	420	420

STANDARD EQUIPMENT:

XE: 2.4-liter 4-cylinder engine, 5-speed manual or 4-speed automatic transmission, driver- and passenger-side air bags, power steering, tilt steering wheel, rear defogger, cupholders, remote fuel door and decklid release, cloth reclining bucket seats, power windows, power mirrors, tachometer, coolant-temperature gauge, trip odometer, intermittent wipers, passenger-side visor mirror, tinted glass, 195/65R15 tires, wheel covers.

GXE adds: air conditioning, cruise control, 4-speaker AM/FM/CD, digital clock, illuminated entry, lockable glove compartment, woodgrain trim, split folding rear seat, dual visor mirrors.

SE adds: 4-wheel disc brakes, front sport seats, leather-wrapped

steering wheel and manual shift knob, white-faced gauges, 6-speaker AM/FM/cassette/CD, power/diversity antenna, remote keyless entry, sport-tuned suspension, theft-deterrent system, fog lights, rear spoiler, 205/60R15 tires, alloy wheels, deletes woodgrain trim.

GLE adds to GXE: 4-speed automatic transmission, leather upholstery, leather-wrapped steering wheel, 8-way power driver seat with adjustable lumbar support, rear center armrest with trunk pass-through, 6-speaker AM/FM/cassette/CD, power/diversity antenna, remote keyless entry, variable intermittent wipers, illuminated visor mirrors, theft-deterrent system.

OPTIONAL EQUIPMENT:	Retail Price	Dealer Invoice
Major Packages		
XE Option Pkg., XE	$1899	$1632
AM/FM/cassette with digital clock, air conditioning, cruise control.		
GXE Security and Convenience Pkg., GXE	549	472
6-speaker AM/FM/cassette/CD, remote keyless entry, theft-deterrent system.		
Safety Features		
Anti-lock brakes	499	450
XE requires Option Pkg.		
Comfort and Convenience		
Leather upholstery, SE	1299	1116
Includes 8-way power driver seat with adjustable lumbar support, rear center armrest with trunk pass-through.		
Power sunroof	849	730
NA XE. GXE requires option pkg.		
Cassette player, GXE	NC	NC
Deletes std. CD player.		
Floormats	79	52
Appearance and Miscellaneous		
Rear spoiler, XE, GXE, GLE	409	287
Mud guards	89	59
Alloy wheels, GLE	299	257
Polished alloy wheels, GXE	599	415

NISSAN FRONTIER

Nissan Frontier SE extended cab 4WD

Rear- or 4-wheel-drive compact pickup

Base price range: NA. Built in Smyrna, Tenn.

Also consider: Chevrolet S-10, Ford Ranger, Toyota Tacoma

FOR • Standard 4-wheel anti-lock brakes (4WD) • Quietness • Control layout

AGAINST • Rear-only ABS on 2WD • Lack of V-6 option

Nissan redesigns its pickup truck for the first time since 1986—and gives it a name. The previous model was known simply as the "Nissan Truck." This one's christened Frontier, and is the seventh-generation small pickup sold by Nissan in the U.S.

Frontier comes as a regular cab with a 6.5-foot-long cargo bed and an extended cab, dubbed King Cab, with a 6.2-foot bed. The only engine offered at this time is a new twin-cam 2.4-liter 4-cylinder with 143 horsepower, 9 more than the previous single-cam version. Nissan says a 3.3-liter V-6 will be available in about a year. Manual transmission is standard, and automatic is optional only on 2-wheel-drive models. Frontiers with automatic transmission get a column-mounted shifter. Both bodies are offered with Nissan's part-time 4WD system, which can be shift-

---

Rating Scale: 5-Excellent; 4-Above average; 3-Average; 2-Below average; 1-Poor

ed between 2WD and 4-High on-the-fly up to 25 mph, but is not for use on dry pavement.

Four-wheel anti-lock brakes are standard on 4WD Frontiers; 2WD models come only with rear anti-lock brakes. Dual air bags are standard and the passenger-side air bag can be deactivated for use with a rear-facing child seat.

Three trim levels are offered: base (regular-cab 2WD only), XE, and SE (King Cab only). Regular-cab models have a bench seat. XE King Cabs have a 60/40 split/folding front bench, SE models get buckets, and both come with side-facing rear jump seats.

Towing capacity is 3500 pounds on manual-transmission models, 2000 pounds with the automatic.

PERFORMANCE Nissan claims its new 2.4-liter twin-cam 4-cylinder engine is the most-powerful standard engine in a compact pickup. Trouble is, it's the only engine currently offered in the Frontier. Even regular-cab 2WD manual-transmission models, the lightest-weight Frontiers, were hardly hot rods. Saddle that engine with the weight of a 4WD King Cab, and it feels lethargic. We did not have an opportunity to measure fuel economy.

On the plus side, manual transmission clutch and shift actions are light and smooth, and the automatic shifts crisply and kicks down quickly for more passing power. The twin-cam four grows coarse at high rpm, but settles down at cruising and road and wind noise are pleasantly muffled for a compact pickup.

Ride and handling are strong points, both ranking with the best small pickups. Bumps are taken in stride, and there's only moderate body lean in corners.

ACCOMMODATIONS Frontier has a fresh, car-like interior. Climate and radio controls are mounted high and within easy reach, and the design is far more modern than that of Nissan's previous pickup.

Front head and leg room are generous for even 6-footers. As in every other extended-cab compact pickup, the King Cab's jump seats are child-sized.

Entry and exit is good to the front, and 4WD Frontiers don't have as high a step-in as some competing 4x4 models. All but the base 2WD model have front-door map pockets.

BUILD QUALITY We've driven only prototypes so far, but paint finishes looked smooth and glossy. There's lots of hard plastic in the interior, but it doesn't look cheap, and cloth trim on seats and door panels is more upscale than in the typical compact pickup.

VALUE FOR THE MONEY Frontier has a rather narrow assortment of available features. For instance, you can't get an automatic transmission with 4WD, bucket seats in a regular-cab, or 4-wheel ABS in 2WD models. And lack of a V-6 really hurts the heavier models' performance. But if one of the models offered fits your needs, Frontier rates among the most refined small pickups.

RATINGS

	Reg. cab 2WD	King Cab 4WD
Acceleration	3	2
Fuel economy	3	2
Ride quality	3	3
Steering/handling	3	3
Braking	3	4
Quietness	4	4
Driver seating	4	4
Instruments/controls	4	4
Room/comfort (front)	3	3
Room/comfort (rear)	—	2
Cargo room	1	2
Value for the money	3	3
Total	34	36

SPECIFICATIONS

	Reg. cab	Ext. cab
Wheelbase, in.	104.3	116.1
Overall length, in.	184.3	196.1
Overall width, in.	66.5	71.9
Overall height, in.	62.8	65.9
Curb weight, lbs.	2911	3685
Maximum payload, lbs.	1400	1400
Fuel capacity, gals.	15.9	15.9

	Reg. cab	Ext. cab
Seating capacity	3	5
Front head room, in.	39.3	39.3
Max. front leg room, in.	40.4	40.8
Rear head room, in.	—	NA
Min. rear leg room, in.	—	NA

ENGINES

	dohc I-4
Size, liters/cu. in.	2.4/146
Horsepower @ rpm	143@ 5200
Torque (lbs./ft.) @ rpm	154@ 4000
Availability	S

EPA city/highway mpg

5-speed OD manual	22/26
4-speed OD automatic	20/24

Prices, standard equipment, and options were unavailable at the time of publication.

Nissan Maxima GLE

Front-wheel-drive midsize car; similar to Infiniti I30
Base price range: $21,499-$26,899. Built in Japan.
Also consider: Ford Taurus, Honda Accord, Toyota Camry

FOR • Air bags, side (optional) • Acceleration • Steering/handling • Ride

AGAINST • Rear seat comfort • Fuel economy • Anti-lock brakes (optional, not standard)

Maxima is the largest car in Nissan's U.S. line. As a midsize sedan it competes with those perennial heavy-hitters on the new-car sales chart, Ford Taurus, Honda Accord, and Toyota Camry. Though Nissan touts Maxima as a "near-luxury" car, we think that title better suits the similar, more upscale I30 sedan from sister division Infiniti.

Last redesigned three years ago, Maxima gets only one significant change for 1998: optional front side air bags for the sporty SE and luxury GLE versions. The entry-level GXE is denied this, at least for now, but anti-lock brakes are again optional for all Maximas.

As before, Nissan's veteran 3.0-liter V-6 links to a manual or optional automatic transmission. Automatic is standard on the GXE. The SE continues with a firm-tune suspension, wider tires on 16-inch wheels (versus 15s), rear spoiler, fog lights, and other "enthusiast" features.

PERFORMANCE We may not put it in the "near-luxury" class, but Maxima could easily belong there for performance and refinement.

The smooth, quick-winding V-6 delivers impressive acceleration. We timed a GXE with automatic at 7.9 seconds to 60 mph—good going even for some V-8 cars. Passing punch is equally strong. Too bad the automatic is slow to downshift at times and can do so with a lurch. Fuel economy depends more than usual on how and where you drive. We averaged 18.2 mpg with one GXE and 21.4 with another, the latter figure inflated by lots of highway driving.

The eager-to-run manual-transmission SE we tested delivered performance that had us thinking BMW 528i at more than $10,000 less. It averaged 20.9 mpg.

Prices are accurate at time of publication; subject to manufacturer's changes.

Maxima has an absorbent and stable ride, precise steering, and capable front-drive handling. Body lean is marked at high cornering speeds in the more softly sprung GXE and GLE models; it's much less noticed in the SE. Grip is secure in any case. The anti-lock brakes provide secure stopping power, but we're dismayed that ABS is still optional here when it's included on so many other cars of similar price. Overall noise levels are modest, with a pleasing lack of engine ruckus.

ACCOMMODATIONS Like so many modern cars, Maxima has adult-size room for four, but not five if the journey will be long. The optional sunroof eats into rear head room, however, and the rear seat cushion is low enough that some people have to ride with their knees up. The trunk is usefully shaped and has a conveniently low sill, but outright volume isn't exceptional.

Instruments and controls are well placed and generally easy to use while driving. One exception is the power seat controls, which are far enough back on the outboard side of the seat cushion as to be partly masked by the lap belt. Visibility is fine to the front and sides, but invisible rear corners can worry in close-quarters maneuvering.

BUILD QUALITY Like most Nissans, Maxima doesn't feel quite as "bank vault solid" as the pricey Europeans, but it's assembled with obvious care from visibly good-quality materials. This car also enjoys a good reliability record.

VALUE FOR THE MONEY Competitors are getting better, but Maxima remains one of the most satisfying midsize sedans you can buy. It performs as well as some costlier cars, matches their refinement, and offers near luxury-class features for far less money. If you're looking for a step up from the usual family 4-door, this is an excellent choice.

RATINGS

	GXE/GLE	SE
Acceleration	4	4
Fuel economy	3	3
Ride quality	4	4
Steering/handling	3	4
Braking	4	4
Quietness	4	4
Driver seating	4	4
Instruments/controls	4	4
Room/comfort (front)	4	4
Room/comfort (rear)	4	4
Cargo room	3	3
Value for the money	5	5
Total	**46**	**47**

SPECIFICATIONS

	4-door sedan
Wheelbase, in.	106.3
Overall length, in.	187.7
Overall width, in.	69.7
Overall height, in.	55.7
Curb weight, lbs.	3001
Cargo vol., cu. ft.	14.5
Fuel capacity, gals.	18.5
Seating capacity	5
Front head room, in.	40.1
Max. front leg room, in.	43.9
Rear head room, in.	37.4
Min. rear leg room, in.	34.3

ENGINES

	dohc V-6
Size, liters/cu. in.	3.0/181
Horsepower @ rpm	190@ 5600
Torque (lbs./ft.) @ rpm	205@ 4000
Availability	S

EPA city/highway mpg
4-speed OD automatic	21/28
5-speed OD manual	22/27

PRICES

Nissan Maxima

	Retail Price	Dealer Invoice
GXE 4-door sedan, 5-speed	$21499	$19470
GXE 4-door sedan, automatic	$23249	$20814
SE 4-door sedan, 5-speed	23499	20916
SE 4-door sedan, automatic	24499	21806
GLE 4-door sedan, automatic	26899	23943
Destination charge	490	490

STANDARD EQUIPMENT:

GXE: 3.0-liter DOHC V-6 engine, 5-speed manual transmission or 4-speed automatic transmission, driver- and passenger-side air bags, 4-wheel disc brakes, air conditioning, power steering, cruise control, cloth reclining front bucket seats, multi-adjustable driver seat w/lumbar support, front storage console, cupholders, folding rear armrest w/trunk pass-through, power windows, power door locks, power mirrors, tilt steering column, tinted glass, tachometer, coolant-temperature gauge, dual trip odometers, digital clock, 4-speaker AM/FM/cassette, diversity antenna, visor mirrors, intermittent wipers, rear defogger, remote decklid and fuel-door releases, map light, bright grille, 205/65R15 tires, wheel covers, deluxe 6-speaker audio system with AM/FM/cassette/CD player, leather-wrapped steering wheel and shifter.

SE adds: sport-tuned suspension, fog lamps, rear spoiler, bright exhaust outlet, color-keyed grille, 215/55R15 tires, alloy wheels.

GLE adds to GXE: 4-speed automatic transmission, automatic air conditioning, 8-way power driver seat, 4-way power passenger seat, leather upholstery, leather-wrapped steering wheel and shifter, simulated-wood interior trim, remote keyless entry, illuminated visor mirrors, variable intermittent wipers, remote keyless entry system with trunk release, theft-deterrent system, Bose 6-speaker audio system with AM/FM/cassette/CD player, Homelink universal garage-door opener, simulated-leather door panels, bright exhaust outlet, 205/65HR15 tires, alloy wheels.

OPTIONAL EQUIPMENT:
Major Packages

	Retail	Dealer
Leather Trim Pkg., SE	1349	1159

Includes leather seats, 4-way power front passenger seat, automatic climate control, simulated-leather door panels. Requires Security and Convenience Pkg. and Bose audio system.

Deluxe Seating Pkg., SE, GLE	449	386

Front-seat side air bags, heated front seats, heated mirrors, low washer fluid warning light, heavy duty battery. GLE requires anti-lock brakes. SE requires anti-lock brakes, Bose audio system, Leather Trim Pkg., and Security and Convenience Pkg.

Security and Convenience Pkg., GXE	699	615
SE	1690	1488

Includes 8-way power driver seat, power sunroof (SE), remote keyless entry system, power trunk release, security system, illuminated visor vanity mirrors, variable intermittent wipers, Homelink universal garage door opener (SE). NA GXE with 5-speed manual transmission.

Safety Features

Anti-lock brakes	499	450

Comfort and Convenience

Bose audio system, SE	899	790

Requires Security and Convenience Pkg.

Power sunroof, GXE, GLE	899	772

GXE requires automatic transmission and Security and Convenience Pkg.

Burlwood trim, GXE, SE	429	292

NA GXE with rear spoiler.

Floormats	79	52

Appearance and Miscellaneous

Rear spoiler, GXE, GLE	429	308

NA GXE with burlwood trim.

Alloy wheels, GXE	849	555

NISSAN PATHFINDER

Rear- or 4-wheel-drive midsize sport-utility vehicle; similar to Infiniti QX4

Base price range: $23,999-$32,849. Built in Japan.

Also consider: Ford Explorer, Mercedes-Benz ML320, Toyota 4Runner

Rating Scale: 5-Excellent; 4-Above average; 3-Average; 2-Below average; 1-Poor

Nissan Pathfinder LE

FOR • Standard anti-lock brakes • Steering/handling • Ride

AGAINST • Rear seat entry/exit • Rear seat room • Engine noise

One of the oldest names among import-brand sport-utility vehicles, the Nissan Pathfinder is all but unchanged for a second year following its stem-to-stern redesign for 1996. Five models continue: 2- and 4-wheel drives in base XE and top LE trim, and a mid-range SE 4x4. All come with dual air bags, 4-wheel anti-lock brakes, and a 3.3-liter overhead-cam V-6 engine.

XEs and SEs come with manual transmission. Automatic is optional for them and standard on LE. Maximum towing weight is 5000 pounds.

Pathfinder's 4WD is a part-time, on-demand setup with floor-mounted transfer case lever. It's not for use on dry pavement, but permits on-the-fly shifts between 2WD and 4WD High.

Nissan's upscale Infiniti division sells a luxury 4x4 Pathfinder called the QX4 with a more-sophisticated drive system, full-house standard equipment, and a higher price.

PERFORMANCE In its latest form, Pathfinder is less truck-like than many rivals, including the best-selling Ford Explorer. The tight suspension and linear steering contribute to a sense of control, but there's a surprising amount of body lean and tire squeal in fast turns. Ride is firm but devoid of harshness over bumps.

The 3.3-liter V-6 is stronger and smoother than Pathfinder's previous engine, but still gruff and growly when worked hard. Low-speed response is good, but Pathfinder can't match V-8-powered domestic SUVs for all-out acceleration. Nissan modestly claims 0-60 mph in about 10.5 seconds for 4x2s, 11.2 for 4x4s. Fuel economy is typical SUV—namely, mediocre. An automatic-equipped SE 4x4 averaged only 14.1 mpg in our city, suburban, and highway driving.

Pathfinder 4x4s don't have pushbutton shifting between 2- and 4WD, whereas many other SUVs offer this at least as an option. Then too, rivals such as Explorer and Grand Cherokee offer more-convenient 4WD that can be used on dry pavement.

ACCOMMODATIONS Pathfinder has a relatively low ride height that makes it easy to get in or out of the front seats. Access to the back is more challenging, as the doors don't open 90 degrees and there's little room to swing your feet and legs through the narrow openings.

All-around head room is good if not exceptional, but the rear seat has barely enough leg room for anyone over 5-foot-10 or so; worse, there's little toe room under the front seats.

The dashboard is a model of simplicity and function, but the air conditioning indicator light tends to wash out in sunshine, and the door-mounted power window and lock switches are too dim at night. Thick roof pillars impeded the over-the-shoulder view of some of our test drivers, but visibility is otherwise good.

So is cargo space. However, folding the rear seats requires tilting the cushion, then removing the head restraints so the backrests can lie flat. We prefer the easier one-step design found on Explorer and the Chevy Blazer/GMC Jimmy.

BUILD QUALITY Our test SE model showed near flawless workmanship. Fit, finish, and materials were all top-notch inside and out.

VALUE FOR THE MONEY Pathfinder costs more than some domestic rivals yet doesn't match their room, power, or available full-time 4WD. Still, it has enough goodness to warrant consideration from anyone who appreciates good road manners.

RATINGS	2WD 5-speed	4WD auto.
Acceleration	3	3
Fuel economy	2	1
Ride quality	3	3
Steering/handling	4	4
Braking	4	4
Quietness	3	3
Driver seating	4	4
Instruments/controls	4	4
Room/comfort (front)	4	4
Room/comfort (rear)	3	3
Cargo room	5	5
Value for the money	3	3
Total	**42**	**41**

SPECIFICATIONS

	4-door wagon
Wheelbase, in.	106.3
Overall length, in.	178.3
Overall width, in.	68.7
Overall height, in.	67.1
Curb weight, lbs.	3675
Cargo vol., cu. ft.	85.0
Fuel capacity, gals.	20.8
Seating capacity	5
Front head room, in.	39.5
Max. front leg room, in.	41.7
Rear head room, in.	37.5
Min. rear leg room, in.	31.8

ENGINES

	ohc V-6
Size, liters/cu. in.	3.3/201
Horsepower @ rpm	168@ 4800
Torque (lbs./ft.) @ rpm	196@ 2800
Availability	S

EPA city/highway mpg

5-speed OD manual	16/18
4-speed OD automatic	15/19

PRICES

Nissan Pathfinder	Retail Price	Dealer Invoice
XE 2WD 4-door wagon, 5-speed	$23999	$21610
XE 2WD 4-door wagon, automatic	24999	22510
XE 4WD 4-door wagon, 5-speed	25999	23410
XE 4WD 4-door wagon, automatic	26999	24311
SE 4WD 4-door wagon, 5-speed	29099	26202
SE 4WD 4-door wagon, automatic	30099	27103
LE 2WD 4-door wagon, automatic	30449	27418
LE 4WD 4-door wagon, automatic	32849	29580
Destination charge	490	490

STANDARD EQUIPMENT:

XE: 3.3-liter V-6 engine, 5-speed manual or 4-speed automatic transmission, driver- and passenger-side air bags, anti-lock brakes, power steering, air conditioning, cloth upholstery, reclining front bucket seats, 60/40 split folding rear seat with reclining seatback and head restraints, center storage console with armrest, cupholders, tilt steering column, AM/FM/CD player, diversity antenna, digital clock, tachometer, coolant-temperature gauge, trip odometer, tinted glass, dual outside mirrors, passenger-side visor mirror, rear defogger, variable intermittent wipers, rear intermittent wiper/washer, remote fuel-door release, auxiliary power outlets, concealed storage bin, rear heat ducts (4WD), map lights, cargo cover (4WD), chrome upper bumpers, front and rear tow hooks, 235/70R15 tires, chromed steel wheels, full-size spare tire.

SE adds: cruise control, automatic air conditioning, moquette upholstery, multi-adjustable driver seat, rear folding armrest, heated power mirrors, power door locks, power windows, remote keyless entry, theft-deterrent system, power antenna, privacy glass, illuminated visor mirrors, luggage rack, tubular step rail, cargo net and cover, fog lamps, rear wind deflector, fender flares, bright grille and bumper, mud guards, 265/70R15 tires, 6-spoke alloy wheels.

Prices are accurate at time of publication; subject to manufacturer's changes.

LE deletes fender flares and tubular step rail and adds: 4-speed automatic transmission, limited-slip differential (4WD), leather upholstery, heated front seats (4WD), leather-wrapped steering wheel, woodgrain interior trim, simulated-leather door trim, digital compass and outside-temperature gauge, Bose AM/FM/cassette/CD player, Homelink universal garage-door opener, bright running boards, 235/70R15 tires, lacy-spoke alloy wheels.

OPTIONAL EQUIPMENT:

	Retail Price	Dealer Invoice

Major Packages

	Retail Price	Dealer Invoice
Convenience Pkg., XE	$1449	$1245

Cruise control, power windows and door locks, heated power mirrors, remote keyless entry and theft-deterrent sytem, cargo cover and net, luggage rack.

Sport Pkg., XE 2WD	1099	944
XE 4WD	499	428

Includes limited slip differential (4WD), black fender flares (2WD), fog lights, rear wind deflector, step rails (2WD), luggage rack, 265/70R15 tires (2WD), six-spoke alloy wheels (2WD). Requires Convenience Pkg.

Leather Trim Pkg., SE	1399	1201

Includes leather upholstery, leather-wrapped steering wheel, heated front seats, simulated leather door trim, compass, outside temperature gauge.

Off-Road Pkg., SE	249	214

Limited-slip rear differential, black bumpers. Requires Bose/Moonroof/Pkg.

Luxury Pkg., LE	1299	1116

Power moonroof, power front seats.

Bose/Moonroof Pkg., SE	1549	1331

Power moonroof, Bose AM/FM/cassette/CD player, power antenna, Homelink universal garage door opener. Requires Sport Pkg.

Comfort and Convenience

Burlwood interior trim, XE, SE	369	252

XE requires Convenience Pkg.

Floormats	79	52

Appearance and Miscellaneous

Rear wind deflector, XE	89	68

Special Purpose, Wheels and Tires

Alloy wheels, XE 2WD	849	588
Spare tire carrier, XE, SE	299	257

XE requires Sport Pkg. SE requires Off-Road Pkg.

Tow hitch	389	292

NISSAN QUEST

Nissan Quest GXE

Front-wheel-drive minivan; similar to Mercury Villager

Base price range: (1997 model) $21,249-$26,049. Built in Avon Lake, Ohio.

Also consider: Dodge Caravan, Ford Windstar, Toyota Sienna

FOR • Passenger and cargo room • Steering/handling • Anti-lock brakes

AGAINST • Control layout

This American-built minivan gets a third model and a few other changes for its sixth season. Wearing Nissan's luxury GLE badge, the added Quest slots in above the GXE and entry-level

XE models because of its standard leather upholstery, power right-front seat, power moonroof, semi-automatic climate control, and CD changer. All but the leather and power seat are optionally available on the GXE. A power driver's seat and anti-lock brakes are standard for GXE and GLE; ABS is available for XE in a package option.

As before, Quest is a near-twin to the Mercury Villager, sharing a Nissan design built by Ford in Ohio that's sized like the shorter Chrysler and General Motors minivans. A left-side rear passenger door still isn't available, but will be next year as part of a major update. All Quests (and Villagers) come with a 3.0-liter Nissan V-6, automatic transmission, two front bucket seats, and a 2-place third-row bench that slides on integrated floor tracks. A 3-person middle bench is standard on XE; other Quests have a pair of individual "captain's chairs." A second-row bench with twin integrated child seats is optional except on the GLE.

See the Mercury Villager report for an evaluation of the Quest.

RATINGS

	XE	GXE	GLE
Acceleration	3	3	3
Fuel economy	2	2	2
Ride quality	3	3	3
Steering/handling	3	3	3
Braking	3	4	4
Quietness	3	3	3
Driver seating	4	4	4
Instruments/controls	3	3	3
Room/comfort (front)	4	4	4
Room/comfort (rear)	3	3	3
Cargo room	5	5	5
Value for the money	3	3	3
Total	**39**	**40**	**40**

SPECIFICATIONS

	3-door van
Wheelbase, in.	112.2
Overall length, in.	189.9
Overall width, in.	73.7
Overall height, in.	65.6
Curb weight, lbs.	3865
Cargo vol., cu. ft.	114.8
Fuel capacity, gals.	20.0
Seating capacity	7
Front head room, in.	39.5
Max. front leg room, in.	39.9
Rear head room, in.	39.7
Min. rear leg room, in.	36.3

ENGINES

	ohc V-6
Size, liters/cu. in.	3.0/181
Horsepower @ rpm	151@ 4800
Torque (lbs./ft.) @ rpm	174@ 4400
Availability	S

EPA city/highway mpg

4-speed OD automatic	17/23

PRICES

1997 Nissan Quest	Retail Price	Dealer Invoice
XE 3-door van	$21249	$18913
GXE 3-door van	26049	23186
Destination charge	470	470

STANDARD EQUIPMENT:

XE: 3.0-liter V-6 engine, 4-speed automatic transmission, driver- and passenger-side air bags, front air conditioning, power steering, cloth upholstery, reclining front bucket seats, 2-passenger second-row bench seat and 3-passenger rear bench seat, front storage console, tilt steering column, tachometer, trip odometer, coolant-temperature gauge, AM/FM/cassette/CD player, diversity antenna, digital clock, tinted glass, dual outside mirrors, rear defogger, visor mirrors, variable intermittent wipers, intermittent rear wiper/washer, cor-

Rating Scale: 5-Excellent; 4-Above average; 3-Average; 2-Below average; 1-Poor

nering lamps, floormats, 205/75R15 tires, wheel covers.

GXE adds: anti-lock 4-wheel disc brakes, rear air conditioning, rear climate controls, cruise control, upgraded cloth upholstery, 8-way power driver seat, second row captain's chairs, power windows, power door locks, heated power mirrors, illuminated visor mirrors, rear audio controls, power antenna, leather-wrapped steering wheel w/audio controls, remote keyless entry, theft-deterrent system, roof rack, side and rear privacy glass, map lights, automatic headlamps, rear auxiliary power outlets, lockable underseat storage, cargo net, alloy wheels.

OPTIONAL EQUIPMENT:	Retail Price	Dealer Invoice
Major Packages		
Handling Pkg., GXE	$549	$472
Power and Glass Pkg., XE	1249	1074
Convenience Pkg., XE	649	558
Touring Pkg., XE	999	858
Leather Trim Pkg., GXE	1299	1116
Luxury Pkg., GXE	1249	1074
Safety Features		
Anti-lock 4-wheel disc brakes, XE	499	428
Comfort and Convenience		
Rear air conditioning, XE	649	558
Second-row captain's chairs, XE	599	514
Integrated child seats,	199	170
Appearance and Miscellaneous		
2-tone paint	299	257

NISSAN SENTRA

Nissan Sentra SE

Front-wheel-drive subcompact

Base price range: $11,499-$16549. Built in Smyrna, Tenn.

Also consider: Chevrolet Prizm, Ford Escort, Honda Civic

FOR • Fuel economy • Ride • Anti-lock brakes (optional GXE, GLE, SE)

AGAINST • Rear seat room • Rear seat entry/exit • Seat comfort

Last redesigned for 1995, Nissan's entry in the hard-fought small-sedan market gets a minor facelift and a fifth model for 1998. Badged SE, the newcomer is a sportier Sentra with the same 2.0-liter 4-cylinder engine that powers the top SE-R version of the related 200SX coupe. (Sentra and 200SX share the same basic chassis, structure, and front-end sheetmetal.) The SE also comes with 15-inch alloy wheels (versus 14s), wider tires, rear-disc brakes, aero body addenda, fog lights, and a special grille with body-color applique.

Other '98 Sentras have their own new-design grille, revised bumpers, and a carryover 1.6-liter 4-cylinder, also with dual overhead camshafts and four valves per cylinder. Base, XE, GXE and GLE trim levels continue. All have standard manual transmission; automatic is optional except on the base Sentra. Anti-lock brakes are optional for GXE, GLE and SE, and include rear disc brakes on GXE and GLE.

PERFORMANCE We haven't driven the SE yet, but it should be much livelier than other Sentras. We'd guess 0-60 mph in the region of 8 seconds with manual shift. The SE also promises to

have markedly sportier handling with its bigger wheels and tires and dual stabilizer bars; other Sentras except the base model have a rear bar only.

As for the 1.6-liter models, they just don't have much low-rpm grunt, so they need lots of throttle to deliver only so-so acceleration. Nissan claims a brisk 8.5 seconds 0-60 mph with manual shift, but our experience suggests that figure is optimistic. The automatic transmission certainly saps enough power to make freeway merging seem dodgy at times, and full-throttle downshifts can be rude and abrupt. At least fuel economy averages a likable 25-30 mpg on any of the 1.6-liter models.

Ride is agreeable too: supple and well controlled for a small sedan. A very solid structure enhances the sense of comfort. Alas, non-SE Sentras have fairly soft damping that allows pronounced body lean in tight corners, where grip runs out early on the relatively skinny tires. Steering is quick and responsive though, and handling is safe and front-drive predictable within the car's modest limits.

We wish noise were more modest. Though smooth and not too boomy, both Sentra engines become quite vocal at higher rpm, and tire thrum can be irritating on coarse pavement.

ACCOMMODATIONS Sentra's interior is slightly below par even for the subcompact class. There's good room up front for average-size adults, but head room is skimpy in back, as are leg and foot room unless the front seats are moved up some. Most adults will also find the fit tight through the narrow rear doors, and all seats are flat and somewhat thin on padding.

Cargo space is a bit sub-par for the class, but adequate. The trunk has a large, low-lip aperture, plus a floor that extends fairly far forward.

Drivers face a friendly and functional dashboard, though it's not remarkable in any way. Outward vision is okay, but invisible rear corners don't help when parallel parking.

BUILD QUALITY Our last test Sentra, a volume-selling GXE, looked rather plain inside and out, but its fit and finish were of a high order. Doors closed with a solid thunk, and interior trim looked tasteful and durable, though not upscale.

VALUE FOR THE MONEY Sentra is a solid, refined subcompact that deserves a look despite the 1.6-liter engine's relative lack of oomph. Dealers should be discounting to win your business, even on the quicker new SE version.

RATINGS	Base/XE 5-speed	GXE/LE auto
Acceleration	3	3
Fuel economy	5	4
Ride quality	4	4
Steering/handling	3	3
Braking	4	4
Quietness	3	3
Driver seating	4	4
Instruments/controls	3	3
Room/comfort (front)	3	3
Room/comfort (rear)	3	3
Cargo room	2	2
Value for the money	3	2
Total	**40**	**38**

SPECIFICATIONS	4-door sedan
Wheelbase, in.	99.8
Overall length, in.	171.1
Overall width, in.	66.6
Overall height, in.	54.5
Curb weight, lbs.	2315
Cargo vol., cu. ft.	10.7
Fuel capacity, gals.	13.2
Seating capacity	5
Front head room, in.	39.1
Max. front leg room, in.	42.3
Rear head room, in.	36.5
Min. rear leg room, in.	32.4

ENGINES	dohc I-4	dohc I-4
Size, liters/cu. in.	1.6/97	2.0/122
Horsepower @ rpm	115@ 6000	140@ 6400

Prices are accurate at time of publication; subject to manufacturer's changes.

	dohc I-4	dohc I-4
Torque (lbs./ft.) @ rpm.............................	108@	132@
	4000	4800
Availability	S	S[1]
EPA city/highway mpg		
5-speed OD manual..	30/40	23/31
4-speed OD automatic....................................	28/37	23/30

1. SE.

PRICES

Nissan Sentra

	Retail Price	Dealer Invoice
Base 4-door sedan, 5-speed	$11499	$10950
XE 4-door sedan, 5-speed	13699	12761
XE 4-door sedan, automatic	14499	13506
GXE 4-door sedan, 5-speed	14899	13494
GXE 4-door sedan, automatic	15699	14218
GLE 4-door sedan, 5-speed	15749	14263
GLE 4-door sedan, automatic	16549	14987
SE 4-door sedan, 5-speed	—	—
SE 4-door sedan, automatic.........................	—	—
Destination charge	490	490

SE prices not available at time of publication.

STANDARD EQUIPMENT:

Base: 1.6-liter dohc 4-cylinder engine, 5-speed manual transmission, driver- and passenger-side air bags, cloth reclining front bucket seats, front console, cupholders, tilt steering column, coolant-temperature gauge, trip odometer, rear defogger, auxiliary power outlet, tinted glass, driver-side outside mirror, 155/80R13 tires.

XE adds: 5-speed manual or 4-speed automatic transmission, power steering, air conditioning, AM/FM/cassette, digital clock, intermittent wipers, remote decklid and fuel-door releases, dual outside mirrors, 175/70R13 tires, wheel covers.

GXE adds: cruise control, split folding rear seat, upgraded cloth upholstery, power windows, power door locks, power mirrors, passenger-side visor mirror, cargo light, bodyside moldings.

GLE adds: velour upholstery, fold front armrest (w/automatic), remote keyless entry, CD/cassette player, tachometer, theft-deterrent system, 175/65R14 tires, alloy wheels.

SE adds: 2.0-liter dohc 4-cylinder engine, variable-assist power steering, leather-wrapped steering wheel, floormats, front stabilizer bar, front air dam, rear spoiler, lower bodyside moldings, fog lights, 195/55R15 tires.

OPTIONAL EQUIPMENT:
Major Packages

SE Option Pkg., SE..	—	—
Power moonroof, remote keyless entry, theft-deterrent system.		

Safety Features

Anti-lock brakes, GXE, GLE, SE..............................	499	450
Includes 4-wheel disc brakes.		

Comfort and Convenience

Power moonroof, GLE...	449	386
3-disc CD changer, XE, GXE	559	408
CD player, XE, GXE	469	307
Rosewood trim, Base, XE, GXE, GLE	319	221

Appearance and Miscellaneous

Rear spoiler, Base, XE, GXE, GLE	339	246

NISSAN 200SX

Front-wheel-drive sports coupe

Base price range: (1997 models) $12,999-$17,549. Built in Smyrna, Tenn.

Also consider: Ford Escort ZX2, Mitsubishi Eclipse, Toyota Paseo

FOR • Anti-lock brakes (optional SE, SE-R) • Acceleration (SE-R) • Steering/handling • Fuel economy

AGAINST • Rear visibility • Ride • Noise

Before 1995, Nissan offered 2- and 4-door Sentra subcompact

Nissan 200SX SE-R

sedans, which sold well, plus related NX "budget coupes," which hardly sold at all. Accordingly, Nissan decided to replace the NX with a more stylish 2-door Sentra with the old 200SX nameplate.

The 200SX has changed little since, including this year. However, the '98s do get minor revisions to bumpers and grille, and, as on other of Nissan's sportier cars, white-face gauges.

The base and step-up SE models retain a 1.6-liter 4-cylinder engine with dual overhead camshafts and four valves per cylinder. The top-line SE-R has a 2.0-liter version. All offer manual and optional automatic transmissions. Anti-lock brakes with rear discs are optional for SE and SE-R.

In other news, the base model is upgraded from standard 13- to 14-inch wheels and tires, and the SE-R gains speed-variable power steering (versus fixed-rate assist).

PERFORMANCE The 200SX comes in two distinct flavors. The SE-R is the spicy model. We timed our manual-shift test example at a speedy 8.4 seconds 0-60 mph—quicker than most class rivals. And the 2.0-liter engine has enough torque for breezy highway passing even with automatic. By comparison, the 1.6-liter base and SE models are mild stuff: adequately zesty with manual shift but none too vigorous with automatic. With either engine the automatic tends to hunt a lot between gears in normal driving. Fuel economy is good with any 200SX. Even our hot-shot SE-R managed 28 mpg overall despite lots of city driving. Lesser 200s are thriftier still.

The SE-R has above-average grip and modest body lean, which make for safe, enjoyable going on twisty roads. Other models have softer damping and narrower tires, so they suffer more cornering lean and front-end plowing. Steering is firm and responsive across the board. The SE-R has a jumpy ride over rough pavement.

None of these cars is peaceful on a long cruise. Vibrations from powertrain and road send a tingle through the structure, engines are boomy and tire noise is prominent.

ACCOMMODATIONS The 200SX offers better-than-average passenger and cargo room for a small coupe. In most such cars, the rear seat is a lost cause except for toddlers or pets. Instruments are clear and well placed, and the dashboard puts most controls close by. Visibility is good except dead-astern, where a narrow rear window and a bulky rear spoiler impede the view.

BUILD QUALITY Like the related Sentra, the 200SX has a substantial on-road feel and commendable overall fit and finish. Still, this is an econocar at heart, so materials are serviceable, not upscale.

VALUE FOR THE MONEY Demand for all sporty coupes is flagging, so Nissan dealers should offer good discounts on the 200SX of your choice. We'd choose the SE-R as the most enjoyable of this bunch, but consider a base or SE if you're on a budget.

RATINGS	Base/SE	SE-R
Acceleration	3	4
Fuel economy	4	4
Ride quality	3	3
Steering/handling	3	4
Braking	4	4
Quietness	3	3
Driver seating	3	3
Instruments/controls	3	3
Room/comfort (front)	4	4
Room/comfort (rear)	3	3
Cargo room	3	3
Value for the money	4	4
Total	40	42

Rating Scale: 5-Excellent; 4-Above average; 3-Average; 2-Below average; 1-Poor

CONSUMER GUIDE™

SPECIFICATIONS

	2-door coupe
Wheelbase, in.	99.8
Overall length, in.	170.1
Overall width, in.	66.6
Overall height, in.	54.2
Curb weight, lbs.	2363
Cargo vol., cu. ft.	10.4
Fuel capacity, gals.	13.2
Seating capacity	4
Front head room, in.	39.1
Max. front leg room, in.	42.3
Rear head room, in.	35.4
Min. rear leg room, in.	31.4

ENGINES

	dohc I-4	dohc I-4
Size, liters/cu. in.	1.6/97	2.0/122
Horsepower @ rpm	115@ 6000	140@ 6400
Torque (lbs./ft.) @ rpm	108@ 4000	132@ 4800
Availability	S[1]	S[2]
EPA city/highway mpg		
4-speed OD automatic	27/36	23/30
5-speed OD manual	29/39	23/31

1. Base, SE. 2. SE-R.

PRICES

1997 Nissan 200SX

	Retail Price	Dealer Invoice
2-door notchback, 5-speed	$12999	$12377
2-door notchback, automatic	13799	13139
SE 2-door notchback, 5-speed	15349	13980
SE 2-door notchback, automatic	16149	14708
SE-R 2-door notchback, 5-speed	16749	15255
SE-R 2-door notchback, automatic	17549	15984
Destination charge	470	470

Prices are for vehicles distributed by Toyota Motor Sales, U.S.A., Inc. The dealer invoice and destination charge may be higher in areas served by independent distributors.

STANDARD EQUIPMENT:

1.6-liter DOHC 4-cylinder, 5-speed manual or 4-speed automatic transmission, driver- and passenger-side air bags, cloth upholstery, reclining front bucket seats, cupholders, power mirrors, tinted glass, tilt steering column, tachometer, coolant temperture gauge, trip odometer, rear defogger, intermittent wipers, remote decklid and fuel-door releases, rear spoiler, 175/70R13 tires, wheel covers.
SE adds: air conditioning, cruise control, upgraded cloth upholstery, front sport bucket seats, split folding rear seat, AM/FM/cassette, digital clock, power windows, power door locks, fog lights, color-keyed bodyside moldings and door handles, 175/65R14 tires, alloy wheels.
SE-R adds: 2.0-liter DOHC 4-cylinder engine, 4-wheel disc brakes, limited-slip differential, remote keyless entry, theft-deterrent system, leather-wrapped steering wheel and shifter, 195/55R15 tires.

OPTIONAL EQUIPMENT:
Major Packages

Value Option Pkg., base	999	858
Air conditioning, AM/FM/cassette.		
Special Edition Sport Pkg., SE	499	455
CD player, remote keyless entry, theft-deterrent system, sport graphics, armrest, floormats. NA with 3-disc CD changer.		

Safety Features

Anti-lock brakes, SE, SE-R	499	450
SE includes 4-wheel disc brakes.		

Comfort and Convenience

Power sunroof, SE, SE-R	449	386
3-disc CD changer	669	511
CD player	469	349

Appearance and Miscellaneous

Rosewood trim	319	221
Floormats	79	52

NISSAN 240SX

Nissan 240SX LE

Rear-wheel-drive sports coupe
Base price range: (1997 models) $18,359-$25,249. Built in Japan.
Also consider: Honda Prelude, Mitsubishi Eclipse, Toyota Celica

FOR • Visibility • Steering/handling
AGAINST • Noise • Rear seat room • Ride (SE) • Cargo room

Nissan's rear-drive compact coupe is unchanged for what may be its last year in America. The 240SX has been a consistent sales disappointment since its 1995 redesign, partly because buyers have turned so strongly toward sport-utility vehicles and even sporty sedans and away from sporty coupes. Critics also blame the 240's conservative styling, which was slightly dressed up last year. Informed sources say Nissan is working on a new "sports car" for 1999, but no one knows whether it will be a direct replacement for the 240 or something more ambitious along the lines of the late, lamented 300ZX.

For now, the 240 returns in base, SE, and LE trim. The LE was added during 1997 as basically an SE with the extra standard luxuries of leather upholstery, power moonroof, remote keyless entry, and high-power CD/cassette audio. All retain a 2.4-liter 4-cylinder engine hooked to manual or optional automatic transmission. Anti-lock brakes are optional for SE and LE.

PERFORMANCE Despite a relatively large engine, 240SX performance is nothing special for a sports coupe. We timed a base model with automatic at 10 seconds to 60 mph, slower than some 4-cylinder family compacts. A 5-speed SE was nearly a second quicker. The engine makes a sporty-but-loud snarl when worked hard. Also, like most big-displacement fours, it's somewhat throbby; you can feel a minor vibration through the gas pedal and even your pants-seat. Prominent road noise further detracts from refinement, putting the 240 well behind the silken Honda Prelude in this respect.

Fuel economy, at least, is satisfying. We averaged 20.8 mpg with our automatic base model and 26.5 with the manual SE.

The 240SX is unique in its class for having rear-wheel drive, which makes for sharp steering and agile handling, but also poor traction in rain and snow compared to front-wheel drive. Ride in any model is firm, becoming jiggly over tar strips, broken pavement and such. It's even livelier in the SE and LE because of their stiffer suspension and wider V-rated tires, though that pays off with greater grip and less body lean in dry-road cornering.

ACCOMMODATIONS Like Prelude and most other rivals, the 240SX provides only "2+2" seating. The snug cabin feels even cozier because of the cockpit-like dashboard that wraps into the doors. The rear seat is a joke. Even toddlers might feel cramped, particularly for leg room.

Up-front head clearance is limited for tall folks, and they'll find even less with the available sunroof. Leg room is ample, though, and drivers have a good view out thanks to the square, glassy roof design; even the rear corners are easily seen for parking.

Trunk space is puny, with most of it in a small rectangular well. The rear seatback folds, but the trunk opening is fairly high and too small for object much bigger than a medium suitcase. Interior small-items stowage is meager too.

BUILD QUALITY The 240SX has a tight, solid on-road feel,

Prices are accurate at time of publication; subject to manufacturer's changes.

plus the tidy, thorough workmanship we expect in Japanese cars. Still, interior decor seems surprisingly plain for a car with sporting ambitions, and some molded plastics don't look "quality."

VALUE FOR THE MONEY We're not impressed by the performance or pricing of the 240SX. Neither are most buyers, apparently. If you are a fan, though, you should be able to work a sizable discount on this slow-selling car that's now fast running out of time.

RATINGS

	Base/ LE	SE 5-speed
Acceleration	3	4
Fuel economy	3	4
Ride quality	3	2
Steering/handling	3	4
Braking	3	4
Quietness	3	3
Driver seating	4	4
Instruments/controls	3	3
Room/comfort (front)	4	4
Room/comfort (rear)	1	1
Cargo room	2	2
Value for the money	3	3
Total	35	38

SPECIFICATIONS

	2-door coupe
Wheelbase, in.	99.4
Overall length, in.	177.2
Overall width, in.	68.1
Overall height, in.	51.0
Curb weight, lbs.	2800
Cargo vol., cu. ft.	8.6
Fuel capacity, gals.	17.2
Seating capacity	4
Front head room, in.	38.3
Max. front leg room, in.	42.6
Rear head room, in.	34.3
Min. rear leg room, in.	20.8

ENGINES

	dohc I-4
Size, liters/cu. in.	2.4/146
Horsepower @ rpm	155@ 5600
Torque (lbs./ft.) @ rpm	160@ 4400
Availability	S

EPA city/highway mpg

5-speed OD manual	22/28
4-speed OD automatic	21/27

PRICES

1997 Nissan 240SX	Retail Price	Dealer Invoice
Base 2-door notchback, 5-speed	$18359	$16437
Base 2-door notchback, automatic	19159	17153
SE 2-door notchback, 5-speed	21999	19695
SE 2-door notchback, automatic	22799	20411
LE 2-door notchback, 5-speed	24449	21888
LE 2-door notchback, automatic	25249	22605
Destination charge	470	470

STANDARD EQUIPMENT:

Base: 2.4-liter DOHC 4-cylinder engine, 5-speed manual or 4-speed automatic transmission, 4-wheel disc brakes, driver- and passenger-side air bags, power steering, cloth reclining front bucket seats, folding rear seat w/trunk pass-through, center storage console, power windows, power mirrors, tachometer, trip odometer, digital clock, tinted glass, rear defogger, remote fuel-door release, 195/60HR15 tires, wheel covers.

SE adds: air conditioning, cruise control, tilt steering column, power door locks, AM/FM/cassette w/four speakers, intermittent wipers, remote decklid release, passenger-side visor mirror, cloth door trim, rear spoiler, fog lamps, sport-tuned suspension, rear stabilizer bar, dual chrome exhaust outlets, 205/55VR16 tires, alloy wheels.

LE adds: leather upholstery, leather-wrapped steering wheel and shifter, power sunroof, CD player w/six speakers, power diversity

antenna, remote keyless entry, theft-deterrent system.

OPTIONAL EQUIPMENT:	Retail Price	Dealer Invoice
Safety Features		
Anti-lock brakes, SE, LE	$699	$629
Includes limited-slip differential		
Major Packages		
Popular Equipment Pkg., base	1449	1245
Air conditioning, cruise control, cassettte player. Requires Power and Convenience Pkg.		
Power and Convenience Pkg., base	649	558
Tilt steering wheel, power door locks and mirrors, passenger-side visor mirror, cloth door trim, intermittent wipers, remote decklid release, alloy wheels.		
Comfort and Convenience		
Air conditioning, base	999	858
Power sunroof, base, SE	899	772
Base requires Popular Equipment Pkg. and Power and Convenience Pkg.		
Leather Pkg., SE	999	858
Leather upholstery, leather-wrapped steering wheel.		
Rosewood trim	399	276
CD player, base, SE	469	349
Base requires Popular Equipment Pkg.		
3-disc CD changer	669	511
Base requires Popular Equipment Pkg.		
Floormats	79	52
Appearance and Miscellaneous		
Pearlglow paint	399	343

OLDSMOBILE AURORA

Oldsmobile Aurora

Front-wheel-drive near-luxury car; similar to Buick Park Avenue and Buick Riviera

Base price: $35,960. Built in Orion, Mich.

Also consider: Acura TL, Cadillac Catera, Infiniti I30, Lexus ES 300

FOR • Standard anti-lock brakes and traction control • Acceleration • Steering/handling • Passenger room

AGAINST • Fuel economy • Wind noise

Introduced for 1995, Aurora symbolizes Oldsmobile's new aspirations as an upscale import-fighting brand. Changes in the car have been few, with suspension and steering revisions, and the optional OnStar system, new for '98.

This 4-door sedan shares its underskin architecture with the 2-door Buick Riviera and 4-door Buick Park Avenue, but has different styling and interior features. Aurora also has a V-8 engine, while the Buicks use a V-6.

Automatic transmission, anti-lock brakes (ABS), and traction control are standard. the dual front air bags are depowered to deploy with less force, but side air bags are unavailable.

Changes to the suspension include increased wheel travel. The steering has been recalibrated for more on-center feel and reduced effort at low speeds. And Olds says the ABS sensors are more accurate.

OnStar links the car via cell phone and satellite with a 24-hour General Motors center from which operators can dispense travel advice, summon emergency help, and offer other services.

Rating Scale: 5-Excellent; 4-Above average; 3-Average; 2-Below average; 1-Poor

The dealer-installed option includes a cell phone, but not installation or monthly service fees.

PERFORMANCE Aurora sounds and feels more like a European sports sedan than an American luxury car. It's a heavy car, though, and while its V-8 doesn't snap your head back under full throttle, it delivers brisk acceleration and ample passing power. We timed our test car at 8.2 seconds 0-60 mph. In a city/highway mix, we averaged 15.6 mpg with one car, 16.6 with another, and 24.3 mpg on a freeway trip. Premium fuel is required. The transmission changes gears smoothly and downshifts promptly for passing. The V-8 has a refined, aggressive growl under hard throttle. Road noise is noticeable without being excessive, but wind noise is prominent around the side windows.

Ride control at high speeds is commendable, but we caution against ordering the optional V-rated tires (for speeds up to 149 mph). They make the ride harsh and jittery on patchy pavement. With the standard H-rated tires (for speeds up to 130 mph) Aurora's ride is firm but more forgiving.

This sedan doesn't feel as nimble as some smaller import rivals, but body lean is well checked in turns, and Aurora is poised on twisting roads. This year's suspension changes reduce some of the clunking over bumps that used to echo through the passenger compartment. Stopping power is impressive, though some of our drivers feel pedal effort is too high. The revised steering works as advertised, proving more assist when parking and firming up as speed increases.

ACCOMMODATIONS Room is ample for four adults, but the body design gives the cabin a closed-in feel. Head and leg room are ample at all outboard positions, and the driver's seat is comfortable. However, squeezing a third passenger in the back is no recipe for comfort.

The well-designed dashboard has large gauges and controls that are easy to reach and clearly labeled. Aurora's styling limits over-the-shoulder visibility, a problem made worse by undersized outside mirrors. Large doors ease entry and exit to all seating positions.

There's ample luggage space, but the trunk's opening is too small to easily load bulky objects, the liftover is high, and the rear seats do not fold to increase cargo space.

BUILD QUALITY Our most-recent test car's structure felt stout, the materials were of high quality inside and outside, and the paint was smooth. However, several earlier versions suffered a few squeaks and rattles, and the pop-out twin cupholder assembly seems fragile.

VALUE FOR THE MONEY Aurora is unmistakably American in character while being competitive in performance and features with Japanese and European sedans costing thousands more. Its V-8 engine is a selling point in this class of mostly 6-cylinder cars. Include it on your shopping list.

RATINGS

	Base
Acceleration	4
Fuel economy	2
Ride quality	4
Steering/handling	4
Braking	5
Quietness	3
Driver seating	5
Instruments/controls	4
Room/comfort (front)	4
Room/comfort (rear)	4
Cargo room	4
Value for the money	4
Total	**47**

SPECIFICATIONS

	4-door sedan
Wheelbase, in.	113.8
Overall length, in.	205.4
Overall width, in.	74.4
Overall height, in.	55.4
Curb weight, lbs.	3967
Cargo vol., cu. ft.	16.1
Fuel capacity, gals.	20.0
Seating capacity	5

	4-door sedan
Front head room, in.	38.4
Max. front leg room, in.	42.6
Rear head room, in.	36.9
Min. rear leg room, in.	38.4

ENGINES

	dohc V-8
Size, liters/cu. in.	4.0/244
Horsepower @ rpm	250@ 5600
Torque (lbs./ft.) @ rpm	260@ 4400
Availability	S

EPA city/highway mpg

4-speed OD automatic	17/26

PRICES

Oldsmobile Aurora	Retail Price	Dealer Invoice
Base 4-door sedan	$35960	$32543
Destination charge	665	665

STANDARD EQUIPMENT:

Base: 4.0-liter dohc V-8 engine, 4-speed automatic transmission, traction control, driver- and passenger-side air bags, anti-lock 4-wheel disc brakes, air conditioning w/automatic climate control system , inside/outside temperature indicator, variable-assist power steering, tilt steering wheel, leather-wrapped steering wheel, steering-wheel climate and radio, cruise control, leather upholstery, power front bucket seats with power lumbar support and driver-side 2-position memory, center storage console with leather-wrapped shifter, interior wood trim, auxiliary power source, overhead storage console, folding rear armrest with trunk pass-through, power memory mirrors with defoggers, power windows, automatic programmable door locks, remote keyless illuminated entry/exit system, automatic day/night rear-view mirror with compass, AM/FM/cassette/CD player, integrated antenna, illuminated visor mirrors, power fuel-door and deck-lid release, intermittent wipers, Driver Information System, tachometer, engine-coolant temperature gauge, trip odometer, oil level sensor, universal garage-door opener, rear defogger, Twilight Sentinel automatic headlamp control, cargo net, floormats, solar-control tinted glass, Pass-Key theft deterrent system, fog lights, cornering lamps, dual exhaust outlets, 235/60R16 tires, alloy wheels.

OPTIONAL EQUIPMENT:
Major Packages

Autobahn Pkg.	395	352
Includes 3.71 axle ratio and 235/60VR16 tires.		

Comfort and Convenience

OnStar System	895	761
Includes global positioning sytem, voice-activated cellular telephone, roadside assistance, emergency services. Requires dealer installation charge and monthly service charges.		
Power sunroof	995	886
Heated driver and front passenger seats	295	263
Bose Acoustimass Sound System	871	775
12-disc CD changer	460	409

Appearance and Miscellaneous

White diamond paint	395	352
Chrome wheels	800	712

OLDSMOBILE BRAVADA

All-wheel-drive midsize sport-utility vehicle; similar to Chevrolet Blazer and GMC Jimmy

Base price: (1997 model) $30,385. Built in Moraine, Ohio.

Also consider: Infiniti QX4, Jeep Grand Cherokee, Land Rover Discovery, Mercury Mountaineer

FOR • Standard anti-lock brakes • Acceleration • Passenger and cargo room • Ride • Standard full-time 4WD

AGAINST • Fuel economy • Rear seat comfort

It's similar to the Chevrolet Blazer and GMC Jimmy, but

Prices are accurate at time of publication; subject to manufacturer's changes.

Oldsmobile Bravada

Bravada stands as the luxury leader of this trio of sport-utility vehicles. The basic design, V-6 engine, and automatic transmission are shared, but Bravada has its own exterior trim, standard leather upholstery, and wood interior accents. And it's now the only one of the three with 4-wheel drive that operates in all surfaces and conditions.

Changes to the '98 Bravada include a new grille, headlights, and bumpers. A redesigned instrument panel adds a passenger-side air bag and new radio. A power-reclining driver seat is a new feature, as are folding headrests for outboard rear-seat passengers. Anti-lock brakes are standard.

Bravada's standard permanently-engaged 4WD system, which Olds calls SmartTrak, is revised. It formerly split engine power 35 front/65 rear under normal conditions, then redistributed it to quell tire slip. This year, it runs in rear-wheel drive and automatically sends power to the wheels with the most traction when slippage occurs. Olds says the new system is quieter, more fuel efficient, and can react faster to changing road conditions. Blazer and Jimmy offer only part-time 4WD that can't be used on dry pavement. Bravada's towing capacity is 5000 pounds.

PERFORMANCE Bravada's V-6 has ample power, and is quiet once it's warm. On cold mornings the engine's coarse and gruff.

The new SmartTrak system should improve fuel economy. Last year's model returned only 15.1 mpg over 600 miles of test driving. This is about average for an SUV.

The automatic transmission shifts smoothly, and ride quality is impressive. Bravada's suspension absorbs bumps better than that of the Ford Explorer or Jeep Grand Cherokee, and handling is near the top of the SUV class, but steering feel is still a little numb on the highway. The anti-lock 4-wheel disc brakes stop the Olds wagon with authority.

SmartTrak lets you concentrate on driving while a computer apportions power among the four wheels. It lacks a low range for serious off-road driving, but if you want a GM midsize SUV with 4WD that matches the convenience of systems offered by the Ford and Mercury or Jeep rivals, Bravada is your only choice.

Visibility is good, however, the tinted rear glass makes backing up difficult at night.

ACCOMMODATIONS Bravada's new dashboard design is shared with the Blazer and Jimmy and features radio and air conditioning controls at the top of the class for ease of use. Gauges are large and clear, and there's a handy center storage console and a new passenger grab handle. Power window, lock, and mirror switches are located high on the door armrest.

Bravada works best as transport for four people. The front bucket seats are comfortable on long drives, but the rear bench still has a low cushion, so you're forced to sit with your knees pointed at the ceiling. Unlike the old ones, the new rear headrests fold automatically and don't have to be removed to fold down the rear seatback—a nice touch.

BUILD QUALITY A lot of hard plastic interior parts have been replaced with pieces that have a softer feel, though we'll await a full test drive of a '98 to declare the absence of small-but-annoying rattles in previous Bravadas we tested. The paint was smooth on '98 models we saw, and exterior panel gaps were even.

VALUE FOR THE MONEY It doesn't have a V-8, but Bravada is otherwise a good match for Explorer and Grand Cherokee. And Oldsmobile is trying to copy Saturn's success in the way it treats customers, so there may be some indirect benefits to choosing a Bravada.

RATINGS

	Bravada
Acceleration	4
Fuel economy	2
Ride quality	4
Steering/handling	3
Braking	3
Quietness	3
Driver seating	3
Instruments/controls	4
Room/comfort (front)	4
Room/comfort (rear)	3
Cargo room	5
Value for the money	3
Total	41

SPECIFICATIONS

	4-door wagon
Wheelbase, in.	107.0
Overall length, in.	183.7
Overall width, in.	67.8
Overall height, in.	63.2
Curb weight, lbs.	4049
Cargo vol., cu. ft.	37.3
Fuel capacity, gals.	18.0
Seating capacity	5
Front head room, in.	39.6
Max. front leg room, in.	42.4
Rear head room, in.	38.2
Min. rear leg room, in.	36.3

ENGINES

	ohv V-6
Size, liters/cu. in.	4.3/262
Horsepower @ rpm	190@ 4400
Torque (lbs./ft.) @ rpm	250@ 2800
Availability	S

EPA city/highway mpg

4-speed OD automatic	16/21

PRICES

1997 Oldsmobile Bravada	Retail Price	Dealer Invoice
4-door wagon	$30385	$27498
Destination charge	515	515

STANDARD EQUIPMENT:

4.3-liter V-6 engine, 4-speed automatic transmission, 4-wheel drive, anti-lock 4-wheel disc brakes, driver-side air bag, air conditioning, power steering, cruise control, leather upholstery, front reclining bucket seats with power lumbar adjustment, 6-way power driver's seat, split folding rear bench seat, center console with storage armrest, cupholders, overhead storage console (trip computer, compass, reading lamps, outside temperature gauge, universal garage-door opener), AM/FM/cassette with equalizer, power antenna, digital clock, tilt steering wheel, power windows, rear defogger, tachometer, oil-pressure, coolant-temperature gauges, voltmeter, trip odometer, power mirrors, tinted windows, illuminated visor mirrors, remote keyless entry, intermittent wipers, auxiliary power outlets, front tow hooks, 5-wire trailer-towing electrical harness, luggage rack, fog lamps, daytime running lamps, floormats, cargo net and cover, striping, 235/70R15 all-season tires, alloy wheels.

OPTIONAL EQUIPMENT:

Major Packages

Towing Pkg.	210	181

Heavy-duty suspension and hazard lights, 8-wire electrical harness, platform hitch, engine oil cooler.

Gold Pkg.	50	43

Gold badging, gold wheel trim, beige striping.

Rating Scale: 5-Excellent; 4-Above average; 3-Average; 2-Below average; 1-Poor

Comfort and Convenience	Retail Price	Dealer Invoice
Cloth upholstery	NC	NC
Power sunroof..................................	$695	$598
CD player	124	107
Includes six speakers.		

Appearance and Miscellaneous

	Retail Price	Dealer Invoice
Engine block heater..............................	33	28
White letter tires...............................	133	114

OLDSMOBILE CUTLASS

Oldsmobile Cutlass GLS

Front-wheel-drive midsize car; similar to Chevrolet Malibu

Base price range: $17,800-$19,425. Built in Oklahoma City, Okla.

Also consider: Honda Accord, Nissan Altima, Toyota Camry

FOR • Standard anti-lock brakes • Acceleration • Passenger and cargo room

AGAINST • Engine noise

Oldsmobile unveiled its all-new midsize Cutlass last year and this year clears the air by dropping its older Cutlass Supreme. That leaves the Cutlass at the entry-level end of the midsize class, while Oldsmobile's new Intrigue occupies the upper rungs.

Cutlass shares its design with the new Chevrolet Malibu, though styling and trim are slighly different and Malibu offers 4- and 6-cylinder engines; Cutlass comes only with a V-6 and automatic transmission. The V-6 has 155 horsepower, down 5 from last year.

Cutlass comes in two price levels, GL and GLS. GL replaces last year's base model. Dual air bags and anti-lock brakes are standard. For '98, the instrument-panel background color changes from gray to black for more contrast and GL includes a cassette player and smoker's kit (ashtray and lighter) as standard; these were option's on last year's base Cutlass. Performance and accommodations are interchangeable with those of a similarly equipped V-6 Malibu.

See the Chevrolet Malibu for an evaluation of the Cutlass.

RATINGS	GL/GLS
Acceleration	4
Fuel economy	3
Ride quality	4
Steering/handling	3
Braking	5
Quietness	3
Driver seating	4
Instruments/controls	4
Room/comfort (front)	4
Room/comfort (rear)	3
Cargo room	4
Value for the money	3
Total	**44**

SPECIFICATIONS

	4-door sedan
Wheelbase, in.	107.0
Overall length, in.	192.0
Overall width, in.	69.4
Overall height, in.	56.9
Curb weight, lbs.	2982
Cargo vol., cu. ft.	17.0
Fuel capacity, gals.	15.2
Seating capacity	5
Front head room, in.	39.4
Max. front leg room, in.	42.2
Rear head room, in.	37.6
Min. rear leg room, in.	38.0

ENGINES

	ohv V-6
Size, liters/cu. in.	3.1/191
Horsepower @ rpm..............................	150@ 4800
Torque (lbs./ft.) @ rpm.........................	180@ 3200
Availability	S
EPA city/highway mpg	
4-speed OD automatic...........................	20/29

PRICES

Oldsmobile Cutlass	Retail Price	Dealer Invoice
GL 4-door notchback	$17800	$16287
GLS 4-door notchback	19425	17773

STANDARD EQUIPMENT:

GL: 3.1-liter V-6 engine, 4-speed automatic transmission, anti-lock brakes, driver- and passenger-side air bags, air conditioning, cruise control, cloth upholstery, reclining front bucket seats, split folding rear seat w/trunk pass-through, storage console w/armrest, front and rear cupholders, tilt steering column, power door locks, dual outside mirrors w/driver-side remote, tachometer, coolant-temperature gauge, trip odometer, tinted glass, AM/FM cassette, digital clock, rear defogger, PASS-Lock II theft-deterrent system, remote decklid release, visor mirrors, auxiliary power outlets, map/reading lights, intermittent wipers, automatic headlamps, daytime running lights, fog lamps, floormats, 215/60R15 tires, bolt-on wheel covers.

GLS adds: leather upholstery, 6-way power driver seat, power windows, power mirrors, remote keyless entry, illuminated passenger-side visor mirrors, passenger-assist handles, cargo net, alloy wheels.

OPTIONAL EQUIPMENT:

Major Packages

	Retail Price	Dealer Invoice
Convenience Pkg., GL	$625	$556
Power windows and mirrors, remote keyless entry, cargo net.		

Comfort and Convenience

	Retail Price	Dealer Invoice
6-way power driver seat, base	305	271
Cloth upholstery, GLS..	NC	NC
Sunroof, GLS..	595	530
GLS..	200	178
Remote keyless entry, base	150	134

Appearance and Miscellaneous

	Retail Price	Dealer Invoice
Alloy wheels, base	315	280
Engine-block heater..	20	18

OLDSMOBILE EIGHTY EIGHT/ LSS/REGENCY

✓ BEST BUY

1997 Oldsmobile LSS

Front-wheel-drive full-size car; similar to Buick LeSabre and Pontiac Bonneville
Base price range: $22,795-$28,395. Built in Orion, Mich.
Also consider: Chrysler Concorde, Dodge Intrepid, Ford Crown Victoria, Toyota Avalon

FOR • Standard anti-lock brakes • Traction control (LS, LSS, Regency) • Acceleration • Passenger and cargo room

AGAINST • Steering feel • Fuel economy (supercharged engine)

Oldsmobile aims at four niches in the full-size car segment with a quartet of trim and equipment variations on a single sedan. The Eighty Eight is the price leader in this line and offers family oriented seating for six. The sportier LS and LSS models adds bucket seats with a floor console for five passenger seating, plus a sport suspension and larger tires. At the top of the line is the luxury Regency. It comes with slightly different styling and a power sunroof as its sole major option.

Standard on all is an automatic transmission and a 205 horsepower 3.8-liter V-6. Optional on the LSS is a supercharged version of this engine with 240 horsepower. Olds sites internal changes to the transmission for '98 designed to make it run more smoothly.

Dual air bags and anti-lock brakes are standard. Traction control is standard on all models except the base Eighty Eight. Oldsmobile's full-size sedans are based on the same platform and share similar mechanical components with the Buick LeSabre and Pontiac Bonneville.

PERFORMANCE The 3.8-liter V-6 develops most of its strength at lower speeds, where it provides ample power for strong take-offs and safe passing. With that engine we were able to reach 60 mph in 9.1 seconds, which is good but not nearly as quick as a supercharged model, which took just 6.8 seconds. We averaged 17.2 mpg in mainly urban rush-hour commuting with the naturally aspirated engine and 18.7 with a supercharged LSS, including lots of highway travel.

General Motors' automatic is one of the world's smoothest-shifting transmissions. It changes gears almost imperceptibly, even in full-throttle acceleration, and downshifts quickly on the highway for passing. Engine noise is moderate even in foot-to-the-floor driving, when the V-6 produces a muted, pleasant growl. Road and wind noise also are low.

The LSS package includes 16-inch tires and a firmer suspension that make this full-size car feel stable and reassuring at highway speeds. It corners with little body lean and has commendable grip for a car its size. However, large bumps pound right through into the passenger compartment and you feel every tar strip and expansion joint.

The Eighty Eight, LS, and Regency do a better job of soaking up bad pavement, though you'll still feel most bumps and the ride is rather jumpy on washboard surfaces and over tar strips. In addition, the base suspension allows more bouncing and bobbing. The power steering on the base, LS, and Regency is too light and lacks feel. The LSS's firmer steering improves control. Stopping power and stability are good, though the brake pedal isn't as sensative to modulation as on many import cars in this price range.

ACCOMMODATIONS Even with bench seats front and rear, Eighty Eight is best suited to carrying four adults, five in a pinch. The middle positions have limited leg room and the car isn't wide enough to accommodate three sets of adult shoulders in comfort.

The bucket seats are comfortable, but don't have much lateral support. Entry/exit is easy front and rear.

Large, round gauges are clearly displayed before the driver. Climate and audio controls are conveniently located. Visibility is clear all around and it's easy to see the trunk for parking. However the small outside mirrors are of marginal use.

Trunk volume is a generous and a bumper-height opening makes loading and unloading easy. Interior storage includes a large glovebox, roomy map pockets on the front doors, and a covered console bin with cupholders.

BUILD QUALITY Most Eighty Eights we've tested have been well assembled. All body panels fit evenly, and the paint is nearly free of bumpy orange-peel texture. However, all had a couple of minor rattles and some interior trim pieces that were not firmly seated.

VALUE FOR THE MONEY They're eclipsed in styling by the big Chrysler Corporation sedans, but the proven Eighty Eight and its GM siblings are still reliable, reasonably priced full-size cars. The supercharged V-6 is a star. Best of all, dealers should be willing to discount prices.

RATINGS

	Eighty Eight	LSS/Super-charged	Regency
Acceleration	4	5	4
Fuel economy	2	2	2
Ride quality	4	3	4
Steering/handling	3	4	3
Braking	4	4	4
Quietness	4	4	4
Driver seating	3	3	3
Instruments/controls	4	4	4
Room/comfort (front)	4	4	4
Room/comfort (rear)	4	4	4
Cargo room	4	4	4
Value for the money	4	4	4
Total	**44**	**45**	**44**

SPECIFICATIONS

	4-door sedan
Wheelbase, in.	110.8
Overall length, in.	200.4
Overall width, in.	74.1
Overall height, in.	55.7
Curb weight, lbs.	3455
Cargo vol., cu. ft.	18.0
Fuel capacity, gals.	18.0
Seating capacity	6
Front head room, in.	38.7
Max. front leg room, in.	42.5
Rear head room, in.	38.3
Min. rear leg room, in.	38.7

ENGINES

	ohv V-6	Supercharged ohv V-6
Size, liters/cu. in.	3.8/231	3.8/231
Horsepower @ rpm	205@ 5200	240@ 5200
Torque (lbs./ft.) @ rpm	230@ 4000	280@ 3200
Availability	S	O[1]

EPA city/highway mpg

4-speed OD automatic	19/29	18/27

1. LSS.

PRICES

Oldsmobile Eighty Eight/LSS/Regency	Retail Price	Dealer Invoice
4-door notchback	$22795	$20857
LS 4-door notchback	24195	22138
LSS 4-door notchback	28095	25706
Regency 4-door notchback	28395	25981

Rating Scale: 5-Excellent; 4-Above average; 3-Average; 2-Below average; 1-Poor

	Retail Price	Dealer Invoice
Destination charge	$605	$605

STANDARD EQUIPMENT:

3.8-liter V-6 engine, 4-speed automatic transmission, driver- and passenger-side air bags, anti-lock brakes, power steering, air conditioning, cruise control, 55/45 cloth front seat with reclining seatback, storage armrest w/cupholders, 8-way power driver seat, tilt steering wheel, power windows, left remote and right manual outside mirrors, tinted glass with solar-control windshield and rear window, rear defogger, AM/FM/cassette player w/6-speaker sound system, digital clock, power antenna, auxiliary power outlet, Pass-Key theft-deterrent system, remote decklid release, power door locks, coolant-temperature gauge, trip odometer, courtesy/reading lights, visor mirrors, intermittent wipers, Twilight Sentinel headlight control, daytime running lamps, floormats, tool kit, 205/70R15 tires, bolt-on wheel covers.

LS adds: traction control system, front bucket seats, remote keyless entry, programmable door locks, power mirrors, illuminated visor mirrors, 215/65R15 touring tires, alloy wheels.

LSS adds: dual-zone air conditioning with inside/outside temperature indicator, variable-assist power steering, automatic load-leveling touring suspension, leather upholstery, manual lumbar support, 8-way power passenger seat, floor console, overhead storage console, rear seat w/trunk pass-through, rear-seat storage armrest, tachometer, leather-wrapped steering wheel w/radio and climate controls, cassette/CD player, automatic day/night rearview and driver-side outside mirror, illuminated entry/exit, fog lamps, cargo net, 225/60R16 tires.

Regency adds to base: traction control system, dual-zone air conditioner with inside/outside temperature indicator, automatic load-leveling touring suspension, leather upholstery, 6-way power front seats with power recliners and lumbar-support adjusters, front and rear storage armrests w/cupholders, overhead storage console w/reading lamps, power mirrors, automatic day/night inside mirror w/compass, driver-seat, outside-mirror memory controls, automatic day/night heated driver-side outside mirror, AM/FM/cassette/CD player, leather-wrapped steering wheel w/radio and climate controls, remote keyless entry, illuminated visor mirrors, illuminated entry/exit system, cargo net, 205/70R15 whitewall tires, alloy wheels.

OPTIONAL EQUIPMENT:

Powertrains

Supercharged 3.8-liter V-6 engine, LSS	1022	909

Comfort and Convenience

8-way power passenger seat, LS............................	350	312
Split bench seat, LS	NC	NC
Includes 205/70R15 tires.		
Power sunroof, LSS,		
Regency	995	886
Cloth seat trim, Regency	NC	NC
Leather upholstery, LS	515	458
Cassette/CD player, LS..	200	178

Appearance and Miscellaneous

Alloy wheels, base	330	294
LS	150	134
LS includes 225/60R16 tires.		
Chrome wheels, LSS	600	534
Engine block heater	20	18

OLDSMOBILE INTRIGUE

Front-wheel-drive midsize; similar to Buick Regal and Pontiac Grand Prix

Base price range: $20,700-$22,100. Built in Fairfax, Kan.
Also consider: Honda Accord, Nissan Maxima, Toyota Camry

FOR • Standard anti-lock brakes and traction control
• Acceleration • Passenger and cargo room • Ride
• Steering/handling

Oldsmobile Intrigue GL

AGAINST • Engine noise

With one bodystyle, one powertrain, one seating configuration, and one suspension setup, Olds pitches the Intrigue as a "tightly focused" car designed to take on the world's best midsize import sedans.

Introduced in May 1997 as an early '98 model, Intrigue replaces the Cutlass Supreme in Oldsmobile's lineup. It shares its front-drive platform with the Pontiac Grand Prix and Buick Regal, but has different styling inside and out. It also differs in chassis tuning, equipment, even some dimensions. At 109 inches, for example, the wheelbase is 1.5-inches shorter than the Grand Prix's.

Base and upscale GL models are offered, both with General Motors' 3.8-liter V-6 and automatic transmission, a console-mounted shifter, and front bucket seats. Dual air bags, anti-lock 4-wheel disc brakes, traction control, and 16-inch touring tires on aluminum wheels also are standard.

PERFORMANCE Intrigue comes as close as any domestic sedan to equalling the feeling and philosophy of formidable import designs such as the Nissan Maxima and Toyota Camry.

It's inviting to drive, with little body lean and stable handling along twisty stretches, plus plenty of pull from the 3.8-liter V-6. Expect fuel economy to be similar to that of an Olds Eighty Eight with this engine, meaning about 17-18 mpg overall. Intrigue has better steering feel than the Camry and a more controlled ride than either the Maxima or Camry. The ride remains comfortably absorbent even with the Autobahn Package, an option on the GL that includes firmer tires and larger brakes. The tires in the Autobahn Package provide better grip and crisper cornering behavior.

With all this plus strong anti-lock brakes, a responsive automatic transmission, and little road or wind noise, Intrigue comes across as a surprisingly sporty and competent family sedan. One small gripe: Hard acceleration brought out more engine noise than in the Intrigue's rivals.

ACCOMMODATIONS The front bucket seats, which are firm and supportive, have ample fore/aft travel, giving tall folks room to stretch. The rear seat isn't as spacious, though there's more than adequate head and leg room for most adults, and the doors are wide enough for easy entry/exit.

Intrigue's driving position is comfortable, commanding, and should suit most people. A tilt steering wheel is standard and a power driver's seat is optional.

Lexus could have designed the dashboard, which puts everything within easy sight and reach in a modern, attractive design. Among the thoughtful touches are map pockets on all doors, a bi-level center console bin, dual cupholders front and rear, a dashboard-mounted ignition switch, and a prop-less hood. Cargo space is more than competitive for the class. The trunk floor is flat and wide, and there are no bulky hinges to intrude into the cargo area.

BUILD QUALITY All early production models we drove felt rock-solid, had precise panel fits, and were generally well finished. The molded interior plastic was smooth and richer-looking than the material found in many domestic cars.

VALUE FOR THE MONEY Intrigue is more sophisticated than the brash Grand Prix and more nimble and poised than the Ford Taurus or Camry V-6. If you're looking for a midsize car with a thoughtful blend of features and performance, don't decide until you've driven this pleasant and surprising new Olds.

Prices are accurate at time of publication; subject to manufacturer's changes.

RATINGS

	Base/GL
Acceleration	4
Fuel economy	3
Ride quality	4
Steering/handling	4
Braking	4
Quietness	4
Driver seating	4
Instruments/controls	5
Room/comfort (front)	4
Room/comfort (rear)	4
Cargo room	4
Value for the money	4
Total	**48**

SPECIFICATIONS

	4-door sedan
Wheelbase, in.	109.0
Overall length, in.	195.6
Overall width, in.	73.6
Overall height, in.	56.6
Curb weight, lbs.	3455
Cargo vol., cu. ft.	16.0
Fuel capacity, gals.	18.0
Seating capacity	5
Front head room, in.	39.3
Max. front leg room, in.	42.4
Rear head room, in.	37.4
Min. rear leg room, in.	36.9

ENGINES

	ohv V-6
Size, liters/cu. in.	3.8/231
Horsepower @ rpm	195@ 5200
Torque (lbs./ft.) @ rpm	220@ 4000
Availability	S

EPA city/highway mpg

4-speed OD automatic	19/30

PRICES

Oldsmobile Intrigue

	Retail Price	Dealer Invoice
Base 4-door sedan	$20700	$18941
GL 4-door sedan	22100	20222
Destination charge	550	550

STANDARD EQUIPMENT:

Base: 3.8-liter V-6 engine, 4-speed automatic transmission, traction control, anti-lock 4-wheel disc brakes, driver- and passenger side air bags, daytime running lamps, shoulder belt adjusters, childproof rear door locks, variable-effort power steering, air conditioning, AM/FM/cassette, cruise control on steering wheel, cloth reclining front bucket seats, tilt steering wheel, center console, front and rear cupholders, power door locks, power windows, power mirrors, remote trunk and fuel door release, map pockets, auxiliary electrical outlets, reading lights, Pass-Lock theft-deterrent system, 225/60SR16 tires, alloy wheels.

GL adds: Comfort and Security Pkg. (remote keyless entry, illuminated entry, tire inflation monitor), automatic dual-zone air conditioning, heated power outside mirrors, 6-way power driver seat, leather-wrapped steering wheel/armrest/shifter, 6-speaker sound system, rear window grid-antenna, split-folding rear seat, illuminated visor mirrors, trunk cargo net, fog lamps.

OPTIONAL EQUIPMENT:
Major Packages

	Retail Price	Dealer Invoice
Autobahn Pkg., GL	230	205
Heavy-duty brakes, 225/60HR16 tires.		

Comfort and Convenience

Sunroof	695	619
6-way power driver seat, Base	305	271
Air filtration system	25	22
CD/cassette player, Base	270	240

	Retail Price	Dealer Invoice
GL	$200	$178
Includes six speakers, seek/scan, digital clock.		
Bose CD/cassette player	500	445
Includes eight speakers, seek/scan, automatic tone control, amplifier, digital clock.		
12-disc CD changer	460	409
Six speaker sound system, Base	70	62
Rear window grid-antenna, Base	25	22
Steering wheel radio controls, GL	125	111
Remote keyless entry, Base	150	134
Leather-wrapped steering wheel, Base	120	107
Includes leather shifter and armrest.		
Leather upholstery, GL	995	886
Split folding rear seat, Base	150	134

Appearance and Miscellaneous

Rear spoiler	150	134
Base requires rear window grid-antenna.		
Engine block heater	20	18
Chrome alloy wheels, GL	600	534

OLDSMOBILE SILHOUETTE

RECOMMENDED

Oldsmobile Silhouette

Front-wheel-drive minivan; similar to Chevrolet Venture and Pontiac Trans Sport

Base price range: (1997 model) $21,675-$26,235. Built in Doraville, Ga.

Also consider: Chrysler Town & Country, Ford Windstar, Mercury Villager, Toyota Sienna

FOR • Standard anti-lock brakes • Ride • Passenger and cargo room • Side air bags

AGAINST • Fuel economy

Standard front side air bags and the availability of 8-passenger seating and General Motors' OnStar navigation system are newsmakers for Silhouette. This is Oldsmobile's version of a van also sold, with slight trim changes, as the Chevrolet Venture and Pontiac Trans Sport.

Silhouette offers regular- and extended-length versions, both with sliding doors on both sides, the passenger-side door being GM's exclusive power-sliding unit. GS, GL, and GLS models are available, the last an extended-length van with leather upholstery, a touring suspension, traction control, rear climate controls, and rear audio controls. The sole powertrain is a 3.4-liter V-6 and automatic transmission.

Anti-lock brakes are standard and the front air bags this year are supplemented by front-seat mounted side air bags. Up to two integrated rear child seats are optional. There's standard seating for seven on two front buckets, a 2-place middle bench or dual middle buckets, and a 3-passenger rear bench. GS and GL models can seat eight for '98 with an available 3-passenger middle bench.

OnStar is a dealer-installed option that links the vehicle by cellular phone and satellite to a 24-hour GM center from which operators can dispense travel information, summon emergency help, and perform other services. The price includes a cell phone, but does not cover installation or monthly service fees.

PERFORMANCE Olds tries to make Silhouette drive like a mid-size sedan, and it mostly succeeded. The ride is comfortable and handling is at the very top of the minivan class, helped by particularly communicative steering. A firm suspension means

---

Rating Scale: 5-Excellent; 4-Above average; 3-Average; 2-Below average; 1-Poor

you'll feel more bumps in a Silhouette than in a Chrysler Town & Country, but the ride is never harsh.

The 3.4-liter V-6 engine provides adequate acceleration, but it doesn't have as much low-speed power as the 3.8-liter V-6 engines offered by Chrysler and Ford. However, GM's automatic transmission is among the smoothest on the market, with prompt downshifts that help get the most out of the engine when a burst of power is needed.

A Silhouette we recently tested returned 19.2 mpg, including several highway trips. That's exceptional for a large minivan, but in a more even mix of urban and open-road driven, expect to average the 15.3 mph we got with our test Chevy Venture.

Visibility is excellent and the large outside mirrors help eliminate blind spots. The standard anti-lock brakes stop this minivan with little drama, but the pedal feels slightly mushy.

ACCOMMODATIONS The dashboard places radio and climate controls where their large buttons and knobs are easy to see and reach. Gauges are sizable and unobstructed. There's plenty of storage space inside, including a handy cargo net attached to the sides of the front seats and a multitude of cupholders. Cargo room behind the rear seats is good in the extended-length model, but only average in the regular version.

The dual sliding doors are a terrific convenience. Even more inviting is the standard power-sliding passenger door, which powers open or closed at the touch of a button on the remote keyfob or inside the cabin. Entry and exit to the rear seats is awkward, however, and the pass-through between the front buckets is narrow.

The driving position is comfortable, and offers a commanding view of the road. Passenger space is good, though taller adults may find leg room a problem—especially in the rear-most seats. Head room is excellent all around. The middle and rear seats are low to the floor and don't feel as substantial or supportive as those in rival Chrysler, Ford, and Toyota vans.

BUILD QUALITY Silhouette and its GM siblings seem solid, and while the paint was smooth and glossy on our test examples, many body-panel gaps were uneven. Interior materials are of pleasing quality.

VALUE FOR THE MONEY Silhouette's very reasonable pricing delivers an impressive array of safety equipment, the convenience of dual sliding doors (one powered), and a driving manner that's friendly, even sporty. Don't buy a minivan without test driving one of these.

RATINGS

	Regular length	Extended length
Acceleration	3	3
Fuel economy	2	2
Ride quality	3	4
Steering/handling	4	4
Braking	4	4
Quietness	4	4
Driver seating	4	4
Instruments/controls	4	4
Room/comfort (front)	4	4
Room/comfort (rear)	3	3
Cargo room	5	5
Value for the money	4	4
Total	**44**	**45**

SPECIFICATIONS

	4-door van	4-door van
Wheelbase, in.	112.0	120.0
Overall length, in.	187.4	201.4
Overall width, in.	72.2	72.2
Overall height, in.	67.4	68.1
Curb weight, lbs.	3746	3942
Cargo vol., cu. ft.	133.0	155.9
Fuel capacity, gals.	20.0	25.0
Seating capacity	8	8
Front head room, in.	39.9	39.9
Max. front leg room, in.	39.9	39.9
Rear head room, in.	39.3	39.3
Min. rear leg room, in.	36.9	39.0

ENGINES

	ohv V-6
Size, liters/cu. in.	3.4/207
Horsepower @ rpm	180@ 5200
Torque (lbs./ft.) @ rpm	205@ 4000
Availability	S
EPA city/highway mpg	
4-speed OD automatic	18/25

PRICES

1997 Oldsmobile Silhouette	Retail Price	Dealer Invoice
3-door van, SWB	$21675	$19616
3-door van, extended	22505	20367
GL 3-door van, extended	24025	21743
GL 4-door van, extended	24575	22240
GLS 3-door van, extended	25685	23245
GLS 4-door van, extended	26235	23743
Destination charge	570	570

SWB denotes standard wheelbase.

STANDARD EQUIPMENT:

3.4-liter V-6 engine, 4-speed automatic transmission, anti-lock brakes, driver- and passenger-side air bags, power steering, front air conditioning, cruise control, reclining front bucket seats w/lumbar adjustment and folding armrests, 4-way adjustable driver seat, second-row 60/40 split folding bench seat, third-row 50/50 split folding bench seat, front storage console, overhead console w/map lights, front and rear cupholders, power windows, power door locks, power mirrors, tilt steering wheel, tachometer, coolant-temperature gauge, trip odometer, digital clock, AM/FM/cassette, integrated antenna, under-passenger-seat storage drawer, solar control windshield, intermittent wipers, rear wiper/washer, remote keyless entry, theft-deterrent system, rear defogger, visor mirrors, interior air filter daytime running lights, rear reading lights, fog lamps, front and rear auxiliary power outlets, roof rack, floormats, 205/70R15 tires (SWB), 215/70R15 (extended), wheel covers.

GL adds: power sliding passenger-side door, 6-way power driver seat, overhead storage console (includes compass, outside temperature indicator, driver information center), deep-tinted glass, cargo net.

GLS adds: touring suspension w/automatic load leveling, traction control, rear air conditioning and heater, second-row captain's chairs, steering-wheel radio controls, rear-seat radio controls, illuminated visor mirrors, 215/70R15 touring tires, alloy wheels.

4-door models add: power sliding driver-side door.

OPTIONAL EQUIPMENT:
Major Packages

Towing Pkg., base, GL	355	305
GLS	85	73

Includes touring suspension, automatic load leveling, engine- and transmission-oil coolers, 5-lead wiring harness, 215/70R15 touring tires.

Rear Convenience Pkg., GL	525	452

Rear air conditioning and heater, rear-seat radio controls.

Comfort and Convenience

Touring suspension, GL	270	232

Includes automatic load leveling, 215/70R15 touring tires.

Traction control, GL	175	151
Power moonroof, GL 3-door, GLS 3-door	695	598

GL requires Rear Convenience Pkg.

Leather upholstery, GLS	870	748

Includes leather-wrapped steering wheel.

Integrated child seat, GL	125	108
Dual integrated child seats, GL	225	194
Deep-tinted glass, base	245	211
CD player, GL, GLS	100	86

Includes automatic tone control.

Cassette/CD player, GL, GLS	200	172

Includes automatic tone control.

Appearance and Miscellaneous

Alloy wheels, GL	285	245
Engine block heater	18	15

Prices are accurate at time of publication; subject to manufacturer's changes.

PLYMOUTH BREEZE

BUDGET BUY

Plymouth Breeze

Front-wheel-drive midsize car; similar to Chrysler Cirrus and Dodge Stratus

Base price: (1997 model) $14,825. Built in Sterling Heights, Mich.

Also consider: Chevrolet Malibu, Honda Accord, Hyundai Sonata

FOR • Optional anti-lock brakes • Steering/handling • Passenger and cargo room • Ride

AGAINST • Noise • Rear visibility

Breeze is the bargain-basement version of a design also used for the Chrysler Cirrus and Dodge Stratus. It gets jazzed up for '98 with a more-potent available engine and an "Expresso" trim package.

Breeze comes with a 132-horsepower 2.0-liter 4-cylinder with manual or optional automatic transmission. New for '98 is an optional twin-cam 2.4-liter 4-cylinder with 150 horsepower and automatic transmission. These engines are also installed in the Dodge Stratus, but Breeze doesn't offer the V-6 that's available on the Stratus and Cirrus.

Standard are dual air bags, depowered this year to deploy with less force. Anti-lock 4-wheel disc brakes and an integrated rear child seat are optional.

There's a single model, but its base price includes amenities such as air conditioning, tilt steering column, rear defroster, and a folding rear seatback. The new Expresso option package includes specific wheel covers, nameplates, exterior accent stripes, and specific seat fabric.

Performance and accommodations of the Breeze duplicate those of a similarly equipped Stratus.

See the Dodge Stratus report for an evaluation of the Breeze.

RATINGS

	2.0-liter	2.4-liter
Acceleration	3	3
Fuel economy	4	4
Ride quality	3	3
Steering/handling	4	4
Braking	3	3
Quietness	2	3
Driver seating	4	4
Instruments/controls	4	4
Room/comfort (front)	4	4
Room/comfort (rear)	4	4
Cargo room	4	3
Value for the money	4	4
Total	**43**	**43**

SPECIFICATIONS

	4-door sedan
Wheelbase, in.	108.0
Overall length, in.	186.7
Overall width, in.	71.7
Overall height, in.	51.9
Curb weight, lbs.	2929
Cargo vol., cu. ft.	15.7
Fuel capacity, gals.	16.0
Seating capacity	5
Front head room, in.	38.1
Max. front leg room, in.	42.3
Rear head room, in.	36.8
Min. rear leg room, in.	37.8

ENGINES

	ohc I-4	dohc I-4
Size, liters/cu. in.	2.0/122	2.4/148
Horsepower @ rpm	132@ 6000	150@ 5200
Torque (lbs./ft.) @ rpm	129@ 5000	167@ 4000
Availability	S	O
EPA city/highway mpg		
5-speed OD manual	26/37	
4-speed OD automatic	22/32	21/30

PRICES

1997 Plymouth Breeze	Retail Price	Dealer Invoice
4-door notchback	$14825	$13599
Destination charge	535	535

STANDARD EQUIPMENT:

2.0-liter 4-cylinder engine, 5-speed manual transmission, driver- and passenger-side air bags, air conditioning, power steering, cloth reclining front bucket seats, folding rear seat, center storage console, tilt steering column, dual remote mirrors, trip odometer, tachometer, voltmeter, oil-pressure gauge, coolant-temperature gauge, tinted glass, 4-speaker AM/FM radio, digital clock, cupholders, rear defogger, speed-sensitive intermittent wipers, auxiliary power outlet, remote decklid release, tinted glass, visor mirrors, front floormats, 195/70R14 tires, wheel covers.

OPTIONAL EQUIPMENT:

Powertrains

4-speed automatic transmission	1050	935
Includes cruise control.		

Major Packages

Pkg. 21B/22B	676	609
4-way manual driver-seat height adjuster, power heated mirrors, power door locks and windows, rear floormats.		
Cold Weather Pkg.	30	27
Engine block heater, battery heater.		
Personal Security Pkg.	170	151
Remote keyless entry w/alarm, illiminated entry. Requires Pkg. 21B/22B.		
Smoker's Pkg.	20	18
Lighter, ash tray.		

Safety Features

Anti-lock 4-wheel disc brakes	565	503
Integrated child seat	100	89
Includes fixed rear seat.		

Comfort and Convenience

Cassette player	180	160
Premium CD player	380	338
Premium AM/FM/cassette and 6-disc CD changer	730	650

Appearance and Miscellaneous

Full-size spare	125	111
Candy-apple red paint	200	178

PLYMOUTH PROWLER

Rear-wheel-drive Sports and GT car

Base price: (1997 model) $38,300. Built in Detroit, Mich.

Also consider: Chevrolet Camaro, Ford Mustang, Pontiac Firebird

FOR • Acceleration • Steering/handling

AGAINST • Cargo space • Visibility • Entry/exit • Anti-lock brakes not available

Prowler is Chrysler Corporation's modern interpretation of a '50s hot rod. It was introduced as a 1997 model, with a produc-

Rating Scale: 5-Excellent; 4-Above average; 3-Average; 2-Below average; 1-Poor

1997 Plymouth Prowler

tion of 1500-2000 planned. But the quality of parts from suppliers and other delays held output to around 700. Prowler will skip the 1998 model year, then re-emerge in early calendar '98 as a 1999 model.

The main change will be a switch in engines, from the 214-horsepower 3.5-liter cast-iron V-6 used in the outgoing generation of Chrysler's full-size cars to the new 3.5-liter aluminum V-6 of the upcoming Chrysler LHS and 300M sedans. It'll have about 250 horsepower but still use a rear-mounted automatic transmission with Chrysler's Autostick manual-shift capability.

All '97 Prowlers were purple; expect one or two additional color choices for '99, including bright yellow. Dual air bags are standard, but anti-lock brakes and traction control will continue to be unavailable. The car has a manual folding cloth top with a glass rear window and defroster. Some body panels and suspension parts are made of aluminum, with plastic compound for the rear body section and front fenders.

PERFORMANCE As might be expected of a professionally engineered car, Prowler accelerates more smoothly, rides softer, and take corners with more control than any home-built hot rod. But the feeling from behind the wheel is still unique among production automobiles.

Though the V-6 doesn't pin you to your seat, it offers plenty of power and the exhaust note is a hearty, rumbling roar. Tire and wind noise are prominent at highway speeds, but only seem to add to the excitement. We averaged 17.2 mpg in a mix of city, suburban, and highway driving.

Prowler may look like a dragster hot rod, but its handling is quite sports-car like. It's nearly flat in turns, with unexpected balance and grip, and firm, no-surprises steering. The brakes are strong and easily modulated, and the 4-wheel independent suspension steps deftly over small bumps. Bigger bumps pitch occupants around in their seats.

ACCOMMODATIONS You sit close to the floor in supportive buckets with the pointed prow visible through the narrow windshield but the front fenders are invisible as they turn with the wheels and bob with the suspension.

Slit-like side windows and the baby-bonnet roof kill any useful views with the top up. You have to be outside the car to fold the fabric roof, but it hides neatly beneath the hard rear deck, which is high enough to quell much of the wind buffeting that affects other convertibles.

The retro instrumentation straps a small tachometer to the steering column and strings other gauges across the center of the dashboard; reading those requires a conscious look away from the road. Controls are standard Chrysler fare and easy to use.

Two or three small, soft bags can pancake into the cargo space enveloped between the rear bulkhead and the decklid.

BUILD QUALITY Prowlers we've tested exhibited cowl shake, but no more than, say, a Mustang convertible. Fit and finish were very good inside and out, cabin materials were of a high grade, and the paint looked exceptionally deep and glossy.

VALUE FOR THE MONEY Once well-heeled buyers paying well over list are sated, prices should stabilize near sticker. Lack of cargo room excepted, Prowler is as practical as most any $40,000 2-seat roadster, which is to say, not very. Still, few cars generate more smiles per mile, and you don't even have to drive it to enjoy it.

RATINGS

	Prowler
Acceleration	4
Fuel economy	2
Ride quality	2
Steering/handling	4
Braking	3
Quietness	2
Driver seating	3
Instruments/controls	2
Room/comfort (front)	3
Room/comfort (rear)	—
Cargo room	1
Value for the money	2
Total	**28**

SPECIFICATIONS

	2-door conv.
Wheelbase, in.	113.0
Overall length, in.	165.0
Overall width, in.	76.5
Overall height, in.	51.0
Curb weight, lbs.	2860
Cargo vol., cu. ft.	1.8
Fuel capacity, gals.	12.0
Seating capacity	2
Front head room, in.	38.0
Max. front leg room, in.	43.0
Rear head room, in.	—
Min. rear leg room, in.	—

ENGINES

	ohc V-6
Size, liters/cu. in.	3.5/215
Horsepower @ rpm	214@ 5850
Torque (lbs./ft.) @ rpm	221@ 3100
Availability	S

EPA city/highway mpg	
4-speed OD automatic	22/32

PRICES

1997 Plymouth Prowler	Retail Price	Dealer Invoice
2-door convertible	$38300	$35863
Destination charge	700	700

STANDARD EQUIPMENT:

3.5-liter V-6 engine, 4-speed automatic transmission w/Autostick, driver- and passenger-air bags, power 4-wheel disc brakes, power steering, tilt steering wheel with radio contols, air conditioning, leather bucket seats, 6-way manual driver-side height adjuster, 2-way passenger-side height adjuster, leather-wrapped steering wheel and shifter, cruise control, center console w/armrest, storage, and cupholder, dual power mirrors, power windows, power door locks, tachometer, voltmeter, engine temperature gauge, oil pressure gauge, trip odometer, AM/FM cassette player, 6-disc CD changer, remote keyless entry, theft-deterrent system, intermittent wipers, rear window defogger, power remote decklid release, floormats, tinted windshield w/integral antenna, manual cloth convertible top w/glass rear window, 225/45HR17 extended mobility front tires w/low-pressure sensors, 295/40HR20 extended mobility rear tires w/low-pressure sensors, alloy wheels.

Options are available as dealer-installed accessories.

PLYMOUTH VOYAGER

Front-wheel-drive minivan; similar to Chrysler Town & Country and Dodge Caravan

Base price range: $17,235-$20,755. Built in St. Louis, Mo., and Canada.

Also consider: Chevrolet Venture, Ford Windstar, Honda Odyssey

FOR • Anti-lock brakes • Ride • Passenger and cargo room

AGAINST • Fuel economy • Wind noise

Prices are accurate at time of publication; subject to manufacturer's changes.

Plymouth Voyager SE

In Chrysler Corporation's script, Plymouth plays the entry-level role and its Voyager minivan stays in character by offering fewer engine and powertrain choices than the similar Dodge Caravan and Chrysler Town & Country.

Voyager is available in the same two body lengths as the others—regular and extended Grand—and with seats for up to seven and sliding doors on both sides, though the doors are options rather than standard features. It doesn't offer the largest Chrysler minivan engine, a 3.8-liter V-6, or the permanently engaged 4-wheel-drive system available on its siblings.

Caravan features five levels of trim, Voyager just two, base and SE, in both body lengths. Base models have a 4-cylinder engine and a 3-speed automatic transmission. Standard on the SE models and optional on base Voyagers is a 3.0-liter V-6. SEs with the 3.0 get a 4-speed automatic for '98; base models stay with the 3-speed. Optional on all is a 3.3-liter V-6 with a 4-speed automatic.

Dual air bags are standard, anti-lock brakes are optional. Two integrated rear child safety seats are available when the middle-row bench seat is specified, and this year, that middle bench's backrest gains hooks for hanging grocery bags. With the available middle-row buckets for '98, the left seat gets the same tip-forward easy-entry feature as the right one.

Newly optional on Voyager SE is the Expresso Decor Package, which includes specific badges and wheelcovers, remote keyless entry, deep-tinted glass, a CD player, and other features.

Voyager's performance and accommodations mirror those of similarly equipped Dodge Caravans.

See the Dodge Caravan report for an evaluation of the Voyager.

RATINGS

	Base 4-cyl.	Grand 3.3-liter V6
Acceleration	2	3
Fuel economy	3	2
Ride quality	3	4
Steering/handling	3	3
Braking	3	3
Quietness	3	3
Driver seating	4	4
Instruments/controls	4	4
Room/comfort (front)	4	4
Room/comfort (rear)	5	5
Cargo room	5	5
Value for the money	4	4
Total	43	44

SPECIFICATIONS

	3-door van	4-door van
Wheelbase, in.	113.3	119.3
Overall length, in.	186.3	199.6
Overall width, in.	76.8	76.8
Overall height, in.	68.5	68.5
Curb weight, lbs.	3516	3683
Cargo vol., cu. ft.	142.9	168.5
Fuel capacity, gals.	20.0	20.0
Seating capacity	7	7
Front head room, in.	39.8	39.8
Max. front leg room, in.	40.6	40.6
Rear head room, in.	40.0	40.0
Min. rear leg room, in.	42.3	39.6

ENGINES

	dohc I-4	ohc V-6	ohv V-6
Size, liters/cu. in.	2.4/148	3.0/181	3.3/202
Horsepower @ rpm	150@ 5200	150@ 5200	158@ 4850
Torque (lbs./ft.) @ rpm	167@ 4000	176@ 4000	203@ 3250
Availability	S[1]	S[2]	O
EPA city/highway mpg			
3-speed automatic	20/25	19/24	
4-speed OD automatic			18/24

PRICES

Plymouth Voyager	Retail Price	Dealer Invoice
Base 3-door van, SWB	$17415	$15845
Base Grand 4-door van	20125	18270
SE 4-door van, SWB	21290	19255
Grand SE 3-door van	22285	20171
Destination charge	580	580

SWB denotes short wheelbase.

STANDARD EQUIPMENT:

Base SWB: 2.4-liter DOHC 4-cylinder engine, 3-speed automatic transmission, driver- and passenger-side air bags, power steering, cloth reclining front bucket seats, 3-passenger rear bench seat, AM/FM radio, digital clock, trip odometer, variable intermittent wipers, variable intermittent rear wiper/washer, visor mirrors, auxiliary power outlet, tinted glass, dual exterior mirrors, 205/75R14 tires, wheel covers.

Base Grand adds: 3.0-liter V-6 engine, sliding driver side door, folding 2-passenger middle bench seat, folding 3-passenger rear bench seat.

SE adds: 4-speed automatic transmission, anti-lock brakes, folding 2-passenger middle bench seat with armrest (SWB), deluxe cloth upholstery, cassette player, tachometer, storage drawer below passenger seat, dual horns, additional sound insulation, cargo net, 215/65R15 tires.

OPTIONAL EQUIPMENT:
Major Packages

Pkg. 22T/24T/28T, Base SWB	1610	1369
Manufacturer's discount price	375	319
Pkg. 22T/24T/28T, Base Grand	885	752
Manufacturer's discount price	25	21

Air conditioning, CYE 7-passenger Seating Group (folding 2-passenger middle bench seat, folding 3-passenger rear bench seat) (SWB), rear sound insulation, storage drawer below passenger seat, dual horns.

Pkg. 25B/25B/28B, SE	1205	1024
Manufacturer's discount price	195	165

Air conditioning, CYN 7-passenger Deluxe Seating Group (reclining/folding 2-passenger middle bench seat and 3-passenger rear bench seat with adjustable headrests), rear defogger.

Pkg. 25C/28C (Expresso), SE	2080	1768
Manufacturer's discount price	885	752

Pkg. 25B/26B/28B plus Expresso Pkg. (solar-control glass, Expresso decals, striping, AM/FM/CD). Requires 3.3-liter V-6 engine.

Pkg. 25D/26D/28D, SE	2240	1904
Manufacturer's discount price	930	790

Pkg. 25B/26B/28B plus tilt steering wheel, cruise control, heated power mirrors, power windows and door locks, Light Group (courtesy lights, illuminated ignition w/time delay), illuminated visor mirrors, added sound insulation, floormats.

Pkg. 28E (Expresso), SE	3115	2648
Manufacturer's discount price	1620	1377

Pkg. 25D/26D/28D plus Expresso Pkg. Requires 3.3-liter V-6 engine.

Pkg. 25L/28L, SE	3545	3013
Manufacturer's discount price	2235	1899

Pkg. 25D/26D/28D plus CYS Deluxe 7-passenger Seating Group (reclining/folding middle bucket seats, and rear 3-passenger bench seat with adjustable headrests), premium cloth upholstery, 8-way power driver seat, overhead console w/trip computer, intermediate map/courtesy lights. Requires 3.3-liter V-6 engine.

Rating Scale: 5-Excellent; 4-Above average; 3-Average; 2-Below average; 1-Poor

CONSUMER GUIDE™

	Retail Price	Dealer Invoice
Pkg. 25N/28N (Expresso), SE..............	$4420	$2925
Manufacturer's discount price	2925	2486
Pkg. 28L plus Expresso Pkg. Requires 3.3-liter V-6 engine.		
Climate Group 2	450	383
Solar-control glass, windshield wiper de-icer. Requires option pkg.		
Climate Group 3,		
Grand SE w/Pkg. 25B/26B/28B..............	1130	961
Grand SE w/Pkg. 25/C28C..............	680	578
10-speaker cassette/CD w/equalizer, SE..............	720	612
Requires Pkg. 25D/26D/28D, 28E, 28L, or 28N.		
Climate Group 3,		
Grand SE w/Pkg. 25D/26D/28D	1020	867
Grand SE w/Pkg. 28E	570	485
Grand SE w/Pkg. 28L	940	799
Grand SE w/Pkg. 25N/28N	490	417
Rear heater and air conditioning, overhead console.		
Convenience/Security Group 1, Base	435	370
Cruise control, tilt steering column, power mirrors. Requires option pkg.		
Convenience/Security Group 2, Base	750	638
SE	315	268
Group 1 plus power locks. Requires option pkg.		
Convenience/Security Group 3, SE	685	582
Group 1 plus power windows and rear quarter vent windows. Requires option pkg.		
Convenience/Security Group 4, SE	235	200
Remote keyless entry, illuminated entry, headlight-off delay. Requires Pkg. 24D/28D, 28E, 28L, or 28N.		
Convenience/Security Group 5, SE	385	327
Group 3 plus theft-deterrent system. Requires Pkg. 25D/26D/28D, 28E, 28L, or 28N.		
Loading & Towing Group 2, SE..............	180	153
Group 1 plus heavy load/firm ride suspension. Requires option pkg.		
Loading & Towing Group 3, Grand SE	445	378
ordered w/Climate Group III	380	323
Group 2 plus Heavy Duty Trailer Tow Group (heavy-duty battery, alternator, brakes, and radiator, heavy-duty transmission-oil cooler, trailer wiring harness). Requires Pkg. 28D, 28E, 28L, or 28N. Requires 3.3-liter V-6 engine.		

Powertrains

3.0-liter V-6 engine, Base SWB	770	655
NA with 4-speed automatic transmission. Base requires option pkg. NA SE Pkgs. 28C, 28E, 28L, or 28N.		
3.3-liter V-6 engine, Base SWB	970	825
Base Grand, SE..............	200	170
Requires 4-speed automatic transmission (std. on SE) and option pkg.		
4-speed automatic transmission, Base	250	213
Requires 3.3-liter V-6 engine and option pkg.		

Safety Features

Anti-lock brakes, Base	565	480

Comfort and Convenience

CYE 7-passenger Seating Group, Base SWB	350	298
Folding 2-passenger middle bench seat, folding 3-passenger rear bench seat.		
CYK 7-passenger Seating Group, Base	285	242
Reclining/folding 2-passenger middle bench seat with two integrated child seats and adjustable headrests, folding 3-passenger rear bench seat. Requires option pkg.		
CYR Deluxe 7-passenger Seating Group, SE	225	191
CYN Deluxe 7-passenger Seating Group with two integrated child seats in middle bench. Requires option pkg. (NA with Pkg. 28L or 28N).		
CYS Deluxe 7-passenger Seating Group, SE	650	553
Reclining/folding middle bucket seats and rear 3-passenger bench seat with adjustable headrests. Requires Pkg. 24D/28D or 28E. Requires sliding driver-side door.		
Air conditioning..............	860	731
Rear defogger,		
Base w/o Convenience/Security Group..............	195	166
Base w/Convenience/Security Group, SE	230	196
Includes windshield wiper de-icer.		

	Retail Price	Dealer Invoice
Sliding driver-side door, Base SWB	$595	$506
Requires option pkg.		
AM/FM/cassette, Base	180	153
Requires option pkg.		
10-speaker cassette player w/equalizer, SE	325	276
Requires Pkg. 25D/28D, 28E, 28L, or 28N.		

Appearance and Miscellaneous

Roof rack	175	149
Requires option pkg.		
Smoker's Group	20	17
Cigarette lighter, ash trays.		
Engine-block heater	35	30
Load-leveling suspension, Grand SE	290	247
Requires Pkg. 25D/26D/28D, 28E, 28L, or 28N.		
Alloy wheels, Grand SE	415	353
Requires Pkg. 25B/26B/28B, 25D/26D/28D, or 28L.		
Full-size spare tire	110	94

PONTIAC BONNEVILLE

✓ BEST BUY

Pontiac Bonneville SE

Front-wheel-drive full-size car; similar to Buick LeSabre and Oldsmobile Eighty Eight/LSS/Regency

Base price range: $22,390-$29,390. Built in Lake Orion, Mich., and Flint, Mich.

Also consider: Dodge Intrepid, Toyota Avalon

FOR • Standard anti-lock brakes • Acceleration • Passenger and cargo room

AGAINST • Fuel economy (supercharged engine) • Ride (SSEi)

Bonneville is the sportiest of the trio of General Motors sedans that also includes the Buick LeSabre and Oldsmobile Eighty Eight. These cars are similar beneath the skin and share powertrains, but have different styling inside and out.

Pontiac's version comes in SE and SSE models, the SSE boasting a longer list of standard equipment and a sport suspension with automatic rear level control. Most of the SSE's equipment is available on the SE as separate options or in packages.

Both models come with a 205-horsepower 3.8-liter V-6 and automatic transmission. A supercharged, 240-horsepower version of the V-6 is optional on SSE models as part of the SSEi option group; last year, the supercharged engine was also available on SE models. A front bench seat gives the SE 6-passenger capacity. Bucket seats are standard on the SSE and optional on the SE.

For '98, the rear spoiler that had been optional on the SE is made standard, and SSE versions come with an 8-speaker Bose audio system. Pontiac's Eyecue Head-up Display, which projects speedometer readings and other information onto the windshield in front of the driver, is now standard instead of optional on the SSE.

Anti-lock brakes are standard, and as on most GM cars, Bonneville's standard front air bags this year are depowered to deploy with less force.

PERFORMANCE You don't have to floor the throttle to get good acceleration from the base V-6, while the supercharged version's performance rivals that of some V-8s. With either engine, the transmission shifts seamlessly and downshifts quickly for passing. We averaged 19.1 mpg in a test of one SSEi driven mostly on the highway, while another got 16.7 mpg in a mix of

Prices are accurate at time of publication; subject to manufacturer's changes.

city and highway use, which is more representative. Unfortunately, the supercharged engine requires premium fuel. Base-engine models average about 17-18 mpg.

The base suspension provides a good balance between a smooth, controlled ride and confident handling. We're less impressed with the available sportier suspensions and with the SSE's optional Computer Command Ride system, which adjusts damping to suit road conditions. All seem unnecessarily stiff for the slight handling improvement they bring, so try before you buy.

On the highway, wind noise is evident but there's little tire or engine noise.

ACCOMMODATIONS Bonneville's interior is spacious for adults front and rear. Some of our testers find rear-seat support lacking on long trips, and we can't seem to get comfortable in the SSE's optional articulating bucket seat, despite 12 separate power adjustments.

Instruments are large and well lit, but the driver must stretch to reach the climate and radio controls in the center of the dashboard. Like the 12-way power seat, the head-up display is a gadget we can do without, but now it's standard. One feature we like is the redundant steering-wheel-mounted radio controls, which are especially handy since the dash-mounted radio controls aren't.

Wide, tall doors make it easy to get in or out at all points. A narrow window and high parcel shelf block the rear view, but visibility is otherwise good.

The trunk is roomy but the opening is oddly shaped.

BUILD QUALITY Fit and finish were good on our test cars, with smoothly applied paint and even gaps between most body and interior pieces.

VALUE FOR THE MONEY Based on their roominess, performance, proven reliability, and pricing, we put Bonneville and its GM cousins at the top of the full-size car list. The Pontiac version's sporty bent makes it no less functional than the others, but go easy on options; it's easy to push a Bonneville well past $30,000.

RATINGS

	SE	SSEi
Acceleration	4	5
Fuel economy	2	2
Ride quality	4	3
Steering/handling	4	4
Braking	4	4
Quietness	4	4
Driver seating	3	3
Instruments/controls	4	4
Room/comfort (front)	4	4
Room/comfort (rear)	4	4
Cargo room	4	4
Value for the money	4	4
Total	**45**	**45**

SPECIFICATIONS

	4-door sedan
Wheelbase, in.	110.8
Overall length, in.	200.5
Overall width, in.	74.5
Overall height, in.	55.7
Curb weight, lbs.	3446
Cargo vol., cu. ft.	18.0
Fuel capacity, gals.	18.0
Seating capacity	6
Front head room, in.	39.2
Max. front leg room, in.	42.6
Rear head room, in.	38.3
Min. rear leg room, in.	38.0

ENGINES

	ohv V-6	Supercharged ohv V-6
Size, liters/cu. in.	3.8/231	3.8/231
Horsepower @ rpm	205@ 5200	240@ 5200
Torque (lbs./ft.) @ rpm	230@ 4000	280@ 3200
Availability	S	O

EPA city/highway mpg

4-speed OD automatic	19/29	17/25

PRICES

Pontiac Bonneville

	Retail Price	Dealer Invoice
SE 4-door sedan	$22390	$20487
SSE 4-door sedan	29390	26892
Destination charge	605	605

Prices for Computer Command Ride/Handling Pkg. not available at time of publication.

STANDARD EQUIPMENT:

SE: 3.8-liter V-6 engine, 4-speed automatic transmission, driver- and passenger-side air bags, anti-lock brakes, daytime running lamps, air conditioning, power steering, tilt steering wheel, cruise control, cloth 45/55 split bench seat with storage armrest, cupholders, power windows, power door locks, 4-speaker AM/FM radio, digital clock, coolant-temperature gauge, oil-pressure gauge, voltmeter, tachometer, trip odometer, rear defogger, intermittent wipers, visor mirrors, Twilight Sentinel, Lamp Group (includes rear courtesy lights, rear assist handles, headlamp-on warning, trunk light), floormats, tinted glass, left remote and right manual outside mirrors, Pass-Key II theft-deterrent system, fog lights, decklid spoiler, 215/65R15 touring tires, bolt-on wheel covers.

SSE adds: traction control, dual exhaust, automatic climate control w/outside temperature indicator, variable-assist power steering, 45/45 leather bucket seats with center storage console, 6-way power driver seat, power passenger seat, rear vents, rear armrest w/cupholders, overhead console with power outlet, heated power mirrors, automatic day/night inside mirror, CD player with equalizer and Bose 8-speaker sound system, leather-wrapped steering wheel with radio controls, power antenna, Eyecue heads-up instrument display, Driver Information Center, remote keyless entry, illuminated entry, remote decklid release, illuminated visor mirrors, cargo net, electronic load leveling, theft-deterrent system w/alarm, lower-body cladding, emergency road kit (includes spot light, first aid kit, air hose, windshield scraper, gloves), 225/60R16 touring tires, 3-spoke alloy wheels.

OPTIONAL EQUIPMENT:

Major Packages

Option Group 2, 1SB, SE 1125 1001
Variable-effort power steering, illuminated entry, remote keyless entry, cassette player, 6-way power driver's seat, illuminated visor mirrors, power mirrors, remote decklid release, cargo net.

Option Group 3, 1SC, SE 2030 1807
Group 1SB plus bucket seats, Radio Enhancement Pkg. (leather-wrapped steering wheel w/radio controls, 6-speaker sound system), 225/60R16 tires, alloy wheels.

Option Group 4, 1SD, SE 3135 2790
Group 1SC plus automatic climate control, power antenna, leather upholstery.

SLE Special Edition Pkg., SE 1100 946
Manufacturer's discount price 600 516
Fog lights, special bumpers and grille, dual exhausts.

Powertrains

SSEi Supercharger Pkg., SSE 1170 1041
Includes supercharged 3.8-liter V-6 engine, driver selectable shift, boost gauge, unique floormats, 225/60HR16 tires.

Traction control, SE 175 156
Requires option group, bucket seats, and alloy wheels.

Comfort and Convenience

Power glass sunroof, SE 995 886
  SE with bucket seats, SSE 980 872
SE includes illuminated visor mirrors. SE requires alloy wheels.

Cloth 45/45 bucket seats, SE 220 196
Includes center storage console and rear vents, illuminated visor mirrors, overhead console w/power outlet.

Leather 45/45 bucket seats,
  SE with Group 1SB 1345 1197
  SE with Group 1SC 850 757
Includes center storage console and rear vents, rear seat storage armrest, leather-wrapped steering wheel, overhead console with power outlet.

Rating Scale: 5-Excellent; 4-Above average; 3-Average; 2-Below average; 1-Poor

	Retail Price	Dealer Invoice
45/45 articulating leather bucket seats, SSE	$245	$218
6-way power passenger seat, SE	305	271
SE requires option group and alloy wheels when ordered with group 1SC.		
Radio Enhancement Pkg., SE w/Group 1SB	275	245
Includes leather-wrapped steering wheel w/radio controls, 6-speaker sound system. Requires alloy wheels.		
Cassette player, SE	220	196
Includes graphic equalizer and Radio Enhancement Pkg.		
CD player, SE	320	285
Includes graphic equalizer and Radio Enhancement Pkg.		
Power antenna, SE	85	76
Requires option group.		

Appearance and Miscellaneous

Theft-deterrent system w/alarm, SE	190	169
Includes locking fuel filler door. Requires Group 1SD.		
Engine block heater	20	18
Computer Command Ride, SSE	380	338
Computer Command Ride/Handling Pkg., SSE	—	—
Computer Command Ride, 3.05 rear axle ratio, 225/60HR16 touring tires.		
16-inch 5-blade alloy wheels, SE	325	289
Requires 225/60R16 tires.		
16-inch gold or silver crosslace alloy wheels, SE	325	289
Requires 225/60R16 tires.		
16-inch Chrome Torque Star alloy wheels, SE	920	819
SE w/Group 1SD, SSE	595	530
SE requires 225/60R16 tires.		
225/60R16 blackwall touring tires, SE	85	76
Requires alloy wheels.		

PONTIAC FIREBIRD

BUDGET BUY

Pontiac Firebird Trans Am convertible

Rear-wheel-drive Sports and GT car; similar to Chevrolet Camaro

Base price range: (1997 model) $17,174-$28,444. Built in Canada.

Also consider: Ford Mustang, Mitsubishi 3000GT

FOR • Standard anti-lock brakes • Acceleration (V-8 models) • Handling

AGAINST • Fuel economy (V-8 models) • Ride (V-8 models) • Rear seat room • Rear visibility • Wet weather traction (without traction control)

Like its Camaro sibling, Firebird gets a new V-8 engine and revised styling for 1998. Camaro sales are double those of the Firebird, but both have declined the past few years.

Firebird coupes come in base, Formula, and Trans Am guise. Convertibles are offered in base and Trans Am form and have a power top with a glass rear window.

The new V-8 is used on Formula and Trans Am models and is based on the Chevrolet Corvette's aluminum engine. It still displaces 5.7 liters and uses overhead valves, but horsepower is up by 20 over last year, to 305. The WS6 Ram Air option boosts it to 320 and includes a functional hood scoop and 17-inch wheels instead of 16s. The base Firebird retains its 3.8-liter 200-horsepower V-6. A 5-speed manual transmission is standard with the V-6 and a 4-speed automatic optional. With the V-8, the automatic is standard and a 6-speed manual is optional.

Firebird's front end is restyled with a shorter, more rounded beak; base and Formula share one design, while Trans Am gets its own look. Taillamps have a new homeycomb appearance.

Four-wheel anti-lock disc brakes are standard, and traction control is available on V-8s. The standard dual air bags are depowered units that deploy with less force for '98.

PERFORMANCE Firebirds are hardly practical cars, but they're still a good performance value. Few automobiles match the acceleration of the V-8 models, and even the V-6 is surprisingly lively. The biggest drawbacks of the Formula and Trans Am are the amount of premium fuel they guzzle and the high insurance rates they trigger. Try the V-6; you might decide you don't need more power.

Base Firebirds hold the road well, though not with the tenacious grip of the wide-tire Formula and Trans Am. They also ride slightly better. The low-profile tires on the V-8s combine with their stiffer suspension for a less-forgiving ride over bumps, though the '98 Trans Am we tested was not annoyingly harsh on bad pavement. The wider tires howl and rumble, too, and the V-8 models' prominent exhaust note and heavy low-speed steering can grow tiresome.

No matter where you live, spring for the optional traction control if you buy a V-8. The combination of rear-wheel drive, wide tires, and abundant power make the car skittish on wet roads. On models we've tested, the traction control allowed us to keep moving in snow and rain.

ACCOMMODATIONS A low build means you fall into the Firebird's front seats, and the wide doors can be a problem in tight spaces. As in the Camaro, the front passenger's leg room is reduced by a bulge in the floorboard. There's a rear seat, but it's a token gesture and tight even for pre-teens.

Instruments are well-placed and controls are clear, though the radio and climate systems are mounted too low for easiest access. Visibility suffers from the low seating position, wide roof pillars, and a high tail. Cargo room is adequate, given that this isn't a family car, but the cargo area is oddly shaped on the coupes and tiny on the convertibles.

BUILD QUALITY Firebirds we've tested recently have been well assembled and generally free from rattles, though the '98 Trans Am we drove exhibited some body-panel creaking associated with its T-tops. The convertible body flexes over bumps more most modern ragtops.

VALUE FOR THE MONEY Firebird's strength is its dollar-to-performance ratio, which soundly beats rival Mustang's. However, the Mustang is more comfortable and easier to live with on a daily basis.

RATINGS

	Base	Formula/ Trans Am
Acceleration	4	5
Fuel economy	2	1
Ride quality	3	2
Steering/handling	4	5
Braking	4	4
Quietness	2	2
Driver seating	3	3
Instruments/controls	4	4
Room/comfort (front)	4	4
Room/comfort (rear)	2	2
Cargo room	3	3
Value for the money	3	3
Total	**38**	**38**

SPECIFICATIONS

	2-door hatchback	2-door conv.
Wheelbase, in.	101.1	101.1
Overall length, in.	193.4	193.4
Overall width, in.	74.5	74.5
Overall height, in.	52.0	52.7
Curb weight, lbs.	3340	3492
Cargo vol., cu. ft.	33.7	12.9
Fuel capacity, gals.	15.5	15.5
Seating capacity	4	4

Prices are accurate at time of publication; subject to manufacturer's changes.

	2-door hatchback	2-door conv.
Front head room, in.	37.2	37.2
Max. front leg room, in.	43.0	43.0
Rear head room, in.	35.3	35.3
Min. rear leg room, in.	28.9	28.9

ENGINES

	ohv V-6	ohv V-8	ohv V-8
Size, liters/cu. in.	3.8/231	5.7/346	5.7/346
Horsepower @ rpm	200@ 5200	305@ 5200	320@ 5200
Torque (lbs./ft.) @ rpm	225@ 4000	335@ 4000	345@ 4400
Availability	S[1]	S[2]	O[2]

EPA city/highway mpg

4-speed OD automatic	19/28	18/24	18/24
5-speed OD manual	19/28		
6-speed OD manual		16/26	16/26

1. Base. 2. Formula, Trans Am.

PRICES

1997 Pontiac Firebird	Retail Price	Dealer Invoice
2-door hatchback	$17174	$15714
2-door convertible	23084	21122
Formula 2-door hatchback	20724	18962
Formula 2-door convertible	26524	24269
Trans Am 2-door hatchback	22884	20939
Trans Am 2-door convertible	28444	26026
Destination charge	525	525

STANDARD EQUIPMENT:

Base: 3.8-liter V-6 engine, 5-speed manual transmission, anti-lock brakes, air conditioning, power steering, driver- and passenger-side air bags, cloth reclining front bucket seats, folding rear bench seat, tilt steering wheel, center console (storage, auxiliary power outlet, cupholder), 4-speaker AM/FM/cassette player with equalizer, intermittent wipers, tinted glass, left remote and right manual mirrors, coolant-temperature and oil-pressure gauges, tachometer, voltmeter, trip odometer, Pass-Key II theft-deterrent system, dual reading lamps, visor mirrors, remote hatch release, floormats, daytime running lamps, front air dam, decklid spoiler, 215/60R16 touring tires, alloy wheels.

Convertible adds: cruise control, power door locks, power windows, power mirrors, power top with glass rear window and rear window defogger, 6-speaker sound system, rear decklid release.

Formula adds to base hatchback: 5.7-liter V-8 engine, 4-speed automatic transmission, anti-lock 4-wheel disc brakes, air conditioning, performance suspension, 235/55R16 touring tires.

Formula convertible includes Formula and base convertible standard equipment.

Trans Am adds to Formula hatchback: cruise control, 4-way adjustable driver seat, leather-wrapped steering wheel, shift knob, parking brake handle, power windows, power mirrors, power door locks, rear defogger, decklid spoiler, fog lights.

Trans Am convertible adds to Trans Am and base convertible: power antenna, steering-wheel radio controls, remote keyless entry system, 245/50ZR16 all-weather performance tires.

OPTIONAL EQUIPMENT:
Major Packages

	Retail Price	Dealer Invoice
Option Group 1SB, base and Formula hatchbacks	1121	998

Cruise control, power mirrors, power windows, power door locks, 4-speaker CD player with equalizer, rear defogger.

base and Formula convertibles	435	387

Remote keyless entry, power antenna, steering-wheel with radio controls, leather-wrapped steering wheel and shifter.

3800 Performance Pkg., base	550	490

Limited-slip differential, 4-wheel disc brakes, faster-ratio steering gear, dual exhaust outlets, 3.42 rear axle ratio (with automatic transmission), 235/55R16 touring tires.

Sport Appearance Pkg., base	1449	1290

Sport Appearance, fog lights, dual exhaust outlets. Requires 235/55R16 touring tires.

	Retail Price	Dealer Invoice
1LE Performance Pkg., Formula hatchback	$1175	$1046

Requires 6-speed manual transmission and Ram Air Performance and Handling Pkg. Rear defogger is the only available option with this pkg.

Ram Air Performance and Handling Pkg., Formula and Trans Am hatchbacks	3345	2977

Ram Air induction system, upgraded suspension, dual bright exhaust outlets, 275/40ZR17 tires, high-polished alloy wheels.

Ram Air Performance Pkg., Formula and Trans Am convertibles	2995	2666

Ram Air induction system, dual exhaust outlets, 245/50ZR16 high-performance tires, chromed alloy wheels.

Powertrains

4-speed automatic transmission, base	815	725
6-speed manual transmission, Formula, Trans Am	NC	NC

NA on Formula 2-door with group 1SB.

Traction control, Formula, Trans Am	450	401

Requires 235/55R16 touring tires or 245/50ZR16 all-weather performance tires.

Rear performance axle, Formula, Trans Am	225	200

Includes 3.23 axle ratio. Requires 4-speed automatic transmission and 245/50ZR16 or 275/40ZR17 tires (in Ram Air Performance and Handling Pkg.).

Comfort and Convenience

Cruise control, base and Formula hatchbacks	$235	$209
Rear defogger, base and Formula hatchbacks	180	160
Removable locking hatch roof, hatchbacks	995	886

Includes sunshades, lock, and stowage.

Content theft alarm	90	80

Requires remote keyless entry system.

Power mirrors, base and Formula hatchbacks	96	85

Requires power door locks and windows.

Power door locks, base and Formula hatchbacks	220	196
Power windows, base and Formula hatchbacks	290	258

Requires power door locks and mirrors.

CD player with equalizer	100	89
Cassette player with equalizer and amplifier, hatchbacks	230	205

Includes 10-speaker sound system. Base and Formula require power door locks and windows.

CD player with equalizer and amplifier, hatchbacks	330	294

Includes 10-speaker sound system. Base and Formula require power door locks and windows.

Trunk-mounted 12-disc CD changer	595	530

NA with CD players.

Power antenna	85	76
Steering-wheel radio controls, base, Formula	200	178
Trans Am hatchback	125	111

Includes leather-wrapped steering wheel and shifter.

Leather articulating bucket seats, base and Formula hatchbacks, convertibles	804	716
Trans Am hatchback	829	738

Base and Formula require Group 1SB. Hatchbacks require cassette or CD player with equalizer and amplifier.

6-way power driver seat	270	240
Remote keyless entry system	150	134

Base and Formula require power windows, power door locks, and mirrors.

Special Purpose, Wheels and Tires

235/55R16 touring tires, base	132	117
245/50ZR16 high-performance tires, Formula, Trans Am	245	218

NA with traction control.

245/50ZR16 all-weather performance tires, Formula, Trans Am hatchback	245	218
Chromed alloy wheels	595	530

Rating Scale: 5-Excellent; 4-Above average; 3-Average; 2-Below average; 1-Poor

PONTIAC GRAND AM

Pontiac Grand Am GT coupe

Front-wheel-drive compact car

Base price range: $14,874-$16,474. Built in Lansing, Mich.

Also consider: Dodge Avenger, Ford Contour, Mazda 626, Nissan Altima

FOR • Acceleration • Steering/handling • Standard anti-lock brakes

AGAINST • Ride (GT) • Rear entry/exit • Noise

Grand Am is the sole survivor of a General Motors trio that included the Buick Skylark and Olds Achieva, less-sporty-looking cars that are no longer in showrooms due to lack of sales. Grand Am, on the other hand, is by far Pontiac's most-popular model.

Little changes for '98, as Pontiac readies a heavily revised Grand Am for the '99 model year.

Coupes and sedans come in SE and GT trim levels. GTs have a sport suspension and a higher level of standard equipment. The base powertrain for both is a 2.4-liter 4-cylinder engine and a manual transmission or optional automatic. Optional on both models is a 3.1-liter V-6 with automatic transmission. Models with automatic transmission include traction control. Anti-lock brakes are standard and for '98, the dual front air bags deploy with less force.

PERFORMANCE We used to recommend the optional V-6 engine, but no longer are convinced it's worth the extra cost over the 4-cylinder. The 4-cylinder is smoother and quieter than it used to be, and while it's still not as refined as similar Japanese engines, it does deliver adequate acceleration and decent passing power, even with automatic transmission. The automatic shifts smoothly and downshifts promptly for passing and our 4-cylinder/automatic SE test car averaged 20.4 mpg in a mix of urban rush-hour commuting and highway driving.

The V-6's edge in smoothness and speed is not a great one. In a test of a V-6 GT heavy on highway miles we averaged 20.3 mpg.

Try an SE before signing for a GT. The GT has crisp handling, but its stiff suspension and low-profile 16-inch tires make for a jolting ride over bumps and more noise on the road. The SE's more modest tires and suspension settings allow it to absorb bumps much better and to ride somewhat more quietly. On both models, the front end continues to bob after encountering a swell or dip in the pavement.

ACCOMMODATIONS Grand Am's instruments are legible, its switchgear generally well located. The radio is positioned above the climate controls, and both are mounted in a panel that protrudes slightly from the dashboard, making them easily accessible to the driver.

There's adequate leg and head room for four average-size adults. The low seating position gives the interior a claustrophobic feel, however, and some of our drivers find the seat uncomfortable on longer trips. As with most coupes, the long doors are hard to open fully in tight places, and getting to the rear seat is a challenge.

Grand Am's trunk is wide at the rear and opens at bumper level, though the opening isn't big enough to easily load large boxes or suitcases. Small map pockets on the doors, a pair of cupholders, open and covered bins in the console, and a medi-um-size glovebox provide adequate interior storage.

BUILD QUALITY The doors on our test Grand Ams closed easily and all body panels fit evenly. Paintwork was smooth and glossy. Much of the interior trim is hard, molded plastic, but it doesn't look cheap.

VALUE FOR THE MONEY Grand Am survived where its corporate cousins didn't because it combined reasonable prices with a sporty attitude. Now, however, it feels old next to the newer Pontiac Sunfire, and lacks the refinement of many Japanese competitors.

RATINGS

	4-cyl. SE sedan	V-6 GT coupe
Acceleration	3	4
Fuel economy	3	3
Ride quality	3	2
Steering/handling	3	4
Braking	4	4
Quietness	3	3
Driver seating	4	4
Instruments/controls	4	4
Room/comfort (front)	3	3
Room/comfort (rear)	3	2
Cargo room	3	3
Value for the money	3	3
Total	**39**	**39**

SPECIFICATIONS

	2-door coupe	4-door sedan
Wheelbase, in.	103.4	103.4
Overall length, in.	186.9	186.9
Overall width, in.	68.3	68.3
Overall height, in.	53.5	53.5
Curb weight, lbs.	2835	2877
Cargo vol., cu. ft.	13.4	13.4
Fuel capacity, gals.	15.2	15.2
Seating capacity	5	5
Front head room, in.	37.8	37.8
Max. front leg room, in.	43.1	43.1
Rear head room, in.	36.5	37.0
Min. rear leg room, in.	33.9	34.9

ENGINES

	dohc I-4	ohv V-6
Size, liters/cu. in.	2.4/146	3.1/191
Horsepower @ rpm	150@ 6000	155@ 5200
Torque (lbs./ft.) @ rpm	155@ 4400	185@ 4000
Availability	S	O

EPA city/highway mpg

4-speed OD automatic	22/32	21/29
5-speed OD manual	22/33	

PRICES

Pontiac Grand Am	Retail Price	Dealer Invoice
SE 2-door notchback	$14874	$13610
SE 4-door sedan	15024	13746
GT 2-door notchback	16324	14936
GT 4-door sedan	16474	15074
Destination charge	525	525

STANDARD EQUIPMENT:

SE: 2.4-liter DOHC 4-cylinder engine, 5-speed manual transmission, driver- and passenger-side air bags, anti-lock brakes, daytime running lamps, air conditioning, power steering, cloth reclining front bucket seats, center console (armrest, storage, cupholders), overhead compartment, rear-seat headrests, AM/FM radio, power door locks, remote fuel-door and decklid release, tachometer, coolant-temperature gauge, trip odometer, illuminated entry, visor mirrors, floormats, left remote and right manual outside mirrors, Passlock theft-deterrent system, tinted glass, fog lights, 195/70R14 tires, wheel covers.

GT adds: leather-wrapped steering wheel, shifter, parking-brake handle, tilt steering wheel, intermittent wipers, dual exhaust, decklid spoiler, 205/55R16 performance tires, alloy wheels.

Prices are accurate at time of publication; subject to manufacturer's changes.

PONTIAC

OPTIONAL EQUIPMENT:
Major Packages

	Retail Price	Dealer Invoice
Option Group 1SB, SE	$545	$485
Cassette player, rear defogger, spoiler.		
Option Group 1SC, SE	995	886
Group 1SB plus 4-speed automatic transmission, tilt steering wheel, cruise control, intermittent wipers.		
Option Group 1SD, SE 2-door	1870	1664
SE 4-door	1935	1722
Group 1SC plus 3.1-liter V-6 engine, power mirrors, power windows, CD player, remote keyless entry, 195/65R15 tires.		
Option Group 1SE, SE 2-door	2575	2292
SE 4-door	2640	2350
Group 1SD plus split folding rear seat, steering wheel radio controls, 205/55R16 tires, alloy wheels.		
Option Group 1SB, GT	375	324
Cassette player, rear defogger, spoiler.		
Option Group 1SC, GT 2-door	1415	1259
GT 4-door	1480	1317
Group 1SB plus 3.1-liter V-6 engine, 4-speed automatic transmission, variable-assist power steering, CD player, power windows, power mirrors, cruise control, remote keyless entry.		
Option Group 1SD, GT 2-door	2470	2198
GT 4-door	2535	2256
Group 1SC plus sunroof, steering wheel radio controls, Sport Interior Group (upgraded cloth upholstery, driver seat lumbar adjuster, seat back pockets, map lights), split folding rear seat,		
Sport Interior Group, GT	170	151
Upgraded cloth upholstery, driver-seat lumbar adjuster, seat back pockets, map lights. Requires Group 1SC.		
Sport Interior Group w/leather upholstery,		
GT w/Group 1SC	810	721
GT w/Group 1SD	475	423
Includes split folding back seat.		

Powertrains

3.1-liter V-6 engine, SE	450	401
Requires 4-speed automatic transmission. Requires Option Group 1SB or 1SC.		
4-speed automatic transmission	810	721
Includes traction control. Requires Option Group 1SB.		

Comfort and Convenience

Rear defogger	180	160
6-way power driver's seat, GT	340	303
Requires Group 1SD.		
Power sunroof	595	530
SE requires Group 1SD or 1SE. GT requires Group 1SB or 1SC.		
Cassette player with equalizer,		
with option group	110	98
Includes six speakers.		
CD player with equalizer,		
with option group	210	187
Includes six speakers.		
Cassette and CD players with equalizer,		
SE w/Group 1SB or 1SC, GT w/Group 1SB	405	360
SE w/Group 1SD or 1SE,		
GT w/Group 1SC or 1SD	195	174
Smokers Pkg.	170	151
Lighter, ashtray.		

Appearance and Miscellaneous

Engine block heater	20	18
195/65R15 touring tires, SE	135	120
Requires Group 1SB or 1SC.		
205/55R16 touring tires, SE	225	200
Requires Group 1SD and 16-inch alloy wheels		
15-inch crosslace alloy wheels, SE	300	267
16-inch alloy wheels, SE	325	289

PONTIAC GRAND PRIX

Front-wheel-drive midsize car; similar to Buick Century, Buick Regal, and Oldsmobile Intrigue

Base price range: $18,795-$20,665. Built in Built in Fairfax, Kan.

Pontiac Grand Prix GT sedan

Also consider: Ford Taurus, Honda Accord, Toyota Camry

FOR • Acceleration • Steering/handling • Passenger and cargo room

AGAINST • Fuel economy (supercharged engine)

After a 1997 redesign, Grand Prix returns with few changes. It shares its platform with Buick's Century and Regal, and Oldsmobile's new Intrigue, but is the only one that also offers a 2-door coupe body style. The new design has been a hit, with sales of the '97 model running more than 50 percent ahead of '96 levels.

The base SE Grand Prix is a sedan, while the sportier GT model is available in both body styles. A performance-oriented GTP package is optional on the GT.

A 3.1-liter V-6 is standard on the SE, and a 3.8-liter V-6 is standard on the GT and optional on the SE. A supercharged version of the 3.8 is included with the GTP package. Standard equipment includes, automatic transmission, anti-lock 4-wheel disc brakes, and traction control; last year, traction control was unavailable with the supercharged engine. The dual front air bags are depowered to deploy with less force for '98.

PERFORMANCE Acceleration from a standing start is adequate with the 3.1-liter V-6, strong with the 3.8, and almost ferocious with the supercharged engine. The transmission changes gears with world-class smoothness and downshifts quickly for passing.

Our test 3.8-liter SE averaged 22.7 mpg in mostly highway driving, including a high of 27 on the highway and a low of 15 in urban commuting. A GTP returned only 17.1 mpg—on the required premium gas—so its supercharged performance doesn't come cheap. We haven't had an opportunity to measure fuel economy with the 3.1-liter V-6.

On all models, road noise is prominent at highway speeds, enough to make it hard to hear the stereo in the front seats because the speakers are low on the doors.

The SE and GT have a stable, comfortable ride with little bouncing over wavy surfaces. Their firm suspension absorbs most bumps well and provides capable handling with little body lean. The GTP's tauter suspension gives slightly sharper handling and it reacts more abruptly to potholes, but does not make the too harsh.

ACCOMMODATIONS There's ample room for four adults, and a fifth can squeeze into the rear seat. The doors open wide to allow easy entry and exit.

Gauges and controls are well illuminated by Pontiac's orange lighting, and most switchgear is clearly labeled and easy to find and use. The up-level stereos have small buttons that are haphazardly arranged, making it hard to pick out any particular one in a hurry. The optional steering-wheel radio controls are helpful.

Visibility is good to the front and sides, but the high parcel shelf blocks the driver's view of the trunk when backing up. Large outside mirrors improve over-the-shoulder visibility.

The trunk's opening is narrow and liftover is high, but the cargo bay is wide and has a long, flat cargo floor. Interior storage space is good.

BUILD QUALITY Our test cars felt impressively solid over rough roads, and the doors and trunk lid closed with a satisfying "thunk." The interior has plastic trim, but it does not feel cheap or flimsy.

VALUE FOR THE MONEY Grand Prix is a highly capable, sporty midsize car that challenges the class leaders in overall value.

Rating Scale: 5-Excellent; 4-Above average; 3-Average; 2-Below average; 1-Poor

CONSUMER GUIDE™

RATINGS

	GT sedan (3.8-liter V-6)	SE sedan (3.1-liter V-6)	GTP coupe
Acceleration	4	3	5
Fuel economy	3	3	2
Ride quality	3	3	3
Steering/handling	4	3	4
Braking	4	4	4
Quietness	3	3	3
Driver seating	4	4	4
Instruments/controls	4	4	4
Room/comfort (front)	4	4	4
Room/comfort (rear)	4	4	4
Cargo room	4	4	4
Value for the money	4	4	4
Total	**45**	**43**	**45**

SPECIFICATIONS

	2-door coupe	4-door sedan
Wheelbase, in.	110.5	110.5
Overall length, in.	196.5	196.5
Overall width, in.	72.7	72.7
Overall height, in.	54.7	54.7
Curb weight, lbs.	3396	3414
Cargo vol., cu. ft.	16.0	16.0
Fuel capacity, gals.	18.0	18.0
Seating capacity	5	6
Front head room, in.	38.3	38.3
Max. front leg room, in.	42.4	42.4
Rear head room, in.	36.5	36.7
Min. rear leg room, in.	36.1	35.8

ENGINES

	ohv V-6	ohv V-6	Super ohv V-6
Size, liters/cu. in.	3.1/191	3.8/231	3.8/231
Horsepower @ rpm	160@ 5200	195@ 5200	240@ 5200
Torque (lbs./ft.) @ rpm	185@ 4000	220@ 4000	280@ 3200
Availability	S[1]	S[2]	O[3]

EPA city/highway mpg

4-speed OD automatic	20/29	19/30	18/28

1SE. 2. GT; optional, SE. 3. GT.

PRICES

Pontiac Grand Prix

	Retail Price	Dealer Invoice
SE 4-door sedan	$18795	$17197
GT 2-door coupe	20415	18680
GT 4-door sedan	20665	18908
Destination charge	550	550

STANDARD EQUIPMENT:

SE: 3.1-liter V-6 engine, 4-speed automatic transmission, Enhanced Traction System, anti-lock 4-wheel disc brakes, driver- and passenger-side air bags, daytime running lights, air conditioning, power steering, cloth front bucket seats, front floor console, auxiliary power outlet, integrated rear seat headrests, AM/FM radio, power windows, power door locks, tachometer, trip odometer, coolant temperature gauge, Driver Information Center, tilt steering wheel, power mirrors, visor mirrors, door map pockets, tinted glass, intermittent wipers, rear window defogger, fog lights, bright exhaust outlets, 205/70R15 tires, wheel covers.

GT adds: 3.8-liter V-6 engine, dual exhaust outlets, MAGNASTEER variable-effort steering, cruise control, cassette player, leather-wrapped steering wheel, remote decklid release, overhead console, 225/60R16 tires, 5-spoke alloy wheels.

OPTIONAL EQUIPMENT:

Major Packages

	Retail Price	Dealer Invoice
Option Group 1SB, SE	540	481

Cruise control, rear-seat pass-through, cassette player, remote decklid release.

Option Group 1SC, SE	1665	1482

Group 1SB plus overhead console, leaer-wrapped steering wheel with radio controls, 6-way power driver's seat, cargo net, remote keyless entry, 225/60R16 tires, machine-faced alloy wheels.

	Retail Price	Dealer Invoice
Option Group 1SD, SE	$2905	$2585

Group 1SC plus MAGNASTEER variable-effort power steering, trip computer, Eyecue head-up instrument display, automatic air conditioning, leather upholstery.

Option Group 1SB, GT	755	672

Rear-seat pass-through, steering-wheel radio controls, 6-way power driver's seat, cargo net, remote keyless entry.

Option Group 1SC, GT 2-door	2085	1856
GT 4-door	2115	1882

Group 1SB plus trip computer, Eyecue head-up instrument display, automatic air conditioning, leather upholstery, Premium Lighting Pkg.

GTP Performance Pkg., GT w/Group 1SB	1610	1433
GT w/Group 1SC	1410	1255

3.8-liter supercharged V-6 engine, 4-speed automatic transmission, full-function traction control, trip computer, rear decklid spoiler, 225/60R16 performance tires, silver 5-spoke alloy wheels.

Premium Lighting Pkg., 4-door	215	191
2-door	185	165

Lighted visor mirrors, front-door courtesy lamps, rear reading lamps, assist grip, automatic day/night rearview mirror. SE requires Group 1SD. GT requires Group 1SB.

Powertrains

3.8-liter V-6 engine, SE w/option group	415	369

Safety Features

Child seat, GT	125	111
SE w/option group, GT w/option group	75	67

NA with leather seats.

Comfort and Convenience

Automatic air conditioning, GT w/Group 1SB	195	174
6-way power driver seat, SE w/Group 1SB	270	240
Power driver seat lumbar support adjuster	100	89

Includes heated driver seat when ordered with leather upholstery. Requires option group and bucket seats.

Leather seats,		
SE w/Group 1SC, GT w/Group 1SB	475	423
45/55 split front bench seat, SE	NC	NC
Heated driver seat	50	45

Requires bucket seats.

Cassette player w/graphic equalizer	190	169

Includes steering-wheel radio controls, premium sound system. Requires option group. NA SE w/Group 1SB.

CD player	140	125

Requires option group.

CD player w/graphic equalizer	290	258

Requires option group. NA SE w/Group 1SB.

Multi-disc CD changer	595	530

Requires option group. NA SE w/Group 1SB.

Premium sound system	125	111

Requires cassette or CD player. SE requires Group 1SC or 1SD.

Overhead console, SE w/Group 1SB	80	71

NA with power sunroof.

Power sunroof	650	579
with overhead console	570	507

SE requires option group. Deletes overhead console.

Remote keyless entry, SE w/Group 1SB	150	134
Theft deterrent system	60	53

Requires option group.

Appearance and Miscellaneous

Rear decklid spoiler	175	156

SE requires option group.

Engine block heater	20	18
Machine faced alloy wheels, SE w/Group 1SB	260	231

Requires 225/60R16 tires.

Crosslace alloy wheels, SE	260	231
GT	NC	NC

SE requires option group, 225/60R16 tires.

5-spoke high-polished alloy wheels, GT	325	289
5-spoke white alloy wheels, GT	NC	NC

Requires white exterior paint.

225/60R16 tires, SE	160	142

Prices are accurate at time of publication; subject to manufacturer's changes.

PONTIAC SUNFIRE

RECOMMENDED

Pontiac Sunfire SE convertible

Front-wheel-drive subcompact car; similar to Chevrolet Cavalier

Base price range: $12,495-$19,495. Built in Lordstown, Ohio, and Lansing, Mich.

Also consider: Chevrolet Prizm, Ford Escort/Escort ZX2, Honda Civic

FOR • Standard anti-lock brakes • Fuel economy • Acceleration (2.4-liter engine)

AGAINST • Rear visibility • Rear seat comfort

Sunfire, which has carried its current design since 1995 with few changes, enters 1998 with...few changes. It shares its mechanicals with the Chevrolet Cavalier, but has different styling.

Sunfire offers 2-door coupe and convertible body styles and a 4-door sedan. All come in an SE trim level, with the coupe also available in GT guise. The convertible has a power top with glass rear window and defogger.

A 2.2-liter 4-cylinder engine is standard on SEs and a 2.4-liter 4-cylinder is standard on the GT coupe, optional on the others. Manual transmission is standard on all but the SE convertible. A 3-speed automatic is optional with the 2.2 on SE coupe and sedan. A 4-speed automatic is available with both engines and includes traction control. Anti-lock brakes are standard, and the dual air bags are new depowered units that deploy with less force.

Sunfire has the same performance and accommodations as similarly equipped versions of the Cavalier.

See the Chevrolet Cavalier report for an evaluation of the Sunfire.

RATINGS

	SE 4-dr.(2.2)	SE conv. (2.2)	GT 2-dr.
Acceleration	2	2	4
Fuel economy	4	4	4
Ride quality	3	3	3
Steering/handling	3	3	4
Braking	4	4	4
Quietness	3	3	3
Driver seating	3	3	3
Instruments/controls	4	4	4
Room/comfort (front)	3	3	3
Room/comfort (rear)	3	2	2
Cargo room	3	2	3
Value for the money	4	4	4
Total	**39**	**37**	**41**

SPECIFICATIONS

	2-door coupe	4-door sedan	2-door conv.
Wheelbase, in.	104.1	104.1	104.1
Overall length, in.	181.9	181.9	181.9
Overall width, in.	67.4	67.3	68.4
Overall height, in.	53.0	54.7	53.9
Curb weight, lbs.	2637	2674	2868
Cargo vol., cu. ft.	12.4	13.1	9.9
Fuel capacity, gals.	15.2	15.2	15.2
Seating capacity	5	5	4
Front head room, in.	37.6	38.9	38.8
Max. front leg room, in.	42.1	42.1	42.1
Rear head room, in.	36.6	37.2	38.5
Min. rear leg room, in.	32.6	34.3	32.6

ENGINES

	ohv I-4	dohc I-4
Size, liters/cu. in.	2.2/133	2.4/146
Horsepower @ RPM	115@ 5000	150@ 5600
Torque (lbs./ft.) @ RPM	135@ 3600	155@ 4400
Availability	S[1]	S[2]
EPA city/highway mpg		
3-speed automatic	24/31	
4-speed OD automatic	25/34	22/32
5-speed OD manual	25/37	23/33

1. SE. 2. GT; optional, SE.

PRICES

Pontiac Sunfire	Retail Price	Dealer Invoice
SE 2-door coupe	$12495	$11558
SE 4-door sedan	12495	11558
SE 2-door convertible	19495	18033
GT 2-door coupe	15495	14332
Destination charge	500	500

STANDARD EQUIPMENT:

SE: 2.2-liter 4-cylinder engine, 5-speed manual transmission, driver- and passenger-side air bags, anti-lock brakes, daytime running lamps, power steering, cloth reclining front bucket seats, center console with storage armrest, folding rear seat w/headrests, AM/FM radio, tachometer, coolant-temperature and oil-pressure gauges, trip odometer, visor mirrors, rear heat ducts, floormats, tinted glass, left remote and right remote outside mirrors, Pass-Lock theft-deterrent system, rear spoiler (coupe), 195/70R14 tires, bolt-on wheel covers.

SE convertible adds: 4-speed automatic transmission, traction control, air conditioning, power top, cruise control, tilt steering wheel, rear defogger, intermittent wipers, Convenience Pkg. (overhead storage console, remote decklid release, assist handles, trunk net, reading lights), rear spoiler, 195/65R15 tires.

GT adds to SE 2-door: 2.4-liter dohc 4-cylinder engine, air conditioning, tilt steering wheel, rear defogger, 205/55R16 tires, alloy wheels.

OPTIONAL EQUIPMENT:
Major Packages

Option Group 1SB, SE sedan/coupe	2130	1896

Air conditioning, 3-speed automatic transmission, CD player, tilt steering-wheel, rear defogger.

Option Group 1SC, SE coupe	3015	2683
SE sedan	3055	2719

Group 1SB plus cruise control, intermittent wipers, Convenience Pkg. (cargo net, overhead console, map lights), power door locks remote keyless entry, rear spoiler, 195/65R15 tires.

Option Group 1SD, SE coupe	3700	3293
SE sedan	3740	3329

Group 1SC plus 4-speed automatic transmission, traction control, alloy wheels.

Option Group 1SE, SE coupe	4655	4143
SE sedan	4760	4236

Group 1SD plus 2.4-liter 4-cylinder engine, power windows, power mirrors, steering wheel radio controls,

Option Group 1SB, convertible	1800	1602

2.4-liter 4-cylinder engine, CD player, steering-wheel radio controls, power windows, power door locks, remote keyless entry, power mirrors, sport bucket seats, leather-wrapped steering wheel, driver seat lumbar adjustment..

Option Group 1SB, GT	1740	1549

4-speed manual transmission, traction control, cruise control, power door locks, remote keyless entry, CD player, intermittent wipers, rear defogger, Convenience Pkg. (cargo net, overhead console, map lights).

Option Group 1SC, GT	2245	1998

Group 1SB plus power windows, power mirrors, steering-wheel radio controls, sport bucket seats, leather-wrapped steering wheel, driver seat lumbar adjustment.

Powertrains

3-speed automatic transmission, SE coupe, sedan	600	534

NA with option groups.

Rating Scale: 5-Excellent; 4-Above average; 3-Average; 2-Below average; 1-Poor

	Retail Price	Dealer Invoice
4-speed automatic transmission, GT	$810	$721
SE sedan/coupe w/Group 1SC	210	187
Includes traction control.		
5-speed manual transmission, SE sedan/coupe w/Group 1SD or 1SE, convertible, GT (credit)	(810)	(721)
SE sedan/coupe w/Group 1SB or 1SC (credit)	(600)	(534)
Requires 2.4-liter DOHC 4-cylinder engine.		

Comfort and Convenience

Air conditioning, SE sedan/coupe	830	739
Rear defogger, SE sedan/coupe	180	160
Cassette player	195	174
Not available with option groups.		
Power sunroof, GT	595	530
SE coupe w/Group 1SB/1SC, GT wGroup 1SB	556	495
Replaces overhead console when ordered with Convenience Pkg.		
Smoker Pkg.	15	13
Lighter and ash tray.		

Appearance and Miscellaneous

Engine block heater	20	18
Alloy wheels, SE sedan/coupe	295	263
Requires 195/65R15 tires and Group 1SC.		
195/65R15 touring tires, SE sedan/coupe	135	120

PONTIAC TRANS SPORT

RECOMMENDED

Pontiac Trans Sport Montana

Front-wheel-drive minivan; similar to Chevrolet Venture and Oldsmobile Silhouette

Base price range: $20,840-$23,090. Built in Doraville, Ga.

Also consider: Dodge Caravan, Ford Windstar, Toyota Sienna

FOR • Standard anti-lock brakes • Ride • Passenger and cargo room • Side air bags

AGAINST • Fuel economy

This is Pontiac's version of General Motors' three front-drive minivans, and like the others, it gains front side air bags for '98. Chevrolet's Venture and Oldsmobile's Silhouette have slightly more-conservative styling but are nearly identical under the skin. Trans Sport sales nearly doubled from '96 to '97, when these minivans were redesigned, but the Dodge Caravan still outsells the Pontiac by about 4-1.

Trans Sport comes in regular and extended lengths. Regular models come with a right-side sliding door, but can now be ordered with dual sliding side doors. The dual doors were previously optional only on extended-length Trans Sports; those models now have them as standard. Both versions can also be ordered with a powered right-side sliding door.

Like most GM vehicles, Trans Sport gets depowered front air bags for '98. Its new side air bags are mounted outboard on the front passenger seats.

Seven-passenger seating is standard, eight-passenger seating is optional. Up to two middle-row integrated child seats are optional.

A V-6 engine and automatic transmission constitute the sole powertrain. Anti-lock brakes are standard and traction control is optional.

Major options include the Montana Package, which counts among its features two-tone paint, a firmer suspension, and tires designed to seal leaks after small punctures.

PERFORMANCE The 3.4-liter V-6 provides Trans Sport with adequate acceleration and is aided by a smooth-shifting automatic transmission that downshifts quickly for passing. Our test Trans Am averaged 18.7 mpg in a mix of driving slightly heavy on highway miles. That fuel economy is a little better than par for a minivan.

As with its Chevy and Olds cousins, Trans Am's ride and handling mirror those of a midsize sedan. These are among the most road-worthy minvians, leading only moderately in turns, and easily taking most bumps in stride.

There is noticeable wind noise around the mirrors on the highway, but little road or engine noise.

ACCOMMODATIONS Trans Sport's low step-in height makes entry and exit as easy as in most cars. The dual sliding doors and the optional power door are valuable conveniences; the power door is found only on these GM vans and on the new Toyota Sienna.

Gauges are unobstructed, and the driver can reach the large radio and climate controls without undue stretching.

The front seats are roomy and while there's adequate space for adults in the rear rows, those seats are low to the floor, making for some awkward bending of the kness and less-than-optimal comfort, The individual bucket seats are light enough to be removed by one person, as is the rear bench. On the extended model, there's good cargo room in back even with all seats in place, unlike on the standard-wheelbase model.

Depending on model and interior furnishings, Trans Sport provides at least nine cupholders and as many as 17. All doors have map pockets, and there are covered bins in the side panels and rear armrests, plus a small cargo net that can be strung between the front seats.

BUILD QUALITY Trans Ams we've tested have been generally well-assembled, though one had a rattle in the driver's door. Exterior fit and finish were of a high standard, and interior materials felt solid, with smooth-acting controls.

VALUE FOR THE MONEY Chrysler Corporation's minivans edge out the GM trio in our rankings, but Trans Sport and its companions shouldn't be overlooked. They offer lots of clever features and are good value.

RATINGS

	3-dr. reg. length	4-dr. ext. length
Acceleration	3	3
Fuel economy	2	2
Ride quality	3	4
Steering/handling	4	4
Braking	4	4
Quietness	4	4
Driver seating	4	4
Instruments/controls	4	4
Room/comfort (front)	4	4
Room/comfort (rear)	3	3
Cargo room	5	5
Value for the money	4	4
Total	44	45

SPECIFICATIONS

	3-door van	3-door van
Wheelbase, in.	112.0	120.0
Overall length, in.	187.3	201.3
Overall width, in.	72.7	72.7
Overall height, in.	67.4	68.1
Curb weight, lbs.	3730	3942
Cargo vol., cu. ft.	126.6	155.9
Fuel capacity, gals.	20.0	25.0
Seating capacity	8	8
Front head room, in.	39.9	39.9
Max. front leg room, in.	39.9	39.9
Rear head room, in.	39.3	39.3
Min. rear leg room, in.	36.9	39.0

ENGINES

	ohv V-6
Size, liters/cu. in.	3.4/207
Horsepower @ rpm	180@ 5200

Prices are accurate at time of publication; subject to manufacturer's changes.

	ohv V-6
Torque (lbs./ft.) @ rpm	205@
	4000
Availability	S

EPA city/highway mpg

4-speed OD automatic	18/25

PRICES

Pontiac Trans Sport	Retail Price	Dealer Invoice
SWB 3-door van	$20840	$18860
SWB 4-door van	22380	20254
Extended wheelbase 4-door van	23090	20896
Destination charge	570	570

SWB denotes standard wheelbase.

STANDARD EQUIPMENT:

SWB 3-door: 3.4-liter V-6 engine, 4-speed automatic transmission, driver- and passenger-side side air bags, front side-impact air bags, anti-lock brakes, daytime running lights, power steering, tilt steering wheel, front air conditioning, interior air filter, cloth upholstery, 7-passenger seating (front reclining bucket seats w/manual lumbar adjustment, second- and third-row bench seats), front storage console, cupholders, power mirrors, power door locks, tachometer, coolant-temperature gauge, voltmeter, trip odometer, AM/FM radio, integrated antenna, under-passenger-seat storage, visor mirrors, intermittent wipers, rear wiper/washer, front and rear auxiliary power outlets, Lamp Group (includes front map lights, rear reading lights, cargo-area lights, underhood light), automatic headlights, floormats, tinted glass with solar-control windshield, fog lamps, 205/70R15 tires, wheel covers.

SWB 4-door adds: sliding driver-side door, cruise control, cassette player, perimeter lighting, cargo net.

Extended adds: rear split reclining bench seats, 215/70R15 tires.

OPTIONAL EQUIPMENT:
Major Packages

	Retail	Dealer
Option Pkg. 1SB, 3-door	460	409
Cruise control, cassette player, cargo net.		
Option Pkg. 1SC, 3-door	1450	1291
Group 1SB plus power windows, power rear quarter windows, deep-tint glass, remote keyless entry, rear defogger, perimeter lighting.		
Option Pkg. 1SD, 3-door	2495	2221
Group 1SC plus power driver seat, rear split reclining bench seats (SWB), overhead console (storage, outside-temperature indicator, compass), illuminated visor mirrors, roof rack.		
Option Pkg. 1SC, 4-door	930	828
Power windows, power rear quarter windows, deep-tinted glass, remote keyless entry, rear defogger, perimeter lighting.		
Option Pkg. 1SD, 4-door	1640	1460
Group 1SC plus power driver seat, overhead console, (storage, outside-temperature indicator, compass), illuminated visor mirrors, roof rack.		
Montana Pkg., SWB 4-door w/Pkg. 1SC	1225	1090
SWB 4-door w/Pkg. 1SD	1050	935
Extended w/Pkg. 1SC	1185	1055
Extended w/Pkg. 1SD	1010	899
Traction control, automatic level control, rear split reclining bench seats (SWB), unique exterior appearance, saddle-bag storage, roof rack, sport suspension, self-sealing 215/70R15 outline-white-letter tires, alloy wheels.		
Safety and Security Pkg.	210	187
Ordered w/Montana Pkg.		
or 215/70R15 self-sealing touring tires	60	53
Theft-deterrent system, 215/70R15 self-sealing touring tires. Requires Option Pkg. 1SD.		
Trailer Pkg.	150	134
Trailer wiring harness, heavy-duty cooling, heavy-duty flasher. Requires automatic level control, 215/70R15 touring tires.		

Powertrains

Traction control	195	174
Requires automatic level control.		

Safety Features

	Retail Price	Dealer Invoice
Integrated child seat	$125	$111
NA w/captain's chairs.		
Two integrated child seats	225	200
NA w/captain's chairs.		

Comfort and Convenience

Rear air conditioning, extended	460	409
Extended w/Montana Pkg.		
or automatic level control	450	401
Includes saddle-bag storage, rear heater.		
Power sliding side door	385	343
Includes power rear-quarter windows. 3-door requires Pkg. 1SC, remote keyless entry.		
Power driver seat	270	240
Power front seats	305	271
Requires rear modular bucket seats, second-row captain's chairs w/split reclining third-row bench seat, or 8-passenger seating.		
Rear split reclining bench seats, SWB	335	298
Rear modular bucket seats, SWB	450	401
SWB w/Pkg. 1SD or Montana Pkg.	115	102
Extended	115	102
Second-row captain's chairs w/split reclining third-row bench seat,		
SWB	600	534
SWB w/Pkg. 1SD or Montana Pkg.	265	236
Extended	265	236
8-passenger seating, SWB	600	534
SWB w/Pkg. 1SD or Montana Pkg.	265	236
Extended	265	236
Leather upholstery	1055	939
Includes leather-wrapped steering wheel w/radio controls. Requires power driver's seat.		
Power windows	325	289
Includes rear quarter vents.		
Overhead console	175	156
Includes storage, outside temperature indicator, driver information center, illuminated visor mirrors. Requires Pkg. 1SC and remote keyless entry.		
Cassette player, 3-door	195	174
Cassette player w/equalizer	350	312
Ordered w/leather upholstery	165	147
Includes rear-seat audio controls and earphone jacks, leather-wrapped steering wheel w/radio controls, extended-range coaxial speakers.		
CD player	100	89
Requires option Pkg.		
CD player w/equalizer	450	401
Ordered w/leather upholstery	265	236
Includes rear-seat audio controls and earphone jacks, leather-wrapped steering wheel w/radio controls, extended-range coaxial speakers. Requires option pkg.		
Cassette/CD player w/equalizer	550	490
Ordered w/leather upholstery	365	325
Includes rear-seat audio controls and earphone jacks, leather-wrapped steering wheel w/radio controls, extended-range coaxial speakers. Requires option pkg.		
Extended range coaxial speakers	50	45
Leather-wrapped steering wheel		
w/radio controls	185	165
Rear defogger	180	160
Remote keyless entry	150	134

Appearance and Miscellaneous

Deep-tint glass	275	245
Roof rack	175	156
2-tone paint	125	111
NA w/Montana Pkg.		
Engine block heater	20	18
Automatic level control	180	160
Includes saddle-bag storage, 215/70R15 touring tires.		
215/70R15 touring tires,		
SWB	75	67
Extended	35	31
215/70R15 self-sealing touring tires	150	134
Alloy wheels	280	249
Reqiures 215/70R15 touring tires		

Rating Scale: 5-Excellent; 4-Above average; 3-Average; 2-Below average; 1-Poor

PORSCHE BOXSTER

Porsche Boxster

Rear-wheel-drive Sports and GT

Base price range: (1997 model) $39,980-$43,130. Built in Germany.

Also consider: BMW Z3, Mazda Miata, Mercedes-Benz SLK230

FOR • Steering/handling • Side air bags • Acceleration • Braking

AGAINST • Engine noise • Ride

The Boxster is Porsche's reply to "retro" 2-seaters like the BMW Z3, Mazda Miata, and Mercedes SLK. It differs from those cars in having a mid-engine layout built around a "flat" 6-cylinder engine (horizontally opposed cylinders) mounted just behind the cockpit. Drive is to the rear wheels via manual transmission or optional 5-speed "Tiptronic," Porsche's manually shift-able automatic.

For 1998, the Boxster receives two safety-related changes: standard door-mounted side air bags and an optional child-seat detection system. The latter automatically deactivates the right-side air bags when a special child safety seat is installed; the option requires some minor vehicle modifications by a dealer.

Other standard features include all-disc anti-lock brakes, 16-inch high-performance tires (wider in back), and a power soft top that disappears beneath a hard cover. Options include 17-inch wheels and tires, traction control, cockpit "wind blocker," a 55-pound aluminum hardtop, and a roof storage system for toting skis or bicycles.

One other change for '98 involves base price. It's up $1020.

PERFORMANCE It may be the latest "budget" Porsche, but the Boxster is no less a thoroughbred sports car than big brother 911. It entertains most on twisty roads, tracking with grippy stability, little body lean and sure control, aided by rifle-quick steering with ample feedback. The penalty for this handling prowess is an annoyingly stiff ride, with constant minor pitching on some freeways and lots of thumpy jiggle over tar strips and patches. Add in marked noise from engine, wind and tires, and the Boxster would be wearing on a long Interstate trip.

Although the engine is strongest at higher rpm, there's enough low-end torque for punchy standing starts and quick passing sprints. Still, our manual-shift test car disappointed slightly in the 0-60 mph test at 7.5 seconds (Porsche claims 6.7). Fuel economy is excellent for the performance, though; we averaged 21.7 mpg in spirited city/highway driving. "Panic" braking is arresting-cable swift. Mash the pedal and the Boxster just hunkers down and stops.

ACCOMMODATIONS Our testers divided sharply on Boxster cockpit room. Some felt cramped even with the top down; others had no complaint. None of us liked the handy but confusing audio and climate controls, and most would have preferred a tilt steering wheel instead of the standard telescopic adjustment; as it is, the wheel rim tends to mask part of the tachometer face. Other gripes: an old-fashioned floor-hinged gas pedal; analog AND digital speedometers; no in-dash glovebox; and no topside engine access other than three "service ports" in the rear trunk.

On the plus side, the Boxster's two cargo holds (front and rear) take a fair bit of stuff for a 2-seater, the seats are supportively comfortable, and visibility is okay despite a "bathtub" driving position and the soft top's fairly blind rear quarters. That top works quickly and seals well, but isn't completely covered when folded under its lid, and the plastic rear window seems cheap at

this price. The optional behind-the-seats wind blocker is effective, but cumbersome to remove or install.

BUILD QUALITY Though solid and rattle-free for a modern ragtop, our test car had some mild body-shake over railroad tracks. Gorgeous paint and precise panel fits were a sharp contrast to the thin, cheap-looking black plastic used on the dash and console.

VALUE FOR THE MONEY As a more affordable new Porsche, the Boxster is mainly for those who appreciate a Porsche's special virtues. BMW's 6-cylinder Z3 2.8 is a more "traditional" sports car that's close on performance, while some of our staff tab the Mercedes SLK as the best all-rounder. All are good in their way and cost about the same, so take your pick.

RATINGS

	Boxster
Acceleration	4
Fuel economy	3
Ride quality	2
Steering/handling	5
Braking	5
Quietness	2
Driver seating	3
Instruments/controls	3
Room/comfort (front)	3
Room/comfort (rear)	—
Cargo room	1
Value for the money	3
Total	**34**

SPECIFICATIONS

	2-door conv.
Wheelbase, in.	95.1
Overall length, in.	169.8
Overall width, in.	70.1
Overall height, in.	50.8
Curb weight, lbs.	2755
Cargo vol., cu. ft.	9.1
Fuel capacity, gals.	15.3
Seating capacity	2
Front head room, in.	NA
Max. front leg room, in.	NA
Rear head room, in.	–
Min. rear leg room, in.	–

ENGINES

	dohc Flat-6
Size, liters/cu. in.	2.5/151
Horsepower @ rpm	201@ 6000
Torque (lbs./ft.) @ rpm	180@ 4500
Availability	S

EPA city/highway mpg

5-speed OD manual	19/26
5-speed OD automatic	17/24

PRICES

1997 Porsche Boxster	Retail Price	Dealer Invoice
2-door convertible, 5-speed	$39980	$35005
2-door convertible, automatic	43130	37610
Destination charge	765	765

STANDARD EQUIPMENT:

2.5-liter DOHC 6-cylinder engine, 5-speed manual or Tiptronic 5-speed automatic transmission, anti-lock 4-wheel disc brakes, variable-assist power steering, driver- and passenger-side air bags, automatic air conditioning, power top, partial leather upholstery, front bucket seats w/power recliners and driver-seat height adjustment, storage console, leather-wrapped steering wheel, leather-wrapped handbrake handle, door handles, telescopic steering wheel, power windows, heated power mirrors, tinted glass, tachometer, oil-level and coolant-temperature gauges, detachable AM/FM/cassette w/anti-theft, integrated antenna, heated washer nozzles, theft-deterrent system, interior air filter, dual exhaust, driver- and passenger-side roll bars, hood scoop, adjustable rear spoiler, front and rear fog lights, 205/55ZR16 front tires, 225/50ZR16 rear tires, alloy wheels.

Prices are accurate at time of publication; subject to manufacturer's changes.

OPTIONAL EQUIPMENT:
Major Packages

	Retail Price	Dealer Invoice
Seat Pkg.	$390	$313
Heated front seats.		
Sport Pkg.	3245	2600
Cruise control, Hi-Fi sound system, CD player, remote keyless entry w/theft-deterrent system, wind deflector, Boxster-design wheels, 250/50ZR17 front tires, 255/40ZR17 rear tires.		
Sport Touring Pkg., ordered w/5-speed trans.	7032	5634
ordered w/automatic trans.	6927	5550
Sport Pkg. plus 6-disc CD player, on-board computer, aluminum instrument knobs, aluminum/leather shifter and brake handle (5-speed), aluminum shifter and brake handle (automatic), chrome roll bar, metal door sill w/insignia, oval center exhaust outlet.		
Technic Sport Pkg.	1901	1523
Traction control, sport suspension, 250/50ZR17 front tires, 255/40ZR17 rear tires, special wheels.		

Comfort and Convenience

Cruise control	390	313
Leather upholstery	1951	1563
Traction control	847	678
Special leather upholstery	2324	1862
AM/FM/CD player	315	253
Remote 6-disc CD changer	689	552
Requires Hi-Fi sound system.		
Automatic day/night inside mirror	448	359
Hi-Fi sound system	490	392
Remote keyless entry w/theft-deterrent system	540	432
On-board computer	274	219
Rain-sensing windshield	1351	1083
Headlamp washers	224	180

Appearance and Miscellaneous

Active carbon filter	448	359
Hardtop	2249	1802
Includes rear defogger.		
Tonneau cover	1230	986
Wind deflector	315	253
Roof rack	448	359
Floormats	261	209

Special Purpose, Wheels and Tires

Boxster-design wheels	1195	958
Includes 250/50ZR17 front tires, 255/40ZR17 rear tires.		
Sport Classic wheels	2432	1948
Includes 250/50ZR17 front tires, 255/40ZR17 rear tires.		

SAAB 900

Saab 900 convertible

Front-wheel-drive near-luxury car

Base price range: (1997 model) $25,470-$42,970. Built in Sweden and Finland.

Also consider: Acura TL, Audi A4, Infiniti I30, Volvo S70/V70

FOR • Standard anti-lock brakes • Acceleration (Turbo) • Steering/handling • Passenger and cargo room

AGAINST • Wind noise • Ignition lock location

Saab is owned by General Motors, but that doesn't have much of an affect on this compact-sized Swedish car's idiosyncratic character. Not many hatchbacks are available these days, but the 900 offers two, a 2-door and a 4-door, plus a 2-door convertible with a power top and glass rear window with defroster. And where 6-cylinder engines are the norm in this price range, Saab drops the 900's available V-6 for '98, leaving all models with 4-cylinder power.

All body styles are offered in S and uplevel SE equipment. S model convertibles and 4-doors use a 150-horsepower 2.3-liter engine. New for '98 is an S Turbo Coupe with a 185-horsepower turbocharged 2.0-liter. The S Turbo Coupe marks the 20th anniversary of Saab's first turbocharged production car sold in North America. It's priced $970 below last year's naturally aspirated 2-door hatchback. The SE models also use the turbo 2.0, and all 900s have manual transmission or optional automatic, plus standard dual air bags and anti-lock brakes. Besides the S Turbo Coupe, changes for 1998 include new front and rear bumpers on all models.

Saab will also import about 1300 units of its larger car, the 9000. These are front-wheel-drive 4-door hatchbacks with a 225-horsepower 2.3-liter turbocharged 4-cylinder. The 9000 is to be replaced by the 1999 Saab 9-5 in the spring of 1998.

PERFORMANCE The naturally aspired 4-cylinder has adequate power with manual transmission but feels weak with automatic. Turbos have excellent acceleration with only a small amount of lag before turbo boost kicks in. We tested a 5-speed turbo and averaged 23.7 mpg, just slightly less than our naturally aspirated 900 test cars have delivered.

The automatic transmission shifts smoothly and downshifts promptly in passing situations, but some of our testers found the 5-speed's clutch engagement inconsistent and its pedal return too strong, making it difficult to drive smoothly.

All 900s have precise steering and a taut suspension that provides sporty handling. The ride is firm but never harsh. Road noise is moderate, but the upright design results in an objectionable level of wind noise at highway speeds.

ACCOMMODATIONS These cars have compact-sized exterior dimenions but passenger and cargo room that would do a mid-size car proud. The hatchbacks have ample room for four adults on firmly padded, chairlike seats. The convertible's rear seats are narrower and too upright to be comfortable on long drives.

The hatchbacks have a spacious cargo area that can be expanded by folding the split rear seat. However, you have to remove the rear headrests and lower a heavy seat frame to create a flat cargo floor. Cargo space in the covertible is above average for a ragtop, but compared to other cars it's skimpy and the trunk opening is small.

The well-designed dashboard places gauges and controls conveniently, though some of our testers complained of too many small buttons. Saab loyalists appreciate having the ignition-key lock on the floor between the seats and being forced to put the manual transmission in reverse before removing the key. It's disorienting to most everyone else.

BUILD QUALITY These Saabs are solidly built with high-grade materials and good fit and finish. But our test cars have suffered glitches. On our most recent example, the "check engine" light illuminated intermittently, and turning the steering wheel triggered a humming noise from the engine compartment.

VALUE FOR THE MONEY There are certainly better near-luxury car buys than this unconventional Saab, starting with the Audi A4 and Infiniti I30. But the 900 has its charms and the new S Turbo Coupe is a performance bargain.

SPECIFICATIONS

	2-door hatchback	4-door hatchback	2-door conv.
Wheelbase, in.	102.4	102.4	102.4
Overall length, in.	182.6	182.6	182.6
Overall width, in.	67.4	67.4	67.4
Overall height, in.	56.6	56.6	56.5
Curb weight, lbs.	2980	2980	3090
Cargo vol., cu. ft.	24.0	24.0	10.0
Fuel capacity, gals.	18.0	18.0	18.0
Seating capacity	5	5	4
Front head room, in.	39.3	39.3	39.0
Max. front leg room, in.	42.3	42.3	42.3
Rear head room, in.	37.8	37.8	37.9
Min. rear leg room, in.	34.1	34.1	33.0

Rating Scale: 5-Excellent; 4-Above average; 3-Average; 2-Below average; 1-Poor

CONSUMER GUIDE™

RATINGS

	S 4-dr.	SE 2-dr.	S conv.
Acceleration	3	4	3
Fuel economy	4	4	4
Ride quality	4	4	4
Steering/handling	4	4	4
Braking	5	5	5
Quietness	2	2	2
Driver seating	3	3	3
Instruments/controls	3	3	3
Room/comfort (front)	4	4	4
Room/comfort (rear)	4	3	2
Cargo room	5	5	2
Value for the money	3	2	3
Total	**44**	**43**	**39**

ENGINES

	dohc I-4	turbo dohc I-4	turbo dohc I-4
Size, liters/cu. in.	2.3/140	2.0/121	2.0/121
Horsepower @ rpm	150@ 5700	185@ 5500	185@ 5750
Torque (lbs./ft.) @ rpm	155@ 4300	194@ 2100	170@ 2000
Availability	S[1]	S[2]	S[2]
EPA city/highway mpg			
4-speed OD automatic	20/26		19/25
5-speed OD manual	22/28	20/27	

1. S models. 2. SE models.

PRICES

1997 Saab 900	Retail Price	Dealer Invoice
S 2-door hatchback	$25470	$22923
S 4-door hatchback	26470	23823
S 2-door convertible	35670	32104
SE Turbo 2-door hatchback	30470	27423
SE Turbo Talledaga 2-door hatchback	30995	27663
SE Turbo 4-door hatchback	31470	28322
SE Turbo Talledaga 4-door hatchback	31995	28557
SE V-6 4-door hatchback	32980	29682
SE Turbo 2-door convertible	41470	37115
SE Turbo Talledaga 2-door convertible	41995	36849
SE V-6 2-door convertible	42970	38458
Destination charge	525	525

STANDARD EQUIPMENT:

S: 2.3-liter DOHC 4-cylinder engine, 5-speed manual transmission, anti-lock 4-wheel disc brakes, driver- and passenger-side air bags, power steering, air conditioning, cruise control, power convertible top (convertible), velour upholstery (hatchbacks), leather upholstery (convertible), heated reclining front bucket seats, driver-seat lumbar adjustment, folding rear seat w/trunk pass-through, cupholder, leather-wrapped steering wheel and shifter (convertibile), power windows, power door locks, heated power mirrors, telescopic steering wheel, solar-control tinted glass, coolant temperature gauge, trip odometer, tachometer, analog clock, 6-speaker AM/FM/cassette w/weather band and anti-theft, power antenna, rear defogger, theft-deterrent system, intermittent wipers, illuminated visor mirrors, headlamp wipers/washers, rear wiper/washer (hatchbacks), front and rear fog lamps, daytime running lights, front spoiler, rear spoiler (2-door hatchback), floormats, tool kit, 195/60VR15 tires, alloy wheels.

SE Turbo adds: 2.0-liter turbocharged DOHC 4-cylinder engine, lower sport chassis, automatic air conditioning, leather upholstery, power front seats w/driver-seat memory, leather-wrapped steering wheel and shifter, power sunroof (hatchbacks), rear spoiler (4-door hatchback), turbo-boost gauge, 8-speaker upgraded audio system, 6-disc CD changer (convertible), Saab Car Computer, walnut-trimmed instrument panel, 205/50ZR16 tires.

SE Turbo Talledaga adds: Super Aero alloy wheels, body-colored bumpers, mirrors, and spoilers, 2-tone interior.

SE V-6 deletes turbo-boost gauge and lower sport chassis and adds: 2.5-liter DOHC V-6 engine, 4-speed automatic transmission, traction control.

OPTIONAL EQUIPMENT:

	Retail Price	Dealer Invoice
Powertrains		
4-speed automatic transmission, S, SE Turbo, SE Turbo Talledaga	$1010	$869
Comfort and Convenience		
Power sunroof, S hatchbacks	1010	869
Leather Pkg., S hatchbacks	1295	1114
Leather upholstery, leather-wrapped steering wheel.		
Child booster seats, 4-doors	250	215
Appearance and Miscellaneous		
Extra-cost paint	190	163

SATURN COUPE

Saturn SC1

Front-wheel-drive sports coupe; similar to Saturn Sedan/Wagon

Base price range: $12,595-$14,755. Built in Spring Hill, Tenn.

Also consider: Ford Escort ZX2, Hyundai Tiburon, Mitsubishi Eclipse, Nissan 200SX

FOR • Optional anti-lock brakes and traction control • Fuel economy • Acceleration (SC2)

AGAINST • Engine noise • Acceleration (SC1/automatic) • Rear seat room • Entry/exit

Saturn's coupe rides the same chassis and shares engines with its sedan and wagon and all have dent- and rust-resistant polymer vertical body panels. The coupe was heavily revised for 1997 and gets only minor changes this year.

Two models are offered, the SC1 and SC2, visually differentiated by outside mirrors and door handles that are black on the SC1 and body color on the SC2. The SC2 also has standard fog lamps.

Both have a 1.9-liter 4-cylinder engine but the SC1's has 100 horsepower and the SC2's 124, thanks to a dual-camshaft design. Manual transmission is standard, automatic is optional.

Dual air bags are standard. Anti-lock brakes are optional and include traction control.

Saturn says the engines have stronger blocks and transmissions stouter housings for '98 designed to reduce noise and improve durability. Revised suspension settings, and child-seat belt guides for the rear seats are other changes.

PERFORMANCE The SC1's engine provides adequate acceleration with manual transmission, but it feels overmatched by fast-moving traffic with the automatic. The automatic takes less steam out of the SC2 and its stronger engine. Acceleration from a stop in these models is impressive for a 4-cylinder/automatic combination, though turning on the air conditioning takes its toll. Highway passing power is also good. Saturn's engines have always generated more noise than most 4-cylinders in this class, and that's true despite efforts to quiet the clamor.

Fuel economy is a strong point: We averaged just over 30 mpg with an automatic-equipped SC2, though roughly three-quarters of that was on highways. Previous examples returned about 26 mpg in a more-even city/highway mix. A test of a 5-speed SC1 netted 31.9 mpg in an equal city/highway mix.

The SC2 has sportier handling than the SC1, but the price is paid in ride comfort. A stiffer suspension and lower-profile tires conspire to allow expansion joints to come through to the passenger compartment with a jolt, while lesser pavement imperfections produce a loud "thump." The SC1's softer suspension is

Prices are accurate at time of publication; subject to manufacturer's changes.

more livable on urban roads.

Either model has short stopping distances with good directional control.

ACCOMMODATIONS Unlike most sports coupes, Saturn's provide good visibility to all directions thanks to thin roof pillars and large windows, though it does take a little neck-stretching to see the trunk. The front seats are rather low, surrounded by a high beltline and a vast dashboard top. Like most sports coupes, there's plenty of room for adults in the front seats, but even children will find the rear seat cramped.

Saturn's dashboard has large, clear gauges. Radio and climate controls are in a pod that protrudes from the dashboard and are mounted too low for best access while driving. Power window and mirror controls are on the center console; they're unlit and difficult to find at night.

Interior storage includes a glovebox, cupholder, small console storage bin, and small map pockets on the doors. Trunk space is adequate, and the split rear seatback folds for additional cargo room. A bumper-height opening makes loading and unloading easier.

BUILD QUALITY Though some of the lower body panels feel flimsy, they're made of dent-resistant material that won't rust. One test car had a rattle from the front suspension, but other SCs we've tested have had generally solid construction. The texture and weight of interior materials mimics Japanese rivals without feeling as rich.

VALUE FOR THE MONEY They're noisier and less-refined than some in this class, but Saturn's coupes are reasonably priced and have an impressive reliability record. And Saturn's no-haggle price policy means that the buying experience is relatively painless—a major consideration for many car shoppers.

RATINGS

	SC1	SC2
Acceleration	2	4
Fuel economy	4	4
Ride quality	3	3
Steering/handling	3	4
Braking	4	4
Quietness	2	2
Driver seating	3	4
Instruments/controls	3	3
Room/comfort (front)	3	3
Room/comfort (rear)	2	2
Cargo room	3	3
Value for the money	4	4
Total	**36**	**40**

SPECIFICATIONS

	2-door coupe
Wheelbase, in.	102.4
Overall length, in.	180.0
Overall width, in.	67.3
Overall height, in.	52.4
Curb weight, lbs.	2308
Cargo vol., cu. ft.	11.4
Fuel capacity, gals.	12.1
Seating capacity	4
Front head room, in.	38.5
Max. front leg room, in.	42.6
Rear head room, in.	35.7
Min. rear leg room, in.	31.0

ENGINES

	ohc I-4	dohc I-4
Size, liters/cu. in.	1.9/116	1.9/116
Horsepower @ rpm	100@ 5000	124@ 5600
Torque (lbs./ft.) @ rpm	114@ 2400	122@ 4800
Availability	S[1]	S[2]@
EPA city/highway mpg		
4-speed OD automatic	27/37	24/34
5-speed OD manual	28/39	26/36

1. SC1. 2. SC2.

PRICES

Saturn Coupe

	Retail Price	Dealer Invoice
SC1 2-door notchback, 5-speed	$12595	$11246
SC1 2-door notchback, automatic	$13455	$12002
SC2 2-door notchback, 5-speed	13895	12326
SC2 2-door notchback, automatic	14755	13082
Destination charge	440	440

STANDARD EQUIPMENT:

SC1: 1.9-liter 4-cylinder engine, 5-speed manual or 4-speed automatic transmission, driver- and passenger-side air bags, daytime running lights, power steering, tilt steering wheel, cloth reclining front bucket seats w/lumbar support, 60/40 split folding rear seatback, front and rear consoles, cupholders, coolant-temperature gauge, trip odometer, AM/FM radio, digital clock, tachometer, rear defogger, intermittent wipers, remote fuel-door and decklid releases, passenger-side visor mirror, tinted glass, dual remote outside mirrors, 175/70R14 tires, wheel covers.

SC2 adds: 1.9-liter DOHC engine, variable-assist power steering, driver-seat height adjustment, locking storage armrest, sport suspension, rear spoiler, fog lights, striping, 195/60HR15 tires.

OPTIONAL EQUIPMENT:

Major Packages

Option Pkg. 1, SC1	1930	1679

Air conditioning, cruise control, power windows and door locks, remote keyless entry, theft-deterrent system, power passenger-side outside mirror.

Option Pkg. 2, SC2	2280	1984

Air conditioning, cruise control, power windows and door locks, remote keyless entry, theft-deterrent system, power passenger-side outside mirror, alloy wheels.

Safety Features

Anti-lock brakes	695	626

Includes traction control. SC2 also includes 4-wheel disc brakes.

Comfort and Convenience

Air conditioning	960	837
Power sunroof	695	626
Cassette player	260	226
Cassette player w/equalizer and premium speakers	390	339
CD player w/equalizer and premium speakers	510	446
Cruise control	290	252
Leather upholstery, SC2	700	626

Includes leather-wrapped steering wheel.

Appearance and Miscellaneous

Rear spoiler, SC1	245	221
Double-fin alloy wheels, SC1	450	392

Includes 185/65R15 touring tires.

Teardrop II alloy wheels, SC2	350	305

SATURN SEDAN/WAGON

RECOMMENDED

Saturn SL2

Front-wheel-drive subcompact; similar to Saturn Coupe

Base price range: $10,595-$14,155. Built in Spring Hill, Tenn.

Also consider: Dodge/Plymouth Neon, Ford Escort, Nissan Sentra, Toyota Corolla

FOR • Optional anti-lock brakes and traction control • Fuel economy • Acceleration (SL2/SW2)

Rating Scale: 5-Excellent; 4-Above average; 3-Average; 2-Below average; 1-Poor

AGAINST • Engine and road noise • Acceleration (SL, SL1, and SW1 with automatic transmission)

General Motors' Saturn division has won a devoted following by selling reliable cars via a one-price strategy: What you see on the sticker is what you pay. There's no bargaining.

Saturn's biggest sellers are its sedans and wagons, which are built from the same platform as its coupe. Sedans are offered in base SL, SL1, and top-trim SL2 price levels. Wagons come as SW1 and SW2 models.

All have a 1.9-liter 4-cylinder engine. It makes 100 horsepower in SL, SL1, and SW1 models, and 124 in the SL2 and SW2 thanks to a dual-camshaft design. Manual transmission is standard on all models. Automatic is optionally available except on the SL.

Dual air bags are standard and anti-lock brakes are optional. Traction control, which reduces engine power to control wheel slip, is included with the anti-lock option.

For '98, there are structural changes to the engine blocks and transmission cases designed to reduce noise and increase durability. Two new exterior colors, redesigned wheel covers, revised suspension settings, and new child seatbelt guides for the rear seats round out the changes.

PERFORMANCE The 100-horsepower engine delivers adequate acceleration with the 5-speed manual, and the light clutch and smooth shift linkage make it easy to change gears quickly. With the optional automatic, the SL1 won't be as lively, and keeping pace with traffic often requires flooring the throttle. Our test 5-speed SL1 averaged a commendable 30 mpg.

The dual-camshaft engine in the SL2 and SW2 provides much better acceleration with both transmissions, but is less fuel-efficient. Our test SL2 automatic averaged 22.5 mpg.

Saturn has quieted its engines somewhat, but there's enough road noise at highway speeds to force you to crank up the stereo a couple of notches.

These sedans and wagons corner with pleasing quickness and control. Body lean in turns is less in the SL2 and SW2, and their tires hold out longer before squealing in protest when you try to hurry through a corner. On all models, the suspension absorbs minor bumps well, but rough roads can cause abrupt, even harsh reactions that are felt by the occupants.

ACCOMMODATIONS Front head and leg room is sufficient for taller people, and the firm seats provide good lateral support. Rear-seat room is adequate if you're under 5-foot-10 and the front seats aren't pushed back too far. The rear seat is not particularly comfortable, and getting in and out is awkward because the door opening is narrow at the bottom.

The dashboard has large, clear gauges. Stereo and climate controls are mounted in a pod that protrudes from the dashboard and are mounted too low for best access by the driver.

The low dashboard and deep side windows help visibility to the front and sides. The tail is too high to easily see straight back, but overall visibility is good.

Trunk space is adequate, and a low liftover eases the strain of loading and unloading luggage. The split rear seatback folds for more cargo space. Interior storage consists of small map pockets on the doors, a roomy glovebox, and open bins and cupholders in the center console.

BUILD QUALITY Most of the interior materials look and feel as good as those in more-expensive subcompacts. Paintwork is good, and the dent-resistant side panels make parking-lot dings less likely.

VALUE FOR THE MONEY Saturn's sedan and wagon have improved over the years, but still don't match the overall refinement of class leaders such as the Honda Civic. It's their reasonable prices and Saturn's exceptional record for customer satisfaction that make them well worth considering.

SPECIFICATIONS

	4-door sedan	4-door wagon
Wheelbase, in.	102.4	102.4
Overall length, in.	176.9	176.9
Overall width, in.	66.7	66.7
Overall height, in.	54.5	54.9
Curb weight, lbs.	2326	2392
Cargo vol., cu. ft.	12.1	24.9

	4-door sedan	4-door wagon
Fuel capacity, gals.	12.1	12.1
Seating capacity	5	5
Front head room, in.	39.3	39.3
Max. front leg room, in.	42.5	42.5
Rear head room, in.	38.0	38.7
Min. rear leg room, in.	32.8	32.8

ENGINES

	ohc I-4	dohc I-4
Size, liters/cu. in.	1.9/116	1.9/116
Horsepower @ rpm	100@ 5000	124@ 5600
Torque (lbs./ft.) @ rpm	114@ 2400	122@ 4800
Availability	S[1]	S[2]
EPA city/highway mpg		
4-speed OD automatic	27/37	24/34
5-speed OD manual	28/39	26/36

1. SL, SL1, SW1. 2. SL2, SW2.

RATINGS

	SL/SL1/ SW1	SL2/ SW2
Acceleration	3	4
Fuel economy	5	4
Ride quality	3	3
Steering/handling	3	4
Braking	4	4
Quietness	2	2
Driver seating	4	4
Instruments/controls	3	3
Room/comfort (front)	3	3
Room/comfort (rear)	3	3
Cargo room	3	3
Value for the money	4	4
Total	**40**	**41**

PRICES

Saturn Sedan/Wagon	Retail Price	Dealer Invoice
SL 4-door sedan, 5-speed	$10595	$9536
SL1 4-door sedan, 5-speed	11595	10436
SL1 4-door sedan, automatic	12455	11192
SL2 4-door sedan, 5-speed	12495	11246
SL2 4-door sedan, automatic	13355	12002
SW1 4-door wagon, 5-speed	12295	10976
SW1 4-door wagon, automatic	13155	11732
SW2 4-door wagon, 5-speed	13295	11786
SW2 4-door wagon, automatic	14155	12542
Destination charge	440	440

STANDARD EQUIPMENT:

SL: 1.9-liter 4-cylinder engine, 5-speed manual transmission, driver- and passenger-side air bags, daytime running lamps, cloth reclining front bucket seats w/lumbar support, 60/40 split folding rear seat, front console, cupholders, tilt steering wheel, tachometer, coolant-temperature gauge, trip odometer, AM/FM radio, digital clock, rear defogger, intermittent wipers, remote fuel-door and decklid releases, passenger-side visor mirror, tinted glass, 175/70R14 tires, wheel covers.

SL1 adds: 5-speed manual or 4-speed automatic transmission, power steering, upgraded interior trim, dual outside mirrors.

SL2 adds: 1.9-liter 4-cylinder DOHC engine, variable-assist power steering, upgraded upholstery, driver-seat height adjustment, sport suspension, 185/65TR15 touring tires.

SW1 adds to SL1: rear wiper/washer, remote liftgate release.

SW2 adds to SW1: 1.9-liter DOHC engine, variable-assist power steering, driver-seat height adjustment, cargo cover, sport suspension, upgraded upholstery, 185/65R15 touring tires.

OPTIONAL EQUIPMENT:
Major Packages

Option Pkg. 1, SL1, SW1, SW2	2055	1788

Air conditioning, cruise control, power windows and door locks, power passenger-side outside mirror.

Prices are accurate at time of publication; subject to manufacturer's changes.

	Retail Price	Dealer Invoice
Option Pkg. 2, SL2	$2405	$2092

Option Pkg. 1 plus alloy wheels.

Safety Features
Anti-lock brakes	695	626

Includes traction control. SL2 also includes 4-wheel disc brakes.

Comfort and Convenience
Air conditioning	960	836
Power sunroof, SL1, SL2	695	626
Cassette player, SL	290	252
SL1, SL2, SW1, SW2	260	226
Cassette player w/equalizer and premium speakers,		
SL	420	365
SL1, SL2, SW1, SW2	390	339
CD player w/equalizer and premium speakers,		
SL	540	473
SL1, SL2, SW1, SW2	495	446
Power door locks	370	324

Includes remote keyless entry, theft-deterrent system. NA on SL.

Cruise control	290	252

NA on SL.

Leather upholstery, SL2, SW2	700	626

Includes leather-wrapped steering wheel.

Cargo cover, SW1	75	68
Floormats	60	52

Appearance and Miscellaneous
Passenger-side outside mirror, SL	40	36
Rear spoiler, SL2	205	185
Fog lamps, SL2, SW2	160	144
Alloy wheels, SL2, SW2	350	305

SUBARU FORESTER

Subaru Forester S

All-wheel-drive compact sport-utility vehicle; similar to Subaru Impreza

Base price range: $18,695-$22,195. Built in Japan.

Also consider: Chevrolet Tracker, Honda CR-V, Toyota RAV4

FOR • Visibility • Maneuverability • Ride • Cargo room • Noise

AGAINST • Acceleration (automatic transmission) • Instruments/controls • Engine vibrations • Rear seat room

Subaru didn't start the hybrid sport-utility vehicle movement, but with the new Forester, it covers it from all sides.

The Japanese company's compact Legacy Outback and subcompact Outback Sport are basically tall-built wagons. The Forester is based on the same Impreza platform as the Outback Sport, but is cast as more of a trucky SUV in the spirit of the Honda CR-V and Toyota RAV4.

Subaru literally raised the roof and added a few inches in length and width to the Impreza wagon to create the Forester. However, with a wheelbase increase of only .2 inch, interior dimensions grow only slightly over the Impreza and passenger capacity remains five.

Subaru's horizontally-opposed 165-horsepower 2.5-liter 4-cylinder is the only engine and manual transmission is standadrd, automatic optional. Subaru's all-wheel-drive system senses wheel slip and automatically sends power to the wheel(s) with the most traction. No driver action is required. Like the other hybrids, Forester has no low-range for serious off-roading. Towing capacity is 2000 pounds.

Base, L, and S model are offered. Dual air bags, air conditioning, fog lamps, and split-folding rear seats are standard. L and S add anti-lock brakes, with the S also including rear disc brakes, larger wheels and tires, a chrome grille, larger power mirrors, and an upgraded interior.

PERFORMANCE With all-wheel drive instead of 4-wheel drive and built off a car rather than truck platform, Forester is not a true SUV. But any SUV owner who drives a Forester will immediately be impressed by its blend of car-like manners and all-wheel-drive utility.

Subaru's flat-4 feels more lively with the manual shift, but performs acceptably with the automatic. That transmission shifts smoothly and kicks down promply, but passing power that feels adequate with just a driver aboard feels subpar with a load of passengers and luggage.

We averaged 17 mpg in a test of an automatic-transmission Forester. That's about two mpg better than we average with midsize SUVs, such as the Chevrolet Blazer, and 2-3 mpg less than in our most-recent test Honda CR-V returned.

Road and wind noise are constant highway companions, but to a lesser degree than in most other SUVs of any stripe. Engine is gruff when pushed hard and the idle is lumpy with the air conditioning on.

Handling isn't as nimble as a car, but Forester is less ponderous than truck-based midsize SUVs. Its AWD provides reassuring grip in turns. With a suspension tuned for the street and not the trail, Forester rides softly and doesn't pitch or rock on uneven pavement as do many true SUVs.

ACCOMMODATIONS Forester looks like a small sport-utility but has the cabin space of a compact wagon. The driving position, while higher than in a traditional sedan, doesn't impart the "command-of-the-road" feeling of a true SUV. However, tall, thin roof pillars and a low cowl make for outstanding outward visiblity to all directions.

There's no step-up to speak of and the doors open wide, so entry and exit are inviting. Head room is generous all around. Front leg room is good, but rear seaters are squeezed for knee clearance and foot space.

The dashboard is well designed, but some buttons hide behind the steering wheel and the radio controls are too small and low to operate easily while driving. The most interesting aspect of the Forester might just be its spacious and versatile cargo area. The split rear seats fold both fore and aft, allowing a reclined seating position or a flat cargo floor. And you don't have to flip up the seat cushion to get the seats to fold down.

BUILD QUALITY Because Forester inherits many of the interior bits from the subcompact Impreza, some of the materials seem a bit cheap and flimsy against other SUVs. However, the body is free of squeaks and the exterior finish was excellent.

VALUE FOR THE MONEY Forester is a worthy competitor for the better-publicized CR-V and RAV4. Hybrids are supposed to drive like cars, perform on-road like SUVs, and look like trucks. This one does.

SPECIFICATIONS
	4-door wagon
Wheelbase, in.	99.4
Overall length, in.	175.2
Overall width, in.	68.3
Overall height, in.	65.0
Curb weight, lbs.	3020
Cargo vol., cu. ft.	64.6
Fuel capacity, gals.	15.9
Seating capacity	5
Front head room, in.	40.6
Max. front leg room, in.	43.0
Rear head room, in.	39.6
Min. rear leg room, in.	33.4

Rating Scale: 5-Excellent; 4-Above average; 3-Average; 2-Below average; 1-Poor

ENGINES

	dohc Flat-4
Size, liters/cu. in.	2.5/150
Horsepower @ rpm	165@5600
Torque (lbs./ft.) @ rpm	162@4000
Availability	S

EPA city/highway mpg

5-speed OD manual	21/27
4-speed OD automatic	21/26

RATINGS

	Base	L	S
Acceleration	3	3	3
Fuel economy	3	3	3
Ride quality	4	4	4
Steering/handling	4	4	4
Braking	4	4	4
Quietness	4	4	4
Driver seating	4	4	4
Instruments/controls	3	3	3
Room/comfort (front)	4	4	4
Room/comfort (rear)	2	2	2
Cargo room	4	4	4
Value for the money	3	3	3
Total	**42**	**42**	**42**

PRICES

Subaru Forester	Retail Price	Dealer Invoice
Base 4-door wagon	$18695	$17454
L 4-door wagon	19995	18034
S 4-door wagon	22195	19925
Destination charge	495	495

Prices are for vehicles distributed by Subaru of North America. Prices may be higher in areas serviced by independent distributors.

STANDARD EQUIPMENT:

Base: 2.5-liter DOHC 4-cylinder engine, 5-speed manual transmission, full-time all-wheel drive, driver- and passenger-side air bags, rear seat headrests, air conditioning, variable-assist power steering, tilt steering wheel, reclining cloth bucket seats, reclining split folding rear seat, 4-speaker AM/FM/cassette, cupholders, storage bins, overhead console (map lights, digital clock, and sunglasses storage), tachometer, power windows, intermittent wipers, rear wiper/washer, rear defogger, power outlets, tinted glass, dual manual outside mirrors, 2-tone paint, fog lights, roof rack, bodyside moldings, trailer harness connector, 205/70R15 tires.

L adds: anti-lock brakes, power door and liftgate locks, floormats, mud guards, rear bumper step pad.

S adds: 4-wheel disc brakes, cruise control, power mirrors, upgraded cloth upholstery, front seatback pockets, driver and passenger vanity mirrors, coat hooks, chrome grille, 215/60R16 tires, alloy wheels.

OPTIONAL EQUIPMENT:
Major Packages
Cold Weather Pkg., S	300	266

Includes heated front seats, heated outside mirrors.

Powertrains
4-speed automatic transmission, L, S	800	711

Comfort and Convenience
Cruise control, Base, L	340	222
Leather upholstery	1295	975
CD player	420	315
CD changer	689	517
Remote keyless entry	225	146

Appearance and Miscellaneous
Grille guard	375	282

Special Purpose, Wheels and Tires
Differential protector	159	104
Trailer hitch	295	192

	Retail Price	Dealer Invoice
Alloy wheels, Base, L	$595	$447

Other options are available as port installed items.

SUBARU IMPREZA

Subaru Impreza 2.5 RS

All-wheel-drive subcompact car; similar to Subaru Forester

Base price range: $15,895-$19,195. Built in Japan.

Also consider: Honda Civic, Mazda Protege, Toyota Corolla

FOR • Anti-lock brakes (Outback Sport, 2.5 RS) • All-wheel drive • Acceleration (2.5 RS) • Maneuverability

AGAINST • Rear seat room • Rear entry/exit • Engine noise

For 1998 Subaru injects some life into its subcompact Impreza. New dashboards, instruments, and door panels can be found on all Imprezas, including the racy new 2.5 RS.

Impreza again comes in 2-door coupe, 4-door sedan, and 4-door wagon body styles, the last the basis for the Outback Sport. Gone for '98 is the price-leading Brighton model. All versions have permanently engaged all-wheel drive (AWD) and dual air bags.

Impreza comes in three trim levels. The L model is available in all body styles. The Outback Sport continues as a taller version of the wagon, and the new 2.5 RS is a 2-door.

Subarus use horizontally opposed 4-cylinder engines. L and Outback Sport models have a 137-horsepower 2.2-liter. The 2.5 RS comes with a 165-horsepower 2.5-liter that was previously available only on Subaru's larger Legacy models. Manual transmission is standard and automatic is optional. L models have front-disc and rear-drum brakes, the 2.5 RS and Outback Sport have anti-lock 4-wheel disc brakes.

Interior changes include a new dashboard with larger instruments, new seat fabrics, and revised door panels. The 2.5 RS gets a rear wing, gold-color alloy wheels, a hood with non-functional air intakes, and a sport-tuned suspension.

Subaru's all-wheel drive requires no input from the driver. It automatically sends power to the tire with the most traction when wheel slip occurs.

PERFORMANCE The 2.2-liter engine delivers decent acceleration with manual shift, but sounds gruff and feels rough. It's noticeably smoother with the optional automatic, but that transmission saps enough power that you'll struggle up steep grades and have only adequate pep on the flat.

The 2.5-liter engine in the 2.5 RS is just as noisy, but considerably more powerful. It has good low-speed power and mates well with the automatic transmission to provide ample around-town acceleration.

Our test Outback Sports returned a respectable 21.5 mpg with automatic transmission and 24.8 with manual. We got 23.4 with a 5-speed 2.5 RS test car.

All Imprezas are nimble and surefooted, but the Outback Sport and the 2.5 RS stay glued to the road at speeds that would have other subcompacts in the ditch. Ride quality is firm, but not harsh.

Road noise can get annoying at highway speeds, as can the buzzy engine. Braking power is exceptional on the all-disc 2.5 RS and Sport models, but only adequate on L models. Coupes

Prices are accurate at time of publication; subject to manufacturer's changes.

have a narrow rear window and large rear pillars that make visibility worse than in the sedans and wagons.

ACCOMMODATIONS The revised dashboard places large gauges directly before the driver and moves the radio and climate controls within easy reach. However, the radio still has too many poorly marked tiny buttons.

Front-seat leg room is only adequate, but head room is good. Our taller test drivers would like the front seats to slide back a few more inches. Rear seat leg room is tight, even for a sub-compact car. And rear entry/exit wins no prizes either, as the doors are quite narrow at the bottom and don't open very wide.

Cargo space is a bit lean in all models—even the wagon. However, the rear seats fold and the wagon's rear opening will obviously accept taller items. A new feature this year is a large, covered bin at the top and center of the dashboard.

BUILD QUALITY Impreza's body panels fit well and the paint on our test cars was blemish-free, but door and trunk closings don't sound very substantial. Interiors are average in most ways, balancing solid panels and padded surfaces against the random thin plastic piece.

VALUE FOR THE MONEY The rugged-looking Outback Sport and 2.5 RS seem clever bows to the younger, "active lifestyle" set, but no Impreza model is exactly cheap. Their all-wheel drive is a huge plus, but only if you really need it.

RATINGS

	L 2-dr.	L 4-dr.	2.5 RS	Sport
Acceleration	3	3	4	3
Fuel economy	4	4	4	4
Ride quality	3	3	3	3
Steering/handling	3	3	4	4
Braking	3	3	5	5
Quietness	2	2	2	2
Driver seating	3	3	3	3
Instruments/controls	4	4	4	4
Room/comfort (front)	3	3	3	3
Room/comfort (rear)	2	3	2	3
Cargo room	2	2	2	4
Value for the money	2	3	2	3
Total	**34**	**36**	**38**	**41**

SPECIFICATIONS

	2-door coupe	4-door sedan	4-door wagon	4-door wagon
Wheelbase, in.	99.2	99.2	99.2	99.2
Overall length, in.	172.2	172.2	172.2	172.2
Overall width, in.	67.1	67.1	67.1	67.1
Overall height, in.	55.5	55.5	55.5	60.0
Curb weight, lbs.	2720	2690	2795	2835
Cargo vol., cu. ft.	11.1	11.1	25.5[1]	25.5[1]
Fuel capacity, gals.	13.2	13.2	13.2	13.2
Seating capacity	5	5	5	5
Front head room, in.	39.2	39.2	39.2	39.2
Max. front leg room, in.	43.1	43.1	43.1	43.1
Rear head room, in.	36.7	36.7	37.4	37.4
Min. rear leg room, in.	32.5	32.5	32.4	32.4

ENGINES

	ohc I-4	dohc I-4
Size, liters/cu. in.	2.2/135	2.5/150
Horsepower @ RPM	137@ 5400	165@ 5600
Torque (lbs./ft.) @ RPM	145@ 4000	162@ 4000
Availability	S[2]	S[3]

EPA city/highway mpg

4-speed OD automatic	23/30	NA
5-speed OD manual	23/30	NA

1. 62.1 cu. ft. with rear seats folded. 2. L, Outback Sport. 3. 2.5 RS.

PRICES

Subaru Impreza

	Retail Price	Dealer Invoice
L 2-door notchback	$15895	$14445
L 4-door sedan	15895	14445
L 4-door wagon	16295	14804
Outback Sport 4-door wagon	17995	16321

	Retail Price	Dealer Invoice
2.5 RS 2-door notchback	$19195	$17404
Destination charge	495	495

Prices are for vehicles distributed by Subaru of America. Prices may be higher in areas served by independent distributors.

STANDARD EQUIPMENT:

L: 2.2-liter 4-cylinder engine, 5-speed manual transmission, permanent all-wheel drive, driver- and passenger-side air bags, air conditioning, variable-assist power steering, tilt steering wheel, cloth upholstery, reclining front bucket seats, split folding rear seat (wagon), front storage console, cupholder, AM/FM/cassette, digital clock, power mirrors, power windows, power door locks, rear defogger, remote decklid release (sedan and 2-door), auxiliary power outlet, cargo cover (wagon), rear wiper/washer (wagon), passenger-side visor mirror, tinted glass, rear spoiler (2-door), 195/60H15 tires, wheel covers.

Outback Sport adds to L wagon: anti-lock brakes, cargo tray, raised heavy-duty suspension, roof rack, mud guards, 2-tone paint, rear bumper cover, 205/60S15 outlined white-letter tires.

2.5 RS adds to L 2-door: 2.5-liter DOHC 4-cylinder engine, leather-wrapped steering wheel, sport bucket seats, reading lights, power sunroof, sport suspension, bodyside moldings, tailpipe cover, 205/55H16 tires, alloy wheels.

OPTIONAL EQUIPMENT:

Powertrains

4-speed automatic transmission	800	717

Comfort and Convenience

Cruise control	357	232
CD player	420	315
Remote keyless entry	225	146

Appearance and Miscellaneous

Fog lights, L, Outback Sport	245	160
Roof rack, L wagon	239	156
Alloy wheels, L, Outback Sport	550	413

Other options are available as port installed items.

SUBARU LEGACY

Subaru Legacy Outback Limited

All-wheel-drive compact car

Base price range: $16,895-$24,895. Built in Lafayette, Ind.

Also consider: Mitsubishi Galant, Nissan Altima, Volkswagen Passat

FOR • Standard anti-lock brakes (except Brighton) • Passenger and cargo room • Ride • All-wheel drive

AGAINST • Engine noise (2.2-liter) • Manual shift linkage

Subaru sets its line of compact cars apart from the herd by giving them standard all-wheel drive, then builds on that with the Outback, a sport-utility-flavored wagon that accounts for about half of all Legacy sales.

Sedan offerings are the L, GT, and GT Limited models, the last replacing the LSi model. Wagons consist of the price-leading Brighton, the L, the Outback, Outback Limited, and GT models. Outbacks are distinguished by a raised roof and higher

Rating Scale: 5-Excellent; 4-Above average; 3-Average; 2-Below average; 1-Poor

ground clearance (7.3 inches to the other's 6.5 or 6.1 inches). Gone is last year's LSi wagon.

As do all Subarus, Legacys have 4-cylinder engines with "flat" or horizontally opposed cylinders. The L and Brighton models use a 137-horsepower 2.2-liter version. A 165-horsepower 2.5-liter powers the GT, Outback, and Limited models.

Both engines team with manual or optional automatic transmission, though automatic is standard on the GT Limited.

Dual air bags are standard, and all models except the Brighton come with anti-lock brakes.

For 1998, the Legacy L and Brighton get the same bumper and grille as GT models. The new GT Limited sedan adds a leather interior and an upgraded audio system. The Outback Limited features similar upgrades and can be fitted with an optional ($1200) twin moonroof setup.

PERFORMANCE Most people prefer automatic transmission for its convenience, but Legacy buyers should prefer it for refinement. Both engines are noticeably smoother and quieter with the automatic than with the 5-speed, though they feel peppier with manual.

The 2.5-liter engine in GT and Outback models is stronger than the 2.2 at all speeds and more refined, as well. In our last test of an Outback, we averaged 24.3 mpg with manual transmission and 19.1 with automatic, though the latter figure was the result of mostly city driving. Still, either number is considerably better than the fuel economy we get in tests of midsized 4WD SUVs, which average 14-16 mpg under similar circumstances.

There's little difference in ride quality between the regular Legacys and the Outbacks. Both suspensions strike a fine balance between comfort and handling—and both are and on par with cars in the same class and better than virtually any truck-based SUV. Subaru's AWD system provides terrific grip in wet or snowy conditions, works unobtrusively, and you never worry whether it will be engaged when you need it.

Road noise is the Outback Limited we tested was actually lower than other Legacy models, and about equal to that of a typical compact sedan. The anti-lock brakes on our test car felt strong and had good pedal modulation.

ACCOMMODATIONS Outback's raised roof provides plenty of head room front and rear, and as in all Legacys, there's adequate leg room for four adults. Sedan models have a modest trunk and all the wagons have generous cargo space. The available fold-down rear seatbacks enhance both body styles' versatility. Large door map pockets, a small covered bin between the front seats, a small glovebox, and two cupholders that pop out of the dashboard account for good interior storage.

Gauges are large and legible. Climate controls are clearly marked and easy to reach, but the stereo is mounted too low to adjust without looking away from the road. The power window and lock controls are at an awkward angle on the driver's door and are unlit.

Visibility is excellent to all directions thanks to thin roof pillars and a high seating position. All doors open wide, and the Outback's raised suspension is no hindrance to entry or exit. The rear doors are narrow at the bottom, making it difficult to swing your feet in or out.

BUILD QUALITY Interior materials are a cut above the average for this class, and there were no squeaks or rattles in our test cars. Paintwork was smooth and lustrous.

VALUE FOR THE MONEY Many buyers need AWD traction at times, but almost no one needs a vehicle designed for heavy-duty off-road use. Legacys fill that role in a conventional sedan and wagon format, with the Outback appealing to those who want more SUV flavor. Beyond that, Legacys don't stand out for performance or value in this tough market segment.

SPECIFICATIONS

	4-door sedan	4-door wagon	4-door wagon
Wheelbase, in.	103.5	103.5	103.5
Overall length, in.	181.5	184.5	185.8
Overall width, in.	67.5	67.5	67.5
Overall height, in.	55.3	57.1	63.0
Curb weight, lbs.	2885	2975	3155
Cargo vol., cu. ft.	12.6	36.1	36.5
Fuel capacity, gals.	15.9	15.9	15.9
Seating capacity	5	5	5

	4-door sedan	4-door wagon	4-door wagon
Front head room, in.	38.9	39.5	40.2
Max. front leg room, in.	43.3	43.3	43.3
Rear head room, in.	36.7	38.8	39.2
Min. rear leg room, in.	34.6	34.8	34.8

ENGINES

	ohc Flat-4	dohc Flat-4
Size, liters/cu. in.	2.2/135	2.5/150
Horsepower @ rpm	137@ 5400	165@ 5600
Torque (lbs./ft.) @ rpm	145@ 4000	162@ 4000
Availability	S[1]	S[2]
EPA city/highway mpg		
5-speed OD manual	23/30	21/27
4-speed OD automatic	23/30	21/27

1. Brighton, L. 2. GT, Limited Outback.

RATINGS

	Brighton	L sedan	GT sedan	Outback
Acceleration	3	3	4	4
Fuel economy	4	4	4	4
Ride quality	4	4	4	4
Steering/handling	4	4	4	4
Braking	3	4	4	4
Quietness	3	3	3	3
Driver seating	3	3	3	3
Instruments/controls	4	4	4	4
Room/comfort (front)	4	4	4	4
Room/comfort (rear)	4	3	3	4
Cargo room	4	3	3	4
Value for the money	3	2	2	3
Total	**43**	**41**	**42**	**45**

PRICES

Subaru Legacy	Retail Price	Dealer Invoice
Brighton 4-door wagon	$16895	$15788
L 4-door sedan	19195	17278
L 4-door wagon	19895	17898
Outback 4-door wagon	22495	20183
Outback Limited 4-door wagon	24595	22049
GT 4-door sedan	22795	20453
GT 4-door wagon	23495	21073
GT Limited 4-door wagon	24895	22314
Destination charge	495	495

Prices are for vehicles distributed by Subaru of America. Prices may be higher in areas served by independent distributors.

STANDARD EQUIPMENT:

Brighton: 2.2-liter 4-cylinder engine, 5-speed manual transmission, full-time all-wheel drive, driver- and passenger-side air bags, child safety rear door locks, cloth reclining front bucket seats, split folding rear seat, air conditioning, storage console, cupholder, variable-assist power steering, tilt steering column, 2-speaker AM/FM/cassette, digital clock, trip odometer, temperature gauge, rear defogger, rear wiper/washer, intermittent wipers, remote fuel door and decklid releases, tinted glass, bodyside moldings, 185/70SR14 tires, wheel covers.

L adds: anti-lock 4-wheel disc brakes, cruise control, power mirrors, power windows, power door locks, map light, 4-speaker AM/FM/cassette, right side visor mirror, deletes rear wiper/washer (sedan).

Outback adds: 2.5-liter DOHC 4-cylinder engine, upgraded cloth interior, overhead console, cargo hooks, cargo area power outlet, cargo tray, floormats, hood scoop, mudguards, roof rack, fog lights, 2-tone paint, rear headrests, heavy-duty suspension, tail pipe cover, 205/70SR15 white-lettered tires, alloy wheels.

Outback Limited adds: Cold Weather Pkg. (heated front seats,, heated power outside mirrors, windshield wiper de-icer), leather upholstery, leather-wrapped steering wheel and shifter, AM/FM/cassette/CD, power antenna, woodgrain interior trim, gold badging, special alloy wheels.

GT adds to L: 2.5-liter DOHC 4-cylinder engine, power moonroof w/sunshade, power antenna, leather-wrapped steering wheel and

Prices are accurate at time of publication; subject to manufacturer's changes.

shifter, variable intermittent wipers, illuminated vanity mirror, wood-grain trim, sport suspension, fog lights, hood scoop, rear spoiler, ground effects, roof rack (wagon), 205/55HR16 tires, alloy wheels.

GT Limited adds: 4-speed automatic transmission, leather upholstery, 6-speaker CD player.

OPTIONAL EQUIPMENT:

	Retail Price	Dealer Invoice
Major Packages		
Cold Weather Pkg., Outback	$400	$358
Includes heated front seats, dual heated outside mirrors, windshield wiper de-icer.		
Powertrains		
4-speed automatic transmission, Brighton, L, Outback, Outback Limited, GT	800	714
Comfort and Convenience		
Dual power moonroofs, Outback Limited	1200	1059
Requires automatic transmission.		
Cruise control, Brighton	334	218
CD player, Brighton, L, Outback, GT	420	315
CD changer, Brighton, L, Outback, GT	689	517
Outback Limited, GT Limited	497	373
Remote keyless entry	225	146
NA Brighton.		
Leather upholstery, Outback, GT	1295	975
Appearance and Miscellaneous		
Body-colored rear spoiler, Brighton, L wagon, Outback, Outback Limited	295	192
L sedan	375	282
7-spoke alloy wheels, Brighton, L	595	199
Cross spoke alloy wheels, Brighton, L	635	199

Other options are available as port installed items.

SUZUKI ESTEEM/SWIFT

Suzuki Esteem wagon

Front-wheel-drive subcompact; similar to Chevrolet Metro

Base price range: (1997 model) $8999-$13,999. Built in Canada and Japan.

Also consider: Dodge/Plymouth Neon, Ford Escort, Hyundai Accent, Toyota Tercel

FOR • Fuel economy • Maneuverability • Cargo room (wagon)

AGAINST • Rear visibility • Noise • Ride • Rear seat room (Swift)

Esteem is the name of Suzuki's 4-door sedan and wagon and Swift is what it calls the 2-door hatchback. Esteem rides a longer wheelbase and has a larger engine than the Swift and is built in Japan. The wagon is a new body style for Esteem and comes with roof rails that can accommodate 100 pounds of cargo and rear seats that fold to increase cargo space to 61.0 cubic feet.

Suzuki shares its design for the Swift with General Motors, which sells a version as the Chevrolet Metro in both 2-door hatchback and 4-door sedan form. Swift and Metro are built in Canada at a plant jointly owned by Suzuki and GM.

Esteem sedans and wagons encompass GL, GLX, and top-line GLX with option package model, the last being the only one available with anti-lock brakes (ABS) and cruise control. All use a 98-horsepower 1.6-liter 4-cylinder engine. Manual transmission is standard on the GL and GLX. Automatic is optional on these and standard on the ABS-equipped GLX with option package.

The Swift has a 70-horsepower 1.3-liter 4-cylinder and manual transmission or an optional 3-speed automatic. ABS is optional with either transmission.

PERFORMANCE Handing on both the Esteem and Swift holds up well against rivals in this class—especially around town, where the two cars feel nimble and maneuverable. That's the good news.

An Esteem GLX we tested with automatic transmission had adequate acceleration, but the transmission vibrated when it changed gears and downshifted harshly. We averaged 24.2 mpg with this car, with nearly all our driving urban rush-hour commuting. Expect better fuel economy with more highway miles and the 5-speed manual. Though Esteem's noise levels are lower than those in the Swift or Metro, there's still lots of tire thumping and roar from the road, plus a loud, coarse growl from the engine.

Ride quality leaves much to desire in any of these Suzukis. The suspension doesn't absorb bumps well, so rough pavement means a rough ride, and there's noticeable bouncing on wavy surfaces.

Swift is best considered an around-town runabout, with too little power to stay with fast-moving traffic and a short wheelbase that makes the car pitch fore and aft on concrete expressways. Swift drivers are bombarded by even more road and engine noise at freeway speeds.

The brakes perform adequately on either car, but rear-wheel lock-up is evident in non-ABS models.

ACCOMMODATIONS Esteem has ample head room in front and adequate room for two people in back, as long as they're not over 6-feet tall. The rear seat padding is hard, though, and the narrow rear doors are tough to negotiate. Visibility to the rear is hampered by wide roof pillars, and the narrow rear window limits the driver's view of the trunk.

Things are tighter in every respect inside the hatchback, and it's even more difficult to get in or out of the rear seat.

A simple dashboard layout puts controls where they're easy to see and reach.

Cargo space in all body styles is a little better than average for cars in this class, but the sedan's trunk opening is small.

BUILD QUALITY The Esteem is a more substantial car than the Swift and Metro, yet the body panels still feel tinny. The grade of interior materials is appropriate for the cars' budget mission and are well-assembled.

VALUE FOR THE MONEY An Esteem GLX with the ABS option package is the most-desirable car in this bunch, and also the most expensive. For about the same price, you can buy a Chevrolet Cavalier or Dodge/Plymouth Neon, which are served by stronger dealer networks. We would only consider the Swift as a daily commuter car, but a larger used car would likely be a better value.

RATINGS	2-dr.	4-dr. sedan	4-dr. wagon
Acceleration	2	3	3
Fuel economy	4	4	4
Ride quality	2	3	3
Steering/handling	3	3	3
Braking	2	3	3
Quietness	2	3	3
Driver seating	3	3	3
Instruments/controls	3	3	3
Room/comfort (front)	3	3	3
Room/comfort (rear)	2	3	3
Cargo room	3	3	4
Value for the money	3	3	3
Total	32	37	38

SPECIFICATIONS	2-door hatchback	4-door sedan	4-door wagon
Wheelbase, in.	93.1	97.6	97.6
Overall length, in.	149.4	165.2	171.1

Rating Scale: 5-Excellent; 4-Above average; 3-Average; 2-Below average; 1-Poor

	2-door hatchback	4-door sedan	4-door wagon
Overall width, in.	62.6	65.7	66.5
Overall height, in.	54.7	53.9	55.9
Curb weight, lbs.	1895	2227	2359
Cargo vol., cu. ft.	8.4	12.0	24.0
Fuel capacity, gals.	10.3	13.5	13.5
Seating capacity	4	5	5
Front head room, in.	39.1	39.1	38.8
Max. front leg room, in.	42.5	42.3	42.3
Rear head room, in.	36.0	37.2	38.0
Min. rear leg room, in.	32.2	34.1	36.6

ENGINES

	ohc I-4	ohc I-4
Size, liters/cu. in.	1.3/79	1.6/97
Horsepower @ rpm	79@ 6000	95@ 6000
Torque (lbs./ft.) @ rpm	75@ 3000	99@ 3000
Availability	S[1]	S[2]

EPA city/highway mpg

	ohc I-4	ohc I-4
5-speed OD manual	39/43	30/37
3-speed OD automatic	30/34	
4-speed OD automatic		27/33

1. Swift. 2. Esteem.

PRICES

1997 Suzuki Esteem

	Retail Price	Dealer Invoice
Swift 3-door hatchback, 5-speed	$8999	$8369
Swift 3-door hatchback, automatic	9649	8973
Esteem GL 4-door notchback, 5-speed	11899	11304
Esteem GL 4-door notchback, automatic	12899	12254
Esteem GLX 4-door notchback, 5-speed	12999	12349
Esteem GLX 4-door notchback, automatic	13999	13299
Esteem GLX 4-door notchback w/option pkg., automatic	14799	14059
Destination charge (Swift)	360	360
Destination charge (Esteem)	420	420

STANDARD EQUIPMENT:

Swift: 1.3-liter 4-cylinder engine, 5-speed manual or 3-speed automatic transmission, driver- and passenger-side air bags, cloth reclining front bucket seats, folding rear seat, tinted glass, intermittent wipers, rear defogger, trip odometer, front console, dual outside mirrors, daytime running lights, wheel covers, 155/80R13 tires.

Esteem GL deletes wheel covers and adds: 1.6-liter 4-cylinder engine, 5-speed manual or 4-speed automatic transmission, air conditioning, power steering, cloth/vinyl upholstery, cupholders, AM/FM/cassette, remote fuel-door and decklid releases.

Esteem GLX adds: cloth upholstery, split folding rear seat, power windows, power door locks, power mirrors, tachometer, passenger-side visor mirror, mud guards, trunk light, 175/70R13 tires, wheel covers.

Esteem GLX with option pkg. adds: anti-lock brakes, cruise control.

OPTIONAL EQUIPMENT:
Safety Features

Anti-lock brakes, Swift	560	504

Comfort and Convenience

Air conditioning, Swift	850	—
AM/FM radio with front speakers, Swift	318	—
Rear speakers, Swift	55	—
CD player, Swift	400	—
6-disc CD changer, Swift	429	—

SUZUKI SIDEKICK

Rear- or 4-wheel-drive compact sport-utility vehicle; similar to Chevrolet Tracker

Base price range: (1997 model) $12,899-$20,199. Built in Canada and Japan.

Also consider: Honda CR-V, Jeep Wrangler, Kia Sportage, Subaru Forester, Toyota RAV4

FOR • Fuel economy • Maneuverability

Suzuki Sidekick JLX Sport

AGAINST • Ride • Noise • Rear seat room (convertible)

The Sidekick accounts for most of Suzuki's U.S. sales. Suzuki added the Sport model two years ago and it quickly became the best-seller in the lineup.

Sidekick returns with 2-door convertible and larger 4-door wagon body styles in 2-wheel-drive JS and 4-wheel-drive JX price levels. All but the Sport use a 1.6-liter 4-cylinder engine with 95 horsepower. A 1.8-liter dual-camshaft engine with 120 horsepower is used in the Sidekick Sport wagon, which returns for its third year in 4WD JX and JLX models, plus a price leader 2WD JS.

The Sport has a longer nose and wider stance than regular Sidekick wagons, plus standard fender flares, 2-tone paint, and 16-inch wheels and tires. This year 4-wheel anti-lock brakes that operate in 2- and 4WD are standard on JLX and optional on all other models.

Sidekicks have standard dual air bags and a 5-speed manual transmission. A 3-speed automatic is optional on convertibles and a 4-speed automatic is optional on wagons.

Sidekick's part-time 4WD system is not for use on dry pavement and requires that the vehicle be stopped when switching from 2WD to 4WD. Automatic-locking front hubs are standard on the Sport JLX; other models have manual front hubs. Other changes for 1998 include a new line of radios and a revised grille on the Sport models.

Sidekick is sold in slightly different form as the Chevrolet Tracker, and Suzuki sells a scaled-down version of the Sidekick as the X-90.

PERFORMANCE The Sport's larger 1.8-liter engine addresses a major shortcoming of the 1.6-liter Sidekick: meager performance. The Sport feels spunky enough to stay abreast of most traffic and even works well with automatic transmission, which shifts crisply and promptly.

We averaged 20.2 mpg with our test Sport in mostly city and suburban commuting, with a high of 26 mpg on one highway trip. That's higher than we've seen with most other SUVs and is one advantage of Sidekick's relatively light weight and small engine.

Unfortunately, the engine emits a nasty growl under throttle and is never really quiet or refined. This also is true of the 1.6-liter. All Sidekicks also suffer lots of road noise and abundant wind noise at highway speeds.

Ride quality is better on the Sport than other Sidekicks, though it's still not in the luxury class. The Sport's wider stance imparts a feeling of security absent from the other Sidekick models. No 4x4 should be driven as quickly as passenger cars in turns, but at least the Sport feels more at ease in spirited maneuvers than some others.

Braking power was more than adequate on our test vehicle.

ACCOMMODATIONS There's plenty of head room all around but mediocre rear leg room, and the narrow interior lacks shoulder room. Four people is all that will fit, and if they're all adults, some will likely be cramped.

Cargo space is poor unless you fold the rear seat. With the seat folded, there's still less cargo space than in most SUVs but far more than in any passenger car. The gauges and controls are clearly marked and easy to see and use.

Visibility to the rear is hampered by the outside-mounted spare tire and the rear head rests. The driver's view is otherwise unobstructed.

BUILD QUALITY Our test vehicle was rattle-free, but the furnishings look and feel as if they were chosen for low cost, and

---

Prices are accurate at time of publication; subject to manufacturer's changes.

there's a flimsiness that comes through in things like doors that close with a tinny clang.

VALUE FOR THE MONEY Aside from better fuel economy and lower prices, the Sidekick is a questionable substitute for a more-substantial 4x4. While the Sport is an improvement over lesser Sidekicks, our nod for a small SUV would go to Toyota's RAV4 or the new Honda CR-V.

RATINGS

	JS 2-dr.	JX 4-dr.	Sport
Acceleration	2	2	3
Fuel economy	4	4	4
Ride quality	2	3	3
Steering/handling	3	3	3
Braking	3	3	4
Quietness	2	2	2
Driver seating	3	3	3
Instruments/controls	4	4	4
Room/comfort (front)	3	3	3
Room/comfort (rear)	2	3	3
Cargo room	3	4	4
Value for the money	3	3	3
Total	**34**	**37**	**39**

SPECIFICATIONS

	2-door conv.	4-door wagon	4-door wagon
Wheelbase, in.	86.6	97.6	97.6
Overall length, in.	143.7	158.7	162.4
Overall width, in.	65.2	64.4	66.7
Overall height, in.	64.3	65.7	66.3
Curb weight, lbs.	2337	2624	2811
Cargo vol., cu. ft.	8.1	21.0	21.0
Fuel capacity, gals.	11.1	14.5	18.5
Seating capacity	4	4	4
Front head room, in.	39.5	40.6	40.6
Max. front leg room, in.	42.1	42.1	42.1
Rear head room, in.	39.0	40.0	38.6
Min. rear leg room, in.	31.7	32.7	32.7

ENGINES

	ohc I-4	dohc I-4
Size, liters/cu. in.	1.6/97	1.8/112
Horsepower @ rpm	95 @ 5600	120@ 6500
Torque (lbs./ft.) @ rpm	98 @ 4000	114@ 3500
Availability	S	S[1]

EPA city/highway mpg

5-speed OD manual	23/26	22/25
3-speed automatic	23/24	
4-speed OD automatic		21/24

1. Sport.

PRICES

1997 Suzuki Sidekick	Retail Price	Dealer Invoice
JS 2WD 2-door convertible, 5-speed	$12899	$12254
JS 2WD 2-door convertible, automatic	13499	12824
JX 4WD 2-door convertible, 5-speed	14669	13642
JX 4WD 2-door convertible, automatic	15269	14200
JS 2WD 4-door wagon, 5-speed	14399	13391
JS 2 WD 4-door wagon, automatic	15349	14274
JX 4WD 4-door wagon, 5-speed	15999	14559
JX 4 WD 4-door wagon, automatic	16949	15423
JS Sport 2WD 4-door wagon, 5-speed	16699	15195
JS Sport 2WD 4-door wagon, automatic	17699	16106
JX Sport 4WD 4-door wagon, 5-speed	17699	16106
JX Sport 4WD 4-door wagon, automatic	18699	17016
JLX Sport 4WD 4-door wagon, 5-speed	19199	17471
JLX Sport 4WD 4-door wagon automatic	20199	18381
Destination charge, 2-door	400	400
Destination charge, 4-door	420	420

STANDARD EQUIPMENT:

JS 2-door: 1.6-liter 4-cylinder engine, 5-speed manual or 3-speed automatic transmission, driver- and passenger-side air bags, folding canvas top, cloth reclining front bucket seats, folding rear seat, cupholders, dual outside mirrors, trip odometer, tinted glass, intermittent wipers, daytime running lights, fuel-tank skid plate, carpeting,

spare-tire carrier w/full-size spare tire, 195/75R15 tires. **JX 2-door** adds: power steering, tachometer, 205/75R15 tires. **JS/JX 4-door** deletes folding canvas top and adds: 5-speed manual or 4-speed automatic transmission, split folding rear seat, AM/FM/cassette, rear defogger, 195/75R15 tires (JS), 205/75R15 tires (JX). **JS/JX Sport** adds: 1.8-liter DOHC 4-cylinder engine, air conditioning, power windows, power door locks, power mirrors, passenger-side visor mirror, remote fuel-door release, theft-deterrent system, map lights, 215/65R16 tires. **JLX Sport** adds: anti-lock brakes, automatic locking front hubs, cruise control, cloth door trim, rear wiper/washer, spare-tire cover w/wheel lock, alloy wheels. **4WD models** add: part-time 4-wheel drive, 2-speed transfer case. **JS 2-door:** 1.6-liter 4-cylinder engine, 5-speed manual or 3-speed automatic transmission, driver- and passenger-side air bags, folding canvas top.

OPTIONAL EQUIPMENT:

Safety Features	Retail Price	Dealer Invoice
Anti-lock brakes, (std. JLX Sport)	$600	$540

SUZUKI X-90

Subaru X-90

Rear- or 4-wheel-drive compact sport-utility vehicle; similar to Chevrolet Tracker and Suzuki Sidekick

Base price range: (1997 model) $13,199-$15,549. Built in Japan.

Also consider: Jeep Wrangler, Kia Sportage

FOR • Standard anti-lock brakes • Entry/exit

AGAINST • Acceleration • Noise • Ride • Cargo space

Suzuki tried plowing new ground two years ago with this cross between a sporty coupe and a compact sport-utility vehicle. The odd-looking little X-90 has been a slow mover, though, with fewer than 3000 sold in 1997.

The X-90 is basically a 2-seat version of the Suzuki Sidekick convertible; it's got the same wheelbase, suspension, and engine, but wears unique T-top styling with a separate trunk.

Its 1.6-liter 4-cylinder makes 95 horsepower. There's a choice of rear-wheel drive or a 4-wheel-drive system that's not for use on dry pavement. Manual transmission is standard, and automatic is optional.

Dual air bags and anti-lock brakes are standard, as are such amenities as power windows and door locks, and twin lift out glass roof panels.

PERFORMANCE The X-90 feels like a tall, crude sports car from the 1960s that could use a semester or two of finishing school. There's intrusive wind noise around the removable roof panels at speeds over 35 mph, and at highway speeds, X-90 occupants are assaulted by excessive road rumble and even more wind howl. The engine produces a loud, coarse growl under throttle.

It's a lively ride, too, with lots of bouncing and pitching on highways, and stiff, jarring reactions to bumpy pavement. The tall, lightweight X-90 also is easily buffeted by crosswinds.

Acceleration and passing power are adequate with the manual transmission, though you often have to floor the throttle to achieve decent results, which, of course, generates considerable noise and vibration. The pace slows considerably on models equipped with automatic transmission but noise levels don't abate.

Rating Scale: 5-Excellent; 4-Above average; 3-Average; 2-Below average; 1-Poor

Our 5-speed 4WD test model averaged 23.5 mpg. That's good compared to most 4x4s, but the X-90 is not meant for even gentle off-road driving and isn't really an SUV.

ACCOMMODATIONS The tall body has adequate head room and leg room for 6-footers, and, unlike many 4WD vehicles, easy entry/exit, with almost no step-up into the interior. The driver's view to the front and sides is good, but the wide rear pillars create large obstacles over both shoulders.

The dashboard has simple, well-marked climate controls. The stereo's buttons are tiny, however, and nearly impossible to use in the dark.

There's a sliver of storage space behind the seats and no map pockets on the doors. The trunk is narrow and shallow and the spare tire eats up valuable luggage space.

BUILD QUALITY We were unimpressed by the quality of interior materials and their assembly. The exterior had glossy paint and good fit and finish.

VALUE FOR THE MONEY Whether you think of it as a sport-utility or a car, the X-90 is a questionable value and a questionable vehicle. Want a reasonably-priced, sporty small car? Look at the Dodge/Plymouth Neon or Chevy Cavalier/Pontiac Sunfire. Looking for a small SUV? Consider the Toyota RAV4 or Jeep Wrangler.

SPECIFICATIONS

	2-door coupe
Wheelbase, in.	86.6
Overall length, in.	146.1
Overall width, in.	66.7
Overall height, in.	60.5
Curb weight, lbs.	2326
Cargo vol., cu. ft.	8.4
Fuel capacity, gals.	11.1
Seating capacity	2
Front head room, in.	34.2
Max. front leg room, in.	41.5
Rear head room, in.	—
Min. rear leg room, in.	—

ENGINES

	ohc I-4
Size, liters/cu. in.	1.6/97
Horsepower @ RPM	95 @ 5600
Torque (lbs./ft.) @ RPM	98 @ 4000
Availability	S

EPA city/highway mpg

5-speed OD manual	25/28
4-speed OD automatic	23/27

PRICES

1997 Suzuki X-90	Retail Price	Dealer Invoice
2WD 2-door, 5-speed	$13199	$12407
2WD 2-door, automatic	14149	13300
4WD 2-door, 5-speed	14599	13577
4WD 2-door, automatic	15549	14460
Destination charge	420	420

STANDARD EQUIPMENT:

2WD: 1.6-liter SOHC 4-cylinder engine, 5-speed manual transmission or 4-speed automatic transmission, driver- and passenger-side air bags, daytime running lights, power steering, cloth front bucket seats, front console w/cupholders, power windows, power door locks, dual outside mirrors, rear defogger, intermittent wipers, T-top, tinted glass, tachometer, trip odometer, rear spoiler, 195/65R15 tires, alloy wheels.

4WD adds: part-time 4WD, 2-speed transfer case, automatic locking front hubs, AM/FM/cassette, theft-deterrent system.

OPTIONAL EQUIPMENT
Safety Features

Anti-lock brakes, 2WD	600	540
4WD	800	700

4WD includes cruise control.

TOYOTA AVALON

RECOMMENDED

Toyota Avalon XLS

Front-wheel-drive full-size car

Base price range: $24,278-$28,128. Built in Georgetown, Ky.

Also consider: Buick LeSabre, Oldsmobile Eighty Eight/LSS/Regency, Pontiac Bonneville

FOR • Side air bags • Quietness • Acceleration

AGAINST • Fuel economy

The flagship sedan for Toyota's U.S. fleet gains standard seat-mounted front side air bags for '98.

Built only at Toyota's Georgetown, Kentucky, plant, Avalon is derived from the popular midsize Camry, but has a longer wheelbase, different styling, and a choice of a front bench seat or buckets. Avalon was designed mainly for the U.S. and is the only import-brand car positioned as a rival to American-style full-size sedans. XL and step-up XLS models are offered and both use a 3.0-liter V-6 and automatic transmission.

In addition to the new side air bags for both models are heated leather seats with driver's memory feature as a new XLS option.

Outside, Avalon gets multi-reflector "jewelled" headlamps, a 9-inch wider lower-trunk opening, integral rear "lip" spoiler, reshaped taillamps, and a bit more chrome on bumper fascias, bodyside moldings, and rear license plate frame. An engine immobilizer (to prevent "hot wiring") is added to the anti-theft system (standard on XLS, optional on XL).

PERFORMANCE Though it's bigger than a V-6 Camry, Avalon is only some 50 pounds heavier and compensates with a bit more horsepower. With that, it's a brisk performer, able to hit 60 mph from rest in about 8 seconds. Mid-range passing punch is equally satisfying. Too bad fuel economy isn't. Though we averaged 21 mpg in our last test, that figure included a lot of moderate-speed highway work that can yield up to 28 mpg by itself. In urban slogging we typically got a so-so 17-18 mpg.

Not surprisingly, Toyota's 3.0-liter V-6 works as well in the Avalon as it does in the Camry: silky smooth, nearly silent at idle, and quite hushed even when working hard. It's nicely complemented by the automatic transmission's prompt, buttery shifts up and down the gears. Wind and road noise are a little more prominent than the engine, but still quite well muted.

For ride and handling, the Avalon falls between, say, a Buick LeSabre's conservative nature and a Dodge Intrepid's sporty aspirations, mainly because of its in-between suspension damping. Hard cornering induces moderate body lean, while big humps and dips allow minor float. Even so, handling is grippier and more precise than is usual for full-size sedans, and the suspension absorbs most bumps with good body control. Less steering boost and more road feel would be appreciated, though.

ACCOMMODATIONS Avalon has plenty of space for four adults, but being narrower than full-size domestic sedans, it isn't a practical 6-seater unless those grownups are willing to rub shoulders. Another problem is lack of knee space for middle-seaters. Outboard riders won't be shy on head or leg room, however.

Avalon also trails Detroit's biggest cars for cargo space, but the trunk is wide, deep, and with a long, flat floor. A low liftover and this year's expanded aperture eases loading and unloading.

Prices are accurate at time of publication; subject to manufacturer's changes.

Drivers are presented with an attractive, well-arranged dashboard that could have come from one of Toyota's premium Lexus models, and there are enough adjustments for most anyone to get comfortable behind the wheel. Outward vision is fine except for invisible rear corners, a minor nuisance on many modern cars.

BUILD QUALITY Toyotas usually rate high in this area. The Avalon certainly does. Paint and panel finish, interior materials, and overall execution leave little to be desired.

VALUE FOR THE MONEY Avalon is priced to reflect its "flagship" role, and it doesn't deliver as much metal for the money as you can get with some full-size Detroiters. Even so, this is a roomy, competent sedan with few faults and the bonus of Toyota's reputation for near-bulletproof reliability—reasons enough to check it out.

RATINGS

	XL	XLS
Acceleration	4	4
Fuel economy	3	3
Ride quality	4	4
Steering/handling	3	3
Braking	4	4
Quietness	4	4
Driver seating	4	4
Instruments/controls	4	4
Room/comfort (front)	4	4
Room/comfort (rear)	4	4
Cargo room	3	3
Value for the money	4	4
Total	45	45

SPECIFICATIONS

	4-door sedan
Wheelbase, in.	107.1
Overall length, in.	191.9
Overall width, in.	70.5
Overall height, in.	56.7
Curb weight, lbs.	3340
Cargo vol., cu. ft.	15.4
Fuel capacity, gals.	18.5
Seating capacity	6
Front head room, in.	39.1
Max. front leg room, in.	44.1
Rear head room, in.	37.8
Min. rear leg room, in.	38.3

ENGINES

	dohc V-6
Size, liters/cu. in.	3.0/183
Horsepower @ rom	200@ 5200
Torque (lbs./ft.) @ rpm	214@ 4400
Availability	S

EPA city/highway mpg

4-speed OD automatic	21/31

PRICES

Toyota Avalon	Retail Price	Dealer Invoice
XL 4-door sedan, front bucket seats	$24278	$21254
XL 4-door sedan, front bench seat	25108	21981
XLS 4-door sedan	28128	24336
Destination charge	420	420

Prices are for vehicles distributed by Toyota Motor Sales, U.S.A., Inc. The dealer invoice and destination charge may be higher in areas served by independent distributors.

STANDARD EQUIPMENT:

XL: 3.0-liter dohc V-6 engine, 4-speed automatic transmission, driver- and passenger-side air bags, front side-impact air bags, anti-lock 4-wheel disc brakes, heated power mirrors, air conditioning, power steering, reading lights, tilt steering wheel, cruise control, cloth 6-way adjustable front bucket seats or power split bench seat with storage armrest, cupholders, tachometer, AM/FM/cassette, power windows, power door locks, power mirrors, remote fuel-door

and decklid releases, illuminated visor mirrors, intermittent wipers, automatic headlamps, rear defogger, tinted glass, full-size spare tire, 205/65HR15 tires, wheel covers.

XLS adds: automatic climate control, outside temperature display, 7-way power front bucket seats or power split bench seat with storage armrest, leather-wrapped steering wheel, premium CD player, remote keyless entry, variable intermittent wipers, fog lights, theft-deterrent system, alloy wheels.

OPTIONAL EQUIPMENT:

Major Packages	Retail Price	Dealer Invoice
Leather Trim Pkg., XL		
with bucket seats	$1910	$1562
XL with bench seat	1060	848
XLS	1005	804
Leather upholstery, simulated-leather door trim. XL adds leather-wrapped steering wheel.		
Leather Trim Pkg. w/memory,		
XLS with bucket seats	1310	1048
XLS with bench seat	1255	1004
Leather Trim Pkg. plus driver seat memory.		
Leather Trim Pkg. w/memory and heat,		
XLS with bucket seats	1555	1288
XLS with bench seat	1555	1244
Leather Trim Pkg. w/memory plus heated front seats.		

Powertrains		
Traction control	300	240

Comfort and Convenience		
7-way power front bucket seats,		
XL with bucket seats	850	714
Power moonroof,		
XL	1000	800
XLS	980	784
Premium cassette player, XL	290	218
CD player, XL	100	75
Premium CD player,		
XL	390	293
Premium cassette/CD player,		
XL	570	428
XLS	180	135
Heated power mirrors, XL	30	24

Appearance and Miscellaneous		
Theft-deterrent system,		
XL	320	256
Mud guards	60	48
Diamond white pearlescent paint	210	179
Alloy wheels,		
XL	435	348

TOYOTA CAMRY

✓ BEST BUY

Toyota Camry LE

Front-wheel-drive midsize car; similar to Lexus ES 300

Base price range: $16,938-$24,868. Built in Georgetown, Ky.

Rating Scale: 5-Excellent; 4-Above average; 3-Average; 2-Below average; 1-Poor

Also consider: Ford Taurus, Honda Accord, Nissan Maxima

FOR • Optional side air bags • Acceleration (V-6) • Ride • Quietness • Passenger and cargo room

AGAINST • Rear visibility • Steering feel

Toyota's mainstream midsize was redesigned last year, losing coupe and wagon models but gaining some size and lots of sales. In fact, Camry was America's best-selling car line for most of 1997, besting usual champs Ford Taurus and Honda Accord.

New-design cars generally don't change much in their second year, especially when sales are hot, so Camry is a virtual rerun for '98. The sedan-only line again comprises CE, LE, and top-shelf XLE models with 4-cylinder or V-6 power. Automatic transmission is standard except on two versions: the 4-cylinder CE, where it's optional in lieu of manual; and the V-6 CE, which is sold with manual only.

This year, seat-mounted front side air bags are a new option for all models. Like big brother Avalon, Camry's anti-theft system (standard XLE, optional LE) is also upgraded with an engine immobilizer that prevents "hot-wiring." Finally, 4-cylinder models now qualify as Low Emission Vehicles (LEVs) in California; V-6s were already so certified. Both Camry engines have slightly lower rated horsepower and torque with California emissions equipment.

Camry remains a close cousin of the Lexus ES 300; both use the same basic design and V-6 powertrain. The Lexus has more standard features and a higher price, however, and is sourced from Japan, whereas most Camrys sold in the U.S. are built at Toyota's Kentucky plant.

PERFORMANCE Camry might seem dull to drive, but only because it's so suave and undemanding. All models have below-average wind and road noise, plus a suspension that readily irons out rough stuff while providing a stable highway ride. Cornering is marked by moderate body lean, good grip, and safe front-drive responses, though the Camry can only be pushed so far before unproductive nose-plowing sets in. The steering is quick and centers wells, but effort is too low and road feel too numb for best control.

Anti-lock brakes are standard on all Camrys bar the 4-cylinder CEs, where they're optional. They work beautifully, capable of short, arrow-straight panic stops with little nosedive.

Camry's base engine is smooth and quiet for a 4-cylinder, and provides adequate acceleration even with automatic. Still, the silky V-6 is far more impressive, launching our test LE to 60 mph in under 7.9 seconds while averaging a passable 20.4 mpg in hard city/freeway driving. A 4-cylinder model returned 22.5 despite more urban driving. The V-6 is unobtrusive except at higher rpm, where it makes a delightful muted growl, and is complemented by the automatic's mostly seamless switch-like shift action.

ACCOMMODATIONS Though last year's redesign gave Camry more back seat space, the comfortable adult passenger load is four, not five. Like most midsize cars, Camry doesn't have quite enough rear cabin width for uncrowded three-abreast travel. It does, however, have ample head and leg room front and rear. Entry/exit is no problem either. Cargo space is competitive, and all models come with a handy split-fold rear seatback.

Camry's dash is typical Toyota: attractively styled and conveniently organized. A small exception involves the climate panel, which is too low in the center for easiest operation. Visibility is good except for a minor over-the-shoulder blind spot from the wide rear roof posts.

BUILD QUALITY Toyota removed weight and complexity from the latest Camry, but it doesn't show. Our test LE was the tightest, most carefully assembled Camry we've ever driven, all but identical in quality to a Lexus ES 300 except for less luxurious trappings.

VALUE FOR THE MONEY It's hard to fault the Camry, and it's hard to find a better choice in a midsize family sedan. No wonder it's been selling so well. All it lacks is a bit of personality and the lowest sticker prices in the class.

RATINGS

	CE	LE/ XLE	LE V-6/XLE V-6
Acceleration	3	3	4
Fuel economy	4	4	3
Ride quality	4	4	4
Steering/handling	3	3	3
Braking	3	4	4
Quietness	3	3	4
Driver seating	4	4	4
Instruments/controls	4	4	4
Room/comfort (front)	4	4	4
Room/comfort (rear)	3	3	3
Cargo room	3	3	3
Value for the money	5	5	5
Total	**43**	**44**	**45**

SPECIFICATIONS

	4-door sedan
Wheelbase, in.	105.2
Overall length, in.	188.5
Overall width, in.	70.1
Overall height, in.	55.4
Curb weight, lbs.	3042
Cargo vol., cu. ft.	14.1
Fuel capacity, gals.	18.5
Seating capacity	5
Front head room, in.	38.6
Max. front leg room, in.	43.5
Rear head room, in.	37.6
Min. rear leg room, in.	35.5

ENGINES

	dohc I-4	dohc V-6
Size, liters/cu. in.	2.2/132	3.0/183
Horsepower @ rpm	133@ 5200	194@ 5200
Torque (lbs./ft.) @ rpm	147@ 4400	209@ 4400
Availability	S	S
EPA city/highway mpg		
5-speed OD manual	23/31	20/28
4-speed OD automatic	23/30	19/26

PRICES

Toyota Camry	Retail Price	Dealer Invoice
CE 4-cylinder 4-door sedan, 5-speed	$16938	$15003
CE 4-cylinder 4-door sedan, automatic	17738	15712
CE V-6 4-door sedan, 5-speed	19828	17563
LE 4-cylinder 4-door sedan, automatic	20218	17699
LE V-6 4-door sedan, automatic	22558	19848
XLE 4-cylinder 4-door sedan, automatic	22628	19810
XLE V-6 4-door sedan, automatic	24868	21771
Destination charge	420	420

Prices are for vehicles distributed by Toyota Motor Sales, U.S.A., Inc. The dealer invoice and destination charge may be higher in areas served by independent distributors.

STANDARD EQUIPMENT:

CE: 2.2-liter DOHC 4-cylinder or 3.0-liter DOHC V-6 engine, 5-speed manual or 4-speed automatic transmission, anti-lock 4-wheel disc brakes (V-6), driver- and passenger-side air bags, power steering, split folding rear seat w/armrest, cloth reclining front bucket seats, front and rear storage consoles, overhead storage console, front and rear cupholders, tilt steering column, tachometer, coolant-temperature gauge, two trip odometers, AM/FM radio w/four speakers, tinted glass, dual remote outside mirrors, remote fuel-door and trunk releases, rear defogger, illuminated visor mirrors, auxiliary power outlet, 205/65HR15 tires (V-6), 195/70R14 tires (4-cylinder), wheel covers.

LE adds: 4-speed automatic transmission, anti-lock brakes, 4-wheel disc brakes (V-6), power door locks, air conditioning, cruise control, power windows, power mirrors, cassette player, integrated antenna, intermittent wipers.

XLE adds to LE: power front seats, driver-seat manual lumbar sup-

Prices are accurate at time of publication; subject to manufacturer's changes.

port, CD player, variable intermittent wipers, theft-deterrent system, alloy wheels.

OPTIONAL EQUIPMENT:

Major Packages

	Retail Price	Dealer Invoice
Black Pearl Elite Pkg.	$820	$452
Black Pearl Emblems, wood dashboard, floormats, trunk mat.		
Gold Elite Pkg.	835	475
Gold badging, wood dashboard, floormats, trunk mat.		
Leather Trim Pkg., LE	1100	880
XLE	1005	804
Leather upholstery, driver-seat lumbar support, leather-wrapped steering wheel and shifter, seatback map pockets. NA with integrated child seat.		
Power Pkg., CE	780	624
Power windows, door locks, and mirrors.		

Powertrains

Traction control, LE V-6, XLE V-6	300	240

Safety Features

Anti-lock 4-wheel brakes, CE w/4-cylinder engine	550	473
Side-impact air bags	250	215
CE requires Power Pkg.		
Integrated child seat	125	100
NA w/Leather Trim Pkg.		

Comfort and Convenience

Air conditioning, CE	1005	804
Cruise control, CE	290	232
Power moonroof, LE, XLE	1000	800
Includes map lights, sunshade.		
Variable intermittent wipers, CE	20	16
Premium AM/FM/cassette, LE	220	165
Includes six speakers, diversity antenna.		
Premium CD player, CE, LE	320	240
NA with Premium AM/FM/cassette		
Premium cassette/CD player, LE	500	375
Includes six speakers, equalizer, diversity antenna.		
XLE	180	135
6-disc CD autochanger	550	385
Remote keyless entry, CE, LE	299	149
Wood dashboard	499	335

Appearance and Miscellaneous

Theft-deterrent system, LE	540	432
Fog lamps	399	249
Mudguards	60	48
Rear spoiler	539	329
Alloy wheels, CE 4-cylinder	755	560
LE 4-cylinder	415	332
LE V-6	435	348

Other options are available as port installed items.

TOYOTA CELICA

1997 Toyota Celica GT

Front-wheel-drive sports coupe

Base price range: (1997 model) $17,178-$26,858. Built in Japan.

Also consider: Dodge Avenger, Honda Prelude, Nissan 240SX

FOR • Steering/handling

AGAINST • Engine noise • Rear seat room

Toyota's sporty coupe is up for a redesign, which may be why Celica is sitting out the first part of the '98 model year. Another reason is that sporty cars have lately been in the sales doldrums—enough to kill two Celica rivals, the Ford Probe and Mazda MX-6. Toyota, meantime, has a pile of unsold '97 Celicas that it hoped to clear by the New Year.

Though Toyota would not disclose '98 plans at presstime, one of two scenarios is probable. Either the current Celica will get very few changes, or a redesigned replacement will appear as an early 1999 model. It's also possible that Celica will be canned altogether for the new Canadian-built coupe version of the hot-selling midsize Camry that's due for 1999. Whatever Toyota decides, it'll sell '97 Celicas until supplies run out.

Last overhauled for 1994, Celica offers ST coupes with a hatchback or trunk and a GT hatchback and convertible. All have a 4-cylinder engine, STs carry a 1.8-liter, GTs a 2.2. All come with manual transmission and offer an extra-cost automatic. Anti-lock brakes are optional on cars equipped with cruise control.

PERFORMANCE For acceleration, all Celicas are not created equal. The ST's 1.8-liter engine (borrowed from the small Corolla sedan) is smooth and fairly quiet except when pushed. But weak low-rpm torque prevents it from pulling strongly with automatic transmission. GTs pack a decent punch with automatic—9.0 seconds to 60 mph in our test—but their 2.2 engine is loud and coarse at full throttle. At least fuel economy is line with engine size. Note, though, that while STs earn higher EPA ratings than GTs, they're not much thriftier in practice because you have to drive them that much harder more of the time.

Handling remains a Celica plus: agile and responsive with no surprises. The GT's available Sport Package includes firmer damping that provides a little extra cornering power in exchange for a markedly choppier ride. The optional anti-lock brakes are more worthwhile, being reasonably priced and quite effective, though we wish they were standard on GTs at least. Road noise is fairly high in any model. Wind rush tends to get drowned out by both engine and tires.

ACCOMMODATIONS Typical of small sporty cars, Celica's back seat is no fit place for adults, especially the convertible's. Front head clearance in coupes is marginal for 6-footers beneath a power moonroof. Hatchbacks are the roomiest, most-versatile cargo carriers here, but all Celicas suffer an awkwardly high load sill. The aperture on convertibles and "trunked" coupes is too small for large hard-sided suitcases—which won't fit anyway.

Though Celica's driving stance is predictably cozy and low-slung, major and minor controls are well spaced for most pilots. Visibility is good in coupes but not so good when traveling roof-up in the ragtop, owing to wide, "blind" rear quarters and a small-ish rear window. At least that window is glass (complete with electric defroster), and the power top mechanism works easily and seals well.

BUILD QUALITY Like other Toyotas, Celica feels solid and shows careful detail finish inside and out. Cabin trim is not that classy, though, and the convertible suffers more body shake than most drop-tops over railroad tracks and other rough stuff.

VALUE FOR THE MONEY Celica is a bit underpowered as an ST and overpriced as a GT, but it's the only such car with Toyota's renowned quality and high resale value. Still, sluggish sporty-car demand should be encouraging Toyota dealers to offer sizable discounts, so don't leave the showroom without one.

SPECIFICATIONS	2-door coupe	2-door hatchback	2-door conv.
Wheelbase, in.	99.9	99.9	99.9
Overall length, in.	177.0	174.2	177.0
Overall width, in.	68.9	68.9	68.9
Overall height, in.	51.0	50.8	51.0
Curb weight, lbs.	2395	2415	2755
Cargo vol., cu. ft.	10.6	16.2	6.8
Fuel capacity, gals.	15.9	15.9	15.9
Seating capacity	4	4	4

Rating Scale: 5-Excellent; 4-Above average; 3-Average; 2-Below average; 1-Poor

	2-door coupe	2-door hatchback	2-door conv.
Front head room, in.	34.3	34.3	38.7
Max. front leg room, in.	43.1	43.1	43.1
Rear head room, in.	29.2	29.2	34.1
Min. rear leg room, in.	26.6	26.6	18.9

ENGINES

	dohc I-4	dohc I-4
Size, liters/cu. in.	1.8/108	2.2/132
Horsepower @ rpm	105@ 5200	135@ 5400
Torque (lbs./ft.) @ rpm	117@ 2800	145@ 4400
Availability	S[1]	S[2]
EPA city/highway mpg		
5-speed OD manual	29/35	22/28
4-speed OD automatic	27/34	22/29

1. ST. 2. GT

RATINGS

	ST	GT
Acceleration	3	4
Fuel economy	4	3
Ride quality	3	3
Steering/handling	4	4
Braking	4	4
Quietness	3	3
Driver seating	3	3
Instruments/controls	3	3
Room/comfort (front)	3	3
Room/comfort (rear)	2	2
Cargo room	2	2
Value for the money	3	3
Total	**37**	**37**

PRICES

1997 Toyota Celica

	Retail Price	Dealer Invoice
ST 2-door notchback, 5-speed	$17178	$15126
ST 2-door notchback, automatic	17978	15831
ST 2-door hatchback, 5-speed	17538	15443
ST 2-door hatchback, automatic	18338	16148
Limited Edition ST 2-door hatchback 5-speed	19605	17359
Limited Edition ST 2-door hatchback automatic	20405	18063
GT 2-door hatchback 5-speed	20238	17718
GT 2-door hatchback, automatic	21038	18417
GT 2-door convertible, 5-speed	24438	21639
GT 2-door convertible, automatic	25238	22338
Limited Edition GT 2-door convertible, 5-speed	26058	23141
Limited Edition GT 2-door convertible, automatic	26858	23839
Destination charge	420	420

Prices are for vehicles distributed by Toyota Motor Sales, U.S.A., Inc. The dealer invoice and destination charge may be higher in areas served by independent distributors.

STANDARD EQUIPMENT:

ST: 1.8-liter DOHC 4-cylinder engine, 5-speed manual or 4-speed automatic transmission, driver- and passenger-side air bags, variable-assist power steering, cloth front bucket seats, 4-way adjustable driver seat, front console with armrest, split folding rear seat, cupholders, tilt steering wheel, digital clock, coolant-temperature gauge, tachometer, trip odometer, intermittent wipers, tinted glass, power mirrors, AM/FM radio with four speakers, rear defogger, remote fuel-door and trunk/hatch releases, map lights, visor mirrors, automatic headlamps, cargo-area cover (hatchback), 185/70R14 tires, wheel covers.

Limited Edition ST adds: air conditioning, power door locks, power windows, rear wiper, rear spoiler, AM/FM/cassette/CD player, four speakers and diversity antenna, alloy wheels, black chrome trim, floormats.

GT hatchback adds to ST: 2.2-liter DOHC 4-cylinder engine, 4-wheel disc brakes, upgraded door and interior trim, cassette player, power antenna, power windows, power door locks, intermittent rear wiper, engine-oil cooler, fog lamps, 205/55R15 tires.

Convertible deletes split folding rear seat and intermittent rear wiper and adds: power top w/glass rear window, contoured rocker panels.

Limited Edition Convertible adds: air conditioning, rear spoiler, premium AM/FM/cassette/CD player, six speakers and diversity antenna, cruise control, deep jewel green paint, alloy wheels, black chrome trim, floormats.

OPTIONAL EQUIPMENT:

	Retail Price	Dealer Invoice
Safety Features		
Anti-lock brakes	$550	$473
Requires cruise control. NA Limited Edition.		
Major Packages		
Power Pkg., ST	525	420
Power windows and door locks. Requires cruise control.		
Leather Pkg., convertible	1085	868
Leather sport seats, leather-wrapped steering wheel and manual shift knob, leather door trim. Requires cruise control.		
Sport Pkg., GT hatchback	970	776
Front sport suspension, front sport seats, leather-wrapped steering wheel and shifter, 205/55R15 summer tires, alloy wheels. Requires cruise control.		
Leather Sport Pkg., GT hatchback	1630	1304
Sport Pkg. plus leather sport seats. Requires cruise control.		
Comfort and Convenience		
Air conditioning	1005	804
Intermittent rear wiper, ST hatchback	170	139
NA Limited Edition.		
Power moonroof	760	608
NA convertible or Limited Edition.		
Moonroof wind deflector	53	32
Cruise control	290	232
ST includes leather-wrapped steering wheel and shifter.		
Auto-reverse cassette player, ST, ST Limited Edition	279	195
Cassette player, ST	335	257
Includes power antenna.		
Premium cassette player, GT hatchback	250	190
convertible	195	146
Includes diversity antenna, graphic equalizer, and six speakers.		
CD player	457	320
3-disc CD changer	699	489
NA with cassette and CD player.		
6-disc CD changer	799	559
NA with cassette and CD player.		
Cassette and CD player, GT hatchback	1335	1004
convertible	1280	960
Includes diversity antenna, graphic equalizer, and eight speakers.		
Remote keyless entry	395	149
ST requires Power Pkg.		
Fog lamps, ST	100	80
NA Limited Edition.		
Center armrest	73	43
Cargo net	42	27
Floormats, ST, GT	78	49
Appearance and Miscellaneous		
Rear spoiler, ST notchback	519	310
ST, GT hatchbacks	415	332
ST requires intermittent rear wiper. NA GT convertible.		
Contoured rocker panels (std. convertible)	200	160
NA Limited Edition ST 2-door hatchback.		
Mud guards	85	51
NA convertibles or with contoured rocker panels.		
Burlwood dashboard	495	225
Theft-deterrent system	695	209
ST requires Power Pkg. NA convertibles.		
Wheel locks	52	31
Alloy wheels, GT	435	348
ST	675	540
ST includes 205/55R15 tires.		

Prices are accurate at time of publication; subject to manufacturer's changes.

TOYOTA COROLLA

Toyota Corolla LE

Front-wheel-drive subcompact car; similar to Chevrolet Prizm

Base price range: $11,908-$15,598. Built in Fremont, Calif., and Canada.

Also consider: Honda Civic, Mazda Protege, Saturn Sedan/Wagon,

FOR • Optional anti-lock brakes • Fuel economy • Ride • Optional side air bags

AGAINST • Rear seat room

Corolla recently surpassed the venerable Volkswagen Beetle as the best-selling automotive nameplate in history, with more than 24 million sold worldwide since the first one rolled off the line in 1966.

Toyota celebrates '98 with a redesigned Corolla that's slightly larger and more powerful than the one it replaces. And it offers front side air bags, a rarity in this class.

Offered only as a 4-door sedan, the new model rides the same wheelbase as before, but its body is two inches longer and most interior dimensions are fractionally larger.

Base VE, CE, and top-line LE models are offered. A CE and LE Touring Package option includes white-faced gauges and color-keyed body trim among its features.

All models use a new 120-horsepower 1.8-liter 4-cylinder engine. It replaces a 100-horsepower 1.6-liter four and a 105-horsepower 1.8. Manual transmission is standard. A 3-speed automatic is optional on the VE, and a 4-speed automatic is optional on the CE and LE.

The new side air bags are mounted to the front seatbacks and are optional on all models. Anti-lock brakes are optional on all models.

VE models start about $1000 below last year's base Corolla; the CE and LE are slighly more expensive than last year's counterparts. Corolla's design and powertrain originates with Toyota but are shared with the Chevrolet Prizm. Both vehicles are built at a joint GM/Toyota plant in California.

PERFORMANCE Toyota claims the new, more-powerful engine cuts Corolla's 0-60 mph time by more than a second, to 9.1 seconds with manual transmission and 10.5 with automatic. We haven't clocked one yet, but while the new car feels stronger at higher engine speeds, automatic models don't get a sharp jump off the line. We rate their acceleration as average for a subcompact—and that's with the 4-speed automatic on the CE and LE. We didn't get a chance to try a VE with its 3-speed automatic, but suspect it's a bit slower. Also, turning on the air conditioning noticeably deadens acceleration. The 4-speed automatic provids smooth, timely upshifts and prompt downshifts for passing, but seems to cut engine power slightly during gear changes.

The suspension is tuned to provide a comfortable ride rather than sporty handling. Bumps are absorbed well, but high-speed turns bring on lots of body roll. This is particularly noticeable in the VE and CE, which lack the LE's front stabilizer bar (which is included in the Touring Package on CEs).

Past Corollas have impressed us with their quiet ride, and this version is no exception. In fact, it's even quieter than before, with little wind or road noise at highway speeds.

ACCOMMODATIONS One of the former Corolla's few faults was a shortage of rear-seat space. Because the new car's

wheelbase is unchanged, the problem persists. With average-sized folks in the front seats, medium-sized adults can squeeze into the rear seats, but knee room will be tight. If the front seats are moved more than halfway back, rear leg room becomes extremely tight. However, Corolla's rear doors are wide enough at the bottom so that average-sized shoes slip easily through the openings.

A low cowl and beltline make for a commanding driving position. It's a slight stretch to the radio and climate controls, but they're simple to use and clearly marked. The redesigned interior incorporates lots of little storage bins and a large glove box. The trunk is usefully sized, but the hinges dip down into the load space when the lid is closed.

BUILD QUALITY We had driven only pre-production Corollas at this writing, but their paint was smooth and glossy and the interior was well-assembled. There's lots of hard plastic trim inside, but it feels reasonably solid and doesn't look cheap.

VALUE FOR THE MONEY Corolla's been a Best Buy choice for several years, and the new car continues the string. And by cutting entry-level prices, Toyota makes it easier to get into one of the best little sedans around.

RATINGS

	VE, CE, LE
Acceleration	3
Fuel economy	4
Ride quality	3
Steering/handling	4
Braking	4
Quietness	4
Driver seating	4
Instruments/controls	4
Room/comfort (front)	4
Room/comfort (rear)	3
Cargo room	3
Value for the money	5
Total	**45**

SPECIFICATIONS

	4-door sedan
Wheelbase, in.	97.0
Overall length, in.	174.0
Overall width, in.	66.7
Overall height, in.	54.5
Curb weight, lbs.	2414
Cargo vol., cu. ft.	12.1
Fuel capacity, gals.	13.2
Seating capacity	5
Front head room, in.	39.3
Max. front leg room, in.	42.5
Rear head room, in.	36.9
Min. rear leg room, in.	33.2

ENGINES

	dohc I-4
Size, liters/cu. in.	1.8/110
Horsepower @ rpm	120@5600
Torque (lbs./ft.) @ rpm	122@4400
Availability	S

EPA city/highway mpg

4-speed OD automatic	28/36
5-speed OD manual	31/38

PRICES

Toyota Corolla	Retail Price	Dealer Invoice
VE 4-door sedan, 5-speed	$11908	$10854
VE 4-door sedan, automatic	12408	11309
CE 4-door sedan, 5-speed	13788	12568
CE 4-door sedan, automatic	14588	13298
LE 4-door sedan, 5-speed	14798	13107
LE 4-door sedan, automatic	15598	13816
Destination charge	420	420

Prices are for vehicles distributed by Toyota Motor Sales, U.S.A., Inc. The dealer invoice and destination charge may be higher in

Rating Scale: 5-Excellent; 4-Above average; 3-Average; 2-Below average; 1-Poor

areas served by independent distributors.

STANDARD EQUIPMENT:

VE 1.8-liter dohc 4-cylinder engine, 5-speed manual or 3-speed automatic transmission, driver- and passenger-side air bags, daytime running lights, power steering, cloth reclining front bucket seats w/lumbar support, front storage console with storage, cupholders, visor mirrors, trip odometer, automatic headlights, remote fuel door release, 175/65R14 tires.

CE adds: 5-speed manual or 4-speed automatic transmission, air conditioning, power windows, power door locks, AM/FM/cassette w/four speakers, digital clock, intermittent wipers, rear defogger, 60/40 split folding rear seat w/headrests, remote trunk release, dual remote mirrors, wheel covers.

LE adds: power mirrors, tachometer, variable intermittent wipers, outside temperature display, color-keyed bodyside moldings, 185/65R14 tires.

OPTIONAL EQUIPMENT:

Major Packages

	Retail Price	Dealer Invoice
All-Weather Guard Pkg., VE	$265	$215
CE, LE	80	67
Heavy-duty rear defogger, starter, and heater, rear heater. ducts		
Touring Pkg., CE	290	232
LE	140	112
Front stabilizer bar, mud guards, rocker panel extensions, tachometer (CE), 185/65SR14 tires.		
Touring Pkg w/alloy wheels, LE	555	444
Power Pkg., CE	640	512
Power windows and door locks, power mirrors.		

Safety Features

Anti-lock brakes	550	473
Side-impact air bags	250	215
Integrated child seat, CE, LE	125	100

Comfort and Convenience

Air conditioning, VE	950	760
Power sunroof, LE	735	588
Rear defogger, VE	185	148
Cruise control, CE, LE.......................................	290	232
Digital clock, VE	65	52
Radio Prep Pkg., VE	100	75
Includes four speakers, wiring harness, antenna.		
AM/FM/cassette, VE..	450	338
Requires Radio Prep Pkg.		
AM/FM/CD, VE..	550	413
CE, LE	100	75
Requires Radio Prep Pkg.		
3-disc CD changer	641	449
Requires AM/FM/cassette or CD		
6-disc CD autochanger	550	385
Requires AM/FM/cassette or CD		
Remote keyless entry, CE, LE	229	149
Requires Power Pkg.		
Burlwood dashboard, VE, CE	325	215
CE w/Power Pkg., LE	425	275

Appearance and Miscellaneous

Theft-deterrent system, CE, LE.............................	399	249
Rear Spoiler	499	299
Mud guards	60	48
NA with bodyside moldings.		
Alloy wheels, VE, CE	755	560
LE	415	332

Other options available as port installed items.

TOYOTA LAND CRUISER

All-wheel-drive full-size sport-utility vehicle; similar to Lexus LX 450

Base price: (1997 model) $41,188. Built in Japan.

Also consider: Ford Expedition, Isuzu Trooper, Mitsubishi Montero

1997 Toyota Land Cruiser

FOR • Passenger and cargo room

AGAINST • Fuel economy • Ride • Entry/exit

A redesigned Land Cruiser debuts in the Spring with rounded styling and slightly larger dimensions. This also applies to the Cruiser's upscale cousin at Toyota's Lexus division, but the Cruiser may not get the Lexus model's new V-8, continuing with 6-cylinder power instead.

Meanwhile, Toyota will sell '97 Land Cruisers. Last redesigned for 1991, this big Japanese-built SUV uses permanent 4-wheel drive with separate low-range gearing. Seating for five is standard and two third-row jump seats are optional.

PERFORMANCE Like the outgoing Lexus LX 450, the current Land Cruiser is an elderly 4x4 that's truck-tough and quite capable off-road. In the daily grind, however, it's much less acceptable than newer, more car-like SUVs like the Ford Expedition. Acceleration, for instance, is too leisurely for carefree two-lane-road passing and easy expressway merging. Though the 6-cylinder engine is willing and fairly smooth, it just doesn't have enough muscle for the Cruiser's two-and-a-half-ton heft. Weight is also the enemy of fuel economy, as shown by the abysmal 13 mpg we averaged in our last test.

Land Cruiser is not only heavy but fairly narrow for its height and thus has a high center of gravity. As a result, it feels tippy in quick direction changes. Vague power steering doesn't help. The permanent 4WD provides great traction with no driver input, but the bouncy on-road ride is tiring.

Though engine noise isn't excessive except at higher speeds, the big tires "sing" loudly most all the time, and the body shape generates plenty of wind rush even in gentle cruising. "Panic" stops are stable, but despite standard anti-lock brakes, distances are relatively long, another penalty of so much weight.

ACCOMMODATIONS Bountiful interior room is a plus, but the narrowish body limits the practical adult passenger load to four, not five. The available third-row seats are hard to reach and big enough only for kids. Cargo space is tight unless those seats are folded up.

Entry/exit requires some high stepping in this tall-riding rig. On the other hand, the driver enjoys a commanding view out, plus ample working room behind the wheel. Unfortunately, the driving posture is the bus-like, and some switches aren't logically deployed.

BUILD QUALITY Excellent workmanship is expected of Toyota, and the Cruiser doesn't disappoint. It also enjoys a near cult-like reputation for rugged dependability that seems well deserved.

VALUE FOR THE MONEY Spy photos suggest the new Cruiser will look something like the popular Jeep Grand Cherokee. We hope it also acts a lot like that polished SUV. Meantime, the old-soldier model should again be a sellout in its final season, appealing to those who value size and off-road toughness over on-road comfort and car-like civility.

SPECIFICATIONS

	4-door wagon
Wheelbase, in.	112.2
Overall length, in.	189.8
Overall width, in.	76.0
Overall height, in.	73.6
Curb weight, lbs.	4834
Cargo vol., cu. ft.	90.9
Fuel capacity, gals.	25.1
Seating capacity	5/7
Front head room, in.	40.3

Prices are accurate at time of publication; subject to manufacturer's changes.

	4-door wagon
Max. front leg room, in.	42.2
Rear head room, in.	39.7
Min. rear leg room, in.	33.6

ENGINES

	dohc I-6
Size, liters/cu. in.	4.5/275
Horsepower @ rpm.................................	212@ 4600
Torque (lbs./ft.) @ rpm...........................	275@ 3200
Availability	S
EPA city/highway mpg	
4-speed OD automatic.............................	13/15

RATINGS

	Land Cruiser
Acceleration	3
Fuel economy	1
Ride quality	3
Steering/handling	3
Braking	3
Quietness	3
Driver seating	3
Instruments/controls	3
Room/comfort (front)	5
Room/comfort (rear)	5
Cargo room	5
Value for the money	2
Total	**39**

PRICES

1997 Toyota Land Cruiser	Retail Price	Dealer Invoice
4-door 4WD wagon	$41188	$35422
Destination charge	420	420

Prices are for vehicles distributed by Toyota Motor Sales, U.S.A., Inc. The dealer invoice and destination charge may be higher in areas served by independent distributors.

STANDARD EQUIPMENT:

4.5-liter DOHC 6-cylinder engine, 4-speed automatic transmission, permanent 4-wheel drive, anti-lock 4-wheel disc brakes, driver- and passenger-side air bags, air conditioning, power steering, cruise control, cloth reclining front bucket seats, folding rear seat, front storage console, middle-seat armrests, power windows, power door locks, power mirrors, tilt steering column, tinted glass, tachometer, voltmeter, oil-pressure and coolant-temperature gauges, trip odometer, AM/FM/cassette, power antenna, digital clock with stopwatch and alarm, remote fuel-door release, rear heater, rear defogger, variable intermittent wipers, rear intermittent wiper/washer, automatic headlamps, front and rear tow hooks, passenger-side illuminated visor mirror, skid plates for fuel tank and transfer case, rear step bumper, trailer wiring harness, 275/70R16 tires.

OPTIONAL EQUIPMENT:
Major Packages

40th Anniversary Edition	5549	4471

Automatic air conditioning, leather upholstery, black pearl emblems, floormats, alloy wheels.

Leather Trim Pkg.......................................	4280	3455

Leather upholstery, power seats, leather-wrapped steering wheel and transfer-case knob, leather-covered center console, Third Seat Pkg.

Third Seat Pkg.	1515	1212

Includes split folding rear third seat, rear 3-point seatbelts, cloth headrests, child-safety hatch lock, privacy glass, rear assist grip, sliding rear quarter windows. NA Leather Trim Pkg.

Comfort and Convenience

Power moonroof.......................................	1185	948
Premium cassette w/CD player	945	709

Includes equalizer.

Appearance and Miscellaneous	Retail Price	Dealer Invoice
2-tone paint	$285	$228
Special Purpose, Wheels and Tires		
Differential locks	825	681
Locking front and rear differentials.		
Alloy wheels	525	420

TOYOTA PASEO

1997 Toyota Paseo notchback

Front-wheel-drive sports coupe

Base price range: (1997 model) $13,248-$17,568. Built in Japan.

Also consider: Ford Escort ZX2, Hyundai Tiburon, Nissan 200SX

FOR • Fuel economy

AGAINST • Noise • Rear seat room • Acceleration (automatic transmission)

The 1998 editions of Toyota's smallest and most-affordable sporty cars don't go on sale until the New Year, but should see few if any changes. Though Toyota wouldn't confirm details in time for this issue, the Paseo will definitely be less-available for '98. Like most sporty 2-doors, this one was a tough sell in 1997, with demand way down from '96 levels. Meantime, Toyota sport-utility vehicles and the midsize Camry sedans are red hot. Toyota is thus cutting cut back imports of the Japanese-built Paseo so it can bring in more of those better-selling models, which are also bigger profit-makers.

Beyond 1998, Paseo's U.S. future is uncertain, especially as it's due to be redesigned along with the subcompact Tercel on which it's based. Industry analysts think Toyota will drop the Paseo from its U.S. line next year, while selling the new-design successor model in other markets.

For now, Paseo offers coupe and convertible body styles with a 4-cylinder engine and manual or optional automatic transmissions. The convertible, new for '97, is a coupe conversion performed in California by an outside contractor; it features a manual folding top with glass rear window.

PERFORMANCE Being based on a budget-priced sedan, the Paseo is basically economy transportation in sports togs. Our last test model was an automatic-transmission convertible and it averaged 25 mpg in a mix of driving heavy on city commuting. Highway mileage was in the 30-mpg range.

Acceleration numbers are much less impressive. Though adequately peppy with manual transmission, the Paseo's 1.5-liter engine just can't pull the automatic with sufficient vigor for no-sweat hillclimbing, freeway merging, or two-lane-road passing. The engine is also a buzzbox even at moderate cruising pace, and the automatic can produce a lurchy bang on full-throttle kickdown changes from high rpm. Also typical of econocars, tire drone is too audible except on glassy asphalt, and wind noise suppression is so-so at best.

Despite fairly soft damping, the Paseo excels at neither ride nor handling. Most bumps register with a thump or jolt, yet the suspension and tires don't come close to furnishing sports-car moves, though the pleasantly quick steering has good road feel. Stopping ability is fine even without the optional anti-lock brakes,

---

Rating Scale: 5-Excellent; 4-Above average; 3-Average; 2-Below average; 1-Poor

but we recommend ABS for the superior straightline stability it affords.

ACCOMMODATIONS Like most sporty small cars, Paseo is a "2+2"—which means the back seat is too small except for toddlers or groceries. Rear leg room disappears if the front seats are moved even halfway back, and upfront head room is limited for 6-footers. Cargo space wins no prizes either, especially on the convertible.

The dash is similar to the Tercel's, but Paseo's driver sits closer to the ground. Even so, all-round visibility is good in the coupe and passable top-up in the convertible. Back seat access is none too easy except for pre-teens.

BUILD QUALITY Paseo benefits from Toyota's usual neat, through fit and finish. Furnishings are anything but lavish, though they're appropriate for an entry-level car.

VALUE FOR THE MONEY Though Toyota's great reliability record is a plus, Paseo has little going for it even as a cheap sportster—and it's not that cheap anyway. For better value and more fun (but no convertible option), look at Ford's new Escort ZX2 or a Nissan 200SX.

RATINGS

	Coupe 5-speed	Conv. w/auto
Acceleration	3	2
Fuel economy	5	5
Ride quality	3	3
Steering/handling	3	3
Braking	4	4
Quietness	2	2
Driver seating	3	3
Instruments/controls	3	3
Room/comfort (front)	3	3
Room/comfort (rear)	1	1
Cargo room	2	2
Value for the money	3	3
Total	**35**	**34**

SPECIFICATIONS

	2-door coupe	2-door conv.
Wheelbase, in.	93.7	93.7
Overall length, in.	163.6	163.6
Overall width, in.	65.4	65.4
Overall height, in.	51.0	51.0
Curb weight, lbs.	2025	2160
Cargo vol., cu. ft.	7.5	6.6
Fuel capacity, gals.	11.9	11.9
Seating capacity	4	4
Front head room, in.	37.8	37.8
Max. front leg room, in.	41.1	41.1
Rear head room, in.	32.0	NA
Min. rear leg room, in.	30.0	NA

ENGINES

	dohc I-4
Size, liters/cu. in.	1.5/90
Horsepower @ rpm	93 @ 5400
Torque (lbs./ft.) @ rpm	100 @ 4400
Availability	S

EPA city/highway mpg

5-speed OD manual	31/37
4-speed OD automatic	27/32

PRICES

1997 Toyota Paseo

	Retail Price	Dealer Invoice
2-door notchback, 5-speed	$13248	$11871
2-door notchback, automatic	14048	12588
2-door convertible, 5-speed	16768	15427
2-door convertible, automatic	17568	16144
Destination charge	420	420

Prices are for vehicles distributed by Toyota Motor Sales, U.S.A., Inc. The dealer invoice and destination charge may be higher in areas served by independent distributors.

STANDARD EQUIPMENT:

1.5-liter DOHC 4-cylinder engine, 5-speed manual or 4-speed automatic transmission, power steering, driver- and passenger-side air bags, manual folding top w/glass rear window (convertible), cloth reclining bucket seats, folding rear seat, cupholders, tinted glass, tachometer, coolant temperature gauge, trip odometer, AM/FM radio, digital clock, intermittent wipers, remote outside mirrors, visor mirrors, rear defogger, remote trunk and fuel-door releases, 185/60R14 tires, wheel covers.

OPTIONAL EQUIPMENT:

	Retail Price	Dealer Invoice
Safety Features		
Anti-lock brakes	$550	$473
NA with cruise control.		
Major Packages		
Power Pkg.	525	420
Power windows and door locks.		
All-Weather Guard Pkg.	70	59
Heavy-duty battery, rear defogger, and heater.		
Comfort and Convenience		
Air conditioning	925	740
Cruise control	290	232
NA with anti-lock brakes.		
Pop-up glass moonroof, notchback	410	328
Includes sunshade and storage pouch.		
Cassette player with four speakers	225	169
Cassette player	279	195
CD player	457	320
3-disc CD changer	699	489
6-disc CD changer	799	559
Remote keyless entry	395	149
Requires Power Pkg.		
Cargo net	42	27
Floormats	72	44
Appearance and Miscellaneous		
Theft-deterrent system, notchback	295	99
Requires Power Pkg.		
Deluxe theft-deterrent system, notchback	695	209
Requires Power Pkg.		
Rear spoiler, notchback	415	332
Mud guards	90	57
Poly-cast wheels	115	92
Alloy wheels	415	332
Wheel locks	52	31

TOYOTA RAV4

Toyota RAV4 4-door

Front- or 4-wheel-drive compact sport-utility vehicle
Base price range: $15,388-$18,708. Built in Japan.
Also consider: Honda CR-V, Jeep Wrangler, Kia Sportage

FOR • Steering/handling • Visibility

AGAINST • Engine noise • Rear seat room (2-door) • Cargo space (2-door)

Toyota's pint-size sport-utility vehicle enters its third season with a few new features. RAV4 offers 2- and 4-door wagons with front-wheel drive or permanently engaged 4-wheel drive. The only engine is a 2.0-liter 4-cylinder. Manual transmission is stan-

Prices are accurate at time of publication; subject to manufacturer's changes.

dard and automatic is optional for all models save the 2-door 4x4. Anti-lock brakes are optional across the board.

Based loosely on the sporty Celica coupe platform, the RAV departs from truck-based SUVs by having all-independent suspension, unitized construction, and no separate low-range 4WD gearing. However, manual-shift 4x4s come with a center differential lock that's useful off-road.

RAV4's engine picks up 2 horsepower and 2 foot-pounds of torque for '98. Outside are a new grille, multi-reflector headlamps, and bolder taillights. All models gain front seatbelt pretensioners that take up belt slack in an impact, plus "force limiters" that allow some post-impact "give" to reduce prolonged belt pressure. Also on hand are upgraded audio systems and a revised gauge cluster with digital odometers. New options include a swing-open left-rear side window for 2-doors and power windows for 4-doors.

PERFORMANCE Compact wagon or mini-SUV? The RAV4 is both—and neither. Though it fills the role of daily commuter as well as any small SUV, the RAV4 is much noisier than the average compact car. Tire roar is always noticed, wind rush rises sharply with speed, and the engine becomes boomy when worked hard. Toyota claims the engine is quieter this year, but there's really not much difference.

On the other hand, the RAV is quieter and more car-like to drive than a Chevrolet Tracker/Suzuki Sidekick, with less body lean and better stability in fast cornering, plus a smoother ride. Even so, there's some choppiness on scalloped freeways and patchy pavement, especially on the shorter-length 2-door.

RAV4 also lags behind most small cars for performance. We timed a manual-shift 4WD 2-door at 10.5 seconds 0-60 mph, but the automatic 4-door needs about 13, marginal for the urban grind—and that's without a load. You thus find yourself driving the RAV foot-to-the-floor most all the time, and that hurts fuel economy. We averaged a disappointing 20.8 mpg from an automatic 4WD 4-door in an even city/highway driving mix. The lighter-weight front-drive models should be a bit thriftier, as well as quicker.

As for off-road prowess, even Toyota admits the RAV is not designed for severe situations. It just doesn't have the ruggedness or pulling power of a Jeep Wrangler or truck-based SUVs like Toyota's own 4Runner.

ACCOMMODATIONS Though four adults will fit comfortably in a 4-door RAV, back-seaters don't have much leg or knee room, and rear entry/exit is a squeeze for larger folk. The 2-door best enjoyed with two adults fore and two children aft because its rear seat is even tighter than the 4-door's and rear access is more difficult despite a slide-forward feature on the right-front seat.

Both body styles provide good cargo space for their exterior size, though most users likely will often resort to folding down the 50/50 split rear seats. Too bad the backrest releases are reachable only from outside on the 2-door.

Though not as commanding as in some SUVs, the RAV's driving stance allows clear views all around and caters well to most people, though more rearward seat travel wouldn't go amiss for tall types. The car-like dash is simple and convenient.

BUILD QUALITY Despite some added sound-deadening last year, the RAV4 is a relatively lightweight rig with little padding and lots of visible painted metal inside. Interior materials are attractive, but in an "econocar" sort of way. With those qualifiers, the RAV is as soundly put together as any Toyota product.

VALUE FOR THE MONEY The RAV4 has its points, but it's been eclipsed by Honda's CR-V, which is roomier, quieter, and a better compact wagon and mini-SUV both. Shop each to see which best suits your needs.

SPECIFICATIONS

	2-door wagon	4-door wagon
Wheelbase, in.	86.6	94.9
Overall length, in.	147.6	163.8
Overall width, in.	66.7	66.7
Overall height, in.	65.2	65.4
Curb weight, lbs.	2701	2789
Cargo vol., cu. ft.	34.7	57.9
Fuel capacity, gals.	15.3	15.3

	2-door wagon	4-door wagon
Seating capacity	4	4
Front head room, in.	40.0	40.3
Max. front leg room, in.	39.5	39.5
Rear head room, in.	38.6	39.0
Min. rear leg room, in.	33.9	33.9

ENGINES

	dohc I-4
Size, liters/cu. in.	2.0/122
Horsepower @ rpm	127@ 5400
Torque (lbs./ft.) @ rpm	132@ 4600
Availability	S

EPA city/highway mpg

4-speed OD automatic	22/26
5-speed OD manual	22/26

RATINGS

	2-door 5-speed	4-door w/auto.
Acceleration	3	2
Fuel economy	3	3
Ride quality	3	3
Steering/handling	4	4
Braking	4	4
Quietness	3	3
Driver seating	3	3
Instruments/controls	3	3
Room/comfort (front)	3	3
Room/comfort (rear)	2	3
Cargo room	2	3
Value for the money	3	3
Total	**36**	**37**

PRICES

Toyota RAV4	Retail Price	Dealer Invoice
2WD 2-door wagon, 5-speed	$15388	$14026
2WD 2-door wagon, automatic	16438	14983
2WD 4-door wagon, 5-speed	16248	14809
2WD 4-door wagon, automatic	17298	15768
4WD 2-door wagon, 5-speed	16798	15052
4WD 4-door wagon, 5-speed	17658	15822
4WD 4-door wagon, automatic	18708	16763
Destination charge	420	420

Prices are for vehicles distributed by Toyota Motor Sales, U.S.A., Inc. The dealer invoice and destination charge may be higher in areas served by independent distributors.

STANDARD EQUIPMENT:

Base: 2.0-liter dohc 4-cylinder engine, 5-speed manual transmission or 4-speed automatic transmission, driver- and passenger-side air bags, power steering, tilt steering wheel (4-door), reclining cloth front bucket seats, split folding and reclining rear seat, front storage console, cupholders, tachometer, trip odometer, coolant-temperature gauge, digital clock, rear defogger, intermittent front and rear wipers, rear auxiliary power outlet, dual outside mirrors, front tow hook, 215/70R16 tires. 4WD models add: permanent 4WD.

OPTIONAL EQUIPMENT:
Major Packages

Value Pkg. 1, 4-door	1672	1505

Air conditioning, AM/FM/cassette player, tilt steering wheel, cruise control, power windows, doors, and mirrors, carpeted floor mats, trunk mat.

Value Pkg. 2, 4-door	1772	1595

Pkg. 1 plus AM/FM/CD player, cloth front and rear headrests, spare tire cover, body cladding graphic.

Upgrade Pkg., 4-door	930	744

Power windows, door locks, and mirrors. Requires AM/FM/cassette or CD player.

All-Weather Guard Pkg.	70	59

Heavy-duty battery, rear heater ducts, heavy-duty starter motor, large windshield washer reservoir.

Rating Scale: 5-Excellent; 4-Above average; 3-Average; 2-Below average; 1-Poor

Powertrains

	Retail Price	Dealer Invoice
Limited slip differential, 4WD	$375	$309

Safety Features

Anti-lock brakes	590	507

Comfort and Convenience

Air conditioning	985	788
Power moonroof, 4-door	915	732
Cruise control	290	232
Tilt steering wheel, 2-door	170	145
AM/FM/CD player	450	338
AM/FM/cassette player	350	263

Appearance and Miscellaneous

Privacy glass, 2-door	220	176
4-door	295	236

Special Purpose, Wheels and Tires

Alloy wheels	685	548
Alloy wheels w/fender flares, 4WD	1140	912

TOYOTA SIENNA

Toyota Sienna XLE

Front-wheel-drive minivan

Base price range: $21,140-$27,100. Built in Georgetown, Ky.

Also consider: Dodge Caravan, Chevrolet Venture, Ford Windstar

FOR • Standard anti-lock brakes • Refinement • Side air bags (LE, XLE)

AGAINST • Fuel economy • Radio placement

Toyota replaces its slow-selling Previa minivan with a more-conventional minivan based on the Camry sedan platform. Previa had a futuristic egg-shaped profile, mid-mounted 4-cylinder engine, and rear-wheel drive. The new Sienna has a less-rounded shape, a front-mounted V-6 engine, and front-wheel-drive.

It comes in a single body length in three levels of trim: CE, LE, and XLE. All have a 3.0-liter V-6 and automatic transmission that's also used in the Camry. Anti-lock brakes are standard, as are dual front air bags. LE and XLE add front side air bags.

A passenger-side sliding door is standard on CE and LE. Dual sliding doors are standard on the XLE and optional on the LE. Power control for the passenger-side door on LE and XLE models is planned for sometime during the model year.

Seats for seven are standard and include either a middle-row bench or two captain's chairs. The third-row split bench can be "tumbled" forward to provide more cargo space. Among the standard features is a low-tire-pressure warning light in the instrument panel. Sienna is built at the same Toyota plant in Kentucky as the Camry.

PERFORMANCE With several hundred pounds more weight to carry, the V-6 that feels strong in the Camry feels merely adequate in the Sienna—and loses some of its snap with the air conditioning on. The transmission shifts smoothly and down-shifts quickly for passing, so Sienna seldom feels underpowered. Chrysler, Ford, and General Motors' competitors offer traction control; Sienna does not, leaving it more susceptible to

wheel slip in snow and rain. In a mix of driving that favored urban commuting, we averaged 15.9 mpg in a test of a Sienna. Toyota recommends premium fuel.

Suspension settings favor a smooth ride over sporty handling, but that's appropriate for this type of vehicle. Bumps are absorbed with little fanfare, and body lean in turns is moderate. Overall road manners are composed and predictable, though Sienna can feel a little nose-heavy when entering freeway on-ramps. Road and wind noise are subdued, leaving the cabin serene at highway speeds.

ACCOMMODATIONS Sienna's is a well-thought-out and pleasant cabin. The low floor makes it disarmingly easy to climb in and out, yet the standard height-adjustable driver's seat affords a commanding view of the road. Some of our testers said the cloth seats were too soft for long-distance comfort; others found them supportive. There's plenty of head room all around the front seats are spacious. Second-row passengers don't have an abundance of legroom if the front seats are pushed very far back, but knee clearance is generally good, even in the rear row.

Climate controls are easily accessed, but the radio is mounted low and recessed into the dash, requiring a long look away from the road to reach while driving. Other controls, such as light and wiper switches, are handy. The roof pillars inturrupt outward visibility to certain quarters and the rear headrests interfer with it to the back; larger outside mirrors would also make for safer lane changes.

Numerous storage bins and drink holders of various sizes handle interior storage nicely. There's room for a double row of grocery bags in the back with all seats in place. The individual seats can be removed fairly easily, and the tumble-folding rear seat makes it easy to expand the cargo area.

BUILD QUALITY Tight, rattle-free construction, a precise fit to the body panels, and interior materials richer-looking than the minivan norm testify to Sienna's Toyota heritage.

VALUE FOR THE MONEY Toyota fired a blank with its Previa, bit hits the bull's eye with Sienna. Priced to compete with similarly equipped domestic rivals, this highly refined new minivan is a formidable force right out of the box.

RATINGS

	CE, LE, XLE
Acceleration	3
Fuel economy	2
Ride quality	4
Steering/handling	3
Braking	4
Quietness	4
Driver seating	4
Instruments/controls	3
Room/comfort (front)	4
Room/comfort (rear)	5
Cargo room	5
Value for the money	4
Total	**45**

SPECIFICATIONS

	4-door van
Wheelbase, in.	114.2
Overall length, in.	193.5
Overall width, in.	73.4
Overall height, in.	67.3
Curb weight, lbs.	3759
Cargo vol., cu. ft.	143.0
Fuel capacity, gals.	21.0
Seating capacity	7
Front head room, in.	40.6
Max. front leg room, in.	41.9
Rear head room, in.	37.7
Min. rear leg room, in.	34.0

ENGINES

	dohc V-6
Size, liters/cu. in.	3.0/183
Horsepower @ rpm	194@ 5200
Torque (lbs./ft.) @ rpm	209@ 4400
Availability	S

Prices are accurate at time of publication; subject to manufacturer's changes.

EPA city/highway mpg
4-speed OD automatic.. 18/24

PRICES

Toyota Sienna	Retail Price	Dealer Invoice
CE 3-door van	$21140	$18724
LE 3-door van	23500	20573
LE 4-door van	23975	20989
XLE 4-door van	27100	23514
Destination charge	420	420

STANDARD EQUIPMENT:

CE: 3.0-liter dohc V-6 engine, 4-speed automatic transmission, driver- and passenger-side air bags, anti-lock brakes, air conditioning, variable-assist power steering, tilt steering wheel, cloth reclining front bucket seats, console with storage, overhead console, 2-passenger second-row seat, 3-passenger split-folding third row seat, cupholders, AM/FM/cassette, digital clock, visor mirrors, auxiliary power outlets, variable intermittent wipers, automatic headlights, tinted glass, daul outside mirrors, 205/70R15 tires, wheel covers.

LE adds: front side-impact air bags, front and rear air conditioning, power windows, power door locks, power mirrors, cruise control, rear defogger, tachometer, illuminated visor mirrors, privacy glass.

XLE adds: power driver seat, heated power mirrors, CD player, quad captain's chairs, leather-wrapped steering wheel, remote keyless entry, floormats, roof rack, theft-deterrent system, 215/65R15 tires, alloy wheels.

OPTIONAL EQUIPMENT:
Major Packages

Pkg. 1, LE..	$430	$333
Cassette player, privacy glass, roof rack.		
Pkg. 2, LE	1690	1341
Pkg. 2 plus captain's chairs, alloy wheels.		
Pkg. 3, XLE	2390	1912
Leather upholstery, power sunroof.		
Leather Pkg., XLE	1410	1128
Leather uphostery.		
Security Pkg., LE	440	352
Theft-deterrent system, remote keyless entry.		
Power Pkg., CE	895	716
Cruise control, Power windows and door locks.		
Towing Pkg., CE	600	480
Includes rear air conditioning. Requires full-size spare tire.		
LE, XLE	120	150
Includes rear air conditioning. CE requires full-size spare tire.		
Towing Pkg. 2, CE	150	120
Not available with rear air conditioning. Requires full-size spare tire.		

Safety Features

Integrated child seat, CE, LE	250	200
NA with quad captain's chairs.		

Comfort and Convenience

Rear air conditioning, CE	450	360
Power mirrors, CE	180	144
Heated power mirrors, CE......................	180	144
Rear defogger, CE	195	156
Remote keyless entry.............................	229	149
CE requires Power Pkg.		
Cassette player, CE	231	162
CD player, CE, LE	335	235
3-disc CD player, CE, LE	641	449
Power sliding door, LE, XLE	375	300
Requires Security Pkg.		
Quad captain's chairs, LE	650	520
Power sunroof, XLE	980	784

Appearance and Miscellaneous

Rear Privacy glass, CE, LE	360	288
Roof rack, CE, LE	210	168
Deluxe theft-deterrent system	399	249
CE requires Power Pkg.		
Full-size spare tire, CE, LE	85	68
Alloy wheels, LE	610	488

Other options are available as port installed items.

TOYOTA T100

1997 Toyota T100 4WD Xtracab

Rear- or 4-wheel-drive compact pickup
Base price range: (1997 model) $14,678–$24,898. Built in Japan.

Also consider: Dodge Dakota, Ford Ranger, Mazda B-Series Pickup

FOR • Optional anti-lock brakes • Acceleration (V-6/2WD) • Quietness

AGAINST • Acceleration (4-cylinder) • No passenger-side air bag • Rear-seat room (Xtracab)

Five years ago, Toyota went where no import-brand truckmaker had gone before with the T100, a larger-than-compact pickup intended to compete with full-size Ford, Dodge, and General Motors models. Sales were minuscule until more power and extended "Xtracab" models were added for 1995, but stiff prices and the lack of a V-8 keep T100 a very minor player in the pickup market.

Except for revised sound systems, this year's T100 is a '97 rerun. A 4-cylinder regular-cab with 2-wheel drive continues as a price-leader. Other models are extended Xtracabs with V-6 power, 2WD or 4WD, and base or deluxe SR5 trim. Manual transmission is standard across the board and automatic is optional. Next year, T100 production will move from Japan to a new plant in Indiana, at which time Toyota is expected to offer a V-8 engine and 4-door models.

PERFORMANCE Until that V-8 arrives, the T100 is better thought of as a personal-use pickup rather than work-oriented full-size. For one thing, its payload and tow ratings are more like those of domestic compacts, with respective ranges of 1680-2150 pounds and 4000-5000 pounds. Then too, the base 4-cylinder model has modest performance at best. A torquey 3.4-liter V-6 makes the 2WD Xtracabs much livelier with or without a load, but the heavier 4x4s really need the manual transmission for adequate punch in passing situations and hillclimbing; with automatic they're rather lethargic.

At least that automatic is a mostly smooth operator. The same goes for engines, which are quiet until marked fan noise intrudes at higher rpm. Furthering this refinement, wind noise is moderate for a bluff-built truck and road roar well controlled.

In ride and handling, the T100 is pleasant but predictable. The 4x4s are fairly bouncy, but 2WDs smother most bumps well and corner with more stability than a lot of big pickups. Steering is also more precise than the class norm. The 4WD is a conventional part-time setup with 2-speed transfer case and on-the-fly shifting between 2- and 4-wheel High.

Overall, the T100 trails most domestic rivals in two important areas. First, anti-lock brakes are optional instead of standard. Second, there's no passenger air bag available, a telling omission these days.

ACCOMMODATIONS All T100s are wide enough for three adults in front, though the middle passenger must assume an awkward knees-up posture. Xtracabs have a front-facing 50/50 rear bench that can be folded up for extra cargo room, but it's too narrow for three grownups. The Xtracab also lacks a third door like Ford and Chevy offer, so rear access isn't that easy, especially in the high-riding 4x4s.

On the plus side, the Xtracab's standard 60/40 split bench is comfortably supportive, as are the front bucket seats available on SR5s. The dash is user-friendly, but deploying the pull-out dual cupholders prevents reaching the climate controls.

The Xtracab's 6.3-foot-long cargo bed will be too small for some users; the lone regular cab has an 8-foot box. Still, floors are wide enough to carry the obligatory 4x8 sheet of plywood. Xtracabs offer up

Rating Scale: 5-Excellent; 4-Above average; 3-Average; 2-Below average; 1-Poor

to 21.4 cubic feet of storage behind the front seats; again, most extended-cab domestics do better.

BUILD QUALITY T100s are a bit plain even in SR5 trim, but there's no doubting their solid, thorough craftsmanship. The T100 also carries Toyota's reputation for reliability, and rates high among all pickups in independent customer satisfaction surveys.

VALUE FOR THE MONEY If you want a bigger-than-compact truck, don't need a V-8, and are willing to pay for finesse, the T100 is a good choice. Otherwise, a domestic full-size pickup offers better value and overall utility.

RATINGS

	Reg. cab 2WD	Xtracab 4WD
Acceleration	3	2
Fuel economy	2	1
Ride quality	3	2
Steering/handling	3	3
Braking	3	3
Quietness	3	3
Driver seating	4	4
Instruments/controls	4	4
Room/comfort (front)	4	4
Room/comfort (rear)	—	2
Cargo room	1	2
Value for the money	3	3
Total	**33**	**33**

SPECIFICATIONS

	Reg. cab	Extended cab
Wheelbase, in.	121.8	121.8
Overall length, in.	209.1	209.1
Overall width, in.	75.2	75.2
Overall height, in.	67.2	68.6
Curb weight, lbs.	3320	3550
Maximum payload, lbs.	1680	2150
Fuel capacity, gals.	24.0	24.0
Seating capacity	3	6
Front head room, in.	39.6	39.6
Max. front leg room, in.	42.9	42.9
Rear head room, in.	—	37.8
Min. rear leg room, in.	—	29.6

ENGINES

	dohc I-4	dohc V-6
Size, liters/cu. in.	2.7/163	3.4/191
Horsepower @ rpm	150@ 4800	190@ 4800
Torque (lbs./ft.) @ rpm	177@ 4000	220@ 3600
Availability	S	S

EPA city/highway mpg
5-speed OD manual	20/24	17/21
4-speed OD automatic	19/22	17/20

PRICES

1997 Toyota T100

	Retail Price	Dealer Invoice
2WD 4-cylinder regular cab, 5-speed	$14678	$13606
2WD 4-cylinder regular cab, automatic	15578	14440
2WD V-6 Xtracab, 5-speed	18608	16673
2WD V-6 Xtracab, automatic	19508	17480
2WD SR5 V-6 Xtracab, 5-speed	20068	17879
2WD SR5 V-6 Xtracab, automatic	20968	18680
4WD V-6 Xtracab, 5-speed	22418	19856
4WD V-6 Xtracab, automatic	23318	20654
4WD SR5 V-6 Xtracab, 5-speed	23998	21133
4WD SR5 V-6 Xtracab, automatic	24898	21925
Destination charge	420	420

Prices are for vehicles distributed by Toyota Motor Sales, U.S.A., Inc. The dealer invoice and destination charge may be higher in areas served by independent distributors.

STANDARD EQUIPMENT:

2.7-liter 4-cylinder engine, 5-speed manual or 4-speed automatic, driver-side air bag, power steering, vinyl bench seat, cupholders, tinted glass, radio prep, 215/75R15 tires, full-size spare tire.

V-6 adds: 3.4-liter V-6 engine, cloth 60/40 split bench seat w/arm-rest, cloth rear jumpseats, dual outside mirrors, digital clock, tachometer, day/night inside mirror, cloth door panels, swing-out rear quarter windows, All-Weather Guard Pkg. (heavy-duty battery and starter, heavy-duty heater, anti-chip paint), mud guards, carpeting, 235/75R15 tires, wheel covers.

SR5 adds: Convenience Pkg. (tilt steering wheel, sliding rear window, variable intermittent wipers, rear privacy glass), voltmeter, oil-pressure gauge, coolant temperature gauge, deluxe AM/FM radio w/four speakers, map lights, illuminated passenger-side visor mirror, Chrome Pkg. (chrome front bumper, grille, and door handles), chrome wheel opening moldings.

4WD models add: 4WDemand 4-wheel drive, Hi-Trac front suspension, styled steel wheels.

OPTIONAL EQUIPMENT:

	Retail Price	Dealer Invoice
Safety Features		
Anti-lock brakes, V-6 models	$590	$507

Base V-6 requires cruise control. SR5 requires cruise control or Value Pkg.

Major Packages
Upgrade Pkg., 4-cylinder	650	530

Tilt steering wheel, cloth upholstery, center armrest, digital clock, variable intermittent wipers, dual outside mirrors, day/night mirror, carpeting, wheel covers.

Value Pkg., base V-6	556	500

Air conditioner, tilt steering wheel, sliding rear window, variable intermittent wipers, rear grey privacy glass, Chrome Pkg. (chrome front bumper, grille, and door handles), chrome rear bumper, floormats, bodyside moldings.

SR5	446	401

Air conditioner, cruise control, Power Pkg. (power windows and door locks, chrome power mirrors), chrome rear bumper, floormats, bodyside moldings.

Convenience Pkg., base V-6	505	414

Tilt steering wheel, sliding rear window, variable intermittent wipers, rear privacy glass.

Cruise Control Pkg., base V-6	310	248
SR5	395	316

SR5 includes leather-wrapped steering wheel. Base V-6 requires Convenience Pkg., tilt steering wheel, or Value Pkg.

Power Pkg., V-6 models	660	528

Power windows and door locks, chrome power mirrors. Requires cruise control.

Chrome Pkg., 4-cylinder, 2WD base V-6	160	128

Chrome front bumper, grille, and door handles. 4-cylinder requires Upgrade Pkg.

All-Weather Guard Pkg., 4-cylinder	130	110

Heavy-duty battery and starter, heavy-duty heater, anti-chip paint.

Comfort and Convenience
Sport Seats, SR5	330	264
Tilt steering wheel, base V-6	235	198

Includes variable intermittent wipers.

AM/FM radio, 4-cylinder base, 2WD base V-6	245	184

Includes two speakers.

Deluxe AM/FM radio, 4-cylinder, base V-6	380	285

Includes four speakers.

Deluxe AM/FM/cassette, base V-6	605	454
SR5	225	169

Includes four speakers.

Premium cassette player, SR5	420	315

Includes six speakers.

Sliding rear window, 4-cylinder	150	120
base V-6	270	216

Base V-6 includes rear privacy glass.

Appearance and Miscellaneous
Metallic paint	NC	NC
2-tone paint, V-6 models	365	292

Requires Value Pkg.

Wheel covers, 4-cylinder	90	72
Styled steel wheels, 2WD V-6 models	110	88

Includes 235/75R15 tires.

265/70R16 tires, 4WD base V-6	325	260

Prices are accurate at time of publication; subject to manufacturer's changes.

	Retail Price	Dealer Invoice
4WD SR5...	$285	$228
Includes styled steel wheels.		
Chrome wheels, 4WD base V-6..............	230	264
4WD SR5...	220	176
Includes 265/70R16 tires, chrome wheel-opening moldings (base V-6).		
Alloy wheels, 2WD base V-6..................	605	484
SR5 2WD...	535	428
4WD base V-6..................................	825	660
4WD SR5...	715	572
Includes chrome wheel-opening moldings, 235/75R15 tires (2WD), 265/70R16 tires (4WD).		
235/75R15 tires, 4-cylinder	125	100
Requires Upgrade Pkg. or wheel covers.		

TOYOTA TACOMA

Toyota Tacoma 4WD Limited extended cab

Rear- or 4-wheel-drive compact pickup

Base price range: $12,538-$24,928. Built in Fremont, Calif.

Also consider: Dodge Dakota, Ford Ranger, Mazda B-Series Pickup

FOR • Passenger side air bag • Acceleration (V-6)

AGAINST • Ride (4WD models) • Rear seat room (Xtracab) • Step-in height (4WD models)

Three years ago, Toyota redesigned its compact pickup and gave it a name. This year, the California-built Tacoma gets a standard passenger-side air bag, plus minor styling and lineup changes.

Regular and extended Xtracab models are offered with 2- or 4-wheel drive. A 2.4-liter 4-cylinder engine is standard; 4x4s get a 2.7-liter 4-cylinder. A V-6 is optional linewide. All team with manual or automatic transmission.

Last year's top SR5 trim level is renamed Limited, and SR5 replaces LX on an upgrade package for base Xtracabs. The Limited comes only as a V-6 Xtracab.

As on other pickups, Tacoma's passenger-side air bag includes a key-operated off switch for use when a child seat is in place. Body-color bumpers and grille are a new option for some models, while 4WD Xtracabs (except 4-cylinder/automatics) can be ordered with a new Off-Road Package.

Tacomas use Toyota's 4WDemand system. It's not for use on dry pavement but has shift-on-the-fly and an available locking rear differential.

PERFORMANCE Typical of small pickups, Tacomas range from lively to lethargic depending on drivetrain. The 2.4-liter has more power than the base 4-cylinders in domestic compacts and provides adequate acceleration with manual transmission in 4x2s. However, the V-6 is almost mandatory on 4WDs; their standard 2.7 four is a bit overburdened by the extra weight. Tacoma's V-6 is on a par with domestic V-6s for standing-start snap, though it isn't quite as muscular in mid-range passing situations. Mileage isn't great in any case. We got only 16.1 mpg with a 4WD V-6 Xtracab, though a V-6/automatic 4x2 returned a creditable 19.4 and ran 0-60 in a brisk 8.7 seconds.

Payload ratings are competitive, but towing limits fall short of domestic rivals by at least 1000 pounds. And anti-lock brakes are optional. Most rivals have standard rear-wheel ABS at least.

Tacoma 4x2s are pleasant to drive, with precise steering,

composed handling, and a fairly comfortable ride. The 4x4s can be uncomfortably bouncy with their stiff damping and big tires. They also ride higher and thus feel tippier in quick direction changes. Noise levels are relatively low across the board, though 4x4s suffer marked tire thrum.

ACCOMMODATIONS Tacoma is the best-selling import-brand pickup, but is no leader in utility. It has only a 6.2-foot-long cargo box, versus the 7- or 7.5-foot beds available on most other compact pickups. The Xtracab doesn't have enough "xtra" rear space to accommodate grownups, but credit Toyota for rear 3-point seatbelts and the ability to mount a rear child seat. Main-cabin room is adult-sized, though middle-riders are hemmed in on the base bench. The optional buckets are a better bet for comfort.

Interior step-in is steep on 4x4s, though Tacoma is little if any worse in this regard than most rivals. The dash is logical and convenient, though the climate controls are obstructed when using the pull-out cupholders.

BUILD QUALITY Exacting fit and finish is a Toyota trademark, and Tacoma does nothing to change that. However, base-trim vehicles have a "stripped" low-buck look, and it takes expensive options to change that.

VALUE FOR THE MONEY Tacoma is a quality small truck for sure, but it's costly to begin with and gets really pricey when you start adding extras. For better dollar value with no great loss in quality, check our suggested alternatives.

RATINGS	4WD reg. cab	V-6 2WD ext. cab	V-6 4WD ext. cab
Acceleration	3	4	3
Fuel economy	2	3	2
Ride quality	2	3	2
Steering/handling	3	4	3
Braking	3	3	3
Quietness	3	4	3
Driver seating	4	4	4
Instruments/controls	3	3	3
Room/comfort (front)	3	3	3
Room/comfort (rear)	—	2	2
Cargo room	1	3	3
Value for the money	3	3	3
Total	30	39	34

SPECIFICATIONS

	Reg. cab	Ext. cab
Wheelbase, in.	103.3	121.9
Overall length, in.	184.5	203.1
Overall width, in.	66.5	66.5
Overall height, in.	61.8	62.0
Curb weight, lbs.	2560	2745
Maximum payload, lbs.	1914	1759
Fuel capacity, gals.	15.1	15.1
Seating capacity	3	5
Front head room, in.	38.2	38.4
Max. front leg room, in.	41.7	42.8
Rear head room, in.	—	35.5
Min. rear leg room, in.	—	27.2

ENGINES

	dohc I-4	dohc I-4	dohc V-6
Size, liters/cu. in.	2.4/144	2.7/163	3.4/181
Horsepower @ rpm.........	142@ 5000	150@ 4800	190@ 4800
Torque (lbs./ft.) @ rpm.....	160@ 4000	177@ 4000	220@ 3600
Availability	S	S	O
EPA city/highway mpg			
5-speed OD manual	22/27	17/21	19/23
4-speed OD automatic.......	21/24	18/21	19/22

PRICES

Toyota Tacoma

	Retail Price	Dealer Invoice
2WD 4-cylinder regular cab, 5-speed	$12538	$11493
2WD 4-cylinder regular cab, automatic	13258	12154
2WD 4-cylinder Xtracab, 5-speed	14708	13330
2WD 4-cylinder Xtracab, automatic	15428	13983
2WD V-6 Xtracab, 5-speed	16048	14545

Rating Scale: 5-Excellent; 4-Above average; 3-Average; 2-Below average; 1-Poor

	Retail Price	Dealer Invoice
2WD V-6 Xtracab, automatic	$16948	$15361
4WD 4-cylinder regular cab, 5-speed	17428	15616
4WD 4-cylinder regular cab, automatic	18328	16422
4WD 4-cylinder Xtracab, 5-speed	18878	16916
4WD 4-cylinder Xtracab, automatic	19778	17723
4WD V-6 Xtracab, 5-speed	19968	17892
4WD V-6 Xtracab, automatic	20868	18699
4WD Limited V-6 Xtracab, 5-speed	24028	21531
4WD Limited V-6 Xtracab, automatic	24928	22336
Destination charge	420	420

Prices are for vehicles distributed by Toyota Motor Sales, U.S.A., Inc. The dealer invoice and destination chrarge may be higher in areas served by independent distributors.

STANDARD EQUIPMENT:

2WD regular cab: 2.4-liter 4-cylinder, 5-speed manual or 4-speed automatic transmission, driver-side air bag, cloth bench seat, cupholders, carpeting, tinted glass, dual outside mirrors, 195/75R14 tires, full-size spare, wheel covers.

2WD 4-cylinder Xtracab adds: 60/40 split bench seat, rear jump seats, swing-out rear quarter windows, 215/70R14 tires.

2WD V-6 Xtracab adds: 3.4-liter V-6 engine, power steering.

4WD regular cab adds to 2WD regular cab: 2.7-liter 4-cylinder engine, part-time 4-wheel-drive system, manually locking hubs, power steering, mud guards, skid plates, 225/75R15 tires.

4WD 4-cylinder Xtracab adds: 60/40 split bench seat, rear jump seats, swing out rear quarter windows.

4WD V-6 Xtracab adds: 3.4-liter V-6 engine, gas shock absorbers.

Limited adds: 4WDemand transfer case, automatic locking hubs, cruise control, power windows, power door locks, adjustable bucket seats, tilt steering wheel, tachometer, coolant-temperature gauge, Deluxe AM/FM/cassette w/four speakers, digital clock, variable intermittent wipers, passenger-side visor mirror, map lights, Chrome Pkg. (chrome bumpers, grille, and door handles), striping, sliding rear window, alloy wheels.

OPTIONAL EQUIPMENT:
Major Packages

	Retail	Dealer
Value Edition Pkg., 2WD regular cab	265	238

Includes power steering, painted rear step bumper, AM/FM/cassette, floormats.

Value Edition Plus Pkg., 2WD regular cab	835	751
4WD regular cab	555	499

Includes air conditioning, power steering (2WD 4-cylinder), AM/FM/cassette, Chrome Pkg. (chrome front bumper, rear step bumper, grille, door handles) (2WD), floormats.

Value Edition Plus Pkg. With Color Key Pkg., 2WD regular cab	815	733

Includes Color Key Pkg. (color-keyed front bumper, valance panel, grille), air conditioning, power steering, AM/FM/cassette, floormats.

SR5 Pkg., 2WD 4-cylinder Xtracab	930	837
2WD V-6 Xtracab	780	702
4WD Xtracab	1280	1152

Includes air conditioning, power steering (2WD 4-cylinder), Deluxe AM/FM/cassette w/4-speakers, sliding rear window w/privacy glass, Chrome Pkg. (chrome front bumper, rear step bumper, grille, and door handles) (2WD).

SR5 Pkg. with Color-Key Pkg., 2WD 4-cylinder Xtracab	910	819
2WD V-6 Xtracab	710	639
4WD Xtracab	1210	1089

Includes air conditioning, power steering (2WD 4-cylinder), Deluxe AM/FM/cassette w/4-speakers, sliding rear window w/privacy glass, chrome rear step bumper, color-keyed front bumper, valance panel, and grille.

Chrome Pkg., 2WD regular cab	380	304
2WD Xtracab, 4WD	235	188

Chrome front bumper, rear step bumper, grille, door handles.

Color-Key Pkg., 2WD	90	72
4WD	165	132

Color-keyed front bumper, valance panel, and grille, chrome rear bumper. NA w/Sport Value Pkg., Limited.

	Retail Price	Dealer Invoice
All-Weather Guard Pkg.	$70	$59

Heavy-duty battery (4-cylinder), heavy-duty starter (2WD V-6, 4WD), heavy-duty wiper motor, rain channeled windshield molding.

Sport Value Pkg., 4WD regular cab	980	882

Includes Chrome Pkg., sliding rear window, cloth bucket seats, center console, wheel arch moldings, alloy wheels, 265/75R15 tires.

Off-Road Pkg.,		
4WD 4-cylinder Xtracab w/5-speed, 4WD V-6	1690	1362
Limited	805	654

Off-road suspension, differential locks, black overfenders (NA Limited), tachometer, trip meter, alloy wheels, 10.5R15 tires. V-6 requires 4WDemand transfer case.

Power Pkg., (Std. Limited)	470	376

Power windows and door locks. Requires cruise control or Convenience Pkg.

Convenience Pkg., (Std. Limited)	710	581

Cruise control, tilt steering wheel, tachometer, trip meter, digital clock, glove compartment light, ignition light, ashtray light.

Powertrains

Differential locks, 4WD	325	268

NA 4-cylinder w/automatic. Requires tachometer, alloy wheels w/265/75R15 tires.

4WDemand transfer case,		
4WD (std. Limited)	230	190
4WD selector switch, Limited	130	107

Safety Features

Anti-lock brakes	590	507

Comfort and Convenience

Air conditioning	985	788
Power steering, 2WD 4-cylinder	300	257
Tilt steering wheel, (std. Limited)	235	201

Includes variable intermittent wipers.

Cruise control, (std. Limited)	290	232
Moonroof, Xtracab, Limited	390	312
Radio Prep, Xtracab	230	173

Wiring harness, four speakers, antenna. NA Limited.

AM/FM radio, Regular cab	270	203
AM/FM/cassette, Regular cab	370	278
Deluxe AM/FM/cassette, Xtracab	580	435

Includes four speakers.

Sliding rear window, regular cab	150	120
Xtracab (std. Limited)	270	216

Xtracab includes privacy glass.

Cloth bucket seats, regular cab	290	232
Xtracab	60	48

Includes console box. NA Limited.

Special Purpose, Wheels and Tires

Alloy wheels, 2WD regular cab	600	480
2WD Xtracab	420	336
4WD (std. Limited)	455	364
Alloy wheels w/265/75R15 tires, 4WD	995	796
Limited	400	320

Includes wheel lip moldings.

215/70R14 tires, 2WD 4-cylinder regular cab	180	144

Includes wheel covers.

TOYOTA TERCEL
Front-wheel-drive subcompact car

Base price range: (1997 model) $10,698-$12,878. Built in Japan.

Also consider: Chrysler Sebring Convertible, Ford Escort, Honda Civic, Mitsubishi Eclipse, Saturn Sedan/Wagon, Toyota Celica

FOR • Fuel economy • Optional front side air bags • Steering/handling

AGAINST • Noise • Rear seat room • Cargo space • Rear visibility

Prices are accurate at time of publication; subject to manufacturer's changes.

1997 Toyota Tercel CE 4-door

Toyota's "cheap wheels" sedan is smaller and less costly than Corolla, but also less powerful and refined. This year, Tercel is both a late arrival and less available. The '98 wasn't set to go on sale until mid-winter, and though Toyota wouldn't release details for this issue, the car should be a virtual '97 rerun. That means single trim-level 4-cylinder 2- and 4-door models in a basic design introduced for 1992.

Tercel sales slumped some 40 percent during 1997, in part, Toyota admits, because many would-be buyers choose a used Corolla instead. A downpriced 1998 base Corolla makes Tercel even less important to Toyota's U.S. profit picture.

Industry watchers expect 1998 Tercel imports to be fewer than 10,000, less than half the '97 total. Toyota may also trim some optional features to maintain Tercel's strict entry-level price position. As for the future, a new-design Tercel has been spied testing in Europe, but whether it will come here is unclear.

PERFORMANCE Tercel remains minimalist transportation for the budget-minded, a fact apparent in many areas. For example, the engine provides marginal acceleration with the optional and ornery-shifting automatic transmission. Note, too, that while 4-doors offer a 4-speed automatic, 2-door buyers must settle for a less-flexible 3-speed. That leaves the standard, slick-shifting manual as the best transmission for performance and quieter highway cruising.

Mileage is excellent with any model; our automatic 4-door got 30 mpg overall. But if Tercel is skimpy with gas, it's also stingy on ride comfort and refinement. There's more wavy-surface bounce and rough-pavement hop than in most other econocars and enough engine and tire noise to all but drown out wind rush at most any speed. The softish damping conspires with relatively skinny tires for modest cornering power and early nose-plowing. Within its limits, though, handling is front-drive safe and predictable. "Panic" stops are shortest and straightest with the optional anti-lock brakes, but premature wheel locking isn't a big problem with the standard setup, and nosedive is modest either way.

ACCOMMODATIONS As with most of the smaller small cars, adults have room enough in front, but the back seat is tight for anyone over 5-foot-10. Rear-seaters have no easy time getting there either, as entryways are tight on both body styles. There's also no surfeit of trunk room, though what's there is usable. A 60/40 split-fold rear seat is available to augment the space.

Drivers get a conveniently arranged dash, but taller ones may wish for more rearward seat travel to get further from the steering wheel. They might also complain about the lack of any wheel adjustment, even as an option. At least the squarish body styling provides good visibility to all quadrants.

BUILD QUALITY Though built with typical Toyota precision, Tercel is built down to a price, with lots of painted metal inside and rather utilitarian trim and equipment. In addition, door closings are on the tinny side and paint finish is ordinary.

VALUE FOR THE MONEY It's an okay errand-runner, but Tercel just isn't up to most driving demands. It's also shy on features; even a remote trunk release costs extra. No wonder would-be buyers find a used Corolla more appealingly. We do.

SPECIFICATIONS

	2-door coupe	4-door sedan
Wheelbase, in.	93.7	93.7
Overall length, in.	161.8	161.8
Overall width, in.	64.8	64.8

	2-door coupe	4-door sedan
Overall height, in.	53.2	53.2
Curb weight, lbs.	2010	2035
Cargo vol., cu. ft.	9.3	9.3
Fuel capacity, gals.	11.9	11.9
Seating capacity	5	5
Front head room, in.	38.6	38.6
Max. front leg room, in.	41.2	41.2
Rear head room, in.	36.5	36.5
Min. rear leg room, in.	31.9	31.9

ENGINES

	dohc I-4
Size, liters/cu. in.	1.5/89
Horsepower @ rpm	93 @ 5400
Torque (lbs./ft.) @ rpm	100@ 4400
Availability	S

EPA city/highway mpg

5-speed OD manual	32/39
3-speed automatic	29/34
4-speed OD automatic	30/37

RATINGS

	2-door/4-door
Acceleration	3
Fuel economy	5
Ride quality	3
Steering/handling	3
Braking	4
Quietness	3
Driver seating	3
Instruments/controls	3
Room/comfort (front)	3
Room/comfort (rear)	2
Cargo room	3
Value for the money	2
Total	**37**

PRICES

1997 Toyota Tercel	Retail Price	Dealer Invoice
CE 2-door notchback, 5-speed	$10698	$10080
CE 2-door notchback, automatic	11198	10551
Limited Edition 2-door notchback 5-speed	10698	10080
Limited Edition 2-door notchback 5-speed	11198	10551
CE 4-door notchback, 5-speed	12168	11279
CE 4-door notchback, automatic	12878	11936
Base 2-door convertible	17925	16244
Highline 2-door convertible	21675	19688
Destination charge	420	420

Limited Edition requires Hawk Value Pkg. Prices are for vehicles distributed by Toyota Motor Sales, U.S.A., Inc. The dealer invoice and destination charge may be higher in areas served by independent distributors.

STANDARD EQUIPMENT:

1.5-liter DOHC 4-cylinder engine, 5-speed manual transmission or 3-speed automatic transmission (2-door) or 4-speed automatic transmission (4-door), driver- and passenger-side air bags, cloth upholstery, reclining front bucket seats, front storage console, cupholders, trip odometer, dual outside mirrors, 175/65R14 tires, wheel covers.

Base: 2.0-liter 4-cylinder engine, 5-speed manual transmission, anti-lock brakes, driver- and passenger-side air bags, integral roll bar, power steering, 195/60HR14 tires, cloth reclining front sport seats with driver-side height adjustment, folding rear seat, console, cupholders, power door locks, tinted glass, tilt steering column, digital clock, trip odometer, tachometer, coolant-temperature gauge, service indicator, front door storage pockets, AM/FM/cassette, rear defogger, theft-deterrent system, variable intermittent wipers, daytime running lights, manual folding top, wheel covers.

Highline adds: air conditioning, cruise control, upgraded cloth top, leather upholstery, heated front seats, power windows, heated power mirrors, illuminated visor mirrors, fog lights, alloy wheels.

Rating Scale: 5-Excellent; 4-Above average; 3-Average; 2-Below average; 1-Poor

CONSUMER GUIDE™

OPTIONAL EQUIPMENT:

	Retail Price	Dealer Invoice
Safety Features		
Anti-lock brakes....................................	$550	$473
Major Packages		
Power Pkg., 4-door	640	512
2-door	525	420
Power windows and door locks.		
Convenience Pkg., CE...........................	365	293
Intermittent wipers, digital clock, remote outside mirrors, 60/40 split folding rear seat, remote fuel-door and decklid releases.		
Value Equipment Pkg. 1, CE..................	857	771
Air conditioning, power steering, floormats.		
Value Equipment Pkg. 2, CE 2-door	1287	1158
4-door	1357	1221
Air conditioning, power steering, remote trunk/fuel release, color-keyed bumpers, AM/FM radio with four speakers, 60/40 split folding rear seats, digital clock, intermittent wipers, dual manual remote outside mirrors (4-door), bodyside molding, floormats.		
Hawk Value Pkg., Limited Edition	1711	1540
Air conditioning, power steering, AM/FM radio with four speakers, 60/40 split folding rear seat, digital clock, intermittent wipers, bodyside molding, P185/60R14 tires, floormats, color-keyed bumpers, color-keyed spoiler.		
All-Weather Guard Pkg.	255	215
Heavy-duty battery, heater, starter, and rear defogger.		

	Retail Price	Dealer Invoice
Comfort and Convenience		
Air conditioning, CE...............................	$925	$740
Rear defogger	185	148
Power steering, CE	270	231
AM/FM radio with two speakers, CE........	245	184
AM/FM radio with four speakers, CE.......	390	293
Auto reverse cassette player..................	279	195
CE requires AM/FM radio or Value Equipment Pkg. 2.		
AM/FM/cassette with two speakers.........	340	232
Midline AM/FM/cassette with two speakers	467	327
Midline AM/FM/Cassette with four speakers	570	399
Deluxe AM/FM/cassette with four speakers............	615	461
CD player	457	320
CE requires AM/FM radio with four speakers or AM/FM/cassette with four speakers		
3-disc CD changer	699	489
CE requires AM/FM radio with four speakers or AM/FM/cassette with four speakers		
6-disc CD changer	799	559
CE requires AM/FM radio with four speakers or AM/FM/cassette with four speakers		
Remote keyless entry............................	395	149
Requires Power Pkg.		
Digital clock, CE	82	50
Console box	70	41
Cargo net..	42	27
Foormats, CE	62	37
Appearance and Miscellaneous		
Theft-deterrent system	295	99
Deluxe theft-deterrent system	695	209
Requires Power Pkg.		
Rear Spoiler, CE	519	310
Color-keyed bumpers	95	76
Includes bodyside moldings.		
Bodyside moldings	50	40
Mud guards	85	51
Wheel locks	90	72
Tire upgrade, CE	90	72
Powertrains		
4-speed automatic transmission	875	856

TOYOTA 4RUNNER `RECOMMENDED`

Rear- or 4-wheel-drive midsize sport-utility vehicle
Base price range: $20,558-$34,618. Built in Japan.

Toyota 4Runner Limited

Also consider: Ford Explorer, Mercedes-Benz ML320, Nissan Pathfinder

FOR • Standard anti-lock brakes (exc. base) • Ride • Quietness

AGAINST • Entry/exit • Fuel economy

Toyota's midrange sport-utility vehicle broke the 100,000-unit sales mark for the first time last year. With things going so well, the 4Runner gets only detail changes for this third run of its current design. As in '97 there are 2- and 4-wheel-drive models in 4-cylinder base form and in V-6 SR5 and Limited trim. Automatic transmission is standard on Limiteds and the 2WD SR5, available elsewhere. Anti-lock brakes are standard except on base models, where they're optional.

Among the few changes for '98 are a four-spoke steering wheel, revised audio systems, and dial-type climate controls in place of sliding levers. In addition, AM/FM/CD audio is now standard for Limiteds (replacing a cassette system).

Toyota's 4WDemand is a part-time 4WD system that isn't for use on dry pavement but allows on-the-fly shifts between 2WD and 4-High modes. Limiteds go a step further with electronic "One-Touch Hi-4," which engages 4WD by pushbutton instead of a lever. All 4WDs have a 2-speed transfer case with separate low-range gearing.

PERFORMANCE Based on our long-term test of a 4WD Limited, we suggest you avoid the 2.7-liter base 4-cylinder 'Runner unless you want 2WD, are willing to shift for yourself, and need only light-duty hauling ability. With automatic, 4WD and/or heavy routine loads, the 4-cylinder provides only so-so performance at best.

The smooth, revvy 3.4-liter V-6 delivers snappy takeoffs and feels pretty lively around town, though highway passing power is unexceptional in the heavier 4x4s. The automatic transmission shifts smoothly and doesn't hesitate much on full-throttle downshifts.

Mileage is an SUV weakness, and the 4Runner is no exception. Though our Limited returned 17.2 mpg overall, that included lots of highway driving, which seldom exceeded 20 mpg. Around town we typically got 15, about par for 6-cylinder SUVs.

The V-6 is noticeably quieter than the four, especially in hard running, but road roar is well muffled in any model. This leaves wind rush as the dominant noise source—no surprise in a tall, boxy vehicle.

Like most SUVs, 4Runner is engineered like a truck, yet it doesn't ride with much bouncy stiffness. Even so, the ride is not car-like, especially on 4WD versions. The same goes for the steering, though it's quick and precise for an SUV. Handling sets no standards, but 4Runner feels more stable in tight turns than some rivals. Our simulated panic stops were safe and undramatic with ABS.

ACCOMMODATIONS With their tall build and big tires, 4WD 4Runners have an unusually high step-in, especially uncomfortable for shorter people. Once aboard, there's room aplenty for four adults, plus better-than-average comfort for a small middle passenger in back.

Cargo room is generous even with the rear seat up. The full-size spare mounts beneath the vehicle to keep the load area relatively clear. The split rear seat double-folds to extend the deck, and the power liftgate window is a convenience not offered by any other midsize SUV. A variety of bins and pockets provides ample small-items storage.

Prices are accurate at time of publication; subject to manufacturer's changes.

4Runner's no-nonsense dash and fine visibility ease driving tasks. One glitch, though, is that using the pop-out dual cupholders blocks the climate controls.

BUILD QUALITY If our long-term Limited is any indication—and we think it is—the 4Runner is virtually trouble-free. Also as expected of Toyotas, workmanship is impressive inside and out.

VALUE FOR THE MONEY 4Runner remains one of the priciest midsize SUVs, but a test drive might convince you that its top-notch quality, reliability, and V-6 refinement are worth the extra money. Still, check into alternatives, especially the improved Ford Explorer and the aggressively priced new Mercedes-Benz ML320.

RATINGS

	4-cyl. 2WD	4-cyl. 4WD	V-6 2WD	V-6 4WD
Acceleration	3	2	3	3
Fuel economy	3	3	1	1
Ride quality	4	3	4	3
Steering/handling	3	3	3	3
Braking	4	4	4	4
Quietness	3	3	4	4
Driver seating	4	5	4	4
Instruments/controls	4	3	3	3
Room/comfort (front)	4	4	4	4
Room/comfort (rear)	4	4	4	4
Cargo room	4	4	4	4
Value for the money	3	3	3	3
Total	**43**	**41**	**41**	**40**

SPECIFICATIONS

	4-door wagon
Wheelbase, in.	105.3
Overall length, in.	178.7
Overall width, in.	66.5
Overall height, in.	67.5
Curb weight, lbs.	3850
Cargo vol., cu. ft.	79.7
Fuel capacity, gals.	18.5
Seating capacity	5
Front head room, in.	39.2
Max. front leg room, in.	43.1
Rear head room, in.	38.7
Min. rear leg room, in.	34.9

ENGINES

	dohc I-4	dohc V-6
Size, liters/cu. in.	2.7/164	3.4/207
Horsepower @ rpm	150@ 4800	183@ 4800
Torque (lbs./ft.) @ rpm	177@ 4000	217@ 3600
Availability	S[1]	S[2]

EPA city/highway mpg

4-speed OD automatic	19/22	17/20
5-speed OD manual	17/21	16/19

1. Base. 2. SR5, Limited.

PRICES

Toyota 4Runner

	Retail Price	Dealer Invoice
Base 2WD 4-door wagon, 5-speed	$20558	$17997
Base 2WD 4-door wagon, automatic	21458	18785
Base 4WD 4-door wagon, 5-speed	22708	19881
Base 4WD 4-door wagon, automatic	23608	20668
SR5 2WD 4-door wagon, automatic	25118	21990
SR5 4WD 4-door wagon, 5-speed	26268	22997
SR5 4WD 4-door wagon, automatic	27168	23784
Limited 2WD 4-door wagon, automatic	32248	28233
Limited 4WD 4-door wagon, automatic	34618	30307
Destination charge	420	420

Prices are for vehicles distributed by Toyota Motor Sales, U.S.A., Inc. The dealer invoice and destination charge may be higher in areas served by independent distributors.

STANDARD EQUIPMENT:

Base: 2.7-liter dohc 4-cylinder engine, 5-speed manual or 4-speed automatic transmission, driver- and passenger-side air bags, power steering, cloth bucket seats, 50/50 split folding rear seat, oil-pressure gauge, front and rear cupholders, tachometer, voltmeter, trip odometer, AM/FM radio with four speakers, power tailgate window, intermittent wipers, passenger-side visor mirror, remote fuel-door release, tinted glass, mudguards, 225/75R15 tires, 4WD models add 4WDemand part-time 4WD.

SR5 adds: 3.4-liter dohc V-6 engine, anti-lock brakes, tilt steering wheel, power door locks, power mirrors, cassette player, spring rear antenna, digital clock, rear defogger, rear wiper/washer, rear cupholders, variable intermittent wipers, map and courtesy lights, privacy glass, chrome bumpers and grille, 4WD models add 4WDemand part-time 4WD.

Limited adds: 4-speed automatic transmission, air conditioning, cruise control, power front sport seats, leather upholstery, premium CD player with six speakers, power antenna, leather-wrapped steering wheel and shift knob, power windows, illuminated passenger-side visor mirror, wood interior trim, tonneau cover, floormats, body-side cladding, fender flares, running boards, 265/70R16 tires, alloy wheels, 4WD adds 4WDemand part-time 4WD, One-Touch Hi-4 4WD, remote 4-wheel drive selector, All-Weather Guard Pkg..

OPTIONAL EQUIPMENT:

Major Packages	Retail Price	Dealer Invoice
Upgrade Pkg., Base	$2275	$1805

Air conditioner, cruise control, power windows and door locks, power mirrors, deluxe cassette, power antenna, additional lighting, floormats.

Preferred Equipment Group 1, SR5	2720	2165

Air conditioning, power windows, premium cassette player with six speakers, power antenna, alloy wheels with 31-inch tires (265/70R16 tires).

Preferred Equipment Group 2, SR5	2105	1673

Group 1 without 31-inch tires.

Convenience Pkg., Base	705	577
SR5	375	300

Tilt steering wheel, variable intermittent wipers, digital clock, intermittent rear wiper/washer (Base), rear defogger, map light.

Power Pkg. #1, Base	810	648

Power door locks, power mirrors, additional lighting.

Power Pkg. #2, Base	920	736
SR5	505	404

Power windows and door locks, power mirrors, power antenna SR5 requires premium cassette player or cassette/CD player.

Sports Pkg., SR5	1760	1422

Sports Seat Pkg., leather-wrapped steering wheel, leather-wrapped shifter (5-speed), fender flares, P265/70R16 tires, alloy wheels.

Sports Pkg. w/locking rear differential,		
4WD SR5 w/automatic	2085	1690
Sports Seat Pkg., SR5	685	548

Cloth sport seats, cruise control, upgraded door trim, leather-wrapped steering wheel, leather-wrapped shift knob (4WD SR5 w/5-speed).

Leather Trim Pkg., SR5	1535	1228

Leather sports seats, leather door trim, leather-wrapped steering wheel, leather-wrapped shift knob (4WD SR5 w/5-speed), cruise control.

All-Weather Guard Pkg.	70	59

Heavy-duty battery, heavy-duty wiper motor and starter motor, large windshield washer reservoir. Base requires rear heater, and rear wiper/defogger or Convenience Pkg. 2WD SR5 and 2WD Limited require rear heater. Std. Limited 4WD.

Powertrains

Locking rear differential,		
Base 4WD, SR5 4WD w/5-speed, Limited 4WD.	325	268

Base requires styled steel wheels or alloy wheels w/31-inch tires (265/70R16 tires). 4WD SR5 w/5-speed requires alloy wheels w/31-inch tires, Sports Pkg., or Group 1.

Alloy wheels w/locking rear differential,		
SR5 4WD w/automatic	1355	1092

Safety Features

Anti-lock brakes, Base	590	507

Comfort and Convenience

Air conditioning, Base, SR5	985	788

Rating Scale: 5-Excellent; 4-Above average; 3-Average; 2-Below average; 1-Poor

	Retail Price	Dealer Invoice
Rear heater	$165	$132
Includes rear storage console w/cupholders.		
Cruise control, Base, SR5............................	290	232
Tilt steering column, Base...........................	235	201
Includes variable intermittent wipers.		
Rear defogger, wiper/washer, Base	365	292
Power sunroof, SR5, Limited	915	732
Tonneau cover, Base, SR5............................	85	68
Premium cassette player, SR5......................	220	165
Includes six speakers. Requires Power Pkg. #2.		
Deluxe CD player, Base, SR5........................	100	75
Includes four speakers.		
Premium CD player, SR5..............................	320	240
Requires Power Pkg. #2.		
Premium Cassette/CD player, SR5.................	500	375
Limited	180	135
Includes six speakers. Requires Power Pkg. #2.		

Appearance and Miscellaneous

Privacy glass, Base.....................................	295	236

Special Purpose, Wheels and Tires

Styled steel wheels, Base	600	480
Includes 265/70R16 tires, 4.56 axle ratio. 2WD requires anti-lock brakes.		
Alloy wheels w/31-inch tires.........................	1030	824
Includes 265/70R16 tires. Base 2WD requires anti-lock brakes.		
Alloy wheels, Base, SR5	415	332

VOLKSWAGEN GOLF

Volkswagen Golf GTI 2-door

Front-wheel-drive subcompact car; similar to Volkswagen Jetta

Base price range: (1997 model) $13,740-$20,070. Built in Puebla, Mexico.

Also consider: Chevrolet Prizm, Honda Civic, Toyota Corolla

FOR • Optional side air bags • Acceleration (GTI VR6) • Steering/handling • Cargo space

AGAINST • Automatic transmission performance • Rear passenger room • Road noise

A new version of VW's hatchback Golf bowed last September in Europe, but won't come Stateside until the fall as a 1999 model. Still, the familiar third-generation Golf and its sporty GTI spinoffs get some changes for swan-song '98. Chief among these are seat-mounted front side air bags as a first-time option. Additionally, GTIs get red interior trim accents, silver-faced gauges, and new 7-spoke alloy wheels.

The mainstay Golf GL comes with four doors, the GTIs with two. GL and the base GTI have a 4-cylinder engine and manual or optional automatic transmission. The GTI VR6 uses VW's compact V-6 and is sold with manual shift only. Standard low-speed traction control is exclusive to the VR6 model. Anti-lock brakes are standard on GTIs and optional for GL. All models have dual air bags and daytime running lights.

VW's Jetta is essentially a Golf/GTI with a trunk and thus performs similarly with comparable equipment.

See the Volkswagen Jetta report for an evaluation of the Golf.

RATINGS

	GL	GTI	GTI VR6
Acceleration	3	3	4
Fuel economy	4	4	3
Ride quality	4	3	3
Steering/handling	4	4	4
Braking	3	4	3
Quietness	3	3	3
Driver seating	3	3	3
Instruments/controls	3	3	3
Room/comfort (front)	3	3	3
Room/comfort (rear)	3	3	3
Cargo room	4	4	4
Value for the money	4	4	3
Total	41	41	40

SPECIFICATIONS

	4-door hatchback	2-door hatchback
Wheelbase, in.	97.4	97.4
Overall length, in.	160.4	160.4
Overall width, in.	66.7	66.7
Overall height, in.	56.2	56.2
Curb weight, lbs.	2544	2565
Cargo vol., cu. ft.	16.9	17.5
Fuel capacity, gals.	14.5	14.5
Seating capacity...............................	5	5
Front head room, in.	39.2	37.4
Max. front leg room, in.	42.3	42.3
Rear head room, in.	37.4	37.2
Min. rear leg room, in.	31.5	31.5

ENGINES

	ohc I-4	dohc V-6
Size, liters/cu. in.	2.0/121	2.8/170
Horsepower @ rpm...........................	115@ 5400	172@ 5800
Torque (lbs./ft.) @ rpm.......................	122@ 3200	173@ 4200
Availability	S[1]	S[2]

EPA city/highway mpg

4-speed OD automatic.........................	22/29	18/24
5-speed OD manual............................	24/31	19/25

1. GL and GTI. 2. GTI VR6.

Golf standard equipment, options, and prices are included in the Volkswagen Jetta price section.

VOLKSWAGEN JETTA

Volkswagen Jetta GL

Front-wheel-drive subcompact car; similar to Volkswagen Golf

Base price range: (1997 model) $13,470-$20,930. Built in Mexico.

Also consider: Chevrolet Prizm, Honda Civic, Toyota Corolla

FOR • Optional side air bags • Acceleration (GLX) • Steering/handling • Fuel economy (TDI)

AGAINST • Automatic transmission performance • Road noise • Rear passenger room

This 4-door sedan version of the hatchback Golf is VW's top U.S. seller, though the Golf is more popular in most other markets. Next year brings a redesigned Jetta based on the new Golf

---

Prices are accurate at time of publication; subject to manufacturer's changes.

that's already out in Europe and will come Stateside for '99. Meantime, the current Jetta makes a last stand with seat-mounted front side air bags as a new option and a remote central locking system integrated with the standard anti-theft alarm.

Jetta GL, GT, and GLS have a 2.0-liter 4-cylinder, while the TDI uses a 1.9-liter Turbo Direct Injection diesel. Exclusive to GLX is VW's compact V-6 engine. All models come with manual transmission; automatic is optional except on the TDI. Anti-lock brakes and low-speed traction control are standard on GLX, with ABS optional on other models.

Jettas with power windows gain all-around one-touch up/down operation, plus a feature that opens or closes windows and sunroof from outside the vehicle by holding the key in the driver's door lock.

PERFORMANCE In mainstream 2.0-liter form, both the Jetta and Golf offer good pickup and passing power with manual shift, but the optional automatic saps a lot of oomph and tends to be harsh on full-throttle "kickdown" gear changes. VW says this transmission is smoother for '98, but the difference isn't likely to be major. The V-6 Golf GTI and Jetta GLX are real flyers, scaling 0-60 mph in under 8 seconds with manual in our tests. That 5-speed works well in all models, apart from some vagueness when engaging 5th or Reverse, and it helps you get the best from the turbodiesel engine, which has loads of low-rpm power but is slightly slower overall than the gas 4-cylinder.

The TDI really shines for fuel economy, though, as its EPA numbers suggest. In our tests of gas-powered models, a 5-speed GLX returned 21.3 mpg in hard driving—not bad for the performance—while our 2.0-liter cars have averaged 22.7 with automatic and 27.2 with manual.

All these VWs have sporty road manners for such practical cars, especially the GTI/GLX with their wider tires and firmer damping. Steering is meaty and precise, while cornering is crisp enough yet front-drive safe and predictable. Ride is comfortably supple on 4-cylinder models, a bit jiggly on V-6s. Road noise remains a problem at highway speeds, as does 4-cylinder engine noise.

ACCOMMODATIONS As with most smaller cars, the Golf/Jetta interior favors front-seaters for room and comfort. Back seats are too narrow for three-abreast grownup travel, and there's not much knee room with the front seats moved back. Aft entry/exit is also tight, even on 4-doors. Cargo room is a high point. Jettas have huge trunks for their external size, while Golfs offer the extra versatility that goes with being hatchbacks. All Golf/Jettas have folding rear seats, but only top-trim models have split backrests.

Drivers sit tall in the saddle, but thick rear roof posts inhibit over-the-shoulder visibility, some minor controls aren't logically placed, and nighttime dash illumination is a bit dim. At least all models have a tilt-adjustable steering column.

BUILD QUALITY VWs score none too well in surveys of customer satisfaction and "things gone wrong." Still, Golf/Jetta workmanship is generally solid and thorough, though some interior materials don't look that nice.

VALUE FOR THE MONEY With competitive pricing and a 10-year powertrain warranty, the Golf and Jetta offer good value for the long haul. V-6 models aren't cheap, though, and none of these cars hold their value as well as most rivals.

RATINGS

	GL/GLS/GT	TDI	GLX
Acceleration	3	2	4
Fuel economy	4	5	3
Ride quality	4	4	3
Steering/handling	4	4	4
Braking	4	4	4
Quietness	3	3	3
Driver seating	3	3	3
Instruments/controls	3	3	3
Room/comfort (front)	3	3	3
Room/comfort (rear)	2	2	2
Cargo room	4	4	4
Value for the money	4	4	3
Total	**41**	**41**	**39**

SPECIFICATIONS

	4-door sedan
Wheelbase, in.	97.4
Overall length, in.	173.4
Overall width, in.	66.7
Overall height, in.	56.1
Curb weight, lbs.	2590
Cargo vol., cu. ft.	15.0
Fuel capacity, gals.	14.5
Seating capacity	5
Front head room, in.	39.2
Max. front leg room, in.	42.3
Rear head room, in.	37.3
Min. rear leg room, in.	31.5

ENGINES

	ohc I-4	dohc V-6	turbodiesel ohc I-4
Size, liters/cu. in.	2.0/121	2.8/170	1.9/116
Horsepower @ rpm	115@ 5400	172@ 5800	90 @ 4000
Torque (lbs./ft.) @ rpm	122@ 3200	173@ 4200	149@ 1900
Availability	S[1]	S[2]	S[3]
EPA city/highway mpg			
4-speed OD automatic	22/29	18/24	
5-speed OD manual	24/31	19/25	40/49

1. Jetta GL and GLS. 2. Jetta GLX. 3. TDI.

PRICES

1997 Volkswagen Jetta	Retail Price	Dealer Invoice
Golf GL 4-door hatchback	$13470	$12432
Golf Jazz 4-door hatchback	14270	13260
Golf Trek 4-door hatchback	14350	13343
GTI 2-door hatchback	16320	15032
GTI VR6 2-door hatchback	19710	18198
GTI VR6 Driver's Edition 2-door hatchback	20070	18750
Jetta GL 4-door notchback	14570	13219
Jetta Jazz 4-door notchback	15370	14048
Jetta Trek 4-door notchback	15530	14214
Jetta GT 4-door notchback	14965	13628
Jetta TDI 4-door notchback	15745	14499
Jetta GLS 4-door notchback	16920	15318
Jetta GLX 4-door notchback	20930	19312
Destination charge	500	500

STANDARD EQUIPMENT:

Golf GL and Jetta GL: 2.0-liter 4-cylinder engine, 5-speed manual transmission, driver- and passenger-side air bags, power steering, cloth reclining bucket seats, driver-seat height adjustment, 60/40 split folding rear seat, front storage console, cupholders, tilt steering wheel (Jetta), power door locks, manual outside mirrors, tachometer, remote hatch and fuel-door releases, variable intermittent wipers, rear defogger, rear wiper/washer (Golf), theft-deterrent system, visor mirrors, daytime running lights, rear spoiler (Golf), cargo cover, trunk light, 195/60HR14 tires, wheel covers.

Golf Trek and Jetta Trek add to Golf GL and Jetta GL: special cloth seats, leather-wrapped steering wheel and shifter, sport instrument gauges, delay-off interior light (Jetta), floormats, cargo net, roof-mounted whip antenna, dark-tinted taillight lenses, fog lamps, alloy wheels, roof-mounted bicycle rack, Trek mountain bicycle.

Golf Jazz and Jetta Jazz add to Golf GL and Jetta GL: AM/FM/cassette player w/6-disc CD changer, special cloth seats, alloy wheels.

GTI adds to Golf GL: anti-lock 4-wheel disc brakes, air conditioning, AM/FM/cassette, cloth sport seats, power sunroof, dark-tinted taillight lenses, reading light, rear spoiler, 5-spoke alloy wheels.

GTI VR6 adds: 2.8-liter V-6 engine, close-ratio 5-speed manual transmission, sport suspension, traction control, cruise control, power windows, heated power mirrors, tilt steering wheel, leather-wrapped steering wheel, trip computer, 205/50HR15 tires, Pinanfarina-style alloy wheels.

GTI VR6 Driver's Eddition adds: remote keyless entry, special interior trim, sport instrument gauges, red-painted brake calipers, bright exhaust pipe tips, 7-spoke alloy wheels.

Jetta GT adds to Jetta GL: cloth sport seats, dark-tinted taillight lenses, rear spoiler, fog lamps, alloy wheels.

Rating Scale: 5-Excellent; 4-Above average; 3-Average; 2-Below average; 1-Poor

Jetta TDI adds to Jetta GL: 1.9-liter turbodiesel engine, cruise control.

Jetta GLS adds to Jetta GL: air conditioning, cruise control, AM/FM/cassette, power windows, heated power mirrors, tilt steering wheel.

Jetta GLX adds: 2.8-liter V-6 engine, close-ratio 5-speed manual transmission, anti-lock 4-wheel disc brakes, sport suspension, traction control, cloth sport seats, power sunroof, leather-wrapped steering wheel, Bose sound system, trip computer, reading lights, rear spoiler, fog lamps, 205/50HR15 tires, Bugatti-style alloy wheels.

OPTIONAL EQUIPMENT:

	Retail Price	Dealer Invoice
Powertrains		
4-speed automatic transmission	$875	$856
NA GTI VR6.		
Safety Features		
Anti-lock brakes, GL, GT, TDI, GLS, Jetta Jazz	775	727
NA Trek, Golf Jazz.		
Convenience Group, Jetta Trek, Golf Jazz	400	349
Heated power mirrors, power windows.		
Cold Weather Pkg., GLS, GLX	250	218
Heated front seats and windshield washer nozzles. GLX requires leather upholstery.		
Comfort and Convenience		
Air conditioning, GL, Trek, Jazz, GT, TDI	860	750
Power sunroof, GL, Trek, Jazz, GT, TDI, GLS	590	516
Leather upholstery, GTI VR6	550	480
Jetta GLX	800	698
AM/FM/cassette, GL, Trek, GT, TDI	485	423
Includes eight speakers.		
Bose sound system, GLS	375	313
6-disc CD changer	495	412
Cruise control, Jetta GL, Jetta Trek, Jetta Jazz, GT	225	197
Appearance and Miscellaneous		
Clearcoat metallic paint, Trek	175	153

VOLKSWAGEN PASSAT

Volkswagen Passat GLS sedan

Front-wheel-drive compact car

Base price range: (1997 model) $19,430-$22,320. Built in Germany.

Also consider: Ford Contour, Mazda 626, Nissan Altima

FOR • Standard front side air bags • Standard traction control • Ride • Passenger and cargo room • Available all-wheel drive

AGAINST • Acceleration (GLS 1.8T w/automatic, TDI) • Tire noise

Volkswagen's largest sedan is redesigned for 1998, borrowing pieces from the smaller Audi A4 and larger Audi A6 to emerge as a less-expensive family sedan with sporty ambitions.

Passat's new look reflects the crescent-form styling first seen on sedans from Audi, which is owned by VW. Compared to the previous Passat, the new model is longer by about three inches in wheelbase and four inches overall, and about an inch wider and taller.

The new Passat debuts as a GLS model with Audi's 1.8-liter turbocharged 4-cylinder engine. A TDI version arrives by spring '98 with VW's Turbo Direct Injection diesel 1.9-liter 4-cylinder. Unveiled at the same time will be GLS V-6 and top-line GLX models powered by the Audi 2.8-liter V-6. And due by summer are wagon models and the option of Audi Quattro-type all-wheel drive, which VW calls "Syncro." All models come with manual transmission; the Porsche-designed 5-speed Tiptronic is available except on the TDI, where the automatic option is a 4-speed. Other linewide standards include low-speed traction control, anti-lock brakes, seat-mounted front side air bags, and "depowered" in-dash air bags.

PERFORMANCE Though the Passat is more family oriented than the A4, it has similarly crisp handling; responsive steering with good feedback; arrow-true highway stability—and, unfortunately, marked road rumble from all-season tires that also squeal too easily in exuberant cornering. On the other hand, the Passat has a marginally softer ride than the A4. The suspension smothers all but the worst bumps and dips, and a tangibly solid structure only adds to the sense of comfort. Braking? Swift and undramatic from most any speed.

All this should apply to any '98 Passat, though we've so far only driven the front-drive GLS with the gas turbo-four. It's quiet enough and generally free of "turbo lag" hesitation, but with automatic transmission, it just doesn't have the brawn for quick getaways and easy high-gear climbing up long, steep grades. The Tiptronic's manual-shift capability helps some, but the 1.8T Passat feels transformed with the standard 5-speed manual transmission, being lively, eager, and genuinely sporty.

The V-6 adds $2440 to the GLS 1.8T's base price, and we'd recommend it if you're not amenable to manual transmission.

ACCOMMODATIONS Passat's ace in the hole has always been generous interior room and the new one continues that tradition. There's spacious comfort for four adults (even five on short hops), plus an almost cavernous trunk and easy entry/exit. Six-footers have only about a half-inch of head clearance beneath the available moonroof, but leg room is plentiful all around.

The new Passat also mimics the A4 with a comfortably tall driving stance that's easily tailored via a standard tilt/telescope steering wheel, rangy fore/aft seat travel and a handy rachet-type driver's-seat height adjuster. Less convenient are the hard-to-reach knobs that operate the backrest recline and lumbar support. The dash is Audi-like too, except for simpler climate controls and different, but still very legible gauges. Visibility is fine except to the rear, where the styling hides the car's corners.

BUILD QUALITY Like the A4, Passat feels impressively stout even on the worst roads. Overall fit and finish are equally satisfying, but interior decor looks a bit drab.

VALUE FOR THE MONEY Gas or diesel, the turbo-fours don't have much guts for a modern family 4-door, so try the different engine/transmission combos to see which fits your needs. Otherwise, VW's newest is suave, sporty, spacious, and solid. It's also strong on features per dollar and "European" personality. We'd give it a good, long look.

RATINGS	GLS	TDI	GLS/GLX V-6
Acceleration	3	3	4
Fuel economy	3	5	2
Ride quality	4	4	4
Steering/handling	4	4	4
Braking	4	4	4
Quietness	3	3	4
Driver seating	4	4	4
Instruments/controls	4	4	4
Room/comfort (front)	4	4	4
Room/comfort (rear)	4	4	4
Cargo room	4	4	4
Value for the money	4	4	4
Total	45	47	46

Prices are accurate at time of publication; subject to manufacturer's changes.

SPECIFICATIONS

	4-door sedan
Wheelbase, in.	106.4
Overall length, in.	184.1
Overall width, in.	68.5
Overall height, in.	57.4
Curb weight, lbs.	3120
Cargo vol., cu. ft.	15.0
Fuel capacity, gals.	18.5
Seating capacity	5
Front head room, in.	39.7
Max. front leg room, in.	41.5
Rear head room, in.	37.8
Min. rear leg room, in.	35.3

ENGINES	turbo dohc I-4	turbodiesel ohc I-4	dohc V-6
Size, liters/cu. in.	1.8/109	1.9/116	2.8/169
Horsepower @ rpm	150@ 5700	90@ 4000	200@ 6000
Torque (lbs./ft.) @ rpm	155@ 1750	149@ 1900	207@ 3200
Availability	S[1]	S[2]	S[3]
EPA city/highway mpg			
5-speed OD manual	23/32	NA	NA
4-speed OD automatic		NA	
5-speed OD automatic	21/31		NA

1. GLS. 2. TDI. 3. GLS V-6, GLS.

Passat prices, standard equipment, and options not avai of publication.

VOLVO C70

Volvo C70 convertible

Front-wheel-drive luxury coupe; similar to Volvo S70/V70

Base price range: $38,995-$39,970. Built in Sweden.

Also consider: Audi Cabriolet, Buick Riviera, Lexus SC 300/400, Mercedes-Benz CLK

FOR • Side air bags • Acceleration • Steering/handling • Standard anti-lock brakes

AGAINST • Rear seat room • Rear seat entry/exit

Volvo made its name with conservative and boxy sedans and wagons. It's trying to update its image and this swoopy new coupe is spearheading the charge. The C70, Volvo's first coupe in seven years, went on sale this fall. A companion convertible should be available by June 1998.

The C70 is based on Volvo's front-wheel-drive S70 sedan and V70 wagon, which are 1998 updates of the 850 line, and has similar exterior dimensions. The coupe sports curvier 2-door styling and seats four instead of five.

Unlike the S70/V70, which offer a choice of three 5-cylinder engines, the new coupe comes only with the most powerful of those engines, a turbocharged 2.3 liter with 236 horsepower. Manual transmission is standard, but Volvo expects most buyers to order the optional automatic, which has Sport, Economy, and Winter shift modes.

One well-equipped model is offered and includes among its standard features front and side air bags, anti-lock brakes, 17-inch alloy wheels, and a power tilt/slide moonroof.

Factory options are limited to a firmer sport suspension with 18-inch wheels, and a package comprising traction control, heated front seats,

full leather upholstery and a 425-watt, 14-speaker audio system.

The convertible will have a leather interior, plus a one-button power top with a glass rear window and electric defroster and small rollover hoops that pop up automatically behind the back seats.

PERFORMANCE The C70 performs much like the other front-drive turbocharged Volvos. That means a stout, almost heavy feel to the structure and reassuring highway stability even in gusty crosswinds. As on the performance-oriented T5 versions of the S70/V70, the coupe has a firm but acceptably supple ride without the prominent tire thumping that plagued performance-oriented 850s. The C70 has ample grip and little body lean in turns. The steering is numb on center, but provides good feel otherwise.

Volvo claims a 0-60 mph time of 6.9 seconds, but neither of our preview C70s felt quite that fleet. The inline 5-cylinder isn't as smooth or sweet sounding as some of today's V-6s, and "turbo lag"—a moment's delay in power delivery—is still bothersome, especially with the automatic transmission.

Brake performance is commendable apart from spongy, long pedal action.

ACCOMMODATIONS The coupe styling extracts a price in more ways than one. For starters, the back seat is tighter than in sedan models, and it's much harder to get into or out of. Volvo tries to improve rear entry/exit with a power sliding feature for both front seats, but the seats move forward like snails. The C70 has reasonable trunk space for a coupe but less than the S70 sedan.

Yet, this is a practical car as coupes go. Leg room is ample in front, and head room is good despite the standard power moonroof. The driver's seat is comfortable and supportive, and visibility is good to all directions.

The power window and door-lock switches have been moved from the center console on the S and V cars to the doors, a more convenient location. We also like the coupe's flip open rear side windows, something few rivals offer.

BUILD QUALITY The flimsy dual cupholder that pulls out from the front center armrest looks and feels like an afterthought in the otherwise classy cabin. Overall, all Volvo models we've tested recently were solid and well built and the coupe's no different.

VALUE FOR THE MONEY Volvo aims the C70 at young-thinking empty nesters ready for something with more style and sizzle than a minivan, sport utility vehicle—or a Volvo sedan. Our experience so far suggests the C70 is a strong entry into that market and should be considered.

RATINGS

	C70
Acceleration	4
Fuel economy	3
Ride quality	4
Steering/handling	4
Braking	5
Quietness	3
Driver seating	3
Instruments/controls	3
Room/comfort (front)	4
Room/comfort (rear)	2
Cargo room	2
Value for the money	2
Total	**39**

SPECIFICATIONS

	2-door coupe
Wheelbase, in.	104.7
Overall length, in.	185.8
Overall width, in.	71.7
Overall height, in.	55.1
Curb weight, lbs.	3325
Cargo vol., cu. ft.	13.1
Fuel capacity, gals.	18.5
Seating capacity	4
Front head room, in.	NA
Max. front leg room, in.	NA
Rear head room, in.	NA
Min. rear leg room, in.	NA

ENGINES	Turbo dohc I-5
Size, liters/cu. in.	2.3/141

Rating Scale: 5-Excellent; 4-Above average; 3-Average; 2-Below average; 1-Poor

	Turbo dohc I-5
Horsepower @ rpm	236@ 5100
Torque (lbs./ft.) @ rpm	243@ 2100
Availability	S
EPA city/highway mpg	
4-speed OD automatic	19/26

PRICES

Volvo C70	Retail Price	Dealer Invoice
2-door notchback coupe, 5-speed	$38995	$34795
2-door notchback coupe, automatic	39970	35470
Destination charge	575	575

STANDARD EQUIPMENT:

C70 2.3-liter DOHC turbocharged 5-cylinder engine, 5-speed manual or 4-speed automatic transmission, driver- and passenger-side air bags, front side-impact air bags, anti-lock 4-wheel disc brakes, daytime running lights, air conditioning w/dual automatic climate control, variable-assist power steering, tilt/telescoping steering wheel, leather-wrapped steering wheel, cruise control, cloth reclining front bucket seats, 8-way power driver seat w/memory feature, 8-way power passenger seat, front armrest w/cupholder, 60/40 split folding rear seat, power windows, power door locks, power remote decklid/fuel filler release, power moonroof, heated power mirrors, automatic day/night inside mirror, tachometer, coolant temperature gauge, trip odometer, digital clock, outside temperature indicator, trip computer, intermittent wipers, 6-speaker AM/FM/cassette/3-disc CD changer w/anti-theft, power antenna, remote keyless entry, rear defogger, reading light, illuminated visor mirrors, floormats, theft-deterrent system, tinted glass, front and rear fog lights, headlight wiper/washer, 225/45ZR17 tires, alloy wheels.

OPTIONAL EQUIPMENT:
Powertrains
Traction control system	450	360

Comfort and Convenience
Dolby Pro Logic sound system	595	475
Leather upholstery	1495	1195
Heated front seats	235	185

Appearance and Miscellaneous
Multi-spoke alloy wheels	1995	1595

VOLVO S70/V70

Volvo S70 GLT

Front- or all-wheel-drive near-luxury car; similar to Volvo C70

Base price range: $26,985-$40,995. Built in Sweden, Belgium, and Canada.

Also consider: Acura TL, Audi A4, Infiniti I30, Saab 900

FOR • Side air bags • Standard anti-lock brakes • Acceleration (turbo models) • Steering/handling • Cargo room

AGAINST • Road noise • Fuel economy (turbo models)

Volvo replaced the 850 sedan and wagon in the spring of 1997 with two early 1998 models, the S70 sedan and the V70 wagon. Both are built off the same platform as the 850, but they have new styling and revised suspensions. The S70 comes with front-wheel drive and the V70 with front- or all-wheel drive.

The most noticeable exterior change from the 850 is a more rounded front end with a reshaped hood and new headlamps. Inside, the S/V70 models have new interiors with standard dual front and side air bags.

Sedans and wagons are available in four models: Base, GL, GLT, and T5. The sporty R model is available only as a wagon, as is the new Cross Country (or V70 XC).

Powering the base models is a 2.4-liter 5-cylinder engine with 168 horsepower. The GLT models get a turbocharged version of that engine that produces 190 horsepower. A 2.3-liter turbocharged 5-cylinder that makes 236 horsepower is standard on the T5 and R models. Base and T5 models are available with either manual or automatic transmission; all others come only with automatic.

Wagons are available with Volvo's all-wheel-drive (AWD) system. It normally powers the front wheels and when the front wheels begin to slip, power is automatically transmitted to the rear to improve traction. The V70 XC's suspension gives it 6.5 inches of ground clearance, about 1 inch more than the other wagons.

Optional on front-drive models and standard on the AWD wagons is TRACS, a traction control system that applies the front brakes to limit wheel slip at speeds under 25 mph. Anti-lock 4-wheel disc brakes are standard on all models.

PERFORMANCE Acceleration with the base engine is adequate, however things pick up considerably in the turbocharged models. Their passing punch is outstanding, but turbo lag—a momentary delay in power delivery—is evident at low speeds. The turbo engines are well suited to the automatic transmission, which shifts smoothly and downshifts promptly.

Fuel economy was better than expected. On a T5 sedan we got 20.3 mpg, and with an AWD wagon we averaged 18.4 mpg. While those numbers aren't outstanding, they are very good for the near-luxury class.

Wind noise is subdued, but the engines are vocal in hard acceleration and road noise can be prominent.

All S/V70s handle well. Body lean is minimal, and the tires grip securely in the turns. Ride quality varies greatly depending on model. The base and GLT models ride smoothly over broken pavement and skim over highway expansion joints. However, the T5 and R models have a stiffer suspension and tires, and they ride harshly on rough pavement.

The AWD provides terrific traction in all conditions without requiring any special effort from the driver, and the standard anti-lock brakes have good stopping power.

ACCOMMODATIONS Compared to the 850 series, the C/V70 has a more hospitable interior, and one that looks more contemporary. The biggest changes are climate and radio controls that make both systems easier to use. Also, the switches for the power windows and door locks are conveniently located on the door armrests instead of the center console. However, some other controls are hidden behind the steering wheel.

Front and rear passenger room is altered only slightly, with the biggest additions coming in rear leg room. That translates into ample space for front-seat occupants and adequate room for two passengers in back. A standard tilt/telescopic steering column makes it easy to get comfortable behind the wheel.

At 15.1 cubic feet for the sedan, cargo space is more than adequate. The sedan also has a 60/40 split folding rear seat that expands cargo capacity. Wagons have a generous cargo hold made more versatile by standard folding rear seatbacks.

Visibility is excellent to all directions thanks to the large side and rear windows.

BUILD QUALITY Fit and finish both inside and outside are good, and we didn't noticed any interior rattles on any of the models we drove.

VALUE FOR THE MONEY S/V70 models are competitively priced against other near-luxury sedans, such as the Cadillac Catera and Infiniti I30, and offer wagon and AWD choices the

---

Prices are accurate at time of publication; subject to manufacturer's changes.

VOLVO

other's ignore. The GLT versions, with their strong turbo engine, are the best all-around values in this line of younger-feeling new Volvos.

RATINGS

	S70 base	V70 GLT	T5/R
Acceleration	3	4	5
Fuel economy	4	4	3
Ride quality	4	4	3
Steering/handling	4	4	4
Braking	5	5	5
Quietness	3	3	3
Driver seating	4	4	4
Instruments/controls	4	4	4
Room/comfort (front)	4	4	4
Room/comfort (rear)	4	4	4
Cargo room	4	5	4
Value for the money	3	3	2
Total	**46**	**48**	**45**

SPECIFICATIONS

	4-door sedan	4-door wagon
Wheelbase, in.	104.9	104.9
Overall length, in.	185.9	185.9
Overall width, in.	69.3	69.3
Overall height, in.	55.2	56.2
Curb weight, lbs.	3152	3259
Cargo vol., cu. ft.	15.1	77.2
Fuel capacity, gals.	18.5	18.5
Seating capacity	5	5
Front head room, in.	39.1	39.1
Max. front leg room, in.	41.4	41.4
Rear head room, in.	37.8	37.9
Min. rear leg room, in.	35.2	35.2

ENGINES

	dohc I-5	Turbo dohc I-5	Turbo dohc I-5
Size, liters/cu. in.	2.4/149	2.4/149	2.3/141
Horsepower @ rpm	168@ 6100	190@ 5200	236@ 5100
Torque (lbs./ft.) @ rpm	162@ 4700	199@ 1800	243@ 2100
Availability	S[1]	S[2]	S[3]
EPA city/highway mpg			
4-speed OD automatic	20/29	20/29	19/26
5-speed OD manual	20/29		NA

1. Base, GT. 2. GLT, AWD, XC AWD. 3. T5, R.

PRICES

Volvo S70/V70

	Retail Price	Dealer Invoice
Base 4-door sedan, 5-speed	$26985	$24785
Base 4-door sedan, automatic	27960	25760
Base 4-door wagon, 5-speed	28285	26085
Base 4-door wagon, automatic	29260	27060
GT 4-door sedan, 5-speed	29540	27240
GT 4-door sedan, automatic	30515	28215
GT 4-door wagon, 5-speed	30840	28540
GT 4-door wagon, automatic	31815	29515
GLT 4-door sedan	32440	30040
GLT 4-door wagon	33740	31340
AWD 4-door wagon	34420	31720
AWD 4-door wagon w/moonroof	35620	32920
XC AWD 4-door wagon	36420	33470
XC AWD 4-door wagon w/moonroof	37620	34670
T-5 4-door sedan, 5-speed	34010	31060
T-5 4-door sedan, automatic	34985	32035
T-5 4-door wagon, 5-speed	35310	32360
T-5 4-door wagon, automatic	36285	33335
R AWD 4-door wagon	40995	36795
Destination charge	575	575

STANDARD EQUIPMENT:

Base: 2.4-liter DOHC 5-cylinder engine, 5-speed manual or 4-speed automatic transmission, driver- and passenger-side air bags, front side-impact air bags, anti-lock 4-wheel disc brakes, daytime running lights, child-proof rear door locks, air conditioning w/dual manual climate control, variable-assist power steering, cruise control, intermit-

tent wipers, velour upholstery, reclining front bucket seats, 8-way manually adjustable driver seat, fully folding passenger seat, 60/40 split folding rear seat, rear-seat trunk pass-through (sedan), front armrest w/cupholder, tilt/telescoping steering column, power windows, power door locks, remote keyless entry, remote decklid/tailgate release, heated power mirrors, coolant temperature gauge, trip odometer, tachometer, digital clock, outside temperature indicator, 6-speaker AM/FM/cassette w/anti-theft, power antenna (sedan), integrated window antenna (wagon), rear defogger, rear wiper/washer (wagon), illuminated visor mirrors, front and rear reading lights, floormats, theft-deterrent system, tinted glass, rear fog lights, front mud guards, tool kit, 195/60VR15 tires, wheel covers.

GT adds: power glass moonroof, 8-way power driver's seat w/memory feature, 6-spoke alloy wheels.

GLT adds: 2.4-liter DOHC turbocharged 5-cylinder 190-horsepower engine, 4-speed automatic transmission, automatic climate control, premium AM/FM/cassette.

AWD adds to GLT wagon: automatic 4-wheel drive, locking rear differential, traction control, heated front seats, automatic load leveling suspension, headlight wipers/washers, 205/55R16 tires, deletes power moonroof.

XC AWD adds: leather-wrapped steering wheel, trip computer, leather and cloth upholstery, AM/FM/cassette w/3-disc CD changer, cargo net, raised suspension, roof rack, front fog lights.

T5 adds to GLT: 2.3-liter DOHC turbocharged 5-cylinder 236 horsepower engine, 5-speed manual or 4-speed automatic transmission, CD player, leather-wrapped steering wheel, trip computer, 205/50ZR16 tires, 5-spoke alloy wheels.

R AWD adds to XC AWD: 2.3-liter DOHC turbocharged 5-cylinder 236-horsepower engine, power moonroof, leather and suede upholstery, leather and suede-wrapped steering wheel, 8-way power passenger seat, alloy instrument panel inserts, front spoiler, deletes raised suspension.

OPTIONAL EQUIPMENT:

Major Packages	Retail Price	Dealer Invoice
Touring Pkg., Base, GT, GLT	$395	$315
Trip computer, leather-wrapped steering wheel.		
Grand Touring Pkg., Base, GT	1780	1420
GLT	1285	1025
8-way power driver's seat w/memory feature (Base), power passenger seat, CD player, burled walnut interior trim.		
Sport Pkg., Base, GT, GLT, T-5	595	475
Front fog lights, rear spoiler.		
TRACS/Cold Weather Pkg., Base, GT, GLT, T-5	785	625
Traction control, heated front seats, headlight wiper/washer.		

Comfort and Convenience		
AM/FM/cassette/CD, Base, GT, GLT, AWD, XC AWD	485	385
Dolby Pro Logic sound system, R AWD	595	475
Leather upholstery, Base, GT, GLT, T-5	1195	955
XC AWD	595	475
8-way power driver's seat w/memory feature, Base	495	395
Burled walnut interior trim, T-5	575	460
R AWD	NC	NC
Replaces alloy dash inserts on R AWD.		

Appearance and Miscellaneous		
Automatic load leveling, 2WD wagons	495	395
Sport suspension, Base, GT, GLT, T-5	175	140
Alloy wheels, Base	450	360
205/50ZR16 high performance tires, T-5	NC	NC

VOLVO S90/V90

Rear-wheel-drive luxury car

Base price range: $34,300-$35,850. Built in Sweden.

Also consider: Acura RL, BMW 5-Series, Lexus GS 300/400, Mercedes-Benz E-Class, Saab 9-5

FOR • Side air bags • Standard anti-lock brakes • Passenger and cargo room • Acceleration

Rating Scale: 5-Excellent; 4-Above average; 3-Average; 2-Below average; 1-Poor

CONSUMER GUIDE™

Volvo S90

AGAINST • Ride (sedan) • Road noise

Volvo's flagship 960 series has been renamed for 1998 to use the company's new S designation for sedans and V for wagons. Still, the S90 and V90, which went on sale in the spring of 1997, aren't long for this world. In mid-1998 Volvo plans to replace these rear-wheel-drive sedans and wagons with an all-new front-drive sedan. It will retain a 6-cylinder engine, but will be the biggest-ever Volvo car offered in the United States.

Along with their nomenclature adjustment, the S90 and V90 also got a new center console and minor suspension upgrades. Both use a 181-horsepower 2.9-liter inline 6-cylinder engine teamed with automatic transmission.

Standard safety equipment includes dual front air bags, side air bags for the front seats, anti-lock brakes, and daytime running lights. The wagon has a standard integrated child booster seat that folds out of the rear seat's center armrest.

PERFORMANCE On paper, the S/V90's 181-horsepower engine would look to have trouble moving a car this heavy with much vigor. However, it performs better than we expected. We timed a 1997 960 sedan at a brisk 8.6 seconds to 60 mph. There was also good passing power and the transmission shifted crisply but smoothly.

Fuel economy was less impressive, averaging 17.9 mpg and just 20.4 on the highway, suggesting the upright stance of the S90 is not so aerodynamic.

Snow-belt drivers take note: Volvo does not offer traction control on these rear-drive sedans, though a limited-slip differential is part of the optional Cold Weather Package, which also includes heated seats and an outside temperature gauge. The transmission also has a "winter" mode that locks out the two lowest gears for enhanced traction on slippery surfaces.

The sedan rides on stiff 16-inch tires rated for speeds up to 149 mph. They make the ride harsh and lumpy except on glass-smooth pavement and generate lots of road noise. These tires improve the sedan's cornering ability a little, but the harsher ride makes the wagon a clear choice for comfort seekers. The wagon has softer 15-inch tires rated for speeds up to 129 mph.

The steering is sharp and direct with a pleasantly tight turning radius. Braking power is excellent, however it is accompanied by lots of nose dive and heavy chatter from the anti-lock system.

ACCOMMODATIONS Both body styles have a roomy, functional interior that holds four adults comfortably and five with a little squeezing. Wide, tall doorways allow easy entry and exit. However, the driver's seat is a little too high and some staffers found it difficult to get comfortable behind the wheel.

The gauges are easy to read and placed right in front of the driver. Radio and climate controls are up high and feature large buttons and knobs.

Visibility is good to all sides, though larger side mirrors would make lane-changing easier. Interior storage is good.

The trunk of the sedan is roomy and the opening large. Cargo space can be expanded by folding down the rear seats of the wagon, a feature the sedan lacks.

BUILD QUALITY Most of the interior materials don't feel as expensive we expect in this class. However, there were no squeaks or rattles in our test cars, and their exterior finish was excellent.

VALUE FOR THE MONEY We rate the big Volvo sedan and wagon highly in most areas, but there are good alternatives in the same price range. Good deals should be available, however, as introduction of the successor model approaches.

RATINGS

	S90	V90
Acceleration	4	4
Fuel economy	2	2
Ride quality	3	4
Steering/handling	4	3
Braking	4	4
Quietness	3	3
Driver seating	3	3
Instruments/controls	4	4
Room/comfort (front)	4	4
Room/comfort (rear)	4	4
Cargo room	5	5
Value for the money	2	2
Total	**41**	**42**

SPECIFICATIONS

	4-door sedan	4-door wagon
Wheelbase, in.	109.1	109.1
Overall length, in.	191.8	191.4
Overall width, in.	68.9	68.9
Overall height, in.	56.6	57.6
Curb weight, lbs.	3461	3547
Cargo vol., cu. ft.	16.6	74.9
Fuel capacity, gals.	20.3	20.3
Seating capacity	5	5
Front head room, in.	37.4	38.1
Max. front leg room, in.	41.0	41.0
Rear head room, in.	36.9	36.7
Min. rear leg room, in.	34.7	34.7

ENGINES

	dohc I-6
Size, liters/cu. in.	2.9/178
Horsepower @ rpm	181@ 5200
Torque (lbs./ft.) @ rpm	199@ 4100
Availability	S

EPA city/highway mpg

4-speed OD automatic	18/26

PRICES

Volvo S90/V90

	Retail Price	Dealer Invoice
4-door sedan	$34300	$31600
4-door wagon	35850	33150
Destination charge	575	575

STANDARD EQUIPMENT:

S90/V90: 2.9-liter dohc 6-cylinder engine, 4-speed automatic transmission, automatic locking differential, driver- and passenger-side air bags, front side-impact air bags, anti-lock 4-wheel disc brakes, integrated child booster seat (wagon), daytime running lights, power steering, automatic climate control, cruise control, leather upholstery, reclining front bucket seats w/lumbar adjuster, 8-way power front seats w/memory feature, rear-seat trunk pass through (sedan), 60/40 split folding rear seat (wagon), power sunroof, power windows, power door locks, heated power mirrors, leather-wrapped tilt steering wheel, AM/FM/cassette w/amplifier and anti-theft, power antenna (sedan), integrated antenna (wagon), remote keyless entry, remote trunk/hatch release, wood interior trim, illuminated visor mirrors, front and rear reading lights, floormats, tinted glass, theft-deterrent system, headlight wiper/washers, front and rear fog lamps, lug-

Prices are accurate at time of publication; subject to manufacturer's changes.

gage rack (wagon), tool kit, 195/65HR15 tires (wagon), 205/55VR16 tires (sedan), alloy wheels.

OPTIONAL EQUIPMENT:
Major Packages

	Retail Price	Dealer Invoice
Cold Weather Pkg.	$645	$415

Heated front seats, locking differential, outside temperature indicator.

Comfort and Convenience

	Retail Price	Dealer Invoice
CD player	$485	$385

Appearance and Miscellaneous

	Retail Price	Dealer Invoice
Automatic load-leveling suspension, wagon	495	320

Rating Scale: 5-Excellent; 4-Above average; 3-Average; 2-Below average; 1-Poor